Praise for

UNWARRA

"Barry Friedman unravels the current state of out-of-control policing in an incisive, provocative and beguiling overview and remedy."
—*Shelf Awareness*

"Friedman's lively writing and clarity of expression enable him to make the thicket of applicable Fourth Amendment law readily understandable for general readers, helpfully illuminated by the personal stories behind the case law. At once creative and conservative, Friedman offers a timely blueprint for recovering democratic control of local and national law enforcement."
—*Kirkus Reviews* (starred review)

"Drawing on landmark court cases, extensive history, and incisive analysis, Friedman takes a hard look at current problems and proposes astute and well-researched solutions in favor of more "democratic and constitutional" policing . . . [*Unwarranted*] is the definitive guide to contemporary policing and its necessary reforms."
—*Publishers Weekly*

"A powerful manifesto against unbalanced policing methodologies and an illuminating and sobering critique of political and legal forces in the U.S."
—*Booklist*

"This important, accessible book diagnoses the many pathologies of modern policing in contexts ranging from inner-city crime to terrorism. Barry Friedman lays the responsibility for our policing ills somewhat on courts but primarily on us, the policed. He provides fresh, concrete guidance for how judges and the American people can make modern policing democratically accountable, lawful, and effective."
—Jack Goldsmith, Henry L. Shattuck Professor of Law at Harvard University

"The relationship between citizens and the police is one of the most urgent constitutional questions in American life today. In this pathbreaking book, Barry Friedman argues that instead of judges reviewing police conduct after the fact, citizens should take responsibility for police conduct before the fact. By insisting that all citizens reflect about the constitutional provisions that govern how the police act, Friedman makes a passionate case that the responsibility for policing the police is a job for all of us."　　　　—Jeffrey Rosen, President and CEO of the National Constitution Center

"In *Unwarranted*, Barry Friedman takes us on a journey through America's problems with policing and surveillance to confront a hard but necessary truth. Our nation's problem with policing reflects a failure of democratic engagement. This book makes a necessary and, until now, missing contribution to our national conversation about policing reform."
—Sherrilyn Ifill, President and Director-Counsel of the NAACP Legal Defense and Educational Fund

BARRY FRIEDMAN
UNWARRANTED

Barry Friedman is the Jacob D. Fuchsberg Professor of Law at New York University School of Law and the director of the Policing Project. For thirty years he has taught, written about, and litigated issues of constitutional law and criminal procedure. He is the author of *The Will of the People* (FSG, 2009). His writing has appeared in *The New York Times*, *Slate*, and *The New Republic*, among other publications. He lives in New York City.

ALSO BY BARRY FRIEDMAN

The Will of the People

UNWARRANTED

Policing Without Permission

———◆———

BARRY FRIEDMAN

Farrar, Straus and Giroux   New York

To Simon and Samara

Farrar, Straus and Giroux
175 Varick Street, New York 10014

Copyright © 2017 by Barry Friedman
All rights reserved
Printed in the United States of America
Published in 2017 by Farrar, Straus and Giroux
First paperback edition, 2018

The Library of Congress has cataloged the hardcover edition as follows:
Names: Friedman, Barry, 1958– author.
Title: Unwarranted : policing without permission / Barry Friedman.
Description: New York : Farrar, Straus and Giroux, 2017. | Includes index.
Identifiers: LCCN 2016033246 | ISBN 9780374280451 (hardback) |
    ISBN 9780374710903 (e-book)
Subjects: LCSH: Electronic surveillance—Law and legislation—United States. |
    Intelligence service—United States. | Espionage—United States. | Civil
    rights—United States. | Privacy, Right of—United States. | Law
    enforcement—United States. | BISAC: LAW / Constitutional.
Classification: LCC KF5399 .F75 2017 | DDC 344.7305/2—dc23
LC record available at https://lccn.loc.gov/2016033246

Paperback ISBN: 978-0-374-53745-6

Our books may be purchased in bulk for promotional, educational, or business
use. Please contact your local bookseller or the Macmillan Corporate and
Premium Sales Department at 1-800-221-7945, extension 5442, or by e-mail at
MacmillanSpecialMarkets@macmillan.com.

www.fsgbooks.com
www.twitter.com/fsgbooks • www.facebook.com/fsgbooks

1   3   5   7   9   10   8   6   4   2

You must first enable the government to control the governed; and in the next place oblige it to control itself.

—James Madison, *The Federalist No. 51*

CONTENTS

PREFACE

I resolved to write a book about policing after September 11, 2001. I live in lower Manhattan, not far from where the Twin Towers stood. I spent that day on the streets of New York, rushing to the hospital to give blood, only to learn none was needed; searching for my future father-in-law, who had been on business near the World Trade Center site, but fortunately made his way to his daughter's place in Greenwich Village; and watching those awful and surreal events—as did so many—in a state of shock and dismay. On that day, and those that followed, I joined groups standing along the West Side Highway, choked up, offering whatever moral support we could to our early and continuing responders. They were (and remain) our heroes.

And yet, in the weeks after 9/11, something I was hearing troubled me no end. People would say we needed to relinquish our liberties in order to give the government more leeway to protect us. Even Supreme Court justices were saying it. On September 29, 2001, while the acrid and unforgettable smell of destruction still hung in the air around us, Justice Sandra Day O'Connor came to New York University School of Law, where I teach, for the groundbreaking of Furman Hall. "[W]e're likely to experience more restriction on our personal freedom than has ever been the case in this country," she warned the somber group gathered there. The events of September 11, she said, would "cause us to reexamine some of our laws pertaining to criminal surveillance, wire-tapping, immigration and so on."

I've taught Constitutional Law and Criminal Procedure for thirty years, so I'm no novice to the much-discussed tension between keeping society secure and safeguarding our liberties. But having studied the law governing policing for three decades, I wondered exactly what everyone was talking about. I'd ask people what it was that they felt the government should now be allowed to do. If they could come up with any example—often they could not—I'd point out, "But the police *already* are allowed to do that. The Supreme Court said so ages ago." Then it was their turn to be surprised—most of them had no idea how permissive the courts were toward policing.

As a practical matter, much of policing in this country is governed today by the Supreme Court's (and lower courts') pronouncements about the Constitution. Of particular importance is the Fourth Amendment, which prohibits "unreasonable searches and seizures." Whether it is the use of force by police on the streets, or surveillance of citizens from the air, police officials will tell you that the courts set the rules they must follow. I'd long believed the judiciary's record on protecting our vital liberties was disappointing at best. I resolved to find a way to say so, to explain how important it was to get policing right.

But while I was searching for precisely what I wanted to say, I had a realization: Why don't the most basic of rules that apply in the rest of government also govern the police? Why is policing treated so differently?

For the rest of government—which is to say, for environmental protection or workplace safety, or tax collection, or all the countless things that local, state, and federal governments do every day—*democratic governance* is paramount. Before government officials act, we require rules that are written down in advance, that are public so everyone can know what they are, and that are adopted after the public has had a chance to weigh in. That is what democracy requires.

But when it comes to policing, the ordinary rules of democratic governance seem to evaporate. Policing officials decide for themselves how to enforce the law. The rules governing policing often are not public. Even more rarely are they adopted with public input. Instead, with policing, we try to fix things *after the fact*, after they go wrong: with civilian review boards, inspectors general, and especially with review by the courts.

This is an enormous failure of democracy. And it's also counterproductive. If our attention to policing is always after the fact, we're always mopping up messes instead of figuring out how to prevent them in the first place.

At a deep level what this book is about is getting the people to take responsibility for how policing occurs in this country. By developing rules and policies that are in place before police act. And by encouraging us all to think about what the Constitution's provisions that cover policing should mean. Because it is not and cannot be the job of the courts and the police alone to decide how we are policed as a society—it is the responsibility of all of us.

Recent events have made clear that getting policing right is one of the most pressing challenges we face as a society. Whether it is omnipresent surveillance, or the use of force on the streets, or concerns about fairness and discrimination and race, it is now apparent to many people that change is needed. The question is how we get there.

Given the nature of this book—and the unfortunate reality of twenty-first-century America—you are about to read one story after another about some way in which policing went off the rails. These stories implicate everyone from cops on the beat to the head of the National Security Agency. And you will meet many perfectly innocent people who did not deserve what happened to them. (You'll meet plenty of guilty people, too, though we still should ask questions about the methods used to apprehend them.)

Even so, this is *not* a book about the failures of the police. I want to make that clear at the outset. I am going to call out two responsible parties repeatedly throughout this book, and neither are the police themselves.

The first actors responsible for the woes of policing today are the courts, which have done a perfectly appalling job of one of the chief tasks we have given them: protecting our basic liberties. I spend my life around judges, many of whom are good friends. Even so, I think the judiciary should be ashamed. Confronted with situations in which the police have done the most inappropriate and untoward things, too many judges simply cannot bring themselves to cry foul. To be fair, judging the police is tough. I'll explain why that is, and why it is wrong to expect judges to do the job alone. One of the chief lessons here is that they should not have to. But still.

The second party is the rest of us. We have abdicated our most fundamental responsibility as citizens in a democracy: to be in charge of those who act in our name. The authority to use force on citizens and to conduct surveillance of them—the powers that define policing and set it apart—may be necessary to maintain order, but those are the most awesome powers we grant any public servants. If we should be superintending anything in our society, that is it. Instead, we've dropped the ball.

The real problem with policing is not the police; it is us. We need to take responsibility for what is done in our names. We need to make decisions and give guidance, even if it is—as it surely is—a difficult thing to do. We need to take an active role in governing policing.

I've put my time and energy (and money) where my mouth is. Besides writing this book, with the help of many individuals and groups I've begun the Policing Project at New York University School of Law, to try to put some of the lessons here into action. Working with the Policing Project has been one of the most personally rewarding things I've done.

And here's the thing: Our constant partners in the Policing Project are law enforcement personnel. I've been privileged over the last couple years to meet and work with some of the most inspiring, dedicated, open-minded, innovative, committed people I've ever met. Some things *are* off the rails in law enforcement land. But they know it. They are working hard to put it right. It's just that they can't do it without the rest of us. Nor should they have to. They deserve—and require—our support.

That's why I've written this book.

Barry Friedman
June 2016

UNWARRANTED

INTRODUCTION:
THE PROBLEMS OF POLICING

AN ANNIVERSARY TO REMEMBER

Charles and Etta Carter celebrated their fortieth wedding anniversary with the Maryland State Patrol.

Charles, sixty-five years old, worked for twenty-nine years at the same retail store. Etta, sixty-four, spent more than twenty-three years as a kindergarten assistant, helping kids with their "reading, writing, and math." Their pride in their only child—who earned her PhD in developmental psychology—was abundant. So when their daughter married, moved into a new house, and started working long hours as a school psychologist, the Carters, ever the loving parents, loaded up a rental van with furniture and drove to Florida to help set up her new home. When they finished the job, they loaded up another rental van full of belongings they would store for the newlyweds, and headed back to their own home, in Philadelphia.[1]

It was just before noon on a hot July day, as the Carters were making their way north, when Corporal Paul Quill of the Maryland State Police pulled them over. He said that Charles—who had a perfect driving record and had made the trip to Florida frequently—was "wobbling" or "weaving." Quill called in a K-9 unit, a drug dog. The elderly couple was ordered to sit on a slippery embankment in the hot sun while the officers unloaded all of their personal belongings from their rental truck onto the roadway. Another officer happened by and was invited to join in. The officers went through everything. They unscrewed panels of the van, took apart a small refrigerator, broke open a brand-new vat of detergent, inspected six boxes of wedding invitations, and opened a sealed bag of peanuts and a box of breakfast cereal. (Quill later described the van as filled with "junk.") One of the officers even rested for a while in a chair the Carters were transporting. They found nothing—because there never was anything to find, and never any reason to believe otherwise.[2]

But that was not the half of it. As the drug dog, Spider, raced about, he relieved himself around the Carters' luggage. The police tossed their daughter's wedding dress on the ground. Had Etta not packed it so well, "it would have been ruined." Etta required frequent bathroom stops, so the Carters carried a portable toilet in the van. After a while, Etta rose to ask permission to relieve herself. She was told that if she stood up again they would both be handcuffed. Forced to wait (unlike Spider), Etta urinated in her clothes and had to sit in them until the ordeal ended. Only her loose blouse spared her further embarrassment when they finally were released and could pull into a rest stop to collect themselves.[3]

In retrospect, no Maryland official could identify any problem with what the police officers had done. The Superintendent of the State Police testified he was not aware of any action the troopers had taken that was inappropriate, or inconsistent with state policy. An Internal Affairs investigation found no wrongdoing. Lieutenant Colonel Ernest Leatherbury, the head of the state patrol's uniformed cops, likewise believed everything that happened was entirely justified.[4]

The lawyer for the State Police, fighting hard for her client when the Carters finally sought redress, was fixated on whether any damage had been done to the Carters' property. But it was not property that got destroyed that July day—it was the Carters' sense of security, faith in the integrity of the law, and confidence in law enforcement. In many sleepless nights and anxious moments afterward, turning the events of that day over and over in their heads, the word the Carters kept coming back to was "humiliated."[5]

THE TIP OF THE POLICING ICEBERG

In his sworn affidavit, Charles Carter said, "It is inconceivable to us that, as American citizens of the late twentieth century, we would be treated in this manner by officers of the law on the day of our fortieth wedding anniversary." But for anyone who has lived through the last few years, it is—unfortunately—not so hard to imagine. To the contrary, it is difficult to miss the fact that something is seriously amiss with policing in the United States.[6]

Policing is just one function of government, and yet it is special. Policing officials are granted remarkable powers. They are allowed to use force on us. And to conduct surveillance of us. This is true not just of *the* police, the folks you see in uniform on patrol, but of all those who work hard every day to keep us safe, from the FBI to the analysts at the NSA.

Possession of these powers—of force and surveillance—is what defines policing, what sets it apart. Officials are granted these powers because policing is vital: Society cannot function in the absence of basic order. But the constant risk we face is that power of this awesome nature will be misused. As it has been.

In June 2013 the nation learned, courtesy of Edward Snowden, that for many years the federal government had surreptitiously gathered up the phone, email, and Internet transaction records of as many Americans as it could. Just two months later, a federal judge found that the NYPD had violated the rights of potentially hundreds of thousands of New Yorkers with its aggressive "stop, question, and frisk" policy. Some eight months later, in April 2014, the Los Angeles County Sheriff's Department made headlines by deciding, without telling anyone until they got caught, to conduct aerial surveillance of an entire city, Compton, California.[7]

Then, in the summer of 2014, the issue of policing exploded in the national consciousness, etched there by the video of one African American after another—often unarmed—dying at the hands of the police. From street protests over the shooting of Michael Brown in Ferguson, Missouri—where the nation also witnessed a highly militarized police force training weapons on the civilian population—to Eric Garner being choked to death by a police officer on a Staten Island street while gasping, "I can't breathe," to a North Charleston officer slaying a fleeing Walter Scott by shooting him in the back repeatedly, to a police officer in Chicago firing at Laquan McDonald sixteen times in fewer seconds, even after he was down, and then officials hiding the truth about it for over a year, it's fair to say the bloom had come off the rose. Scarcely a week would pass without some new revelation of policing gone awry. In a particularly horrific week in July 2016, the nation watched a live stream on Facebook of the aftermath of police shooting an African American man in Minnesota, a cell phone video of another such shooting in Baton Rouge—and then, shocking footage out of Dallas, where a lunatic (claiming retaliation) gunned down five police officers who were guarding a peaceful protest. What for so many years managed to escape unnoticed has now fully captured the country's consciousness. It has spawned popular movements such as Black Lives Matter and Million Hoodies for Justice, congressional hearings, special investigations, town halls all over the country, and a presidential Task Force on 21st Century Policing.[8]

The fact that the misuse of policing power—from the beat cop to the NSA—has been in the news almost nonstop for the last three years suggests something must be done. What may be more difficult to grasp is that all of this is still but the tip of a very large iceberg.

LOOKING BELOW THE SURFACE

Physics tells us that 90 percent of an iceberg is below the water's surface. It's a lot harder to say how much of what goes on with policing is obscured from view. It is difficult to get firm data—or often any data at all. After the shooting in Ferguson, FBI Director James Comey asked his staff a seemingly simple question: "How many people shot by police were African-American?" They could not answer. Despite the country's vast administrative machinery, you can't learn how often police discharge their weapons or how frequently, where, and against whom force is used. Part of the difficulty, to be sure, is antiquated recordkeeping and the sheer volume of the task.[9]

But let's face it: A good deal of the problem is that many officials prefer that policing occur outside the public eye. At every level of government, they have made a fetish of secrecy. When the government gets a court order for cell site records from a telecom company, it usually insists the order be kept secret. The disciplinary records of police officers are often protected from disclosure by special state laws, even though police early intervention systems rely on records of prior instances of abuse to predict future problems. The FBI and police forces nationwide have engaged in a massive conspiracy to cover up the use of Stingray cell phone tracking technology, which scoops up data on countless Americans with no cause. The problem goes all the way to the top. President George W. Bush—discussing national security surveillance—assured the country that "any time you hear the United States Government talking about wiretap, it . . . *requires a court order. Nothing has changed . . . constitutional guarantees are in place when it comes to doing what is necessary to protect our homeland, because we value the Constitution."* That was in 2004. In 2005 the nation learned of the National Security Agency's secret wiretapping program doing just what the president said it was not.[10]

Eight Million Searches a Year . . . and More

Despite the veil of secrecy, state legislation and court decrees have forced police to reveal some small bit of information about what they do, why they do it, and how successful they are. The picture that emerges is not pretty.

In a country of just over 300 million people, a rough analysis suggests state and local police conduct more than 8 million searches annually of pedestrians and automobiles alone. That sizable number doesn't include searches of homes or workplaces, or searches by the federal government.[11]

The number also doesn't include a vast amount of police activity people commonly would call a "search" or "seizure," but that doesn't get labeled that way by the courts. For example, it is a typical practice in some states—like Florida—for officers to board interstate buses to perform drug interdiction. Basically it goes like this: With the passengers seated and ready to depart, sheriff's department officials show up at the door. The driver hops off, the officers climb on, the door is shut. One officer stands in front, hand on his holstered weapon, facing the passengers. Another officer asks passengers to identify their carry-on luggage. All the while, the passengers are forced to sit, waiting. One Florida police officer testified that "during the previous nine months, he, himself, had searched in excess of three thousand bags."[12] Another court record indicated some 78,000 bus passengers had been searched this way.[13]

Courts say incidents like these are not "searches" or "seizures" because people unhappy with these encounters are free to simply disregard the officers and go about their business. In legalese, they say people have "consented" to the intrusion, a notion that is one of the single greatest farces of the law today. People "consent" to being searched by police in such high numbers that even some judges cannot bring themselves to use that word to describe what is happening. Take Los Angeles. In one six-month period in 2006 the LAPD asked 16,228 drivers for consent to search their vehicles: 16,225 said yes, while just 3 said no. Over the same period, 99.9 percent of pedestrians who were stopped consented to searches when asked. People "consent" when they have nothing incriminating on them. They also "consent" when they have trunks full of drugs.[14]

People succumb to these intrusions because they feel they have no choice. One bus interdiction officer conceded that it was "very rare for passengers to decline to be searched" and that "the overwhelming number . . . feel it is their duty to cooperate." When Charles Carter said he was "ordered" out of his car, Maryland's lawyer challenged the description, asking: "[W]hy do you perceive a question . . . 'Would you please step out of the van?'—to be the same as an order?" Carter's reply mirrors what most of us think: "If a policeman is to ask me something or tell me something, that's an order."[15]

The Use of Force

The use of force is arguably the most serious thing the government can do to its citizens. Force is central to policing; it is part of what cops are asked to do, part of the job. But today we have a culture of using force now, asking questions later. High-profile shootings have alerted us all to the issue, but the full extent of the problem sits hidden from our view.

For shootings alone, the numbers are far too high. In 2015, police killed almost one thousand people, 10 percent of whom were unarmed. Take Houston, where on- and off-duty police killed some thirty-two people between 2013 and 2015, including four teenagers. A twenty-six-year-old student wearing a hoodie, who fled from an off-duty cop, was shot and killed. An officer with a prior shooting in his past killed a wheelchair-bound double amputee holding only a pen.[16]

The problem goes well beyond guns, however. Lieutenant John Pike of the University of California Police became an Internet meme after coolly pepper-spraying peaceful protesters at UC Davis. He's hardly alone. *High school* officials regularly pepper-spray students; a lawsuit in Alabama charges the use, on more than three hundred high school students, of a spray designed to cause "severe pain," including "coughing, burning, blindness, [and] skin peeling." Tasers can be a sensible alternative to lethal force; still, hundreds of Taser deaths occur, in part because police use them—against the manufacturer's directions—on pregnant women, the disabled, and people lying in water. A babysitter called South Dakota police because an eight-year-old had a paring knife and supposedly had stabbed herself in the leg (she hadn't); with four officers present, including a training instructor, they fired a Taser into the eight-year-old's chest, the electrical charge throwing her against a wall.[17]

Nothing is so revealing as the frequent use of SWAT raids—*some 50,000 to 80,000 a year* (again, no one can say for sure). Iraq War vet Alex Horton awoke on a Sunday morning to find himself on the muzzle end of the sort of raid he conducted in a war zone, simply because his landlord failed to notify suspicious neighbors that Horton was sleeping in another apartment while his was repaired. Why not investigate before bursting in, Horton asked the shift commander later. The reply? "It's not standard to conduct investigations beforehand because that delays the apprehension of suspects." Responding to a report of a drug deal, a Georgia SWAT team rammed their way into a home, unintentionally tossing a "flash-bang grenade into a playpen" of a baby. There was no suspect there (he was apprehended elsewhere without the use of SWAT). The child has undergone countless operations and is scarred for life. "Is it going to make us more careful in the next one?" the police said to a reporter. "Yes ma'am it is."[18]

Surveillance (and the Double Edge of Technology)
Surveillance, too, has always been essential to police work. But government spying poses an enormous threat to liberty and free expression.

Aided by the same advancing technology that makes it easier for us to communicate with one another, government snooping has become pervasive.

The NSA has been collecting our phone call data for years, invoking national security as justification. However, it emerged in 2013 that, as part of Operation Hemisphere, the Drug Enforcement Administration (DEA) was doing the same, working closely with AT&T to access records for every call made through the AT&T system since as early as 1987.[19]

Today, the government is able to track you through the cell phone in your hand, record your most private thoughts via the computer on your desk, and keep tabs on you from the skies above. Cops can extract the contents of cell phones in minutes, and download them into FBI-managed "kiosks." Government spies use malware to hack and monitor computers, or watch people after secretly activating their webcams. Police forces use aircraft to spy on entire neighborhoods, with cameras able to track individual pedestrians. Pilotless aircraft soon will be omnipresent, from battlefield-tested Predator drones to hummingbird and mosquito drones, which can take a DNA sample without you knowing it. Closed-circuit television cameras and license plate readers are common; the use of facial recognition software is on the rise.[20]

The product of all this surveillance is vast, barely regulated government databases storing records on all of us. The federal government has spent $2 billion to build an NSA data storage facility roughly five times larger than the U.S. Capitol Building. With federal money, state and local police forces have been creating "fusion centers" to collect and merge together existing databases that have our credit history, driver information, real estate information, criminal records (for those who have them), and more.[21]

The Really Crazy Stuff

All this is part of the humdrum, everyday policing; it doesn't even begin to deal with the truly outrageous stuff—much of which flies entirely below the radar. Two professors, conducting a "ride-along" study with the police in the anonymous town of "Middleburg," estimated that some 6–7 illegal searches per 100 residents happen each year. In one case, officers stopped a bicycle rider for no reason whatsoever and threatened to "fuck up his balls" unless he consented to a cavity search.[22]

The invasions of people's bodies are revolting. Officers throughout the country have conducted roadside digital anal and vaginal exams on the thinnest of pretexts. Two twenty-something women were cavity searched with children in the backseat. Another pair of women received the same treatment, the officer not bothering to change gloves between searches; nothing was found. People suspected of being under the influence who could not or would not urinate on demand have been tied to gurneys and forcibly catheterized. One man who would not sit still for catheterization was tased into submission.[23]

People are needlessly humiliated and their lives inappropriately endangered. An NYPD helicopter filming a nighttime, unpermitted group bike ride paused to shoot four minutes of a couple making love on a rooftop. The man involved said he was "usually in favor of surveillance"—it was "more the sensibility that the police think it's O.K. that they do that—it's about their professionalism." Police have taken teenagers caught in possession of drugs and scared them into being informants, only to have them end up dead in grotesque gangland killings. Federal agents obtained a cell phone from a woman complicit in a drug offense and without her knowledge used her photos, including a picture of her in underwear and a photo of her minor son, to create a fake Facebook account to catch other suspects.[24]

One wishes things like this could be attributed solely to bad apples, but incidents like these are all too common.

Policing for Profit

It's important not to lose sight of a troubling motive for much of this conduct, something that is the antithesis of what policing should be about: raising money.

The events in Ferguson brought to the country's attention the extent to which municipalities use police to obtain funds, often from the least well-off. In Ferguson, the U.S. Department of Justice (DOJ) found that "law enforcement practices are shaped by the City's focus on revenue rather than by public safety needs." Missouri's Attorney General has since sued thirteen suburbs, claiming they were raising revenue beyond what state law permitted, by imposing undue traffic fines; Normandy, Missouri, brought in almost 40 percent of its revenue that way. What's happening in Missouri goes on throughout the country.[25]

But municipal fund-raising doesn't hold a hat to the disgrace that the nation's forfeiture laws have become. The original rationale behind forfeiture was that crime would be deterred if the government deprived the bad guys of their ill-gotten gains. So the law allows police forces to grab the goods and keep a share of the proceeds themselves. In the usual criminal case the government must prove guilt beyond a reasonable doubt. With forfeiture the standard is much lower, and the burden generally falls on the victim to get the property back. These laws have been subjected to extraordinary abuse; property has been seized on the thinnest of pretenses, feathering the pockets of law enforcement agencies. A twenty-two-year-old man left Michigan bound for a new career in Los Angeles carrying his life savings of $16,000 in cash; DEA agents took the money away with absolutely no evidence of wrongdoing. The DEA explained, "We don't have to prove that the person is guilty. It's the money that is presumed to be guilty."[26]

Annually, local, state, and federal police seize homes, cars, and millions of dollars in cash, much of it from innocent people. For many, these seizures are debilitating; this isn't extra cash, it's the sole means of transportation, hard-earned wages earmarked for medical procedures, the family home. At the same time departments have spent forfeiture proceeds on a range of remarkable things, including a $90,000 sports car; a quarter of a million dollars in donations to a sheriff's alma mater; $20,000 for campaign ads; football tickets; and liquor and kegs for an employee barbecue.[27]

Who Gets Policed

You may be sitting there thinking, "This isn't about me; I'm not a criminal." Neither were the Carters nor most of the people you've read about thus far. That sort of complacency is a big part of the problem. The way policing is conducted today, everyone is a target, and we should all take it seriously.

Of course, we'd be lying to ourselves if we do not recognize that policing often falls hardest on racial minorities, on the lower classes. Study after careful study confirms this. Perhaps this is the right moment to point out that the Carters were African American. They also were salt-of-the-earth, hardworking people who did not deserve what happened to them. Lieutenant Colonel Leatherbury—the supervisor who defended the actions of the cops in that case (and who was African American himself)—conceded that the racial disparities in traffic stops in Maryland were "glaring." He did not think they were defensible. As FBI Director Comey recently had the courage to say, it's time to face the "hard truths"—pointing to the role that unconscious (and conscious) racial bias has played in policing. If the head of the FBI can acknowledge this publicly, it is time we all do.[28]

While this book is primarily about policing as it applies to all of us, it should be impossible to read the pages that follow and miss the undeniable role race and class play in policing. One chapter is devoted to the problem of racial profiling, and racial issues are omnipresent elsewhere. Still, as my beloved colleague the critical race theorist Derrick Bell, who passed away in 2011, would have said, the best way to tackle racism in policing may well be to understand that the problems of policing can and do affect everyone. What Bell recognized—he called this "interest convergence"—is that many more people get engaged to address a problem if they see how it has an impact on them directly.[29]

It is simply naïve to think the sort of policing described here is something happening to "other" people, that it can't affect you. You don't ride the Greyhound bus, and aren't worried about *those* searches? How about Amtrak? The mathematician Aaron Heuser was taking an Amtrak sleeper from his old position at the National Institutes of Health to a new job. The DEA came by and insisted he allow them to search his compartment. When he would not agree, they forced him to leave the room, certain he was transporting drugs. How did they "know"? (They were wrong.) Because he booked a sleeper car and traveled alone without checking luggage. Isn't that what sleepers are for? When this story was published in *The Atlantic*, numerous other people wrote in to say the same sort of thing had happened to them.[30]

Much of policing today is intentionally indiscriminate: it is aimed at all of us. The NSA's data collection is in "bulk," meaning the agency wants everyone's information. We all are subjected to drunk-driving roadblocks and airport security; our location is recorded by license plate readers as we drive around town. Even when supposedly targeting just the guilty, law enforcement's lack of care ensnares countless innocents. *Millions* of Americans are being subjected to this sort of policing.[31]

The "war on drugs" has accounted for a great deal of aggressive policing, some of it utterly misguided. For example, the DEA's "Operation Pipeline" emboldened state and local police to conduct as many ordinary vehicle stops as possible to try to ferret out drug couriers.[32] Kansas's Operation Pipeline manual is particularly eyebrow-lifting. It tells officers to rely on "high volume traffic stops" to catch those carrying drugs, and explains it "puts excitement into ordinary patrol." Officers are instructed not to "profile" but to look for "indicators" of drug use or transportation, including "luggage," "fast food wrapper[s]," "car phone/pager *everyone has them*" (how the fact that "everyone has them" helps identify traffickers is mystifying), and affixed "disclaimers" such as "police or religious symbols." Officers are told to be watchful for "visual indicators" such as "eyes: *the window to the soul.*" Yet it seems almost anything you do with your eyes signals involvement with drugs: "eyes wide open (bug-eyed)" or "closes eyes *hopes you'll go away.*" There is also "dry mouth," "tugs at ears" or "plays with mustache," and so on. A California legislative report—based on videotape of stops relying on just this sort of amateur psychology—concluded: "It was not uncommon to see travelers spending 30 minutes or more standing on the side of the road, fielding repeated questions about their family members, their occupations, their marital status, their immigration status, their criminal histories and their recreational use of drugs and alcohol."[33]

The war on terror has led to equally unjustified and undiscriminating intrusions. The federal government encourages local officials to file SARs—suspicious activity reports—that get fed into a nationwide database. Among the criteria utilized in Los Angeles are "using binoculars," "taking notes," and "drawing diagrams." An accomplished photographer was stopped for trying to capture a piece of famous public art near Boston; a journalism student was interrogated in New York after taking photographs in front of a Veterans Affairs building, which the police erased.[34]

In countless cases, law enforcement officials subject ordinary citizens to these sorts of personal invasions, based on little or no evidence. In protesting their treatment to those who seemed to think the Maryland State Police had done nothing wrong, the Carters felt compelled to volunteer "to submit to lie detector tests and furnish a legion of character references to attest to [their] reputation." This seems to have the burden of proof rather backward, doesn't it?[35]

POLICING, OUT OF (POPULAR) CONTROL

The question is, what should be done about all of this?

As urgent as that question is, we cannot begin to answer it until we can see the problem clearly. And we do not. Despite all the media attention to the issues described here, all the task forces and government reports, the television talk shows, community forums, and academic gatherings, we remain blind to the central difficulty with policing today.

We don't even think about all these various practices, troubling as they are, as a single phenomenon. Each is a pinprick, an isolated issue, looking for its own solution. Officers involved in shootings of civilians draw attention to racial bias. Drones and cell phone tracking raise questions about individual privacy and technology. The events in Ferguson caused consternation about the militarization of policing. Forfeiture highlights the problem of policing for financial gain. The NSA's activities are considered an entirely different thing altogether.[36]

And yet, if we "connect the dots"—to use a phrase popularized by the 9/11 Commission report regarding intelligence gathering—we can see something fundamental that unites all of this.[37]

It is a complete failure of democratic governance.

Consider this: In California, there is an entire code of regulations for barbers and barbers' colleges. Similarly, the Golden State heavily regulates "Roadside Rest Areas and Vista Points," with precise rules for newspaper dispensing machines. Across the country in Florida, there is an administrative code devoted to (you might have guessed it) the Department of Citrus, which describes the allowable coloration of "Midseason Varieties," and several provisions set out guidelines for distinguishing a Murcott Honey Tangerine from a Sunburst Tangerine or a Tangelo.[38]

In neither of these states, though, is there much on the books about warrantless searches. Most policing happens without a warrant, but neither state legislature has seen fit to give anything but cursory guidance to the police, who are left to decide when and how to thrust themselves into people's lives.[39]

So ask yourself, which is more important: regulating vaginal and anal searches of citizens by the side of the road, or specifying the size of newsstands and classifying Sunburst Tangerines?

To put it plainly, policing in the United States—from the overzealous beat cop all the way to the NSA—is out of control. That's not intended as hyperbole; it's a careful and deliberate statement of fact. And it is assuredly not aimed at the police, who have an incredibly difficult job to do, often without the support they need to do it. The problem is the rest of us.

Call the problem *policing without permission*. We have categorically failed to offer clear guidance to policing agencies as to what they are to do (or refrain from doing). If anything, we've sent mixed messages. We insist that above all we want safety and low crime. But then, when the police do their best to deliver, we start casting blame about the way they went about it. It is we who are at fault, for failing to specify how we wish to be policed, for largely ducking the question altogether.

There is nothing—nothing—more destructive of individual liberty than unbridled executive power, and no greater and more terrifying executive power exists than the power to conduct surveillance and exercise coercive force. The entire history of democratic governance and constitutionalism throughout the world has been one long struggle to devise systems to keep such power in check. That is why, although lumping together the NSA's intelligence gathering and metropolitan forces' stop-and-frisk under the rubric of "policing" may seem to be mixing apples and oranges, it's not. The authority to use force and conduct surveillance is, again, what sets policing apart from the rest of government.

When it comes to policing and its governance, our much-admired system of democratic accountability and transparency is largely cast aside. Policing agencies in this country—from your local police force to the Federal Bureau of Investigation—operate with very little democratic guidance. The typical enabling statute of a policing agency simply authorizes it to enforce the criminal law—but says little or nothing about *how* to do so. We have adopted a few laws on the "how" of policing—such as federal rules governing wiretapping or the occasional state or local regulations of drones or drunk-driving roadblocks—but these form a woefully incomplete framework.[40]

You might think that policing is special, different in some way that justifies this shortcut on democracy. But you'd be wrong. To be sure, there are times—though fewer than you think—when secrecy is essential to policing. To the extent that is the case, policing may demand some special procedures. For the most part, though, the free pass on democratic governance given to policing agencies is habit, not necessity. Some police forces, in places such as Chicago or Seattle, have their manuals readily available to the public on the Internet. And there are even cities, like Los Angeles, where policing policy is set by a board of commissioners with regular public input. Just like the rest of government operates.[41]

Democratic policing can be done; we just don't do it.

HOW WE GOT HERE

It is not entirely an accident that policing today is left largely free from democratic governance. And yet it's not like we planned it that way either. Rather, a series of occasional and not fully thought-out decisions, reacting to historical, social, and technological developments, has resulted in the highly militarized and intrusive Leviathan over which we exercise far too little control.

Until the mid-nineteenth century, we didn't have anything that remotely resembled the organized police forces of today. But soon after the advent of large metropolitan departments, the police became entwined in the sort of municipal graft and corruption that was all too common at the turn of the twentieth century. Cops collected the money that fed the political machine. And so, in order to address that problem, we decided that policing should be separated from politics, and professionalized. Police departments took on their military bearing, and police officers came within the civil service.[42]

By the 1960s, though, the ill effects of disconnecting law enforcement from adequate public control were so glaring that the idea of community policing—about which we hear so much today—was born. As ghettos burned, and civil rights and Vietnam War protesters battled officers on urban streets and university campuses, it became clear that the police were altogether too autonomous, and insufficiently professional. A presidential commission appointed by Lyndon Johnson concluded that what was needed was a closer connection between the police and their local communities. Many agreed. Cops should get out of their patrol cars and walk the beat, get to know the people they served, help them solve problems. And *listen* to the local residents.[43]

But community policing was never entirely popular in cop culture, and was easily displaced. When financial times got tight and police budgets were cut, community policing officers often were the first to go. Nixon declared the war on drugs in the 1970s; law enforcement agencies went into full battle mode during the crack cocaine epidemic of the 1980s. Just as the drug war appeared to be falling out of popular favor, terrorism provided yet another justification for policing agencies maintaining a war footing.[44]

And during all of this—over the last three decades or so—a fundamental shift occurred in how we are policed.

Up until the 1980s, policing was largely reactive. It was about finding the bad guys, and locking them up when you did. It was all pretty familiar, and a lack of democratic governance is a lot less glaring when nothing new or different is happening. Police would conduct searches of people and homes, they would take individuals into custody and question them. Even when things went wrong, it didn't occur to anyone to think an elaborate rule book was needed to try to get them under control.[45]

Today, though, policing is increasingly complex, and proactive in a way that affects all of us, every day. It is about deterring anyone from even thinking about committing a bad act. That means conducting widespread surveillance, and wielding massive force. Which is why closed-circuit television (CCTV) cameras are omnipresent, we snake through airport security lines and wait our turn at drunk-driving roadblocks, and the NSA collects our data in bulk. In the new policing, departments across the country are ramping up to employ automatic license plate readers and facial recognition software—and soon enough drones—to be able to track us everywhere we go. They are utilizing software to predict where crime will occur next, and by whom. It is also why it has become utterly commonplace to see the police dressed in military fatigues, carrying heavy armament. Policing today is *regulatory*: it is about shaping behavior on the front end, not capturing crooks after the fact—and we have all become its targets.[46]

Let's be clear: Some of these policing practices may be altogether appropriate; others may not. The point is that we cannot begin to know the difference—indeed, as a matter of democratic governance there *is* no difference—until the citizenry is given a chance to weigh in.

That is what has gotten lost almost entirely from policing.

THE CONSTITUTION OF POLICING

The lesson here is not simply that policing without popular input is a bad idea—though it certainly is. Rather, I argue that *as a matter of constitutional law*, policing without permission is altogether illegitimate.

For most people, to mention the Constitution and policing in the same breath is to conjure up images of the courts, and judicial enforcement of the Bill of Rights. It is commonly believed that when it comes to the Constitution and policing, the judges are in charge—and should be.

It ought to be evident by now that I believe that common understanding to be a huge mistake.

Our Constitution is about *popular* control of government. The Bill of Rights was an afterthought, ratified four years following the Constitution itself, because some refused to support the original Constitution without a promise to add these additional protections. What is central under our constitutional scheme, what matters most, is the will of the people—as implemented by the officials we elect and appoint.

In three related parts, this book explains how the Constitution (and, for that matter, many state constitutions as well) should be understood to regulate policing.

Part I of this book is about what I call *democratic policing*. I suggest that too much of policing today is misguided because we, the people, have failed to take responsibility for it. Undue secrecy and a lack of democratic regulation have led to the poor use, and misuse, of policing power. And I offer some ways to address this.[47]

Only then, in Part II, will we turn to the Bill of Rights (as well as other amendments to the Constitution that place limitations on policing). And even here, the argument will be that enforcing those rights is not the sole job of courts, which have made a muck of their responsibility. The restrictions on government imposed by the Constitution must be respected by all government officials—under the watchful eye of the citizenry—no matter what courts say is permissible.

Finally, Part III integrates these two aspects of American constitutionalism, popular control and individual rights, explaining how they can help us tackle the great challenges faced by policing in the twenty-first century: technology and terrorism.

WHAT POLICING "ACCOUNTABILITY" SHOULD LOOK LIKE

Despite all the talk about making police "accountable," policing officials would tell you they already are awash in rules and oversight. Increasingly, Inspectors General, civilian complaint boards, and special monitors oversee policing agencies, both local and federal. And of course there are the courts. Judges have written many of the rules that regulate the police—on matters such as search and seizure, or interrogation.

While all these are *forms* of accountability, every one of them suffers from at least one of two serious defects. The goal of the first part of the book, on democratic policing, is to make this clear, and explain how to fix the problem.

First, most of what passes for accountability in policing today is *not* democratic control. There is an altogether appalling lack of transparency; we have far too little information on what the rules of policing even are. In the all-too-rare instances in which policing rules are open to public view, the public's input simply has not been solicited in formulating them. Civilian complaint boards involve at most a minuscule part · of the public, and mostly limit themselves to investigating complaints of police misconduct. Inspector Generals' offices are not democratic bodies at all. Nor are courts, which are supposed to be independent of democratic control. Even the mayors who can hire and fire police chiefs are no substitute for democratically adopted rules about how policing is to take place.

Closely related, most of the oversight in policing today is *after-the-fact* review, when what we need are policies put in place *before* things go wrong. Most oversight is about *mis*conduct, when it is the regular conduct of policing agencies that needs attention as well. That's how the rest of government runs. Yes, when a police officer shoots and kills a civilian, some official body should look into it. And when a group of government officials decide on their own to start collecting information on all our private telephone or Internet communications, there darn sure should be an inquiry.

But what is urgently needed—and is glaringly absent from much of policing—is not reviews but rules: rules that are written *before* officials act, rules that are *public*, rules that are written with *public participation*.

Legislative bodies could write these rules—and undoubtedly should do more of it—but the policing agencies also could do it themselves. Yes, the police. They are, after all, the experts. That is how much of administrative government operates, by having the relevant agency write its own rules. But most agency rules are both public and fashioned with public participation. Which is to say, after the agency drafts a preliminary version of the rules, the public is invited to comment—and then agency officials revise the final rules to take account of what the public has had to say. There is no reason policing agencies should not act in the same way.[48]

CONSTITUTIONAL LIMITATIONS ON POLICING

Of course, under our Constitution—and the constitutions of the states as well—democratic rule is not the end of the matter. Which brings us to the second part of the book, about *constitutional policing*.

Other parts of our federal and state constitutions—typically in a bill of rights—limit what policing officials can do. Chief among these in the federal Constitution is the Fourth Amendment, which governs "searches" and "seizures." Also relevant are the free speech and assembly provisions of the First Amendment, the Due Process Clause (no person "shall be deprived of life, liberty, or property without due process of law"), and the Constitution's fundamental guarantee of equality and against discrimination, the Equal Protection Clause.

In Part II I argue that when it comes to interpreting how the Constitution applies to policing, the courts have made an utter hash of things. They've failed to require warrants when they should, they've watered down the "probable cause" standard in the Fourth Amendment to the point that it fails to serve as an appreciable restraint on who is a proper target of policing and who is not, they've allowed the most blatant invasions of person and property, and they've done little to address pervasive racial profiling. More than anything else, though, the courts simply have failed to come to grips with how policing has changed over the last decades, from a time when policing was reactive and all about catching bad guys, to today's proactive monitoring of all of us in the name of deterring crime. In some ways the courts are stuck back in the halcyon days of *The Andy Griffith Show*, when present-day policing increasingly looks more like the sci-fi thriller *Minority Report*.[49]

And so, in a sense, Part II is a prescription to courts on how to get right the limitations and restraints the Constitution imposes on policing. It is about things like warrants, and probable cause, and racial profiling, stop-and-frisk, drug interdiction, roadblocks, and even airport security.

The limits in the Constitution become all the more important given the first part's argument for more involvement by popular majorities in policing. That is because while democratic governance has its strengths—and is a fundamental requisite under our Constitution—majorities also at times step on minority rights. Indeed, it is fair to ask whether democratic policing will improve things for those minorities—a question tackled in the Conclusion.[50] For now, though, two points should suffice. First, leaving policing in the hands of the police and the courts, rather than insisting on democratic participation, has not worked out so well for minorities as it is. It's time to give democracy a chance, while always remembering that basic constitutional liberties cannot be infringed by majorities.

And second, it's essential to remember that the prescriptions in Part II are not *just* for courts, not by any measure. Enforcing the Constitution is the responsibility of all the branches of government: legislatures and executive officials as well. More to the point, the Framers wrote our state and federal constitutions precisely so that we *all* would understand and be watchful for our liberties. The idea was that when elected officials violated those liberties, the people themselves would serve as a restraint, sounding the alarm and voting those officials out of office.[51]

WHAT WE GET WRONG ABOUT POLICING IN THE TWENTY-FIRST CENTURY

Finally, Part III puts this all together to tackle the twin problems of twenty-first-century policing: technology and terrorism. It explains how we can make headway on seemingly intractable challenges by combining the ideas of democratic and constitutional policing.

Central to the third part of the book is recognizing that we are off base in some of the most basic ways that we discuss the Constitution and policing. Although these themes resonate most strongly in discussions about safeguarding our national security, the truth is they pervade almost every aspect of policing today.

Security over Privacy

It is often assumed that the Fourth Amendment, the primary constitutional provision governing policing, guarantees privacy. One of the big breakthroughs in Fourth Amendment law supposedly happened in the 1960s, when the Supreme Court concluded that your rights didn't depend simply on whether the police happened to trespass on or damage your property. "[T]he Fourth Amendment protects people, not places," the justices said, noting for the first time that what a person "seeks to preserve as private" is worthy of protection as well.[52]

Unfortunately, this focus on privacy has done more harm than good. It leads people to say, as they often do when arguing that police should not be fettered, "I've got nothing to hide." The British government relied on this logic in a campaign to rouse public support for its vast closed-circuit television network. Their slogan: "If you've got nothing to hide, you've got nothing to fear." Or, as Eric Schmidt, the CEO of Google, offered, "If you have something that you don't want anyone to know, then maybe you shouldn't be doing it in the first place."[53]

None of us should feel guilty for wanting privacy. Some argue that privacy simply can't be protected in a world in which we give it all up to Facebook, Instagram, and others. As early as 1999 the then-CEO of Sun Microsystems, Scott McNealy, famously said, "You have zero privacy anyway. Get over it." But polls show that people haven't gotten over it. Majorities of Americans don't want stores and online retailers to monitor their online activity or collect data on them. They want more control over their information. And this instinct is right. Lots of things we do, and want to do, and are entitled to do, still may look maudlin or foolish or embarrassing when made public beyond our intended audience. It's one thing to decide what you want to post on Facebook and another to resist the great personal data grab that is American society. There's no crime in that, and you should not be made to feel like a criminal for wanting to keep your personal life to yourself.[54]

Still, despite what everyone says, the Fourth Amendment is not just about privacy, it's about security. *Read* it. It says, "The right of the people to be *secure* in their persons, houses, papers, and effects, against unreasonable searches and seizures, shall not be violated." To say that forcing you to sit in your own urine, collecting the data on all the phone calls you make, or piling into your home with a heavily armed SWAT team is about "privacy" trivializes what the Constitution is supposed to guard against. It's about your personal security, and your sense of it. Even if we have, as a society, given a lot of our privacy up to Facebook, Google, and their ilk, they aren't going to use the information to come take you away. But the government might. And it is just that sense of personal security that must be kept in mind when regulating policing.[55]

Security v. Security

One of the great dangers of talking about the Fourth Amendment in terms of privacy is that it leads to discussions about whether we should or must trade that privacy for greater security. This sort of talk about a privacy-security or liberty-security tradeoff is common, and yet it is far too simpleminded. Sometimes there *is* a tradeoff, and to the extent this is true then obviously we need to take our security seriously. "The Constitution," as wise judges have observed, "is not a suicide pact." Nor should it be. To insist upon constitutional principles that limit the ability of the government to protect us from serious threats would be sheer folly.[56]

But constitutional rules are not there to hobble us; they were designed to enhance our security by preventing precipitate or foolish action. The Framers were neither stupid nor reckless, and many had risked their lives fighting for independence. They fundamentally understood the value of liberty, and equally well understood the necessity of government's ability to act decisively, out of expedience.[57]

Let's put emergencies aside and consider how the ordinary rules of constitutional law actually aid sensible decisions. Things like separation of powers and checks and balances, judicial review, warrants and probable cause—these are not simply obstacles to getting the job done. They are tools to make sure the job gets done properly. Our constitutional system was designed to slow down intemperate thinking on the notion that most of the time deliberation—public deliberation—would lead to better ideas and results. It is human nature to act rashly at times, and it is particularly understandable with policing, which is mission-oriented and aimed at our greatest threats. That's what these constitutional systems are designed to guard against.

Even in real emergencies, though, constitutional procedures can be enabling rather than crippling. In making this very point, my colleague Stephen Holmes—a political scientist specializing in constitutionalism and national security—tells the gripping story of his daughter's horrific accident, after which she was rushed to the emergency room. She needed blood *fast* and he was eager to see the infusion started. Instead, the emergency room personnel went through an elaborate and time-consuming ritual of reading her name and blood type from her wristband, and comparing it with the donor blood. Then, maddeningly (hurry up!), they switched roles and did it all again. To the uninitiated this looked like a foolish, potentially deadly delay. But these seemingly annoying protocols exist because careful decision-makers had come to realize that more people die from transfusions with the wrong blood type than they do during the delay to get it right. It is precisely in times of emergency that people act rashly, make mistakes, injure people, or even get themselves killed. This is why emergency responders are encumbered by detailed rules and procedures, in which they drill endlessly. In emergencies, preplanned and broadly agreed-upon procedures are more important, not less so. Really protecting our liberty—our security from government—means having rules in place that guide (and, yes, limit) government, so that it does not react badly, or overreact, when things are going wrong.[58]

Efficacy

Finally, one of the strongest arguments for taking the Constitution seriously insofar as it relates to policing is that doing so might actually make us *safer*. This, too, is a point that often gets missed in the usual privacy v. security debates. Does allowing the government to collect all our phone information bolster security? Or is it a hugely costly and time-consuming exercise that seems appealing given modern technology, but actually is of very little value? There are experts—people who, like the rest of us, don't want their families blown to bits—who believe it is the latter. Given the secrecy surrounding policing, it is often hard to assess whether what is being done is working. In the rest of government, we rely on cost-benefit analysis (CBA) to evaluate policy. Yet, as the Vera Institute of Justice, a respected think tank, said in a 2014 report, "Although CBA is a well-established economic method, it has not been widely used in criminal justice."[59]

The question that should concern all of us is *efficacy*. Are those responsible for policing this country doing so in the most effective and efficient way? In a way that is most calculated to keep us safe and secure, while intruding into our liberty no more than necessary? No one expects perfection by the police, but are we even coming close? It is precisely for this reason that we need democratic examination of policing up front, and a set of constitutional rules that work to ensure efficacy, not simply giving police a blank check. A constant theme of what follows is that democratic and constitutional policing may well make us more safe.[60]

FIXING POLICING, TOGETHER

Given the extent of government overreaching—which by now should be plainly apparent, and there is much more to come—and serious questions about the efficacy of these practices, it is time to set aside labels and politics and join together to fix the problem. Powerful voices, usually on opposite sides of the political divide, today are unified in expressing concern about our criminal justice system. This is a healthy sign.[61]

Fixing policing is the responsibility of all of us—*including the police*. One of the most hopeful aspects of the current situation is that increasingly a growing number of thoughtful, dedicated law enforcement personnel are acknowledging the problems and challenges we face. They realize that for policing to work best, it must have the trust of the people. To have that trust, the people must participate in policing decisions. But it is also the case that the people cannot possibly make sensible decisions about policing without respectful and serious conversations with the police themselves.

This, ultimately, is the lesson: It's time we all take responsibility for governing policing. For too long now, we've been cowed by threats (real and imagined) to our safety and security, and beguiled by overwrought assertions of the need for secrecy and flexibility. We've chosen not to be bothered by the grimy task of figuring out where the lines of proper policing rest. By failing to do so, we have jeopardized our liberty and security both. It's time to take the Constitution seriously when it comes to policing—not just as a baseline set of rules for what is and is not allowed, but as a guidebook on the democratic governance of one of society's most vital functions.

PART I

Democratic Policing

Democratic policing is the idea that the people should take responsibility for policing, as they do for the rest of their government, and that policing agencies should be responsive to the people's will. Of course, democracy in the United States does not mean the people make all the decisions all of the time. If that were the case, no one would have time to lead their everyday lives. It means, rather, that our representatives make decisions for us, in an open and transparent way. Those representatives can include policing officials themselves, who have expertise in what needs to be done. But what democratic policing requires, at bottom, is that rules are in place before policing officials take action, that the public has an opportunity to participate in the formulation of those rules, and that the rules are available for all to see.

Applying this familiar model of government to policing poses certain challenges. In part those challenges are historical; we've left policing officials to make decisions on their own for a long time now. Fundamentally changing how we do things is going to be a big shift. All the more so because part of the reason policing is not subjected to close democratic control is that our representatives don't see much profit in writing rules for the police. So we are going to need to find a way to motivate the process of popular participation in the governance of policing. Then, even after we overcome those hurdles, we have to take account of the special nature of policing. Popular governance requires transparency, but policing sometimes needs a certain amount of secrecy. So we have to figure out how to accommodate those competing considerations.

This first part is about how we tackle these challenges in order to achieve democratic policing. Chapter 1 discusses the history of policing and the problem of transparency v. secrecy. Chapter 2 talks about the need for public rules to regulate policing, why legislators don't deliver them, and how policing agencies themselves could. Chapter 3 answers the question many may have, and that needs to be addressed sooner rather than later—why can't the courts just supervise the police? Chapter 4 then explains how judges actually could help spark the process that is needed to democratize policing.

1

POLICING IN SECRET

The public can't participate in setting policing policy if people don't know what is going on. It's as simple as that. If anything should be obvious, it is that transparency is essential to democratic governance. Yet a veil of secrecy has shrouded policing for much of its history. Some of this is necessary, but much of it is habit. If democratic policing is to be a reality, we need to start by sorting out when secrecy is appropriate in policing, and when the veil must drop.

THE SECRET

February 11, 2014, was "The Day We Fight Back." Around the globe, a raft of consumer-friendly Internet companies, like Reddit, Tumblr, and Mozilla, and groups such as the Electronic Frontier Foundation, Human Rights Watch, and Amnesty International, sponsored a loosely knit series of events against mass surveillance. Chicago's event—a march starting at Daley Plaza, in Chicago's Loop, and ending in a dinner at Timothy O'Toole's Pub—was hosted by Restore the Fourth Chicago, "a non-partisan political group of concerned individuals dedicated to restoring our Fourth Amendment rights."[1]

Among those in attendance in Chicago was Freddy Martinez. Martinez, a youthful techie with a degree in physics, had developed a preoccupation with a law enforcement device he'd read about, one that scoops up cell phone transmissions. The device works by tricking cell phones into thinking it is a cell tower. The cell phones then ping it, revealing their unique identity numbers—their IMSI, or international mobile subscriber identity—as well as their locations.[2]

Although it goes by many names—including cell site simulator and IMSI catcher—the device is mostly called a "Stingray." It's one of many brands made for law enforcement by the Harris Corporation, a large defense contractor. Stingrays can even capture content from cell phones—effectively wiretapping them. It is indiscriminate, though: when being used, a Stingray captures the data of all cell phones in the vicinity.[3]

Martinez's interest was part technical and part political. He had come to suspect that the Chicago police were using the device to conduct mass surveillance, and in particular to spy on peaceful protests. He was hardly alone in his suspicion. Now-public documents reveal the Miami police used a Stingray during demonstrations over the proposed Free Trade Area of the Americas. A *Christian Science Monitor* story suggested the same was occurring in Chicago. Martinez had begun to wonder whether, by fighting fire with technology fire, the Stingray could be defeated.[4]

While Martinez was struggling with the technical problem of countering the Stingray, a friend suggested filing a Freedom of Information request. And so he shot off an email to the Chicago Police Department (CPD): "I am seeking records pertaining to the purchase or reception of any IMSI catchers, commonly known as Stingrays (a trademark of Harris Corporation)."[5]

Eventually Martinez, aided by his attorney Matt Topic, sued the City of Chicago for the information. In return they got a handful of IMSI-catcher invoices. As the local CBS affiliate reported, "The Chicago Police Department has finally acknowledged that it had purchased cellphone interceptor devices back in 2008." The story noted that when CBS asked the very same question ten months earlier the CPD had "denied it."[6]

Martinez and Topic filed more requests, trying to get answers to a host of important questions about the use of Stingray devices. What sorts of surveillance were they being used for? Do the police get warrants, or other permission from judges, first? Are judges being told the truth about what devices the police are using? Is the data that is captured stored somewhere? How is that data being used? Who has access to it? Are there protocols governing how and when a Stingray can be used? Has the CPD done any analysis of whether using a Stingray is even constitutional?[7]

It was like pulling teeth. The CPD hired a fancy law firm and quickly spent over $100,000 fighting off the requests. The deflections came shotgun style: No responsive documents exist. If they do exist, they are sealed from public view by court order. In any event, the information is a national security secret that is protected by federal law. Besides, it's a trade secret. And so on.[8]

The CPD's responses raised more questions than they answered. Court records do get sealed away from the public, but then they regularly get unsealed to respond to FOIA requests when the events are over—so why not these records? How is it a trade secret when Harris had filed public patent documents with much of the requested information? Given major constitutional questions about Stingray use, why was there no legal opinion in place?[9]

But the really odd thing was this: while the CPD was playing "I've got a secret" with Martinez and Topic, news about the use of Stingrays by law enforcement was popping up all over the country. Like mushrooms after a downpour. The secret they were struggling to keep was hardly a secret at all.

As details emerged, things got more curious still. The Anaheim Police Department released a letter on Stingrays (basically saying they couldn't say anything). Journalists noticed that Anaheim's letter looked an awful lot like one released in San Diego. And in Gwinnet County, Georgia, too, for that matter. In Martinez's case, the CPD offered up an affidavit of an FBI agent named Morrison about why this all must be kept under wraps. A Google search revealed Morrison was filing similar affidavits throughout the country.[10]

It turns out that for at least a decade the federal government had been subsidizing state and local law enforcement purchases of Stingrays—but with that money came a big catch: law enforcement could not divulge anything about the device. To anyone: to judges, to public officials, in court, under oath, nothing. It was in the contract with the Harris Corporation. And just to make sure matters were clear, the FBI made local law enforcement sign nondisclosure agreements (NDAs) as well. As the story leaked out, it became obvious the FBI was orchestrating a campaign of noninformation.[11]

Policing officials argue that this game of cat-and-mouse makes us safer. They can't answer questions about Stingray use because "much like a jigsaw puzzle, each detail may aid in piecing together other bits of information" on what the government is doing. It would, as the FBI stated in a prepared press release to be used by local law enforcement, "provid[e] criminal elements with the ability to circumvent these devices." Not everyone sees it that way. "It's ridiculous," argues Hanni Fakhoury, an attorney at the Electronic Frontier Foundation. "It's secrecy for the sake of secrecy. It's not actually a public safety issue now."[12]

SECRECY'S COSTS

Stingrays indisputably have a role to play in law enforcement. One St. Louis judge, who does seem troubled by the "broad" way law enforcement is using them today, says they nonetheless are doing "miracle work." He had a case where a Stingray was used to catch a murderer. The FBI claims the technology is used in a variety of contexts: "It's how we find killers, it's how we find kidnappers, it's how we find drug dealers, it's how we find missing children, it's how we find pedophiles."[13]

But like many things in life, the question is whether all this sneaking around is worth the costs. Or even whether the secrecy surrounding the use of Stingrays is necessary. And it is at that level that Freddy Martinez and Matt Topic aren't buying it.

For one thing, Martinez and Topic are leery of how the Stingrays are being deployed, and in particular of whether the police are spying on peaceful, lawful protesters. The Chicago Police Department has a bad history this way. For decades its "Red Squad"—to quote a rather conservative judge—"spied on, infiltrated, and harassed a wide variety of political groups," including those that "were not only lawful . . . but also harmless." Martinez and Topic both worry the CPD is using Stingray technology to build up a database of protesters. "We just don't know," Topic says. "They aren't disclosing any information."[14]

Even if the Stingray is used only for perfectly legitimate criminal cases, Topic and Martinez had plenty of reason to suspect the police were not being straight with judges. To conduct most electronic surveillance, the government needs some sort of a court order—a warrant, even. Given the secrecy provisions in the contract with the Harris Corporation and the FBI's nondisclosure agreement, were cops accurately explaining to judges what they wanted to do? In Charlotte, North Carolina, the judges themselves learned the answer was no after the local media obtained some documents through a FOIA request. It turned out that the Charlotte-Mecklenburg Police Department (CMPD) had had a Stingray since 2006, yet the police didn't even bother to go to court for an order until 2010. Then, when they did go to court—between 2010 and 2014—they didn't come clean with the judges about what they were doing. Court records suggest that a Stingray may have been used in more than five hundred cases, but law enforcement still didn't quite say so. (Since this all became public, the *Charlotte Observer* reported, the CMPD has "revised" its court filings to—these are the CMPD's words—"improve the effectiveness of the process and provide greater transparency.")[15]

Secrecy has threatened to overturn criminal convictions. If judges granted orders without accurate information—or if people were spied on unconstitutionally without any court order at all—then anything the police discovered as a result had to be thrown out at trial. The Charlotte prosecutor has had to go through those five hundred files to ensure nothing in them will require a reversal of a conviction. "That is our fervent hope," said the deputy district attorney. A similar situation confronts prosecutors in Tacoma, Washington.[16]

It is also clear that because of the demand for secrecy, some defendants are getting off easy—or even scot-free. Under the nondisclosure agreements, the FBI has the right to force local prosecutors to drop a case instead of revealing evidence of Stingray usage. The Bureau claims it's never done this, but the evidence is that, acting on those NDAs, cases have been dropped or generous plea bargains given to defendants. In Tallahassee, Florida, a couple of guys toting BB guns stole a cell phone and $130 worth of pot. They were quickly apprehended. When a defense lawyer asked how the heck the police caught their clients so quickly, the witness—a sergeant named Corbitt—claimed it was through a subscription database. Can't be, pointed out the lawyers, it was a prepaid "burner" phone. Under pressure, Corbitt admitted, "We do have specific equipment that allows us to . . . direction find on a handset if necessary." When pressed yet further, he clammed up "[d]ue to a non-disclosure agreement with the FBI." Result: for a crime that carries a minimum of four years in prison, the defendants walked with six months' probation.[17]

Then there's the loss of trust in law enforcement generally. Matt Topic says of the faux-secrecy, "This is something that harms the credibility of law enforcement as they come in asking for the benefit of the doubt on other issues." Some judges have been apoplectic. In Baltimore—where records show a Stingray was used more than four thousand times between 2007 and 2015—a judge threatened the police with contempt if they did not detail the method of tracking cell phones. The prosecutors elected to do without the evidence. Since then, a Maryland appellate court has ruled that police are required to have probable cause and a warrant before they can track a phone with a Stingray. In the Tallahassee case, stymied by the NDA, defense counsel subpoenaed the device. The government argued it was exempt from Florida's open records statute. Judge Frank Sheffield demanded from the bench: "What right does law enforcement have to hide behind the rules and listen in and take people's information like the NSA?"[18]

But beyond all this there is something even more fundamental at risk: democratic governance itself. How can we govern something we don't know about? When shown a copy of the NDA in Florida, Bruce Jacob—the former dean of Florida's Stetson Law School—said, "It reminds me of what happens in totalitarian countries: you don't know what the hell is going on." In a FOIA suit brought by the ACLU in Erie County, New York, the judge referred to the secret agreements to dismiss criminal prosecutions when the FBI snapped its fingers, saying, "If that is not an instruction that affects the public, nothing is."[19]

Concern for democratic accountability, more than anything else, is what drives Martinez and Topic. It turns out Chicago actually has had Stingrays since 2005. Martinez worries that by the time we discuss this, it will be a fait accompli. "We should have had the discussion ten years ago." Topic insists, even if Stingray use is constitutional, "I reject the idea that you can use it without discussion."[20]

Just as Stingrays can play a real role in law enforcement, secrecy has its place too. The committed people who work to keep us safe do, on some occasions, just need us to trust them. To leave them to do their job. The problem, as Matt Topic would say, is where to draw the line.

EARLY DAYS

Because of the muddled history of policing in this country, the question of how much autonomy law enforcement needs may seem tougher than it actually is. We've simply gotten into the bad habit of granting law enforcement more space than it requires.

Our Constitution does an inadequate job of regulating the police in large part because at the time it was written no one anticipated the sort of organized police forces we have today. The issues the Framers had with "policing"—and some were serious enough to be precipitating factors in the American Revolution, and to lead to ratification of the Fourth Amendment—were mostly about taxes and tax collection.

Early Americans didn't like being policed: law enforcement in the eighteenth century was, at best, a loose collection of sheriffs, constables, and night watchmen. They often lacked the most basic tools to do their job, as was evident in the case of the hapless Sheriff Hermanus Schuyler of Albany. A court fined Schuyler twenty pounds for failing to arrest two trespassers, though Schuyler kept trying to explain that the fellows really were quite dangerous. Proving Schuyler's point, court records indicate that the very day the fine was imposed, one of the men was sought for "assaulting and wounding the Sheriff of Albany, Hermanus Schuyler." (Poor Schuyler was then ordered to arrest him for that as well.) The night watch—a civic duty one could buy one's way out of in some jurisdictions—was the butt of many jokes. The *New York Gazette* of 1757 dubbed its watch a "[p]arcel of idle, drunken, vigilant Snorers, who never quelled any nocturnal Tumult in their lives . . . as ready to join in a Burglary as any Thief in Christendom." A half century later, the *Louisiana Gazette* said of the watch, "It is like setting wolves to guard the sheep."[21]

By the mid-1800s, though, civic disorder—or perceptions of it—led Americans to overcome their worries about "absolute police despotism." And so it "became necessary" to create urban forces, as an 1833 report explained, to have "in every large town . . . several intelligent and experienced men devoting their time and skill to the pursuit and arrest of . . . [r]obbers, housebreakers, pickpockets and other felons." The model—only loosely followed here in the United States—was London's police force, which was created in 1829 under the guidance of Sir Robert Peel (hence the name "bobbies").[22]

These early forces, though, were little better than the night watch. Police were given a uniform, a club, handcuffs, and a whistle, and sent out to patrol for crime. (Guns came later.) They were ill-paid, and so it was understandable if they took the chance to slip off for a drink or a little nap. When Theodore Roosevelt became one of the commissioners of the New York police force in 1895, he went out to observe the troops and was startled to find them "in restaurants, asleep, or otherwise away from their posts." One late night, Roosevelt even found an officer "asleep on a butter-tub in the middle of the sidewalk, his snoring loud enough to be heard across the street."[23]

Nineteenth-century cops could be incompetent and brutal both. Philadelphia's first marshal of the city police had to let one-third of the force go only a year into the job, deeming his own troops "worthless, drunken, and totally unfit." Almost twenty-five years later, an 1872 *Philadelphia Ledger* article described a certain type of officer, "the men who upon merest whim, or the slightest show of resistance, fly into a gust of passion, pull out their revolver and make a serious affray out of what might have passed off as an unimportant incident."[24]

THE SEEDS OF UNACCOUNTABILITY

As for how this ragtag bunch became today's militarized, independent, and secretive forces—the die was cast on that roughly one hundred years ago. The trigger was corruption, which ran so deep and stank so bad that eventually it could no longer be ignored—corruption that threatened democratic governance itself.

On May 24, 1875, Inspector Alexander S. "Clubber" Williams retired from the New York police force. On March 25, 1917, he died. Both events occasioned long stories in *The New York Times*, for Inspector Williams was no ordinary officer.[25]

Williams got his nickname for his work on patrol and his "energetic action at popular gatherings." Famously, he said, "There is more law in the end of a policeman's nightstick than in a decision of the Supreme

Court." He was placed into one of New York's toughest precincts; on his first day on the job he tossed two of its biggest troublemakers through plate-glass windows. He didn't like the moniker—he went by Alex, and enjoyed "Czar of the Tenderloin," which is what the obituary called him—but he also defended his record when called "Clubber" by the mayor: "Just ask the Mayor if he can point to a single person I ever clubbed that did not deserve it. He can't name one and he knows it."[26]

When Williams retired from the force, however, he did not do so voluntarily, and clubbing was not the reason for his demise. It was the take. At the time he retired—on a half pension of $1,750 per year— Williams was a wealthy man, with a net worth well beyond the sum of his modest wages. Among his properties was an estate in Connecticut, *avec* yacht. When asked by the Lexow Commission, charged to investigate vice and corruption in New York, how he came by all this, he replied only, "I bought real estate in Japan and it has increased in value."[27]

Williams's path to the Lexow Commission was complex, but if it was paved by any one man, that man was the Reverend Charles Henry Parkhurst. Parkhurst held the pulpit at the Madison Square Presbyterian Church at a time when the Democratic political machine Tammany Hall ruled the city. Parkhurst became the head of the Society for the Prevention of Crime, a group of do-good New York citizens appalled by sprawling vice. At first Parkhurst thought the police were simply not doing enough, and hoped publicity would fix that. But then, it "began to dawn on me" that the police "protect and foster crime and make capital out of it." And that the corruption ran all the way to the top. In a sermon, Parkhurst called the mayor and his staff "a lying, perjuring, rum-soaked and libidinous lot of polluted harpies." The Lexow Commission was appointed when growing indignation—particularly among Republicans—got a bill passed in Albany and funding from private sources.[28]

Once the Lexow Commission got going, it uncovered a level of violence and graft that was breathtaking. Nearly ten thousand pages of transcripts detailed a system of police "blackmail, extortion and corruption." On a regular basis citizens were "abused, clubbed and imprisoned, and even convicted of crime on false testimony by policemen and their accomplices." There were prices, fixed prices, for everything, from police jobs, to keeping open a brothel, to the "protection" money paid by honest business owners. Stolen property was "recovered" at a price set to pay off the pawnbroker and the cops. Owners of houses of prostitution were forced to stay open even when they wanted to close, to feed the yawning maw of the police.[29]

But it was the next thing the Lexow Commission discovered that called for immediate attention: widespread electoral fraud. "[I]n a very large number of the election districts of the city of New York," pronounced the Commission, "almost every conceivable crime against the elective franchise was either committed or permitted *by the police*, invariably in the interest of the dominant Democratic organization of the city of New York, commonly called Tammany Hall."[30]

New York, it turned out, was one cesspool of collusion between the city's machine and its police force. Cops bought their jobs, which they were placed into as a matter of political patronage. They then shook down the citizenry for money that feathered the nests of their superiors and fed back into the political machinery of the city, assuring its continued political domination.[31]

The phenomenon of a police force overly beholden to elected leaders was commonplace in many places in the country, even if Tammany's malfeasance could not be matched. In places not nearly as corrupt, the connection between political leadership and the police was still thought to foster deep ills. August Vollmer, the first police chief of Berkeley, California, was one of the great police reform figures of his time. In a 1917 report, he condemned the "era of incivility, ignorance, brutality and graft," noting that too often "the only requirement necessary for appointment as a policeman was political pull and brute strength."[32]

"PROFESSIONALISM" AND AUTONOMY

If the problem was that the police were corrupt, that they were uncivilized, that they were too close to the politicians, then the answer was clear: separate them from politics. Police forces would become autonomous, and above all else "professional." The independence of a professional police from political control became the fundamental operating assumption regarding policing, one that—despite many reforms since— has proven difficult to shake off. To this day, it's part of the reason we are so reluctant to govern and restrain the police. It's one of the reasons we don't have democratic policing.[33]

For reformers like Vollmer—and his protégé O. W. Wilson, the chief of several major police forces such as Chicago—the point of police professionalism was "scientific" and "efficient" policing. Much of what seems familiar to us today had its start in the early twentieth century. Police began formal recordkeeping, including the Uniform Crime Reports that still are kept. Crime labs were created and forensic technology was taking hold, the most ubiquitous aspect of which today is fingerprinting. Hiring standards for the police—and training once they got on the force— were on the upswing.[34]

Even if this new "professional" model was the right one, getting there wasn't easy. As late as 1931, the National Commission on Law Enforcement and Observance, commonly named the Wickersham Commission after the Attorney General who was its chair, found that corruption pervaded Prohibition-era policing. Police regularly employed the "third degree"—extracting confessions by engaging in practices all too akin to torture. In New York, which supposedly had been rescued by do-gooders, the Wickersham Commission heard reports of "fixed" charges, "shakedown arrests," and a force still all too in the thrall of Tammany.[35]

The cities were practically oases of professional policing compared with what went on in more rural parts of America such as the South or West, where vigilante justice often took on a nauseating form, particularly if the targets were African American. In 1936, in *Brown v. Mississippi*, the Supreme Court took what was then the remarkable step of overturning a state murder conviction. One defendant had been hung twice from a tree. He and others were whipped till their backs were in shreds, escaping further punishment only by confessing. After the war, in 1946, Isaac Woodard's name became a rallying cry for the nascent civil rights movement after South Carolina law enforcement beat him to blindness for displaying insufficient deference to his white bus driver.[36]

Still, by fits and by starts, policing changed. "Professionalism" may not have been exactly the right word for it, conjuring as it does images of highly trained individuals who do their work free of supervision. In truth, police agencies were hierarchical bureaucracies, organized along military lines. Orders came down from above. But Progressive-era innovations such as the civil service allowed the police to break free of partisan politics. Officers could be hired on something approaching merit. When bipartisan police commissions proved an unwieldy way to manage the force, the chiefs themselves were granted substantial autonomy as well.[37]

Gradually, these scientific, educated, efficient—professional—police were cut free from other responsibilities to focus their efforts single-mindedly on crime fighting. In the late nineteenth and early twentieth centuries, the police had been expected to deal not only with criminals, but also with the castoffs of an industrializing society. They performed a variety of social services, including even housing the homeless. But as the nation faced crime waves both real and manufactured—none more gripping than the tommy-gun-laden hijinks of Prohibition—society came to accept that the singular job of the police should be going after the bad guys.[38]

By the 1950s, if any single iconic image captured reform-era policing, it was the shiny squad car, with its two-way radio. Police patrolling their communities on foot was seen as passé. Mobile police would be freed up from their neighborhoods and all their social problems, and turned loose to quell crime and quickly nab offenders. Radio technology allowed a centralized HQ to maintain control, dispatching officers to answer emergency calls. Success could now be captured in measurable statistics: call response times and crime rates.[39]

PROFESSIONALISM'S FAILURE

And then it all went south.

The façade of professional policing crumbled entirely during the turbulent 1960s. Between 1963 and 1968 America's ghettos were set ablaze by riots during a series of "long, hot summers." The Kerner Commission—charged by President Lyndon Johnson to assess what had happened—pointed a sharp finger: It found "deep hostility between police and ghetto communities as a primary cause of the disorders." Police were "not merely the spark": "abrasive relationships between the police and . . . minority groups have been a major and explosive source of grievance, tension and, ultimately, disorder."[40]

The situation on America's campuses was not much prettier; in the face of student protests, police struck out aggressively at the intelligentsia and children of the Establishment. A neoconservative academic described how "thanks to the New York City Police Department, a large part of the Columbia campus had become radicalized" because of police who "simply ran wild," giving the treatment not only to protesters but also to "[t]hose who tried to say they were innocent bystanders or faculty."[41]

The obvious problem with "autonomy," it turned out, was that it left the police free to make their own decisions, many of which were hardly "professional." This was clear in a number of disasters brought to the nation's attention courtesy of television. Viewers watched Southern police in Birmingham and Selma turn fire hoses, whips, and vicious dogs on peaceful protesters, adults and children alike. During the 1968 Democratic Convention, Chicago's police—"professionalized" by O. W. Wilson—used Mace and "unrestrained and indiscriminate police violence" against people, especially reporters and photographers, who had "broken no law, disobeyed no order, made no threat," in conduct an official report decided "only can be called a police riot."[42]

Above all, having set up crime statistics as the metric of success, police failed by their own measure: Crime rates rose at levels that alarmed the public. Fear of crime seemed to skyrocket even faster than crime rates themselves; the subject gripped the nation so firmly it became one of the two defining issues in the presidential election of 1968. (The other issue was the Vietnam War.)[43]

And so, the hunt was on for a new paradigm, some other way to understand and implement policing.

COMMUNITY POLICING

In the midst of all the chaos of the 1960s, "recognizing the urgency of the Nation's crime problem and the depth of ignorance about it," President Johnson appointed another blue-ribbon committee, his Crime Commission, to examine its causes and make recommendations. The report of the President's Commission, *The Challenge of Crime in a Free Society*, was revealing of what professionalism and reform had wrought.[44]

The problem was a lack of trust brought about by police misconduct. "Police agencies cannot preserve the public peace and control crime unless the public participates more fully than it now does in law enforcement," explained the Crime Commission. Yet "[t]here is much distrust of the police, especially among boys and young men, among the people the police often deal with." As a result, "[i]t is common in those neighborhoods for citizens to fail to report crimes or refuse to cooperate with investigations." The Crime Commission was as clear as the Kerner Commission in stating the reason for the distrust: "Commission observers in high-crime neighborhoods . . . have seen instances of unambiguous physical abuse," "[t]hey have heard verbal abuse," they "have seen a certain amount of harassment."[45]

The Commission was firm in insisting that the wounds had to be healed, that the police and the communities had to learn to work together. And while the Commission was clear that "[c]itizen hostility toward the police is every bit as disruptive of peace and order . . . as police indifference to or mistreatment of citizens," still "the duty of taking the initiative clearly devolves on the police, both because they are organized and disciplined and because they are public servants sworn to protect every part of the community." The Commission recommended creating community relations "machinery," especially in minority communities. It also said there should be a "citizens' advisory committee" that is "broadly representative of the community" to "work out solutions to problems of conflict between the police and the community." "It is an urgent duty," the commissioners insisted.[46]

Nothing in the policing world changes quickly, but by the late 1980s progressive forces were embracing the idea of "community policing." Houston's police commissioner Lee P. Brown—the first African American chief of a major city department—set this all out in a 1989 manifesto that was a complete rejection of what the earlier professionalism movement had stood for. Those squad cars buzzing through the metropolis responding to emergency calls, controlled by centralized management—they turned out to be the problem, not the solution. Officers spent their time racing from pillar to post when what they needed to do was get out of their cars, walk the beat, and engage with their communities. They should be "encouraged to initiate creative responses to community problems." Police forces should "recognize the merits of community involvement," and should decentralize authority so that officers can "interact with residents on a routine basis and keep them informed." Brown also advocated "power-sharing," meaning "the community is allowed to participate in the decision-making process."[47]

This vision of community policing got a boost when, in his 1994 State of the Union address, President Bill Clinton vowed to put 100,000 new police officers on the streets. Later that year the Community Oriented Policing Services (COPS) office opened in the Department of Justice. Over the next six years nearly $9 billion was disbursed to state and local government to support community policing efforts. By 1999, the Bureau of Justice Statistics was reporting that fully one quarter of the police were "community policing" officers or their equivalent.[48]

There was a new sheriff in town, and this one was talking a real good game of police-community partnership. Perhaps the wall between the people and the police was about to come down.

THE FAILURE OF COMMUNITY POLICING

Even before Clinton focused national attention and resources on community policing, detractors rushed to call the concept into question. Manhattan's crusty longtime District Attorney, Robert M. Morgenthau, poured cold water on all the optimism about policing's new direction. To the extent "[c]ommunity policing . . . harks back to the halcyon days when an officer was permanently assigned to the same areas so that he came to know its residents and their problems," then—he wrote in an 1990 op-ed piece in *The New York Times*—"[n]o sensible law enforcement official" could disagree. Reforms like these were "long overdue."[49]

But community policing, Morgenthau argued, was asking too much of officers, more than their employers were prepared to train them to handle. "The new patrol cop is to be a municipal ombudsman—a conduit for the services of other city agencies and a catalyst for community self-help efforts." "[F]or this awesome task," Morgenthau proclaimed, "no one can seriously believe that five months at a police academy is adequate training."[50]

Morgenthau was hardly alone in his skepticism. As numerous observers pointed out, community policing was, like beauty, in the eyes of the beholder. It was variously described as "a hodge-podge of unintegrated programs, absent central purpose or theme," and "a buzzword," for which "the variety of activities associated with it seem to have little in common." Community policing programs came to be so amorphous, so all encompassing, that they even included hiring SWAT teams.[51]

To be sure, there was a buzz of activity, some of it admirable and effectual. With that much federal money being tossed around, one certainly hoped so. One strand of community policing, perhaps its most prominent, emphasized problem solving, in which the police would work with the community to address root problems. For example, after lawsuits stopped the Colorado Springs Police Department (CSPD) from simply arresting homeless camp residents, a unit of the CSPD managed to eliminate the camps by leading a network of social service providers to help relocate residents. A remarkable collaboration in Los Angeles reduced gang violence in 2010. Police began athletic leagues; programs like Neighborhood Watch became regular features throughout the country.[52]

But community policing also had a dark side, what came to be known as "order maintenance" policing. In a game-changing article in the March 1982 issue of *The Atlantic* titled "Broken Windows," George Kelling and James Q. Wilson argued that disorder cannot be left alone because it breeds more disorder. "[I]f a window in a building is broken and is left unrepaired, all the rest of the windows will soon be broken." Then, disorder breeds fear of crime, which in turn creates an environment in which crime can prosper—"many residents will think that crime, especially violent crime, is on the rise, and they will modify their behavior accordingly. They will use the streets less often, and when on the streets will stay apart from their fellows, moving with averted eyes, silent lips, and hurried steps." The answer was to go after disorder the moment it showed its face.[53]

As applied, order maintenance policing's aggressive approach served only to worsen police-community relations. In New York City, Mayor Rudy Giuliani brought it front and center, cracking down on turnstile jumpers and squeegee men, but also harassing local residents with the frequent use of stop-and-frisk. Measures like these, across the country, "undermine[d] the legitimacy of the criminal justice system" and bred yet further hostility in communities deeply in need of help from the police. As George Mason's Center for Evidence-Based Crime Policy explained, not only was there a serious debate about whether order maintenance policing reduced crime, "there is the concern that any effectiveness of broken windows policing . . . may come at the expense of reduced citizen satisfaction and damage to citizen perceptions of the legitimacy of police."[54]

Community policing, as people like Lee Brown promoted it, called for deep philosophical change, but most police forces simply did not buy in. In 2008, Wesley Skogan, a Chicagoan and longtime student of policing, wrote "Why Reforms Fail," a lament about the demise of community policing aspirations. "Police," he wrote—echoing conclusions reached by many others—"are skeptical about programs invented by civilians." He attributed this to "police culture": "American policing is dominated by a 'we versus they,' or 'insider versus outsider' orientation that assumes that the academics, politicians, and community activists who plan policing programs cannot possibly understand their job." In short, "[t]hey do not like civilians influencing their operational priorities, or deciding if they are effective."[55]

As a result, the same lack of trust between police and policed communities that caused so much trouble in the 1960s once again reared its head publicly beginning in the summer of 2014, with the shooting of Michael Brown in Ferguson, Missouri. In the face of one "officer-involved" shooting after another, of riots and protests throughout the country, the distrust was plain to see. The country could no longer ignore the fact that policing still retained its "we versus they" perspective, aloof from the community, autonomous if not always professional, and not particularly welcoming to meddling or criticism.

And so, in the wake of the latest national turmoil over policing yet another president appointed yet another committee—the Task Force on 21st Century Policing—to make yet more recommendations. "Given the urgency of the issues," said Barack Obama (perhaps unintentionally echoing Lyndon Johnson), the group would report back in ninety days as to what should be done. Those recommendations were telling. Finding there was still a severe lack of trust between police and the communities they police, the Task Force called on law enforcement "to establish a culture of transparency and accountability to build trust and legitimacy." "[L]aw enforcement," it emphasized, cannot build community trust if it is seen as an occupying force coming from outside to impose control on the community."[56]

SECRECY FOR SECRECY'S SAKE

The problem is there will never be trust and accountability without transparency. Anyone who thinks otherwise is dreaming. To the extent we believe things are being hidden from us, we will not trust. And unless we can know what law enforcement is doing, we cannot govern. Transparency is essential if the people are going to have a say in what the police do.

Yet, despite this basic truth, policing today remains shrouded in secrecy to a degree that is often difficult to comprehend.

In the early days of 2012, the Los Angeles County Sheriff's Department flew a plane over the ten-square-mile city of Compton, California, using a high-resolution camera to record what went on below. For nine days the plane captured video so fine the deputies could see auto accidents, a necklace snatching—and much else. None of the residents knew; even the mayor was kept in the dark. When the surveillance was discovered, a sergeant with the LACSD told a journalist, "This system was kind of kept confidential from everybody in the public. A lot of people have a problem with the eye in the sky, the Big Brother, so in order to mitigate those kinds of complaints we basically kept it pretty hush-hush."[57]

A statement like that—people would be upset, so we kept it secret— would be jaw-dropping if any other public official had said the same. Conor Friedersdorf, writing in *The Atlantic*, declared, "That attitude ought to get a public employee summarily terminated." Imagine the head of the school board saying, "We decided to send the best teachers to a school where we thought kids would benefit the most, but we knew it would bother people so we kept it quiet."[58]

It's not just the secrecy; it's the public prevarication, the outright lying. Cops shade the truth so much in court hearings that there is a colloquial name for it—"testilying." A 1987 study in Chicago found 76 percent of officers said they frequently "bent the facts" to establish probable cause; a 1992 survey of judges and lawyers in the same city estimated that in evidence exclusion cases there is outright perjury by the police 20 percent of the time. It is justified on the grounds that if cops are honest in court about what they did, bad guys will walk. (One cop described such lying as "God's work.") New York's 1994 Mollen Commission termed police perjury "probably the most common form of police corruption facing the criminal justice system." But this very same sort of misrepresentation is also seen at the highest levels—like when the president lied to the country about tapping Americans' overseas calls without a warrant, or when the head of national intelligence lied to Congress about bulk data collection.[59]

It's not just bad cops; it's a culture. When things go wrong in the policing world, the "Blue Wall of Silence" goes up to keep it in the family. In September 2010, a federal judge awarded the victim of a beating by a DEA agent $830,000. She made a point of calling out the police for their treatment of the Kansas City police detective Max Seifert, who labored to fight a cover-up of the incident. Seifert was subsequently drummed out of the force, losing part of his retirement benefits. The judge called the treatment of Seifert "shameful," saying he was "shunned, subjected to gossip . . . and treated as a pariah." A federal grand jury in Chicago fingered a similar "code of silence" in a case involving a drunken off-duty cop who beat a woman bartender for refusing to serve him more. A local reporter covering the case described the "underbelly of a police subculture": "the blue curtain, an understanding between police officers that they should cover for each other unconditionally and that testimony against a fellow cop amounts to a betrayal of their fellow bond." When the Department of Justice was investigating racial profiling along the New Jersey Turnpike, the New Jersey State Police worked hard to keep the data from federal investigators.[60]

But put aside the really ugly stuff and acknowledge that the most basic information about law enforcement, essential to sound oversight, is regularly kept from public view. The Task Force on 21st Century Policing decried the deplorable lack of data available even about the use of force. How can communities be expected to trust when they can't get the facts on how often guns are drawn, shots fired? It has taken reporting by *The Guardian* and *The Washington Post* to shame government into doing a better job of gathering this information. When plaintiffs asked a New York court to turn over New York Police Department stop-and-frisk data, the Department objected this would "give away information about specific policing methods, such as location, frequency of stops, and patterns." The ACLU conducted an analysis of the use of SWAT teams nationally; over half of the policing agencies contacted wouldn't answer. A UCLA law professor reported that when conducting an important study on the extent to which officers are indemnified if they are held liable for misconduct—after all, how can you develop a system of accountability if no one ever pays?—she was startled by the refusal to provide data or describe local policies.[61]

What's happened is an inversion of what should be the ordinary state of public affairs, in which government officials report to the people for whom they work. The noted legal philosopher Jeremy Waldron puts matters bluntly: "In a democracy, the accountable agents of the people owe the people an account of what they have been doing, and a refusal to provide this is simple insolence."[62]

In the 1960s, Kenneth Culp Davis—America's foremost scholar of administrative governance—did an in-depth study of the Chicago Police Department. He concluded that the top officers of the CPD failed to understand that "they are not the proprietors of a private business. They work for the public. In a democratic system, the members of the public—the electorate—are their bosses. And the bosses have a right to know what is going on."[63]

What should be clear by now is that the more things change, the more they remain the same. Speaking of Stingrays, Freddy Martinez and Matt Topic would say that Kenneth Culp Davis's observation is a continuing problem. And they're right. In August 2015, *The Wall Street Journal* reported that law enforcement is using new devices—called "Wolfhounds" and "Jugulars"—that are cheaper than Stingrays but do basically the same thing. Given the difference in technology between Wolfhounds and Stingrays, law enforcement appears to be arguing that no judicial review is needed before deploying these devices. Not that they are saying much publicly. "We can't disclose any legal requirements associated with the use of this equipment," said a Baltimore Police Department spokesperson. "Doing so may disclose how we use it, which in turn interferes with its public-safety purpose." Doesn't this begin to sound awfully familiar?[64]

DRAWING LINES

The police are always going to say what they said about Stingrays—and now Wolfhounds. That they can't answer questions, because explaining things in public will allow criminals to more skillfully evade police detection.[65] Policing, they explain, is like a game of cat and mouse—as the cats get smarter, the mice adapt. The longer police are able to keep their investigative strategies secret, the longer they can maintain the upper hand.

Fair enough—sometimes, at least. But what's important is to make sure we aren't the mice, from whom unnecessary secrets are kept. That's why it is important to draw workable lines.

In reality, the need for secrecy is not nearly as acute as it may seem. When it comes to many of the police tactics that currently escape regulation—from protocols for the deployment of SWAT teams, to what police must do to obtain consent to search, to whether and for what Stingrays are used, there simply is no plausible case for keeping the public in the dark.

The key distinction, the one we should be making, is between the policy that governs policing, and some of its operational details. Operational details—both pertaining to a specific investigation and to investigative techniques that, if revealed, would encourage circumvention—are the sorts of things that ought not to be revealed. Police should not have to announce where they hide listening devices, or the specifics on how they conduct undercover operations. The last thing we would expect, or want to see, on a police department website is the protocol on how active shooter situations will be handled. But whether those tactics are to be used at all—surely that much can and must be made public and be publicly debated without undermining law enforcement.[66]

Take Stingrays. There may be some operational aspects that need to be kept secret. (It would be easier to have a sense of this if the entire matter were not under wraps.) But surely the public has the right—and the responsibility—to participate in answering questions like whether they will be used at all (some jurisdictions and law enforcement agencies have, by court decision or law enforcement policy, banned their warrantless use), whether they may be employed to collect data on protesters, where data is stored and accessible by whom, and whether and when the police need warrants or other court orders to use them.[67]

Most important, there's one clear place the line between secrecy and transparency should *never* rest, and that is with an argument such as the Compton cop made: that people would be mad if we told them what we were up to, maybe make us stop, so we didn't tell them. It should never, ever be an acceptable argument that if people knew what the police were doing, they would keep them from doing it, so the people cannot know.

That, for what it is worth, is precisely what Matt Topic and Freddy Martinez think the Stingray fight is all about. Martinez scoffs at the idea that secrecy is about tipping off the bad guys. "It is not about the techniques, everyone knows the techniques, tapping phones, the tried and true techniques are all public . . . But they are illegitimate and people would say no." Topic concurs: "It is a thin, made-up justification to keep people from debating this stuff, which may lead to curtailing its use." "If we let people know what we are doing, people will argue with what we are doing and then they may limit our using it and jeopardize our national security." "But that," he says, "is just not how we do things in a democracy."[68]

Beginning in June 2014, Senators Patrick Leahy and Charles Grassley—the ranking members of the Senate Judiciary Committee—began asking probing questions of the Attorney General about what was going on with Stingrays. These two, a leading Democrat and Republican, often disagree. But on the necessary transparency of the Stingray policy, they were united.[69]

Since then, the FBI has been doing a slow about-face. First, it declared that its nondisclosure agreements "should not be construed to prevent a law enforcement officer from disclosing to the court or a prosecutor that this technology was used." Never mind that this is the opposite of how those agreements read. Next came a top-to-bottom policy review. Finally, the Department of Justice announced that the Bureau henceforth would obtain court warrants before using the device. (One can only speculate what local forces like Chicago are doing.)[70]

Time and again we'll see this. When there is transparency and disclosure, policy changes. That's how it is supposed to be in a democracy. Trust is built on transparency. And accountability requires it.

This is true even if the decision to limit the police would make us less safe. One can assume in all good faith that the police have our best interests at heart. That they believe what they are doing is necessary. They may even be right. But democracy means we get to make these decisions ourselves. Even if they are rotten ones.

Of course, transparency is only the beginning of the story. Transparency is the way we can see what our officials—those who work for us—are doing. But all the transparency in the world is only going to get us so far unless we do something with the information we obtain. What we should do is the subject of the next chapter.

2

LEGISLATURES THAT WON'T LEGISLATE

What makes policing unique—what defines it—is a government monopoly on the use of force and surveillance to enforce the law. When those awesome powers are used incorrectly, and things go wrong, the consequences can be devastating. Given the tragedy that policing can leave in its wake, it is troubling, to say the least, that so much of policing occurs without any clear rules or policies in place, let alone rules that are vetted publicly to make sure they are sensible and meet with popular approval. There's a reason for this serious omission: it proves remarkably difficult to get legislators, who should be doing the job, to write rules for policing.

THE RAID

In late July 2008, Corporal Shawn Scarlata of the Narcotic Enforcement Division Interdiction Squad of the Prince George's (PG) County, Maryland, police received a tip that a FedEx package containing nearly thirty pounds of marijuana had been sent to an address in Berwyn Heights, a small bedroom community just outside Washington, D.C.[1]

Because the package was sent FedEx Ground rather than via overnight air, Scarlata had some time to investigate. He drove by the address, finding a tidy brick home situated on a suburban street corner. He learned from vehicle registration and consumer database records that the house was owned by Trinity Tomsic—the addressee of the package—and a Cheye Calvo. Scarlata got a warrant to search the package once it arrived at FedEx. It did in fact contain drugs.[2]

So it was that on July 29, a SWAT team from the PG County Sheriff's Office mustered at staging grounds near the Tomsic-Calvo residence. The plan was to have a police officer posing as a FedEx driver deliver the package. Once the package was inside, the narcotics team would get another warrant to enter and search the home.[3]

After Scarlata's colleague Sergeant David Martini briefed the SWAT and narcotics teams, a detective attempted to deliver the package. The woman who came to the door explained she had some rambunctious dogs—they jumped against the screen door as this happened—and asked the detective to leave the package on the porch. There it sat for some fifteen minutes, till a man came out with two black Labrador retrievers on leashes.[4]

Conducting surveillance from a nearby vehicle, Martini watched the man walk the dogs up and down the street. Thinking there was something odd about the man's actions—he was looking at a number of the cars on the street—Martini concluded he was engaged in "counter-surveillance." Martini and the man actually made eye contact with each other, at which point Martini waved and said hello. Returning with the dogs, the man picked up the package on the porch and brought it inside the house. Once the package was inside, a judge issued a warrant to enter the residence.[5]

The SWAT team set off decked out in full battle gear—black hoods, protective goggles, Kevlar helmets, bullet-resistant SWAT vests—carrying a battering ram, bullet-resistant body shields, MP5 and M16 submachine guns, and Glock 23 .40-caliber handguns. Corporal Wilbert Yarbrough, Jr., led the five-man team around the back of the house, at which point a middle-aged woman in the kitchen spotted them. Team members screamed "Sheriff's office" and pointed a submachine gun at her. Through the window they could see she was plainly alarmed and appeared to be screaming.[6]

Concluding that they were "compromised" by having been seen by the woman, Yarbrough decided to take his men in through the front door. Despite having been issued a knock-and-announce warrant, which required the officers to knock on the door and give the residents time to answer it, the team's two "breachers" simply burst the door down with the battering ram. Entering, the team immediately spied the woman, who turned out to be Georgia Porter, Tomsic's mother, cooking in the kitchen. (She was making tomato sauce in a frying pan.) Pointing their submachine guns at her, they ordered Porter to the floor. Paralyzed, she failed to follow instructions and was taken to the ground, handcuffed, and physically searched.[7]

Before the men could get to Porter the dogs appeared, barking. The officers said they were showing their teeth and advancing. Yarbrough shot the older dog, Payton, named after legendary running back Walter Payton, twice in the chest. When Payton looked to the officers to still be coming at them, Corporal Edward Sagin shot him through the head. Chase—the younger, more timid Lab—ran off, clearly terrified.[8]

While Sagin was securing Porter in the kitchen, Chase ran back in. Both dog and Sagin were "startled" to see each other; the dog immediately turned tail and ran away. Sagin then heard more shots—Chase had been shot as well, likely while he was fleeing.[9]

Cheye (pronounced "shy") Calvo was upstairs changing into business clothes for an evening meeting when he was startled by the events below. Hearing the police say they were coming upstairs, he shouted "Please don't shoot!" The SWAT team ordered Calvo to walk backward down the stairs with his hands up—not an easy task. Then Calvo, too, was taken to the ground, his hands bound in plastic cuffs behind his back. He was wearing only boxer shorts.[10]

Shortly thereafter, Trinity Tomsic returned home from her job with the Maryland State government as a finance officer. Told what had happened—house raided, husband and mother cuffed, dogs shot and killed—she became hysterical. Although hers was the name on the FedEx package, she was never restrained.[11]

Calvo and Georgia Porter remained bound for two hours while the Drug Interdiction Unit ransacked the entire house seeking evidence of drug dealing. They tracked the dogs' blood all over. Calvo was moved to the kitchen, within sight of one of his dogs' dead bodies. He asked Scarlata to remove the cuffs, saying they'd been set up; no one at his house was responsible for the drugs. Scarlata refused. He deemed Calvo a risk sitting among the kitchen knives—where Scarlata, oddly, had kept him—because he was "emotionally erratic." This was based on the fact that Calvo had expressed anger at his dogs being shot, wept when Animal Control carried the dogs' bodies off, and otherwise tried to reason with the officers. (Martini, on the other hand, testified Calvo was too "calm" for someone who was innocent and had just had his dogs shot.)[12]

There was an exuberant moment when the drug team thought they'd found something; it turned out to be $68 in cash in an envelope marked "yard sale."[13]

Scarlata eventually concluded there was a good chance no one at the house was guilty of anything. This was not so crazy. PG County officers, including both Sagin and Martini, were well aware that drug dealers were mailing parcels to innocent people—sometimes fake addressees, sometimes real ones—and then grabbing the packages off the porches before they were picked up.[14]

And so the police traipsed out, leaving Calvo and Tomsic to deal with their shattered home and lives. They did their best to restore order, mopping the dogs' blood, replacing belongings strewn throughout. The front door had been knocked off its hinges; the couple spent the night on an air mattress downstairs, worried that a drug dealer might show up for the marijuana. The police neither apologized nor offered to help.[15]

A couple days later, Scarlata arrested the FedEx contract driver— two of them, actually—for delivering more than four hundred pounds of marijuana in two separate drug-dealing conspiracies. Neither was ever charged; they "cooperated" and helped the police track down the people actually dealing the drugs.[16]

Despite the arrest of the FedEx driver who would have delivered the parcel to the Tomsic-Calvo residence, Maryland state officials were slow to clear Calvo's name. They told the media that he and his family were "persons of interest." PG County Police Chief Melvin High, who came under fire for the raid, justified it thus: "In some quarters this has been viewed as a flawed police operation . . . which it is not. This is about an address; this was about a name on a package."[17]

"JUST DOING THE ORDINARY"

And there the matter would have rested, as it does with so many SWAT raids gone bad, were it not for one other fact the police learned while

Calvo was subdued in handcuffs and boxer shorts: he was the mayor of Berwyn Heights. Scarlata said it didn't matter, he would not have done anything differently if he had known; plenty of politicians, he said, are corrupted by drugs.[18]

It turned out it did matter, though, because Calvo had both the need and the means to do something about it. Calvo's an earnest, tall, good-looking guy with a wry sense of humor. And by his own account, he's a policy wonk. In addition to being Berwyn Heights's mayor, a part-time job he does for one hundred and fifty bucks a month, he's worked full-time for years on government and policy issues. As the police continued to refuse to concede his innocence, Calvo decided early on that he had to get on top of the story. And Trinity and Cheye found that to move on with their lives they needed to understand why their beloved pets were murdered and the serenity of their home invaded by heavily armed men who happened to work for the government. So policy wonk Calvo, who to this point didn't have much knowledge about SWAT practices, set about understanding.[19]

What Calvo learned was that, much to his surprise, there was nothing special about him—the sort of thing that he and Trinity and her mother, Georgia, experienced was all too common, routine even. Lying on the floor at the bottom of the stairs, in the early moments of chaos, Calvo's thought was that there had been some "terrible mistake." But in a speech afterward, to New Hampshire's Liberty Alliance, Calvo explained that he was wrong. "It wasn't a mistake. It was, in fact, business as usual." "They were just doing their jobs . . . They were just doing the ordinary."[20]

In the last few decades, highly militarized SWAT teams have spread like kudzu throughout the United States. SWAT—short for Special Weapons and Tactics—was the brainchild of Daryl Gates, then a commander of the Los Angeles Police Department, and later the LAPD's chief. Faced with urban turmoil in the 1960s, what seemed to him guerrilla warfare, Gates consulted veterans back from Vietnam, and implemented the SWAT concept. For two decades such teams were few, and their mission limited, but then the federal money spigot opened in the 1980s in the war on drugs, and the Department of Defense started giving civilian forces military equipment and training like chocolate bars to the kids of countries they'd invaded. By the mid-2000s, nearly 80 percent of small towns had SWAT teams, and as of the late 1990s, nearly 90 percent of large cities had them. In fact, the reason the PG County Sheriff's team was used was that the PG County Police team already was busy when Scarlata needed them, and so was another local team.[21]

It's hard to justify having a SWAT team if you aren't going to use it, which is why today SWAT raids are as common as breakfast cereal. In the early days SWAT teams were reserved for the exceptional: barricades, hostage takings, hijackings, prison escapes. Now they mobilize as many as 50,000 to 80,000 times a year. They mostly get called out to serve warrants, what the ordinary police used to do. In the entire state of Maryland, 93 percent of SWAT deployments in 2014 were for serving search warrants. It was standard operating procedure in PG County to serve narcotics warrants with a SWAT team. Scarlata testified he did this routine an average of three times a week; the PG County Police Department's SWAT team does more than one mission *a day*. It's good business for the cops, because under current forfeiture laws, the police departments get to keep a chunk of the drug proceeds they rake in. In a recent year, Prince George's County's budget showed at least $2.5 million dollars of drug money.[22]

It stands to reason that when you multiply SWAT teams like this, there's the risk that talent will drop and training will suffer. These guys were not the Navy SEALs. The Prince George's Sheriff's SWAT team had been formed because a bunch of officers lobbied hard for it, plainly finding it more exciting than the work they were doing guarding war memorials and serving eviction notices. Some of them had spent frustrated years stocking inventory or working as security guards before they even got on the force. They were hungry to do something sexier. They attended a two- or three-week "basic SWAT school: [e]ntry, room clearing . . . the range, gas deployment . . . [d]iversionary flash bang," and not a lot beyond that. The briefing for the Tomsic-Calvo mission was all of ten minutes. Corporal Yarbrough, who fired the first two shots into Payton's chest, could not even recite the use-of-force continuum that strictly governs how police are to deal with escalating violence by civilians.[23]

When heavily armed forces are tasked with domestic policing, a military mind-set takes over. Cheye Calvo was not a person walking his dogs, curious why there were unfamiliar cars on his street; he was conducting "counter-surveillance." Georgia Porter was not a woman cooking dinner for her family; she was a "suspect" who had to be "secured." She did not look up from her stove, terrified at the sight of a squadron of armed men racing at her; she "compromised" the team, threatening their "objective." Officer safety is paramount, as perhaps it should be, but so too is the "operation." Testified Sagin: "The team's flow into the house cannot be interrupted by human being or dog . . . If there is a threat, whether it be a dog or a human, the threat has to be taken care of."[24]

It's inevitable that things go wrong and people get hurt. Radley Balko, a journalist, author, and leading expert on militarization of the police, has an online raid map displaying all the SWAT missions gone bad. Law enforcement officers get shot by people believing they are intruders—they even get shot (and killed) by fellow officers. Civilians' lives are shattered. In 1994, Boston's seventy-five-year-old Reverend Accelyne Williams dropped dead when his home was invaded. In 2006, Jerry Agee of Elyria, Ohio, had his door shattered with a battering ram while he was cooking eggs, a mistake that left his girlfriend utterly humiliated. ("She was naked, and they didn't even let her put nothing on," Agee said. "I was mad because I felt like she was being violated.") In 2008, Kristy Cohn of Woodhaven, Michigan, was dragged out of the shower and also forced to stand naked until police saw her engagement photo and realized they were in the wrong place. In January 2011, a SWAT team in Framingham, Massachusetts, killed a sixty-eight-year-old grandfather when an officer's gun accidentally discharged during a raid. Officers had already arrested the suspect they were looking for—outside and without incident—but decided to proceed with the raid anyway. Later in 2011, a veteran of the war in Iraq was shot twenty-two times when he mistook a nighttime SWAT raid for a burglary; the team had conducted several raids that night and ultimately turned up a small bag of marijuana in a different house.[25]

And yet the cops sometimes can be remarkably blasé about the whole thing. Calvo was right: what seems extraordinary, chilling even, to us "civilians" is just business as usual to the police. Scarlata was asked why he didn't conduct more investigation before sending a SWAT team into the Tomsic-Calvo residence, why he didn't even google the name Cheye Calvo. Scarlata's reply: the SWAT invasion *was* his investigation. "In order for me to determine if the recipient of the parcel . . . is involved or not involved," and to "gather evidence . . . in a manner that is safe to the officers . . . that is the technique and tool that I use . . . And I don't know another way that I could have done that without utilizing that tool." When Sagin was questioned about why he shot at the dogs, he explained, "[T]here was no time for me to transition from my submachine gun to using pepper spray." But—Calvo's lawyer followed up—what about Georgia Porter, who was in the line of fire—what was done to protect her? Responded Sagin: "That wasn't an option."[26]

The question we all need to be asking is *why* it's business as usual for government forces, using urban warfare tactics, to be bursting into American homes some fifty thousand times a year. Why are police regularly executing warrants by battering down doors, using diversionary flash-bang grenades, and carrying weaponry well beyond what the job plausibly requires in most instances? What's occurring in large- and small-town America, says Calvo, too often looks like footage from a "war zone," from "Afghanistan or Iraq."[27]

A FAILURE OF OVERSIGHT

There's a reason this is happening, and Cheye Calvo, after all his investigation, was able to put his finger right on it. It wasn't the cops' fault, he decided. As much as he wanted to, he could not hate them or blame them; they were just doing their jobs. Rather, the problem was a complete failure of "leadership," of "oversight."[28]

The mistake we make, Calvo concluded, is that we "rely on the police to oversee themselves." We only get involved after the fact, to "blame someone, or fire someone." Our goal, he suggested, should not be "to get people who do things that are bad"; it should be to "prevent them from doing things that are bad" in the first place. And to do that we need to "challeng[e] the police, not because they are bad people, [but] because we live in a place where government working successfully is based on checks and balances."[29]

In leaving the police "to oversee themselves" we abandon time-honored checks and balances, and thus violate the most bedrock principle of democratic governance. We are given to saying that we have a government of laws, not of men. These words were penned by John Adams, who enshrined them in the Massachusetts Constitution of 1780. While the phrase was catchy, the idea was common. *Common*

Sense, even. In the revolutionary pamphlet by that very name, Thomas Paine explained, "[I]n America, *the law is king.* For as in absolute governments the King is law, so in free countries the law *ought* to be king; and there ought to be no other."[30]

Making the law king, rather than the other way around, means having rules in place—instructions, if you will—telling those who run things what they may and may not do. Consider the familiar slogans of democracy, things like government must rest on the "consent of the governed" or "officials are accountable to the people." These things can't happen without rules—public, democratically approved rules—telling those who police us what is in and what is out.[31]

From matters as mundane as getting a driver's license to more complex ones such as curtailing greenhouse gases, America is governed by rules. Government officials cannot act without reasonably clear legislative authorization. If the legislature delegates power to those officials, they must develop their own rules—rules we can all read and see, comment on and challenge—regarding how they will exercise their power. Absent some unanticipated emergency, the rules must be put in place in advance of action, not offered as post hoc explanations, so that we—and courts—can measure what the officials did against the yardstick of what they were told they could do and what they said they would do. This is what it means to be a government of laws, in which officials are accountable to the people they serve.[32]

Yet ironically, when it comes to policing, we have forsaken this very basic principle. *Ironically,* because policing—the use of force and surveillance to govern society—is the most grave and threatening of all the governmental functions. That much should be clear by now. If the person who issues driver's licenses gets out of line, it is not likely to destroy anyone's life. There's time to correct things. But not so with policing. The use of force and coercion, surveillance and spying, these are serious, serious matters. And yet, of all of government, we have left police agencies, which utilize these weapons on a regular basis, to do as they wish without publicly vetted rules.

Although there are of course some statutes in place, overall there is remarkably little legislative direction for America's policing officials. The typical enabling statute of a policing agency simply authorizes it to enforce the criminal laws on the books in the broadest of terms, saying little or nothing about what methods the police are permitted to use in doing so. Take the FBI. A federal statute creates a Bureau of Investigation within the Department of Justice and authorizes the Attorney General to appoint officers to "detect . . . crimes against the United States." That is pretty much it. The New York City charter tells police to "preserve the public peace, prevent crime, detect and arrest offenders, suppress riots, mobs, and insurrections, disperse unlawful or dangerous assemblages [and] protect the rights of persons and property." That's awfully wide authority, and there's not much additional legislative direction.[33]

What is needed is a thoughtful, thorough set of instructions telling police officers and agents how to exercise their incredibly broad discretion. Discretion's an important and unavoidable part of policing, but it can and should be guided by rules. Can a cop set up a roadblock just anywhere? Or are there guidelines for when and where and how, and a chain of command for approval? Can anyone caught using drugs be flipped and turned into an informant? Or should there be limits on using juveniles, or putting people in harm's way? When should SWAT teams be called out? How should they be trained and equipped?

What happened to Cheye Calvo—especially his two Labradors being shot—happened because of a gaping lack of government rule making. Although the team understood it was "common" for drug dealers to have "aggressive dogs," there were no rules or instructions governing what to do. None of them had received any animal training. When the commander on the scene realized there were dogs present, he improvised, handing Sagin pepper spray. It was not standard issue. When these same guys were busy being regular PG County cops, they carried a variety of nonlethal force, such as pepper spray, batons, Tasers. It was *regulation*. But on the SWAT team there were no regulations, they made their own decisions about what to carry, and nonlethal tools were apparently not high on the list.[34]

Time and again during the depositions in the Calvo case, Cheye Calvo's lawyer asked this question: Were there any "rules, regulations, policies, or general orders" governing what the officers did? His point was: Had anyone authorized what happened? Had anyone thought about it in advance and made rules to ensure things went properly, that people were not injured? And time and again the answer was no. No on the constant deployment of force to serve warrants on civilians; no on the training; no on the preparation to deal with animals; no on the equipment to be used.[35]

WHY THE BUCK GETS PASSED

It's no accident that things are this way. It is not like we just forgot to adopt rules to govern policing. There are structural forces at work that cause us, as a society, to leave the police free to do as they will. At best we tell ourselves the courts are doing the job—though as we will see in the next chapter, they can't and they don't. So the police are left minding their own shop.

Legislatures avoid regulating the police because they don't see any advantage in doing so. Consider matters from the perspective of your ordinary lawmaker. When legislators make laws, they create winners and losers. People who, come reelection time, will be friends or enemies. When deciding what legislative agenda to pursue—and what to leave alone—there is an ongoing calculus of how this is going to play at the polls.[36]

Legislative politics is all about being organized. The people who have something big at stake get together and lobby the legislature, letting them know what they'd like done—and what they'd like left alone. This lobbying process informs lawmakers of just which friends or enemies they are likely to be making if they pass a particular bill. As a consequence, the unorganized multitude sometimes takes it on the chin. That's what people mean when they talk about "special interests" winning out.[37]

When it comes to policing, the most organized interests are the police themselves—and their close cousins, prosecutors. Police unions, in particular, are very powerful. When laws are proposed that affect policing, these groups jump into action. Prosecutors and police officials knock on lawmakers' doors, or testify in legislative hearings. Their goal in lobbying is to be left alone to do their jobs: more power and less regulation. From the mission-driven perspective of police and prosecutors this only makes sense.[38]

On the other hand, the people affected by policing aren't usually as organized—or organized at all. It's no secret that the heaviest burden of aggressive policing falls disproportionately on the shoulders of minorities, on the less well-off. Those folks always struggle in the legislative process. But the problem goes well beyond that. You might think, "What happened to Calvo could happen to any of us." It could. The problem is we don't tend to think about that until after the fact, but by then it is too late.[39]

To the extent most people worry about policing at all, it usually is a generalized concern about being a crime *victim*. For the last fifty years or so—even at times when crime rates were falling—the bugaboo of American politics has been crime and the fear of crime. And so legislators have made their careers and ensured their continued tenure by being "tough on crime," engaging in "zero tolerance," and enacting laws like "three strikes and you're out."[40]

Given societal fear of crime, you can see why lawmakers are reluctant to take steps that tie police hands. No one wants to go into an election with their opponent running ads saying they've been soft on crime.[41] If legislators do something to regulate the police—even in the smallest of ways—and then something goes wrong, they are open to the charge that the latest horrific crime was their fault.[42]

After the raid on his house, Cheye Calvo actually managed to get passed the very mildest form of police regulation; the story of that law is an object lesson in all that is wrong here. Calvo, who had worked with the legislative process throughout his professional life, thought a good starting point would be a law requiring reports on how often SWAT teams mustered. Perhaps if that information were public, SWAT overuse would be kept in check, or the people would respond with some other measures. But it was a struggle getting even this baby step passed; law enforcement fought it tooth and nail. Eric Sterling, the head of the Criminal Justice Policy Foundation, noted that "[i]t took raiding the mayor and killing his dogs and their being completely innocent white people to get relatively minor legislative action . . . and there was [a] very decided knee-jerk law enforcement opposition to it." That law isn't even on the books anymore; it expired in 2014 and was not renewed.[43] Apparently it was just too much for Maryland law enforcement to keep track of how many SWAT raids occur.

Some may shrug off legislative neglect of policing, arguing there is accountability in the system. Many sheriffs stand for election. Mayors or city councils can let their police chief go. The head of the FBI serves at the will of the president. The idea seems to be that if something is wrong with policing, these police officials will lose their jobs.[44]

In truth, though, this sort of electoral accountability only exacerbates the problem. Elected officials are the obvious targets of society's anxiety about crime. If crime rates go up, the voters get angry, and mayors or other elected officials find their jobs in jeopardy. Thus, mayors sensibly take it as their job to hold down crime, and are likely to give the police free rein so long as that is the case.[45]

Rarely—rarely—is it the case that a mayor gets asked to toughen up on the police. In 2013, Bill de Blasio was elected mayor of New York, in an election that was very much about policing, particularly the use of stop-and-frisk on people of color. But how many elections can you think of in which the candidate ran against aggressive policing? Even in New York, it took years of media attention to the practices of the NYPD to get there. And de Blasio, as mayor, still needs the police. A year after his election, the country was treated to television images of ranks of police turning their backs on him, a problem he has had to work hard to remedy.[46]

All of us would prefer to avoid responsibility for what the police do. And most of us can be forgiven for just wanting to go to bed at night knowing our families are safe. For not asking a lot of questions.

The problem is that our elected officials aren't doing the job of supervising the cops either. And while it may be that those officials would rather play the ostrich when it comes to policing issues, it also is completely unacceptable. It violates our most fundamental principles. And it is a large part of the reason for why things go wrong.

POLICE POLICING THE POLICE

There is another solution available: the police could make rules to govern themselves. That, actually, is the primary way that most executive agencies are brought within the rule of law. Legislatures are too busy to write all the rules that government needs to function. So they pass laws telling executive officials in broad strokes what they are supposed to accomplish, and delegate power to those officials to write their own rules.[47]

There would be some real advantages to police writing their own rules. Courts and legislatures often grant law enforcement officials deference based on their expertise; to the extent they possess it, they are in the best position to write rules for themselves. Besides, the police will be more inclined to follow their own rules. As one advocate for police rule-making put it years ago: "The police, organized in a semi-military tradition, work in that tradition's responsiveness to going by the book, which is always less grudging if one has a role in writing the book."[48]

There was one brief moment in this country's history when the idea of police rule-making was fashionable. In the 1950s, amid complaints that policing was not doing its job, the American Bar Foundation—the research arm of the national lawyers' organization, the American Bar Association—set out to study the problem, sending many researchers out into the field. But by the time the researchers were recalled to home base some thirteen weeks later for "clean-up" retraining, it was clear to everyone involved that everything they thought they knew about policing needed to be tossed in the trash. The first night out in the field in Milwaukee, the ABF investigator spent the night with on-duty cops drinking in bars. In Detroit, the investigator saw "police routinely breaking into buildings to obtain evidence or make arrests," as well as "harassing homosexuals" and setting the "whore squad" loose on prostitutes. In Pontiac, Michigan, police officers were observed beating and severely injuring an African American who took pictures of them while bowling, as part of an Urban League effort to identify officers associated with "police brutality."[49]

Participants in the ABF study were surprised—one hardly can understand today how this was news—to learn that as police went about their daily duties, they exercised a tremendous amount of discretion. Contrary to the "top-down" image of professional policing so prominent in that period, it turned out the real rules were made "bottom-up" by patrol officers. This was confirmed in study after study that followed on the ABF project's heels.[50]

Once discovered, the concern about police discretion continued unabated, playing prominently in the 1967 report of President Johnson's Crime Commission, which suggested rule-making as the antidote. The Commission pointed out that "[f]ew legislatures and police administrators have defined in detail how and under what conditions certain police practices are to be used." Thus, "[t]he need for legislative and administrative policies to guide police through the changing world of permissible activity is pressing." The Commission recommended that "[p]olice departments should develop and enunciate polices that give police personnel specific guidance for the common situations requiring exercise of police discretion."[51]

The notion that police forces must operate subject to rules quickly won prominent adherents. Noted academics and judges argued for police rule-making. Lawyers and criminologists at Boston University partnered with the Boston Police Department to draft and implement rules on various investigative procedures; a second group of academics at Arizona State worked with representatives from police departments across the country on still another model rules project. The American Law Institute and the American Bar Association both drafted sets of model rules and principles to guide the police.[52]

Ultimately, though, the rule-making movement fizzled. Part of the reason undoubtedly was that as crime rates continued to climb and the country took a more conservative turn after the Johnson years, arguments for more constraints on policing largely fell on deaf ears. But— for the reasons we've just seen—it turned out that no one was really motivated to govern policing, to insist that police be governed by rules, and to provide the resources necessary to make this happen. And so the problem of vast police discretion persists.[53]

To be clear, the police *do* have rules—one positive result of the rule-making moment is that police certainly have more than they did in the 1960s—but still it is not the comprehensive set of rules they should have. Police officials govern their forces with internal rule manuals, standard operating procedures, or what are called General Orders. Unfortunately, the whole process is pretty haphazard. Depending on what jurisdiction you're in, there may be protocols on the use of force, on the storage and disposition of confiscated property, even on strip searches of arrestees—but then little or nothing on informants, consent searches, SWAT teams, or drones.[54]

It is not like each police force, from Podunk, Indiana, to Keokuck, Iowa, would have to write its own rule book. That would be an impossible burden on the more than 15,000 police forces in the United States, many with twenty-five officers or fewer. When legislatures come to passing statutes they often copy one another, or begin with model statutes drafted by reputable bodies such as the American Law Institute or the National Conference of Commissioners on Uniform State Laws. They then tailor those model laws to meet their own local needs. In the world of policing, there are similar policy-writing entities. While the rules drafted in the 1960s and 1970s are hopelessly out of date—

and, to be honest, were often not the sort of rules easily implemented by police anyway—there still are model policies available on pressing issues. For example, when the use of drones came into vogue for the police, and became worrisome to communities, the International Association of Police Chiefs issued guidelines for adopting a drone policy, including soliciting community input, banning drones armed with any weaponry, and urging that images recorded by drones either be erased or made available for public scrutiny.[55]

Unfortunately, though, even when model rules are readily available, police often fail to adopt them because—again—there's nothing making this happen. Take Tasers. In 2004, two Seattle police officers stopped Malaika Brooks for going twelve miles over the speed limit in a school zone. They wrote her a ticket, but she refused to sign it. Signing didn't admit to anything except that she had received the ticket, but Brooks was either confused or just plain obstinate. She was also seven months pregnant, a fact of which she informed the officers when they decided to arrest her. After Brooks refused to get out of her car, and after they failed at physically removing her, the officers then actually had a side conversation about where best to use a Taser on a pregnant woman. Fortunately, they figured out the answer was not her stomach—so they shocked her on the leg and neck until she fell from the car, immobile. Much litigation ensued. All this could have been avoided: The Police Executive Research Forum, working in conjunction with the U.S. Department of Justice, has since drafted model Taser guidelines. Under those guidelines Brooks, pregnant and a passive resister, would not have been tased at all. But no one was compelling Seattle's police to adopt a policy on the subject.[56]

THE WILL OF THE PEOPLE

Even when police forces do have rules, those rules still flunk the basic test of democratic accountability. If the police are deciding for themselves what to do, there is none of what Cheye Calvo referred to as "oversight." We have no idea if what the police do is what the people would choose, given a choice as to how their society is policed.

The FBI is an excellent case in point. As we've seen, Congress has given the Bureau little in the way of formal legislative direction. But the

Attorney General has stepped up, writing rules to govern what FBI agents can and cannot do: the Attorney General's Guidelines for Domestic FBI Operations (AGG). Better yet, acting pursuant to those guidelines, the FBI has promulgated its own extremely detailed (maybe too detailed) rulebook, the Domestic Investigations and Operations Guide, or DIOG. And to its credit, even though the FBI has blacked out big portions of those rules, for the most part the DIOG itself is public. You can find it on the Internet.[57]

Just because you can read chunks of the rules governing the FBI, however, doesn't mean that you get any say in what they do. And for that very reason, we can't be confident that the FBI is behaving as most Americans think it should. To the contrary, there is plenty of evidence that the FBI's rules would look different in important ways if the public had some say.

Here's one significant example. In 2002—in the aftermath of 9/11 and as the United States was contemplating foreign military action in Iraq—an FBI agent attended an antiwar rally hosted by the Thomas Merton Center, "Pittsburgh's Peace and Social Justice Center." On his return he wrote a memo to his supervisor captioned "To report results of Pittsburgh anti-war activity." When the FBI publicly released the memo pursuant to a Freedom of Information Act (FOIA) request, Director Robert Mueller was grilled about it at a congressional hearing. Senator Patrick Leahy, the senior Democrat on the Judiciary Committee, demanded, "What possible business does the F.B.I. have spying on law-abiding citizens simply because they oppose the war in Iraq?" He's right. Isn't this exactly why we have a First Amendment?[58]

Pressed to explain why the FBI was investigating domestic political activity, Director Mueller said the event had been misinterpreted: it was part of an ongoing terrorism inquiry. The agent was present not because of antiwar activity but because the FBI was on the trail of a "person of interest." Mueller told Congress: "We were attempting to identify an individual. The agents were not concerned about the political dissent."[59]

It turned out, though, that Mueller's story was completely bogus. According to the Department of Justice's Inspector General, what happened was that the Special Agent who attended the rally was a new employee who needed work, and the supervisor, noting that the day after Thanksgiving was "one of those slow work days," sent him down there "to see what they were doing." (Which does sound an awful lot like the FBI was investigating an antiwar rally.)[60]

Spying on a domestic peace rally was not bad enough; once the incident became public, FBI officials then fabricated elaborate explanations to cover up their tracks. The richest of them was that the Special Agent was investigating one Farooq Hussaini, who supposedly was a terrorism suspect with ties to the Thomas Merton Center. The Inspector General, however, concluded that those "assertions were not true" and noted that when Hussaini died several years later, Pittsburgh designated a day in his honor because of his contributions to the community. (The IG exonerated the Director completely in the falsehood, but plainly implicated many FBI officials at various levels in a string of conduct that was at best revolting, and perhaps downright illegal. Highlighting the lack of oversight here, we have no clue what, if any, discipline was imposed.)[61]

What's notable about this story for present purposes is that although attending an antiwar rally clearly violated FBI rules at the time, and caused a big stir, under today's rules, it would be perfectly legal. The Attorney General has gone from barring the FBI from investigating lawful demonstrations to welcoming it doing so. This, despite a long history of public disapproval of the FBI spying on domestic political movements. But that is not the half of it. By a wave of his hand—again, without any formal congressional intervention—the Director of the FBI converted the Bureau from a law enforcement agency charged to investigate "discrete matters" to an intelligence agency authorized to gather "critical information needed for broader analytic and intelligence purposes." It is difficult even to understand how such a fundamental shift in mission can occur without formal democratic approval, but that is just the way things go in the policing world.[62]

As a consequence, what required a cover-up by the FBI in 2002 because it was such a flagrant violation of the rules is today perfectly acceptable. The Attorney General's Guidelines now provide that FBI agents are entitled to attend whatever demonstrations or gatherings they wish—even religious services. And they can do it without any sort of factual predicate or suspicion at all. We don't know how common this sort of activity is, but it is definitely happening. Members of an

Orange County, California, mosque contacted the FBI in 2007 to alert the Bureau that an individual had begun attending their mosque and was promoting terrorist plots and trying to recruit others. As a result of his behavior he had been banned from the mosque. How surprised were those mosque members to learn he was an FBI informant, an ex-con the FBI had retained to spy on the mosques, using electronic equipment the FBI provided. The informant was paid at one point as much as $11,000 a month. He'd even been given leave to lure women he met in the community into sexual relationships and record their pillow talk.[63]

If there had been some public lawmaking process, it is not at all clear the Attorney General's most recent guidelines—and the FBI's own rules implementing them—would have been approved. Maybe they would. Public concerns about terrorism often give the government great leeway. But when police officers in the District of Columbia engaged in similar investigations of peaceful protest activity, the City Council condemned the conduct and passed legislation banning it. Similarly, under the DIOG agents may now map "locations of concentrated ethnic communities." At one point, Director Mueller authorized agents to count mosques. When the LAPD announced a public program to do this, people went nuts, and the whole thing went in the trash.[64]

The Attorney General has authorized the FBI to engage in conduct that we can be certain many people find problematic, and that may not at all reflect the popular will. It is that latter factor that is critical, and in general is absent from policing. There's a difference between the police having rules, and having rules of which the public approves.

RULES THAT MAKE SENSE

We don't just need public participation in rule-making so that the rules police follow are consistent with the popular will: participation also helps ensure those rules make sense. One of the great advantages of public vetting is that if there are arguments that government rules are counterproductive—or even harmful—those arguments will emerge and be considered. Indeed, one thing judges do well—when dealing with parts of government other than the police—is to bounce rules that the agencies can't justify on the facts. When other parts of government adopt rules, not only may the public put in its own two cents; if affected individuals think the agency rules aren't rational, they can challenge them in court. Because police rules aren't made publicly—or aren't made at all—this sort of review by judges just doesn't exist.[65]

It is not at all clear, for example, that the new rules governing FBI investigations are making us any safer. Under the old rules, FBI agents needed a factual basis for beginning certain investigations, or engaging in particularly intrusive surveillance. Now, though, many of those investigative tactics don't require any factual predicate whatsoever. The FBI argues it needs to conduct this sort of information collection without any factual basis because "detecting and interrupting criminal activities at their early stages, and preventing crimes from occurring in the first place, is preferable to allowing criminal plots and activities to come to fruition."[66]

It's hard to argue with the idea of uncovering criminal plots before they are brought to fruition—but allowing investigations to proceed with no basis whatsoever may be squandering limited resources when they are needed elsewhere. The FBI, as one commentator pointed out, "vacuums up all the information" it can get its hands on—including from commercial vendors collecting information on us—and then "disseminates the information to other government agencies and retains it indefinitely." That's a lot of information; more than the Bureau or other government agencies can hope to process. Not only do factual predicates such as the Constitution's standard of "probable cause" (a phrase which notably does not appear in the Attorney General's Guidelines for the FBI) protect our rights, they also make sure police don't spend all their time on a wild goose chase, looking under every prayer rug for bad guys who don't exist. Many today argue the government's antiterrorism tactics lack focus, to the detriment of us all.[67]

The problem is that absent public rule-making, the FBI is left free to do as it wishes, and never mind the contrarians—even if the contrarians turn out to be right about what keeps us safe, and what causes us harm. Maybe the FBI is right—but the problem is that the public does not get to weigh in, and simply does not know.

The very same sort of problem is apparent in the multitude of SWAT missions like the one that descended on Trinity Tomsic and Cheye Calvo's house. It's undeniable that the 50,000 to 80,000 SWAT raids a year leave a hurricane's worth of destroyed property and sundered lives in their wake. The question we should be asking—that is asked of virtually every other part of government when it acts—is whether the benefits of this sort of policing justify the costs.[68]

Cost-benefit analysis is—outside the area of policing—one of the primary tools of good government. It is what is used to ensure the public that rules made in their name actually make sense. Yet applying cost-benefit analysis to policing is very much in its infancy. For example, there is no measure whatsoever that counts the costs of police tactics like stop-and-frisk, or consent searches—or SWAT.[69]

Evidence suggests that our frequent use of SWAT teams may well be misguided. The long-standing rule is that before police enter a residence they must knock and give the occupants time to come to the door. Yet SWAT teams, by their nature, obtain and execute "no knock" warrants; surprise entry is their calling card. In Denver, in 1999, 146 no-knock warrants were executed. Of that number, charges were filed in only 49 cases, and only in 2 of them did jail time result. In ordinary felony cases, some 21 percent of defendants end up going to prison; in Denver's no-knock cases, only 4 percent.[70] In other words, it's not obvious that the victims of SWAT raids are even guilty in many of these cases, let alone unusually dangerous.

Experts on policing and the use of SWAT teams offer up a litany of proposals that legislatures should consider to get SWAT use under control: from basic training standards, to special warrants for the use of SWAT teams, to higher intelligence thresholds and better threat matrices before a SWAT team is deployed (too many of these raids happen on bad intelligence from unreliable police snitches; too often the raids are executed at the wrong address). These things aren't crazy: the more advanced police forces use them already. Some within the SWAT community are debating whether to shift toward strategies such as "contain and call-out": muster force and order the residents to come out so they can be dealt with safely outside. Sometimes surprise is important, but how often, really, would suspects not surrender themselves to overwhelming force?[71]

Again, the point here is not certainty about the right answers. It is that because of the lack of public input and debate, and the sort of cost-benefit analysis this often prompts, we don't know what is right. This is precisely the problem Cheye Calvo put his finger on.

Even if there is public rule-making, that doesn't mean the police have to listen to everything the public has to say. When courts review rule-making by other agencies, they defer—as they should—to rules that have a rational basis. But the point is that courts are deferring to a process that is public, and reaches conclusions that make basic sense. In the 1970s, when the District of Columbia police decided to get into the business of writing rules, they sought and incorporated feedback from public defenders and civil liberties lawyers. One author, who did not support requiring the police to gather public feedback, still acknowledged, "Such public access will promote the production of sophisticated, balanced policy positions."[72]

Isn't that exactly what we're after?

NO MATTER HOW, THERE MUST BE
DEMOCRATICALLY ACCOUNTABLE RULES

By its very nature, policing is an intrusive and forceful enterprise. That's what we pay police to do: use their presence, but also surveillance and force when necessary, to deter crime and take violators into custody. This is an extraordinary responsibility. Even when policing goes right, the toll can be devastating. And as we have seen, policing often goes wrong.

It would be inconceivable for any other part of government to exercise this sort of power absent popular input and strict controls. It is an immense failure of democracy that policing is left so ungoverned. Whether adopted by a legislative body, or by policing agencies themselves, what is needed are transparent, democratically accountable rules.

You may be fighting this conclusion. Indeed, you may be engaging in one last dodge, the same dodge the country has engaged in for at least half a century: Isn't supervising the police the job of the courts? Can't we trust the judges to police the police, leaving the rest of us free to focus on other things?

As we are about to see, this idea of courts controlling the police is a fairy tale we tell ourselves to avoid our responsibilities. It is pure fiction. Once that is clear, we will have no more excuses to avoid the serious work of regulating policing ourselves.

3

COURTS THAT CAN'T JUDGE

Many people seem to believe that it is the responsibility of judges to supervise law enforcement. In this view, the Constitution says what the police may and may not do, and the courts interpret the Constitution. As we saw in the prior two chapters, the real explanations for why policing escapes democratic regulation are in part historical (the corruption of policing and politics in the late nineteenth and early twentieth centuries) and in part because politicians just don't want to do the job. But the widespread notion that courts are supervising the police has allowed the rest of us to avoid taking responsibility for policing.

It is time to face the facts. The courts are not up to the task of regulating policing. At best, all courts can do is declare, after the fact, whether what the police did was consistent with the Constitution. They can't (and really shouldn't) write detailed policing policies designed to keep things from going wrong in the first place. And even if they could—and did—write such rules, that still is not the same as *democratic* control of policing. Indeed, the courts are even less democratically accountable than the police themselves.

The courts are acutely aware of their shortcomings—maybe too much so. When it comes to regulating the police, judges are far more likely to roll over than they are to defend your rights. While the rest of us have been imagining that the courts are supervising the police, the judges actually have been letting policing agencies do mostly anything they want. That explains a lot of why we are where we are today.

THE STRIP SEARCH

Clayton County, Georgia, sits just south of Atlanta. On October 31, 1996, Officer Zannie Billingslea of the Clayton County Police was scheduled to teach the antidrug D.A.R.E. program to Tracey Morgan's class of fifth-graders at West Clayton Elementary. As Billingslea arrived, a student reported to Morgan that an envelope of money containing $26 that he had brought in for a field trip had disappeared from the teacher's table. When a search of the classroom failed to produce the money, Morgan, with permission from the assistant principal, turned her attention to the students. She had them empty out their desks, book bags, and pockets—still nothing.[1]

Morgan and Billingslea decided to take the students to the restrooms to search them more thoroughly. In the men's room, Officer Billingslea undid his trousers and dropped them, in a demonstration of what he expected them to do. Then Billingslea "visually inspected the boys' underwear to ensure the envelope was not inside." In the girls' room, "Morgan made them lower their pants and raise their dresses or shirts. Most of the girls were also asked to lift their brassieres and expose their breasts to ensure the envelope was not hidden under their bras." Several of the girls said they were touched in the process. Other students, coming to use the restroom, stopped and watched. Several students said they were threatened with suspension or even jail time unless they complied.[2]

The federal judges who heard the case, *Thomas ex rel. Thomas v. Roberts*, found that the "highly intrusive" searches violated the students' constitutional rights.[3] That much seems obvious. But they also decided they would do nothing to hold anyone responsible for the unlawful searches. The judges concluded that the law was not clear enough to put Billingslea and school officials on notice that schoolchildren could not be strip-searched in this way. There was something more than a little puzzling about that conclusion, given that just four years earlier the very same court, in a quite similar case, had said the same thing: strip searches of schoolchildren violated the Constitution, but the law was too unclear to hold anyone responsible.[4] What, after all, does it take for the law to become clear?

But here's the truly remarkable thing. In February 2012, the very same lawyer who sued Clayton County in the *Thomas* case brought yet another lawsuit involving yet another strip search in yet another Clayton County school—this time of a seventh-grade boy named D.H. Three boys who themselves were strip-searched on accusations of possessing marijuana falsely accused D.H. of having drugs. When the police brought D.H. in and started to search him in front of the other boys, one of the boys admitted they were lying about D.H. The cop responded, "Why didn't you tell me this before we brought him into the office?" but ordered D.H. to take off his clothes anyway. All of them. D.H. "begged to be taken to the restroom for the search," but was forced to do it in front of his accusers, the vice principal, and the police. Nothing was found (of course).[5]

Police and school officials keep strip-searching students in violation of the Constitution because courts cannot bring themselves to impose a penalty upon them for doing so.[6] It's just that simple. The law books are bursting with reports of such searches. Kids from preschool to the twelfth grade get searched. Kids are searched in private, but also in front of other students, teachers, police, and administrators. They are searched for as little as three dollars that has gone missing, and searched because a teacher decides a student is "too well-endowed" and therefore "crotching" drugs. Children are humiliated, and their rights are violated, with no reason. This happens again and again.[7]

In 2011, the Supreme Court had a strip-search case of its own, and it, too, declined to provide any relief, despite finding a clear violation of rights. In that case, *Safford Unified School District v. Redding*, thirteen-year-old Savana Redding was told to unclothe, and then had her bra and underpants examined on the allegation that she had nonnarcotic painkillers. The Supreme Court voted 8–1 that "because there were no reasons to suspect the drugs presented a danger or were concealed in her underwear," the search violated Redding's Fourth Amendment rights. But once again the defendants paid no price, because—even after all these prior cases holding strip searches of schoolchildren unconstitutional—the law supposedly was still not clear enough to let them know they were doing anything wrong. Dissenting, Justice Stevens pointed out, somewhat facetiously, "'It does not require a constitutional scholar to conclude that a nude search of a 13-year-old child is an invasion of constitutional rights of some magnitude.'"[8]

If government officials pay no price for violating the Constitution, those violations will continue. Yet courts cannot bring themselves to do their job and impose these penalties. Indeed, contrary to popular impression, courts find it extremely difficult to regulate policing activity such as surveillance and the use of force at all. To be fair, it is not just that judges lack the will to do the job (though it certainly is partly that). They also realize they are ill suited to it.

Policing the police has fallen on courts because no one else wants to do it. But leaving this job to courts has proven a distinct failure.

THE GOLDEN MOMENT

The common assumption that the courts are responsible for patrolling the police has its roots in one brief historical moment. That moment has come and gone, but apparently endures in the popular mind.

In the 1950s and 1960s, the Supreme Court—headed at the time by Chief Justice Earl Warren—set out to reform state criminal justice systems. In one landmark decision after another, the justices set benchmarks—minimal constitutional rules—that states would have to abide by. There were rulings on search and seizure, on the way police obtained confessions, and on the right to a lawyer for criminal defendants.[9]

There were two reasons the justices took this task upon themselves. First, and most obviously, it was because no one else would do it. Herbert Packer, one of the nation's leading criminal law professors, deemed it "naive or disingenuous" to think the Court could sit by silently when "its hand is the only one raised or raisable."[10]

Second, many of the defendants in the pathbreaking cases were black, and much of the Warren Court's self-assigned mission was to eliminate gross inequality in American society. In the mind of some, the criminal procedure decisions were just one element of a much broader agenda of racial justice.[11]

These two reasons also explain why so much of this criminal justice "revolution" was surprisingly popular. When police complained about having to follow one of these decisions, *The New York Times*'s Anthony Lewis said the decision reflected "a national moral sentiment" that refused "to tolerate police misbehavior." The decision in *Gideon v. Wainwright*, requiring lawyers for criminal defendants, was widely hailed as a matter of evident and simple justice. Even the governor of Florida, where Gideon was an inmate, conceded the point: "In this era of social consciousness, it is unthinkable that an innocent man may be condemned to penal servitude because he is . . . unable to provide counsel for his defense."[12]

But the tide turned against the Supreme Court's effort to reform the police and state criminal justice in the late 1960s. With the ghettos burning and violent offenses on the rise, "crime replaced communism," remarked correspondent Fred Graham, "as the hobgoblin of American politics." "Fear" was the word on everyone's lips. Appointing his Crime Commission to study the matter, Lyndon Johnson said, "Fear haunts . . . too many American communities. It assails us all, no matter where we live, no matter how little we own."[13]

Richard Nixon took advantage of this climate of fear in his campaign of 1968, running against the Court. "[S]ome of our courts and their decisions," he argued, "have gone too far in weakening the peace forces as against the criminal forces in this country." During the election, Congress also went after the Court: the leading visual display at congressional hearings was a graph that charted rising crime rates against the Warren Court's major defendant-protecting decisions.[14]

After Nixon won, the justices began to dismantle and back away from the protections they had afforded us. While Nixon was president numerous vacancies opened up on the Supreme Court, and he filled them with people who had expressed concern about crime rates and the mollycoddling of criminal defendants. The law began to shift, gradually at first, but then faster. And almost always in the direction of leaving the police free to do as they would.[15]

REMEDYING THE CONSTITUTION

When it comes to how the Constitution applies to the police, two things matter. The first is what lawyers call "substantive law," meaning the actual rules. Can police or school officials strip-search children, and under what circumstances? Equally important, though, as the story of the Clayton County schools makes clear, is the second, the "remedy." What happens to the defendants if they have violated someone's rights? In the eyes of many, a right without any remedy is no right at all. What does it matter if strip searches are prohibited if, because there is no penalty, they still continue?[16]

The story of the Supreme Court's failure to regulate the police is as much about the remedies as the rights themselves.

The Constitution doesn't say a word about what happens if the Fourth Amendment is violated, mostly because at the time the amendment was adopted, everyone knew. If someone violated your rights, you sued them—for money. If the conduct was particularly bad, you also could recover punitive damages. Back then they were called "exemplary" damages—meaning they made an "example" of the wrongdoer, warning others not to engage in the same conduct.[17]

The common law could be shockingly unforgiving when government officials violated people's rights, even if they made honest mistakes or if the officials were just following orders—including those of the president himself. Captain George Little, commander of the U.S. frigate *Boston*, learned this the hard way. In 1799, the United States was in the middle of an undeclared naval war with France, and the president had issued a directive to ship captains like Little to seize any ships believed to be United States vessels that were headed to or from a French port. Following orders, Little seized the *Flying Fish*, traveling *from* a French port, and acting very suspiciously. But the president was implementing a congressional law that only allowed seizures of ships traveling *to* French ports that were undeniably United States vessels. The *Flying Fish* turned out to be Danish, so under Congress's rules Little was twice in the wrong. In *Little v. Barreme*, the Supreme Court ordered Little to pay the sum of more than $8,000 (some $170,000 today) for his error. The Chief Justice acknowledged he had agonized over this, but the president's orders "cannot change the nature of the transaction, or legalize an act which without those instructions would have been a plain trespass."[18]

Pretty tough. But also pretty effective if you don't want people's rights violated. Ultimately, Captain Little got Congress to pick up the tab for him; governments then and now often indemnify their officers in this way. Still, indemnification was in those days by no means certain, and in any event *someone* had to pay the freight when rights were violated.[19]

By the middle of the twentieth century, though, for a variety of reasons that remain somewhat unclear to this day, the common law system of remedies was breaking down. The result was that the police were doing as they wished, with impunity—to the point that police would feel comfortable testifying brazenly at a criminal trial that they had kicked open the door to a home without a warrant.[20]

And so the Supreme Court decided to intervene.

ENTER THE EXCLUSIONARY RULE

The case on remedies that made Supreme Court history began in Cleveland, Ohio, on May 23, 1957. Two things were big in Cleveland in those days: the numbers racket and boxing. Their uncomfortable collision found the police breaking and entering the home of Dollree Mapp. Mapp was a unique and determined person. ("[C]unning" and "audacious" was how Sergeant Carl Delau, the lead officer in the operation, described her.) She'd been married to the Cleveland boxing legend Jimmy Bivens; she divorced him for abusiveness, but she still ran in boxing circles.[21]

On May 20, 1957, a bomb exploded at the home of Don "The Kid" King. King would go on to become one of boxing's legendary promoters, but at the time he was deeply involved in Cleveland's numbers (or "policy") racket. Afraid for his life, King called the police, whose investigation led to one Virgil Ogeltree. Three days later, police received an anonymous tip that Ogeltree was staying at a particular address. That was where Dollree Mapp lived with her fifteen-year-old daughter; she rented out the first-floor apartment to boarders. So Sergeant Delau and two other members of Cleveland's notorious "Special Investigations" squad set off to investigate.[22]

When the police showed up at Mapp's house, she was alarmed and called her attorney. He told her not to let the officers in without a warrant. Delau had no warrant, so she didn't. The lawyer rushed over to protect Mapp's rights, but the police wouldn't let him enter either. A few hours and more cops later, Sergeant Delau got tired of waiting and decided to end the standoff. The police pried open a screen and broke a window. When Mapp demanded a warrant, Delau waived a piece of paper in her face. Mapp grabbed it and shoved it down her bosom; Delau went in after it. (Only after much litigation did the government admit there never had been a warrant.)[23]

Because they viewed Mapp as "belligerent" in demanding to see a real warrant, the cops handcuffed her to another officer—and then to the bannister—while they searched her home. They eventually found their man—not in Mapp's house, but in the renter's apartment downstairs. That didn't keep them from tearing Mapp's place apart. Mapp describes the search: "They searched the drawers, the kitchen cabinets, the closets, in the pills—I had some diet pills. I guess they were looking there for some man in the pill package. They went all over."[24]

The next thing Mapp knew, she was on trial herself. In a piece of luggage in Mapp's bedroom the police found numbers paraphernalia and four "lewd" books, including *Memoirs of a Hotel Man*. The luggage was that of a former tenant; Mapp had simply cleared out his stuff, which is why she later was acquitted of possessing the numbers materials in the luggage. Strangely, although the books were in the very same suitcase, she nonetheless was convicted of possessing trashy literature, and sentenced to one to seven in the state reformatory.[25]

The Supreme Court originally took Mapp's case to decide whether Ohio's obscenity law—which didn't require proof that she'd even looked at the stuff—was constitutional. But prompted by a stray paragraph in the brief of the Ohio and American Civil Liberties Unions, the justices decided the time was ripe to answer a long-standing question: whether state courts should have to throw out any evidence that was seized by police in violation of the Constitution. *Memoirs of a Hotel Man* and the other "lewd" books plainly were seized in violation of Mapp's rights; if they were inadmissible into evidence for that reason, Ohio had no case against Mapp.[26]

This rule barring from evidence anything unlawfully seized—called the *exclusionary rule*—had been applied in federal courts since 1914. As the justices explained when adopting the rule, if evidence can be seized in violation of the Fourth Amendment and then entered in court, "the protection of the Fourth Amendment . . . is of no value, and . . . might as well be stricken from the Constitution." Here again is the idea we've seen, that rights without remedies are meaningless. But applying the exclusionary rule to the federal courts was one thing; making all the states follow suit was going to be a big deal. And so even as late as 1949, in a case called *Wolf v. Colorado*, the justices refrained from imposing the exclusionary rule on the states, hoping they would work to adopt their own effective remedies for unlawful search and seizure.[27]

By the time *Mapp v. Ohio* made its way to the Supreme Court, in 1961, the justices had given up on the notion that states were going to take responsibility for reining in their cops. Writing for the Court, Justice Clark said it was now time "to close the only courtroom door remaining open to evidence secured by official lawlessness in flagrant abuse of that basic right." So in *Mapp* the justices imposed the exclusionary rule on the states.[28]

WHAT'S WRONG WITH THE EXCLUSIONARY RULE?

Remedies are difficult to calibrate. If there is no adequate remedy, police and the governments for which they work will violate rights at will. But if the penalty imposed seems too harsh, judges will shy away from applying it. Either of these alternatives speaks poorly to protecting our rights. Indeed, the perceived problems with the exclusionary rule have led judges to approve a lot of bad policing just to avoid imposing it.

People—including some judges—hate the exclusionary rule. Despise it. And it is not difficult to see why. The police catch someone with a carload full of drugs—or worse yet, nab a rapist or murderer—and a judge tosses out the evidence because the police broke a rule, often described in these circumstances as a "technicality." The very fact that otherwise good evidence is being tossed out only goes to show that the defendant is guilty—and yet without that evidence likely will walk.[29]

What people seem to miss, consistently, is that the price they are paying in letting these defendants off is not because of the exclusionary rule—it is the cost of having a Fourth Amendment in the first place. When *Mapp v. Ohio* was decided, police officials were outraged. New York's police commissioner Michael J. Murphy was notably blunt: "I can think of no decision in recent times in the field of law enforcement which had such a dramatic and traumatic effect as this . . . Retraining sessions had to be held from the very top administrators down to each of the thousands of foot patrolmen." But why, after *Mapp*, did the police require *any* police retraining? *Mapp* didn't change the Fourth Amendment, which already bound the state and local police. All *Mapp* held was that the government could not use evidence seized in violation of that amendment. What these outraged officials really were saying was that before *Mapp* they were violating people's rights willy-nilly—and getting away with it without consequence. Commissioner Murphy's Deputy Commissioner Leonard Reisman was candid about this to *The New York Times*, perhaps more so than he meant to be. Describing *Mapp* as a "shock" that required the police to "reorganize our thinking," he said, "Before this, nobody bothered to take out search warrants . . . the feeling was, why bother?"[30]

It's true that the exclusionary rule lets off some bad people, but it's supposed to. As the Supreme Court tells us, it works by "deterrence." The idea is that the threat of depriving society of convictions that everyone agrees should stick will cause the police to clean up their act. Or lead the rest of us to make them do so. If you don't want evidence thrown out, follow the constitutional rules. If the exclusionary rule were taken seriously, and convictions were tossed out regularly when the Constitution was violated, problematic actions and policies would be changed.[31]

There *are* serious problems with the exclusionary rule; they are just different than what bothers most people about it. All these problems emerge from the fact that in exclusionary rule cases, judges see a biased sample. Think of it this way: Cops are out in the world doing what they do. Sometimes it works, sometimes it doesn't. But in an exclusionary rule case the judges see only an instance in which the cops' tactic worked. They got the bad guy. Judges almost never see any of the cases in which the tactic proves ineffective.[32]

The first problem with the biased sample is that because judges don't want to let a bad guy go, they bless what the police did in that case, no matter how out of line it was. Take as an example the 1988 decision in *Murray v. United States*. In that case, officers suspected that the defendants had drugs in a warehouse. So they—as the Supreme Court tells us—"forced entry." Seeing that drugs were indeed there, only then did they do what they should have done beforehand: they went to a judge for a warrant to search the warehouse. The initial entry was an egregious violation of the law and the Constitution, and the evidence should have been tossed out. But the courts didn't: they approved the subsequent search based on the warrant. Faced with the fact that the defendants had 270 bales of marijuana, you can see why the judicial system, especially at the height of the war on drugs, was reluctant to toss all this evidence out and let the defendants walk. But still.[33]

The second problem is worse: once a court approves what the police did in the case, it effectively grants permission to the police to keep using the same tactic in all subsequent cases. Each of these cases is not just one instance of bending over backward to send a bad guy to jail. It serves as a precedent for the next case. The *Murray* decision effectively told cops: Sure, go ahead and peek without a warrant, what the heck. Or, as the dissent pointed out, the Court "emasculates the Warrant Clause and undermines the deterrence function of the exclusionary rule."[34]

What's unsettling is that because judges are ruling in these cases based on a biased sample, they have no clue whatsoever whether the tactic they are blessing really works, or whether police are using it to invade the liberty of countless unknown and unseen people and in this one instance just happened to get lucky. All the judge sees is that it worked to catch this bad guy. As you'll recall from the Introduction, cops often are using these tactics on countless people with little success. When police admit they search fifteen hundred bus passengers per week, and have caught no one in months, that is a whopping lot of people intruded upon for no apparent return. But judges don't see aggregate data like this in most exclusionary rule cases; they just see the one guy who happened to get caught. If they saw how ineffective the tactics were overall, their rulings might differ substantially.[35]

Not only does judicial distaste for the effect of the exclusionary rule lead to bad decisions, it also is leading the Supreme Court to systematically dismantle the exclusionary rule itself. For example, if the police seize evidence illegally but can argue that they would have found it anyway had they not broken the law—as in the *Murray* warehouse case— courts will admit it. And if the police violate the law but can persuade the court it was just a "good faith" mistake, often the evidence they seize will be admitted. In 2011, in *Davis v. United States*, the justices referred to the exclusionary rule as a "bitter pill" that society should swallow only as a "last resort"—and that is certainly the trend of the Court's decisions.[36]

MONEY DAMAGES, AND WHY THEY FAIL

So what about the old-fashioned remedy: sue the cops for money damages? A lot of notable people who purport to care about the underlying constitutional rights—including some prominent judges—argue money damages is a better alternative than the exclusionary rule. By forcing cops, police forces, and governments to pay the victim of errant policing, we will ensure the police don't violate the rules in the first place. And at least now the winner in court can be someone who wasn't guilty of anything.[37]

On paper at least, there is a federal money damages remedy. Around the same time the justices were deciding *Mapp v. Ohio*, they also decided that if state law was an obstacle to the innocent recovering money damages in court, they'd create a way to do this under federal law.[38]

In reality, though, the Supreme Court has made it almost impossible to get these money damages.

One wants to be careful before imposing money damages on cops. It's that familiar problem of calibrating the remedy. On the one hand, if we don't attach meaningful penalties to misconduct, then, as we've seen, the misconduct won't stop. On the other hand, if the penalties are too harsh we will "overdeter" the police—someone will be screaming "help" inside a building and the cops will think, "Gosh, if I run in and a court later decides I should not have, I could lose the family house." We don't want that, either. Like Goldilocks's porridge, when it comes to deterring police misconduct, one wants to get it exactly right.[39]

The Supreme Court has tried to deal with this problem by giving government employees who are bound by the Fourth Amendment (be they cops or school officials) what is called "good faith" immunity—the very thing that has let off the hook all those people who conducted strip searches. If individual officials violate a rule that is "clearly established," then they pay money damages; but if the law was uncertain at the time they acted, then it seems unfair to make them pay.[40]

The problem is that, as we saw in the strip-search cases, the judges' discomfort with punishing the police leads them frequently to claim that the law was not clear enough to award money damages. It turns out that before an official can be held liable there has to be a decision dealing with virtually the exact same facts from an appellate court in the exact same jurisdiction. And even here, courts bend over backward not to hold the cops liable.

Examples of judges' unwillingness to call a spade a spade abound. When Seattle police officers tased pregnant Malaika Brooks three times for refusing to leave her vehicle after a speeding violation, the federal appellate court held that the officers were entitled to good faith immunity because the relevant case law did not establish that "every reasonable official would have understood . . . beyond debate that tasing Brooks in these circumstances constituted excessive force." When an Idaho state trooper suspected Jason Miller of driving under the influence, he had a catheter forcibly inserted into him, with no warrant to back that up. Yet the trooper was not liable because "American search-and-seizure law is undeveloped as to when an officer may administer an involuntary warrantless catheterization on a suspect." When seventeen-year-old Demarius Steen sped away from a Florida police officer on his bike, the officer tased Steen from his moving window. Steen crashed his bike, fell under the tires of the police car, and was killed. Although Steen's death was "tragic and unfortunate," a federal court nonetheless granted the officer immunity because there was no case "stak[ing] out a bright line and holding that it is excessive force for a police officer in a vehicle to tase someone who is fleeing on a bicycle." In a case strikingly similar to the Supreme Court's *Stafford* strip-search decision, Kansas school officials in 2011 responded to a "tip" from a student that another student, a fifteen-year-old tenth-grader, was hiding marijuana in her bra. Against the student's protests, officials touched her breasts, and coerced her to "lift up her shirt and bra away from her body exposing her breasts." No drugs were found. The federal court found that neither *Stafford*, nor other precedent, "clearly establish[ed] this more particularized issue." What does that even mean?[41]

This all seems nuts—right? Now you see the heart of the problem. Courts just can't face holding officers liable, no matter how outrageous the conduct or how clear the law that prohibited it. But cops are only human: if courts are willing to sign off on what they do, then they keep doing it. This is precisely how policing gets out of control.

You'd think that even if the courts are unwilling to stick individual police officers with money damages, they'd be willing to hold the departments responsible—or maybe the state or city itself. In the world of private employment, if your employee runs over me with a truck, you pay. You hired the guy, you gave him the truck, and if you have to pay to make things right, you and all other employers will make sure their employees are more careful in the next case. That is how deterrence works.

Unfortunately, the Supreme Court has largely given the employers of police a free pass as well. The justices have decided that under the Constitution state governments for the most part cannot be forced to pay money damages at all. And before a local government entity—a town or a police force itself—can be held liable, it has to have an official policy in place. Now, there's a Catch-22 if ever one existed. As we've seen time and again, these policies don't exist, which is why the bad stuff keeps happening. But under the Supreme Court's rules, the governments are rewarded for not having policies by not having to pay. (Maybe this is part of the reason we don't have the policing policies we so desperately need.)[42]

INSECURE JUDGES AND UNCLEAR RESTRICTIONS

It may seem at this point like the judges just don't care about our rights, or want to protect the police at any cost. But that's not it—or one hopes that is not it. It is just that the judges find themselves in a very difficult position. Policing is complicated, and judges lack information to know whether their tactics are necessary or not. So, in the name of public safety, and uncertain what is right, they let the cops do as they wish.

The problem is that when judges refuse to say no, the police are left without the regulations they so desperately need. Or that the rest of us need them to have. All of government needs rules to operate, but especially the police. For a paramilitary organization, clear rules—what the law sometimes calls "bright line" rules—are of the utmost importance. Confronted with one difficult emergency situation after another, the police need to know what they can and cannot do.

As it happens, the Supreme Court is happy to fashion clear rules telling the police what they *can* do, but terrified of telling them what they *cannot*. There are all kinds of clear-line rules giving the police leeway to search. When police stop a car they can order everyone out, even if there is no reason to suspect any of them of wrongdoing. If the driver of a car has violated the law—even in the most trivial of ways, such as driving without a seat belt—police may arrest her. When police choose in their discretion to arrest someone—again, no matter how minor the offense—they can search the person's body. When the person is put into a facility, a strip search, including visual cavity search, is always fine. And so on.[43]

When fashioning these "yes" rules, the justices tell us (as is true) that the police need clear rules to know what they are allowed to do. They say things like "A single, familiar standard is essential to guide police officers, who have limited time and expertise to reflect on and balance the social and individual interests involved in the specific circumstances they confront."[44]

But when asked to formulate a rule for what police may *not* do, the justices invariably choke. All of a sudden, clear rules are a problem. The justices tell us what the police did can only be evaluated after the fact, after the harm is done, based on the "totality of all the circumstances." Do police have to tell people they needn't consent to having their person or property searched? No. The facts of each case must be examined to determine "from the totality of all the circumstances" whether consent was voluntary. Are there specific training guidelines or records that must be kept before treating the alert of a drug dog as probable cause to search? No. "We have rejected rigid rules, bright-line tests, and mechanistic inquiries in favor of a more flexible, all-things-considered approach."[45]

The consequence of this failure to adopt clear rules is all around us. Take the so-called consent searches, where as we have seen tens if not hundreds of thousands of people each year agree to be searched. As Justice Stevens said in one case—in which his colleagues refused even to require the police to tell drivers they are free to go before asking them to consent to searches—"Repeated decisions by ordinary citizens to" agree to the searches "cannot be satisfactorily explained on any hypothesis other than an assumption that they believed they had a legal duty to do so."[46]

Ironically, Supreme Court justices seem most unable to say no; their colleagues on the state high courts sometimes do, only to find their decisions restricting the police reversed by the justices. Perhaps the justices' reluctance is understandable: they make law for the entire country in one fell swoop, and plainly are concerned that with their limited knowledge they not handicap the cops. But it is sheer delusion to believe the courts are regulating the police when no one else does. The courts aren't either.[47]

THE NEW WORLD OF POLICING

Whatever capacity the courts once had to regulate police behavior has been seriously undermined by fundamental changes in how policing takes place today. Well into the twentieth century, policing was reactive—the goal was to apprehend people who violated (or were about to violate) the law. But now, aided by technology, policing is increasingly proactive, increasing its reach deep into society, and making it extremely difficult for courts to draw lines about what is permissible and what is not. And so, once again, they mostly say yes.[48]

Policing today often relies on what law professor Christopher Slobogin calls "panvasive" surveillance, by which he means it is aimed at "keeping tabs on the citizenry routinely . . . across huge numbers of people, most of whom are innocent of wrongdoing." Closed-circuit television (CCTV) cameras stare down at us in public spaces, and license plate readers capture us on the roads, while aircraft—and soon drones—patrol the skies. We are stopped at all sorts of roadblocks, from drunk-driving to immigration to license-and-registration checks. "Administrative" searches—by surprise and without cause—are conducted on bars, nightclubs, junkyards, and even barber shops. Our data is collected in bulk by all levels of government and "fused" together to create dossiers on us. The new policing is focused on surveillance and intelligence gathering to a degree unimaginable even a generation ago.[49]

Under reactive catch-the-criminals policing, what the police did was based on suspicion—was there sufficient reason ("probable cause") to think this or that person was up to no good. But under the new policing, because there are no suspects and thus no suspicion, constitutional protections such as probable cause are of no value. Instead, courts have concluded it is their job simply to balance competing values. Courts consider (on the one hand) how much the police tactics intrude upon an individual's privacy. On the other, they assess the degree to which the intrusion helps the government deter or ferret out crime.[50]

Making the tradeoffs of the new policing is a deeply value-laden endeavor. Are drug testing of students or employees, or dog sniffs in public places, bulk data collection, or highway roadblocks worth it to protect public safety, or conduct the war on drugs, or the war on terror? The things being weighed against one another often are "incommensurable"—

apples and oranges. In the law, these types of balancing tests often are derided as notoriously subjective. If values are to be weighed like this, isn't the democratic process better than leaving the decision in the hands of the judges? That sort of thinking is doubly correct when policing is at issue, because there's no reason to think judges have adequate data or can evaluate either side of this balance.[51]

Take the question of how to weigh the intrusiveness of a given police practice, like a dog sniff or a search of one's trash. Professor Christopher Slobogin and a colleague decided to test how much the Supreme Court's intuitions in this regard matched what ordinary people think, by administering a survey to a variety of students and citizens (including, somewhat inexplicably, some Australian students). Many of the Supreme Court's and popular impressions matched—looking in the bushes in a public park is not a big deal, nor is having to go through the metal detector at the airport, while a body cavity search is very serious. Still, on some things that are a familiar part of the new policing, the justices' intuitions are way off from that of the public at large. In a variety of cases, the justices have deemed a dog sniff not even a "search" triggering Fourth Amendment protections. They have called the intrusion of compelled urine tests for drugs "negligible." Yet, on a scale of 1 (not serious) to 100 (serious), the public found being forced to urinate while someone listened to be a 72.49 and even the dog sniff is a 58.33.[52]

As for efficacy—whether these tactics are necessary, or work—as we've seen, judges rarely have sufficient evidence to decide, and so they just favor the government. For example, the justices signed off on the drug testing of all students in Tecumseh, Oklahoma, schools who participated in extracurricular activities. On what evidence? Under federal law, the school district was required to fill out paperwork to get federal drug-free-schools money. That paperwork indicated that between 1994 and 1996 "[l]ess than five percent" of the students said they'd used any illegal drugs, and between 1996 and 1998 "drugs were present but [were] not identified . . . as major problems." The evidence of a drug problem was flimsy at best, largely based on the testimony of a few teachers who felt some students were acting oddly. Still, that was enough for the justices to say compelled drug testing was fine.[53]

The justices seem so eager at times to approve the new police practices that rather than even trying to balance apples against apples, or even oranges, they balance one apple against the whole orchard. In the school drug testing case, the Supreme Court weighed the "minimally intrusive nature of the sample collection" for one person against "[t]he drug abuse problem among our Nation's youth." In a drunk-driving roadblock case the court weighed the intrusion on the (single) "average motorist" against the "magnitude of the drunken driving problem [and] the State's interest in eradicating it."[54]

Rapid technological advance has only made the Supreme Court's job more impossible. In 1971, Justice William O. Douglas observed that "[w]hat the ancients knew as 'eavesdropping,' we now call 'electronic surveillance'; but to equate the two is to treat man's first gunpowder on the same level as the nuclear bomb." Justice Douglas was talking about an informant wearing a wire. If a wired informant was a "nuclear bomb," it is hard even to come up with an apt metaphor to describe the NSA scooping up all our phone records, or a drone planting itself over someone's backyard.[55]

The tactics and technology of today's policing cry out for detailed data-driven rules. In what circumstance is Taser use appropriate or not? How long should CCTV video be stored, and who may view it? When should SWAT teams be deployed, and with what equipment? What is a policy for drones that accommodates privacy concerns while maximizing their value? Courts can bite around the edges here, but that is about it. And so, yet again, they tend to defer to the police and no one is left minding the shop.

A FAILURE OF DEMOCRATIC ACCOUNTABILITY

Even if courts could resolve these intricate policy-oriented questions, there is one requirement of democratic policing they can never fulfill: a popular pedigree. Rules on things like the strip-searching of school children, the use of Tasers, the deployment of SWAT teams, and the recording of people on the street, all are (at least in the first instance, which is to say as a matter of policy and before we even get to questions of constitutional law) properly the responsibility of the people, not their courts. Most federal judges and many state and local judges are not elected by the people. And even when judges are elected, their job still is to rule after the fact on the constitutionality of policing actions. Judges are never paid to write rules in the first instance.

California's governor, Jerry Brown, has had some trouble appreciating this critical lesson. Twice in three years he vetoed legislative measures aimed at regulating policing, arguing the job should be left to the courts and the Constitution, not the people. In 2011, the California legislature passed a law overturning a decision by the California Supreme Court allowing police to search the cell phones of arrestees. Why veto that? Because, Brown explained in his veto message, "courts are better suited to resolve the complex and case-specific issues relating to constitutional search-and-seizure protections." Then, in 2014, the legislature passed a measure prohibiting the use of drones without a search warrant, absent certain specified exceptions. No good, said the governor. While "[t]here are undoubtedly circumstances where a warrant is acceptable," this law "could impose requirements beyond what is required" by the federal or state constitutions.[56]

This tendency to turn policing over to the courts is one of our unhealthiest habits of a country that deems itself a democracy. If the governor thought the measures were wrongheaded on the merits, he should have said so, instead of playing coy and putting it off on courts. Policing agencies pry into our private lives and use force to coerce compliance of our friends, neighbors, and families. This use of force and surveillance may well be necessary in an orderly society of our size, but they are necessary evils and should never be used lightly or without forethought. It is our responsibility to regulate these things. We do not meet that responsibility by trying to foist the job off on judges—and in particular on judges who lack the capacity and will to do the job.

The challenge we face, in light of the political logjam discussed in Chapter 2, is how to get ourselves—as a society—to take up the job of regulating the police. It is a tough, tough problem. But as we are about to see, despite all their other shortcomings, it turns out there may well be a way for the judges to help us all out here.

4

FOSTERING
DEMOCRATIC POLICING

What we need are rules and policies to govern policing, written in advance, with public input. Sometimes we get them, particularly after policing hits the news in a big and troubling way, but usually we don't. As we've seen, legislators and the police are not anxious to provide such rules, and the courts can't. So, what is to be done?

It turns out the courts have a vital role to play here, one that they ought to find easier and more congenial than ruling on the constitutionality of police practices—they can force the rest of us to take responsibility for policing. This chapter closes out our discussion of democratic policing by illustrating how courts can prod legislative and executive bodies to do their jobs. Because policing that occurs without democratic authorization is simply unacceptable.

THE REPORT

Anyone who, in August 2014, picked up a newspaper or turned on a television, is all too familiar with the following events. They saw images so powerful it justified retrospectives in many publications a year later. What matters now, though, is not so much what happened that month as what preceded it. And what followed.[1]

On August 9, 2014, Officer Darren Wilson of the Ferguson, Missouri, Police Department shot and killed Michael Brown, an unarmed black teenager. Demonstrations began a day later, in and around West Florissant Avenue, in Ferguson. While many of the protesters were peaceful, some turned violent. Projectiles were thrown at the police. Looting occurred.[2]

Still, wrote Jamelle Bouie in *Slate*, capturing the dominant sentiment of the nation, "[t]he most striking photos from Ferguson, MO aren't of Saturday's demonstrations or Sunday night's riots; they're of the police." There's the picture of a sniper set up atop a military vehicle. There is the phalanx of soldiers—correction, make that police officers, but in the photographs they seem indistinguishable from images of American troops in Iraq or Afghanistan—decked out in camouflage, pointing automatic weapons at a tall, thin black guy in dreadlocks, his arms raised to the air. There are the Kevlar helmets, the night vision goggles, the rubber bullets raining on unarmed civilians. And everywhere the fog of tear gas fired indiscriminately.[3]

It looked, proclaimed voice after voice, like a war zone. All of the sudden, Ferguson was dropped in the same breath as places like Gaza or Ukraine, like—as *The New York Times* put it—"a chaos stricken corner of Eastern Europe, not like the American Midwest." Prior to Ferguson, those who worried over the "militarization" of the police were voices in the wilderness. Overnight that changed. Republican State Senator Branden Peters of Minnesota said, "You get these pictures that just shock the conscience." His fellow Republican, and libertarian, Senator Rand Paul of Kentucky, declared, "The images and scenes we continue to see in Ferguson resemble war more than traditional police action.[4]

Indeed, focus for just a moment on what a select few had to say, those in what one might call Ferguson's political chain of command. The governor of Missouri, Jay Nixon, was "thunderstruck by the pictures we saw—the overmilitarization, the MRAPs rolling in, the guns pointed at kids in the street." (MRAP stands for "mine resistant ambush protected"—the sorts of vehicles that were on everyone's minds following the televised images from Ferguson, though what we saw on the street there was actually a BearCat.) The district's Representative in Congress, William Lacy Clay, announced, with apparent outrage, "I witnessed firsthand, high-powered sniper rifles with night scopes being

pointed at my constituents who were peacefully exercising their constitutional rights." "We need to demilitarize this situation—this kind of
response by the police has become the problem instead of the solution,"
insisted Missouri Senator Claire McCaskill. "At a time when we must
seek to rebuild trust between law enforcement and the local community," weighed in Attorney General Eric Holder, "I am deeply concerned
that the deployment of military equipment and vehicles sends a con-
flicting message." Even the president spoke up, saying at a press conference at which Ferguson shared double billing with conflict in Iraq, "I
know that many Americans have been deeply disturbed by the images
that we've seen in the heartland of our country."[5]

While their concern was undoubtedly sincere, they—among all
others—should hardly have been surprised.

Beginning in the 1990s, the U.S. government gave away to state
and local law enforcement—or otherwise subsidized the purchase of—
billions of dollars of military equipment. While the laws that enabled this
giveaway originally were adopted as part of the war on drugs, the war on
terror provided the primary justification after September 11. From 2009
to 2014 alone, some $18 billion of money or materiel was transferred from
the military to domestic policing agencies. Nick Gragnani, of St. Louis's
Area Regional Response System, which did the acquisition for Ferguson,
explained that "[t]he focus is terrorism, but it's allowed to do a crossover
for other types of responses . . . There was no restriction put on that by
the federal government." The primary vessel was the Department of
Defense's "1033" program, dispensed through the Defense Logistics
Agency's Law Enforcement Support Office (motto: "From warfighter to
crimefighter"). But there were at least eleven others, including grants
from the Department of Homeland Security and the Department of
Justice.[6]

Although the vast majority of this equipment was uncontroversial—
from binders to computers to desks—a large portion of it was military
grade, what the federal government calls "controlled equipment." Almost
five hundred thousand pieces of it. Aircraft, armored vehicles, muni-
tions, grenade launchers. MRAPs. Weapons above .50 caliber, which
Stars and Stripes magazine says "can crack an engine block without breaking a sweat, so getting hit by one would ruin your day." And bayonets—
though what conceivable use law enforcement could have for bayonets
on American streets was a question many felt worth asking.[7]

The equipment was distributed like Halloween candy. North Carolina got sixteen military helicopters and twenty-two grenade launchers; Tennessee got thirty-one MRAPs and seven grenade launchers; Florida did particularly well, garnering forty-seven MRAPs, thirty-six grenade launchers, and more than seven thousand rifles. Then there were the schools: five districts in Texas and five in California received materiel, including MRAPs and grenade launchers. Mississippi's Hinds Community College and the University of Central Florida each got grenade launchers; Hinds got two M16s as well.[8]

The nation aghast, the president ordered a review of these programs. His office brought in representatives from federal agencies, law enforcement, the academy, and civil rights organizations. In December 2014, he issued a report. The report explained that, particularly in light of local budget cuts, the programs have "been valuable" in helping law enforcement "carry out their critical missions in helping to keep the American people safe." But from there it went downhill fast.[9]

In a very few pages, and couched in bland bureaucratese, the report was nonetheless searing. There was "insufficient transparency" in the programs, which took place "outside of a local government's standard budget process and without civilian (non-police) government approval." One result: often local officials and the general public were in the dark. Another: "the proliferation of equipment in amounts . . . inconsistent with the size and training capacity" of law enforcement. The Department of Defense, dispensing the goods, could not assess what was necessary, as it "does not have expertise in civilian law enforcement operations." Yet law enforcement itself expressed concern that "police chiefs" and others responsible "lack proper training to understand when and how" the equipment should be deployed. "[T]raining has not been institutionalized, specifically with respect to civil rights and civil liberties protections, or the safe use of equipment." What training there was may have "unintentionally incentivize[d] the use of military-like tactics and equipment when unnecessary." There was no effective coordination among the various federal programs; "[a]s a result, there may be no single entity in the federal government able to track" the equipment, and if a particular police force is cut off by one program because of "misusing funds or equipment or violating the Constitution" the force could simply go somewhere else.[10]

Perhaps it pays to simplify. The federal government spent billions of dollars putting military equipment in the hands of local law enforcement. It did it behind the backs of civilian authorities, and without assessing the need for the equipment. Local police authorities took the equipment even though they lacked proper training in how to deploy or use it. But deploy it they did; indeed, one of the all-too-few requirements of the program was "use it or lose it": the equipment had to be deployed within a year of receiving it.[11]

POLICY CHANGES AFTER FERGUSON

Although for the most part the acquisition by local law enforcement of military-grade equipment had happened outside the public's consciousness, in the aftermath of Ferguson that changed. "The August, 2014 clashes between protesters and heavily equipped police in Ferguson, Missouri," explained the Bozeman (Montana) *Daily Chronicle*, "led to a national conversation about the militarization of police forces." That national discussion was not nearly as consequential as the many local ones taking place in state legislatures and town councils, in neighborhood and community associations. American democracy is layered: absent some overriding national necessity, state and local governments are free to make their own choices. After Ferguson, many of those units started to do so, adopting policies that differed in significant ways from one locale to the next—the sign of a healthy democratic process at work.[12]

State Senator Nia Gill represents New Jersey's 34th legislative district. She hails from Montclair, a suburban college town just outside of New York. Gill is African American and a Democrat. After graduating from law school she served as a public defender. Then she went into politics. She served seven years in the State Assembly before moving to the State Senate, where she is now President Pro Tempore.[13]

Following Ferguson, Gill asked the New Jersey Attorney General for information about what military-grade equipment was in the state, and where. It took a little persistence, but what she finally found out both troubled and surprised her. Not only was there a great deal of equipment "more suited to a war zone than community policing," but "most of the military equipment like the assault rifles and grenade launchers . . . were in suburban communities, and the communities knew nothing about them." So Gill set out to do something about that.[14]

As a result of Gill's efforts, on March 16, 2015, Republican Governor Chris Christie signed into law S2364, which passed both houses of the New Jersey legislature *unanimously*. The trick to such bipartisan success? Her bill was agnostic on whether communities should possess 1033 material. Instead what it did was set up a requirement that before any police force registered for 1033 equipment or acquired any particular items, it "shall be approved by a resolution adopted by a majority of the full membership of the governing body of a local unit." The "community local government factor," she says, "was something everyone could agree with," be it a rural Republican, a representative from a major urban area, and even the police themselves. Law enforcement, she explained, "wanted to have a system so if they needed training, or to have the equipment housed, they would know how it would happen. By making it transparent they were on board."[15]

New Jersey was the first state in the nation to act; Montana was the second. There the primary mover was a free-market, small-government Republican from Superior, Representative Nicholas Schwaderer. His approach was different: the Montana law bans law enforcement from receiving any of a list of materials—including armed or weaponized drones, grenades and grenade launchers, silencers, militarized armored vehicles—from the federal government (though they can still buy the same with their own funds). In addition, if law enforcement "requests property from a military equipment surplus program," public notice must be provided two weeks beforehand.[16]

What happened in New Jersey and Montana took place in other states and cities and towns throughout the United States. The Davis, California, City Council gave its police chief sixty days to come up with a plan to get rid of the city's MRAP. "When it comes to help from Washington," said Davis's mayor, "we have a long wish list. But a tank, or MRAP, or whatever you choose to call it, is not on the list." San Diego's Unified School District returned its MRAP also. Superintendent Cindy Marten said school safety issues should be addressed with input from "students, staff, parents, community members, law enforcement and others." The district's police chief, Rueben Littlejohn, concurred: "The value that this defensive tool would bring cannot exceed the value of retaining the public's trust, confidence, and perceptions of how we will protect our students." The Town Board of Woodstock, New

York, passed a resolution "declar[ing] it has never accepted, nor will accept or procure military arms and/or heavy armor for its police department now or in the future." Cathy Mararelli, a board member, was "shocked" to learn that Ferguson, population twenty thousand, had $4 million worth of military-type equipment. "It's ridiculous to have that much armor for a small town."[17]

WHEN PEOPLE PARTICIPATE, POLICING CHANGES

The people can come together and make decisions about policing. And when they do, policy often changes.

The first thing you notice about these many efforts is how they traversed the ideological spectrum. The Pew Charitable Trust observed that legislative responses to Ferguson were "backed by Democrats and Republicans, in red states and blue states." The ACLU was a key player in New Jersey; Montana's effort was publicized and promoted by the Tenth Amendment Center, a states-rights organization. (The Tenth Amendment Center also supported State Senator Gill's measure.) The same phenomenon was true of another set of reforms occurring in Ferguson's aftermath: limiting the funds municipalities can collect from traffic fines. When the Missouri legislature passed a bill doing so, the primary sponsor was a white Republican; another sponsor was an African American Democrat who'd been arrested during the protests in Ferguson. "If the St. Louis Tea Party coalition and the ACLU are on the same page," said Bill Hennessy, a leader of the Tea Party coalition, "we must be going down the right path."[18]

When people focus their attention on policing, vibrant policy conversations occur. In 2012, the City of Seattle bought two Draganflyer X6 drones with Homeland Security money. It was on the city's consent calendar—intended for adoption without debate—but someone noticed and a firestorm erupted. Several public hearings then ensued, at which opponents called council members "idiots," "crooks," and even "Nazis." Enough, cried Seattle's mayor, and ordered disposal of the drones. This proved more difficult than expected—the manufacturer would not take them back—but eventually Seattle pawned them off on Los Angeles. Lesson learned? The Seattle Police Department's spokesperson said, "It's important to have an open conversation with the public on what your plans are when you're talking about drones."[19]

When Seattle's drones moved to LA, the lesson about public discussion traveled with them. Police Chief Beck insisted the drones remain under lock and key until there was a public process. "The Los Angeles Police Department will never, ever give up public confidence for a piece of police equipment." He handed the drones over to the LAPD's inspector general, and the president of the LA Police Commission tweeted, "Putting the two hot potatoes in the freezer while we do public process." That process proved contentious. The organization Drone-Free LAPD No Drones, LA! formed in response. A year and a half later, the drones remained grounded.[20]

Upstate from Los Angeles, in San Jose, a proper public process led to a very different result—one favoring law enforcement. As in Seattle, public anger grew on word of an impending drone acquisition. But the San Jose Police Department got the message fast, repeatedly apologizing for not having "done a better job of communicating" about the purchase of the drone. Ultimately, the San Jose Neighborhoods Commission, which initially had been very concerned, came around. It authorized a yearlong pilot project, concluding "the UAS [unmanned aerial system] can be a useful tool," and "that if the department continues to work openly with the council, the commission and the public, the public's concerns can be alleviated." The Commission was proud of its involvement and its role in the eventual result. "We're participating in a really important process here," said Commissioner Nick Labosky. "We're showing the template for how it's done."[21]

These conversations reinforce the proper political hierarchy: the people on top, governing, working with the police in making decisions. In Menlo Park, California, the police got upset at legislation limiting data retention from drones and red light cameras. Chief Robert Jonsen told the city council, "I personally do not feel an ordinance is necessary for this department. It's a matter of trust." Council member Ray Mueller shot back, "We've been aggressive when it comes to using technology. If we didn't trust you, we wouldn't give them to you. It's about having a prudent check on power." The city of Durham, North Carolina, adopted special rules for consent searches after data showed police were twice as likely to search blacks as whites, despite turning up no greater amount of contraband. Police Chief Jose L. Lopez, Sr., was frustrated. "You have a Puerto Rican police chief in the City of Durham, and you are going to accuse him of racism?" Replied Pastor

Mark-Anthony Middleton, a leader in the Durham Congregations, Associations & Neighborhoods group, "[H]e has to understand who runs the city. He sure does now."[22]

These sorts of conversations are essential because the answers are not always easy, although they may seem so to committed partisans. As New Jersey's Nia Gill points out, "I was not trying to eliminate participation in the program if the community felt it was necessary; maybe they want their police to have night goggles but not bayonets and assault weapons." The Ferguson backlash caused many places to return their MRAPs. But those vehicles actually can serve valuable purposes. The chief of the University of Texas's police force, Michael Heidingsfield, explained to the press that his community went through an elaborate process of discussing how to deal with armed shooters, and ultimately decided the MRAP was essential. "What we have here is really an armored container on wheels, it has no weapons associated with it whatsoever, it has our graphics on its side." ("Emergency Rescue" is what it says.) Similarly, after Gill's legislation was adopted, many New Jersey shore towns decided to acquire more military vehicles to help in high winds and water. Around the country, military vehicles have been credited with playing a critical role in rescuing flood victims during a storm.[23]

Indeed, it is a sign of a vibrant democracy that—after debate—jurisdictions reach different conclusions. Says Gill, "In fact we found that there was varying opinion. Some local people wanted to get certain things; some wanted to get others." That proved true throughout the country. Davis gave up its MRAP, as did Sangamon County in Illinois, but the Edinburg Consolidated Independent School District in Texas kept its two Humvees, cargo truck, and M4 and AR-15 assault rifles. The Aledo, Texas, School District got rid of its M16 (and M14) rifles, while Utah's Granite School District and Nevada's Washoe County School District had no plans to get rid of theirs. The Los Angeles Unified School District held on to its rifles, but got rid of three grenade launchers, and eventually its MRAP.[24]

What matters, as UT's Chief Heidingsfield makes clear, is an open process leading to reasoned outcomes. "The question that communities need to ask is how are their police agencies going to use this equipment and if there's been a deliberative, thoughtful, rational process . . . I think that's where the judgment should be made, not simply the fact that the agency received a certain piece of equipment."[25]

What's notable is that when there is transparency, when public dialogue occurs, policy unequivocally does change. We've now seem plenty of examples of this, but there are many more. For example, when citizens of Washington State learned that some of their police were using a Stingray cell phone tracker, the state legislature passed a law not only requiring a warrant, but specifically requiring that police describe the technology and its impact in detail to judges. It unanimously passed both houses. Stingray legislation also has passed in Virginia, Minnesota, and Utah. When news stories surfaced in Texas that officers were conducting roadside body cavity exams, the Texas legislature adopted a bill banning such searches without a judicially issued warrant.[26]

All of this suggests that the secrecy and lack of debate so common around policing is deleterious. If, given public discussions, things would be different, then democracy demands those discussions occur.

MOVING THE ELEPHANT

The problem is that sparking the sort of public action witnessed here is tough. The list of policing issues untouched in most places by any sort of public conversation and popularly vetted rules is long: the use of informants, the protocols for consent searches, the circumstances under which stop-and-frisk is appropriate, vehicle chases, the retention and collection of images from public cameras, deployment of roadblocks (sobriety and otherwise). One could go on and on.[27]

This should come as little surprise. As we have seen, left to their own devices, lawmakers who must stand for election would rather not regulate the police. So how to change this calculus? What will cause legislative bodies to take up their responsibilities, even if they would prefer not to?

The Policy Director for the ACLU of New Jersey, Ari Rosmarin, can give you one answer. Before Ferguson, Rosmarin had been working in New Jersey on the issue of militarization. His efforts even to get the basic information he needed—like what equipment was in the hands of New Jersey police forces—were stymied. He'd tried Freedom of Information requests only to have them denied.[28]

And then, he explained, Ferguson happened, and "it shifted the way we talked about it." Before Ferguson the issue was "esoteric," but "people now had a visual sense of the concern we talked about. The projection of the imagery from Ferguson undoubtedly shifted how people thought about the issue and changed the political calculus as well." It became a "hot story" in New Jersey, and as it did the state "started releasing more data that it had refused to provide before. All this stuff came out: grenade launchers, bayonets, M16s—it became a local issue, people engaged with it in a way they had not before. It would not have, but for this idea of 'militarization' becoming a dominant narrative after Ferguson."[29]

Rosmarin puts his finger on a primary lesson of legislative politics: salience is everything. Public attention is the lever that can pry loose many a stuck rock. Once the public cares, and the media is engaged, then legislators no longer can avoid the issue: they are forced to take positions, to listen, and perhaps to act.

The news and the media can affect salience; but so too can interest groups. If they are prominent enough they can start the legislative ball rolling. Take the federal law that governs law enforcement use of electronic surveillance, the Electronic Communications Privacy Act. We'd never have that legislation except for the fact that the telecommunications industry did not want to continue spending time and money responding to government data requests. So they made an issue of the problem and they lobbied hard for the legislation.[30]

Of course, interest groups can stop legislation also, and in that regard, as we've discussed, law enforcement is a powerful player. When the Electronic Communications Privacy Act needed updating, even the tech lobby found it difficult to get action, because significant elements of law enforcement continued to oppose the proposed fixes.[31]

It takes pretty solid momentum to overcome law enforcement resistance. Rosmarin notes there are other bills pending in New Jersey that interest the ACLU—from an independent prosecutor for police shootings, to police training, to body cameras. But in the hearings on these measures, "every gradation of policing, from police unions, to superior officers, to patrolmen" will come to talk about the "threat to public safety, the damage to police morale" if the bill is passed. There are the "optics: guys with badges coming into the hearing room telling you there will be blood in the street."[32]

The police unions, in particular, are a potent force—perhaps even more so than police chiefs. They bring "endorsement, money, votes," explains Rosmarin. "They will do canvassing, phone banks, they are engaged in a way the police reform movement isn't and cannot be." As a legislator, you don't want the "average voter to get a mailer saying Senator X voted against the police, who are trying to protect you." That sort of pressure is "difficult to stand up to absent an upsurge of momentum in the other direction."[33]

By now, the nub of the problem should be screamingly evident. There's lots of room for rule-making on policing. But it's difficult to gather the sort of "momentum" to get the ball rolling, to generate consensus, to overcome law enforcement opposition. In part, Senator Gill accomplished it by cleverly framing her bill as simply moving the issue down the legislative ladder. But in part it took a Ferguson. And a Ferguson is a rare event.[34]

It turns out, though, that there may be an entirely different solution. A surprising one.

PRODDING THE LEGISLATURE

Several years ago, two law professors had a disagreement. Both taught at the same law school—George Washington University, in the District of Columbia. Both are experts in criminal procedure.[35]

The disagreement was over how to handle the rules for government searching in a world of rapidly changing technology. Orin Kerr, who had spent time at the Department of Justice working on computer crime issues, argued that courts should step out and let the legislature do the job. Technology is complicated, it changes quickly, courts aren't competent to know what to do, and they can't fashion the sort of broad rules we need to regulate matters. Not so, responded his colleague Daniel Solove, whose specialty is privacy law: courts can get all the information they need from the parties before them, and besides, legislatures are not doing a very good job of keeping up anyway.[36]

Their debate was reminiscent of a 1980s advertising campaign. A disagreement breaks out in a bar. Over beer. But not, as you'd think, over which beer is better—no, this is a fight over what attributes made a particular beer (Miller Lite) best. "Less filling," hollered one part of the crowd. "No," the others shouted back, "tastes great."[37]

The answer, of course—for Miller Lite, and for Kerr and Solove—is, why can't it be both? Why shouldn't courts and legislatures work together on policing?

This, in fact, is how some of our most important legislation on policing has been made. Here's an example. In 1928, in a case called *Olmstead v. United States*, the Supreme Court held that the Fourth Amendment had nothing to say about government wiretapping. As far as the Constitution was concerned, the government could do as it wished. "Congress soon thereafter, and some say in answer to *Olmstead*, specifically prohibited the interception without authorization, and the divulging or publishing of the contents of telephonic communications." That was the Supreme Court talking, in the 1967 decision in *Berger v. New York*, referring to congressional enactment of a provision in the Federal Communications Act of 1934. The point was that the Supreme Court's refusal to regulate wiretapping forced Congress into the act.[38]

It turns out the *Berger* decision had the same effect of provoking legislation as *Olmstead*. In *Berger* the Supreme Court struck down New York's wiretapping and eavesdropping law, holding that it flunked the Fourth Amendment in a number of ways. The response to *Berger* was to trigger one of the more important federal statutes in this area ever adopted, Title III of the Omnibus Crime Control and Safe Streets Act of 1968, commonly referred to as the Wiretap Act. Title III comprehensively regulates police wiretapping practice throughout the nation. The statute uses the Supreme Court's opinion in *Berger* as a road map, though it exceeds in some aspects what the Supreme Court said the Fourth Amendment required.[39]

There are three very interesting lessons to this pattern of judicial-legislative interaction. They relate directly to the problem of how difficult it is to motivate a legislative body, and why.

First, although the courts have proven disappointing at protecting constitutional liberties and regulating the police, they can play an important role in forcing democratic action around these same issues.

Second, as the Court's opinions in *Berger* and *Olmstead* indicate, what seems to trigger legislative action in response to a judicial decision is for the judges to take somewhat of an extreme position. It almost doesn't matter in which direction. *Olmstead* left wiretapping entirely unregulated by constitutional standards. *Berger*, on the other hand, took a stringent view regarding wiretaps under the Constitution. Both caused—in a sense forced—Congress to enact legislation in response.[40]

But finally, although an extreme decision in either direction may work to elicit legislation, given the nature of interest-group politics around policing, there is reason to think the best tool will be rights-protective rulings that limit what government can do. That's because, as we've seen, the most focused and successful interest group around policing is the police themselves—and their partners in crime prevention, prosecutors.[41]

Stated directly: If the courts say the police cannot do something, at least absent some sort of legislative regulation, and if the police think it is important that they have this power, they will come to the legislature and demand action. Gore the government's ox, and it will rise and respond. And then we will have the democratic debate that is so desperately needed in this area.

While this strategy works to motivate legislative action, there's a big problem with it. We've already seen how courts are extremely reluctant to rule against the police, concerned that they lack a certain amount of information and expertise. But it is worse yet.[42]

The difficulty is that with constitutional rulings—including those under the Fourth Amendment—legislatures can't move them out of the way, even if those court rulings prove silly or counterproductive. We are stuck with constitutional rulings unless and until we pass a constitutional amendment, or the Supreme Court changes its own mind and reverses itself. The first almost never happens and the second is pretty rare as well.

That's yet another reason judges are so cautious about saying no to the police on the basis of the Constitution. We can see how rights-protective rulings can spur legislative action. But judges are reluctant to do it very often, because it may tie the hands of the police in ways that prove troubling.

AUTHORIZING THE POLICE

What, though, if instead of saying "aye" or "nay" to the police, the courts could somehow require popularly accountable bodies to consider the issue themselves? In other words, what if the courts could simply insist that before the police act, the lawmakers adopt democratically accountable rules regulating police behavior?

That's what happened in *Utah v. Sims*.[43]

At about 9:30 a.m. on July 27, 1988, Louie Sims was tooling down Highway 15 just outside Nephi, Utah, when he encountered an "all purpose" roadblock being run by the Utah Highway Patrol. UHP Sergeant Paul Mangelson, a somewhat hyperactive drug enforcer, was in charge. Sims stopped, and was asked for his license and registration. At that point, Trooper Carl Howard smelled alcohol and saw an open container in the backseat. He had Sims exit the car, and asked permission to search. Sims consented. In the rear passenger ashtray Howard found the remains of a couple of joints, so he asked to search the trunk, too. There, in a suitcase, Mangelson found two plastic bags of marijuana. At that point Sims said "no more," but—believing he now had sufficient probable cause—Mangelson kept going. In the spare tire well he found a kilogram brick of cocaine.[44]

Sims argued that no Utah law authorized the roadblock, so it was invalid and all the evidence against him had to be thrown out. In most other jurisdictions, Sims would be on his way to the hoosegow. The roadblock was stopping everyone to check license and registration; Sims was plainly in violation of an open container law; he consented; and it was a pretty big haul. This is precisely the situation in which courts are reluctant to toss out evidence, and so they bend over backward to approve what the police have done. As the Utah Supreme Court noted, courts in other states had inferred permission to maintain such roadblocks from the sorts of general authority given to the police to enforce the criminal law that we have seen are common.[45]

But not only did Sims walk, the Utah Supreme Court ruled he did not even have to pay the $400,000 tax bill imposed by the state. The Utah courts—there were opinions from the Utah Court of Appeals and the Supreme Court—noted that other sorts of roadblocks in the state had specific legislative approval. Whether it was to search large trucks carrying livestock, or all cars to enforce the fish and game laws, "the collective will of the people is expressed" through "their elected representatives." But here, there was no law whatsoever in place, a complete lack of "political accountability." Thus: search invalid.[46]

In striking down the search of Sims, the Utah courts stressed how important it was to have some sort of check on law enforcement. The courts pointed out that the requirement that police obtain warrants before searching was taken seriously in that state as a way to curb police excesses. But roadblocks typically happen without warrants, because there is no "probable cause" to believe that anyone has done anything wrong. Thus, said the Utah courts, it was doubly important to have a preexisting statute in place. "Both warrants and statutes originate outside the executive branch, serving to check abuses of that branch's law enforcement power." The Court of Appeals made much of the fact that "no written policy, from the Highway Patrol or from any other source, existed to guide the conduct of the roadblock."[47]

These sorts of decisions requiring legislative authorization of policing are all too rare here in the United States, although they are hardwired into the system in other countries. In *R. v. Spencer*, for example—a decision of the Canada Supreme Court—the defendant was caught with gobs of child pornography on his hard drive. At that point, though, all the police had was an anonymous user account they knew held unlawful images. The question in the case was whether the police needed a warrant before going to the account holders' Internet service provider (ISP) to find out who the actual user was. In analyzing the question, the *Spencer* court set out the standard approach in Canada. There, a search is "reasonable" if (a) it was authorized by law; (b) the law itself was reasonable [i.e., constitutional]; and (c) the search was carried out in a reasonable manner. Note the critical first inquiry.[48]

Skipping over the initial question—whether what the police did was authorized by law—is strange in a country like ours that's so full of pride about its democratic heritage, so ostensibly reliant on the will of the people. There's little explanation for it save force of habit. Courts are so used to ruling in constitutional terms that they don't stop to ask whether what policing agencies are doing has any clear authorization.

Rather than cluttering up policing with a lot of ill-considered constitutional rules, courts should force democratic deliberation and legislative action. That is easy enough to do if they would just stop to ask the simplest of questions: "Is what happened here authorized by some existing, democratically accountable rule?" If there is clear authorization, then courts must move to the constitutional question. But if not, that alone is sufficient basis to invalidate what the police did. Not for all time, as a constitutional ruling would. But until the policing agency has obtained clear democratic authority—either from the legislature, or by promulgating its own rule with popular input.

WHEN SPECIFIC AUTHORITY IS REQUIRED

To the extent there is no law at all giving policing officials authority to do something, it is obvious courts should refuse to allow them to do it. After all, no government official can act without formal authority. But as we've seen, there typically are extremely broad grants of authority to police agencies that tell them to go forth and enforce the criminal law. Ought these to suffice, or is there still room for courts to step in?[49]

The question courts should be asking themselves in each case is whether an existing blanket authorization is sufficient to cover what the police did. For familiar policing tactics with a long pedigree—such as traffic stops based on probable cause—the answer likely is yes. But there are a number of situations, increasingly common, in which such age-old authorizations dubiously cover what has happened. For example, when police employ invasive technologies, such as drones and heat sensors, that were beyond the wildest imagination of anyone, including the legislators, at the time the general authority was conveyed, it seems entirely plausible to require the government to go back to the legislature and get specific permission. Similarly, all the vehicles of the new programmatic, proactive, deterrent policing—roadblocks, CCTV, administrative searches—these, too, could not have been in the minds of those who authorized policing in the most general of terms. So, yet again—as the Utah courts concluded in *Sims*—legislative authorization should be obtained, or at least the police should develop public rules.

What courts in the United States often do in circumstances like these—at least outside the area of policing—is express "constitutional doubt" that the seemingly broad statute covers the specific circumstances in question. They say, in effect, we're not sure if the Constitution allows this, so absent clear evidence that the action was democratically authorized we aren't going to allow it. In *Kent v. Dulles*, for example, the Supreme Court was asked whether a law that left the authority to issue passports "to the discretion of the Secretary of State" included the Secretary's decision to deny a passport on the ground someone was a Communist. Kent argued that denying him a passport on this basis violated his First Amendment right to associate with any political movement he chose. Rather than answer this First Amendment question, the Supreme Court ducked it by denying the power the administration wanted, saying it would not "readily infer that Congress gave the Secretary of State unbridled discretion to grant or deny" passports on this basis. In other words, unless and until Congress came out explicitly and gave the power to the Secretary of State to deny passports to Communists, the Supreme Court would just assume there was no such power.[50]

This same tactic—of narrowly construing authority until a legislature speaks clearly—was evident in the Canadian child pornography case. There was a statute on the books that allowed "lawful authority" to get the information about who the anonymous user was, but did that reference to "lawful authority" include asking the ISP without getting a warrant first? In resolving that question, the court realized it needed to look beyond the scoundrel in that particular case. "[T]he issue is not whether Mr. Spencer had a legitimate privacy interest in concealing his use of the Internet for the purpose of accessing child pornography, but whether people generally have a privacy interest in subscriber information with respect to computers which they use in their home for private purposes." Given the privacy interests at stake, the court decided it must interpret "'lawful authority' as requiring more than a bare request by law enforcement" to the ISP. If that was wrong, then the government could go back to the Parliament and get clear authorization first.[51]

Note the favor this sort of ruling—based on a narrow interpretation of the existing statute rather than on the Constitution—does for all of us. To conclude that no warrant was required would put everyone's privacy in Internet use at risk. On the other hand, to insist on a warrant as a constitutional matter might strike the balance the wrong way, for the court only has in front of it one case and can't imagine all the others where warrants might be a real problem. By simply interpreting the law on the books in a narrow way, and nothing more, the legislature is free to think through the problem, and if necessary or appropriate come up with a set of circumstances in which a warrant is required, and those in which it is not—or even adopt some other sort of procedure for decoding ISP addresses.

The constitutional law of policing is chock-a-block with examples in which it would seem to make abundant sense to ask what the legislature has in mind. Yet the Supreme Court disregards or ignores the views of rule-making bodies as often as it respects them. For example, in order to even invoke the Fourth Amendment, something must be a "search" or "seizure." In Virginia, police arrested a man for something that was not an arrestable offense; they then searched him "incident to a lawful arrest" and found drugs. One would think the arrest was not "lawful" and thus the search invalid. Instead, the Supreme Court said, "We are aware of no historical indication that those who ratified the Fourth Amendment understood it as a redundant guarantee of whatever limits on search and seizure legislatures might have enacted." What? One would think what the "legislature enacted" specified precisely what was reasonable and what was not.[52]

Similarly, the Supreme Court's test for whether police surveillance constitutes a "search" governed by the Fourth Amendment is whether a person has a "reasonable expectation of privacy" in the situation. It would seem that if the state said particular prying conduct—like trespassing on someone's property or digging through someone's trash—was forbidden, that would be a pretty clear statement about what privacy rights we have, and thus what the police may or may not do. Instead, in ruling on police activity the Supreme Court explicitly ignores state law protecting privacy in favor of its own view of what the police should and should not be allowed to do.[53]

The Supreme Court's fetish for governing policing through constitutional rulings, rather than putting the ball in the legislature's court, is radically inconsistent with the democratic principles on which this Republic rests. Here, the People are to rule. Not the police, and not the courts either. When policing issues arise, the first role of courts must be to ensure that the people have had their voice, and if not, then insist that they do.

ENCOURAGING DEMOCRATIC POLICING

What's needed is for courts to see themselves not as the final word on policing, but as partners with rule-makers—be they legislatures, administrative bodies, or the police themselves—in ensuring that policing not only is constitutional but is democratic. Rather than being so quick to jump in and declare something unconstitutional or constitutional, the courts should focus instead on helping the democratic process work to reach sound rules for governing the police.

The Supreme Court has done this to great effect in some critical cases by explicitly inviting legislative action, and even providing a bit of a road map about what can be done. In the *Berger* case discussed previously, even though the Supreme Court struck down New York's wiretapping law as lacking in sufficient constitutional protections, the justices made it clear that wiretapping had its place, and they were quite specific about what needed to be done. In another case, called *Keith*, the government had spied on the defendant as part of a national security investigation, but without a warrant. *Keith* held that domestic security investigations still required warrants, but the justices were responsive to the government's arguments about what was special about national security. They even offered particular suggestions as to what might work, leading to adoption of the Foreign Intelligence Surveillance Act (FISA).[54]

When it happens, this sort of interbranch interaction has been extremely successful. Federal statutes like the Wiretap Act and FISA—though perhaps outdated today—were in their time great bipartisan victories of sensible lawmaking. They occurred precisely because the justices, while acting as a prod, still were open to a cooperative decision-making process to ensure guidelines for the police that met constitutional muster.[55]

Indeed, courts can provide incentives to the police to seek democratic authorization. As we have seen, courts often simply "defer" to what the police have done. Deference, however, should not be dispensed so liberally. Granting or withholding it can serve as a powerful vehicle for getting the police to obtain popular input before proceeding.[56]

It is one thing for courts to defer to governmental decisions adopted transparently with an opportunity for public input; it is quite another to defer to the often nontransparent decisions of police officials. There are some aspects of policing in which deference may be appropriate. For example, the Supreme Court has said that judges should give "due weight" to an officer's "experience and expertise" on whether a particular set of facts are suspicious enough to equal probable cause to search. On the other hand, it hardly makes sense to defer to decisions by policing agencies about things like whether to put drones in the sky, employ SWAT teams to serve most warrants, set up roadblocks on public highways, or collect the phone records of all Americans. Although we certainly want to hear from policing agencies on these issues, ultimately they are questions crying out for public judgment, not police diktat.[57]

The courts should learn to use deference as a tool—to create a safe harbor for the police when they adopt rules before acting. A 1970s case decided by the District of Columbia federal appellate court shows how the job should be done. The question in the case was whether the police were correct to bring a suspect back to the scene of a crime for an identification by witnesses. Such identification evidence is extremely unreliable, and only gets more so as time wears on. Still, because the police had taken the trouble to put a rule into place that seemed reasonable enough, the judges were happy to defer and not substitute their own judgment. Said the judges:

> [A]fter this case arose, [the police] put into operation a regulation restricting on- and near-the-scene identification confrontations" to sixty minutes. "We see in this regulation a careful and commendable administrative effort to balance the freshness of such a confrontation against its inherent suggestiveness, and to balance both actors against the need to pick up the trail while fresh if the suspect is not the offender. We see no need for interposing at this time any more rigid time standard by judicial declaration.[58]

If legislatures or the police are aware courts will defer to well-reasoned public rules, they are more likely to draft them. If they get deference all the time, no matter what, then any incentive to write publicly accountable rules is lost.

There's a real opportunity here, and legislatures as well as courts should seize it. When asked about which legislation governing policing tends to get through the New Jersey legislature and which gets gummed up, Senator Nia Gill gave a surprising answer. "You know, we don't really deal with policing issues," she said. Rather than "direct regulation of policing," all the state legislature typically does is adopt criminal laws and policies; for example: "If we say that it is a third-degree crime, then . . . there is this penalty." For that reason, she concludes, "we don't necessarily have the opportunity to have these broader conversations about policing."[59]

This—from the woman who declares her "abiding faith in government that is close to the people"—represents a lost opportunity. Although much policing is the responsibility of local government and should be regulated there, the same is true at the state level. Local government is, after all, the creature of state law. Laws are needed on a host of subjects, from body cameras and CCTV to roadblocks and SWAT team deployment. The list is very long, and the underlying rights at stake are extremely important. Local government often lacks the capacity to address all these issues, and so it, too, defers to the police. The state legislature needs to step up at times, but something must force it to do so.[60]

We've gotten into a bad, bad habit in this country. We leave policing to the police and, occasionally, to the courts. We've now seen how poor courts are at regulating the police. But they could make a sound contribution if they just began to ask the one simple question: Was this authorized? And if they then refused to allow the police to act without such authorization. In this way, courts can help foster democratic policing.

———————

It should now be apparent both what is needed, and how courts can help us get there. We all need to take responsibility for what the police do, to participate in making policing policy, to give direction. In order for that to happen, the decisions policing agencies make must be public and transparent. And we need to insist that there be rules in place, before police act, that are adopted with democratic input.

Because politicians are so reluctant to take this responsibility, courts can play an important role. They can force politics to operate by refusing to allow the police to act without democratic authorization. And they can reward the police for obtaining public approval before the fact by then deferring to the rules that are put in place.

None of this is to say that every democratically authorized policing rule will be acceptable. Some of those rules still might violate the Constitution. That's the other half of the policing equation, and one we're about to explore. We're going to examine what the Constitution says about how policing agencies must operate. But that question should not even arise unless and until the people have spoken up on the issue. That has been the point of this first part: to make clear how essential it is that we have democratic policing, governed by transparent rules that the public participates in writing.

PART II

Constitutional Policing

The Constitution does not just demand popular engagement around policing. It also limits what government can do. The Fourth Amendment, the most pertinent part of the Constitution when it comes to policing, prohibits "unreasonable searches and seizures." The Equal Protection Clause also plays a role: it provides a strong rule against discrimination.

This part explains how the Constitution's primary safeguards apply to policing. Chapter 5 talks about warrants: why they are necessary and how modern technology makes getting them in advance of police action much easier. Chapter 6 explains that much of what has gone wrong with policing—from stop-and-frisk to overly aggressive drug interdiction—has occurred because the courts were not taking the Constitution's requirement of "probable cause" seriously. Chapter 7 turns to the new policing; it offers a clean and easily applied understanding of how the Constitution's two-hundred-plus-year-old safeguards should govern modern tactics like drunk-driving roadblocks, administrative inspections of businesses, drug interdiction, and airport security. Finally, Chapter 8 tackles the pervasive problem of profiling—racial and otherwise.

A not insubstantial part of what's wrong with policing today results from a failure of courts to implement what the Constitution requires. In light of the last part's critique of courts, one might reasonably wonder: Can we ever depend on courts to get this right? That's a fair question, but there is a reason for hope.

First, the courts may be more open to the argument here than it seems at first blush. Policing has changed in dramatic ways over the last decades. Though the courts have tried to keep up, they have not quite understood how the Constitution should apply to the new policing. On many occasions, judges have gotten things wrong not so much because of reluctance or recalcitrance as simple confusion. Often they are not far off, and with a few course corrections by the judiciary, the constitutional law of policing would look quite different.

Second, the Constitution is not *just* for the courts, though we have fallen into the habit of thinking so. All government actors must adhere to the Constitution's requirements, even if the judges are not doing their job. The points about the Constitution made in this part are as much for policing officials and legislatures as they are for the courts. Policing agencies and legislative bodies should stop assuming that if the courts say something is constitutional, it is fine to go ahead and do it. That is precisely what has led to the realization today that too much policing is "lawful but awful." Policing officials in particular should ask themselves whether what they are about to do really is consistent with how *they* believe the Constitution should operate.

Finally, every citizen ought to have an understanding of what the Constitution requires. There is plenty of evidence that not only government officials but courts as well fall into line with popular understandings about constitutional meaning. This means that the public should have a certain constitutional literacy regarding policing. Part II is about connecting the time-honored principles of the Constitution to the new order of policing.

5

SEARCHES WITHOUT WARRANT

Just as the concept of democratic policing is meant to ensure that policing practices are consistent with the will of the people, warrants are a similar safeguard in individual police actions. Before the police burst into someone's home, or seize them or their property, another branch of government—the judiciary—checks to make sure that the facts justify what is about to occur. Warrants are one way to keep mistakes from happening. That is why, as the Supreme Court has said for over one hundred years, the Fourth Amendment expresses a preference that before police act, they have a judicial warrant.

In actual practice, though, the obligation to get a warrant is far more honored in the breach. Worse yet, of late, some Supreme Court justices have started to argue the Fourth Amendment doesn't really require warrants anyway. Thus, ironically, at the very moment technology is making it easier for the police to get warrants, judges are tripping over themselves to excuse them.

This is a mistake.

A REMARKABLE, UNREMARKABLE CASE

"The facts are remarkable." So began the opinion of the federal appellate judges in the case of *Frunz v. City of Tacoma*. The case is indeed remarkable, but perhaps not for the reason the judges had in mind.[1]

Susan Frunz and her husband, Ted Quandt, had divorced. Quandt had possession of the house and an order restraining Frunz from entering his residence. But when Quandt moved to California, in mid-November 2000, he gave the house back to Frunz, mailing the keys to her divorce lawyer, William Dippolito. After having the phone and power turned back on, Frunz moved in, and—shortly thereafter—had two guests over.[2]

The police enter this story because of Frunz's neighbor, Clinton Staples. On November 18, 2000, Staples called the police and told them that Quandt had asked him to watch the house, and that Quandt's ex-wife (Frunz) had shown up with a companion. Officers responded, and knocked at Frunz's door. When no one answered, they left. Four hours later, Staples called again, to report that someone had come to the door; he had seen Frunz answer it and let the person in. This time Staples told dispatch that there was a restraining order out on Frunz precluding her from entering the premises.[3]

Six or seven officers returned, and observed people in the house. Covering the front door, they broke into the back one. Frunz heard the crash and went to investigate. She encountered an officer, who thrust a gun in her face, just inches from her head. Frunz and her guests were ordered to the floor—one was physically slammed there—and they were handcuffed. One guest was moved to the lawn and hog-tied, his feet secured as well.[4]

Once the officers determined there were no warrants on the men they released them, but—inexplicably—kept Frunz handcuffed. They moved her to a chair, and began to interrogate her. They repeatedly demanded Frunz's name, asked other questions. Every time she tried to explain, someone would say, "Shut up," and insist, "You're a burglar." They threatened to jail her. Even when one officer found some paperwork in the house containing Frunz's name, they refused to believe her. Cold and in tears, Frunz told them just to take her to jail, to end the nightmare.[5]

Finally, Frunz persuaded the officers to call her divorce lawyer. Given that it was a Saturday, and that Dippolito himself was in Florida, it was sheer luck that Dippolito's son answered and connected his father with the police. Eventually, Dippolito confirmed Frunz's story, to the officers' satisfaction. Whereupon they simply up and left. The required incident report was never even filed.[6]

Faced with this set of facts, the judges played "you be the police officer." How else might the officers have handled the situation? The lawyer arguing on behalf of the officers insisted they'd done the only thing possible; they were confronted with an emergency, and so they went in. The judges demurred; they were able to think of a host of other possibilities. For example, the police might have "questioned the neighbor as to his last contact with the husband, in which case they may have learned that the husband had moved out of the house and was living in another state." They even could have knocked at the door, as they had done just an hour and a half earlier, and politely asked the occupants whether they were entitled to be there.[7]

But the last thing the judges pointed to was (in their words) "most important"—*the failure to get a warrant.* "Reasonable officers," the court said, would not have "[b]urst through the back door unannounced with guns drawn and handcuffing the occupants—the owner for a full hour." They would "have tried to obtain a warrant . . . and monitored the house to see if anyone went in and out."[8]

The jury awarded Frunz $27,000 in compensation, and another $111,000 in punitive damages. If anything, the judges thought, this was kind to the officers. "[T]he citizens of Tacoma," they said, "would not want to be treated in their own homes the way the jury found officers . . . treated Frunz and her guests." In addition to fining the defendants for filing a frivolous appeal, the judges ordered that the City Attorney inform the City Council what happened. The author of the court's opinion was one of this country's best-known judges, a conservative with a libertarian streak, Alex Kozinski.[9]

While the court called the facts of Frunz's case "remarkable," police officers conduct searches and seizures without warrants frequently, despite having ample time to obtain them. In fact, these days police officers almost never get warrants before searching. As is true in so many other areas of policing, it is difficult to get hard data. But there is some clear evidence. One study from the 1980s concluded that "the overwhelming majority of criminal investigations are conducted without recourse to a search warrant" and that few law enforcement officers sought warrants. Another study from 1991, looking at seven jurisdictions with a combined population of almost four million, found that only 2,115 search warrants were issued in a six-month period. Two academics conducting fieldwork in 2004 in a mid-sized American city observed 115 searches; none were by warrant. Even warrantless entries of the home—what bothered the judges most in *Frunz*—are common, as but a few minutes on the Internet will reveal.[10]

The reason police don't bother to get warrants is because the Supreme Court has taken a cavalier, if not outright dismissive, attitude toward them. Given the justices' willingness to approve what police do without a warrant, it can come as no surprise that police don't bother to get them.

What happened to Susan Frunz is all too common, and yet quite avoidable. The judges in Frunz's case were right to be angry and to treat the case as remarkable. One wishes that sort of reaction to the failure of police to get a warrant were more typical, and that as a result more warrants were obtained—especially now that technology has made it much easier to do so.

THE IMPORTANCE OF WARRANTS

In the film classic *The Maltese Falcon*, police visit the home of the private detective Sam Spade—played by Humphrey Bogart—suspecting him of having shot his business partner. They ask what kind of gun he carries, and Spade replies, "None. I don't like them much." When pressed on whether he has one at the house, he denies it and urges the officers, "Look around." Then he taunts them: "Turn the dump upside-down if you want. I won't squawk—if you've got a search warrant."[11]

That was 1941, and at the time, Supreme Court precedent squarely supported Spade's insistence on a warrant. Indeed, in 1877, in one of their first Fourth Amendment decisions ever, the justices wrote, "Whilst in the mail, [a person's papers] can only be opened and examined under like warrant, . . . as is required when papers are subjected to search in one's household." The justices have said similar things time and again since—until very recently.[12]

Why warrants? In common parlance, "unwarranted" means unjustified. So, too, when it comes to particular searches or seizures: warrants are a form of approval by a neutral third party—a magistrate or judge—acknowledging good reasons ("probable cause") to allow police to invade someone's life. Police—on a mission to get the bad guys—

may act too hastily. They may, as in Susan Frunz's case, be overly confident in their assessment of the necessity of searching a particular person or place. All this is both predictable and understandable. Thus the importance of warrants. Warrants simply ensure, as Justice Robert Jackson explained in 1948, that the ultimate decision to search is made "by a . . . magistrate instead of being judged by the officer engaged in the often competitive enterprise of ferreting out crime."[13]

Intuition and experience support the requirement to ask permission. How often have you had an idea, one you were persuaded was a really good one, only to have it collapse when you said it out loud to someone else? Even your best friend. Sometimes just the thought of telling someone else what we intend to do can cause us to cringe, to realize what seemed smart a moment ago is actually foolish. Police are no different; the simple fact of having to check in with a judge can cause cops to stop and think. To ask, "Do I have this right?" or "Is this really necessary?" That is exactly why, as the Supreme Court has said, the "informed and deliberate determinations of magistrates" are "to be preferred over the hurried action of officers."[14]

There's lots of social science that supports the idea that asking to search will lead to better decisions. When people are forced to justify their decisions to a third party, research shows, those decisions tend to be more rational and less biased. For example, it turns out to be more likely that legal disputes will settle before trial if the parties are forced to consider the best arguments of their *opponents*; this allows people to see things in a more balanced light.[15]

That's what warrants are about. Giving reasons. And getting approval. From another person, one step removed from the chase. Because, as what happened to Susan Frunz demonstrates all too vividly, mistakes by the police can be traumatic to the innocent people who suffer them.

WATERING DOWN THE WARRANT REQUIREMENT

In 1967, in a case called *Katz v. United States*, the Supreme Court restated the requirement that officers get warrants before searching, in the firmest of terms. Searches without warrants, the justices declared, are "per se unreasonable." That's strong stuff in the law; it means that unless the police get a warrant first, a court simply will presume that what they did was unlawful. Unconstitutional. *Katz* has been cited time and again for the proposition that warrants are required.[16]

Since then, though, the justices have riddled the seemingly strong rule with exception after exception, to the point that the warrant "requirement" now looks like a piece of "Swiss cheese."[17]

To be clear, there have always been exceptions to the warrant requirement, but they were rooted squarely in necessity. The most important exception—the one the police relied on (wrongly) to defend their actions in Frunz's case—is "exigent circumstances." This exception states the obvious: the police need not get a warrant if there is no time to do so. No court has ever demanded a warrant in an emergency.[18]

Two of history's longest-standing exceptions to getting warrants were built squarely on this idea of exigency. It has been the rule for centuries that people can be arrested without a warrant. But that's obviously because people did not tend to stay put while a warrant was procured to take them into custody. Similarly, a search of the person and nearby property was allowed "incident to a lawful arrest," so that police could locate evidence (which otherwise could be quickly destroyed) or weapons (which could be used to injure the police or others).[19]

Of late, though, the Supreme Court has created so many new exceptions to the warrant "requirement" that legal scholars cannot even agree how many: they simply call the number "vast" or a "multitude." Justice Scalia himself claimed there were twenty-two. The exceptions now include immigration checkpoints, administrative searches of regulated businesses, "consent" searches, searches of welfare recipients, students, parolees, and government employees, inventory searches, searches of moveable containers, automobile searches, boat searches, fire investigation searches—the list goes on.[20]

Nothing captures the Supreme Court's current disregard for warrants so much as the so-called automobile exception. Basically the justices have eliminated the need for a warrant whenever a car is searched. Now, cars obviously are mobile: in many circumstances exigency itself may justify a warrantless automobile search. But the Supreme Court has announced a blanket exception for cars—even immobile cars, like one case in which the owner was in custody and the police had the keys.[21]

Although the automobile exception is now firmly ensconced in law, the justices cannot offer a coherent explanation for it, try though they might. They have said that police don't need warrants to search cars, because people are visible in them. But houses have windows too; that doesn't mean the police can simply walk in and search through our stuff. They have made the point that cars are used for transportation, not storage; that hardly covers the trunk of the car, and besides people need personal security when they are traveling just as much as when they are at home. The justices have even suggested that warrants are not necessary because state law requires registering cars—which seems to have nothing to do with anything at all.[22]

In the roughly fifty years from its declaration in *Katz* that warrant-less searches are "per se unreasonable" the Court effectively has reversed direction—in large part under pressure from the war on drugs—dismantling the warrant "requirement." Here's the critical thing, though: *None* of the cases explains why warrants are undesirable or unnecessary. There's not a bad word about warrants to be found. It is just that same phenomenon we saw in Chapter 3, of courts bowing after the fact to what the police have already done, and in the process creating exception after exception until the rule itself is practically obliterated.

CALLING THE WARRANT REQUIREMENT INTO QUESTION

But things are worse than that. There is nowadays an indication the justices—certainly some of them—are ready to say the Constitution doesn't really call for warrants. Again, none of them has even tried to offer any policy reason against warrants. Rather, today's effort by some justices to undermine the use of warrants is based solely on the Fourth Amendment's somewhat oddly written text, and an idiosyncratic inter-pretation of its history. They are wrong in this, and it is important to see why because the argument reverberates well beyond warrants, to the Fourth Amendment's probable cause requirement, and to the question of how we are to regulate most aspects of the new policing.

Begin with the text of the Fourth Amendment (with a couple of numbers inserted)—and note how it does indeed seem to leave some-thing unsaid:

(1) The right of the people to be secure in their persons, homes, papers, and effects, against unreasonable searches and sei-zures, shall not be violated, (2) and no Warrants shall issue, but

upon probable cause, supported by Oath or affirmation, and particularly describing the place to be searched, and the persons or things to be seized.[23]

Clause (1) creates a right to be free from "unreasonable searches and seizures." Then, clause (2) bans the issuance of warrants without probable cause, etc. But, as a Joint Committee of the American Bar Association and the American Law Institute said of that text in 1966, "the amendment nowhere connects the two clauses." Specifically, "it nowhere says in terms what one might expect it to say: that all searches without a warrant . . . are . . . unreasonable." Can you see that? On its face the Amendment does not seem to require warrants explicitly.[24]

This omission has left room to argue that warrants are simply unnecessary. Two noted scholars—Telford Taylor writing in 1969, and Akhil Amar writing in 1994—have done just that. Under their theory, the failure to come right out and insist on warrants was not a mistake. It was quite intentional, they argue, because the Framers of the Fourth Amendment disfavored warrants, and hardly would have insisted upon them.[25]

How this seemingly topsy-turvy reading could make sense requires recalling—Taylor and Amar tell us—that back in olden days the remedy for an unlawful search or seizure was to sue the offender for money damages. But if the searcher had a warrant, that warrant would provide almost complete immunity from liability. In other words, historically warrants were like "Get Out of Jail Free" cards—call them "Search and Seize As You Will" cards. The abuse of warrants to immunize British officials, Taylor and Amar argue, led the framers of the Fourth Amendment to disdain warrants and impose controls on them. Because of this history, Taylor and Amar conclude, it is wrong to read the Fourth Amendment as *requiring* warrants. All the amendment requires is that searches and seizures be "reasonable." And it instructs how to control these dangerous warrants, should they be used.[26]

Now, it is indeed a fact that the colonists loathed the British use of "general warrants"—warrants that did not specify who or what could be searched or seized, but provided immunity to the searchers nonetheless. These warrants were issued indiscriminately. As a result, British officers were given complete discretion, frequently abused, to search who and what they would. Focus closely on this somewhat hysterical message from the Boston Town Meeting in 1772—we'll come back to it—as it gives the sense of how the colonists felt about the British warrants:

> Thus our houses and even our bed chambers, are exposed to be ransacked, our boxes chests & trunks broke open ravaged and plundered by wretches, whom no prudent man would venture to employ even as menial servants; whenever they are pleased to say they suspect there are in the house wares &c for which the dutys have not been paid. Flagrant instances of the wanton exercise of this power, have frequently happened in this and other sea port Towns. By this we are cutoff from that domestic security which renders the lives of the most unhappy in some measure agreeable. Those Officers may under colour of law and the cloak of a general Warrant break thro' the sacred rights of the domicil, ransack mens houses, destroy their securities, carry off their property, and with little danger to themselves commit the most horred murders.[27]

Nonetheless, the problem with Taylor and Amar's theory is that although the colonists hated *general* warrants, they were quite happy with "specific warrants," i.e., those that were based on probable cause and did specify who or what was to be searched. Indeed, by the time the Fourth Amendment was adopted, they had come to insist upon them. But, as we are about to see, Taylor and Amar take no account of this.

THE SUPREME COURT BITES

Taylor and Amar's theory would have remained just what it is—an academic theory—had not Justice Antonin Scalia bought into Taylor and Amar's view of history in a case called *California v. Acevedo*. What he said there should sound quite familiar by now: "The Fourth Amendment does not by its terms require a prior warrant for searches and seizures; it merely prohibits searches and seizures that are 'unreasonable.'" The Warrant Clause provides "limitation upon their issuance rather than requirement of their use." This is because "the warrant was a means of insulating officials from personal liability assessed by colonial juries."[28]

Justice Scalia wrote alone in *Acevedo*, but soon enough he was writing for the Court's majority, making much the same point—or worse. In 1999, in *Wyoming v. Houghton*, he gave a two-part test for whether a government search was lawful. "[W]e inquire first," he said, "whether the action was regarded as an unlawful search or seizure under the common law when the Amendment was framed." If the Framers would have allowed or forbidden warrantless searching, that's the end of the matter. However, "[w]here that inquiry yields no answer, we must evaluate the search or seizure under traditional standards of reasonableness by assessing, on the one hand, the degree to which it intrudes upon an individual's privacy and, on the other, the degree to which it is needed for the promotion of legitimate governmental interests."[29]

Look what just happened. No longer are warrantless searches *per se* unreasonable, as *Katz v. United States* declared. Now warrants aren't needed at all, unless they were required "under the common law when the Amendment was framed." (Obviously, there were no common law rules for things like automobiles or SWAT raids or drug testing or digital surveillance technology when the Fourth Amendment was ratified in 1791.) And if the warrant was not required by the common law, then the fallback question—the entire weight of our liberties—comes down to a generalized assessment by the judges of whether what the police did was "unreasonable." As we saw in Chapter 3, the sort of balancing test Justice Scalia calls for gives judges free license—usually to approve what the government has done.

Katz's insistence on warrants isn't gone completely; recent cases seem to seesaw between the two theories. But *Houghton's* balancing test has been used of late to justify any number of searches, among them the government collecting cell site location data without a warrant, DNA testing of people under arrest for serious offenses, and strip searches of juveniles in private group homes. Warrants have fallen from favor.[30]

So, who's right? Justice Jackson or Justice Scalia? *Katz* or *Houghton*? To figure this out, we are going to take a brief tour of the two most important moments in the history of the young Fourth Amendment: the British "Wilkesite" cases, and the American fight against "writs of assistance" in the 1760s and 1770s.

What we're about to see is that there is no war between history and common sense. To the contrary, it turns out Justice Scalia committed two serious historical errors. The first was in imagining that the law regarding warrants was fixed for all time by the common law as it stood in 1791. The second was in buying into the argument that warrants were disfavored in 1791 anyway. To the contrary, the generation that ratified the Fourth Amendment had precisely the preference for warrants the Supreme Court itself has continually expressed, until very recently.

"WILKES AND LIBERTY" . . . AND LEGAL CHANGE

Britain's suppression of John Wilkes and other opposition pamphleteers in the mid-1760s resulted in some of the most famous judicial precedents regarding government searching in the years leading up to the American Revolution. "Wilkes and Liberty" became a rallying cry for the colonists, especially the Sons of Liberty (of Boston Tea Party fame), whose actions so infuriated the British. The importance of these cases was such that Wilkes, and the judge who decided many of the cases, Lord Camden, had notable American locales named after them—from Wilkes-Barre, Pennsylvania, to Camden Yards where the Baltimore Orioles play.[31]

Wilkes was an unlikely hero. The second son of a well-to-do British distiller, well-educated and cultivated, Wilkes bought himself a seat in Parliament in his early thirties. He was a libertine, a member of a well-connected group dubbed the Hell-Fire Club for its bacchanalia, which involved, at the least, heavy drinking and blasphemy, and perhaps regular orgies. Benjamin Franklin called Wilkes "an outlaw and exile of bad personal character, not worth a farthing."[32]

Wilkes never distinguished himself in Parliament, but made his fame outside it as an anonymous pamphleteer. When King George III's government started publishing the pro-government pamphlet *The Briton*, Wilkes responded by putting out *The North Briton*, a mocking and satirical response to government policy. Freedom of the press wasn't what it is today, and there was plenty of talk of shutting *The North Briton* down. When Wilkes was asked by a notable Frenchman how far liberty of the press extended, he responded, "I cannot tell, but I am trying to know."[33]

In response to issue Number 45 of *The North Briton*—which went after the king in a backhanded way—the government's ministers decided it was time to shut the publication down. Though everyone knew by word of mouth who was publishing *The North Briton*, that and clear proof were two very different things. So the Secretary of State, Lord Halifax, issued a broad, ill-defined warrant for his messengers "to make a strict & diligent Search for the Authors, Printers & Publishers of a Seditious, & Treasonable Paper, intitled, the North Briton, Number 45."[34]

Lord Halifax's general warrant led to the most indiscriminate of searching. On little proof at all, Dryden Leach, publisher of an earlier edition of *The North Briton* but having nothing to do with Number 45, was hauled out of his bed in the middle of the night, subjected to a six-hour search of all his papers, saw fourteen of his journeymen printers and servants arrested, and was held for four days. All and all some forty-nine people were seized. Among them, of course, was Wilkes. His house was torn apart, hundreds of locks broken, numerous papers seized including the most private having nothing to do with *The North Briton* at all. He was taken to the Tower of London, and from there ascended to stardom on behalf of British liberty.[35]

Wilkes and the other victims of the searches sued Halifax and the messengers, in numerous lawsuits, succeeding brilliantly. The government is said to have paid a total of around £100,000 in "costs and judgments."[36]

In deciding these cases, the judges made eloquent statements vilifying "general warrants"—which is to say dragnet warrants that failed to specify their targets, the reason for suspecting them of anything, and precisely what was to be searched or seized. Granting Wilkes his freedom from the Tower of London, Judge Pratt (who later ascended to the peerage as Lord Camden) volunteered that "[t]he warrant I think [is] a very extraordinary one, I know of no law that can authorize it, nor any practice that it can be founded on." When Wilkes's case against the officials came before him, Pratt declared: "If such a power is truly invested in a Secretary of State, and he can delegate this power, it certainly may affect the person and property of every man in this kingdom, and is totally subversive of the liberty of the subject."[37]

The really important part of this story, though, is not that general warrants were condemned—no one disagrees with that. Rather, this became a landmark moment in history precisely because the decisions punishing Halifax and the messengers were an extraordinary *departure* from preexisting precedent. This whole story, central to the adoption of our Fourth Amendment, calls into question Justice Scalia's peculiar notion in *Houghton* that the common law (and thus our rights) is *ever* fixed at any particular point in time.

General warrants—which were better than what long preceded them: forcible intrusion and seizure with no warrant at all—had been in use in Britain for more than 150 years before the Wilkesite cases. The King's ministers who decided to go after Wilkes had not acted lightly; they had consulted the precedents carefully.[38] When lawyers representing the defendants in the Wilkesite cases fashioned their arguments, they relied heavily on these precedents approving general warrants. The Duke of Newcastle, who had served as Secretary of State himself, wrote to a friend, saying, "Pratt [is] (I fancy) a little mistaken . . . If I remember, I have signed many in the same form & words." In the printer Leach's case, *Money v. Leach*, Solicitor General de Grey insisted, "Similar warrants have been brought before this Court for a century past and never disallowed." Pratt himself, when Attorney General, had issued a general warrant.[39]

What's notable is that when the Wilkesite cases came to court, the judges didn't hesitate a moment over these long-existing precedents they felt were incompatible with personal security. In *Money v. Leach* Lord Mansfield said, "It is said that usage will justify it . . . Usage has great weight, but will not hold against clear and solid principles of law." His colleague Justice Yates concurred: the warrant was "[s]o totally bad, that an usage, even from the foundation of Rome itself, would not make them good." In *Wilkes v. Wood*, Pratt himself noted that "[t]he defendants claimed a right, under *precedents*, to force persons houses, break open escrutores, seize their papers, &c. upon a general warrant." But he refused to accept those precedents as governing, deeming them "totally subversive of the liberty of the subject."[40]

These statements must seem a little strange. What does it even mean to say that long "usage" will not hold against "solid principles of law"? Wasn't that long usage the law itself? How could something that had endured from "the foundation of Rome" be suddenly "bad" and thus unlawful?

The answer to this question explains why Justice Scalia was so far off in claiming that the "common law" at the time the Fourth Amendment was adopted necessarily binds us today. What Justice Scalia and his colleagues failed to acknowledge (for surely they knew!) is that the common law is both extant from time immemorial, and yet ever-changing.[41] As Supreme Court Justice Joseph Story, one of the United States' greatest lawyers, wrote in 1837, "In truth, the common law is not in its nature and character an absolutely fixed, inflexible system . . . It is rather a system of elementary principles and of general judicial truths, which are continually expanding with the progress of society." This ability to evolve "with the progress of society" was the "genius" of the common law. While the change was never directly acknowledged—for what gives the common law its fundamental stature is its apparent continuity—if it were incapable of gradual adaptation it would have withered on the vine long ago.[42]

In short, the Wilkesite cases—which mattered so much to those who authored the Fourth Amendment—represented an important shift in the common law. Before, the hated general warrants were in common use. After, as a result of the judges' actions, the Crown was limited in its ability to rely upon them. The common law was not fixed and unchanging, as *Houghton* implied; rather, when "the progress of society" demanded change, the common law adapted.

In light of this understanding of the common law, it is hard to fathom the Supreme Court claiming that our right to be free from a warrantless search is fixed in any way by the common law as it was more than two hundred years ago. Before automobiles (let alone drones and through-the-wall cameras) were invented. One can understand this sort of reasoning from Justice Scalia, who was an "originalist," which is to say he believed the Constitution must be interpreted as it was at the time it was ratified, without taking into account intervening societal change. (With his passing, Clarence Thomas became the sole remaining originalist justice.) But the rest of Scalia's colleagues on the Court don't feel that way at all. In a recent decision, the justices were required to decide whether warrants were necessary before searching cell phones incident to a lawful arrest—one of the historical exceptions to the warrant requirement. The Court's opinion in the cell phone case, *Riley v. California*, written by Chief Justice John Roberts, limited the historical common law exception in light of modern technology. Even Akhil Amar, whose theory Scalia was cribbing, disagrees with him that the common law is fixed in stone. "Reasonableness" under the Fourth

Amendment, Amar insists, "is not some set of specific rules, frozen in 1791 . . . amber."[43]

THE WRITS OF ASSISTANCE . . . AND REVOLUTION

Even if Justice Scalia were correct that our rights were fixed as of 1791, a look at developments across the Atlantic suggests he was wrong anyway about what the common law had to say on the subject of warrants at the time the Fourth Amendment was written.

In some very odd way, what Justice Scalia really seemed to have missed was the American Revolution. He often fixated on the common law in Britain; he seemed to forget the colonists were *rebelling* against the British way of doing things. Two of the most notable sources of their frustration were the continued usage of general warrants by the British in the colonies—in the guise of "writs of assistance" to enforce the customs laws—and the supremacy of Parliament, which allowed that to happen. In the end, the colonists rejected both parliamentary supremacy and general warrants; they came instead to favor constitutional limitations on the legislature, and warrants to control the executive branch.

The rule that eventually emerged in Great Britain was that general warrants were invalid—unless and until Parliament approved them! Narrowing Judge Pratt's decisions on appeal, the King's Bench agreed Crown officials could not use general warrants on their own say-so, but the same was not true in the "many cases where particular Acts of Parliament have given authority to apprehend, under general warrants." In other words: the King could not use general warrants on his own, but could if Parliament gave the okay. What followed was a battle royal in Parliament itself over whether general warrants should ever be allowed. The final result was a ban on their use—"except in cases provided for by act of Parliament." Some progress.[44]

In Britain, once Parliament spoke, that was the end of the matter. As William Blackstone—the great chronicler of British common law—explained at the time of the American Revolution, "[T]here is no court that has the power to defeat the intent of the legislature." This was true even if the parliamentary act was believed to be contrary to Britain's unwritten constitution. Parliament still had the final say: What Parliament chose to do, wrote Blackstone, "no authority upon earth can undo."[45]

But it was precisely this idea of parliamentary supremacy that the colonists ultimately rebelled against. And a critical battle in that fight was over writs of assistance.

Writs of assistance were a tool—not unlike general warrants—used to enforce hated British customs duties. They allowed British customs collectors to search and seize where and when they wished, and to demand help in doing so. This was precisely the sort of thing the Boston meeting complained of so vociferously, in the long quote we read earlier.[46]

The fight over the writs of assistance got under way in about 1755 when Charles Paxton, Boston's much-loathed customs collector, showed up at a warehouse to enforce a writ of assistance. Paxton was searching for Spanish iron on which supposedly duty had not been paid. Thomas Hutchinson, the brother of the warehouse owner, was present at the time. Hutchinson unlocked the door to the storehouse to show that there was no iron, but then told Paxton he could have sued him because his writ was illegal. Hutchinson's argument was that the governor lacked authority to issue writs of assistance, something the governor quickly remedied by arranging for the Superior Court to issue them instead. Soon thereafter, a group of more than sixty Boston merchants petitioned the Superior Court to disallow the writs entirely.[47]

The lawyer for the merchants challenging the writs of assistance, James Otis, famously argued in *Paxton's Case* that the writs were flat out invalid. The judge in the case—none other than Thomas Hutchinson, who since his interaction with Paxton had been appointed to the Massachusetts Superior Court—explained that Otis "objected to the writs, that they were in the nature of general warrants." Or, as Otis himself put it, memorably:

A man's house is his castle; and while he is quiet, he is as well guarded as a prince in his castle.—This writ, if it should be declared legal, would totally annihilate this privilege. *Custom-house officers may enter our houses when they please*—we are commanded to permit their entry—their menial servants may enter—may break locks, bars and everything in their way—and whether they break through malice or revenge, no man, no court may inquire.[48]

Under British law the answer to Otis, of course, was that Parliament had provided for issuance of the writs and so they were perfectly fine. But Otis's understanding of legislative supremacy was quite different from Blackstone's: he informed the Superior Court in the writs of assistance case that "[n]o Acts of Parliament can establish such a writ . . . AN ACT AGAINST THE CONSTITUTION IS VOID." If general warrants and writs of assistance were invalid under Britain's unwritten constitution—as the colonists felt they were—then the fact that Parliament issued them hardly fixed things. This argument formed the very essence of the American Revolution, the notion on the American side of the Atlantic that legislative authority was subject both to the higher will of the people and the higher law of a constitution.[49]

John Adams, who was present in the courtroom that day and heard Otis's argument, said years later (engaging in a bit of hyperbole), "Then and there the child Independence was born." He deemed James Otis's argument "the first scene of the first Act of Opposition to the arbitrary Claims of Great Britain." And one could indeed trace a line from Otis's argument to the decision to rebel and seek independence. Thomas Hutchinson, who as the judge in *Paxton's Case* eventually granted the writs of assistance, had his house burned during the Stamp Act riots of 1765. British authorities soon learned that though they could obtain writs of assistance, enforcing them was another matter entirely. When the customs collectors came to call, Massachusetts residents staged "liberations" of the goods, making the work of those collectors impossible. When Connecticut courts then refused to grant the writs, it led in 1767 to British passage of the Townshend Revenue Acts, which in turn triggered opposition to writs of assistance throughout the colonies. In 1774, in addresses to the American people and to the British Crown, the Continental Congress protested the power "to break open and enter houses *without the authority of any civil magistrate founded on legal information.*"[50]

Edward Thurlow, Attorney General of Great Britain and an opponent of American independence, found it strange that colonial judges who refused to enforce writs of assistance "should think the laws of the mother country too harsh for American Liberty." But so they were.[51]

THE AMERICANS CHOOSE SPECIFIC WARRANTS

Even as he condemned general warrants, Otis told the court that what was needed were "special warrants . . . issued by justices of the peace, to search in places set forth in the warrants" based on "information given upon oath." In other words, Otis was saying that if the government wanted to search it had to get a warrant to search a particular place, based on specific information indicating that what the government sought was in that place. Just like the Fourth Amendment says.[52]

Otis was ahead of his time, but by 1791 when the Fourth Amendment was ratified, such specific warrants were strongly preferred in the new United States. *This* was the emerging common law in the United States at the time of ratification, and to the extent Justice Scalia and his colleagues believed otherwise, they simply were wrong.[53]

Prior to 1760, general warrants were, if anything, more omnipresent in the colonies than in the mother country. But opposition in Massachusetts to general searches flared in response to British naval impressment gangs, the collection of excise taxes, and door-to-door smallpox searches. As a result, Massachusetts's law increasingly came to rely on the specific warrant. The same would occur in the other colonies, then states, in the thirty-year period that saw the Revolution, the Constitution, and then the Bill of Rights.[54]

Sentiment and action against the Townshend Acts confirmed that the distaste for general warrants was being replaced by a preference for specific ones. British officials applying for their writs found themselves frequently stymied by colonial courts that sometimes denied them explicitly, more often simply dragged heels or feigned illness—but would issue them in specific form. When in 1771 Pennsylvania Collector John Sift sought his writ, the court demurred: "Yes, if you will make oath that you have had an information that . . . [smuggled goods] are in any particular place, I will grant you a writ to search that particular place but no general writ to search every house—I would not do that for any consideration."[55]

In the period following the American Revolution, the now-united states gradually abolished all general warrants and displayed their signal preference for specific warrants whenever possible—with some exception for warrantless searches of particular businesses, such as distilleries. The Fourth Amendment was ratified in 1791, and—as documented meticulously by the historian William Cuddihy—between the Revolution and 1791 the states definitively turned against general warrants and in favor of specific ones.[56] Indeed, to the extent there was resistance to the transformation, it was in the Southern states, which adhered, for example, to copious and unregulated search-and-seizure discretion in slave patrols. Hardly a model for our modern Fourth Amendment.[57]

The movement in the United States to adopt a national constitution fostered the insistence on specific warrants, given fears about the power the new central government would possess. Throughout the process of ratification, leading Anti-Federalists demanded a protection against indiscriminate searches and seizures. Patrick Henry—of "Give me liberty or give me death!" fame—may have been the most florid, but the sentiments he expressed were common:

> The officers of Congress may come upon you now, fortified with all the terrors of paramount federal authority. Excisemen may come in multitudes; for the limitation of their numbers no man knows. They may, unless the general government be restrained by a bill of rights, or some other restriction, go into cellars and rooms, and search, ransack, and measure, everything you eat, drink and wear.[58]

Leading treatise writers of the early nineteenth century recognized that following adoption of the Bill of Rights, specific warrants were required. Here is what the Virginian St. George Tucker, a deeply admired law professor and judge, said about the Fourth Amendment, updating Blackstone's Commentaries on the British common law to make them applicable to the United States: "In the administration of preventative justice, the following principles have been held sacred: *that some probable ground of suspicion be exhibited before some judicial authority; that it be supported by oath or affirmation.*" That sure sounds like a warrant *requirement*, a point Tucker made even clearer in his lecture notes:

> What shall be deemed unreasonable searches and seizures. The same article informs us, by declaring, "that no warrant shall issue, but first, upon probable cause—which cause secondly,

must be supplied by oath or affirmation; thirdly the warrant must particularly describe the place to be searched; and fourthly— the persons, or things to be seized. *All other searches or seizures, except such as are thus authorized, are therefore unreasonable and unconstitutional.* And herewith agrees our State bill of rights— Art. 10.[59]

William Rawle, who was appointed the United States Attorney for Pennsylvania in 1791, the year the Bill of Rights was ratified, agreed. In 1825 he published his treatise, *A View of the Constitution of the United States of America.* In it, Rawle is foursquare with Tucker: "*The term unreasonable is used to indicate that the sanction of a legal warrant is to be obtained, before such searches or seizures are made.*"[60]

For these Americans, the meaning of the Fourth Amendment, in light of history, was quite apparent: warrants were required. Although the Amendment was only explicit in what a valid warrant looked like, it was implicit that—absent an established exception rooted in history and based in necessity—a warrant was requisite. After all, how could it be that the favored alternative to a search based on a valid warrant was a search based on no warrant at all?[61] As the law professor Thomas Davies has responded to Amar, after exhaustive historical research, "the Framers expected that warrants would be used . . . [T]hey believed that the only threat to the right to be secure came from the possibility that too-loose warrants might be used."[62]

In 1921, the Supreme Court made clear that it understood history just this way. In *Gouled v. United States,* the justices explained:

> "The wording of the Fourth Amendment implies that search warrants were in familiar use when the Constitution was adopted . . . Searches and seizures are as constitutional under the Amendment when made under valid search warrants as they are unconstitutional, because unreasonable, when made without them—*the permission of the amendment has the same constitutional warrant as the prohibition has,* and the definition of the former restrains the scope of the latter."[63]

The Supreme Court's movement away from warrants is simply bad history. While general warrants were indeed hated, and the Fourth

Amendment was adopted to control them, those who drafted and ratified the Amendment believed the answer to the problem of general warrants was not no warrant at all—it was specific warrants.

MORE WARRANTS, NOT FEWER

Rejecting a warrant requirement is bad policy as well. If anything, insistence on a warrant is more important and more appropriate today than it was at the time of the Fourth Amendment's adoption. There are two reasons for this.

First, today warrants may be the only effective weapon we now have against unlawful searches. Recall that Taylor and Amar's entire argument that warrants were not required by the Fourth Amendment rested on the assumption that if officers search unlawfully without warrants, they will be held liable for money damages. At common law, such liability was a real deterrent to feckless searches. As we saw in Chapter 3, though, the Supreme Court has now made it almost impossible to get money damages for unlawful searches—and has cut way back on the other remedy, the exclusionary rule, as well. Indeed, although Justice Scalia was wont to claim the exclusionary rule was not needed in light of the possibility of obtaining money damages, he voted consistently in favor of limiting money damages also. If Justice Scalia had had his way, we would be left with virtually no remedy for Fourth Amendment violations: no money damages, no exclusion, no warrants.

In law we typically prefer remedies for unlawful conduct to come after the law is violated, not before. We don't lock people up because they might rob a house; we wait until they've robbed it to impose punishment. Similarly, we don't by statute require people to mop the floor of their store, but if someone slips and falls we make them pay for failing to alert the public till it was dry. In this way—the way of deterrence—people learn to avoid imposing harm.

Sometimes, though, after-the-fact remedies are so ineffective, and the potential harms are so great, that we require permission up front. We don't allow people to build buildings and then if things are not in order have them torn down. We require them to get building permits first. We don't let anyone operate surgically on you and then simply impose money damages if they mess up. We do impose damages for medical malpractice, but we also license surgeons on the front end.

Warrants are, in this critical way, a before-the-fact means to prevent Fourth Amendment violations. They are a license to search. Because we are so bad after the fact at saying the police went astray and imposing money damages, or excluding unconstitutionally seized evidence, the right answer is for police to get permission up front. That is what warrants are: before-the-fact permission. In this way, many unlawful searches—like the one Susan Frunz experienced—will be avoided in the first place.[64]

Besides, it seems flat-out strange to limit the requirement to obtain warrants at the very time in history that technology has made getting them quickly so much easier. As we have seen, many of the exceptions to the warrant requirement rest in exigency, the idea that there is simply no time to get a warrant, so we won't require one. That is true of arrests, of searches incident to lawful arrests, and for many automobile searches.

In the old days, it could take a lot of time to prepare a warrant application, get it to a judge, and get it approved. Even as late as 1970, one pictures a cop sitting at a Remington typewriter laboriously hunting and pecking out a warrant application in triplicate.[65]

These are not the old days. As the *Frunz* judges pointed out, the officers could have obtained "a telephone warrant if they believed it was urgent." Telephonic warrants, which actually have been with us since the 1970s, are increasingly the norm. The rules that govern cases in federal court were recently amended to encourage reliance on just this sort of rapid, electronic communication.[66]

Nowadays, jurisdictions are experimenting even more with rapid warrant technology. Some Florida officers use Skype to obtain judicial permission to test drivers for alcohol. Similarly, Louisiana officers at drunk-driving roadblocks request prompt search warrants from judges when authority is needed to take blood samples. In Butte County, California, the judges have iPads so they can issue warrants at all hours, using DocuSign for electronic signatures. The justices themselves have recognized that "[w]ell over a majority of the States allow police officers or prosecutors to apply for search warrants remotely through various means, including telephonic or radio communications, electronic communications such as e-mail, and video-conferencing."[67]

Indeed, given the available technology, it seems apparent we should be requiring warrants in more circumstances rather than fewer, including those in which we do not currently—like for many administrative searches—or even for arrests. Depriving someone of their liberty is a grave, grave thing. Historically we did not demand warrants for arrests, because it was impossible to get them fast enough. Today, police could get electronic permission while the suspect waits in the police cruiser.

There are some hopeful signs on the horizon. In a 2013 drunk-driving case, in which the question was whether officers could take blood without consent or a warrant, the justices said no. Changes in technology making it faster to get warrants demanded the government prove in each case that getting a warrant was impossible. Similarly, in the 2014 case holding that cell phones could not be searched without a warrant, the Chief Justice said, "Our cases have determined that '[w]here a search is undertaken by law enforcement officials to discover evidence of criminal wrongdoing . . . reasonableness generally requires the obtaining of a judicial warrant.'" That's a kindness by the Chief Justice to a body of decisions that have in fact dismantled the warrant requirement. But it is the direction in which we should be moving. Whenever police can get permission—a warrant—before searching or seizing, they should have to do so.[68]

Of course, warrants aren't everything. They are only as good as the "probable cause" that supports them, a topic we turn to next. But getting warrants—authorization before cops act—would go a long way toward protecting our liberties, and avoiding the sort of thing that happened to Susan Frunz, and happens all too often today. Mistakes are part of life, but we should do what we can to avoid them, particularly if it is relatively easy to do.

6

SEARCHES WITHOUT PROBABLE CAUSE

Whether they have a warrant or not, government officials need a good reason before they intrude into people's lives. That's what the Fourth Amendment means when it talks about "probable cause" and prohibits "un*reason*able" searches and seizures. Searches with warrants must be based on probable cause, but so, too, the searches that are excused from the warrant requirement. "Cause" is what spells the line between lawful and lawless policing: without just cause—a good reason—the government's use of coercive force runs the risk of being arbitrary, discriminatory, or just plain senseless. Unfortunately, the Supreme Court has watered down this vital protection, to the point that it has made suspects of us all.

"SHAKE EVERYONE UP"

Consider the case of Nicholas Peart. Nicholas is the sort of young man you'd be proud to call your own. He's soft-spoken, gentle, handsome, and fit, and carries the weight of the world on his shoulders. Nicholas's mother died when he was twenty-one, of lung cancer. He had to take a year off from school to care for her, and for his three younger siblings, whom he is now raising (with some help from an older sister who lives nearby). His younger sister is disabled. Nicholas is working toward his college degree, and holding down a job, all the while making sure he is around for the kids.[1]

On December 18, 2011, Nicholas published a piece in *The New York Times* Sunday Review titled "Why Is the N.Y.P.D. After Me?" Good question. In it he describes three instances over the course of four years in which multiple police officers took possession of him, held guns to his head, pushed him to the ground or against walls, ran their hands over his body, and picked through his pockets, his wallet, and his clothes. The first was his eighteenth birthday, when he was sitting with a cousin and friend on a bench; squad cars suddenly appeared, officers jumped out, held guns on them, and forced them to the ground. One officer took Nicholas's wallet out of his pants, looked through it, found his driver's license, and tossed it back, saying sarcastically, "Happy birthday." The second time, he was leaving his grandmother's house in Flatbush.[2]

The third was the most startling. Walking home from the gym, Peart was accosted by officers who took his cell phone, wallet, and keys. They handcuffed him and put him in the back of an unmarked police car. Then, while Peart was restrained down the block, one of the officers used Peart's keys to enter the building where Nicholas and his family lived, and actually tried to get into their apartment. His younger sister, hysterical, had been warned not to let strangers in and kept the door barred. She tried frantically to call Nicholas, but he could not answer to reassure her: the police had his phone.[3]

Peart, who has never been in any trouble with the law—well, unless you count the law hijacking him repeatedly—is hardly alone. Between 2004 and 2011 there were more than *four million* similar stop-and-frisk actions documented by the NYPD, and apparently countless undocumented ones as well. You'd think these were a lot of bad people getting jumped all over by armed officers, but you'd be wrong. The only legal justification for frisking someone in this manner is that an officer has "articulable suspicion" that the person possesses a dangerous weapon. Yet the NYPD has found weapons roughly 1.5 percent of the time, and guns in less than 0.1 percent of the stops. Barely ever. If the officers were really acting on "articulable suspicion," and still finding this few weapons, we'd worry about their ability to distinguish what is suspicious from what is not. But that's not what is going on here at all. A precinct sergeant was secretly recorded instructing officers, as they headed out to the beat, "Shake everybody up. Anybody moving, anybody coming out of that building . . . Everybody walking around. Stop 'em." Or a deputy inspector, on Halloween night: "[T]hey got any bandanas around their necks, Freddy Krueger masks, I want them stopped, cuffed, aright, brought in here, run for warrants. They're juveniles, we're gonna leave 'em in here till their parents come and pick 'em up."[4]

Let's take this for what it is. In an effort to keep guns off the street and crime rates down, the NYPD—with nothing remotely approaching a legally sufficient reason, or "cause"—subjected people to stop-and-frisks simply to ensure they would not misbehave. The NYPD, which was sued over the practice, denied this is its policy. Yet, at the same time (making for an odd litigation strategy), then-Commissioner Ray Kelly explained that it is a "deterrent to criminal activity, which includes the criminal possession of a gun." What the Commissioner was saying is that if police stop people indiscriminately—meaning without cause—then people will never know when they might be searched, and so they will simply leave weapons and contraband at home.[5]

We condemn this sort of indiscriminate use of government force when it happens in other countries. We like to imagine it doesn't happen here. But it does. And it's not just stop-and-frisks, of which there are millions every year throughout the country.[6] In train terminals and on buses, on the streets and roadways of America, police seize us, and search our persons and possessions, without anything approaching a sufficient reason. It all has happened because the Supreme Court has backed away from the Constitution's requirement of "probable cause."

This sort of activity is not costless. It has turned wide swaths of the American public, innocents as well as guilty, into criminal suspects. As a result, many do not trust the police. Peart explains how it feels, the anger, the fright, how "the mood just changes and your heart kind of drops." Most of all, the humiliation: "Other people see you're being stopped and frisked and they're looking at you saying what did he do." It *is* degrading and humiliating. As often as this cliché gets tossed around inappropriately, it is fair to say that if the Framers of our Constitution were here to see this, they'd be mortified.[7]

Something has gone terribly wrong. Some of these police activities are entirely legitimate, while others are so far off the mark as to be intolerable in any society that calls itself free. The problem is that we've lost the ability to tell the difference. This chapter tells the story of how this happened, how, bit by bit, the Supreme Court loosened the requirement of just cause to the point that government officials were left with no clear guidance of what is in and what is out. And what unguided power in police hands has meant to the rest of us.

WHAT'S CAUSE?

There's nothing in the least bit novel about the idea of requiring just cause before one's body or property is forcibly violated. The concept has been part of our legal tradition for hundreds of years. By the time James Madison penned the Fourth Amendment, the idea of probable cause already had been a feature of English law for almost two centuries.

English judges emphasized the importance of probable cause as early as 1611, in *Sir Anthony Ashley's Case*. Sir Anthony was a minor aristocrat who had fallen into some disgrace, accused of embezzlement, when Sir James Creighton decided he wanted to get his hands on Ashley's holdings and income. When other attempts failed, Creighton and his coconspirators cooked up a plot to accuse Ashley of having murdered a fellow named William Rice, who had died some eighteen years before. The plot failed and the tables were turned on Creighton and the others, who were then tried for conspiracy. At the heart of the case was the question of whether Creighton and his collaborators had been justified in arresting Ashley in the first place. (This was the time before organized police, when private parties enforced the criminal law.) The court's answer was no; an arrest was out of the question unless "he who doth arrest hath suspicion upon probable cause." Such cause was altogether lacking in this instance: "the said William Rice did not die of any poisoning, but of another horrible disease, that he had got by his wicked and dissolute life, which with reverence cannot be spoken."[8]

Sir Anthony Ashley's Case highlights why such a requirement of sufficient cause is so important. Police might act, like Sir James, out of ill motives. Or they might simply act without sufficient care. Either way, if people can be searched or arrested without cause, then everyone is at risk of having their liberty taken away at any moment. That is why, no matter what it has been called—including "probable suspicion," "cause and probability of suspecting the party," and "reasonable cause"—this idea of sufficient cause to intervene has long been part of our tradition.[9]

In 1948, in a case called *Brinegar v. United States*, the Supreme Court offered the definition of probable cause that is used to this very day. At about six o'clock on the evening of March 3, 1947, federal officers watched Virgil Brinegar drive his car heading west toward the Oklahoma-Missouri border. Missouri was a "wet" state, Oklahoma a "dry" one, and federal law made it illegal to transport alcohol from one to the other. The feds had arrested Brinegar for the illegal transport of booze just five months earlier, and in the intervening months had on several occasions observed his loading crates of alcohol in Joplin, Missouri. So when they saw Brinegar in his apparently heavily laden Ford coupe pass them about five miles east of the Oklahoma border, they took off after him, figuring he was up to his usual tricks. Once the feds caught up with Brinegar a mile later, he admitted he had twelve cases of liquor. The issue in the case was whether the federal agents had probable cause to pull him over in the first place. In deciding yes, the Supreme Court explained that probable cause means more than "bare suspicion." It "exists where the facts and circumstances within . . . [the officers'] knowledge and of which they had reasonably trustworthy information [are] sufficient in themselves to warrant a man of reasonable caution in the belief that an offense has been or is being committed."[10]

That's all there is to it: Is there enough evidence to make a reasonable person think a crime is being committed or evidence of a crime will be found? It's a hard call whether there actually was probable cause to pull Brinegar over. The justices of the Supreme Court disagreed with one another vehemently on the question, as did the judges in the lower courts. But the point is that at least in Brinegar's case there *was* a debate—everyone thought that before the police went stopping people they needed good evidence of a reason for doing so.

Within fifty years of *Brinegar*, this most basic rule of criminal procedure had broken down completely. What had endured as a foundational principle of policing for centuries began to unravel in 1968. And it has continued to unravel ever since.

THE JUSTICES' DILEMMA

The NYPD's aggressive stop-and-frisk policy that entangled Nicholas Peart was built on the Supreme Court's 1968 decision in *Terry v. Ohio*. So was much other invasive policing. Yet *Terry* was, from the start, an unstable edifice on which to build. Resolving *Terry* put the justices in a terrible bind. They chose the path they thought would do least harm, but their guess has proven terribly incorrect.

Terry arose on the streets of Cleveland, Ohio, on the afternoon of October 31, 1963. Detective Martin "Mac" McFadden was on his usual beat, patrolling the downtown shopping district in plainclothes. McFadden, a thirty-eight-year veteran of the force, specialized in nabbing pickpockets and thieves of the local department stores; he'd covered this very same shopping area for thirty years.[11]

As he was patrolling his beat that Halloween afternoon, something caught McFadden's eye. Walking northeast on Huron Street, McFadden spotted two men standing on the corner of Huron and Euclid. "Now in this case when I looked over they didn't look right to me at the time."[12]

His suspicions aroused, McFadden hastened his pace until he could slip into the lobby of a nearby store to observe what was happening. "I get more purpose to watch them when I seen their movements." The two men were taking turns walking up and down Huron Street. Each would walk west a few hundred yards, look into a store window, and then walk back. McFadden could not tell which store window exactly, but he "didn't like their actions"; he "suspected them of casing a job, a stick-up." After the two men had walked the circuit two or three times, a third man appeared and spoke with them, then walked away. The two men took another couple trips up and down Huron, then abandoned their task.[13]

McFadden, still suspicious, tailed the two men down Euclid, but he did not have to go far. Soon he watched the two reconnoiter with the third man, in front of Zucker's Department Store. Deciding the time was ripe for action, McFadden approached the men and asked their names. When someone "mumbled something," McFadden grabbed one of the men, who proved to be John Terry, and spun him around so that he was facing the other two. McFadden then "patted" or "tapped" Terry's body and "felt something that seemed like a gun." Unable to pull it out easily, he "ordered the three of them into the store," telling the occupants to call the paddy wagon. McFadden made his prisoners face the wall with their hands up, and frisked the three of them. From Terry's pocket, and from that of his partner Richard Chilton, McFadden pulled out two .38 revolvers.[14]

Both men were charged with possessing concealed weapons. Whether the charges against Terry and Chilton could stick depended entirely on whether McFadden's actions on Euclid Street that day were lawful. Their lawyer argued that McFadden had violated the men's rights under the Fourth Amendment when he seized them and patted them down, and that the guns he recovered should be excluded from evidence.[15]

As Judge Bernard Friedman of the Cuyahoga County Court of Common Pleas saw the question, it was whether "an officer who has long experience as a detective is justified based upon what he saw and observed to stop and frisk an individual." It had long been the rule that police could search someone they were arresting, but Judge Friedman didn't think there had been a lawful arrest at the time the frisk took place. He also believed "it would be stretching the facts beyond reasonable comprehension" to claim there was probable cause to arrest at the time that McFadden stopped the men to question them. Still, the judge believed McFadden was in the right to investigate the activity he'd observed, and he concluded that once McFadden stopped the men to investigate, he was entitled to pat them down for his own protection. No doubt the judge's conclusion was colored by the fact that a week earlier Cleveland had buried a cop who had sprung upon an armed man unawares.[16]

The case arrived at the Supreme Court as both a political and a legal hot potato. At that moment in history the justices were under terrific pressure to defend law and order. Crime rates were skyrocketing, the country was afraid, and the justices were being criticized in heated terms for their pro–defendants' rights decisions. Deciding against the stop-and-frisk practices of McFadden and other officers would be seen as taking away yet another arrow in the beat cop's quiver.[17]

Still, deep down the justices had concerns about stop-and-frisk, which was an increasingly common and increasingly controversial practice on the troubled streets of the United States of America in the 1960s. Between ghetto riots and protests of all sorts—against the Establishment and the Vietnam War; for civil rights—the country's public spaces were seen as out of control. Martin Luther King, Jr.'s assassination triggered widespread rioting and looting in the District of Columbia just months prior to the resolution of the *Terry* case, and Bobby Kennedy was shot and killed just five days before. Police claimed they needed the sort of authority McFadden had used just to keep the peace. But those on the streets resented it. Two crime commissions that decade fingered this very sort of police conduct to be the source of great hostility in minority communities.[18]

While the justices were inclined to okay what McFadden had done—their initial vote on the case was unanimous—justifying it as a legal matter was going to prove no easy matter. The question the justices were forced to answer in *Terry* was whether—even if getting a warrant was impossible given the exigency that someone like Officer McFadden faced—a "search" or "seizure" was ever permissible in the absence of probable cause.

Note that one way to approve McFadden's actions was simply to declare that what he did was neither a "search" nor a "seizure." If this were true, then the Fourth Amendment said nothing about it, and the guns were admissible. Yet calling it neither a "search" nor a "seizure" meant this sort of police conduct would be entirely unregulated by the Constitution. Police could toss people against walls and frisk them as they wished.

On the other hand, if it was a "search" or "seizure," then under precedents going back to the 1600s, McFadden needed probable cause. Yet, as Judge Friedman had noted, it was hardly apparent that McFadden had probable cause at the time he acted.[19]

So, what to do? That was the justices' dilemma.

THE BIRTH OF "REASONABLENESS"

The justices flatly rejected the first fork of this dilemma, refusing to accept that "'stop' and 'frisk' . . . is outside the purview of the Fourth Amendment." Chief Justice Earl Warren's opinion for the Court was positively eloquent on the subject. Fending off arguments that stop-and-frisk was no big deal, he wrote that "it is simply fantastic to urge that such a procedure performed in public by a policeman while the citizen stands helpless, perhaps facing a wall with his hands raised, is a 'petty indignity.'" "[I]t is nothing less than sheer torture of the English language to suggest that a careful exploration of the outer surfaces of a person's clothing all over his or her body in an attempt to find weapons is not a 'search.'" He described how "[a] thorough search must be made of the prisoner's arms and armpits, waistline and back, the groin and area about the testicles, and entire surface of the legs down to the feet." Stop-and-frisk, the Court concluded, is "a serious intrusion upon the sanctity of the person, which may inflict great indignity and arouse strong resentment, and it is not to be undertaken lightly."[20]

But if McFadden had both seized *and* searched Terry, was there probable cause to justify it? On this question the justices, despite their initial agreement, began to splinter. Probable cause of what? Sure, McFadden was suspicious of what was going on, thinking the men were "casing a job, a stick-up." But all they'd done was walk up and down the street looking in a store window. "Store windows," the Court recognized, "are made to be looked in." And as Justice Douglas, who ultimately proved the lone dissenter, pointed out, "[T]he crime here is carrying concealed weapons; and there is no basis for concluding that the officer had 'probable cause' for believing that that crime was being committed."[21]

What really worried the justices—and everyone else watching the case—was that if they called the facts observed by McFadden "probable cause," that would seriously lower the bar on police interfering in people's lives. The Fourth Amendment doesn't kick in until something is a "search" or "seizure." But once there is probable cause, then almost any searching or seizing short of injuring or killing a person, or gratuitous ransacking, is permitted. The Fourth Amendment, up to this point in history, was notoriously short on middle ground. The same cause that would have justified the brief frisk of Terry would also, under existing law at the time, have allowed a full search of his body and anything he was carrying. It would have permitted McFadden, without ever saying a word to Terry, to arrest him then and there. Did McFadden have enough evidence, at the moment he confronted the men outside Zucker's Department Store, to simply load them into the police wagon and imprison them?

So there the justices were, stuck between a "no search and seizure" rock and a "probable cause" hard place.

What the *Terry* Court ultimately did was to toss probable cause overboard. As we have seen, there are two clauses in the Fourth Amendment, one that states the people have a right to be free from "unreasonable searches and seizures" and one that specifies the requirements about warrants, including that any warrant must be based on "probable cause." The separation of these clauses, as we learned last chapter, has allowed some to argue that warrants are not a requirement. But even if the justices have not always insisted on a warrant, until *Terry* they had consistently maintained that probable cause was a necessity.

Breaking with hundreds of years of tradition, the *Terry* Court concluded that rather than requiring probable cause, "the conduct involved in this case must be tested by the Fourth Amendment's general proscription against unreasonable searches and seizures." In other words, rather than looking to see if there was probable cause to stop and frisk Terry and Chilton, they would simply ask whether what Officer McFadden did was "reasonable." Once again, this is precisely the sort of open-ended analysis that inevitably leads to judges reducing our rights.[22]

In fairness, the justices in *Terry* tried hard to make clear that in relying on the Fourth Amendment's "unreasonable" language alone they were making but a tiny inroad into probable cause. The Chief Justice said they were addressing the "quite narrow question" of "whether it is *always* unreasonable for a policeman to seize a person and subject him to a limited search for weapons unless there is probable cause for an arrest."[23]

But despite his attempt to write narrowly, Warren's *Terry* opinion contained the seeds of enormous discretion for law enforcement, which police and prosecutors would capitalize upon—ultimately with the Court's gradual blessing—in the years to come.

THE COSTS OF INSUFFICIENT CAUSE

What the justices in *Terry* failed to do adequately was explain when police could stop people in the first place. The *Terry* opinion's most precise holding was about the frisk: "[T]here must be a narrowly drawn authority to permit a reasonable search for weapons for the protection of the police officer, where he has reason to believe that he is dealing with an armed and dangerous individual." Justice Harlan, concurring, felt the problem with the majority opinion was its failure to explain why the police could engage in a "*forcible* stop." After all, if the police have no reason to hold someone against their will, and thus be in that person's presence, the justification for the frisk—danger to the officer— evaporates as well. The justices' not very helpful guidance was that "[e]ach case of this sort, will, of course, have to be decided on its own facts."[24]

The result of this omission is that the police, unencumbered by any clear standard to limit their discretion, stop unfathomable numbers of people and shake them like fruit trees, hoping something juicy topples out. Back when probable cause mattered, it provided a way of distinguishing those trees that deserved attention, and those that should be left alone. With probable cause out the window, lots of people get stopped and frisked by the police, and comparatively little evidence or contraband is found. This high intrusion and low success rate should surprise no one; the whole point of probable cause is to indicate when a search for evidence might prove fruitful.

Symptomatic of the problem is law enforcement's reliance on a so-called drug courier profile. All over this nation, on highways, on streets, at bus stops and train stations, thousands of government agents are engaged in drug interdiction. When drugs are found on someone, the agents must explain why they detained the person in the first place. What was the "reasonable" basis for the stop? One of the Drug Enforcement Administration's favorite tricks is to tell courts that the suspect they nabbed fit a "drug courier profile"—a set of facts that supposedly yields reasonable suspicion of illegal activity.[25]

In *United States v. Condelee*, for example, Agent Carl B. Hicks of the DEA claimed to have a "tip"—it is never disclosed where it came from, and never verified that he had it at all—that "sharply dressed" women were acting as couriers carrying drugs from Los Angeles through the Kansas City airport. Hicks saw a well-dressed woman arriving there from LAX, and followed her. He then approached her, showed his badge, and asked her for ID. She seemed nervous, opened her purse on a trash can so Hicks couldn't see inside, and handed her ID to him. He showed his badge a second time, informed her he was a DEA agent looking for drugs, and asked if she had any. She responded no. Hicks next asked to search her garment bag, and she agreed. The search again turned up nothing. So he asked to search her purse, at which point Condelee replied that she had no drugs, and told him to get a search warrant if he wanted to bother her further. Hicks persisted nonetheless. Condelee asked to go to the bathroom. Hicks said she could, but also said she couldn't take her purse. The pressure continued, until Condelee broke down crying and owned up to having drugs in the purse.[26]

Forget the drugs for a moment—you'll have reason to be skeptical about the magical detection abilities of DEA agents soon enough—and ask where Hicks was getting the authority to hound someone through an airport like this. What justified his persisting in hassling her when she said "enough" and told him to get a warrant? Where did he get the power to decide who can use the restroom and under what circumstances? What if it were you?

Hicks's argument was that the stopping and harassment of Condelee was justified because she met the "drug courier profile." As he explained, because a "sharply dressed" woman had arrived from the "source city" of LA, and moved rapidly through the airport carrying little luggage and not looking around her, he was entitled to hassle her till she broke down and admitted she had drugs. The court bought Hicks's story, holding that those facts "created a reasonable, articulable suspicion that Condelee had committed or was about to commit a crime."[27]

Really? That's reasonable, articulable suspicion? Those same facts describe most women professionals on out-of-town overnight business. The dissenting judge was flabbergasted, pointing out, among other things, that the tip on which Hicks purportedly was acting said nothing about any particular person or flight. To see how thin Hicks's basis for stopping Condelee was, consider the fact that she went to jail on a 3–2 vote in her *favor*; the magistrate judge who first considered her motion to exclude the evidence, and the trial judge, both agreed with the dissenting judge on the three-judge appellate panel that the facts did not support Hicks's actions.[28]

Agent Hicks and his supposed "drug courier profile," it turns out, was ubiquitous in Kansas City airport drug busts. In another of Hicks's cases, one judge, Richard Arnold, asked the million-dollar question. "It would be interesting to know," Judge Arnold mused, "how many innocent people have been stopped, either for questioning alone, or for search of their luggage. This information, which we never seem to get in these cases, would go far towards enabling us to say whether the kind of police tactic we have before us is reasonable, which is, after all, the controlling criterion in applying the Fourth Amendment."[29]

What Judge Arnold wanted to know, in other words, was Agent Hicks's "hit rate." In what percentage of his stops did his tactics yield contraband? After all, if it was high, then maybe there was something to Hicks's idea of a profile. On the other hand, if not, then maybe the "profile" was simply natural fertilizer.

Judge Arnold got no answer to his critical question, but another judge, in another part of the country, did. In a drug courier profile case out of Buffalo, Judge George Pratt blew the whistle on the DEA. The problem, Judge Pratt boldly stated, was that "the drug courier profile is laughable because it is so fluid that it can be used to justify designating anyone a potential drug courier if the DEA agents so choose." For example, in the case before him the agents justified the seizure, as they did in Condelee's case as well, because the defendant had traveled to Buffalo from a "source city" for narcotics. But at argument in the case "the government conceded . . . that a 'source city' for drug traffic was virtually any city with a major airport." That bit of honesty "was met with deserved laughter in the courtroom."[30]

Judge Pratt did a little research to compile a list of the various factors DEA agents regularly rely upon to justify conduct as falling within the drug courier profile. Here's the list (supported in the original by copious citations to actual cases). People are couriers if they:

> Arrived at night
> Arrived early in the morning
> One of the first to deplane
> One of the last to deplane
> Deplaned in the middle
> Used a one-way ticket
> Used a round-trip ticket
> Carried brand-new luggage
> Carried a small gym bag

Traveled alone
Traveled with a companion
Acted too nervous
Acted too calm
Wore expensive clothing and gold jewelry
Dressed in black corduroys, white pullover shirt, loafers without socks
Dressed in dark slacks, work shirt, and hat
Dressed in brown leather aviator jacket, gold chain, hair down to shoulders
Walked rapidly through airport
Walked aimlessly through airport
Flew to Washington National Airport on the LaGuardia Shuttle[31]

You get the idea.

Not only that, but Judge Pratt got a specific answer to Judge Arnold's question: How often *do* agents stop suspects and hassle them like this, only to come up with nothing? The agents in the case before him testified they "spend their days approaching potential drug suspects at the Greater Buffalo International Airport." In 1989 "they detained 600 suspects . . . yet their hunches that year resulted in only ten arrests." *Ten hits out of six hundred people harassed.* Less than a 2 percent hit rate. Judge Pratt concluded, "It appears that they have sacrificed the fourth amendment by detaining 590 innocent people in order to arrest ten who are not—all in the name of the 'war on drugs.'" In other words, it *could* be you.[32]

This phenomenon that Judges Arnold and Pratt identified is precisely what repeatedly caught Nicholas Peart in the NYPD's relentless snares. In one of the lawsuits against the NYPD for its program of muscling people without cause to ferret out supposed crime, the judge ordered the defendants to produce data on how often people were stopped and how successful those stops were. (The NYPD was already collecting the data, because of an earlier lawsuit challenging similar practices.) Of the "2.8 million documented stops between 2004 and 2009" in almost 90 percent of the cases the police released the target without even a summons for any criminality. Arrests were about 5 percent, the rest received a summons for a minor crime. Only slightly better than in the Buffalo airport.[33]

The reason for these low hit rates—i.e., the reason so many completely innocent people get hassled—is directly attributable to the *Terry* Court's failure to state when stops are permissible. Lower the level of cause enough and we are all susceptible to law enforcement intrusion on something that goes by the name of "hunch," but in common parlance could as easily be whim or caprice. The case law has evolved to allow almost anything to count. In one case, for example, police received an anonymous tip that a car was being driven erratically and had forced someone to the roadside; police located and tailed the vehicle for five minutes seeing no evidence of anything erratic, but the justices okayed a stop of the vehicle anyway.[34]

FRISKING AS THE GOAL

Not long after *Terry*, one of history's most famous judges, Henry Friendly—a man who wasn't much for mollycoddling criminals—worried that "[t]here is too much danger that instead of the stop being the object and the protective frisk an incident thereto, the reverse will be true." Judge Friendly proved prescient; rather than stopping on cause and frisking for protection, over time the search became the goal and the stop merely a means to that end.[35]

In drug cases in particular, the courts almost invariably approve a frisk, on the theory that whenever there might be drugs, there might be guns. Symptomatic was a 1994 District of Columbia case, *United States v. Clark*. Some undercover cops were buying doughnuts (true story) when a person offered to sell them pot. When he produced a ziplock bag full of marijuana, the cops arrested him. The dealer then volunteered to snitch out the guy with the "stash" if the cops would go easy on him. The informant directed the cops to Edward Clark, Jr., who was getting into his car. The police pulled Clark from his car at gunpoint and had him kneel behind the car while they searched him and the car for weapons. Finding none, the cops next threatened to seize the car if there were drugs in it, at which point Clark broke down and revealed where cocaine base (note: not marijuana) was hidden.[36]

The judges agreed there was no probable cause to search Clark, but concluded the tip was suspicion enough for a "stop." And given the alleged crime of drug dealing, the "frisk" was automatically acceptable, with no other facts to think Clark was armed and dangerous. But in explaining why what the police did to Clark was acceptable, you can just hear the ambivalence dripping out of the judges' mouths: "Taking a citizen out of a car, putting him on his knees, and then searching the car . . . [it] gets to a point eventually you wonder what the police are limited in doing at all under our law."[37]

These drug cases have a narcotic effect, leading judges to approve conduct of police officers that most of us would view as simply insane: pulling a man from his car on the word of a drug dealer the cops did not know from Adam, and having him kneel at gunpoint while they searched him.

It's true the police found drugs on Clark, but the question that always needs asking is how often the police are frisking or otherwise searching people and finding nothing. Are they acting on fact-based hunches or stabbing in the dark?

Once again, the NYPD figures are telling.

A stunning number of the arrests actually made by the NYPD following stop-and-frisk were for possessing small amounts of marijuana—stunning because possession of a small amount of marijuana is not an arrest-worthy offense in New York unless the marijuana is burning or in public view. But cops apparently solved this problem by putting their hands into suspects' pockets—as they did repeatedly with Peart—and pulling out marijuana, then arresting people for having it in "public." But when it came to finding weapons, particularly guns—the basis for the frisk in the first place—as we've seen the cops largely were coming up empty.[38]

New York is hardly alone. Lawsuits in Philadelphia and Boston have revealed similar evidence. In Los Angeles, car and pedestrian searches are no more productive. In 2008, a study of LAPD data found not only that racial minorities were far more likely to be stopped, to be frisked when stopped, to be arrested when stopped, and to be searched, but also that they were substantially *less* likely to be found with weapons, drugs, or other contraband after a frisk. In other words, the hit rate was lowest in the groups facing the most police scrutiny. Hit rates vary, but they are low across the boards.[39]

It is plain from what is happening on the nation's streets, and in its airports, that *Terry*'s elimination of the probable cause standard has set the police loose on the rest of us. Not just to stop us, but to place their hands on our bodies and possessions. The police still ostensibly need articulable suspicion to forcibly stop people—that much is clear—but what counts as articulable suspicion is deeply suspect, and the Supreme Court has done virtually nothing to rein in this sort of conduct. The stops occur, the frisks follow almost automatically, and the bodily integrity of millions of people is violated without good cause.

FIXING THE PROBLEM

The Constitution says precisely how much cause is appropriate. *Probable* cause. For roughly four centuries the meaning of what was required before government seized or searched someone or their property was relatively constant. Only in recent decades did the Supreme Court muddy this up, choosing lesser gradations of cause—reasonable cause, articulable suspicion, and the like—that no one quite knows what they mean.[40]

The question is whether there is any reason to tolerate this alteration of the Constitution's precise test for police intrusions.

One reason given to justify the lesser standards is the historical argument debunked in the last chapter: that the Constitution does not require warrants or probable cause, only that searches and seizures not be "unreasonable." But the Constitution certainly tells us in unmistakable terms what *does* make a search or seizure reasonable, and that is probable cause. There is no evidence that the ratifying generation, many of whom were hysterical about government overreaching, thought something less was appropriate.[41]

The other reason is, as we saw in *Terry*, the claim of necessity. If we adhere to the probable cause standard, the concern is we will be unable to investigate and thereby foil real crime.[42]

It's not at all clear that this claim of necessity is accurate either. Probable cause itself is an accommodation between society's need to investigate and the individual's liberty to be free of government intrusion. That's where the Constitution drew the line. But it may be more than that. The probable cause standard spells the line between when following every lead and every suspicion is a waste of time, and when it is worthwhile to investigate. As we've seen—indeed as we keep seeing—all this relentless searching on less than probable cause is turning up very little in the way of misconduct.

It's not just people's liberty at stake; it's resources that could be devoted to something more productive. Neither public budgets nor the size of police forces is infinite. Resources must be allocated. Lowering the cause standard sends officers on wild-goose chases, without many wild geese to show for it. Was it worth the money to plant officers in Buffalo's airport for a year detaining six hundred people to arrest ten? Could they have been doing something else to make us safer?

Having said that, it is not obvious that eliminating stop-and-frisk entirely is the right answer either—or even feasible. Police have long insisted on the need to question people based on their intuition that something is amiss. For years, police relied upon vagrancy and loitering laws to remove people who seemed problematic or out of place. When the law properly clamped down on this practice, finding such laws unconstitutionally vague or otherwise in violation of First Amendment rights, police forces turned to stop-and-frisk. Even before the Supreme Court authorized the practice in *Terry*, some states had stop-and-frisk statutes on the books.[43]

Persistent arguments for investigative stops suggest some core utility. They also suggest that police are likely to continue these practices, lawful or not. As the *Terry* majority seemed to concede, it may be better to accept the inevitability of stop-and-frisk and regulate it rather than relegating it to the realm of lawless police conduct. And in truth, overruling *Terry* would leave an investigative gap: what, precisely, are police supposed to do if they lack probable cause yet believe, to quote *Terry*, that "crime is afoot"?[44]

The question we need to answer is whether there is a way that *Terry* can be limited so that it meets law enforcement's real needs, and not an iota more. There have been a host of suggestions to place controls on stop-and-frisk. Some would restrict the use of *Terry*-type stops to certain contexts, such as felonies or violent crimes. Others focus on recordkeeping, which has been instituted as a result of court-ordered settlements. In order to ensure the integrity of that data, some commentators have suggested giving people a "receipt" explaining why they were stopped and the process for issuing a complaint. Departments also can create early intervention systems and make it "easier to sack bad cops." Obviously, there are prominent calls for expanded use of body cameras.[45]

As a matter of constitutional *law*, though, if stop-and-frisk is to be retained, the best solution is to return it to its roots: as an investigative tool to be used only when the police—as in *Terry* itself—can specify precisely what crime they suspect is in the offing, and have the facts to back it up. Unlike the rampage of unjustifiable stop-and-frisk that has been occurring on the nation's streets, Officer McFadden was quite clear in what he was doing. He suspected Terry and Chilton "of casing a job, a stick-up." He detailed at length the movements of Katz, Chilton, and Terry that justified this suspicion. On review, the Supreme Court explained why those very "specific and articulable facts" led to a reasonable inference that a robbery was about to take place. The *Terry* Court noted that it "would have been poor police work indeed for an officer of 30 years' experience" to watch Terry and Katz casing the store as they were without investigating further.[46]

This critical aspect of *Terry*—that the police identify which crime they have cause to believe is being committed—has gone out the window. Police no longer even try. Between 2004 and 2009, the number of stops in which a NYPD officer failed to articulate suspicion of *any* particular crime rose from 1 percent to 36 percent.[47]

When the police stop pointing to specific crimes as a basis for a stop or frisk, innocents are hassled and officer time is wasted. In 55 percent of the stops in New York, officers identified "high crime area" as a key factor, and in 42 percent of the stops officers indicated a suspect had engaged in "furtive movements." (Furtive movements can encompass such activities as "walking in a certain way" and "stuttering.") Notably, when the police identified furtive movements or high crime area as their primary reason for stopping and frisking, their success rates in finding guns or contraband were actually *lower* than the average.[48]

If reasonable suspicion is to remain as a standard for "less intrusive" measures such as stop-and-frisk, police must be able to articulate a specific, plausible crime that is being committed or is imminent. And the specific evidence that backs that claim up. In *Terry*, the Court warned that if stops were made to turn on the "inarticulate hunches" of an arresting officer alone, "the protections of the Fourth Amendment would evaporate." That is precisely what has happened.[49]

The same has to be true of the frisk. The *Terry* Court required officers to provide additional reason to believe the person is armed and dangerous before frisking. Given the facts of *Terry* it would have been "clearly unreasonable" to ask McFadden to approach the men without allowing him to frisk them if he suspected they were armed. Yet courts now allow officers to frisk any time a drug crime is suspected on the generalized theory that drugs and weapons must go hand in hand. This, too, must stop.[50]

Similarly strict rules should apply to automobile stops. Courts have fallen into the habit of stating that the standard for an auto stop is "reasonable suspicion." But when did probable cause go by the boards as the standard for pulling over automobiles, and why? We already dispense with warrants for car stops; must cause go too? If anything, stopping an automobile is more of an interference than what could be a very quick encounter on the street. Short of specific, articulable facts as to why an officer believes a particular crime is being committed, auto stops and searches should not be allowed. Period.[51]

Probable cause is what the Constitution seems to demand. Perhaps it would have been better, in retrospect, to deem what Officer McFadden had to be "probable cause." The costs of the breach have been enormous. To the extent any deviation from probable cause is allowed, police must be required to specify the crime that they believe is being violated, and provide facts to justify this. Real facts. If not, they make criminals of many of us, for nothing.

Judge Richard Arnold—the judge who wanted to know about Agent Hicks's hit rates—was a sober man, taciturn, learned in the law, hugely respected. President Clinton came within a hair's breadth of nominating him to the Supreme Court. He was hardly a man given to hyperbole. And so it's instructive to hear what he had to say in an uncharacteristically blunt dissent in a drug courier case. Because it is so apt for the millions of stops that are occurring in the United States each year based on insufficient cause.[52]

"It's hard to work up much sympathy for" the defendant in the case, Judge Arnold admitted: "He's getting what he deserves, in a sense." It was the rest of us the judge worried about: "[I]nnocent travelers are stopped and impeded in their lawful activities." These people "go on their way, too busy to bring a lawsuit against the officious agents who have detained them." "Airports," Judge Arnold cautioned, "are on the verge of becoming war zones, where anyone is liable to be stopped, questioned, and even searched merely on the basis of the on-the-spot exercise of discretion by police officers."[53]

Concluded Judge Arnold: "The liberty of the citizen, in my view, is seriously threatened by this practice." What has happened to Nicholas Peart, and so many more like him, certainly confirms this.[54]

The Supreme Court's lowering of the cause threshold from "probable cause" to "reasonable suspicion" has put us all in jeopardy. But that has hardly been the end of the Supreme Court's road in watering down the Fourth Amendment. Today, largely in response to the new, deterrence-driven policing, the Court has eliminated cause as a requirement altogether in many searches. That problem—and what to do about it—are what we tackle next.

7

GENERAL SEARCHES

One of the most complicated questions judges—and all the rest of us—have to grapple with is how to apply the Fourth Amendment to the new order of policing. As we've seen, the Fourth Amendment is all about suspicion. The people who wrote and ratified it abhorred "general searches," which is to say searches aimed at many people, without sufficient cause to suspect any of them. But much of policing today looks like what one might call a general search. In order to deter crime, and prevent terrorist incidents, many policing tactics are aimed at the entire population—without reason to suspect any given individual of anything. That's true of everything from drunk-driving roadblocks to airport security to bulk data collection.

How can today's policing be squared up with the Framers' antipathy of general searches? Answering that question requires us to recall the specific evils that animated the Fourth Amendment: arbitrary, unjustified government intrusions into people's lives. If we focus on what disturbed the Framers about general searches, rather than on the label itself, it is possible to reconcile their concerns with present-day practice. Not only that, but we can simplify Fourth Amendment law greatly.

IS NO SUSPICION EVER BETTER THAN SOME?

On January 15, 2001, officers from the auto trap division of the Orange County, Florida, Sheriff's Office visited Wholesale Auto Advantage, Bill Bruce's auto repair and salvage business. The police say there were eight officers present; employees of Wholesale insist it was closer to twenty. The employees say they were lined up against a fence and patted down, that guns were drawn, that they were kept on the premises against their will for hours. They called it a "raid." The police deny this. But the police concede that officers from the SWAT squad were present, decked out in SWAT gear, carrying weapons ranging from shotguns to Glock 21s.[1]

All of which is odd, because what was supposed to be happening that day was an "administrative" search. Administrative searches are humdrum affairs that occur on a regular basis in order to make sure businesses are complying with applicable regulations—like inspections of restaurants or liquor wholesalers. Or home inspections to ensure they meet the building and electrical codes. For an auto salvage place like Wholesale it's a way of making sure the business is not a "chop shop," trafficking in stolen vehicles and parts. Typically, a couple of plainclothes inspectors show up, check the records, maybe compare them with the cars on the lot, and unless something is seriously awry, they are soon gone. Judy Bass, the office manager at Wholesale, testi-fied that they'd had exactly that happen in the past, that the officers were "very polite" and stayed for fifteen minutes. This time, though, the first cop into her office was in camouflage, armed, and not identifiable as a police officer; she was "deathly scared."[2]

The police spent the entire day taking Wholesale Auto Advantage apart. Literally. Cars were sawed open, drawers and files were searched from top to bottom, then carted off. They hauled away seven pallets of goods, leaving basically nothing behind. Even Judy Bass's calculator and a Shop-Vac were seized as evidence.[3]

Bruce had done nothing wrong, as he and Judy Bass tried to demon-strate to the officers both at the time and for days afterward. It's true that some of the things the police encountered seemed odd. For exam-ple, they found a few vehicle identification number tags—the VIN you can see through a car windshield—that allegedly had been unlawfully removed from vehicles. But "seemed" is the operative word here: if the police had not been so hell-bent on cracking the big one and listened—or even looked at the paperwork—they would have realized that. Salvage businesses have to take off VINs to do their work. As Bruce explained, "This is for a body shop. They did not raid a library or a car wash." Florida law plainly allows for this; the cops evidently had insufficient familiarity with the very statutes they claimed to be enforcing.[4]

There's no need to take Bruce's word that he did nothing wrong. The Sheriff's Office brought a forfeiture action against Bruce, seeking to keep the property it seized, including well over one hundred cars on the lot. The state judge disagreed, ordering almost everything returned to Bruce. The State's Attorney quickly dismissed all of the charges.[5]

The cops basically ruined Bruce. The Sheriff's Office ignored the court order to return all the goods, keeping what they felt they needed to prosecute Bruce—despite the State's Attorney declining to do so. They held on to all the car titles they had taken, so that Bruce could sell nothing. Eventually he went out of business, busted.[6]

Bruce sued, and the federal appeals court judges were clearly irate. They believed the "massive show of force" at Wholesale was both inappropriate and unlawful for an administrative search. They sent the case back for a trial on whether the facts were as the employees alleged, and whether the defendants should be held liable.[7]

But the judges stumbled on the real question in Bruce's case, which was not *the way* the police conducted the raid that January day, but *whether it should have happened in the first place.*

The police showed up at Bruce's business that day because a few days earlier a young man named Zeeshan Mohammed Shaikh came to them to say that his insurance company had told him the VIN on his car's dashboard—a 1985 Mustang he bought from Bill Bruce—did not match the "confidential" VIN. A confidential VIN is hidden inside vehicles precisely to deter stealing cars and selling them for parts; the public and confidential VINs are supposed to match.[8]

As it happened, though, the sale of the Mustang was perfectly legal; it's a fine story, and had the police just knocked on Bruce's door and asked instead of tearing his place apart, he would have told them. It turns out some kid had a 1985 Mustang that he totaled. He then stole a 1993 Mustang, and put the VIN from the original car on the stolen car.

When he broke up with his girlfriend, she ratted him out, and he went to jail. Bruce bought the car at an auto auction; the car was sold as a "theft recovery" vehicle, with the VIN discrepancy noted on the documents. In fact, Florida had issued a new VIN for the car. This was all clearly indicated on the bill of sale: when Bruce resold the car he even made the buyer and his mom sign that they understood it was a theft recovery. Bruce had the papers (including one signed by a police official) documenting the Mustang's status as a theft recovery.[9]

No one—not the cops and not the judges—believed that when the police stormed Bruce's business that day they had probable cause to conduct a search for criminal violations. When Sheriff's Deputy Randall Root was asked, "[C]ould [I] just call you up and say, I think I got a stolen vehicle and can you raid Joe Bob's down the road," he insisted, "No, no." In Root's view, Shaikh was not even "alleging that he had a stolen vehicle." That's why the cops never took a formal complaint from Shaikh, and never sought a warrant. And it is why the judges in Bruce's case concluded that the information the police did have "did not rise to the level of probable cause that would have supported application for a warrant."[10]

Rather, the police simply decided, based on Shaikh's tale about what the insurance company had told him, that they would instead conduct an "administrative search" of Bruce's business. Unlike a criminal investigation, under Florida law police can conduct administrative searches without any cause whatsoever, and without getting a warrant.[11]

So here's the legal conundrum the judges could not solve. If the cops had enough evidence of criminal activity that it equaled probable cause, then they had to get a warrant. If they had no suspicion at all, they could conduct an administrative search without a warrant. But what if—as was the case here—they had a little suspicion, but not enough to equal probable cause? Was a warrantless administrative search acceptable then?

On first glance this question may seem crazy. One of the three judges hearing Bruce's case, Edward Carnes, thought so. Writing alone, he chastised his other colleagues' "hand-wringing" over the matter. After all, if no suspicion is fine, how could some suspicion be worse? "[T]his," Carnes wrote, "is one area covered by Mae West's observation that: 'Too much of a good thing is wonderful.'"[12]

Carnes has a point, right?

THE PROBLEM OF SUSPICIONLESS SEARCHES

Wrong.

Despite the superficial logic of Judge Carnes's position, things are not nearly so simple. After all—as we know—the police could not have gotten a warrant to search Bill Bruce's salvage shop. Warrants require probable cause, and no one thought the police had probable cause. As we've seen, the Constitution's requirements of probable cause and warrants are what keep police from doing what they like, when they like. And they prevent mistakes from happening.

If that's true, should cops be able to get around the probable cause and warrant requirements by just calling what they are doing an "administrative search"?

That's precisely what worried the other two judges in Bruce's case. They didn't believe it really was an administrative search. There was nothing regular about it: the cops came in SWAT gear and tore the place up. If police can call anything they want an administrative search, "the administrative search exception [could] be allowed to swallow whole the Fourth Amendment." This, the judges felt, would "invest law enforcement with the power to invade the privacy of ordinary citizens." It was "cause for general alarm."[13]

Though the two judges were clearly nonplussed, in light of Supreme Court precedent they didn't know what to do about the problem in the case before them. The Supreme Court had said administrative searches without any cause at all were fine. Ultimately, like Judge Carnes, they did not understand how having a little cause—though not enough to get a warrant—could eliminate the right to conduct an administrative search.

What all the judges in Bill Bruce's case failed to consider is precisely *why* administrative searches are okay without any cause whatsoever. Or, indeed, why any search without cause is ever acceptable. Why it is not prohibited as one of the "general searches" condemned by the Framers of the Constitution. Had they done this, they would have seen the problem with the search of Wholesale that day.

Ponder *this* puzzle: The government "seizes" millions of people each year and requires them to go through "searches" at airport security if they want to board a plane. The consensus is that airport searches are perfectly constitutional. That they are not, in the words of the Fourth Amendment, "unreasonable searches and seizures." Yet, why is that exactly? There's no cause, probable or otherwise, to suspect any of these people of doing anything wrong. At first blush, this seems the very sort of general search that the Fourth Amendment was written to prohibit.

In a world in which policing has shifted from a focus on getting the bad guys through suspicion-*based* searches, to conducting surveillance of all of us as a way to make society safer, these sorts of suspicion-*less* searches have become pervasive. That fact forces us to confront the question: Under what conditions are these searches without any suspicion whatsoever permissible? Once we stop caring about cause—about any suspicion of wrongdoing—how can we tell which searches and seizures are barred by the Constitution's prohibition on "unreasonable searches and seizures" and which are not?

This is one of the most significant problems of our day. If subjecting everyone who hops on a plane to a search without cause is okay, what about drug testing or DNA testing of all of us? Is that also fine? How about the National Security Administration grabbing all our phone records in the name of national security? What of roadblocks of all sorts, from drunk driving to auto safety checks? Or administrative searches of our homes and offices?

On questions such as these, the justices of the Supreme Court are deeply confused. But they are hardly alone. Civil libertarians, scholars, mayors and presidents, spymasters and police chiefs, all have found it difficult to figure out a principled way of distinguishing an "unreasonable" search from one that is reasonable, especially when they are contemplating a search on no suspicion at all. One cost of this confusion certainly has been an enormous loss of civil liberties: many searches are permitted that should never occur. But by the same token, the justices also have banned some valuable forms of policing as "unreasonable" when they plainly should be allowed.[14]

Things need not be this complicated. If one returns to first principles and simply recalls that the Fourth Amendment exists in large part to prevent arbitrary, unjustified, and discriminatory government searching, it becomes apparent that searches based on some cause, and entirely suspicionless searches, pose two completely different problems. And for that reason, as we will see, they admit of two very different solutions. What matters in the end is having in place protections to make sure that, in the absence of "probable cause," suspicionless searches are neither arbitrary nor unjustified.

THE DEATH OF "CAUSE"

The justices had billed their 1968 decision in *Terry v. Ohio*—permitting stop-and-frisk on less than probable cause—as a "narrow" exception to the general rule. Over time, though, the justices allowed other, and larger, exceptions, until cause no longer mattered at all anymore. We're not talking about lowering the level of suspicion somewhat to allow for things like stop-and-frisk, like we saw in the last chapter. We're talking about getting rid of cause completely. Each exception on its own may have looked like a "reasonable" little nibble out of the rule requiring probable cause to search or seize people. But like mice with a piece of cheese, nibble by nibble the justices ate up the probable cause rule in its entirety.[15]

The initial damage was done in cases in the mid-1970s involving automobile stops to enforce the immigration laws. These cases followed *Terry*'s lead in recognizing that once the courts let go of probable cause, there is "no ready test for determining reasonableness other than by balancing" the government's need to search against the individual's interest in avoiding "the invasion which the search [or seizure] entails." So balance the justices did, and on this basis they approved roadblocks more than fifty miles from the border—based on no cause at all. While "the potential interference with legitimate traffic is minimal," the justices declared, "[r]outine checkpoint inquiries apprehend many smugglers and illegal aliens who succumb to the lure of such highways." As we've seen time and again, this sort of balancing usually means goodbye to our rights.[16]

By the mid-1980s, the Court was making strong statements about the unimportance of cause. *New Jersey v. TLO*, decided in 1985, involved a school disciplinary investigation. (Because she was a juvenile, TLO's full name was kept out of the records.) Based on a report that TLO was smoking in the bathroom, and faced with her denial, Assistant Vice Principal Theodore Choplick searched TLO's purse and found marijuana, along with some evidence that the fourteen-year-old TLO was dealing. She ended up in Juvenile Court and challenged the constitutionality of the search. It's a fair question whether school officials should have to play by precisely the same Fourth Amendment rules that govern policing. But instead of starting from the principle that probable cause and warrants are required, and explaining why school officials are an exception, the Court instead made the bold declaration that probable cause is not "an irreducible requirement of a valid search." Rather, "the underlying command of the Fourth Amendment" is only "that searches and seizures be reasonable."[17]

Then, in 2002, in the case of *Board of Education v. Earls*, the justices approved the drug testing of all high school students who participated in extracurricular activities, without any evidence to suspect any particular student of using. The justices were quite clear that being made to pee in a bottle with supervision by others, and then having your urine tested for the chemicals it contained, was unequivocally a "search" governed by the Fourth Amendment. But as for the probable cause usually required to justify such a search, the Court stated: "[W]e *have long held* that 'the Fourth Amendment imposes no irreducible requirement of [individualized] suspicion.'" It depends, one supposes, on what "long" means. It took hundreds of years to move from probable cause to something slightly less, in *Terry*. Yet, within decades of *Terry* the justices had become blasé about whether any cause at all was needed before government employees conducted searches.[18]

Suspicion of any sort has now been done away with in a wide variety of contexts, from roadblocks to administrative searches, to secret collection and searching of our data by the FBI and NSA, to DNA testing of people arrested for crimes as minor as engaging in antiwar protests. Effectively, we've all become suspects, whether we've given the government any reason to believe we've done anything wrong or not. Take Lindsay Earls, the plaintiff in the case challenging the drug testing of students involved in extracurricular activities. Earls was a top student who never took drugs, and was in the show choir, the marching band, the Academic Team, and the National Honor Society. She went to college at Dartmouth, and then on to law school. She was, by her own admission, a "Goody Two-Shoes." She just didn't believe government officials could randomly single her out, and humiliate her by making her urinate on command, all to satisfy their own cravings for control over a social problem she had never given any indication of having created or participated in.[19]

Despite the hand-waving balancing test in these cases, what the justices have never managed to do is explain coherently why *some* searches are acceptable without any cause whatsoever, while others are not. The justices had a chance to clear things up in a case coming from Indianapolis, Indiana, decided in 2000. Instead, they muffed things badly. And this time, they didn't limit our rights; instead, they may have made us all less safe.

INDIANAPOLIS ROADBLOCKS

The Near Westside of Indianapolis in the mid-1990s was a tough place. The neighborhoods of Haughville, Hawthorne, and Stringtown were poor, and ridden with crime. The area, which was about 60 percent white and 40 percent black, had a median household income of just under $17,000. Only half of the adults possessed a high school education, and almost a third of the people lived below the poverty line. Drug trafficking was widespread and the gun violence that came with it all too common.[20]

Residents of the Near Westside were begging their elected officials to do something about the crime problem, and those officials were trying. The police chief and the mayor were looking for creative solutions.

Ultimately, the City of Indianapolis decided to experiment with drug interdiction roadblocks. In 1995, and then on a more widespread basis in 1998, the police set up checkpoints on roads leading into the Near Westside. Motorists were asked for their licenses and registration, while K-9s sniffed for signs of narcotics. If the canines alerted, the cars were pulled to the side for full searches.[21]

The roadblocks were announced in a press conference at which community leaders wearing hard hats backed up Mayor Stephen Goldsmith. Some 10 percent of people at the roadblocks turned out to be offenders. There were six checkpoints between August and November 1998, at which a bit more than one thousand cars were stopped, and just over one hundred people were arrested. Half of these were for drug crimes, and the rest for something else. (One man had a pit bull locked in his trunk.) Many had small amounts of drugs, but one of the first cars had more than two hundred pounds of marijuana in the trunk.[22]

Still, the main point of the roadblocks wasn't catching people with drugs and weapons: it was to forestall the problem. It was precisely the sort of deterrent-based policing that is so popular today. As the mayor and police officials explained, given the publicity attendant on the road-blocks they might not catch many drug traffickers, but they would "deter people" from bringing in drugs in the first place. "It's not just the statistics," explained one police official, "it's the message." "It made a statement," said another: "You're not going to be totally safe driving around with drugs in the car, or with guns."[23]

The roadblocks were popular with local residents, but they were challenged in court by the Indiana Civil Liberties Union, representing motorists unhappy that they were stopped. Neighborhood residents stepped up to defend the police, saying they'd asked for aggressive enforcement. "We are the ones who have to lay in bed and listen to the gunshots. We are the ones who can't use our streets because the drug dealers are there. We like these roadblocks."[24]

When the case—*City of Indianapolis v. Edmond*—got to the Supreme Court, the justices shut down the drug roadblocks. In doing so, one hoped they would offer an intelligible reason why some searches without cause were fine, and others were not. Or even why some roadblocks are fine and others are not. But they didn't. Instead they handed down a decision that by wide consensus makes no sense at all—yet continues to reverberate through the law, imposing a significant limitation on what government is allowed to do.

THE POLICE CAN'T SEARCH IF THEIR "PRIMARY PURPOSE" IS LAW ENFORCEMENT?

Roadblocks like those used in Indianapolis are common enough in the United States. They are used to address a variety of problems, from unlawful immigration to drunk driving, to unsafe vehicles on the road. Whether one approves or disapproves, the question is whether such vehicle stops, without any cause to believe any driver has done something wrong, are lawful.

Under preexisting law, one would have thought Indianapolis's road-blocks were perfectly kosher. A full decade before, in a 1990 case called *Michigan Department of State Police v. Sitz*, the Supreme Court had approved of drunk-driving roadblocks. In doing so, in *Sitz*, the justices set out a three-part analysis that was really just a variant on the "reasonableness" balancing test. First, did the government have an important problem it was addressing with the roadblock? Second, how much of an intrusion was the roadblock stop? Finally, was the program reasonably effective? In *Sitz*, the Supreme Court concluded that drunk-driving roadblocks easily met the test. "No one can seriously dispute the magnitude of the drunken driving problem," wrote the Court, noting the "slight" intrusion the roadblock entailed. And while it was true that only 1.6 percent of motorists traveling through the checkpoint were arrested for driving under the influence, that—the justices said—was good enough.[25]

Surely Indianapolis's drug interdiction roadblocks should have been upheld under this test. The justices in *Edmond* acknowledged that "traffic in illegal narcotics creates social harms of the first magnitude," not the least of which was the gun violence rampant in the Near Westside. The searches in Indianapolis took a bit longer than in the Michigan roadblock case, but still were only a couple of minutes or so. As for effectiveness, the number of arrests that resulted from the Indianapolis checkpoints was more than twice as high as the Michigan roadblock if narcotics offenses alone were considered, and five times higher if all crimes were taken into account.[26]

So, what possibly could be wrong?

The failing of the Indiana roadblocks, the justices explained in *Edmond*, was that they were set up for the "primary purpose" of "crime control." All the other roadblocks and general searches that they had approved, the justices said, had been used to address "special needs" of law enforcement *other than* ordinary criminal law enforcement. They had "never approved a checkpoint program whose primary purpose was to detect evidence of ordinary criminal wrongdoing."[27]

What does this even mean? It is a very strange thing, to say the least, to condemn the police for conducting a search whose "primary purpose" is "crime control." Isn't that their job? And isn't that also exactly what the police were doing in Michigan with their drunk-driving roadblocks?

How exactly does one distinguish a roadblock (or almost any other search or seizure) for "ordinary crime control" from one furthering "special needs of law enforcement"? After all, the defendants in both *Sitz* and *Edmond* were headed to jail for violating the law. And if the argument in *Sitz* was that the point of drunk-driving roadblocks was to deter drunk driving as much as catch criminals, well, exactly the same was true in *Edmond*, albeit to deter carrying drugs. Sending people to jail when we catch them is how we deter crime. The Supreme Court's test is so confused that in a case right after *Edmond*, the justices got all tangled up in trying to distinguish an "ultimate goal" from an "immediate objective."[28]

If you are confused at this point, you are hardly alone. In the wake of *Edmond*, the lower courts—and all the rest of us—are left completely clueless about what is permissible and what is not. Just look at what's happened since their decision in 2000. In one case out of Tampa involving a driver's license checkpoint, a cop explained, "If you get drugs that's fine too, but basically it's a driver's license checkpoint." The court did not agree. Yet, in another case DEA agents accompanied state officers from the Department of Consumer Protection on an "administrative" search of a pharmacy; this, the courts deemed okay.[29]

TWO OLD, ODD CASES

There's more than a little irony in the Supreme Court's utter confusion about how to tell a valid search without cause from an invalid one. That's because the secret to unraveling this rampant confusion is found in two of the Supreme Court's earliest cases involving searches without suspicion: *Camara v. Municipal Court* (a 1967 decision involving home inspections) and *Delaware v. Prouse* (a 1979 case involving highway stops). Unlike the *Terry* stop-and-frisk case, in which the justices used the idea of reasonableness to broaden police power, in *Camara* and *Prouse* the Fourth Amendment's prohibition on "unreasonable searches and seizures" was used to limit what searching the government could do without probable cause—or at least the way in which the government went about conducting suspicionless searches.

At first the reasoning in these two cases is going to seem mighty peculiar. But once we revert to first principles, and remember what the Fourth Amendment was designed to protect against, not only will the reasoning make sense, but it will point the way to clearing up all the confusion that has occurred since, and to how we ought to regulate the new policing.

Camara's Dilemma

In 1967, the year before *Terry* was decided, the justices confronted a dilemma involving housing inspectors. Some home owners were unwilling to allow government inspectors to enter their personal castles to check for unsafe wiring and the like without a warrant. But how could the inspectors get a warrant? After all, the Fourth Amendment says "no Warrants shall issue, but upon probable cause," and in the typical housing inspection there is no probable cause of wrongdoing; usually there is no suspicion at all. Most housing inspections—like most safety or administrative inspections of businesses—simply involve inspectors subjecting owners to periodic inspections. You get inspected when it is your turn, not when someone thinks you've done something wrong. Just like Bill Bruce's assistant Judy Bass testified happened on occasion at Wholesale Auto Supply.

In *Camara* the justices required warrants for housing inspections, but in doing so they were forced to redefine the notion of what it means to have "probable cause." After all, the Fourth Amendment says no warrants without probable cause, and in the usual housing inspection there isn't any. The validity of the search, the justices concluded, was to be decided by balancing the need for the housing inspection against the intrusion of the housing inspector. The former was great; the latter small. In light of this balance, there was "probable cause" (the quotes are the Court's) whenever the inspectors can show a magistrate the need for a search of the homes in a given area based on some set of criteria such as "the passage of time" since the last inspection, "the nature of the building," or "the conditions of the entire area."[30]

Heretofore, probable cause meant individual suspicion that someone had done something wrong. Now it meant whenever the need outweighed the intrusion. This new definition of probable cause was quite odd, was it not?

Prouse: Misery Loves Company

Equally perplexing was the logic of the 1979 decision in *Delaware v. Prouse*. In *Prouse*, a cop stopped a car for a license and registration check.

Approaching the car, he smelled pot, and then saw it in plain view. Prouse was arrested for illegal possession. The problem was the police officer had exactly zero reason to stop the car in the first place. "I saw the car in the area and wasn't answering any complaints, so I decided to pull them off."[31]

In deciding that this stop on less than probable cause—indeed no cause at all—was invalid, the Supreme Court used the familiar three-part balancing test. The justices were quick to concede that the state had a "vital interest" in making sure that drivers were properly licensed and cars were registered and safe to drive. But they were not so sanguine about the intrusion that these "random" stops entailed. Such a stop reflects an "unsettling show of authority," it interferes with "freedom of movement," and can be inconvenient and time-consuming. It can create "substantial anxiety."[32]

What really seemed to tilt the Court toward throwing out Prouse's conviction, though, was the third part of the balance: the justices doubted the efficacy of such stops. "It seems common sense that the percentage of all drivers on the road who are driving without a license is very small and that the number of licensed drivers who will be stopped in order to find one unlicensed operator will be large indeed." Wouldn't it be better, they asked, to stop people whose driving is erratic or whose vehicles seem to have a problem? Such stops, based on probable cause—actual suspicion—"occur countless times each day" and "it must be assumed," absent evidence to the contrary, that these stops are far more effective in finding unlicensed drivers.[33]

For this reason, the stop at issue in *Prouse* was deemed invalid. "In terms of actually discovering unlicensed drivers or deterring them from driving, the spot check does not appear sufficiently productive to qualify as a reasonable law enforcement practice under the Fourth Amendment."[34]

So far, so good. But it was just at this moment that the *Prouse* Court took its own odd turn, holding that its ruling "does not preclude the State of Delaware or other States from developing" alternatives, one of which is the "[q]uestioning of *all* oncoming traffic at roadblock-type stops." If the problem with the spot check of motorists like Prouse himself was that it was too intrusive given how unlikely it was to turn up a violation, weren't these roadblocks only going to be worse? Now even larger numbers of people would be inconvenienced, with the same small chance of finding violations.[35]

Justice Rehnquist, dissenting from the Court's ruling, was caustic in pointing out the illogic of *Prouse*: "Because motorists, apparently like sheep, are much less likely to be 'frightened' or 'annoyed' when stopped en masse" a patrol officer can "stop *all* motorists on a particular thorough-fare, but he cannot . . . stop *less* than all" of them. (Coincidentally, the case immediately after *Prouse* in the published Supreme Court decisions is called *Leo Sheep Company v. United States*.) This, he concluded, "elevates the adage 'misery loves company' to a novel role in Fourth Amendment jurisprudence."[36]

Rehnquist seems right: taken at face value, *Prouse* was as strange as *Camara*. In just the way that the state's interest in conducting housing inspections hardly seemed to qualify as "probable cause," how could stopping all these people provide more cause than stopping one?

BACK TO FIRST PRINCIPLES

The peculiarity of *Prouse* and *Camara* slips away, though, when one re-calls that a primary purpose of the Fourth Amendment is avoiding arbi-trary, unjustified police intrusions into our lives. It is about limiting the unbridled discretion of officers—or the government itself—to pick and choose who gets searched. The justices in *Prouse* reminded readers that "[t]he essential purpose of the proscriptions in the Fourth Amendment is . . . 'to safeguard the privacy and security of individuals against arbi-trary invasions.'" This could hardly have come as a surprise: the justices said the same thing ten years earlier in *Camara*—in exactly the same words.[37]

This concern for arbitrary enforcement goes all the way back to the two eighteenth-century incidents (described in Chapter 5) that led us to have a Fourth Amendment in the first place. Arguing against the Writs of Assistance in 1761, James Otis put his finger on the problem, stating that permitting general searches would allow "[e]very man prompted by revenge, ill-humor, or wantonness to inspect the inside of his neighbor's house . . . one arbitrary exertion will provoke another." Across the pond, condemning the general warrants used to search John Wilkes's property, Chief Justice Pratt—later Lord Camden—

condemned the "discretionary power given to messengers to search wherever their suspicions may chance to fall." There's virtually no disagreement that a, if not the, chief purpose of the Fourth Amendment is preventing arbitrary, unjustified searches. Judges and scholars of the Fourth Amendment have said the like, over and over and over, without dissent from the proposition.[38]

When it comes to figuring out whether a search without cause is permissible, the concern for arbitrary and discriminatory policing is what should matter—and not the Supreme Court's impenetrable distinction between "ordinary law enforcement" and the "special needs of law enforcement." As both the *Prouse* and *Camara* Courts made clear, the sine qua non of official arbitrariness is allowing officers unfettered "discretion" to invade our lives and our property whenever the whim strikes. The harm of a warrantless home search in *Camara* was to "leave the occupant subject to the discretion of the officer in the field." Similarly, the spot check at issue in *Prouse* represented the "kind of standardless and unconstrained discretion" that is "the evil the Court has discerned when in previous cases it has insisted that the discretion of the official in the field be circumscribed, at least to some extent."[39]

In light of the concern to avoid arbitrary enforcement, the seemingly bizarre solutions in *Prouse* and *Camara* all of the sudden make perfect sense.

In the ordinary case envisioned by those who wrote the Fourth Amendment, it is the twin requisites of probable cause and a warrant that provide the protection against standardless or arbitrary government action. Probable cause provides the reason for a particular search; it ensures that an officer is not arbitrarily or discriminatorily singling someone out. Then, the warrant ensures that the officer's judgment as to cause is not biased by crime-fighting zeal (or anything else for that matter).

But because there is no suspicion—and thus no probable cause—in housing inspections and license and registration spot checks, the Supreme Court had to come up with a new means of ensuring that the government was not singling out people for no good reason. The *Camara* Court solved this problem by requiring housing inspectors to show some regular plan for choosing who got searched and who did not. The "cause" justifying a safety inspection was area-wide rather than individual. If an area was dilapidated, or had not been searched in a long time, or had a particularly tricky set of structures, this would be enough "cause" to justify the search—precisely because it avoided the possibility of the inspectors targeting someone out of thin suspicion, whim, or malevolence. (And, it is worth noting, the justices also required a warrant by a neutral magistrate, in order to confirm this.)[40]

The *Prouse* Court's choice—subject obvious violators to traffic stops, or stop everyone at roadblocks—makes sense for the same reason. Yes, a checkpoint seems to be a greater intrusion for not much higher odds of finding violators. But it also ensures that no one is being arbitrarily, or discriminatorily, treated to the state's use of force. "At traffic checkpoints the motorist can see that other vehicles are being stopped, he can see visible signs of the officers' authority."[41]

TWO TYPES OF SEARCHES

Once we see that in *Prouse* and *Camara* the justices were putting in place safeguards to prevent arbitrary policing (and its cousins: unjustified and discriminatory policing), we can see that in truth there are two very different kinds of searches, each requiring its own sort of protection: searches that are suspicion-*based*, and those that are suspicion-*less*.

Television shapes the typical image of what the police do. In most television shows, the police are after a particular suspect for a particular crime. Police are *investigating* a violation of the law that has either occurred or is about to occur. The police may know the suspect, but in many cases they are trying to track him (or her) down based on some leads. Think here of Brenda Lee Johnson in *The Closer*, or Jack Webb in *Dragnet*, or *CSI: Crime Scene Investigation* in its many incarnations. In doing their job, the police engage in all kinds of things we might call searches, from looking for information on the Internet or in a police database, to taking fingerprint or DNA samples, to busting down the door of a suspect's house (hopefully with a warrant).[42]

The distinguishing characteristic of this sort of investigative search is that it is suspicion-based. The police have cause to believe that some particular person, known or unknown, has committed or is about to commit some specific crime. And the police are trying to discover the facts and put the culprit away.

But in much of the policing we've been discussing in this chapter, the police are doing something entirely different. They aren't investigating to catch a particular suspect; they are for the most part trying to keep there from being a suspect in the first place. That's what's going on with the searches in airport security. It is not that we put the TSA officers there to look for a bomb in a suitcase (though assuredly they are—and if they find one the person is surely going to prison). Instead, we spend an untold fortune on such elaborate security in the hope that people will simply leave their agents of destruction at home. The same sort of thing is going on with drunk-driving roadblocks. Yes, if a drunk wanders through then the police are going to get them off the road. But the real reason for the roadblocks—and the publicity that always accompanies them—is to discourage people from getting behind the wheel of a car in the first place. (Studies suggest this strategy is successful.)[43]

What distinguishes this second sort of search is that there is *no cause whatsoever*. Because the purpose of the search is deterrence—trying to get people to behave in the first place—there is no suspect and thus no suspicion. A wide swath of society is subjected to policing in order to make people think twice before violating the law.[44]

Suspicion-less v. suspicion-based searches. It doesn't matter whether the police are searching for "ordinary law enforcement" or "special needs." What matters is whether they have suspicion.

TWO TYPES OF PROTECTIONS

Once we see that there are two very different types of searches, it becomes equally apparent we need two different sorts of protections against government arbitrariness. What works for one simply will not work for the other. That's what the Supreme Court understood when it decided *Camara* and *Prouse*, but then seems to have forgotten when it went in a whole new direction with its unworkable approach in the *Edmond* case involving the Indianapolis roadblocks.

Avoiding Arbitrariness I: Cause-Based Searches
When the police search with suspicion, the protection is obvious. The Fourth Amendment tells us exactly what is needed: probable cause and a warrant. Probable cause ensures there is enough suspicion to single

someone out for a search; the warrant confirms the police have it right. And if a search is suspicion-based, but there is inadequate suspicion, then we have the danger of arbitrariness the Fourth Amendment was written to guard against.[45]

The problem of failing to distinguish suspicion-based v. suspicion-less searches is seen in a Supreme Court case that looked remarkably like the one that opened this chapter, only the junkyard owner in this case was named Burger, not Bruce. Burger owned an auto junkyard in New York City. One day the administrative inspectors, who also happened to be police officers, showed up at Burger's junkyard ostensibly conducting an administrative search. They asked to see his license and the book in which he was supposed to log all the cars and parts on the lot. Burger straight off told the police he had neither: he admitted he was operating illegally. At that point the police searched the junkyard, and Burger ultimately was convicted for dealing in stolen vehicles.[46]

On appeal, Burger complained (among other things) that the police didn't have a warrant to search his junkyard. The Supreme Court responded, in a complete non sequitur, that warrantless administrative searches were necessary to achieve an element of surprise. (After all, search warrants are executed all the time by surprise.)[47]

The justices realized, though, that absent a warrant some "constitutionally adequate substitute" was necessary. They identified three that in their view made everything fine. First, New York law only allowed searches during daylight. Second, it put licensed junkyard owners on notice that they could be searched. And finally, it limited the scope of the search: inspectors could only look at records and vehicles.[48]

Note how *none* of those supposed "safeguards" mentioned by the justices is designed in any way to protect against the evil underlying the Fourth Amendment: the police using their unlimited discretion to arbitrarily single out whom to search. Not one of those so-called protections avoids the police picking on someone for the wrong sort of reason or no reason at all.

There's a telling footnote at the start of the *Burger* decision that tips readers off to the real problem here. "It was unclear from the record why, on that particular day, Burger's junkyard was selected for inspection." That turns out to be a darn good question. The justices simply shrugged it off, saying, "The junkyards designated for inspection apparently were selected from a list of such businesses compiled by New York City police detectives." But that can't possibly be correct. After all, recall that when the cops showed up at Burger's junkyard, he told them right off that he wasn't licensed. Without a license, he wouldn't be on any official list of licensees subject to administrative searches. Right?[49]

Aha. Now we can pretty much guess why the police showed up at Burger's junkyard that day: they must have gotten a tip of some sort—like Shaikh's story to the Orange County cops about Bill Bruce and the stolen Mustang—that made them want to search Burger's junkyard. The search of Burger's junkyard—just like Bruce's—was a suspicion-*based* search. It was not a suspicionless administrative search.

What we don't know, and will never know, is whether the suspicion that the police had in Burger's case added up to probable cause. If there was probable cause in Burger's case, then a warrant would have made all fine. But if there was not probable cause, we are back to our old evil: the danger of arbitrarily picking and choosing whom to search.

You might respond, "So what, they got the bad guy, what could be wrong with that?" But this is precisely the problem we dealt with last chapter. If the police were always this good, then maybe we would decide to live with their supernatural powers of ferreting out crime. Of course, if they were that good, and honest about it, we would not need to worry about unjustified, or discriminatory, or arbitrary searching in the first place.

The problem is that, as we saw, the police are often wrong about their hunches, their searches on insufficient cause. Justice Jackson made precisely this point in the *Brinegar* case that defines probable cause: "There may be, and I am convinced that there are, many unlawful searches of homes and automobiles of innocent people which turn up nothing incriminating, in which no arrest is made, about which courts do nothing, and about which we never hear." That's what we have seen time and again: police searches on less than probable cause are often altogether wrong. And when the police are wrong, then innocent people—like Bill Bruce—pay the price.[50]

The Constitution is completely clear about the protections for cause-based searching. Warrants and probable cause. The Supreme Court watered these protections down when it allowed stop-and-frisk on "reasonable suspicion." That alone was problematic—and in the last chapter we explored the fix for that particular problem. But in allowing searches of places like Burger's junkyard on some undefined suspicion, without any protection against arbitrariness, the justices have gone seriously awry.

Avoiding Arbitrariness II: Suspicionless Searches

What, then, to do about suspicion-*less* searches? If the search of Burger's or Bruce's junkyards had been a true regulatory or deterrent search, it would have made zero sense to require probable cause. There would not have been any. We don't have suspicion that any given person in line at airport security has a weapon, or that any driver at a drunk-driving roadblock was drinking.

Some people would prohibit suspicionless searches altogether, viewing them the sort of "general searches" the Framers abhorred. But is it really true we can't have airport security or sobriety roadblocks or bulk data collection, for that matter? That seems to be cutting off our noses to spite our faces.[51]

The alternative is to have some protection—other than cause—to avoid arbitrary, unjustified, discriminatory searches. And at this point we know exactly what that other protection is.

The answer is you subject *everyone* to the same treatment. In that way the risk of arbitrary, discriminatory searches disappears. That's what the *Prouse* Court was saying about roadblocks, and that's pretty much what happens (or should happen) at airports.[52]

Of course, searching everyone can get prohibitively expensive, but there is yet another option available in many circumstances: selecting who gets searched in a truly random way. In *Prouse*, Justice Harry Blackmun joined in the Court's decision but wrote separately to point out it was not necessary to stop *every* car at a checkpoint. It would be perfectly fine to stop every fifth car or every tenth car. If people knew that the police were using roadblocks, this would serve as enough of a deterrent. And from there what matters is only that the police are not picking and choosing based on some possibly illegitimate basis. Random selection does that.[53]

While randomness can help bring down the cost of a regulatory search, and is often appropriate, it is at least worth making the pitch for searching everyone, at least on some occasions. Very broad searches can help solve the problem of knowing whether a suspicionless search is worth the bother. Think about it. With suspicion-*based* searches we get some measure of what works by looking at the "hit rate": the number of times the police come up with the goods. But (and this is a point the Supreme Court has altogether missed) in suspicion-*less* searches, low hit rates are more likely, and perhaps better, than high ones. That is because the purpose of these suspicionless searches is deterrence. We are trying to keep people from violating the law, so in a successful use of such searches we may have a very low hit rate—i.e., it works. But then, how do we know whether inconveniencing people with this sort of suspicionless search is worth it? It turns out that inconveniencing a lot of people actually helps. Misery does indeed love company.[54]

First, if the government is forced to search everyone, and bear the cost of doing so, we will know the government truly believes this form of deterrence is worth the cost. Think about airport security, which is unfathomably expensive. The TSA has a huge budget, money that could be spent on many other antiterrorism approaches. Budgets are not unlimited; choices must be made about what deterrent measures are sufficiently efficacious to make them valuable. The public does not always have a basis for knowing what's worth it or not, but the fact that the government is forced to make these choices provides some guarantee that it has at least considered alternatives and decided this particular intrusion into everyone's life makes sense.

Second, if enough people are searched, the political process itself will serve as a safeguard of our liberty. The more people who are subjected to police searching of this sort, and put up with it, the more we can be comfortable knowing that people at least believe the effort is appropriate and worthwhile.[55]

Face it—going through airport security is a pain in the keister. But while people may grumble about the lines, there is no widespread call to stop the searches. The public is persuaded the inconvenience is worth it to avoid airborne terrorism. Note, though, that when the TSA started to use X-ray machines that were too revealing of people's bodies, there was an immediate outcry and the practice was stopped. The public deemed the intrusion too great given the payoff. With a truly general search, the decision about legitimate government interests and minimal intrusions rests where it should: with the public.[56]

Indeed, consistent with our notion of democratic policing, these sorts of searches should be approved in advance by the public anyway. And with these suspicionless searches, the government has little argument about the need for keeping them secret. The whole point of the searches is deterrence; people knowing only helps the plan succeed.

So, there you have it. By asking a very simple question, the law governing searches and seizures can be simplified greatly. When examining the constitutionality of police tactics, the first question should be: is it suspicion-*based* or suspicion-*less*? If the former, then the protections of sufficient cause (usually probable cause) and warrants are required. If the latter, then we need to ensure that the search is conducted in a way that avoids arbitrariness—usually by making sure everyone is searched.

GETTING IT RIGHT

Now, finally, the answer to the judges' confusion in Bill Bruce's case should be obvious. If the police had sufficient suspicion to search Wholesale Auto Salvage, which they did not, then they should have gotten a warrant based on probable cause. On the other hand, if it was truly an administrative search, it should have been random, which it also was not. What the police did at Wholesale Auto that day violated Bill Bruce's constitutional rights.

Either a search is suspicion-based, and there should be adequate suspicion (plus a warrant when possible). Or a search is suspicionless, and then must be universal, or at least truly random.

The failure to recognize that cause-based and suspicionless searches require very different safeguards against arbitrariness has led the Supreme Court to exacerbate two deeply regrettable problems.

First, allowing suspicion-based searches on something less than probable cause leads to the arbitrary treatment of people like Bill Bruce.

Second, prohibiting suspicionless searches, even for "ordinary law enforcement" (so long as the search is truly general or random), invalidates some searches, like the roadblocks in Indianapolis, that may well be both valuable and appropriate.

The scheme of drug interdiction roadblocks in *Edmond* was set up to avoid officer arbitrariness and discretion. The affidavits in the case explained that the checkpoint locations were chosen by supervisors "weeks in advance," "taking into consideration area crime statistics and the ability to locate the checkpoints in a location which will minimize the interference with normal traffic flow." Cars were stopped in predetermined groups (i.e., five cars at a time), and even if police or fire department vehicles were in that group they were stopped. Most important, the officers were instructed that "every vehicle stopped must be examined in the same manner until particularized suspicion or probable cause develops." It was emphasized that there was "no discretion given to any officer" in terms of which cars were stopped.[57]

Whether such roadblocks are a good or bad idea is for each community to decide, but it is hard to see them as unconstitutional.

We've lost sight of the reason the Fourth Amendment exists in the first place, and having done so we've become confused about what police agencies may and may not do. Yet it is not complicated. Suspicion-based searches should require probable cause. And suspicionless searches need regularity, i.e., subjecting everyone or at least some random set to the search, and avoiding any arbitrariness or discrimination, any whim or caprice.

Two types of searches, two very different protections. In this quite simple way, we can reconcile the Framers' concerns about general searches with the imperatives of the new deterrent-based policing.

There still is one last, important problem we need to solve. Often suspicionless searches are aimed not at everyone, but at a particular group. The next chapter tackles that problem, by turning to another part of the Constitution, the Equal Protection Clause.

8

DISCRIMINATORY SEARCHES

Often, the government singles out a group to search. In common parlance, and in law, some of this is called "profiling." It happens to racial minorities in drug interdiction. It happens to ethnic and religious minorities in the war on terror. There is an ongoing and heated debate about when, or even whether, profiling is justified.[1]

The Fourth Amendment standing alone doesn't really help us much in dealing with these discriminatory practices, but another part of the Constitution does: the Fourteenth Amendment's Equal Protection Clause. When it comes to law enforcement and counterterrorism, though, judges tend to ignore the legal precedents implementing the Constitution's guarantee of equality. Instead they make up a special set of rules under the Fourth Amendment. That's unfortunate. Relying on settled nondiscrimination law not only would help with fraught questions regarding racial and religious profiling, it would clarify our thinking even when the group singled out is more innocuous, such as people who fly on planes rather than taking trains (and thus are subjected to extensive preboarding security), or drug-testing only students who participate in extracurricular activities.

JUSTIFIED PARANOIA

Inside the cluttered, busy office of Linda Sarsour, Executive Director of the Arab American Association of New York, there's a clear—albeit jarring—message. A neglected computer sits in the corner, dusty and covered with papers, including a holiday card from the Obamas. (Sarsour's a White House "Champion of Change.") The walls and surfaces urge visitors to "Organize, Register, Vote." But the dominant motif is spying. Police spying. Posters and cartoons declare: "#sayno2spying," "We are not anti-police, we are anti–police spying," "NYPD stop spying on us." A photograph of the cadet class at the Police Academy contains cutout faces of Muslim women wearing the hijab.[2]

Sarsour, too, wears the hijab, though she proclaims she is not so much religious as nationalist Palestinian. She's in constant motion, a young woman filled with nervous energy, keeping track of a bustling organization and office. The waiting room is full of people, mostly older women, who have come for social services. Eid Al-Adha, the Muslim holy day marking the end of the Hajj, the pilgrimage to Mecca, has come and gone; Islamic Relief is set up outside handing out packets of frozen beef, the product of the holiday's ritual sacrifice, to the needy. And Sarsour is rushing around monitoring it all, while describing how paranoid she is: "I'm paranoid, I'm a paranoid executive director."[3]

Between all the posters, and Sarsour's talk, you might think she was crazy paranoid—except for the documentary record that indicates she's not. After 9/11 the NYPD began "mapping" Muslim communities. It sent informants into mosques and other Muslim or Arab organizations, and set cameras up outside them. NYPD officers went underground as spies. People stopped lingering after prayer services, and imams closed mosques—traditional gathering places for the community—when services were not in session. Student groups doing charity work were shunned by other Muslims when word got out that informants had infiltrated them. Muslim groups of all sorts discouraged any talk of any topic remotely political or controversial.[4]

Sarsour describes with visible stress the time she was told by the Associated Press that it had documents showing attempts by the NYPD to put an undercover agent on her not-for-profit board. All the sudden, the most innocent-seeming events deserved scrutiny, like the guy from

Libya who showed up out of the blue wanting to help, claiming he was getting a master's degree, no apparent day job to go to, and who—after Sarsour drove him off—surfaced again at a Barnard poetry reading among some Muslim friends. She's outraged by it all. Her board, she points out, is not a public place where anyone can enter. It is a private organization. "They have no right to be here." The board discusses financial issues, trips they've taken. But "people get afraid to talk."[5]

Sarsour has a complicated relationship with the NYPD. She feels close to the local precinct, has the captain's cell phone number on hand, believes they are doing their job and doing it with integrity. It's the top brass with whom she has issues; she objects to the creation of the "Demographics Unit"—the ones who did the spying—and the use of training materials like the NYPD's *Radicalization in the West: The Homegrown Threat*, which tars the entire Muslim community. She explains how the people of her community have real needs for the police at times, but she has to reassure them it is okay to call.[6]

It's hard to imagine anyone tolerating this at Catholic churches and welfare organizations in the United States, or Jewish synagogues and schools. If the First Amendment is about anything, it is that we don't take names and pictures of people going to pray, to receive community services, to engage in political activism. Indeed, this was just the very sort of conduct that got the FBI and CIA in trouble in the 1960s and 1970s, spying on domestic organizations, on people doing what they had every right to do under the United States Constitution.[7]

Yet people have defended and will continue to defend what the NYPD was doing here. New York's Mayor Michael Bloomberg did. Though his successor, Mayor Bill de Blasio, was quick to settle litigation involving stop-and-frisk, an ACLU case involving spying in the Muslim community lingered on for quite a while before settling. After all, many people say—and have said since 9/11—Isn't that where the trouble comes from? The conservative commentator Charles Krauthammer made just this point right after 9/11. So did the liberal Michael Kinsley, who in his September 30, 2001, column in *The Washington Post* said, "[T]oday we're at war with a terror network that just killed 6,000 innocents and has sent anonymous agents in our country plotting more slaughter. Are we really supposed to ignore the one identifiable fact we know about them?"[8]

What should the rules be when government takes Krauthammer's and Kinsley's advice—not just in this instance, but generally—and singles out a particular group for surveillance or searching? We've already seen that when the government searches to *deter* crime, the proper constitutional protection is to search everyone. That's what we do at airports, and it is exactly what Krauthammer was complaining about. Why are we patting down female flight attendants, he asked, when we know the bad guys who are part of al-Qaeda are "young, Islamic, Arab and male"?[9]

This sort of selective searching happens all the time. Welfare recipients are subjected to drug tests, while those who do not require government assistance are excused. Cars containing people of Latino appearance are targeted for immigration inquiries. Jurisdictions have mandatory DNA testing for some arrestees but not others.[10] In fact, few searches are truly as general as the last chapter suggests they should be. We search everyone at airports, but not at bus stations or railways. Sometimes the grouping can be subtle: Roadblocks are placed at one location, not on every road, meaning only motorists in a particular neighborhood will be stopped.[11]

The Supreme Court has made a mess of what to do about these sorts of discriminatory searches. It is yet another example of the usual constitutional rules getting twisted beyond recognition when policing is at issue. In constitutional law, no sort of discrimination is more taboo than allowing the government to pick and choose on the basis of race. Yet, beginning with a 1975 immigration-stop case, *Brignoni-Ponce*, the justices have allowed law enforcement officers leeway to rely on racial characteristics in some instances. The Court has shown little confidence as to how to deal with other discriminations, be they subjecting some arrestees but not others to DNA testing, or demanding students who participate in extracurricular activities take drug tests while others need not. The justices have mostly just thrown up their hands, allowing government to choose as it will.[12]

Once again, the courts have lost sight of the proper concern—government arbitrariness. In cases such as these, courts should require the government to answer the perennial question under the Constitution when one is searched or seized: "Why me?" But when the target is a group, not an individual, the most apt part of the Constitution is the Fourteenth Amendment's Equal Protection Clause, not the Fourth

Amendment. Courts reviewing government discrimination among groups in the policing context should engage in the same sort of inquiry that judges employ in nonpolicing discrimination cases.[13]

We'll start by looking at policing aimed at groups that traditionally have been the subjects of discrimination and get special protections under the Constitution—instances of racial, religious, ethnic, and gender and sexual-orientation-based discrimination. With these groups, the rules ordinarily would be quite clear, but the analysis ends up muddled because the issue is law enforcement. We'll then move to even tougher cases, where the groupings don't happen along such sensitive lines, but the constitutional right to be free from arbitrary searching or seizing is put at risk anyway.

A MANHUNT IN ONEONTA

In the wee hours of the morning, on September 4, 1992, an intruder entered a remote home in Oneonta, New York, and attacked an elderly woman who was visiting. Wielding a knife, the intruder stuffed a bandana in her mouth, and sat atop her intending to rape her. She struggled, was cut, the culprit fled. The woman could not identify her assailant, but told the police—based on her view of an arm and hand, and the timbre of voice—that it was a black male. The police concluded that he might have cut his hand. They decided, or she told them, that he was young.[14]

And so the search was on, for a young black man with a cut on a hand. Oneonta, population 10,000, had about 300 black citizens, and another few hundred at the nearby college. The police decided to track them all down. A top college administrator prepared a list at police request—it came to be called "the black list"—and the police then chased after every black male student at the college. Officers burst into dorm rooms, threatened to take students downtown, forced them to show their hands in front of classmates who looked on, certain they'd done something wrong. In town things were yet more chaotic. Blacks were stopped on the street and ordered to put hands on cop cars; there was so little rhyme or reason to the manhunt that some were stopped several times in the dragnet that occurred over the course of several days. So were older black men, even women. One woman, an admissions officer at the college, was told she could not board a bus to visit her grandmother if she did not produce identification. The perpetrator was never found.[15]

"We've tried to examine the hands of all the black people in the community," explained the New York State Police investigator, H. Karl Chandler. No disrespect was intended, he insisted, it only made sense. "If your car has an accident, and there's red paint on it, are you going to look for a green car?"[16]

When it came time for the federal courts to rule, they basically agreed with Investigator Chandler. The judges said they were not "blind to the sense of frustration that was doubtlessly felt by those questioned by the police during the investigation." What happened was "understandably upsetting." But plaintiffs "were not questioned solely on the basis of their race." Rather, the police legitimately were following a "physical description given by the victim."[17]

POLICING AND RACE: THE FIRST MISTAKE

The first of two very wrong things courts say about policing based on racial or other similar characteristics is that the Constitution's equality provision, the guarantee of "equal protection of the laws," is not implicated when police are simply following a description of a culprit given by witnesses or a victim. As we'll see, in most cases it is perfectly consistent with the Constitution for police to pursue such a lead. But to say that the police can do whatever they want when looking into what is reported to them, and that the Equal Protection Clause has nothing to say about it? That's wrong.[18]

The problem is that when it comes to policing, all the usual rules about race, ethnicity, gender, etc., get tossed out the window. Though proper application of those rules will not lead to a different outcome in most cases in which a witness offers a description of a perpetrator, it might well have in Oneonta. And it most certainly would in the sort of case we will be particularly concerned about here, when police are not following a victim description, but are engaging in racial profiling.

The law regarding constitutional equality is not particularly complicated. It asks only two questions. Does the government have an important reason for what it is doing? And does dividing people into groups—classifying them, *discriminating* among them—achieve that goal? What we are trying to figure out is whether the division into groups accomplishes what the government has set out to do in a sensible, rational way. If not, we suspect the government is engaging in discrimination for impermissible reasons, either because it is being irrational or because it is biased by dislike for the disfavored group.

What makes patrolling for discrimination tricky is that it's impossible to govern and not divide people into groups. You have to be sixteen to drive, eighteen to vote, twenty-one to drink. Only people with incomes below a certain level get welfare benefits. Businesses over a certain size have to follow workplace safety rules, while some small businesses get off. You cannot drive over fifty-five miles an hour. Restaurants must store food at a certain temperature.[19]

Worse yet, the lines that government draws, putting people into groups, necessarily are often imperfect. Surely there are young adults seventeen years and nine months old who could vote as sensibly as eighteen-year-olds (and plenty of eighteen-year-olds who are not the most discriminating of voters). Why isn't the speed limit fifty-three, or sixty for that matter? Any one of these choices might be as rational or sensible as the next. If every line could be challenged in court and struck down simply because there was another equally plausible (or imperfect) line, there would be no more laws left. Laws often are the product of interest-group bargaining, and not all the necessary compromises to get a law passed are going to make the most sensible of lines. That's just unavoidable.[20]

For these reasons, the ordinary response to government line drawing and group forming is a certain amount of deference. As long as the lines are sensible enough, the groups roughly the right ones, we give the government the benefit of the doubt. Courts often say they won't "second-guess" government choices.[21]

Under some circumstances, though—such as when the government draws lines among people based on race, religion, ethnicity, gender and sexual orientation, etc.—we look more closely. We call these "suspect classifications." We believe that these categories rarely are or should be relevant to most things government does. Their very use is "suspect": we worry that when government discriminates against someone in one of these groups, it is because of a stereotype or simple dislike, rather than a sound rationale.[22]

This closer look at suspect classifications has a name—"strict scrutiny." Strict scrutiny asks the same two questions: What is government trying to accomplish? And does it need to treat this group differently to do so? But under strict scrutiny the courts are more demanding about the answers. If, say, the government wants to treat one racial or religious group differently than others, it needs a super-strong reason, and the classification must be absolutely necessary to achieve the government's goal. If the government can't meet that test, it must find some other, nondiscriminatory way of meeting its goals. In examining this issue we ask for proof: Is the problem we are concerned about much more prevalent in the disfavored group than any other? And is the incidence of the problem high enough to justify imposing on everyone in the group?[23]

Which brings us back to Oneonta, and the federal court's claim that relying on race in a victim description simply does not implicate the Equal Protection Clause of the Constitution.

CAN THE POLICE USE A RACIAL DESCRIPTION TO FIND A SUSPECT?

The right question in a case like *Oneonta* is not whether the Equal Protection Clause applies—of course it does—but whether the use of a racial description of a suspect meets the test of strict scrutiny. Courts have offered a number of reasons for why policing based on a victim or witness racial description should get a free pass from any analysis under the Constitution's equality guarantee, but none of them are very persuasive. The best one is the argument that the government didn't dream up the racial classification itself, it is just what a witness or victim told the police. Fair enough, but still it is the government that's using race as a basis for choosing who to stop and search. Surely government can't evade the requirements of the Constitution because someone else gave the police the idea of doing it. And it is not like government doesn't make decisions about what exactly to do once it gets this information: witness the dragnet that occurred in Oneonta.[24]

Still, it seems obvious, does it not, that in most cases a witness's description of a suspect that includes race will easily justify police following that description. It passes the Equal Protection Clause's strict scrutiny test. If a crime has been committed, the government's interest in catching the perpetrator is obviously high—"compelling" in the lingo of the Equal Protection Clause. And if the witness says the perpetrator is a person of a particular race dressed in a green coat who limps, that is obviously who the police should be looking for. Looking for a person of a different race would make no more sense than seeking a marathon runner in red.

On the other hand, a suspect description that relies *only* on race will almost always be impermissible. That is one of the problems the Equal Protection Clause is concerned about: blaming a group for the possible actions of some of its members (or worse yet, stereotypes about those members), when most of them are innocent. That was the real problem in *Oneonta*. The suspect was *probably* a youngish black man, and *maybe* he cut his hand, but uncertainty on this score is the only possible explanation (other than out-and-out harassment) why the police were stopping women and older black men as well. In essence, all the police could be sure of was one fact: the culprit was black.

The only thing that made relying on race in Oneonta remotely plausible was the relatively small number of black people who lived there, but still this seems hard to swallow. If a crime was committed somewhere, and all we knew about the suspect was that he was one of a thousand or more white men in the vicinity, would we suppose the police could stop all of them? In the absence of any other information, we would be extremely reluctant to make suspects of all these people. So why were things different in Oneonta, where there were several hundred black men, all of whom were apparently quite innocent?

While the judges upheld what happened in *Oneonta*, lots of other people thought the police got it wrong. One kid at the college who was on the black list explained, "[T]he only list I ever wanted to be on was the Dean's List." In time, many expressed regret about the indignities in Oneonta. The state police apologized. The college did the same; the administrator who turned over the list was demoted. The office of New York Attorney General Eliot Spitzer defended state officials in the case. After they'd prevailed, Spitzer himself read the court opinion and told the press, "We won the case, but it makes your skin crawl."[25]

RACIAL PROFILING

Agreed, then: if a suspect is described as a person of a particular race wearing a green coat, it makes no sense to search for someone of a different race wearing a red coat. But what if the characteristics that define the suspect are part of a profile, not a witness description? Are these the same thing? This was just the sort of argument people were making after 9/11: Why are we searching grandmothers from Topeka, when we should be searching Muslim men or men of some particular heritage or appearance? Should the rules be the same when there is a profile rather than a witness description?

That brings us to some recent history about racial profiling in this country.

In 1999 the then–Attorney General of New Jersey did the unthinkable: he released a report condemning his own state police for rampant racial profiling. (Prosecutors don't succeed at their jobs by pointing fingers at law enforcement.) Troopers on the New Jersey Turnpike had been accused of stopping many more minority motorists, and searching them more often. The problem of "disparate treatment" of minorities, the AG concluded, "is real not imagined."[26]

It's no wonder the New Jersey AG did this, though: by the time he released his report, his hand had been forced by a wealth of evidence of racial profiling by the New Jersey highway patrol, including a quite remarkable study performed in a case called *State v. Soto*. In *Soto* the State of New Jersey had argued that more minorities were stopped either because there were more of them on the highway or because they broke the traffic laws more often. But Dr. John Lamberth, an expert in statistical methods and social psychology, conducted a rigorous study to prove this was not the case. To eliminate these possibilities, Lamberth put spotters by the side of the Turnpike with binoculars to count the racial makeup of drivers on the highway. Then, he utilized rolling survey vehicles to see who was violating the traffic laws. Dr. Lamberth's study established that while some 13 percent of the drivers on the Turnpike were African American, and while some 15 percent of the traffic violators were African American, African Americans constituted from 35.6 percent to 46.2 percent of the stops. Relying on this data, and on the testimony of police officials, the judge in *State v. Soto* found that there was a "de facto policy" on the part of the State Police "of targeting blacks for investigation and arrest."[27]

As it happened, matters in New Jersey were much, much worse than the *Soto* judge thought. Troopers would park their vehicles perpendicular to roadways, rendering their radar guns ineffective but making it easier to see the race of the driver. Some of the troopers pretty much arrested only minorities. Governor Christine Todd Whitman fired the superintendent of the state police, Colonel Carl Williams, for telling the press, "The drug problem is mostly cocaine and marijuana. It is most likely a minority group that's involved with that." State officials hid data from the *Soto* judge and from the U.S. Department of Justice, which conducted its own investigation, ultimately concluding that New Jersey had engaged in a consistent pattern of racial profiling.[28]

The Attorney General's report documented that racial discrimination was particularly prevalent in the use of so-called consent searches. When troopers had no basis to search a vehicle—and traffic stops typically provide none, for what would be the hidden evidence of speeding or having a taillight out?—they frequently would ask the motorist for permission to search. The AG's report found that in some instances, 80 percent of the consent search requests were directed at minorities. The more discretion a trooper had, the more likely there would be disparate treatment of minorities. In one locale, troopers operating radar guns (which can't tell blacks from whites) were issuing tickets to about 18 percent of African Americans, while troopers with the most discretion were issuing tickets to over 34 percent of blacks. "[O]fficers who had more time to devote to drug interdiction," said the AG, "may have been more likely to rely upon racial stereotypes."[29]

New Jersey was hardly unique when it came to racial profiling. In another thorough study, Dr. Lamberth found that in Maryland 17 percent of the drivers were African American and yet a whopping 72 percent of those being stopped and searched also were, a disparity Lamberth called "literally off the charts" of statistical significance. Researchers in Michigan decided to get a peek behind the decision to stop, by examining queries to the mobile data terminals cops have inside their cars. Not only were queries of supposedly suspicious drivers made more often of African Americans, but the number of such queries increased significantly the further blacks were seen driving into whiter neighborhoods. In North Carolina, blacks were 68 percent more likely to be stopped by the North Carolina State Patrol than whites. Colorado officials paid more than $800,000 in damages to motorists stopped on I-70 based on a drug courier profile that targeted minorities, none of whom were ticketed or arrested.[30]

This sort of racial profiling is pervasive in society. A report by Professor Ian Ayres of Yale Law School concerning LAPD stops in 2003–2004 found, after controlling for crime rates and other variables, that "African Americans and Hispanics are over-stopped, over-frisked, over-searched, and over-arrested." Per 10,000 residents, there were 4,500 stops of African Americans, but only 1,750 for nonminority residents. Indeed, in some districts there were more stops in the reporting period than there were residents. In New York, more than 87 percent of the 700,000 people stopped in 2011 by the NYPD were either black or Latino. From 2007 to 2010, in Boston, there were more than 200,000 "Field Interrogation/Observation/Frisk and/or Search Incidents." More than 60 percent of that number were black even though Boston has fewer than 25 percent African Americans.[31]

WHY RACIAL PROFILING HAPPENS

Even if one chooses to ignore the stunning human toll of racial profiling, it is unquestionably ineffective policy. Study after study shows minorities are not carrying or using drugs at higher rates than Caucasians; indeed, just the opposite is true. When police search, the hit rates—the number of times drugs or other contraband are found—are consistently higher for whites than for minorities. In North Carolina, where the State Patrol was stopping far more blacks than whites, the "hit rate" for whites who were searched was 33 percent, while it was 26 percent for blacks. In Illinois, even after years of working on the racial profiling problem, an annual report in 2014 concluded that minority drivers are still about twice as likely to be the subject of a vehicle consent search than other drivers, relative to how frequently they are stopped, yet police officers conducting consent searches are 50 percent more likely to find contraband in a vehicle driven by a white driver than one driven by a minority driver. Ayres's report on the LAPD found that "frisks and searches are systematically less productive when conducted on blacks and Hispanics than when conducted on whites." As the New Jersey AG's report pointed out, "many of the stereotypes about drug use are simply wrong"; among high school students, "white students are actually more likely than black or Hispanic students to report having ever used" drugs or alcohol.[32]

If profiling doesn't work, why is it so pervasive? One possible answer is widespread intentional racism. But that answer is both too simple and too disheartening to accept without considering alternatives. And it turns out that at least one alternative is readily at hand and instructive. It is an answer grounded in the idea of unconscious racial bias.[33]

A chapter of the New Jersey AG's report, titled "The Circular Il-logic of Race-Based Profiles," describes a "self-fulfilling prophecy" that explains why racial profiling occurs. Think about it this way. You like to fish, so you ask people what's a good spot. They say Trout Pond. You go there, and sure enough you catch some fish. Occasionally you go some-where else, and you catch some fish there, too, but you've been told Trout Pond is a surefire bet, and you've seen some evidence of that, so you keep coming back to it. Now, if you'd done a careful study, you'd have learned that Trout Pond was no better than any other spot, and in fact might have been less good. There were more fish in other places, like Town Wharf or Towd Point. But having been told of Trout Pond and had your information confirmed, that is where you went. The AG's report de-scribed the hits officers got by stopping minorities—and then told one another about—as the "statistics . . . used to grease the wheels of a vicious cycle."

> Consistent with our human nature, we in law enforcement proudly display seized drug shipments or 'hits' as a kind of tro-phy, but pay scant attention to far more frequent 'misses,' that is, those instances where stops and searches failed to discover contraband . . . Logically, of course, one cannot hope to judge the overall effectiveness of any practice or program by looking solely at its successes, any more than by looking only at is failures.[34]

By the late 1990s all this was well-enough known that a national consensus against racial profiling had developed. President George W. Bush had condemned the practice, as did many, many others. Congress was considering legislation that would have required state and local police forces to keep statistics that would reveal profiling where it occurred. A whopping 81 percent of respondents told the Gallup poll they disapproved of the practice.[35]

Then came September 11. Radical Islamists attacked the United States and the consensus against racial profiling quickly melted away. On the day of the attack, New Jersey's new Attorney General, John Farmer, Jr., was in Atlantic City at a conference talking about the progress the state was making in addressing the profiling problem. But within two weeks of 9/11 he published an article in *The Star-Ledger* titled "Rethinking Racial Profiling." In it Farmer called the fact that before 9/11 "we were able to condemn universally the practice of racial profiling" a "luxury." "More than 6,000 people are dead, some would argue, because of insufficient attention to racial or ethnic profiles at our airports . . . How can law enforcement not consider ethnicity in investigating these crimes when that identifier is an essential characteristic of the hijackers and their supposed confederates and supporters?"[36]

So, what's right? What we said before 9/11, or after it?

WHEN IS RACIAL PROFILING OKAY?

The second incorrect thing courts—and others—say about race and policing is that profiling is okay so long as race is not the "sole" item in the profile. It's okay to look at race, they say, so long as there are other factors in play as well. But this, too, deviates from the way we usually deal with questions of racial discrimination when the issue is not policing.

The standard rule under the Equal Protection Clause is that if race is *a* "motivating" factor in a government decision, strict scrutiny must be applied, even if it is not the "*sole*" factor. Strict scrutiny requires us to compare the incidence of the problem that the government is concerned about in both the favored and disfavored (here, searched) groups. Although in *very* rare occasions race may be a relevant factor in a profile, it's unlikely to be in most instances.[37]

To see why race or other suspect classifications rarely will be appropriate in a profile, it helps to look at a familiar example: airport drug interdiction cases. Typical was *United States v. Weaver*, yet another case involving our old friend from Chapter 6, DEA Agent Carl Hicks. In this case the police spotted Arthur Weaver getting off a plane in Kansas City, coming from Los Angeles. Hicks explained Weaver was suspect because he was "a 'roughly dressed' young black male who was carrying two bags and walking rapidly, almost running, down the concourse toward a door leading to a taxi stand." Hicks also testified that he "was aware that a number of young roughly dressed black males from street gangs in Los Angeles frequently brought cocaine into the Kansas City area, and "walking quickly towards a taxicab was a common characteristic of narcotics couriers at an airport." So Hicks stopped Weaver. Weaver declined to allow Hicks to search his bags, and told him to get a warrant. Hicks persisted in grabbing at Weaver after he got in a cab, so Hicks and Weaver ended up tussling over Weaver's bags. After Weaver hit Hicks's hand in order to pry it off his bag, Hicks arrested Weaver, patted him down, and—having obtained a warrant—searched the bags and found drugs.[38]

The judges in *Weaver* did what judges do—they said, wrongly, that if race is "a" factor it is fine so long as it is not "the" factor: "We would not hesitate to hold that a solely race-based suspicion of drug courier status would not pass constitutional muster . . . had Hicks relied solely upon the fact of Weaver's race as a basis for his suspicions, we would have a different case before us." But, said the court wistfully, "facts are not to be ignored simply because they may be unpleasant." Here Hicks knew that "young male members of black Los Angeles gangs were flooding the Kansas City area with cocaine." Expressing regret about all the black drug dealers—"We wish it were otherwise, but we take the facts as they are presented to us, not as we would like them to be"— the court washed its hands of this use of race.[39]

The judges went shockingly astray in their analysis. In the rest of equality law, as we already have seen, if race is *a* motivating factor at all, strict scrutiny is to be employed. The same two familiar questions get asked: Does the government have a compelling need here? And does this use of race further the compelling need?

In order to determine whether the use of race in a profile meets strict scrutiny, we must examine the incidence of possible offenders in the two populations, those profiled on the basis of race, and those not. There are two percentages that matter. First, are blacks who meet the profile notably more likely to be drug couriers than whites? And second, what percentage of blacks who meet the profile actually are drug couriers.[40]

As to the first question, if blacks are not substantially more likely to be couriers than whites, then the use of race in the profile is "*under*inclusive" and unconstitutional. Which is to say, by looking only for blacks we are missing a lot of drug couriers of other races who are equally culpable. Thus, the profile is not narrowly tailored in the way required to meet the constitutional test of strict scrutiny.

In this regard, note the critical role race played in Agent Hicks's story. As Judge Richard Arnold pointed out, disagreeing with the other judges in the case, many people on airplanes these days appear to be "roughly dressed." And if walking rapidly from gate to taxicab is cause for suspicion, countless people would be under investigation. Of all the fast-walking, "roughly dressed" people on the plane from LA, it was Weaver's black skin that made him a drug-toting gang member in Hicks's eyes. But why? Do we have any basis for thinking that there were not plenty of whites also carrying drugs in the airport, who did not earn Agent Hicks's attention?[41]

As to the second, how many fast-walking black men not dressed to Agent Hicks's standards of couture are drug couriers? Half of them? One out of a hundred? If there are lots of fast-walking African American guys not dressed as Agent Hicks would like who are not carrying drugs, then Hicks's profile is also "*over*inclusive." It is sweeping in too many innocent people and again fails the strict scrutiny test.

So what were the facts on these vital statistical questions? We don't know, of course. What we do know is that in the airport interdiction cases there is often evidence that minorities are being stopped at a disproportionate rate. But despite this, judges fault the defendants for not having better evidence of discrimination and send them to prison. Yet the government is the one engaging in the conduct—if it is relying on a supposed profile, then the government ought to be able to prove the factual accuracy of what it is doing.[42]

This is the very problem with the argument of those who said, after 9/11, that we should search only Muslims or those of Arab descent in airport security (or otherwise). First, doing so is underinclusive. High-profile arrestees for terror in the United States have hardly all been of

Arab or Middle Eastern descent (not to speak of the fact that it may be impossible to discern who is a Muslim or Arab based on one's appearance). Timothy McVeigh, Richard Reid, Jose Padilla, and John Walker Lindh all were convicted for terrorism, and none obviously met this description by looking at them. But, far more important, any such generalization is unacceptably overinclusive. There are some 3.3 million Muslims in this country and at least 1.8 million Arab Americans. It is wildly implausible that any but a minute fraction of this number has any involvement at all with terrorism. Under the Equal Protection Clause we do not visit the sins of a very few on all those of the same race, religion, or ethnicity. To the contrary, avoiding doing so is a major reason we employ strict scrutiny.[43]

WHAT ABOUT WHEN SUSPECT CLASSIFICATIONS ARE NOT AT ISSUE?

What should happen, though, when government is searching groups, rather than everyone, and the group is *not* chosen based on religion, race, gender, or some other suspect criteria? These sorts of lines get drawn all the time. Student athletes get drug tested, but other students don't. People arrested for sex offenses are DNA tested; other arrestees aren't. Greyhound passengers are subjected to interrogation about carrying drugs, but it doesn't happen on Amtrak's high-speed business-class Acela trains. If the courts have a hard time dealing with policing that discriminates on the basis of a suspect classification, they make an absolute mess of things when the discrimination is along some other sort of line.[44]

In cases like these the Supreme Court has said that judges should perform a balancing act. On the one side of the scale they are to place the privacy interest at stake; on the other is the reason why the government needs to search. When the government interest outweighs the individual privacy interest, the search is okay, even if there is no warrant or any cause at all.[45]

As we've seen over and over again, these kinds of balancing tests are transparently unworkable. Take, as an example, a drug-testing program of student athletes, adopted to help make a school drug-free. Consider how difficult it would be to perform this balance honestly. First, one would need to put a value on student athletes urinating in a supervised setting, and having their urine tested (including any private information it might reveal besides illegal drug use). Then one would have to have some way of knowing if this sort of program achieves any deterrent effect, which means some sort of data on drug use beforehand and afterward. Finally, there would need to be a way to reduce these very different things into the same unit of measurement. It's not impossible to do this, but it is really hard. And we almost never have the necessary data.

That is why real balancing doesn't take place; almost always, when courts say they are balancing, the government just wins. A perfect example is the Supreme Court's decision in *National Treasury Union Employees v. Von Raab*, involving a drug-testing program for certain employees in the Customs Service. The program was adopted in 1986, at the very height of the war on drugs. The Reagan administration had proposed drug testing well over a million federal employees in "sensitive" positions, and the Customs Service effort was the tip of the spear. The Director of the Customs Service, William Von Raab, decided it was necessary to test any Customs official who worked in drug interdiction, carried a firearm, or handled classified information.[46]

It is generous to call the "balancing" test performed by the Supreme Court in *Von Raab* a farce. To begin with, there was no showing of government need at all. When he ordered the program, the Director of the Customs Service said publicly that he thought "Customs is largely drug free." Testing proved this out: after more than three thousand tests only five people proved positive for drugs. So why were we picking on these public servants? Dissenting, Justice Scalia was properly scathing on the point:

> What is absent in the Government's justifications—notably absent, revealingly absent, and as far as I am concerned dispositively absent—is the recitation of even a single instance in which any of the speculated horribles actually occurred: an instance, that is, in which the cause of bribetaking, or of poor aim, or of unsympathetic law enforcement, or of compromise of classified information, was drug use.[47]

In the place of demonstrated need, the Supreme Court majority substituted gibberish. The Court's opinion talked about how Customs officials had been "shot, stabbed, run over by vehicles, and hit with blunt objects" and nine had died in the line of duty since 1974. What any of this had to do with drug testing was a mystery. Obviously the supposed rationale was that people involved in drug interdiction could be corrupted. But it is not clear that officials had to be drug users (which is what was being tested for) to be corrupted, and it is equally unclear why Customs officials dealing with other sorts of smugglers—say of jewels—could not become corrupted as well.[48]

As for the other side of the supposed balance, the officers who were tested, the Supreme Court simply waived away the intrusion. While the justices conceded that having to engage in supervised urination and then having that urine tested was a notable intrusion of privacy, the Supreme Court decided that given the nature of their jobs, Customs Officials had a "diminished expectation of privacy" concerning urine testing. But why would this be? One might think that given their sometimes-dangerous jobs, those officials had done enough for their country without having to be subjected to this.[49]

The whole thing was nothing but a PR stunt to show how serious the government was in the war on drugs. It had zero to do with any problem of drug use in the Customs Service. Dissenting, Justice Scalia pointed to the memorandum setting up the program, explaining that "[i]mplementation . . . would set an important example in our country's struggle with this most serious threat." It is up to the government to decide to have a war on drugs, and symbolism is fine. What the Constitution forbids is doing that on the backs of these officials. If you want to test people for drugs, test all of us (good luck getting that one passed).[50]

What courts should be doing in cases like this is precisely what they do in cases involving suspect classifications. The courts should ask if there is a government interest at play that actually is advanced by what the government is doing. No mushy balancing. A careful analysis of whether there is a reason to be picking on a particular group. As always, the government should be prepared to respond to the question "Why me?"

Another drug testing case decided by the Supreme Court the very same day as *Von Raab* is an object lesson in what proper analysis should look like. This case involved a drug-testing program for train employees mandated by the Federal Railroad Administration. The program required testing train personnel in the case of certain significant train accidents, and also allowed it upon a showing of "cause" in other circumstances. In the event of an accident—as defined by the regulations—all train employees were to be tested forthwith for drug or alcohol impairment.[51]

Many things distinguished the sensible program in the railroad case from the ill-advised one in *Von Raab*. First, in adopting the railway-testing program, public input was solicited, including from those affected by the policy. That participation led to a program more focused in scope than the one the Director of the Customs Service simply mandated. Second, the government documented both the toll taken by major train accidents and the persistent presence of impaired operators as a cause. Train wrecks are a serious threat, impaired train employees are a frequent cause, and testing for impairment is designed both to deter the conduct and inform the public why the problem occurs.[52]

IS THE FOURTH AMENDMENT LESS IMPORTANT THAN OTHER CONSTITUTIONAL RIGHTS?

The only hard question in these cases is how closely the courts should scrutinize what the government is doing when it chooses to search one group rather than another—or everyone for that matter. As we saw above, laws that draw suspect classifications are supposed to be examined quite closely, while all others get pretty much a free pass. When the groups chosen are not based on race, gender, nationality, sexual orientation, or the like, is there nonetheless justification for a closer look?

The very fact that constitutional rights are on the line in an area fraught with arbitrariness ought to be enough to justify closer scrutiny by courts.[53] When other constitutional rights are at stake, such as the right to bear arms or speak freely, the justices mandate a close look at government rationales. As the Supreme Court said in *District of Columbia v. Heller*, involving the Second Amendment right to bear arms, "If all that was required to overcome the right to keep and bear arms was a rational basis, the Second Amendment . . . would have no effect." Similarly, in *Plyler v. Doe*, the Supreme Court applied strict scrutiny to strike down Texas's denial of funds to educate the children of undocumented aliens, even though "[u]ndocumented aliens cannot be treated as a suspect class" and "education [is not] a fundamental right."[54]

Surely the Fourth Amendment interest in avoiding arbitrary searches and seizures is as significant as the interests at stake in *Heller* or *Plyler*. In *Wolf v. Colorado*, in which the Supreme Court held that the Fourth Amendment applied to the states, Justice Frankfurter declared that "[t]he security of one's privacy against arbitrary intrusion by the police—which is at the core of the Fourth Amendment—is basic to a free society." The precise level of scrutiny may be hard to fix, but where arbitrariness is a very real concern, constitutional review needs to be a darn sight more serious than simply deferring to what the government says, as the justices so typically do.[55]

The risk of arbitrariness is particularly high when specific groups are targeted for searching or seizing. Often this occurs in the midst of a social scare, be it terrorism, drugs, or immigration. It is precisely at these moments, when the public is worked up and urging government to do something, that rash actions are possible.

Take Linda Sarsour and her Muslim community. The NYPD's Demographics Unit, responsible for "mapping" Muslims in New York, established in 2001 in the aftermath of 9/11, was disbanded in 2014. Initially lauded for its effectiveness in thwarting terrorist attacks, the unit never actually "helped thwart" anything. In fact, the Assistant Chief of the NYPD Intelligence Unit, Thomas Galati, testified under oath that in his six years in office, the Demographics Unit's work had not provided one single lead or criminal investigation. However, by 2014, the unit had already done its damage, instilling fear in Muslim Americans, suppressing religious expression, and severing the trust between Muslim communities and law enforcement.[56]

The Constitution does not prohibit singling out groups for special treatment, even if it involves searches and seizures. But the Constitution does require that the groups deserve the treatment. That means the government producing evidence that the problem it is addressing is pervasive in that group, as opposed to others. This is precisely what has gone missing in the judiciary's analysis of these issues, turning people into suspects because of their skin color, religion, age, or other status alone.

With that, we come to the end of our discussion of constitutional policing. The next part of the book will pick up these themes, and apply them and the idea of democratic policing to the twenty-first century's issues of technology and terrorism. But by now we should be clear on the basic rules governing policing, and how much the courts have distorted them. That's both peculiar and unfortunate, because nothing need be as complicated as the courts have made it. Warrants are required when time allows. When searches are suspicion-based, there should be probable cause, except for the limited use of reasonable suspicion in stop-and-frisk, subject to the proviso that still officers must say what crime they suspect is afoot. Suspicionless searches must affect everyone or be truly random. To the extent a group, but not everyone, is subjected to searches, the government must justify why members of that group should be searched, by providing evidence that the problem is prevalent in that group compared to everyone else, and that enough people in the group are implicated to justify burdening everyone in the group. Constitutional policing in one paragraph—half a paragraph, even.

It's not that difficult. But two things have distorted this set of rules. The first is judges' inability to sensibly connect old principles to the new policing. The second is judges' zeal to uphold whatever the government does, often because of the distorting effect of the exclusionary rule. Neither of these is a good reason for where the law now stands.

PART III

Twenty-First-Century Policing

In the twenty-first century, policing faces serious challenges. Technology is moving so rapidly it is difficult for policing agencies to stay ahead of those who would do us ill. And a very real, and ongoing, threat of terrorism has made clear to all of us just how much harm can be done. Both advancing technology and terrorism have required those charged with our safety to employ new tools and novel strategies.

With those new tactics and tools, though, come equally great threats to our liberties. Rapid advances in technology mean that the government can get its hands on virtually all our personal information, quickly—and in many instances the government claims it can gather information stored in the cloud or held by third-party providers without probable cause or a warrant. Technological advance also has made it possible for the government to store vast amounts of the information that it collects, compiling dossiers on us, even if we are not suspected of anything. The very real terrorist threat causes the public, understandably, to be more acquiescent even as the government expands its powers.

New policing technologies and strategies pose complex questions. Under what terms should the government be able to access our information stored in the cloud? Is it meaningful to distinguish between the content of that information (like the text of an email) and the "metadata" (the addressing information)? When the government employs new technologies such as license plate readers or facial recognition, is it even a "search" governed by the Fourth Amendment? Does the Constitution have anything to say about "predictive policing"—the practice of gathering and mining vast amounts of data to try to predict criminal behavior before it occurs? What should the rules be for bulk collection of our data as part of the war on terror?

Above all, *are* these new tools and technologies making us safer? Which of these new policing tools and tactics works, and which do policing agencies employ simply because they have access to them?

This final part examines the challenges posed by new policing technologies and the ongoing threat of terrorism. Chapter 9 asks how we begin to figure out whether the use of any given technology even qualifies as a "search," thus bringing the Constitution into play. Chapter 10 calls into question the old rule that allows the government to get all our information from third parties without warrant or probable cause, now that most of our information is held by third parties. Chapter 11 looks into issues surrounding the government's practice of gathering our information and compiling it in vast databases. Here we will meet yet one more constitutional limitation on policing, the Due Process Clause. Finally, Chapter 12 asks what tools are appropriate to counterintelligence and the war on terror when the rights of Americans are at stake as well.

There is one overarching theme here: when considering these questions as they arise, it is essential not to lose track of the basic principles of democratic and constitutional policing. Those principles, if employed in a clearheaded way, will ensure we stay true to our values, and have policing that is effective. Both terrorism and emerging technologies have exacerbated the tendency of policing agencies to keep things hush-hush, to act without permission. Although, as we saw in Chapter 1, there is some room for operational secrecy in policing, a constant theme of this part is that government must get back in the habit of seeking democratic sanction for its actions. Similarly, warrants and probable cause remain essential elements of protection when the government is engaging in suspicion-based searching; they do not simply go out the window when new technologies are employed. And if the government is conducting surveillance without cause, it is essential that it do so in an even-handed way, not singling out groups for special attention without sufficient justification.

It is often claimed—it has been the constant claim throughout history—that shortcuts are needed on these basic protections to keep us safe. But what history has proven, time and again, is that such claims are often incorrect. Democratic deliberation ensures we are doing sensible things. Warrants and probable cause make certain we are not chasing down blind alleys. The Constitution is not at war with our safety; properly understood, it is integral to it.

9

SURVEILLANCE TECHNOLOGY

The Fourth Amendment prohibits "unreasonable searches and seizures." What that means is that if something is not a "search" or a "seizure," the Fourth Amendment provides no protection *at all*. Common sense would seem to dictate that whenever the government comes snooping, that's a search. But the Supreme Court doesn't see it that way. The justices have said the Fourth Amendment does not apply to a host of intrusions, from combing through our trash to trespassing on our property. The Supreme Court already takes too narrow a view of when the Fourth Amendment's protections kick in; the rapid appearance of new technology is only making it more urgent that we get right this central question regarding the Fourth Amendment: "What is a search?"

"SOMETHING CREEPY AND UN-AMERICAN"

In a classic children's story, a hatchling bird tumbles from the nest and goes on an odyssey in search of its mother, who has flown off to find food. The little bird asks everything it comes across—a kitten, a cow, an airplane, even a bulldozer—"Are you my mother?" In the end, the bulldozer answers the question by lifting the bird back into its nest, reuniting it with its mother.[1]

Abdo Alwareeth has long been on a similar odyssey, a real one, with an equally pressing question—but his quest has not resulted in success. What Alwareeth wants to know is which government agency has been spying on him, and why. No one will say, though the fact of the spying has been undeniable ever since Alwareeth discovered and removed a GPS tracking device from his car, which law enforcement promptly demanded he return.[2]

Alwareeth is an American citizen, a self-made immigrant of Yemeni descent. He left his aristocratic family as a teenager and set out to find his way in the world. He was educated in Kuwait, then came to the United States. An Arab Muslim, Alwareeth harbors neither prejudice nor fanaticism. His first job after coming to San Francisco was at Glide Memorial Church, where he made a lifelong friend of his Christian boss. His first wife was Jewish. He's not particularly religious. He established a successful chain of gas stations and grocery stores, remarried, had three children. He served for years as president of the Yemeni Benevolent Society. At a certain point he decided his children should experience Arab culture firsthand, so he sold his business and moved the family to Egypt for several years. Then he brought them back so that the kids could attend college in the United States.[3]

Alwareeth's trouble started when California wrote to him in September 2008 to offer free auto repair services if he enrolled for a day of basic automobile maintenance training. After the classroom session, everyone's car took a turn on the lift. When Alwareeth's Infinity went up, sixth or seventh in the queue, it was hard to miss the device toward the rear, with its antenna, and wires sticking out of it. Alwareeth's classmates started yelling it was a bomb, so the instructor ordered them out. Then he and Alwareeth hammered down what the instructor recognized as a tracking device, and removed the battery. Alwareeth bluntly describes the "humiliation" he felt among his classmates—"He's an Arab, he has a bomb in his car."[4]

Once their surveillance of Alwareeth was interrupted, law enforcement's priority became recovering the device. Alwareeth took his car to his own mechanic the day after the device was discovered, to repair something the auto maintenance class had revealed. When he found the shop busy he booked an appointment a day later. Immediately after Alwareeth departed, unmarked cars descended on the auto repair shop; officers jumped out and demanded return of the GPS tracker. The hapless owner had no clue what they were talking about; they searched the shop anyway. When Alwareeth returned the next day, the law enforcement rodeo repeated itself. Detective Sergeant Raffaello Pata of the San Rafael police gave Alwareeth his card, demanded the device, and apologized, saying it was all a mistake; the device was intended for a drug dealer. (Alwareeth asked them if they thought he was stupid.)[5]

At this point, a guilty person would slink into the darkness, but Alwareeth pursues his inquiry relentlessly. "A clean person," he says, "has nothing to hide." His file holds the business cards of all the officials he has met, and his correspondence with them: the inspector with the District Attorney of Marin County, special agents with the FBI, a social worker with the Marin County Department of Health and Human Services. The DA's investigator warmly promised to find answers. When Alwareeth came back to the DA's office a couple of days later the mood had changed. He told Alwareeth just to drop it. The City of San Rafael's insurer, against whom Alwareeth filed a claim, denied any complicity, stating, "The only interaction between your client and the police department was when Mr. Alwareeth filed the complaint with the City regarding the device." (One is curious, then, how Detective Sergeant Pata's card materialized in Alwareeth's file.) The San Rafael Police Department informed Alwareeth they had no clue which government agency was responsible.[6]

Alwareeth is the loyal, believe-in-the-American-dream sort who brags about the American system of justice and record on human rights when he's back in Yemen, but who is left to wonder: "What happened to *my* human rights?" The short answer is that at the time the government did this to him, the courts had said he didn't have a right—none of us had a right—to be free from government GPS tracking.[7]

The Fourth Amendment prohibits "unreasonable searches and seizures," making the question of what is a "search" (or "seizure") the lynchpin of everything else. As we saw in Part II, if something is a search, law enforcement can still do it, so long as they have probable cause and a warrant. But if it is not a "search," within the meaning of the Fourth Amendment, there are no limits on what the government can do. To any of us.

In a case called *United States v. Pineda-Moreno*, the federal court of appeals with jurisdiction over California, where Alwareeth resides,

decided that when the government engages in long-term GPS surveillance, that is not a "search" subject to constitutional protections. The
government, suspecting Pineda-Moreno of growing and distributing
marijuana, snuck onto his property at night and installed a GPS device
on his car. They tracked his movements for four months, with no warrant. No problem, said the judges: it is not a search because no one has
a "reasonable expectation of privacy" in his or her whereabouts.[8]

No reasonable expectation of privacy in one's whereabouts? That seems
a tad strong. The case brought together in dissent two judges who rarely
agree with each other, Alex Kozinski and Stephen Reinhardt. When
these two see things the same way, it's fair to worry something is seriously
amiss. To call sneaking onto someone's property in the dead of night and
then gathering "the precise locus of all of Pineda-Moreno's movements"
not a "search," Kozinski pointed out, means "police can do it to anybody,
anytime they feel like it." "The needs of law enforcement," Kozinski
noted archly, "to which my colleagues seem inclined to refuse nothing, are
quickly making personal privacy a distant memory." Kozinski was born in
Bucharest, Romania, in 1950, and grew up there until he was twelve, leading him to point out that for those who actually had "lived under a totalitarian regime," this sort of conduct by the government created "an eerie
feeling of déjà vu." "There is something creepy and un-American about
such clandestine and underhanded behavior."[9]

Advances in technology have made this question of what a "search"
is one of the most pressing we face today. Philadelphia's former Police
Commissioner Charles Ramsey, the co-chair of President Obama's Task
Force on 21st Century Policing, has noted that "technology is advancing
faster than policy." "We have to ask ourselves the hard questions," he
insists: "What do these technologies mean for constitutional policing?"
Ramsey was quoted in a report by the Police Executive Research Forum cataloging some of the spy technologies police now possess: "automated license plate readers . . . facial recognition software, predictive
analytics systems." (Predictive analytics systems identify people believed
likely to commit crimes in the future; you last saw this technology star-
ring alongside Tom Cruise in the futuristic *Minority Report*, in which
people were incarcerated for "pre-crime.") That list doesn't begin to cover
it, though. There are radar flashlights that see through walls. There are
drones that fly over our backyards. The government employs software

programs with names like Carnivore and Magic Lantern to install malware on our computers able to record every keystroke, sort through email, even turn on and off the webcam. The microphone on your cell phone can be activated without you knowing. "1984 may have come a bit later than predicted," observed Kozinski, referring to George Orwell's dystopian novel about the surveillance state, "but it's here at last."[10]

Is all of this technology available to the government to spy on anyone it chooses, with no restrictions at all? Or is its use a "search," to which the Fourth Amendment applies? This question, on which so much turns for so many, has tossed the courts into complete and utter disarray. In 2012, two years after *Pineda-Moreno* held that long-term GPS surveillance was not a search, the Supreme Court decided the opposite. But the justices split three ways on why, and were unable to offer a coherent test to govern other technologies. The problem, many of the justices realized, was that technology has altered our "reasonable expectations of privacy" dramatically, leaving them totally at a loss on how to deal with the problem.[11]

Solutions are less elusive than the courts believe, though. For one thing, courts should pay more attention to social convention in determining whether we have a "reasonable expectation of privacy." But for another, this is not the sort of question judges need to resolve on their own. In the GPS case, Justice Samuel Alito, joined by many of his colleagues, practically begged Congress for guidance. As we saw in Chapter 4, however, courts don't have to beg legislatures to weigh in on police use of new technologies. They can insist that it happen. And they should.[12]

IS PHYSICAL INTRUSION REQUIRED FOR A "SEARCH"?

The question of what government activity constitutes a Fourth Amendment "search" has bedeviled the Supreme Court for almost a century.

Until Prohibition, if the government acquired evidence from people—either by stealth or by force—it largely was taken for granted that it constituted a "search." But then the advent of the age of electricity complicated things enormously. What should define a "search" when the government could spy and gather evidence without any physical entry or force whatsoever? The scope of the problem became clear in the wake of the country's first high-profile wiretapping investigation. The target was Roy Olmstead, one of the West Coast's foremost rum-runners, whose life really was the stuff of fiction.[13]

For a long time it seemed like the best thing that ever happened to Roy Olmstead was being busted for smuggling booze into Seattle in 1920. A young, up-and-coming member of the police force—the papers called him the "baby lieutenant"—Olmstead was promptly fired. But noting his aptitude for importing and distributing "the stuff," prominent men helped set him up full time in the liquor business. Seattle at the time was progressive on Prohibition, which is to say alcohol was readily available and many drank it, typically with the sanction of local authorities. Its colorful mayor, Doc Brown, had made clear that "[n]o one is going to die for want of a drink of good spirits frumenti as long as I'm mayor."[14]

In relatively quick order, Olmstead established an operation of remarkable legal and logistical complexity, often with the complicity of local officials. He traveled frequently to Canada to purchase his wares, which made their way down the coast in large ships and were offloaded to the mainland via speedboat. The freight was stored in a ranch outside town, in a cave excavated for this very purpose, over which sat an old garage that had been placed on rollers for access to the stash. The goods then were moved into safe places in town, and delivered to willing buyers. Orders were phoned into an office that operated by code to keep itself clear of any evidence of involvement in the booze trade. Olmstead had much of the municipal police working for him.[15]

If Olmstead was to be shut down, it was the federal Prohibition officials who were going to have to do it, but Olmstead ran the feds in rings—so they resorted to tapping his phones. All of them, home and office, at all hours of the day and night. Whatever there was to hear, business or personal, they could hear it. All told, federal agents accumulated more than 700 pages of transcripts. Never did they seek a warrant. The press tagged Olmstead's trial the case of the "whispering wires." After Olmstead was sentenced to four years and a large fine, his appeal made its way all the way up to the Supreme Court.[16]

The central question in Olmstead's case was whether the wiretapping was a "search," and for Chief Justice William Howard Taft—writing for a five-person majority of the Supreme Court—the answer was an easy one: the language of the Fourth Amendment simply did not cover wiretapping. Taft had been a federal judge before being president of the United States, then returned to the Supreme Court as its Chief, the one job he'd always coveted. He was hell-bent on enforcing Prohibition, and if any case called for the iron arm of the law, it was this one.[17]

As Taft read the Fourth Amendment, unless the government *physically* intruded into one's property or person and took something *tangible* there could be neither a "search" nor a "seizure." The language of "[t]he amendment itself," he explained, indicates it is addressed only to "material things": warrants must specify "the place to be searched and the person or *things* to be seized." Here, by contrast, "[t]he evidence was secured by the use of the sense of hearing and that only." The government, Taft noted, had been careful to place its taps outside of Olmstead's home and office. Thus, "[t]here was no searching. There was no seizure."[18]

Justice Louis Brandeis, dissenting in *Olmstead*, deemed Taft's emphasis on physical intrusion naïve in light of technological change. Brandeis had been Taft's ally in many Prohibition cases, though a split now was emerging in their understandings of government power, prompted in part by the excesses of Prohibition enforcement. For Brandeis, it was simply "immaterial where the physical connection with the telephone wires leading into the defendant's premises was made." Physical intrusion was no longer necessary because "[s]ubtler and more far-reaching means of invading privacy have become available to the government." Brandeis noted that "the tapping of one man's telephone line involves the tapping of the telephone of every other person whom he may call, or who may call him"—most of whom might be entirely innocent.[19]

Brandeis was prescient about the threat technology's march posed for personal security. In words that must have seemed science fiction at the time, he wrote, "Ways may some day be developed by which the government, without removing papers from secret drawers, can reproduce them in court." (A training manual prepared by California prosecutors in 2010 quoted Brandeis's opinion in *Olmstead*, and—in a section on "how to get the good stuff"—bragged that just as Brandeis has predicted, technological breakthroughs like cell technology have made it possible "to obtain disclosure in court of what is whispered in the closet.")[20]

It would take two generations of utter legal foolishness to undo the damage to civil liberty that Taft accomplished by allowing the government to spy in any way it wished, without warrant or cause, so long as there was no physical intrusion. This was made clear by two cases that hopscotched the decades prior to *Olmstead*'s overruling. In 1942, in *Goldman v. United States*, the Supreme Court followed *Olmstead* in holding that police did not violate the Fourth Amendment when they listened in to a private conversation by placing a "detectaphone"—essentially a high-tech cup—against the office wall in which it occurred. Dissenting, Justice Frank Murphy was incredulous. True, he said, "[t]here was no physical entry in this case," but under the Court's interpretation "the most confidential revelations between husband and wife, client and lawyer, patient and physician, and penitent and spiritual advisor" were fair game. But then, in *Silverman v. United States*, decided nineteen years later, the government did much the same, and got called out for it. Rather than listening to the room next door with a detectaphone, it used a "spike mike," which actually penetrated the wall, sitting against a heating duct in the defendant's apartment. A skeptical lower court seemed to believe that "[a] distinction between the detectaphone employed in *Goldman* and the spike mike" was "too fine a one to draw." It was "unwilling to believe that the respective rights are to be measured in fractions of inches." But under the *Olmstead* approach they were. In *Silverman*, the Supreme Court found the evidence inadmissible because there was "an actual intrusion into a constitutionally protected area." For forty years that thin physical line made all the difference.[21]

THE PROTECTION OF "PRIVACY"

Olmstead was finally overruled, in 1967, in a case involving gambling rather than booze. Charles Katz was one of the leading college basketball handicappers of his day; not only did he call college basketball games well, he also bet on them. To elude the authorities—wagering on interstate wires is and was a federal offense—Katz had a routine. When placing a bet, Katz would go to a group of three public telephones on Sunset Boulevard in Los Angeles, and randomly pick one of them to make his call. In this day of cellular communication, public phone booths like the ones Katz used, tall narrow cubes made of glass with a closing door for privacy, are a dying breed.[22]

The FBI nailed Katz by tapping the pay phones. With the telephone company's knowledge, agents placed one of the three phones out of order. Then, the federal agents put a listening device on top of, and between, the remaining two booths. When Katz came down to place his bets, one agent signaled another to activate the listening device.[23]

Ushering in the modern era, the *Katz* Court concluded that henceforth in determining whether the government had conducted a "search," the question would not be whether it had physically intruded onto property, but instead if it had violated one's "privacy." "For the Fourth Amendment protects people, not places." The government had argued that any notion of privacy was foolhardy in *Katz*: after all, the man had stepped into a cube of glass, readily visible to all around him. "But," the Court responded, "what he sought to exclude . . . was not the intruding eye—it was the uninvited ear." "One who occupies [a phone booth], shuts the door behind him, and pays the toll that permits him to place a call is surely entitled to assume that the words he utters into the mouthpiece will not be broadcast to the world."[24]

PRIVACY'S PROTECTION EVAPORATES

Soon enough, though, things went south again. Although the Court was prepared to conclude that the Fourth Amendment's new focus on privacy banned warrantless wiretapping, it has had a very difficult time defining what else the concern for privacy ruled out.[25]

Under what became known as "the *Katz* test," whether something is a search or not depends on whether the government invaded a person's "reasonable expectation of privacy." That's the key phrase. The *Katz* Court said that "[w]hat a person seeks to preserve as private, even in an area accessible to the public, may be constitutionally protected." At the same time, though, "[w]hat a person knowingly exposes to the public, even in his own home or office, is not a subject of Fourth Amendment protection."[26]

Superficially, this "knowingly exposes" test makes sense. Just as it is reasonable to expect privacy for some activities in a public space, like using a pay phone, even in a private place, privacy can be forgone. If you stand in front of a plate glass window in the middle of the day, with pedestrians and police about, and murder someone, you can't really "reasonably" expect the people to avert their eyes and ignore this, even if it is in your own home. You've "knowingly exposed" your actions for the world to see.

Ultimately, though, the Supreme Court's attempt to identify police activity that violated our "reasonable expectations of privacy" collapsed. Two things killed it. The first was the justices' inability, which we have seen consistently, to stand firm anytime a majority of them perceived that protecting our personal security might limit the government's ability to control crime. The second was a flood of new technologies.

It came to pass that no matter what law enforcement did to get itself into position to spy, the Supreme Court would conclude people had "knowingly exposed" their conduct. In *California v. Ciraolo*, an anonymous tipster told the police that the defendants were growing marijuana in their backyard. The defendants had erected not one, but two fences— the outer one at six feet, the inner one at ten—clearly strong measures to keep the backyard private. Conceding that no one could see in from street level, the Supreme Court nonetheless said that the fences "might not shield these plants from the eyes of a citizen or a policeman perched on the top of a truck or a two-level bus." Of course, that isn't what the police did—how frequent are double-decker buses in Santa Clara, California? Rather, they "secured a private plane" and flew over the house at 1,000 feet. Still, the justices decided by a 5–4 vote, the defendants had no "legitimate expectation of privacy" because they had "knowingly exposed" their backyard to the public view: "Any member of the public flying in this airspace who glanced down could have seen everything that these officers observed." Really? The chance that someone would look out of a commercial plane, recognize marijuana, manage to connect that to the specific street address, and decide to notify the police was, as the dissenters pointed out, "virtually nonexistent." "It is no accident," they said, "that, as a matter of common experience, many people build fences around their residential areas, but few build roofs over their backyard."[27]

Similarly, in *California v. Greenwood*, the justices signed off on the police searching through people's trash on the equally imaginary ground that by putting it out for municipal collectors, the defendants "exposed their garbage to the public sufficiently to defeat their claim to Fourth Amendment protection." It "is common knowledge," the justices said, that "plastic garbage bags left on or at the side of a public street are readily accessible to animals, children, scavengers, snoops, and other members of the public." Once again, though, none of that had happened. Rather, the defendants had put their trash out on the curb in opaque bags, precisely as the law required them to do. The police had asked the trash collector to nab the defendant's trash and hand it over to them; they then pawed through it. Had "animals, children, scavengers" or "snoops" strewn the Greenwood trash in the yard so that police or others had seen drug paraphernalia, the government would not have been complicit. But given what actually happened, it is a bit hard to know what the justices meant when they said, "[T]he police cannot reasonably be expected to avert their eyes from evidence of criminal activity that could have been observed by any member of the public."[28]

The GPS tracking of Abdo Alwareeth was built on a similarly shaky foundation. *United States v. Knotts*, decided in 1983, was the first case to sign off on electronic location tracking. Acting on a tip that someone was buying chemicals used to manufacture drugs, the police arranged for a beeper to be placed in a canister of the chemicals, so that after it was picked up they could follow it to its destination. The beeper led the police to a drug lab. The justices said tracking the car containing the chemicals was fine because "[a] person travelling in an automobile on public thoroughfares has no reasonable expectation of privacy in his movements from one place to another." The automobile driver, according to the justices, had "voluntarily conveyed" his whereabouts "to anyone who wanted to look." Yet again, though, this is not what happened. The police lost track of the canister at one point, hardly a surprise given that the driver, deliberately attempting to keep his whereabouts private, engaged in "evasive maneuvers." So the police used a helicopter to relocate the beeper signal. Obviously, members of the public are not flying around like the Jetsons in helicopters tracking one another.[29]

The cake, though, may well go to Chief Justice Burger's opinion in yet another overflight case, in which the justices approved the government's taking pictures inside a Dow Chemical facility after plant officials refused access. The lower court described how the government employed the "finest precision aerial camera available," which cost more than $22,000, and was mounted on an aircraft "able to 'provide photographic stability, fast mobility and flight endurance for precision photography.'" Seeking to make this seem utterly ordinary, the majority described it as a "*standard* floor-mounted precision aerial camera." Explaining the Chief Justice in blasé fashion: "The photographs at issue in this case are essentially like those commonly used in mapmaking. Any person with an airplane and an aerial camera could readily duplicate them." Indeed.[30]

The problem with the justices' approach in these cases should be apparent. The Fourth Amendment only kicks in where people have a "reasonable expectation of privacy"; that expectation does not exist if we "knowingly expose" what we are doing to the public. Fair enough so far. But if by "knowingly expose" it means "[a]ny person with an airplane and an aerial camera," can see us, or the government can install a beeper and follow us via helicopter, it is clear we are not going to have much in the way of Fourth Amendment rights at all.

BACKPEDALING AGAINST TECHNOLOGY

More recent years have seen the justices, frightened by the shadow of their own creation, backpedaling. But even when the justices appear to take the idea of constitutionally protected privacy seriously, they still have something going against them: technology. Modern technology is effectively erasing the distinction so critical in *Katz*: between what we knowingly expose to the public and what we seek to keep private. And it is this problem that the Supreme Court cannot seem to get its collective head around.

In approving the use of the beeper to track the car in *Knotts*, the justices explained that the Fourth Amendment did not prohibit the police from "augmenting the sensory faculties bestowed upon them at birth with such enhancement as science and technology afforded them." "Insofar as respondent's complaint seems to be simply that scientific devices such as the beeper enabled the police to be more effective in detecting crime . . . [w]e have never equated police efficiency with unconstitutionality."[31]

The question is how far one allows law enforcement to go in "augmenting" human senses before it becomes a search requiring at least a warrant and probable cause. After all, that is exactly what technology does. In *Katz* itself, hadn't the agents simply "augment[ed]" their "sensory faculties" by putting a tap on the phone to improve their ability to overhear what Katz was saying as he placed his bets? If there are no limits on the ability of law enforcement to use technology to augment its faculties, we will have no privacy left.[32]

The first serious attempt by the justices to restore privacy in the face of advancing technology came in *Kyllo v. United States*, a 2001 case involving the use of a thermal heat detector. Acting on a tip that Kyllo was growing pot at home, officers used an Agema Thermovision 210 to detect a high level of infrared radiation coming off one part of the roof. This suggested Kyllo was using grow lamps. Armed with that, the tip, and Kyllo's utility bills, they then got a warrant. Four members of the Court were up to their old tricks. "All that the infrared camera did," they said, was what "the ordinary use of the senses might enable a neighbor or passerby" to do—notice the heat emanating from a building. As if a passerby on the street could somehow sense the heat from the grow lamps coming off the roof.[33]

The five-person *Kyllo* majority, though, with Justice Scalia writing the opinion, tried to put limits on law enforcement using technology to "see" inside our homes. Absent a warrant, the Court held, police could not employ "sense-enhancing technology" to obtain "any information regarding the interior of the home" that could not otherwise have been obtained without being physically present inside.[34]

The problem is that, like a radioactive isotope, *Kyllo*'s seemingly rights-protective opinion will necessarily decay. That is because of a critical caveat Justice Scalia added to his test. The ban on sense-enhancing technology to discover what goes on in a house, he wrote, holds only so long as "the technology is not in the general public use."[35]

Given the current pace of technology, soon everything law enforcement possesses might be "in general public use." Thermal heat sensors are readily available for purchase—there's even a smartphone app. Go ahead, google it. Justice Scalia himself dropped a footnote in *Kyllo* to point out that the Department of Justice was working on new surveillance technology, including a "Radar Flashlight" that "will enable law enforcement officers to detect individuals through interior building walls." Drones already are flying all over the place: Does that mean the government is now free to hover them outside our windows and over our backyards?[36]

Ultimately, though, it was Abdo Alwareeth's *bête noir*, GPS tracking, which made clear the limits of the Supreme Court's ability to protect our privacy. In *United States v. Jones*, the government had attached a GPS device to a suspected drug dealer's car, tracking him for a month, using satellites that gave the car's location within 5–100 feet, collecting "more than 2,000 pages of data." Was this a search? Didn't *Knotts* allow the tracking of vehicles?[37]

Although the justices decided unanimously that the GPS tracking in *Jones* was a "search," they found themselves unable to agree on a reason for that result. Hemmed in by the *Knotts* beeper case, which they did not overrule, and which had held that we have no expectation of privacy in our whereabouts on public streets, the justices splintered on the question of what exactly the government had done wrong. They could not even say how much GPS tracking was too much.[38]

Justice Scalia—who again wrote for the majority in *Jones*—went back to the future: because government agents had "physically occupied private property for the purpose of obtaining information" (i.e., installed a GPS device on his car) this was a search. If that sounds just like *Olmstead*, it should. *Katz*, he explained, *added* privacy to the list of things protected by the Fourth Amendment, but it did not take away the importance of actual invasions of property rights in determining whether something was a search. Basically, because the police had trespassed by installing the beeper to track Jones, it was a search.[39]

While this sounds promising—now we have more protection, i.e., privacy plus immunity from physical intrusion—in reality it (like his test in *Kyllo*) offers cold comfort. The government already no longer needs to rely on physical intrusions to track us; most of us carry our GPS trackers in our pocket in the guise of cell phones. The government has installed television cameras in thousands of locations, and many police cars have them also. These systems already are being used, in combination with license plate recognition technology, to determine the whereabouts of individuals. Our own cars have onboard computers that record our location, and we use toll payment systems that do the same.[40]

But at least Justice Scalia had a test. The concurring justices, led by Justice Alito, simply threw up their arms. Reiterating that under *Knotts* "relatively short-term monitoring" of location on public streets poses no constitutional problem, Justice Alito concluded that "use of longer-term GPS monitoring in investigations of most offenses" crossed the line. But he could offer no clue where the line is between "relatively short-term" and "longer-term." He didn't say which of "most offenses" could not be uncovered by long-term GPS surveillance, and which could. The opinion was altogether noteworthy for its inability to say anything specific about what the government could or could not do. The *Jones* decision has left the lower courts in utter disarray as to what sort of location tracking—or any other use of technology for that matter—constitutes a "search."[41]

In his *Jones* opinion, Justice Alito did make an extraordinarily important point about how the decreasing cost of technology was likely to leave us all vulnerable to government spying. "In the pre-computer age," he explained, the greatest impediment to government spying was resources: "Traditional surveillance for any extended period of time was difficult and costly and therefore rarely undertaken." He's right. In 1954, Los Angeles's police chief said keeping a suspect under "constant and close surveillance"—as was done to Jones and Alwareeth—would be "not only more costly than any police department can afford, but in the vast majority of cases it is impossible." Such surveillance, Justice Alito pointed out, would involve "a large team of agents, multiple vehicles, and perhaps aerial assistance." For that reason, it would happen only in "an investigation of unusual importance." But no more. "Devices like the one used in the present case . . . make long-term monitoring relatively easy and cheap."[42]

The problem is clear: the prevalence of increasingly inexpensive technology eliminates the distinction between what we keep private and what we display in public, be it on the street or in the supposed privacy of our homes. Location tracking reveals where we are at all times. Malware, mikes, and cameras make it possible to see and hear us whenever we are near a computer. Radar and thermal devices reveal our movements and our possessions. Overflight haunts us. In technology's hands, we have neither privacy, nor what the Fourth Amendment really protects: security, in our "persons, houses, papers, and effects."

THE OTHER *KATZ* SOLUTION: SOCIAL CONVENTION

For all the apparent confusion it created, *Katz* also contained the seeds of a solution.

Katz can be read as making social convention determinative of when we have a reasonable expectation of privacy. In other words, one interpretation of the *Katz* decision is that whether the government is conducting a "search" that requires it to have probable cause, and get a warrant, properly rests on societal norms about when we all ought to be able to expect to have our privacy respected. "The critical fact in this case," wrote Justice Harlan in *Katz*, "is that [o]ne who occupies" a telephone booth, "shuts the door behind him, and pays the toll that permits him to place a call is surely entitled to" assume that "the words he utters into the mouthpiece will not be broadcast to the world." "Surely entitled" is big talk, but it was not at all out of place—because everyone in *Katz* knew what the social norms of the time were. You went into that phone booth precisely to get the sort of privacy that people would then afford you.[43]

It's both true and unavoidable, as Justice Alito noted in *Jones*, that technology may alter social convention. That is exactly what the law must take account of. Technology invariably is going to shift the way we interact with one another, and what our expectations of appropriate social behavior are. The law must be concerned with how people understand their privacy in the world in which we actually live. And it is to those expectations that law enforcement must adhere.

The telephone provides an apt example of social convention changing the meaning of privacy, even explaining the differing conclusions in *Olmstead* and *Katz*, the cases of the bootlegger and the bettor. Plenty of folks alive today can remember picking up the phone and hearing others' conversations. "Party lines" were familiar well into the 1960s, and more than one nosy neighbor would listen in. Calls were placed through live operators, who—at least in a small town—seemed to know everyone's business. New York City's Police Commissioner Arthur Woods in 1916 made the point that "[t]elephone conversations . . . cannot be private in a way that letters can be, since the employees of the telephone company cannot help hearing parts of conversations and may, if they are inclined, easily hear all." But by 1967 such eavesdropping was frowned upon, and there simply was no way to get around the fact that in nailing Katz, the government was spying in a socially unacceptable fashion: "To read the Constitution more narrowly," said the *Katz* Court, getting it exactly right, "is to ignore the vital role that the public telephone has come to play in private communication."[44]

Because the reasonable expectation of privacy test properly incorporates social convention, it is true that there will be hard cases—even for the most mundane of technologies. In a case out of Washington State, for example, an officer—acting on a report of someone growing pot—looked in the window of a mobile home with a flashlight, discovering marijuana and paraphernalia. The Washington Supreme Court leaned heavily on social convention in concluding this was not a search. "An officer may act as any reasonably respectful citizen." People, the justices said, commonly walk up to one another's front doors and peer in their windows. They also use flashlights: "in this state" it "would be an expected device for someone to use approaching a mobile home in a rural area at dusk or after nightfall." Still, there was room to doubt this seemingly obvious conclusion. The dissent felt the officer—who had also trespassed by going further onto the property to check out a shed, and had peered in a back window of the home as well—had wandered too far off the permissible "access route" to the house. Do "reasonably respectful" citizens do that?[45]

The real problem in this area, though, is not the difficulty of determining social convention in most cases; it is once again the judges' lack of fortitude to make law enforcement adhere to acceptable social norms. Judge Kozinski hit the nail on the head in *Pineda-Moreno* when he said that his colleagues simply lacked the will to constrain law enforcement, the privacy of all of us be damned. In the *Greenwood* trash case, the majority, in support of its argument that we have no expectation of privacy in our trash, quoted an article about "journalistic 'trashpicking,'" which said that "evidently . . . everybody does it," citing as an example Henry Kissinger's trash being combed through by a tabloid when he was Secretary of State. As the dissent pointed out, however, the public "roundly condemned" this, calling it "a disgusting invasion of personal privacy" and "indefensible . . . as civilized behavior." In complete disregard of social convention, courts have approved overflights of glass ceilings, secret video cameras fixed onto poles outside of homes, and the use of night-vision goggles to peer through windows. Though the technology exists for law enforcement to do all these things, none of it is cricket—at least not without probable cause and a warrant.[46]

Lest there be any doubt about where social convention stands, it is instructive to see how the justices and other public officials react when the shoe is on the other foot. In Portland, for example, officials went berserk when a local newspaper decided to paw through their trash to make a point about police spying. The brouhaha began when the Portland police did a "garbage pull" on one of their colleagues with whom they had a vendetta, finding—among other things—a "bloody tampon" that they sent off for a drug screen. A local judge disapproved the trash drop—relying of course on the Oregon Constitution, because, as we have seen, the federal Constitution has nothing to say about this. The local DA and police chief then challenged the wisdom of the judge's decision, believing trash drops a valuable tool. So *Willamette Week* decided to see what was in their trash. When reporters came to show the police chief what they'd found, he said "This is very cheap" and tossed them out of his office. The mayor had stronger things to say: "I consider *Willamette Week*'s actions in this matter to be potentially illegal and absolutely unscrupulous and reprehensible. I will consider all my legal options in response to their actions." The mayor and police chief were right; what *Willamette Week* did was outrageous. But the germane question is why the Supreme Court thinks it is okay for the police to do the same sort of thing, without warrant or probable cause.[47]

Justice Scalia—who was with the majority in allowing trash drops in *Greenwood*—had a similar negative reaction when, in 2009, a Fordham professor had his class engage in a "teaching moment"—assembling a dossier on the justice by trolling the Internet and seeing what they could find. They found a lot: what TV shows and food he likes, his home address and phone number, his wife's email address. Justice Scalia had set himself up for it. At a conference he'd scoffed at Internet and personal privacy. When confronted with the class project, though, Justice Scalia was, to say the least, displeased. He called the exercise "abominably poor judgment," and snidely added that because the professor "was not teaching a course on judgment, I presume he felt no obligation to display any."[48]

There is simply no excuse for courts inviting the police to ignore the norms of society. People can physically stand on toilet seats and peer into the next stall, but it's not at all acceptable, and for that reason cops shouldn't be allowed to either—at least not without probable cause and a warrant. As Judge Kozinski said in *Pineda-Moreno*, lambasting the lackluster diligence of his colleagues, "To say that the police may do to your property what urchins might do spells the end of Fourth Amendment protections."[49]

SOLVING HARD CASES

Because social conventions change, there are going to be hard cases, of course. But neither the police nor the courts need to figure out on their own what social convention permits. The tools for "policing with permission" are available to help, and should be used.

Warrants

To the extent law enforcement wants greater clarity in any given case, there is an easy answer: get a warrant. In many of the cases in which courts have waved a green flag at the police after the fact, a warrant would have been utterly obtainable. The government did get a warrant in *Jones*; they just failed to comply with it by attaching the GPS after the deadline, and in the wrong jurisdiction to boot. And surely in cases like *Rose*, the marijuana flashlight case from Washington State, where the tipster is a known citizen who could be prosecuted for sending the police on a false mission, detailed allegations of why they think the law is being violated should provide the police with ample probable cause. Investigating marijuana growing was hardly an emergency that justified skipping over getting a warrant before snooping around.[50]

If the government decides to spy without getting court permission on the front end, then courts should be extra-reluctant to push the boundaries of the Fourth Amendment on the back end by deeming what the government did in that case not to be a search. If the government can get a warrant in close cases, it should. It is true that in some cases it is tougher to develop probable cause than in others—a problem we'll tackle in the next chapter. Only when cause is absent, though, should courts struggle with this difficult question of whether a search even occurred. If there was probable cause, and doubt about whether a warrant was necessary, the right answer is to get a warrant. If courts are quick to say that what police did was not even a "search"—and thus placing it wholly outside the Fourth Amendment—the police will never bother to get an independent opinion from a magistrate. That is precisely how and why the privacy of all of us is at risk.

The Legislative Solution

Emerging technologies present two very real sorts of problems. If social convention allows something, then the police don't need a warrant. Yet

it can be difficult for courts to know precisely what is socially acceptable. In addition, for some of these technologies, we have to ask whether,
even if the police have probable cause, a warrant is enough protection.

Take drone technology. Drones have the capability of changing our
world, in many ways for the better. They can be used for fire patrol,
traffic snarls, locating lost children. But the fact that drones are remarkably cheaper than their aerial predecessors means there also could
be widespread abuse. The Federal Aviation Administration had licensed
just over 300 drones as of 2013; that number is expected to top 30,000 by
2020. "Hummingbird" drones can hover outside our windows with cameras and microphones. "Mosquito" drones can be remotely controlled and
take blood samples without our knowing. Is a warrant enough to justify
law enforcement in utilizing these technologies, or are further rules
necessary?[51]

Automatic license plate recognition, or ALPR, provides another apt
example. On the one hand, all that ALPRs record are license plates visible
to anyone in public. On the other hand, using nothing but a camera and
an optical character reader, this technology allows law enforcement to har-
vest the location of millions of vehicles, and store that information in
searchable databases. ALPR has enormous potential as a crime-fighting
tool. A 2011 survey found 71 percent of police agencies used license plate
readers. And 85 percent of agencies planned on acquiring or increasing
their use of license plate readers over the next five years. In Montgomery County, Maryland, for example, one officer using an ALPR for some
hundred hours over a twenty-seven-day period collected almost 50,000
license plate "reads." These reads resulted in more than two hundred traffic citations, identified twenty-six suspended licenses, sixteen emission
violations, four stolen and one expired set of plates, and three arrests.[52]

But just as ALPR has promise, it also poses a threat to civil liberties.
The International Association of Chiefs of Police, which has done excellent work in this area, explained that ALPR cameras "may collect the
license plate numbers of vehicles parked at public locations that, even
though public, might be considered sensitive, such as doctor's offices,
clinics, churches, and addiction counseling meetings, among others." A
sergeant with the Los Angeles Sheriff's Department said of ALPR data:
"I'd keep it indefinitely if I could"; it is not "Big Brother"; and "[i]t's doing
what a deputy normally does in his routine duties." That's not true: the

normal deputy can't collect 50,000 license plate numbers, let alone millions, and store them away in a database that can be used to reconstruct a vehicle's movements over a week, month, or year.[53]

What is needed to address the difficult questions with regard to emerging technology is *policy*—the sort courts just can't give, and democratically accountable bodies should, as we saw in Part I. Justice Alito made precisely this point in the *Jones* case. "In circumstances involving dramatic technological change," he wrote, "the best solution to privacy concerns may be legislative." That is because "[a] legislative body is well situated to gauge changing public attitudes, to draw detailed lines, and to balance privacy and public safety in a comprehensive way." The ACLU's chief technologist, Christopher Soghoian, said much the same thing regarding the use of malware: "We have transitioned into a world where law enforcement is hacking into people's computers, and we have never had a public debate."[54]

Where judges and others have gone wrong, though, is in thinking that courts must act if legislatures have not. Soghoian pointed out that in the absence of legislative action, "[j]udges are having to make up these powers as they go along." Alito said the same in *Jones*. Ruing the fact that "[t]o date . . . Congress and most States have not enacted statutes regulating the use of GPS tracking technology for law enforcement purposes," he concluded the justices were forced to do "[t]he best that we can do"—i.e., to decide whether or not it is a search.[55]

This is simply incorrect: there is something else the judges not only could do, but should, which is to refuse to allow emerging technologies to be used by the police for surveillance until rules are in place to regulate them. As we discussed in detail in Chapter 4, courts do not have to say "aye" or "nay" to police activities. All they need do is ask the question "Is the police use of long-term GPS tracking (or malware, or drones) authorized by law?" General statutes authorizing policing agencies to enforce the law, adopted in some cases decades before such technology was even imaginable, ought not to be held to authorize anything the police choose to do. That is particularly the case with regard to the new policing, which uses some of these technologies—such as ALPR—not just when there is probable cause to suspect someone of wrongdoing, but on all of us at any time the police wish, without cause or warrants.

Instead of forcing democratic debate about the use of technology for spying, the justices have done the opposite, choosing to disregard relevant legislative enactments. In *Greenwood*, local law required the trash be put on the curb, it prohibited the trash collector from going through that trash, and the California Supreme Court had held that as a matter of state law, one had a right of privacy in one's trash. No matter, said the Supreme Court: "We have never intimated that whether or not a search is reasonable within the meaning of the Fourth Amendment depends on the law of the particular State in which the search occurs." In *United States v. Dunn* government agents went over a perimeter fence, one interior fence, two additional barbed-wire interior fences, and a final wooden fence on the defendant's 198-acre ranch located half a mile from a public road, then used a flashlight to see a drug lab in a barn located near a private home. The justices ignored the fact that state law prohibited just such trespassing, holding (somewhat incoherently) that it was not a search at all because it occurred in an "open field" rather than the home or its surrounds.[56]

If state law forbids what the cops have done, that should be the end of the matter. What is more telling of social convention than the laws adopted by democratically accountable bodies? It is possible those laws will fall out of date. But the way to discern this is for courts to follow them—even if it means limiting the police—unless and until democratic processes change the law.[57]

As we have seen time and again, giving people a voice makes for very different policy. Take data retention policies for ALPR. Is it a coincidence that under rules drafted by the New Jersey Attorney General, ALPR data can be kept for five years, while under a democratically adopted Maine statute it is twenty-one days? The District of Columbia was set to adopt a widespread system of closed-circuit video surveillance, like that omnipresent in the United Kingdom. The use of such cameras, originally part of the fight against terror, was to be expanded "to deter and/or eliminate crime in residential and commercial areas." Community leaders applauded them as a popular solution to crime. But then the D.C. government did what it should, and engaged in rule-making, inviting public participation. The result was a significantly scaled-down project that included provisions for erasing the recordings on a regular basis.[58]

In the face of rapidly changing technology, what is required of judges is caution, some humility about their ability to understand what expectations of privacy society deems reasonable, and deference to democratic processes. In one of the first of the current era's electronic communications cases to reach the Supreme Court, *City of Ontario v. Quon*, the justices recognized their own limitations. The case involved a police officer's use of a department beeper for private communications—including sending sexually explicit messages. The Court said it must "proceed with care" because "[t]he judiciary risks error by elaborating too fully on the Fourth Amendment implications of emerging technology before its role in society becomes clear." "[I]t is uncertain how workplace norms, and the law's treatment of them, will evolve." The justices concluded, "Prudence counsels caution," lest any single case, with its own peculiar facts, establish "far-reaching premises" about privacy expectations.[59]

The Court in *Quon* had it exactly right. What is needed when technology is at issue is ongoing democratic intervention. The justices should force it to occur by refusing to allow the use of new surveillance technologies until they are authorized by public action.

To be clear, deeming more activity a "search" puts law enforcement in a little bit of a bind. Because searches require probable cause (and often a warrant), there will be instances in which law enforcement officials have reason to suspect something is up, but not enough evidence to add up to probable cause—i.e., enough to search or get a warrant. What do they do then? This has proven a particularly contentious issue in the Internet and cellular age, and so that is where we will turn next.

10

THIRD-PARTY INFORMATION AND THE CLOUD

There's long been a serious chink in the Fourth Amendment's armor: a Supreme Court rule that says if the government demands information about you from a third party, it is not a "search," and therefore doesn't implicate your rights at all. Time and technology have worn that chink into a spyhole on what we hold both intimate and dear.[1] As our lives have moved from actual homes and offices to the virtual world of cyberspace, most everything about us is now sitting in some third party's hands. If the government wants it, the Supreme Court says, it need only subpoena it from whoever happens to be holding it. No warrant is needed and no probable cause required, thank you very much.[2]

There's a growing consensus that giving the government this much leeway can't be right. It's one reason so many companies like the texting giant WhatsApp and iPhone maker Apple have moved to end-to-end encryption—to protect user data by making themselves immune to these government requests. Still, figuring out how the third-party rule should be changed is a daunting task, one that has tied Congress in knots. That's in part because it also implicates the other side of the equation: law enforcement's ability to obtain information it needs in criminal and terrorism investigations.

CYBERSPACE: THE GOVERNMENT'S
OWN FILE CABINET

What's at stake under the third-party rule was made clear in a clash between the government and the social media giant Twitter, during the government's investigation of WikiLeaks, the international organization dedicated to exposing government secrets. In May 2010, U.S. Army Private Bradley (now Chelsea) Manning was arrested for allegedly passing hundreds of thousands of classified documents to WikiLeaks. In December of that same year, as part of its investigation of the massive leak, federal prosecutors issued to Twitter what is known as a 2703(d) order—or simply a D-order—to get records pertaining to three Twitter customers, one of whom—the computer security expert and activist Jacob Appelbaum—was a United States citizen. (The other two were Rop Gonggrijp, who founded the Netherlands' first private Internet service provider, and Birgitta Jonsdottir, a member of Iceland's Parliament.)[3]

At the time, most tech companies simply would have complied. But Twitter, which has made its reputation on protecting user privacy, was different. It has long had a policy of notifying targets so they can defend themselves in court. Ben Lee, Twitter's Vice President, Legal, explains that "modern platforms for communication and expression . . . create a certain level of responsibility . . . for the rest of society." For that reason, he says, it is "hammered into" the minds of people at Twitter: "Protect the user where we can." The goal of notifying the user, Lee emphasizes, is to "hold the government accountable to existing legal requirements before they can obtain user data."[4]

When the government demanded the information from Twitter, it did so in a court filing kept secret from the users and the public. It is common for the government to try to keep such requests under wraps, which, as the WikiLeaks Three later pointed out, makes it difficult "to oppose an order because the individual does not know about it." When Twitter refused to comply until the order was made public and the targets were notified, it was instant front-page news. Barton Gellman, writing in *Time*, wagged his finger at Twitter's competitors: "It is beyond reasonable doubt that authorities asked other companies to supply the same kinds of information sought from Twitter, but none of them admit it."[5]

To be clear, the information the government sought in this case was not public. The government wanted everything Twitter had about the WikiLeaks Three other than their tweets: account names and user IDs, all personal addresses, payment information, session times, and IP addresses for devices from which tweets were sent. The targets complained the information could be "'intensely revealing' as to location" and would let the government create a "map" of their private associations.[6]

Twitter's fight to notify its clients ended in vain, because the court decided, remarkably, that the targets of government inquiry didn't even have legal "standing"—a legal right to come to court to challenge the attempt to gather their data. Instead, the third-party information holder—in this case Twitter—was the only one who could fight their battles for them. Twitter's Lee was "flummoxed" when prosecutors first made this argument. A former Legal Aid defender well used to sitting across the table from lawyers in the District Attorney's office, he was surprised at the "aggressiveness with which they were approaching this." Twitter pointed out in court that even if it had the resources to fight all these battles on behalf of their customers, "Twitter will often know little or nothing about the underlying facts necessary to support their user's argument that the subpoenas may be improper." As the ACLU aptly noted, third-party companies "just don't have the capacity—or the incentives—to go to bat against the government each time there is a challenge to one of their user's rights."[7]

What matters at the moment isn't that the WikiLeaks Three lost, but why. The court ruled that the users could not complain about the government getting hold of their data, because they had "voluntarily" turned the information over to Twitter. "Voluntarily" is the trick word here. Even assuming using Twitter is voluntary, in today's world we have little choice but to give our most intimate information to third parties all the time.[8] Half the time, we don't even know the information is being collected. Indeed, in ruling against the WikiLeaks Three, the court justified its position in part by saying the need to give over information like your IP address is "built directly into the architecture of the Internet." That's right, but it seems to undercut the court's own argument that giving over the information is "voluntary." It quickly becomes clear that "voluntary" in court-speak bears little relation to what ordinary human beings mean when they talk about giving something knowingly and freely to someone else.[9]

Under current Supreme Court decisions, virtually any information you provide to anyone is "voluntarily" given and thus fair game for the government to grab. Unless you plan to keep your cash in a mattress, you need a bank and credit. These institutions have all your financial information. Search engine companies know if you looked into breast cancer symptoms, sought marriage counseling, worried whether your kid was autistic, or wondered how to treat your hemorrhoids. "Smart meters" tell utility companies not only how much electricity you are using, but which appliances are using it and when. Radio-frequency identification tags— "RFID"—implanted in your credit cards, your passport, your customer loyalty cards, even ticket stubs, reveal what you buy and where you go. Your cell phone provider not only knows where you've been, but where you are right at this moment. The "cloud" holds all your music, your photos, your instant messages, your love notes, and your spreadsheets—even if you've done nothing but upload them for your private use. The ACLU's chief technologist Chris Soghoian has written, aptly, "In the cloud, the government is just one subpoena away." In theory it may be possible to go off the grid and avoid opening yourself up to any scrutiny—the Unabomber pulled it off for a while—but for most of us it is impossible to live that way.[10]

Few today doubt this area of the law is ripe for change, but what makes it tough is that the government claims a good argument of its own. As the judge in the WikiLeaks case pointed out, "The purpose of a criminal investigation is to find out whether crimes have occurred." The whole reason "the legal threshold for issuing a subpoena is low," explained a judge in another Twitter user case, is that some investigations would never get off the ground if probable cause were required just to get started in the first place. This sort of worry is in part what has FBI Director James Comey stumping the country fretting about encryption and issuing dire warnings about the government "going dark."[11]

That's the tension: protect the information, and law enforcement says it can't go after some bad guys; weaken protections, and we all can say adios to any shard of security from government prying. Caught in the middle are the tech companies, which—frankly—have long tried to have it both ways. A company like Twitter, *The New York Times* pointed out, has to "play nice with the governments of countries in which it operates." At the same time, the companies feel the need to reassure users of their privacy. Worse yet, says the president of the Electronic Privacy Information Center (EPIC), Marc Rotenberg, while "commercial providers like to act as though they are adjudicating a dispute between the government and users," the truth is that many "want access to the data themselves" for commercial purposes such as promoting advertising. They want to hold it, but then it is right there in their hands when the government wants it. And so, Rotenberg concludes, "we are in this very weird triangular space."[12]

This tension between the needs of law enforcement and user privacy—made worse by tech companies' own complex interests—triggered one of the great legislative standoffs in memory. For over half a decade it has been apparent to *everyone* involved—legislators, law enforcement, courts, the public—that the laws on the books regulating law enforcement access to digital information held by third parties are hopelessly out of date. Everyone is vulnerable at present. But Congress is paralyzed; the most it has even tried to tackle is access to email, the easiest case for privacy protections. And so the battle is fought out in the courts—the very courts that gave away all our data in the first place.

WHAT YOU'VE "VOLUNTARILY" GIVEN AWAY

In a trio of cases from the 1960s and 1970s, the Supreme Court concluded that if you'd given your data to a third party, it was not a Fourth Amendment "search" for the government to acquire it.

The first case, from 1966, involved the notorious Teamsters Union leader Jimmy Hoffa. The government had gone after Hoffa for violating federal labor law. Hoffa was acquitted. Then the government caught him conspiring to bribe jurors. Critical to the government's jury tampering case was the testimony of an informant named Partin. Partin agreed to rat out Hoffa to the feds in order to avoid prison for his own misdeeds. Hoffa complained that the government had placed Partin in his inner circle deliberately in order to gather information; the government insisted Partin was acting on his own initiative. Distinction without a difference, responded the justices: the Fourth Amendment simply doesn't protect a wrongdoer's "misplaced belief that a person to whom he voluntarily confides his wrongdoing will not reveal it."[13]

Many, justifiably, associate the government's use of secret informants with totalitarianism. Still, the *Hoffa* decision has a certain logic to it. Hoffa had blabbed, and in doing so, to paraphrase the Supreme Court's terminology, he'd "assumed the risk" that the third party he told would turn that information over to the government. Surely, if Partin had decided to go to the government on his own initiative with the incriminating information, no one would have had any problem with that.

Pretty soon, though, the justices began to rob the idea of "voluntarily" giving information to third parties of all ordinary meaning. In the early 1970s, the government was investigating a fellow named Mitch Miller (no, not the television bandleader, for those old enough to remember) concerning a king-sized bootlegging operation. As part of its investigation, agents from the Bureau of Alcohol, Tobacco and Firearms used a subpoena to get Miller's financial statements and deposit slips from his banks. Miller cried foul, but—relying on *Hoffa*—the justices concluded Miller had no Fourth Amendment rights. What the government had collected was "only information voluntarily conveyed to the banks and exposed to their employees in the ordinary course of business." Just like Hoffa, the justices claimed, Miller took the "risk, in revealing his affairs to another," that the information would be given to the government.[14]

There are two nontrivial problems with applying *Hoffa* like this to Miller. First, it is not clear any of us "voluntarily" use financial institutions. What is the alternative, exactly? But second, what risk had Miller actually assumed? Sure, he put his money in a bank rather than stashing it in a cupboard. But the risk he took in doing so—that bank officials would reveal his financial records to the government—was close to zero. Bank officials never would have put two and two together, in part because they didn't have half the information—i.e., any suspicion that Miller was bootlegging. What really happened in *Miller* was that a federal law required the bank to retain the records, and then the government used a subpoena to force the bank to turn them over. That all may be fine as an accommodation to the needs of law enforcement— we'll get to that question in just a moment—but to claim the government came across the information "voluntarily" is to torture the English language.[15]

The real crusher happened in the decision in *Smith v. Maryland*. This seemingly limited case from 1979 has become crucial to defining our rights in the information age. A woman was robbed. Then she started getting threatening and obscene phone calls. Once, the caller, who said he was the robber, asked her to step outside while he drove by her place. The police soon spotted the vehicle in her neighborhood, and obtained the car owner's name and address by tracing the license plate number. Then they arranged for the phone company to install a "pen register"—a device that records the phone numbers a caller dials— which showed that Smith was phoning the woman from his home. This information was used in turn to get a warrant to search Smith's house, where yet more evidence was found to convict him. Smith asked to have all the evidence thrown out, on the ground that installing the pen register was a warrantless "search."[16]

The Court held Smith had no expectation of privacy in the phone numbers he dialed, because—as you surely can guess by now—"[w]hen he used his phone, [Smith] voluntarily conveyed numerical information to the telephone company and 'exposed' that information to its equipment in the ordinary course of business." This makes less sense than *Miller*. Unlike the bank, the phone company wasn't even holding the information the government wanted. The government had to have the company attach a device to collect the information. Still, the Court said that it didn't matter whether the phone company chose to collect this sort of information on its own or not: "Regardless of the phone company's election" the company "had facilities for recording it and was free to record." Translated: If a third party is capable of gathering the information the government wants, it can make them collect it and turn it over.[17]

If the logic of *Smith* were solid, it gets very difficult to see why the government can't just ask the phone company to record your conversations whenever it wants. After all, the phone company is every bit as capable of recording conversations as it is phone numbers dialed—the fact that they don't do it doesn't mean they couldn't. The justices in *Smith* distinguished *Katz*, in which—as we saw in the last chapter—they held that wiretapping was out, by stressing that the pen register didn't capture the *content* of conversations, just the phone numbers dialed. But, as Justice Stewart, the author of the *Katz* decision said—dissenting in *Smith*—most people would not "be happy to have broadcast to the world a list of the . . . numbers they have called." Not because it would incriminate them, but "because it easily could reveal . . . the most inti-mate details of a person's life."[18]

Given what a creep Smith was, it is easy to see why the Supreme Court ruled as it did, but nothing can reel back the unfathomable li-cense the decision has been taken to grant the government. *Smith* has been used to justify everything from location tracking to bulk data col-lection by the National Security Agency. Police officials take full advan-tage of this third-party rule, in numerous cases, to obtain big helpings of personal information. In 2012, cell phone companies reported they'd received 1.3 million demands from law enforcement for everything from texts to location information. And, consistent with the "triangular" po-sitioning of the tech companies, it has even turned into a major revenue stream for the businesses. AT&T alone took in more than $8 million dol-lars that very year by turning over its customers' information in response to law enforcement demands. At a private conference held in Washing-ton, D.C., for law enforcement and their vendors, Sprint Nextel's "man-ager of electronic surveillance"—that's quite the job title, no?—described how it had set up a dedicated website so police could access customer information directly from their desks. "The tool has just really caught on fire with law enforcement," he bragged.[19]

SUBPOENAS: A LICENSE TO PRY

What makes matters worse still is how the government gets its hands on most of this third-party information—by using a subpoena. A sub-poena is an order to produce documents or other information at a given place or time, backed up by the threat of being held in contempt of court. Unlike with a warrant, to get a subpoena law enforcement officials need not show probable cause, and they don't even have to get permission from a judge. In the *Miller* case, the Supreme Court blithely described how Treasury agents "presented" the bank presidents "with grand jury sub-poenas *issued in blank by the clerk of the District Court, and filled in by the United States Attorney's office.*"[20]

The origin of prosecutors' "blank check" authority to issue subpoenas rests in the traditional function of the grand jury, an evidence-gathering body that dates back as far as twelfth-century England. Grand juries, usually composed of from twelve to twenty-three people, are empaneled to investigate crime in the community. If the grand jury concludes there is cause to believe a crime has been committed, it hands down an indictment, signaling the start of criminal proceedings. The Supreme Court has said that a grand jury "can investigate merely on suspicion that the law is being violated, or even just because it wants assurance that it is not." Its job "is not fully carried out until every available clue has been run down and all witnesses examined." Given this "broad brush" role, the logic runs, it would make no sense to require probable cause even to begin investigating. As the Twitter court pointed out, requiring probable cause would stop an investigation in its tracks before it got going.[21]

If you are wondering, reasonably, how to square grand jury fishing expeditions with the probable cause requirement of the Fourth Amendment, the answer rests in the fact that historically the grand jury was separate from the government. Just like the Fourth Amendment itself, the grand jury was understood as a *check* on government. The grand jury's "most valuable function," the Supreme Court has said, is "not only to examine into the commission of crimes, but to stand between the prosecutor and the accused."[22]

Part of the reason our federal Constitution contains a right to an indictment by the grand jury stems from the famous trials of John Peter Zenger. Zenger was a printer in the 1700s harshly critical of New York's colonial governor. Thrice the government tried to prosecute Zenger; each time the grand jury refused to issue an indictment. Similarly, grand juries refused to let Stamp Act prosecutions go forward in the run-up to the Revolutionary War. Historically, grand juries—at their own initiative—pursued official wrongdoing and unveiled official corruption. During the Progressive Era, grand juries were the downfall of big city machines like that of Boss Tweed.[23]

Today, though, grand juries are nothing but the tool of prosecutors, who wield the subpoena power in the grand jury's name, but with no real supervision by the jurors themselves. That's why it is said that if a prosecutor asked, the grand jury would "indict a ham sandwich." The country got a vivid taste of this when Special Prosecutor Ken Starr went after President Bill Clinton for perjury and obstruction of justice involving his affair with Monica Lewinsky. Not only did Starr subpoena Lewinsky's semen-stained dress, he also used a subpoena to get his hands on Monica Lewinsky's hard drive containing love letters to Clinton. He even hauled off the computer of one of Lewinsky's friends, ultimately revealing to the world the friend's private, intimate letters about her honeymoon in Tokyo.[24]

Congress eventually dispensed altogether with the pretense that the grand jury is supervising the prosecutor, authorizing government officials to issue subpoenas without a grand jury anywhere in the picture. Whether it was antitrust violations or failure to follow wage and hour laws, the notion was that administrative officials could not find offenders if they had to have probable cause before even beginning to investigate. More recently, the line between administrative agencies and prosecutors was obliterated. Statutes now empower prosecutors to go after health care fraud and child sex offenders by issuing their own subpoenas. Investigating health care fraud, prosecutors—with no showing of probable cause and no grand jury in existence—have forced doctors to turn over not only their financial records, but patient records, lists of magazines and journals they read, information about courses they take, and the financial records of their children. As one doctor fighting off a health care fraud subpoena pointed out, if a government agent came to take his papers without a warrant, that would violate the Fourth Amendment; and if the government agent got a warrant without probable cause, that also would violate the Fourth Amendment; so how come a prosecutor can just write out his own subpoena and demand the same papers?[25]

The failure of all checks on government prying was when Congress decided to give the FBI—not even prosecutors, but a *policing* agency—its own form of subpoena authority, National Security Letters (NSLs). Initially, NSLs were available only if the FBI had "specific and articulable facts" indicating that the person being investigated was "a foreign power or the agent of a foreign power." When Congress passed the USA Patriot Act in the wake of 9/11, though, it substantially broadened the Bureau's NSL powers. Now NSLs can be used to get information from anyone—foreign agent or not—so long as the FBI says the information is "relevant" to an authorized terrorism or intelligence investigation. Using this incredibly loose standard, the FBI is collecting everything from credit information to telephone toll and email subscriber records on American citizens. Following adoption of the Patriot Act, the number of

NSLs skyrocketed to tens of thousands annually. The DOJ Inspector General's office found widespread abuse of the practice, from substantially underreporting the number of requests in reports to Congress, to issuing something called "exigent letters"—for which there was zero authority in law—to gather information quickly without even meeting the minimal requirements for NSLs.[26]

The president's Privacy Review Group on Intelligence and Communications Technologies, appointed by President Obama to investigate government spying in the wake of the Snowden revelations, urged the elimination of the NSL practice. "[I]t is important to emphasize," Group members wrote, "that NSLs are issued directly by the FBI itself, rather than a judge or by a prosecutor acting under the auspices of a grand jury." The Review Group found itself "unable to identify a principled argument why NSLs should be issued by FBI officials." This remains the law, nonetheless.[27]

The rationale for letting law enforcement officials issue their own subpoenas is that—supposedly—the government acts under the ultimate supervision of the courts. Anyone who doesn't think a subpoena is legit can come to court and challenge its validity. If the court agrees, it tosses the subpoena out—"quashes" it, in the lexicon.[28]

The first problem with this supposed justification is that in defending its subpoena in court, the government still does not have to show probable cause. It need only demonstrate that the subpoenaed information is "relevant" to a government investigation. Relevance is a whole lot less than probable cause, which is precisely why the subpoena is likened to a blank check. Probable cause means the government has cause to believe *you* did something wrong; "relevance" just means they think they need it whether you are under suspicion or not.[29]

But the real kicker is this: If the subpoena is served on a third party, like in the *Miller* case or the WikiLeaks case, the target won't know about it, and so wouldn't know to complain to a court in the first place. And even if companies like Twitter want to tell customers about the data hunt, they typically are forbidden by law from doing so. Gag orders are the order of the day. Many of the laws that authorize subpoenas and D-orders have provisions forbidding the recipient from telling the target. One judge, who balked at the practice, said that, in seeking to get a subscriber's emails off its servers, the government wanted "Microsoft gagged for . . . well, forever."[30]

CONGRESS STEPS IN

At the dawn of the digital age, it was clear to all concerned that congressional legislation was needed to regulate law enforcement's access to electronic communications. Under the existing Wiretap Law, adopted in 1968, the government had to get a sort of "superwarrant" before it could listen in on telephone conversations. But no protection at all existed for email or other electronic information. It took no genius to see that given the Supreme Court's third-party rule, and the government's broad subpoena power, all the information in the hands of the new information service providers was going to be easy prey for government poaching. Not only was that bad for individual privacy, it also was bad for business: the burgeoning Internet companies needed to be able to assure customers that their data would remain secure. Even law enforcement needed help: In the face of the Supreme Court's liberal third-party doctrine, states were adopting their own privacy laws to protect third-party disclosures, making a uniform solution essential. So civil libertarians and industry joined together, with support from law enforcement, to get Congress to do something.[31]

In response, in 1986, Congress enacted the Electronic Communications Privacy Act. At the heart of the ECPA rested the distinction, drawn initially by the Supreme Court in the *Smith* case, between what today we call "metadata"—such as the addressing information on an email, or the number that was dialed from a particular phone—and the "content" of those communications. Under the ECPA, the most protection is accorded to the content of communications. Before the government can get this information it generally needs a traditional warrant issued by a judge and based on probable cause. On the other hand, if the government wants noncontent "records" stored with third-party providers, the sort of D-order that was used in the WikiLeaks case will suffice. To obtain such an order the government need only provide a court with "specific and articulable facts" showing the information is potentially "relevant and material" to a criminal investigation. That's not a whole lot; among other things, the government need not show the target has done anything wrong. Finally, armed with nothing but a subpoena issued by the government itself, under the even looser "relevance" standard, agents can get ahold of basic subscriber data such as name, address, log-in, and account information.[32]

Although the ECPA may have made sense in the early days of digital technology, its shortcomings have become glaring in a world no one could even imagine in 1986. The theory was that the more private the information, the higher level of suspicion and judicial supervision required. But it has not worked out that way.

First, the ECPA contains a strange loophole that allows the government to gather a lot of email with nothing but a subpoena. Email—like phone conversations—undeniably contains "content" and thus seems to require the highest level of protection—a probable cause warrant. And under the ECPA, if an email is sitting on a server for less than six months, a warrant is indeed needed before the government can read it. But if the email sits there for more than six months, the government can simply issue a subpoena and get it. Why this bizarre "six month" distinction? Because when the ECPA was adopted in 1986, third-party storage was extremely expensive, and the assumption was that people would download their emails to their own computers to avoid incurring these costs. If they had not downloaded the email, the thought was that the email had been abandoned, and the government should be able to access it. But who, today, doesn't store emails with commercial providers for more than six months?[33]

Then, there's the widespread storage in the cloud of data other than email. In 1986, no one could have anticipated how much of our private lives would be kept on third-party servers—our personal documents, our diaries, our photos. All of this is undeniably "content." Yet, under the ECPA, it appears a warrant is not necessary to get any of this material either.[34]

Finally, there's the underprotection of metadata. The ECPA requires no probable cause to get this information. But metadata is often all the government needs to pry our lives apart. "In the analog world," explains the Electronic Privacy Information Center's Marc Rotenberg, "the transcript of the phone conversation was obviously more valuable than looking at a pattern of phone numbers." That was the "old style" approach to law enforcement investigation." But the "new style . . . is all about data, all about network analysis. In that world the data is more important than the calls. It is more objective, it can't be modified; people can't use a code to hide its meaning."[35]

The best example of the privacy implications of collecting metadata is location tracking. *The New York Times* explained in 2012 that "[i]n most cases, law enforcement officers do not need to hear the actual conversation; what they want to know can be discerned from a suspect's location or travel patterns." Government requests for cell phone location data have skyrocketed even as old-fashioned wiretap requests have become a disappearing breed. That's because, as the *Times* elaborated: "location data can be as revealing of a cellphone owner's associations, activities, and personal tastes as listening in on a conversation, for which a warrant is mandatory."[36]

The ECPA as originally adopted makes little sense today, but in fairness it was simply asking too much of Congress—or anyone else in 1986—to have the faintest clue what the future would hold. In 1984, in the run up to enactment of the ECPA, only 5 percent of homes had a personal computer. The World Wide Web as we know it did not exist. Congress had not authorized the development of the Internet for commercial use, and the first Web browser was seven years away.[37] Email was a novelty to most; those who had it paid for it, and the idea of services such as Gmail was beyond the ken. Similarly with cell phones. The year before the ECPA was passed there were fewer than 1,000 cell sites. By 2010 one estimate put the number at more than 250,000.[38]

By very early in the twenty-first century, though, the overwhelming consensus was that the ECPA was seriously out of date and needed to be fixed. At a 2004 conference on Internet surveillance at George Washington Law School, every commentator who discussed the ECPA, no matter their ideological stripes, called for "changing it in fairly significant ways." In 2010, Digital Due Process, a wide-ranging coalition of tech companies, individuals, and organizations from across the political spectrum, formed to lobby for ECPA reform. By 2015, groups as diverse as the conservative Heritage Action for America and the liberal ACLU even agreed on what needed done, which was to step up the standards by which government obtained information, including—in many cases—requiring a warrant and probable cause.[39]

But Congress was frozen because law enforcement—which also recognized the law needed to be changed—could not get comfortable with the proposed reforms.

LAW ENFORCEMENT'S TECHNOLOGY PROBLEM

By the middle of the second decade of this millennium, law enforcement faced a tough problem of its own. In a high-profile speech given on October 16, 2014, FBI Director Jim Comey explained that developments in communications technology were making it difficult for law enforcement to keep up. The question he asked was "Are Technology, Privacy, and Public Safety on a Collision Course?"[40]

Comey's central point was this: even when law enforcement could and did get orders from judges to engage in surveillance, technological change was rendering those orders "nothing more than a piece of paper." When the Wiretap Act was passed in 1968, if law enforcement needed to know what was said on the telephone call, all it needed were "two alligator clips and a tape recorder." Not only was the technology relatively straightforward, but there was only one provider, the monopoly known as Ma Bell. Now, though, things are more complex: "If a suspected criminal is in his car, and he switches from cellular coverage to Wi-Fi, we may be out of luck. If he switches from one app to another, or from cellular voice service to a voice or messaging app, we may lose him." "The bad guys know this," said Comey. And "they're taking advantage of it every day."[41]

Early in the digital revolution, in 1994, Congress had given law enforcement a hand by enacting the Communications Assistance for Law Enforcement Act, or CALEA, which required communications firms to design their equipment specifically to ensure that law enforcement could conduct surveillance. But, as Comey told his audience, CALEA had been adopted "[t]wenty years ago—a lifetime in the Internet Age." The same problem of unanticipated change that had made the ECPA obsolete in protecting our privacy was doing the same with regard to law enforcement's ability under CALEA to get what it needed. For example, CALEA applied to "communications" companies, but it exempted "information" firms. Obviously, no one in Congress had foreseen the volume of Internet vehicles for communicating that we have today: Google Hangouts, apps that allow people to talk with one another, digital games that permit players to scream and yell but also to send messages. There are thousands of new "information" firms that facilitate communications, many of them start-ups whose hardware and software leave no room for law enforcement to gain access.[42]

And so, Comey declared, law enforcement was at risk of "going dark." "Those charged with protecting our people aren't always able to access the evidence we need to prosecute crime and prevent terrorism even with lawful authority."[43]

Indicative of the problem, in Comey's mind, was Apple's move to encrypt iPhones passcodes so only the owner could unlock the phone and access data on it. With its iOS8 update, Apple told consumers, "it's not technically feasible for us to respond to government warrants for the extraction of this data." Rather, "[w]e've built privacy into the things you use every day." Comey's address came just a month later, and he singled out Apple—as well as its competitor Android, which was following suit. "Both companies are run by good people, responding to what they perceive as market demand. But the place they are leading us is one that we shouldn't go without careful thought and debate as a country."[44]

Soon enough, the country was treated to an example of what Comey said was wrong. Two homegrown terrorists, inspired by Islamist terrorists abroad, attacked a gathering of public health workers in San Bernardino, California, killing and wounding more than thirty people. As part of its investigation, the FBI obtained a court order requiring Apple to develop software so that FBI investigators could get into the telephone used by one of the perpetrators. As an epic court battle attracted the nation's attention, an anonymous third party surfaced to show the FBI how it could gain access to the information it wanted, without Apple's assistance. That resolved the immediate case. But there was no gainsaying the issue would be back before long.[45]

LAW ENFORCEMENT'S POLITICAL PROBLEM

The problem law enforcement faced in 2014 was technical, but—as Comey himself recognized—it was equally political. "In the wake of the Snowden disclosures," he conceded, "the prevailing view is that the government is sweeping up all of our communications." Comey sought to assure people "that is not true," and issued dire warnings about the risks we face from those who would do us harm if law enforcement cannot get the information it needs, even with a warrant.[46]

The wall Comey was running into was that repeated news reports of government snooping on Americans, combined with instances of official dissembling—such as the president of the United States claiming none of it was happening prior to the Snowden revelations proving him wrong—had eroded the trust law enforcement requires to do its job. Law enforcement had gotten so aggressive in grabbing data, that by the time Comey spoke of the challenge of "going dark," many people were no longer in any mood to make it easier for them to do so.

Law enforcement simply has had a hard time hearing the society's concern about government collecting private information from third-party providers. The harm in the Snowden disclosures, Comey said, "has extended—unfairly—to the investigations of law enforcement agencies that obtain individual *warrants*, approved by judges." But the fight is *not* just about warrants, and if it were, then law enforcement might get a lot more of what it wants. The government consistently has taken legal positions—often based on the poor drafting of the ECPA—that would give it access to email communications held by third parties, without a warrant or probable cause.[47] And, if you carefully parse the speeches and testimony of law enforcement officials, they talk about getting "court order[s] *or* warrant[s]." In other words, government still believes it should be able to get information from third parties using only subpoenas or D-orders. This was clear in joint testimony Comey and Deputy Attorney General Sally Quillian Yates gave to the Senate Judiciary Committee in July 2015. They bluntly expressed concern about a world in which "users have sole control over access to their devices and communications," and discussed the need to use court orders "to recover the content of electronic communications from the technology provider." Users, on the other hand, seem to think they *should* have "sole control" over their own devices and communications.[48]

In fairness, a tightening up of the third-party rule could create a problem for law enforcement, what we might call the "investigative gap." As Principal Deputy Assistant Attorney General Elana Tyrangiel told the House Judiciary Committee in September 2015, "non-content information gathered early in investigations is often used to generate the probable cause necessary for a subsequent search warrant. Without the mechanism to obtain non-content information, it may be impossible for an investigation to develop and reach a stage where agents have the evidence necessary to obtain a warrant." In other words, law enforcement says it needs to be able to collect information from third parties using its broad subpoena power, just to uncover probable cause of criminal activity in the first place.[49]

But what law enforcement has proven either unable or unwilling to do is prove how real this problem is—and many people are no longer simply willing to take them at their word. Tyrangiel, for example, gave the absolutely horrifying case of the government getting hold of photographs of a man "sexually abusing his prepubescent son." As she told it, in displaying the photographs he had carefully masked his identity behind the anonymity of the Internet and so court orders were required to discover the IP address of the device he was using, and ultimately his identity. But surely these photographs constituted probable cause of a crime being committed, and so law enforcement ought to be able to get a warrant. Rather than making its case rigorously and empirically, government officials regularly argue by pulling out anecdotes and horror stories. In today's environment, though, the minute law enforcement offers up an anecdote, hecklers and naysayers instantly appear all over the Internet to dispute the claimed need.[50]

More than anything else, law enforcement has lost the help of dependable allies in the communications and tech industries. Recent disclosures have made clear the extent to which, prior to the Snowden and other recent disclosures, some of the telecom and tech firms were playing both sides of the fence—no company more than AT&T. In 2013, in response to a Freedom of Information request, law enforcement turned over a set of slides (apparently by mistake) describing the "Hemisphere Project." Under Hemisphere, AT&T employees teamed up with the federal Drug Enforcement Agency to facilitate the rapid turnover of phone information. The government would pay AT&T to put AT&T employees in-house with the DEA. Then, when the government wanted information, it simply handed over an administrative subpoena to the embedded AT&T employees. In this way, the government could get any phone information it wanted moving through an AT&T switch. By some accounts, the Hemisphere Project was collecting some four *billion* records a day before it was (supposedly) shut down. Through unacceptable subterfuge, this program was kept secret even from courts.[51]

Consumer anger—directed not only at the government but also at the tech and communications companies themselves—has caused those companies to hop squarely on the consumer-driven bandwagon to tighten privacy laws. A series of annual releases by the Electronic Frontier Foundation, titled "Who Has Your Back?," tells the story in a simple chart, on which gold stars are given to companies that "help protect your data from the government." Stars are awarded for things like "Requires a warrant for content," "Tells users about government data requests," and "Fights for users' privacy rights" in courts or in Congress. As recently as 2011, there weren't a lot of stars on that chart, other than those awarded to Twitter and Google. By 2015, however, gold was everywhere (AT&T still being a notable exception).[52]

The ECPA was a compromise, passed in 1986 with the concurrence of private industry, individual rights advocates, and law enforcement. This sort of "competitive cooperation" seems hard to imagine today. Caught in the crossfire between tech companies and consumers on the one hand, and law enforcement on the other, for the better part of a decade Congress has proven unable to deal with pressing issues like access to emails, location tracking, and encryption.

And so the battles have raged in the courts.

SOLVING FOR TECHNOLOGY: WHAT TO DO ABOUT THE THIRD-PARTY DOCTRINE?

Whether by courts or by Congress, lines need to be drawn, and wherever and however they are drawn is likely to be unsatisfying. Anyone who thinks this is easy is engaging in self-delusion. The digital transformation has put law enforcement, and thus all of us, in a kind of bind. The Internet may allow me to exchange sweet nothings I would not want others to hear, or post photos I would share only with my closest friends. But it also allows child abusers to strike unmentionable deals and terrorists to hatch unimaginably destructive plots. Even Twitter recognizes, says Ben Lee, that "[p]seudonymity and anonymity are very important and tricky things on the Internet" and that there is not "a right never to be unmasked." The issue is what "process we need first" to ensure government accountability. The question, in short, is where on a very slippery slope we can draw lines about when the government should be able to get information about us from third parties.[53]

Law tends to move by analogies, but given the rapid technological transformation, those analogies have become perilously strained. In one case, a court reasoned that obtaining cell tower data to track a suspect's location could not possibly be a search: "If a tool used to transport contraband gives off a signal that can be tracked for location, certainly the police can track the signal." Otherwise, the court concluded "dogs could not be used to track a fugitive if the fugitive did not know that the dog hounds had his scent," and "[a] getaway car could not be identified and followed based on the license plate number if the driver reasonably thought he had gotten away unseen." That's quite the stretch—in the hound and license plate examples the government is on the trail without requiring a data dump from a third-party provider of completely private information shared only because one needs to use a phone.[54]

Analogies run out because digital technology not only has altered where we store our data; it has profoundly affected the very way we live our lives. In a 2011 article titled "Home, Home on the Web," a law professor, Kathy Strandburg, described how an earlier technology—the telephone—did the same. All the sudden, people easily had long-distance relationships, and made "different decisions about where to work or live." And thus a "telephone system open to unregulated wiretapping by government (and others)" would have changed the way the world evolved. So too, today, she says, the way our lives are lived is formed as much by the properties of cyberspace as by the physical space that surrounds us. She describes a hypothetical person, Moira, who in the morning collaborates on a report stored in the cloud with colleagues in another state, at lunch shares thoughts on Facebook with family and friends, then in the afternoon texts private messages to a long-distance boyfriend suggesting they stream a movie together on Netflix that night while talking together on Skype. This isn't very hypothetical, is it?[55]

The question we must confront is this: Is all our information really fair game for the government, without warrant or probable cause, simply because a third party holds it? And if not, what's in and what's out?

Content

There is no serious argument that our "content" (as opposed to metadata), even if stored in cyberspace, should be available to law enforcement without a warrant. In their joint testimony to the Senate Judiciary Committee, Director Comey and Deputy Attorney General Yates said,

"The more we as a society rely on electronic devices to communicate and store information, the more likely it is that information that was once found in filing cabinets, letters, and photo albums will now be stored only in electronic form." That's true, but it is not clear how it helps their case. To get that information in the past, what law enforcement needed was a warrant, based on probable cause. Why should it matter that the information is in virtual storage? When you rent an apartment or put things in a storage unit, the government can't just come in and get what it wants on its own say so. Although the government does not seem to like it, even the federal courts finally recognized in 2010 that despite the ECPA, the Constitution forbids collecting our emails from cyberspace—no matter how long they were on the server—without probable cause and a warrant.[56]

Metadata

Nor is it clear the rules should be any different for "metadata" as opposed to content, though here law enforcement has put up a much bigger fight. Relying on the 1979 *Smith* telephone pen register decision, the Department of Justice insists a subpoena should be enough to get "addressing information" for email and other electronic communications. But even assuming *Smith* was right when decided—and there is, as we've seen, reason to doubt that—metadata today is much richer than the "to/from" information of olden days. Today, phone metadata reveals not only what number you called, but whether the call was completed, how long you were on the line, where you made the call from, what equipment you used—and often, the location from which you made the call. Similarly, email metadata can reveal the identities of your correspondents, the computer you wrote from, any attachments, and so forth.[57]

What people, including some judges, are rapidly coming to see is that all these bits and pieces of metadata about people are just as revealing of our lives as content information—and thus deserve similar protection. In a case involving a warrantless search of a cell phone, the Supreme Court pointed out that Web browser history (addressing information, after all) "could reveal an individual's private interests or concerns—perhaps a search for certain symptoms of disease, coupled with frequent visits to WebMD." It said the same about the "apps" you own: "There are apps for Democratic Party news and Republican Party news; apps for alcohol, drug, and gambling addictions . . . for tracking pregnancy symptoms." Some of this may be "content" and some "non-content," but that's the point: the line itself is collapsing, and so giving the government ready access to metadata on a grand scale no longer makes sense.[58]

Information Used by Third Parties

Some courts have suggested the government should have freer access to information we give third parties to use, rather than merely to store. The argument seems to be that if we're allowing the third party to make use of our data, it is no longer private. But it's not obvious this is right either.[59]

Judge Richard Posner points out that it is easy to confuse privacy with secrecy, but—he explains—keeping things private "does not mean refusing to share information with everyone." "The fact that I disclose symptoms of illness to my doctor," says Posner by way of example, "does not make my health a public fact, especially if he promises (where the rules of the medical profession require him) not to disclose my medical history to anyone without my permission." Adds the philosopher Helen Nissenbaum: We talk to teachers about problems our kids are having that we would not share with anyone else; we give financial information to professionals that we expect they will keep to themselves. The sharing of information is contextual, and the law should respect this.[60]

If those entities decide to go to the government on their own that is one thing. It is quite another to claim no Fourth Amendment search occurs when the government shows up demanding the information. Just because Google's Gmail machine-reads your email in order to display targeted ads, that hardly means the government should be able to order Google to turn the information over. As courts have recognized, your landlord may have a right to come into your apartment periodically to fix things or inspect for safety, but that doesn't give her the right to go through your desk, and it surely doesn't allow her to show the government around without a warrant. The hotel housekeeper cleans your room; that has never been seen as license for the government to slip in for a look around either.[61]

The Third Parties' Own Records

A somewhat better argument is that the government should be able to demand access to records that contain your information but are created by the third party itself in its usual course of business. In the *Miller* case, for example, when approving the subpoena for the bootlegger's financial information, the Court stressed, "these are the business records of the banks." The DOJ has relied on this logic to argue in favor of obtaining location tracking information from cell phone providers.[62]

Still, the argument is a tricky one, underscoring the fact that tech companies are being put between a rock and a hard place. On the one hand, they are making a lot of money off user data and want to keep it. On the other hand, consumers are mad that the data is being stored, and thus is so easily accessible to the government. Some consumers already are choosing companies that will guarantee them privacy by making sure the data does not exist.[63]

The hard question we must face—which is as much a matter of policy as constitutional law—is whether we want to hurt the competitiveness of these companies, efficiency gains, and even our own security advantages, in order to give law enforcement the tools it claims to need. This was a point driven home by the former head of the NSA and CIA, Michael Hayden, in the context of the encryption debate. In an op-ed piece, Hayden described how in the late twentieth century the United States tried to protect against the export of high-powered computing power, because our monopoly on that power made us leaders in breaking codes. Eventually, though, we realized that we were undercutting our global competitiveness in the computer industry, and that maintaining our long-term security advantage meant keeping that industry on top. So too, today, said Hayden, pointing a finger at law enforcement's efforts to control the use of encryption: "One wonders what the Russias and Chinas of the world will demand if U.S.-based firms are forbidden to create encryption schemes inaccessible to themselves or the government." His point is that companies are adopting encryption to be competitive in the face of consumer worries, and if the government insists on tunneling in nonetheless, then not only do we undercut competitiveness and efficiency, we may undermine security interests as well.[64]

It may be that there are no constitutional constraints on law enforcement obtaining a third party's own records about us with but a subpoena. Some courts have so held. Still, we should be mindful of the costs in terms of privacy, efficiency, and competitiveness.

Ground Rules

Although at this juncture one might be inclined to think the whole third-party rule needs to be junked, that would fail to take account of law enforcement's needs. Law enforcement forcefully maintains that it requires some of this third-party information, because insisting on warrants might derail important investigations before they get started. Suppose, for example, the government comes across some information that suggests a terrorist plot is in the offing. The information contains a phone number, and the government wants to find out who owns the phone, but doesn't have probable cause. Or consumers tell a state Attorney General they think a company is engaging in fraud, but there's not enough evidence there to get a warrant for anything. In such cases should the government do nothing and just hope probable cause develops? Or should there be some authority to get certain kinds of information from third parties via a subpoena?

While these are inescapably difficult questions, there are a few things that can be said with certainty, and that help frame a resolution.

For one thing, under no circumstances should law enforcement be writing its own blank checks. Without thinking clearly through the problem, we've drifted from grand jury supervision of prosecutors, to administrative agencies authorizing their own subpoenas, to prosecutors doing the same—all the way to the FBI getting its own NSL authority. There are various ways to get the situation back under control. Subpoenas—which, after all, are only a tool to get information—should not be used without prior judicial authorization, as is the case with warrants. This could be true even if what the government must show to get the order is less than probable cause, as with D-orders. It violates every fundamental constitutional precept to allow law enforcement to decide on its own what information to demand.

Similarly, we should require law enforcement to demonstrate how, and to what extent, its ability to detect crime will be substantially hindered before we grant it easy access to private information in third-party hands. Enough with the anecdotes and horror stories; we need real facts and data. We do need a sane policy to allow law enforcement to protect us, but sane policies are based whenever possible on hard facts. Law enforcement officials must develop the case for why they need this information, without pulling out horror stories about child pornographers that are an easy emotional sell but often prove quite uninformative.

Finally, as we have seen time and again, the courts are simply not the best place to resolve these nuanced issues. Their primary tool is the Constitution, which is a blunderbuss, not a scalpel. Deciding questions in constitutional terms casts them in concrete. Rapidly advancing technology has gotten us into this pickle. Hard-to-change rules adopted by judges lacking in expertise is not the way to get us out.

All this would be problematic enough if the question were only the government gaining access to our information in third-party hands. But it turns out the government not only acquires the information when it needs it, it is saving much of the information it obtains to build databases containing our information. This chapter has been about the acquisition of the data; the next chapter tackles the problem of saving the information, and using it for data mining.

11

GOVERNMENT DATABASES

We are living in the age of Big Data—a time of big possibilities but also big problems. With data abundant, the natural urge of government has been to gather and make something of all that information. What could be better than to eliminate crime, terrorism even, with nothing but information? Focus on that hope often has blinded us to the real difficulties and threats posed by this mass data grab.

In assessing the value of data to policing, it is important to pay attention to the countless instances in which the use of databases erroneously causes law enforcement to target a wholly innocent individual; mistakes here can be costly both to the government and the person involved.

Ironically, though, the mass collection of personal data by the government should concern us just as much when the process is error-free and the data used as intended. That is because the whole point of the mass collection of data so common today is to allow the government to build dossiers on as many of us as possible, on the theory that once the accumulated data is analyzed, offenders will pop out. For the system to work, the government must have access to the data of everyone, innocent as well as guilty, in order to search for patterns that point to wrongdoers. What that means in practice is that the government is building vast databases of our personal information. We all are forced to relinquish our privacy and security, and that should be of serious concern.

The endeavor to collect massive amounts of data in an effort to keep us all safe may be a good idea or a bad one, depending on how such data-collection programs are adopted and implemented. The trick is to use the principles of democratic and constitutional policing to maximize the possibilities of databases, while minimizing the threats to our liberties and privacy. That's essential, but it is not at all what the government is doing at present.

THE DANGERS OF DATABASES

Meet Abe Mashal—an average Midwestern guy. He's tall, taciturn, a big fellow with a baby face and a goatee. A dog trainer by profession, on April 20, 2010, Mashal was in Chicago's O'Hare Airport, en route to Spokane to train a customer's pets. The trip, though, had gotten off to a bad start. When Mashal tried to check in online the night before, he was told he had to do it with an agent at the airport. So he got to O'Hare early—faced with squeezing his large frame into an airplane seat, he was eager to make Southwest Airlines's first boarding group. The ticket counter agent typed his name into the computer, gave him a "very strange look," and then disappeared into the back. Minutes later, Mashal was surrounded by some thirty officers from the Chicago Police and Transportation Safety Administration.[1]

That's when the counter agent told him he was on the No Fly List.[2]

Mashal thought this had to be a joke, "some huge mix-up." Told the FBI wanted to interview him, he agreed, provisionally. "I will go in back to answer your questions, but I only have one rule." "What's that?" they asked. "No water boarding!" Everyone tried hard to stay stone-faced, but many couldn't help tittering.[3]

He's like that; Mashal's a jokester. The events that began in O'Hare Airport that day turned into a huge ordeal for him and his family; in the course of it Mashal wrote an autobiographical account of his life and what happened to him that for a novice author is pretty decent reading. In it he describes in elaborate detail how he pranked and joked his way through school, never taking anything too seriously—the consummate "class clown." Like the times he'd set open liquid beverage containers spinning down the school staircase, soaking the unlucky with milk or even urine, to great guffaws from his crew. That lasted until he got busted and was given thirty days janitorial duty in lieu of expulsion, working right alongside the very folks whose lives he'd been making miserable. After a few days of hazing, though, they were all best buddies.[4]

On leaving school, Mashal cleaned up his act. He decided he wanted to go into law enforcement, become an FBI or Secret Service agent. Those jobs are hard to get but the recruiter he spoke to indicated one clear path. So Mashal took it, and to this day it represents to him a singular life accomplishment.[5]

Mashal's a former marine. He made it through boot camp, got married, had a kid (the first of four), got a college degree, became an expert shot, marksmanship instructor, and K-9 handler, and ran a supply shop. Then he left the Corps, deciding against law enforcement—he'd had enough bad bosses in the service to know he wanted to work for himself—and became a private dog trainer. With some others he also started a not-for-profit that trains and provides service dogs to veterans who need them. "Always Faithful Service Dogs." *Semper Fi*, that's Abe.[6]

So there he was, standing in the terminal surrounded by law enforcement "with my Marine Corps luggage bag, and Marine Corps t-shirt being told that I am on the No Fly List."[7]

Several months later, having failed to get himself off the list, despite numerous efforts, including filling out the redress forms the government offered, Mashal became part of an ACLU lawsuit against the Department of Homeland Security. The lawsuit challenged the constitutionality of the way the no-fly list is operated. Mashal is one of a group of plaintiffs, several of whom are U.S. veterans.[8]

Many of the ACLU's no-fly plaintiffs have something else in common too: they are Muslims, or of Arab descent. Mashal is both. His full name is Ibraheim Mashal, though he's always just been known as Abe. Half Palestinian Arab, half Italian. First generation on his dad's side, second on his mom's. An American of immigrant stock, like so many of us. Mashal's book is titled *No Spy No Fly* because, among other indignities, the FBI offered to get him off the list if he'd spy on mosques for them. That apparently has happened a lot, the government using the no-fly list as leverage to recruit spies. [9]

To this day, Mashal can't understand how it is he landed on the list. He is not particularly religious. His dad dragged him to religious school at one point when he was growing up, but that didn't last long. He wonders if it is because, during a short period of tragedy when he sought religious solace, he wrote to an imam asking for advice about raising children in two faiths. (Right after he left the service, his father died, his wife miscarried eight weeks before their second kid was due, and a close friend had a fatal crack-up on a motorcycle.) In his book he wrote that he "felt ignorant for not knowing how bad these watch lists had become and how many innocent people were affected by it." These "sounded like stories that would come out of a place like communist Russia. Not America."[10]

Welcome to Mashal's world—one that is fast becoming the world of all of us. We live in the time of massive government databases that keep track of much of what we do. Under the long-standing "Secure Flight" program, the TSA checked fliers' "name, gender and date of birth" against "terrorist watch lists." In 2013, the TSA announced it was expanding passenger screening, compiling records of property ownership, physical traits, intelligence and law enforcement data, tax IDs, and travel histories and reservations. Our information is handed out to state, local, and even foreign governments, or "private companies for purposes unrelated to security or travel." Those who find themselves accused (rightly or wrongly) of TSA violations can be reported to private debt collection agencies.[11]

In this new world of government databases, once you are caught in the machine, it can prove very hard to set things right. The late Senator Edward Kennedy found himself on the no-fly list. After he was stopped several times before boarding or subjected to additional screening, his staff contacted TSA headquarters. It took over three weeks to get him off the list. Kennedy used a hearing to grill Homeland Security Undersecretary Asa Hutchison: "If they have that kind of difficulty with a member of Congress, how in the world are average Americans, who are getting caught up in this thing . . . going to be treated fairly and not have their rights abused?" It's a good question, and one that to this day the government has not answered adequately.[12]

Even more threatening to our liberty than database screw-ups may be when the database programs work as intended. The government has the means to gather incredible amounts of information on all of us. What it doesn't collect itself it buys from private vendors. During the Johnson and Ford years the suggestion to "link government databases" was met with public protests. Now it happens without us even knowing.

Discussing the TSA's efforts, a lawyer with the Electronic Privacy Information Center said, "The average person doesn't understand how much intelligence-driven matching is going on and how this could be accessed for other purposes."[13]

The government's use of data to monitor and control citizens is likely to prove the largest problem ordinary Americans face in this century regarding our personal privacy and security. Yet it is one about which we know and understand little. The difficulty is that, as the EPIC lawyer told *The New York Times*, all this data collection and data matching is occurring with "no meaningful oversight, transparency, or accountability." There are statutes that govern privacy and data sharing, but most of these have exceptions for law enforcement, eliminating protection just where we need it most.[14]

When it comes to the use of private data for law enforcement purposes, the government pretty much makes it up as it goes along. The consequences for anyone caught up in all this can prove staggering. And all of us are having our personal information gathered, often without our permission. What's needed here is democratic authorization of database systems *before* they are created, transparency throughout the process, and proper constitutional analysis of those programs that exist. Yet these most basic protections are often missing.

THE RISE OF DATA

Databases have been with us for a long time, but comparing the "then" of scribbled notes stored in a file cabinet to the "now" of Big Data is like confusing the metal tube Copernicus used to see the stars with the Hubble Telescope. Take, for example, the FBI's legendary fingerprint capabilities. The project was launched in 1924. That database, even bolstered by an early card sorter, largely was searched manually until 1985, when the Bureau's Automated Fingerprint Identification System (AFIS) allowed what once took thousands of hours to occur in a matter of minutes. Then, in 1999, the database was converted to digital technology, and renamed the *Integrated* Automatic Fingerprint Identification System (IAFIS). By 2014 the FBI announced that IAFIS itself was about to become obsolete; its NGI—"Next Generation Information— system was "fully operational," linking more than 18,000 state, local, and federal forces together to share data on a real-time basis. Today, in a matter of minutes the system can compare tens of millions of criminal and civilian records, along with physical characteristics such as mug shots, scars and tattoos, and aliases.[15]

The database revolution is driven by a trifecta of factors—the proliferation of data, exponential advances in computing speed, and revolutionary miniaturization and growth of storage capability. Today, an Intel microchip is thousands of times faster and tens of thousands of times cheaper than its first chip, manufactured in 1971. Intel's current CEO, Brian Krzanich, observed that if a 1971 Volkswagen Beetle followed the same trajectory, today it would travel 300,000 miles per hour, and go "two million miles per gallon of gas." The same is true of data storage. One estimate says 90 percent of the world's data has been created in the last two years; a similar prediction is that the amount of data stored will double every two years until 2020. You can place the entire printed collection of the Library of Congress on a hard drive that can fit in the palm of your hand.[16]

Aided by this technology, law enforcement's databases are vast and growing. The National Crime Information Center currently holds more than 13 million records ranging from gun control background checks to stolen license plates to sex offenders. On a single day in June 2015, it answered over 14.5 *million* queries. Then there are the terrorism databases. The National Counterterrorism Center's Terrorism Identities Datasmart Environment (TIDE)—the central database for the intelligence agencies—has ballooned to more than a million names, including some 25,000 American permanent residents and citizens. Every night 1,000 or more new names and bits of information come pouring into the FBI's Terrorist Screening Center, where analysts begin deciding who ends up on the watch list.[17]

But it's not just criminals and terrorist suspects—we are all in the government's data clutches. The government has our tax data, property ownership histories, car registration records, and employment data. It keeps track of our physical characteristics, travel activities, and can even hold information gleaned from previous government interactions, such as what book somebody was bringing through airport security when they got stopped for special screening. It maintains intelligence and security files on us. Through an "Automated Targeting System," the Department of Homeland Security (DHS) brings together disparately held data—profiles that are "secret, unreviewable, and maintained by the government for 40 years"—to perform statistical terrorism risk assessments on each person entering or leaving the country.[18]

One of the most ambitious government data-gathering efforts has been "fusion centers," which allow state, local, and tribal government law enforcement agencies to join resources and information—ostensibly to prevent terrorist activity. These were created with federal funds after the 9/11 Commission targeted the failure of government officials to share threat information as a primary cause of the 2001 terrorist attacks. In October 2006, Director of National Intelligence John Negroponte explained in remarks at the FBI National Academy that "the federal government can't be—and should not try to be—everywhere all the time." Rather, "[o]ur state and local colleagues are our eyes and ears throughout the nation."[19]

Although originally about counterterrorism, the mission of most fusion centers quickly morphed to something *much* broader: "all hazards, all crimes, all threats." Everything. This is not entirely surprising. As a Sacramento police lieutenant who conducted a Department of Homeland Security study pointed out, there is "insufficient purely 'terrorist' activity to support a multi-jurisdictional, multi-governmental level fusion center that exclusively processes terrorist activity." Analysts, he pointed out, would get bored and their "skills would atrophy." So the focus of fusion center personnel moved well beyond terrorism. And they share the information they gather widely: with schools, licensing agencies, child-care businesses, and transportation services, even the private sector.[20]

The amount of citizen information being "fused" is staggering. Delaware State Patrol Captain Bill Harris, who ran the Delaware Information and Analysis Center, explained what it entails: "The fusion process is to take law enforcement information and other information—it could be from the Department of Agriculture, the Department of Transportation, the private sector—and fuse it together to look for anomalies and push information out to our stakeholders in Delaware who have both the right and need to know." "I don't want to say it's unlimited, but the ceiling is very high." Rhode Island's Deputy Superintendent of the State Patrol emphasized, "There is never ever enough information . . . That's what post-9/11 is about."[21]

A critical data entry point into fusion center databases is "suspicious activity reports" or SARs. Cops on patrol, and ordinary citizens, are told to provide a tip if something seems off. These reports get entered into the national "Information Sharing Environment." Reasonable suspicion of criminal activity is not required for SARs to enter the system; much innocent conduct will land you in the database. The Los Angeles Police Department lists sixty-five activities indicative of "foreign or domestic terrorism" warranting a SAR, including "using binoculars," "drawing diagrams," "espousing extremist views," and "taking pictures or video footage 'with no apparent esthetic value.'" (Stop and read that last one again.)[22]

What the government doesn't collect on you these days, it buys. Private vendors such as Choicepoint and Acxiom have made vast fortunes harvesting and bundling private data for sale to governments. (Choicepoint was purchased in 2008 for $3.6 billion by Reed Elsevier; formerly an educational publisher, the recently renamed RELX Group is making a killing by providing information for risk management.) The companies also run analytics for the government. For example, Raytheon markets an "extreme scale analytics" program called "RIOT"—for Rapid Information Overlay Technology—that enables the government to create a literal map of a person's life. Pulling photos from social media with embedded location information, RIOT creates charts indicating where you go, and when, while also mapping relationships among people. There's a promotional video where you can watch Raytheon track one of its own employees ("so now we know where Nick has gone, and we know now what Nick looks like . . .")[23]

The real muscle of law enforcement's proactive, deterrence-based efforts is data mining—the practice of trying to discern patterns in all this data it has gathered from public and private sources. The number of law enforcement data-mining programs is large and growing. The software program Beware, sold to law enforcement by the company Intrado, integrates "billions of publicly-available commercial records," to provide "threat scores, headlines and 'Be Aware' statements . . . in a matter of seconds" to police first responders. Given a particular address, Beware can, say, identify the cars registered at the location and provide phone numbers and criminal records of residents; it also searches social media content and online purchases to determine the risk an officer faces.[24]

What's all the rage now, at every level of government, is "predictive policing." Police forces are using software programs with names such as

PredPol and HunchLab to try to identify where crime will happen next. "By looking at the whole picture," says one professor working with the Chicago Police Department, "you can begin to learn what it means for a certain area to be abnormal." (Study policing data programs for a while and you start to notice this word gets used a lot, this relentless hunt for the "abnormal.") Similar programs have sprouted up across the country, enabled by enthusiastic corporate partners. IBM developed a program called BluePALMS (Predictive Analytics Lead Modeling Software) that allows the police to enter details of an unsolved crime and "get a list of 20 suspects within one minute." "This is not science fiction," boasts Miami's Lieutenant Arnold Palmer on an IBM video touting the technology.[25]

All this can get a little spooky, as is evident from the Raytheon video showing how data collection and aggregation allows them to track their employee Nick. The sales pitch moves to its denouement: "Now we want to try to predict where he may be in the future . . . if you ever did want to try to get ahold of Nick, *or maybe get ahold of his laptop*, you might want to visit the gym at 6 a.m. on Monday."[26]

Imagine you are Nick. You may be, soon enough.

THE HUMAN COSTS OF DATABASES

To be clear, there's promise in these new technologies. An employee of Intrado, which sells the Beware product, tells of a case where a man took a woman and her daughter hostage. Police wanted to enter into negotiations, but calls to the woman's home phone went unanswered. Using Beware, they got her cell phone information, which ultimately led to a conversation that defused the situation.[27]

But there's trouble in Big Brother's paradise, too.

Given the enormous volume of information flowing into government hands, and the low standards for ending up in databases and on watch lists, errors are frequent, with just the sort of consequences Abe Mashal and Senator Kennedy faced. Tens of thousands of travelers are stopped wrongly every year because of incorrect information in the terrorism database.[28]

Similar problems exist locally, as horror stories about proliferating "gang" files make clear. Three teenage Vietnamese girls were put into a gang database when stopped at a mall in Orange County, California, for dressing in "baggy pants and tight shirts." One got stopped again; this time—because she was in the database—she had her purse and phonebook searched illegally by a cop who told her, "If you have a problem with this, then don't come to my city." Following a shooting in San Diego, a number of young African American men with no criminal records and no complicity whatsoever were jailed because they'd been placed on a confidential law enforcement list that labeled them gang associates. (In San Diego, as elsewhere, you can land in the gang database if police believe you are wearing gang-related clothing or think they have seen you make a gang sign.)[29]

This lust to gather information on anything that anyone deems "abnormal" or out of place has caused fusion center agents to engage in colossal wrong turns, squandering precious law enforcement resources. Virginia's fusion center concluded that black colleges were "a radicalization node for almost every type of extremist group." It advocated surveillance of students. Across the Potomac in Maryland, a nineteen-month investigation into war protesters nabbed two Catholic nuns and a well-known political activist, labeling them "terrorists." In Missouri, a publication on right-wing militant groups fingered followers of the third-party presidential candidates Bob Barr and Ron Paul as threats, causing a media storm. Nationwide, local, state, and federal authorities have monitored the Black Lives Matter–led protests of police shootings.[30]

Although these incidents underscore the threat to civil liberties from overzealous data collection, the broader danger to many of us comes from the government, overwhelmed by information, missing what's critical. In 2007 alone, the Terrorist Screening Center recommended the removal of more than 22,000 names that did not belong in the database. An audit after 2009's failed Christmas Day airplane terrorist bombing showed that hundreds of people on the no-fly list had been granted visas, which the State Department promptly revoked on the premise that such "individuals could present an immediate threat." Before he was nabbed, the Times Square bomber—who was on the terror list—got on a plane and sat there until just before takeoff. The failed Christmas bomber, on the other hand, was found unsuitable for the no-fly list despite his father's warnings to U.S. officials, who had entered the report into TIDE.[31]

Russ Travers, who ran the government terrorism database, says, "The single biggest worry that I have is long-term quality control."[32]

UNREGULATED DATABASES

It's no wonder quality control is a concern: there is a notable lack of rules regarding the government collecting, storing, analyzing, and sharing our personal data. "[D]ata mining is almost entirely unregulated under current law today," offers one legal expert. Another says that "in contrast to the approach in many other nations, it is unusual in the United States to find any comprehensive privacy laws." Even when privacy laws are on the books, those laws almost universally exempt law enforcement.[33]

In the 2009 case *Herring v. United States* the Supreme Court pretty much eliminated any Fourth Amendment protection for people who are injured by law enforcement reliance on databases. Bennie Herring was arrested after a computerized database said he had an outstanding arrest warrant. A subsequent search of his person turned up drugs and a gun. But the arrest warrant had been recalled months earlier, and should have been removed from the database; the failure to do so was the result of negligence on the part of police department employees. Some of the justices expressed alarm about the damage such errors could cause, and felt the government should be responsible. "Electronic databases form the nervous system of contemporary criminal justice operations," wrote Justice Ruth Bader Ginsburg, and "[t]he risk of error stemming from these databases is not slim." But the majority disagreed; unless "police have been shown to be reckless in maintaining a warrant system, or to have knowingly made false entries to lay the groundwork for future false arrests," there is not much the Constitution has to say about it.[34]

On the one hand, you can see where the Supreme Court majority in *Herring* was coming from. Imagine the impact if the result of any database mistake by law enforcement was that the suspect received a get-out-of-jail-free card. That can't be right.

On the other hand, with no remedy in law, there's no incentive for government to do what it takes to get its databases right. As Justice Ginsburg pointed out, private businesses are held liable for employees' mistakes precisely on the theory that employers will then assure they don't happen.[35]

So what is to be done?

Some argue that the only proper restraint on databases is after-the-fact auditing to ensure there was no misbehavior. That's the view of Stewart Baker, a brilliant lawyer of conservative leanings who served as the

General Counsel of the NSA before 9/11 and later was chief of policy at the Department of Homeland Security. Following his tenure in government Baker wrote *Skating on Stilts*, a take-no-prisoners denunciation of those who oppose security measures in the name of civil liberties. He is bullish on data's promise, and skeptical about most proposed limitations on data mining.

Baker concedes there's an "uncomfortable pattern to the use of data by governments." Government gets data for one reason—be it crime prevention or social security—then, "as time goes on, it becomes attractive to use the data for other, less pressing purposes—collecting child support, perhaps, or enforcing parking tickets." Still, he says, it is "fighting technology" to try to limit the use of data to the purpose for which it was collected. "It's like wearing someone else's dress. Over time, use restrictions end up tight where they should be roomy—and loose where they should be tight." Similarly, he feels that lawyers, trained in traditional Fourth Amendment law, are just too focused on before-the-fact "predicates" such as the probable cause that the government has to meet to allow it to go a-searching.[36]

What Baker's all about—and he is hardly alone in this approach—is management and auditing. "If the lawyer's solution is to put a predicate between government and the data and the bureaucrat's solution is to put use restrictions on the data, then . . . the auditor's solution" is simply to catch those who use data improperly. "Government access to personal data need not be restricted by speed bumps or walls. Instead it can be protected by rules, so long as the rules are enforced." (By "rules" he means restrictions on who can use data for what purposes, such as using the database to gather information for personal reasons.)[37]

The problem is that these sorts of solutions are designed for when things go *wrong* with databases, not when they go *right*. Of course we should punish government employees who sneak a peek at what they should not. And we should have mechanisms—much better than we have now—to purge information in the database that is incorrect.[38]

But after-the-fact auditing is of no help in figuring out how data should be used in the first place. Auditing can do nothing to fix the threat to liberty and security posed by databases holding vast amounts of our personal information that operate all too well.

Take, for example, the urge to collect data to identify communities where trouble might be found. In the 1940s, countless Japanese Americans complied with the United States Census, revealing their personal roots. "[W]ith a growing alliance between Japan and Germany," writes one author, "these visits could not have been comfortable." But the Japanese Americans cooperated, perhaps reassured that "by federal law, census data was subject to strict use restrictions" such that personal data could not be revealed. That was the case until 1942, however, when Congress removed those restrictions and the War Department used that information to sweep them into prison camps. There they languished for years, the victims of government taking advantage of data collected for one purpose, and extending it to another. You can see how auditing would not provide much help here. This country has been tripping over itself ever since to apologize.[39]

Think this can't happen today? In 2004, the Electronic Privacy Information Center revealed that the Census Bureau provided Homeland Security with a "zip-code breakdown" showing where Arab Americans lived and their "country of origin." When news of this broke, DHS argued the information was being used to develop Arabic-language signage at airports. Do *you* believe that?[40]

Yes, we definitely should figure out a way to address database errors. But we also need to think through why we are creating databases in the first place. Like so much else in law enforcement, when it comes to data we spend too much time mopping up after the fact, rather than thinking through things before we proceed.

NEITHER AUTHORIZED NOR TRANSPARENT: FUSION CENTERS

What's needed with regard to databases is a return to the basics: up-front democratic authorization and transparency. Too often, when it comes to collecting data, the rule has been to act now, worry about privacy and personal security later. This is exactly backward. Democratic authorization, including clear limitations on the use of data, meaningful privacy policies, and a mechanism for ongoing transparency, should precede establishment of database programs.

Fusion centers are a stunning example of what goes wrong without clear democratic authorization in place. Congress forked out the money for fusion centers, but it did not and could not authorize their activities. "As state and local entities," a congressional report explained, "the exact missions of individual fusion centers are largely beyond the authority of the federal government." Unfortunately, most states failed to specify those missions either. Colorado is among the few states that actually defines what a fusion center even is, but Colorado law says little about what a fusion center should do. A 2013 study of fusion centers by the Brennan Center for Justice found "organized chaos." The federal government had thrown well over a billion dollars at a "loosely coordinated system" of collecting information "with insufficient quality control, accountability, or oversight."[41]

Little surprise, then, that after years of officials lauding fusion centers as a vital tool, a bipartisan Senate investigation essentially labeled fusion centers a joke. When it came to antiterrorism intelligence gathering, the Senate report concluded they were literally worse than worthless. The "intelligence" (the report's sarcastic quotes) that did flow in was "of uneven quality—oftentimes shoddy, rarely timely." Not infrequently it simply recapitulated old or publicly accessible news that "more often than not" was "unrelated to terrorism." "[W]hat a bunch of crap is coming through," said one intelligence chief; another agreed, "You had a lot of data clogging the system of no value." "[I]n no case," concluded the report, "did a fusion center make a clear and unique intelligence contribution that helped apprehend a terrorist or disrupt a plot." Follow that?: "in *no* case" were fusion centers a help. Worse still, the report flagged three incidents that "raised the possibility that some centers have actually hindered or sidetracked Federal counterterrorism efforts."[42]

On the other hand, the Senate report declared, fusion centers were "endangering citizens' civil liberties and Privacy Act protections." DHS was fully aware that information could not be collected or held "solely for the purpose of monitoring activities protected by the U.S. Constitution," yet such violations were common. A motorcycle gang was investigated for a pamphlet essentially telling "members to obey the law." One fusion center intelligence report was about a U.S. citizen who gave a motivational talk to a Muslim group on "positive parenting." Commented a DHS intelligence analyst: "The number of things that scare me about this report are almost too many to write into this [form]," not the least of which was that "the nature of this event is constitutionally-protected activity (public speaking, freedom of assembly, freedom of religion)."[43]

This is what happens when government is allowed to violate what should be the cardinal rule of policing: explicit, before-the-fact, democratic authorization. Before government sets out to do something, the something it is going to do should be clear—both to government officials and to the public. The federal government shot fusion centers up with piles of taxpayer dollars for one specific reason—counterterrorism— but the centers themselves decided to take the funds and do something else entirely. Not atypical was Michigan's fusion center, which "changed its mission," dropping terrorism entirely and identifying a new goal: to "promote public safety" through a "public-private partnership." That sort of vague, wide-ranging, self-determined mission is precisely what has led to so many of the problems.[44]

Equally absent was the other essential half of democratic governance: transparency. Policy analysts who have studied fusion centers say they run the risk of becoming "a 'one-way mirror,' in which citizens are subject to ever-greater scrutiny by the authorities, even while the authorities are increasingly protected from scrutiny by the public." Or, as an official at one fusion center put it bluntly: "If people knew what we were looking at, they'd throw a fit." An analyst at another center echoed the sentiment, calling it the "wild west," where operators did what they could "before 'politics' catches up and limits options."[45]

CONSTITUTIONAL PROTECTIONS: WHAT'S WRONG WITH OUR DNA TESTING SYSTEM?

Of course, up-front democratic authorization and transparency are just half of what the Constitution demands; when people's lives, liberty, and property are at stake, the protections of the Fourth Amendment, as well as the Due Process and Equal Protection Clauses, apply. Yet, when it comes to government databases, the analysis of these constitutional safeguards often is extremely muddled—if not neglected entirely.

Government-compelled DNA testing makes this point well. Compared with fusion centers, the country's DNA database system seems the picture of law enforcement perfection. The accuracy of DNA analysis is highly acclaimed, and congressional and state statutes alike authorize the country's DNA databases and associated protocols. But the lesson of the DNA testing regime is that even properly authorized databases still must meet the standards of constitutional policing. Our

DNA collection system—despite having received the blessing of the Supreme Court—does not. And the reason should be familiar by now: a failure to distinguish suspicion-based from suspicion-less searches.

An Advertisement for DNA Testing

In 2009 a man named Alonzo King was arrested for assault after brandishing a shotgun at a number of people. His DNA was gathered pursuant to a Maryland law mandating collection from anyone arrested for a "crime of violence," and compared with DNA samples in the cold-case database. That comparison resulted in a match with DNA taken from a violent rape committed some six years previously. King now is serving a prison term of life without parole for that rape.[46]

King argued that the mandated DNA testing violated his Fourth Amendment rights. The Supreme Court upheld the conviction, touting "DNA testing's 'unparalleled ability both to exonerate the wrongly convicted and to identify the guilty.'" It certainly seems hard to argue with a system that puts the Alonzo Kings of this world behind bars for life.[47]

A Supreme (Court) Lie

While DNA technology is worthy of our admiration, the Court's opinion in *Maryland v. King* is not. The decision in *King* is built on a lie.

The question in King was whether the state can mandate the forcible collection and testing of the DNA of all arrestees. Justice Kennedy's opinion for the 5–4 *King* majority said that taking King's DNA was necessary to "identify" the arrestee. He used the analogy of fingerprints. The state needs to know whom it has taken into custody and—in order to set the terms for pretrial release—whether they have a criminal past.

But, as Justice Scalia pointed out in a dissent dripping with sarcasm at the majority's disingenuousness, fingerprinting already accomplishes that task. Besides, under existing systems, it took Maryland four months from the time of arrest to the DNA match in King's case. Identification had nothing to do with why the state of Maryland took and tested King's DNA.[48]

As anyone can plainly see, the DNA of arrestees is being checked to solve cold cases. That's not "identification" as normal people use the word. It is, rather, precisely what Maryland law says: The samples are collected "as part of an official investigation into a crime." Or, as Maryland's governor put it, DNA testing "bolsters our efforts to resolve open investigations and bring them to resolution."[49]

What's at Stake?

You may be thinking, so what? Who cares if the DNA was collected to "identify" King or to solve a crime he committed years earlier? Good for us: they caught the bad guy.

But it matters, because there is much more at stake.

The problem is that there was no probable cause—indeed any cause at all—to believe King had committed the rape, thus justifying collecting his DNA to investigate it. And if there was no probable cause, then the search was flat-out invalid. As we saw in Chapter 7, searches without cause are impermissible unless they are done to all of us. If the government can pick and choose whom to search, without cause, we are all vulnerable.

We'll examine this point about the lack of probable cause, and what to do about it, more closely in just a moment, but first let's get a handle on how the use of the DNA database extends well beyond bad guys like King. Consider Elizabeth Haskell, who was arrested in California during a peace demonstration. She was never charged with anything, but officers refused to release her until she submitted a DNA sample. Once in California's database, it is extraordinarily difficult and costly to get out. So there Elizabeth Haskell sits.[50]

Elizabeth Haskell is hardly alone: behind our backs, and without any authorization for it at all, the government is building a broad DNA database. DNA is taken from members of our armed services, with the solemn rationale of identifying remains if necessary. But their DNA is kept after they leave the military. Police ask volunteers to give up their DNA in order to crack particularly horrific unsolved crimes. But these volunteers then end up in the database, often without recourse. One person agreed to submit DNA to help solve a murder; it took six years and a lawsuit to get out of the database. Police nab DNA from cigarette butts and Breathalyzer mouthpieces; courts have said that's fine too. Hundreds of thousands of blood samples from newborns sit in state hands and there is worry these, too, will be added.[51]

If you are wondering who cares if anyone ends up in the database, the answer—apparently—is that most of us do.

Plenty of respected figures have argued for a universal database, and it is clear from the efforts described above that the government wants one. Law professor Akhil Amar, whom we met in Chapter 3 as author of the argument that the Constitution does not require warrants, wrote on the opinion pages of *The New York Times* that a universal DNA database would represent "a real improvement in the criminal justice system" given that it would "increase the odds of finding the guilty, freeing the innocent, and vindicating victims." For that reason, he concluded, "it makes sense to include all citizens in the database." Even the founder of DNA testing, Alec Jeffreys, himself says that "[i]f we're all on the database, we're all in exactly the same boat—the issue of discrimination disappears."[52]

But we aren't going to have a universal database anytime soon, because people just won't go for it. Popular support is not remotely there for the government collecting and storing all our DNA. And perhaps for good reason.

DNA testing is said to involve the analysis of what is known as "junk DNA." The appellation "junk" refers to the fact that unlike other parts of the DNA strand, which are highly revealing about a person, the information used in cold-case testing supposedly reveals little except the fact of the match. Scientists have figured out how to gather information from some thirteen sites, or loci, on the DNA strand, to create a profile that—when compared with other profiles—is highly accurate in assuring a match while supposedly telling nothing else about the subject whose DNA is taken.[53]

The first problem with the "junk" DNA theory is that even the junk is revealing of our personal traits. It can reveal Type I diabetes. It can reveal ethnicity. Indeed, in some places DNA profiles are stored in some databases with racial coding. Jeffreys has suggested that "further troubling links between DNA fingerprints and disease will emerge."[54]

But it is worse yet, because if the government has your "profile" built on the supposed "junk," it likely also has the sample that the profile was constructed from—and that sample holds your entire genome, meaning everything about your genetic makeup. Samples aren't destroyed after they are used to construct DNA profiles; they are stored away, often into perpetuity. State laws vary and many are silent on the subject of how long.[55]

We're assured the original samples won't be touched—why, then, are they kept?—but that is a blatant falsehood as well. We know this because stored samples already have been accessed for some aspects of "familial" DNA testing. Familial testing works like this: the government runs the profile of an arrestee against cold-case profiles and comes up with a partial match for a murder that occurred years ago. The arrestee isn't the murderer, but someone in his genetic family is. Knowing this fact, the government can try through further investigation to locate the murderer. In order to facilitate familial matching, California has allowed investigators to go back to original DNA samples to conduct a new test used to confirm male familial ties. Although success stories in familial testing are extremely rare, the government has used this method of familial matching to catch some serious bad guys, such as the notorious BTK ("bind torture kill") murderer. But this use of stored DNA samples has occurred without any democratic authorization whatsoever. As a result, entirely innocent people get visited by law enforcement and asked to map their families; many of these innocents live for some time under a debilitating "cloud of suspicion."[56]

If the government can break into the samples for a purpose not properly authorized by law, and certainly not authorized at the time the samples were taken, they can break in for other reasons down the line. Like when some scientist discovers a way to test DNA for a "predisposition" to crime. That is not as farfetched as it sounds, given that—as the privacy scholar Jeffrey Rosen puts it—"genetic research . . . reveals increasing ties between genes and predisposition to violence and other antisocial behavior." Welcome to *Minority Report*.[57]

What we do know is that governments have treated cavalierly DNA samples that supposedly were inviolate. When Iceland sold its citizens' genetic data to deCode Genetics, its founder, Kari Stefansson, said, "We have never claimed that the protection of privacy cannot be broken. The principal element here is trust." That didn't cut it with the Icelandic people; now there are stricter controls in place, including jail time for decoding identity. History confirms that governments have a bad record of protecting data. "Perhaps the construction of such a genetic panopticon is wise," wrote Justice Scalia, dissenting in *King*. "But I doubt that the proud men who wrote the charter of our liberties would have been so eager to open their mouths for royal inspection."[58]

The Costs of Constitutional Dissembling

Which brings us back to the utter failure of constitutional guarantees here. No one disputes the fact that DNA testing is a "search" for Fourth Amendment purposes. Indeed, there are at least two searches: the swab of an arrestee's cheek to collect the DNA, and the testing of the profile against cold cases.

What there is not in these cases is any sort of cause—suspicion—probable or otherwise, to justify these searches. That's why Justice Kennedy had to engage in such disingenuousness to reach the result he wanted. He needed a purpose to justify the search, and "identification" was the one he managed to concoct.

As we learned in Chapters 7 and 8, the government *can* search without any cause at all, but to do so it must meet one of two conditions. Either it must search all of us, in a statute that clearly authorizes the search. Or it must have a statistical basis for searching some subset of us, but not others.

Neither of these is true in the DNA-testing context.

It may possible to develop a constitutionally acceptable statistical basis for some parts of the DNA database. For people who are convicted (not arrested, but convicted) of certain crimes, there may be evidence showing sufficiently high rates of recidivism. One could argue on this basis that collecting their DNA will help deter future crimes once the offenders are released, because they will know DNA might be found to apprehend them. But this doesn't quite work as a basis for collection from all convicts, as the recidivism for some of them, such as nonviolent drug offenders, is comparatively low. On *PBS NewsHour* on July 17, 1998, Benjamin Keehn, a public defender in Boston, made the case that "if we are going to take DNA from prisoners because they are at risk [of committing crimes in the future], why shouldn't we take DNA from teenagers, from homeless people, from Catholic priests, from any subgroup of society that someone is able to make a statistical argument of being at risk?" And there is no statistical case whatsoever for DNA testing of arrestees, who—like Elizabeth Haskell—are entirely innocent of anything, no different from anyone walking the streets.[59]

Equally obviously, we are not all in the DNA database. It is clear some in government would like a universal database, but there's no way the voters are supporting one. So government continues to do what it can: passing statutes that pick on easy targets, such as arrestees, and trapping people in the database once it gets hold of their DNA. But that is flat-out unconstitutional.

As is so often the case when the government acts unconstitutionally, it is acting inefficaciously as well. Does it make sense to continue to stuff the so-called offender database so full of names, many of whom are not offenders at all? Looking at California, the well-respected research not-for-profit RAND Corporation concluded that if the goal is resolving unsolved crimes, "it would seem to be a wiser use of California's resources to devote them to analyzing the backlog of crime-scene evidence." In other words, do a better job of developing cold-case DNA data. But that is expensive, time-consuming, and exacting. Swabbing the cheeks of people who have done nothing to justify it is easy. So government does the cheap and easy thing, rather than the sensible one, and our privacy sits unguarded in a database that contains the genetic code of a growing number of people.[60]

DUE PROCESS OF DATABASES

There's one more part of the Constitution we've not really discussed yet: the Due Process Clause. It is basically the guarantee of transparency for our constitutional rights. The Due Process Clause says that no person may be deprived of "life, liberty, or property, without due process of law." Among other things this means that if the government is doing something bad to you, it has to explain why and give you a chance to respond to its evidence. In legal terms, the government has to give you "notice" and an "opportunity to be heard."

When it comes to databases, the government rarely accords due process and courts rarely do anything about it. To date, this is a pretty gaping hole in your rights.

In the world of databases, algorithms are king. Algorithms are the formulas that tell the computer what to look for when a database is searched. One needs a way to sort through all that data, and an algorithm provides it. Whether it is predicting who will commit crime, deciding whose taxes to audit, granting welfare benefits, or monitoring Americans' communications, the algorithms are making the decisions.

The problem is that although the government is now using those algorithms to decide people's fate based on the pile of information it holds, it likes to keep the algorithms secret. We don't know what the government is looking for, and we certainly don't know whether the use of any particular algorithm makes sense. We are kept at bay by database secrecy, particularly when data analysis is being used to our detriment.

This sort of secrecy is completely untenable, because the protocols used to analyze data in databases are prone to mistakes. Even when it comes to DNA testing and the conclusions drawn from it, there are errors. In the summer of 2015, the Texas Forensic Science Commission came to the conclusion that state crime labs were wrongly stating the probability that DNA evidence matched a particular perpetrator—its new protocol required labs to go from saying there was a one-in-a-million chance the DNA had identified the wrong person, to what was more like one in thirty or one in forty. That's quite the difference. And there are documented cases of people wrongly convicted on DNA evidence, like Josiah Sutton, who was convicted of rape based on DNA, though he was much shorter and lighter than the victim claimed.[61]

Which brings us back to Abe Mashal and the no-fly list. Abe's case finally did go to court, and after years of fighting, he now can fly again. It is because a federal judge called the whole thing for what it was: a flagrant violation of Mashal's most basic constitutional rights. The bad news is that it took five years and huge amounts of time and money to accomplish the constitutionally obvious.[62]

What countless people on the no-fly list do not get is precisely what due process should afford them: notice and an opportunity to be heard. The government won't say whether you are even on the list, let alone why. You get to file a "redress form," but you aren't told what you are rebutting. This sort of Kafkaesque nightmare should scare all of us, right down to our anklebones.[63]

Together, the Fourth Amendment and the Due Process Clause could do a lot of work to protect us where databases and algorithms are concerned, far more than courts have recognized. Every step of the government's use of our data, from collecting it, to holding it, to disseminating it, to analyzing it, is potentially a search. And using that data against us without explaining how the database was used may well violate our due process rights. At present, though, courts pretty much scrutinize only the collection of data, ignoring all the other steps that follow. They rely on the Fourth Amendment's prohibition against unreasonable searches and seizures, and sideline the Due Process Clause almost entirely when it comes to data aggregation, dissemination, and analysis. That needs to change.

Would complying with both these constitutional clauses be a bother for the government? You bet. But our lives, liberty, and property are on the line. So is common sense. The government fights and fights and fights to keep information secret, only to have it come out that its data programs make no sense, the algorithms do not work, the error rates are staggering. This is not making us safer. Often, it is wasting vast amounts of money on fools' errands. "Sunlight," as Justice Brandeis said in a different context, "is the best of disinfectants."[64]

When family tragedy struck Abe Mashal, he sought succor in his faith. When the government ensnared him in its net, he abandoned that faith. His ACLU lawyers told him to do what he wants; the government shouldn't be allowed to crush the practice of his religion. "That's true," Mashal says, resigned, "but you have to live and learn, too." The question is whether *that* is the lesson we all should learn from Abe Mashal's case. That the government can toss us into its databases without sufficient protections, and if our lives are mangled as a result, c'est la vie. Or whether we should get wise, and regulate databases properly.[65]

We're almost at the end of our road. But not quite. We've not yet discussed counterterrorism, and what may be the government's biggest data grab yet, one that captured the nation's full attention: the use of bulk data collection for national security purposes. That problem, our last, deserves its own chapter.

12

COUNTERTERRORISM
AND NATIONAL SECURITY

We live in the age of global terrorism. In response, some in the United States government decided—without the public's knowledge—to adopt a sweeping program that gathered and mined the telephone and Internet data of Americans. When the country learned of these efforts, a sprawling and contentious debate began about the permissible bounds of government spying. Yet, at least as a constitutional matter, these issues are not nearly as complicated as they appeared. There is much the government can do to keep us safe, guided by constitutional principles that should by this point be well familiar. The problem is not so much what those in government did; it is how they went about doing it.

THE RIGHTS OF U.S. PERSONS

The Daily Show—June 10, 2013. John Oliver is sitting in at anchor, hosting for the very first time. On the screen is the graphic "Good News! You're Not Paranoid."[1]

The topic: NSA Oversight.

Oliver plays a video.

It is a hearing before the Senate Select Intelligence Committee. Seated in a padded leather swivel chair behind the rostrum is Senator Ron Wyden, Democrat from Oregon. His chiseled face is deadly earnest (though he's looking rather natty in a blue checked shirt and bright red tie). Speaking into the microphone, Wyden asks the witness:

"So, I want to see if you can give me a yes or no answer to the question: Does the NSA collect any type of data at all on millions or hundreds of millions of Americans?"

And there behind the witness table, is—as the television caption tells us, although the bulldog face and bald pate of America's then top spy already has become quite familiar—Lieutenant General James Clapper (Ret.), Director of National Intelligence. Clapper, as captured on the video, is forced to play the straight man to John Oliver's comedic riff.

Clapper is scratching at the top of his head repeatedly, his body language oozing discomfort, unable to make and keep eye contact with Wyden.

"No, sir," responds Clapper, looking up, looking down, rubbing his head more.

"It does not?" asks Wyden.

"Not wittingly."[2]

Jump back to John Oliver, shaking his head in disbelief, aping Clapper's head-rubbing, as the audience begins a roll of laughter that builds to a roar by the time Oliver puts up a picture of Clapper with a full head of hair. "Here's how much this guy was rubbing his forehead. This is him at the start of the hearing." "No spy," announced Oliver, coming to the punch line, "should have that big a tell."

The video of Clapper, shot three months before the *Daily Show* episode, is funny only because Oliver is showing it five days after the country first heard about the NSA's breathtaking surveillance—of all of us. In a breaking story in *The Guardian*, Glenn Greenwald reported that "under the Obama administration the communications records of millions of US citizens are being collected indiscriminately and in bulk—regardless of whether they are suspected of any wrongdoing." *The Guardian* and *The Washington Post* subsequently reported on another secret spy program, PRISM, by which the NSA tapped into Internet companies such as Google, Facebook, and Apple to obtain personal data including "search history, the contents of emails, file transfers and live chats." Continued disclosures revealed that in programs with names running from the sinister to the sublime—MUSCULAR, EVILOLIVE, HAPPYFOOT,

ROYAL CONCIERGE—the NSA was collecting and collating an al-most unfathomable amount of information. By June 9, a day before Oliver took Clapper on, the world learned the leaker was Edward Snowden, the then twenty-nine-year-old former intelligence consultant who had secreted away thousands of classified intelligence documents and leaked them to the press.[3]

Snowden's revelations kicked off a national dialogue, one Senator Wyden had been trying to provoke for years. In May 2011, Wyden took to the Senate floor and in an impassioned speech delivered a "warning" to his colleagues: "[W]hen the American people find out how their govern-ment has secretly interpreted the Patriot Act," he said, "they are going to be stunned and they are going to be angry." He was right.[4]

Wyden's central and correct point—as true in foreign intelligence gathering as in any other area of policing—is that the American people need to be "in a position to ratify or reject the decisions their elected officials make on their behalf." That's why all-encompassing secrecy is "fundamentally inconsistent with democratic principles." Wyden brushes aside the argument that this sort of information needs to be kept hush-hush, explaining "American citizens recognize" that the details of intelli-gence operations cannot be revealed, but "I do not believe the law should ever be kept secret. Voters have a right and a need to know what the law says and what their government thinks the text of the law means."[5]

Many disagree with Wyden. It is their position that when it comes to national security, to decisions about foreign intelligence gathering, matters should rest in the hands of the executive branch alone. Or, in any event, that these surveillance decisions can and should be kept as a secret between executive branch officials and a small number of mem-bers of Congress who are briefed in, and who will "represent" the rest of us. They believe open debate is inappropriate, and begrudge the par-ticipation of the full Congress, the courts, and the American people.

But the Constitution says otherwise. What matters under the Consti-tution is not the purpose of the surveillance—i.e., national security—but who is spied upon. The moment the American people become targets of government surveillance, all the protections in the Constitution—from open debate and legal authorization of surveillance programs to proper warrants based on probable cause—kick in.

As is so often the case when the government acts in secret, unauthorized ways, there are grave doubts about whether these government programs have been efficacious. Wyden asserts that intelligence community "misstatements have consistently exaggerated the effectiveness of domestic surveillance programs and consistently understated their intrusiveness." There is plenty of evidence that he is right about this as well.[6]

Some—and perhaps much—of what the government set out to do could have been done constitutionally, had it been done openly and properly. Bulk collection may be just fine, so long as we approve it and all are subjected to it. Targeting of particular citizens also is permitted, so long as there are warrants and sufficient cause. But what the executive branch may not do, and yet did on a colossal scale, is decide on its own to conduct surveillance on the American public.

THE PERILS OF INTELLIGENCE GATHERING

Intelligence gathering to protect their security is what nations do, and the United States is no exception. George Washington employed spies to great effect to win the Revolutionary War. During the Civil War telegraph lines were tapped; the Union Army even had an aerial balloon corps for a while, though between camouflage on the ground and the difficulty of moving the equipment it proved not worth the bother.[7]

When it comes to foreign intelligence gathering, the United States often has scrambled to keep up with its foes. Until mid-twentieth century, the oceans surrounding the continent offered a comfort that lowered our guard when it came to developing a sophisticated apparatus to detect what our foes were up to. Both world wars required hasty assembly of intelligence operatives.[8]

Many of our worst moments have been the result of massive intelligence failures. That was true of Pearl Harbor. And it was true of the second war in Iraq as well. The events of 9/11 may have been no exception. It is counterfactual to assert that we definitely could have stopped the attacks had things all gone right. Still, the 9/11 Commission Report is a damning record of missed leads and opportunities.[9]

But some of our most inexcusable failures have involved turning the nation's national-security intelligence-gathering apparatus on the American people themselves.

On December 22, 1974, *The New York Times* published a story by

Seymour Hersh headlined "Huge C.I.A. Operation Reported in U.S. Against Antiwar Forces, Other Dissidents In Nixon Years." Following on the heels of the June 17, 1972, Watergate break-in, Hersh documented how the CIA kept files on more than ten thousand Americans, with information gathered by illegal break-ins, wiretapping, and opening of private mail.[10]

A Senate committee appointed to investigate the government spying—the Church Committee, named after its Chair, Senator Frank Church of Idaho—uncovered jaw-dropping evidence of government malfeasance from the 1940s into the 1970s. In the name of national security, the CIA, NSA, and FBI had gone after Americans notable and ordinary, from senators such as Adlai Stevenson to groups including the John Birch Society and the Socialist Workers' Party. The FBI had files on half a million people; the CIA opened a quarter of a million letters, and the FBI over 100,000 more. In an eerie foreshadowing of the Snowden revelations, the NSA obtained "[m]illions of private telegrams sent from, to, or through the United States . . . under a secret arrangement with three United States telegraph companies." The civil rights movement was a frequent target; the FBI plotted to bring down Martin Luther King, Jr., and replace him with a black leader more to its liking. The CIA launched Operation CHAOS, sending spies to foment distrust among groups deemed "domestic dissidents," including the antiwar movement and the women's liberation movement.[11]

What's most disturbing is how those conducting these activities so easily turned a blind eye on the Constitution. One witness explained how the government started with national security targets and moved to groups expressing political dissent, moving "from the kid with the bomb to the kid with a picket sign, and from the kid with the picket sign to the kid with the bumper sticker of the opposing candidate. And you just keep going down the line." The decade-long head of the FBI Intelligence Division testified that "never once did I hear anybody" ask of what they were doing "is it legal, is it ethical, or moral . . . we were just naturally pragmatic." In one particularly emotional moment, Senator Phillip Hart of Michigan, known as the "conscience of the Senate"—who everyone knew was dying of cancer—came to testify in a tearful mea culpa, saying this is what his family, his kids, had been telling him was going on, but "in my great wisdom and high office . . . I assured them that they were [wrong]—it just wasn't true, it couldn't happen."[12]

In light of what it uncovered, the Church Committee insisted that "[c]lear legal standards and effective oversight and controls are necessary to ensure that domestic intelligence activity does not undermine the democratic system it is intended to protect." Its members did not believe that "mere exposure of what has occurred in the past will prevent its recurrence." The "natural tendency of Government is toward abuse of power" and "[a]buse thrives on secrecy." While "[o]bviously" one cannot reveal "the names of intelligence agents or the technological details of collection . . . in the field of intelligence, secrecy has been extended to inhibit review of the basic programs and practices themselves."[13]

That is absolutely right, and yet history cannot seem to keep from repeating itself.

THE PROTECTIONS IN PLACE

Electronic surveillance of the American public, though often controversial, has long been a staple of intelligence gathering in the name of national security. When Attorney General (and later Supreme Court Justice) Robert Jackson—like some of his predecessors in office—banned wiretapping in 1940, he was quickly overruled by his boss, at least for "matters involving the defense of the nation." FDR authorized wiretapping of people "suspected of subversive activities against the Government of the United States." FDR's policy, with variations, persisted at least until the administration of Lyndon Johnson. During this thirty-some-year stretch, Congress considered legislation to restrict wiretapping, but proved unable to act.[14]

In 1978, prodded by the Church Commission revelations, Congress finally regulated electronic spying for national security purposes. And when it did, it was guided by the only case to date in which the Supreme Court had spoken to the issue.[15]

On September 28, 1968, several sticks of dynamite went off outside the CIA recruitment office on Main Street in Ann Arbor, Michigan. Just over a year later, a grand jury indicted three members of the White Panthers, a far-left group united in goals with the Black Panthers. One of the three, White Panther Minister of Defense Lawrence "Pun" Plamondon, went underground, earning a spot on the FBI's Ten Most Wanted list. He was captured when an occupant of a car he was driving tossed a can out the window, getting them stopped by the police.

Plamondon's lawyers asked to see any electronic surveillance that had been conducted of their client.[16]

The government admitted that it had gathered information on Plamondon without a warrant. But it claimed the warrantless wiretapping was fine. It insisted that it could even withhold the information from the defendant—because it was collected as part of the president's power to protect national security.[17]

The question the Supreme Court was asked to answer in the *Keith* case (so named for the trial judge, Damon Keith, who ordered the information disclosed) was whether the government could engage in warrantless wiretapping of U.S. citizens if it was doing so for national security purposes. The justices were willing to assume that the government had ample reason—cause—to tap Plamondon's conversations. The issue was whether it could do so without "prior judicial approval."[18]

The government's position in *Keith* is precisely the one we hear so much about today in the battle against terrorism. National security cases and criminal cases are two different things, the government argued then and argues now. Unlike in ordinary criminal cases, courts are said to lack the expertise necessary to assess the need for surveillance in the national security context. Besides, the government argued, secrecy is particularly essential in this context, and obtaining warrants risks leaks of sensitive information.[19]

The Supreme Court in *Keith* was sympathetic to the government's concerns, and yet the justices were unequivocal in concluding that the executive branch must get a warrant before wiretapping its citizens. Indeed, they noted that national security investigations present particular dangers "because of the inherent vagueness of the domestic security concept, the necessarily broad and continuing nature of the intelligence gathering, and the temptation to utilize such surveillances to oversee political dissent."[20]

"The warrant clause of the Fourth Amendment is not dead language," the *Keith* Court insisted. Neither "Fourth Amendment freedoms" nor those in the related First Amendment can "properly be guaranteed if domestic surveillance may be conducted solely within the discretion of the executive branch."[21]

Although it had ruled against the government and in favor of warrants, the Supreme Court provided some qualifiers in *Keith* that paved the way for the action Congress subsequently took. First, the justices were clear that their opinion touched only on "the domestic aspects of national security"; they "express[ed] no opinion" regarding "the issues which may be involved with respect to activities of foreign powers or their agents." Second, the Court said Congress was free to adopt different standards even for domestic intelligence gathering. This is because criminal investigation and intelligence gathering are different: "gathering of security intelligence is often long range and involves the interrelation of various sources and types of information," and "the exact targets of such surveillance may be more difficult to identify than in" ordinary criminal cases. Thus, a different sort of showing of "probable cause" might apply in the national security intelligence-gathering context. Finally, the Court suggested that Congress could designate a special court to hear the warrant requests.[22]

When Congress adopted the Foreign Intelligence Surveillance Act (FISA) in 1978, it was with the *Keith* Court's guidance in mind. Although FISA is a complicated statute, its basics are simple enough. FISA provided that a "United States Person" (basically, citizens and those resident in the United States) could not be searched—including by electronic surveillance—without a warrant. The warrant application had to include certifications from high officials that the "purpose" of the surveillance was foreign intelligence gathering and that the target was an "agent of a foreign power." And Congress created a special court—the Foreign Intelligence Surveillance Court (FISC)—to hear warrant applications from the government in the utmost secrecy.[23]

There matters stood, until nineteen Islamist fanatics hijacked four planes on September 11, 2001.

THE PATRIOT ACT, AND THE WALL

In the wake of the 9/11 terrorist attacks, Congress enacted the USA-Patriot Act, which granted the government substantially more freedom in intelligence gathering. It was not just about terrorism: law enforcement used 9/11 to obtain tools that had long been on its wish list. To this day, the Patriot Act remains a subject of huge controversy, with many claiming it allowed the government too much leeway to invade citizens' liberties.[24]

Notably, though, the Patriot Act adhered to FISA's insistence on warrants from the FISC—and indeed relied on them to solve the curious

problem of "the Wall." "The Wall" was a set of information-sharing limitations erected to keep the relatively more permissive standards for national security warrants from eroding the rights of suspects in ordinary
criminal investigations. Because FISA warrants could stay in place longer, with less oversight than ordinary warrants, and could be granted with
a different sort of probable cause, the concern was that law enforcement
would use FISA warrants as a workaround in ordinary criminal prosecutions. In response to these concerns, the Department of Justice put in
place strict rules limiting when investigators on the criminal side of a
case could share information with those on the intelligence side, and
vice versa.[25]

The Wall, already controversial among law enforcement and intelligence officers, was widely condemned after 9/11 when it became clear
that it prevented the sharing of some information that may have contributed to stopping the attacks. Khalid al-Mihdhar was one of the five
hijackers of AA Flight 77, which struck the Pentagon. The CIA had
long been interested in him, tracked him to a meeting in Kuala Lum-
pur, and lost him. A month before the attack, FBI officials realized al-
Mihdhar might be in the United States and sent out a lead for him. An
agent in New York who was investigating the bombing of the U.S.S.
Cole in Yemen, in which al-Mihdhar was believed complicit, jumped
into the search, but was waved off—despite an appeal to high FBI legal
counsel—on the ground that because he was working on a criminal
case, it would violate the Wall. The agent shot off an angry email:

> Whatever has happened to this—someday someone will die—
> and wall or not—the public will not understand why we were
> not more effective and throwing every resource we had at cer-
> tain "problems." Let's hope the National Security Law Unit
> will stand behind their decision then, especially since the big-
> gest threat to us, UBL [Usama Bin Laden], is getting the most
> protection.[26]

Among the many things it did, the Patriot Act was meant to tear
down the Wall. Whereas previously "the purpose" for a FISA warrant
had to be foreign intelligence gathering, the Patriot Act said it only had
to be "a significant purpose." So other purposes—such as criminal

investigation—were fine. It also made clear that prosecutors and foreign intelligence officials could share information with one another.[27]

At some level, the idea of the Wall was always crazy. As we saw in Chapter 7, it's practically impossible to distinguish criminal prosecution from other purposes of government searching. In fact, that is exactly what the FISA Court of Review—the appellate judges that on rare occasion review FISA court decisions—said after some judges on the FISA court tried to put the Wall back in place following enactment of the Patriot Act. The FISA Court of Review judges pointed out that surveillance often will have two key goals—the gathering of foreign intelligence, and the gathering of evidence for a criminal prosecution—and that the two simply cannot be separated.[28]

The right answer, as a matter of law and policy both, is to require effective warrants whenever executive branch officials seek information about citizens, even when national security is at stake. That's exactly what the FISA Court of Review said. Once it overturned the lower court's attempt to reerect the Wall, the Court of Review realized it had to decide whether FISA warrants met Fourth Amendment standards. Otherwise, it understood, national security surveillance of citizens would present a serious constitutional problem. But FISA warrants were just fine, the Court of Review easily concluded, because—like regular warrants—they are "issued by neutral, disinterested magistrates"; there is a showing of cause to believe someone is a foreign agent (which, under the Patriot Act, typically involved a showing of the commission of a U.S. crime); and the warrant was specific about what was to be gathered.[29]

And so the Wall was down for good, warrants were in place, and to the public eye all looked fine and well. Except for what was going on behind our backs. It turned out that a massive system of surveillance was being constructed and deployed—often against the American people—with no proper legal authorization.

TOTAL INFORMATION AWARENESS: A PLAN TOO FAR?

In the immediate aftermath of 9/11, Admiral John M. Poindexter pushed a radical idea with a revealing name: Total Information Awareness (TIA). Poindexter, who had been a submarine hunter in the Navy, later served as Ronald Reagan's National Security Advisor. He was forced to resign after his scheme to sell arms to Iran and use the proceeds to fund Nicaraguan rebels—what became known as the Iran-Contra Affair—was uncovered. After leaving government, tech-savvy Poindexter worked in the defense industry, and it was there that he developed the idea that ultimately led the Bush administration to invite him to head the Information Awareness Office in the Department of Defense after 9/11.[30]

TIA was to be an early-warning system for terrorist incidents. Poindexter and others believed there was a "signature" to the movement of terrorists planning an attack. For a former sub hunter like Poindexter, the concept was familiar: enemy submarines had a "signature" that skilled operators could detect and isolate in an ocean of "nois[e]." So too with terrorists; if one could only identify their signature, then one could search a sea of data and hope to discover the plot in advance.[31]

When TIA became public—and, in fairness to Poindexter, there was no real attempt to keep it secret—people went ballistic. To make the system work, the government had to vacuum up that sea of data, pretty much everything about all of us. The conservative columnist William Safire wrote an outraged piece in November 2002, titled "You Are a Suspect," in which he explained the breadth of TIA: "Every purchase you make with a credit card, every magazine subscription you buy and medical prescription you fill, every Web site you visit and email you send or receive, every academic grade you receive, every bank deposit you make, every trip you book and every event you attend—all these transactions and communications will go into what the Defense Department describes as 'a virtual, centralized grand database.'" "Anyone who deliberately set out to invent a government program with the specific aim of terrifying the Orwell-reading public," opined *The Washington Post*, "could hardly have improved on the Information Awareness Office."[32]

Congress killed TIA (though some pieces were parceled off to the NSA), and Poindexter was shipped back out to private industry. Unknown to the rest of us, though, the NSA already was working toward a vision similar to Poindexter's. General Michael Hayden, who headed the NSA on 9/11, and who was fond of sports metaphors, described it as an agency that had "frankly played a bit back from the line" to avoid the sort of thing uncovered by the Church Committee. Determined to change that, he was fond of saying, "[W]e're going to play inside the foul lines, but there's going to be chalk dust on our cleats."[33]

Hayden, it turned out, had an odd idea of where that constitutional chalk line was—and, more important, who decides what is fair and foul when it comes to the surveillance of Americans. As we now know, he was party to perhaps the largest unauthorized collection of Americans' data in all of history.

COLLECTING A GIGANTIC HAYSTACK, ON THE OFF-CHANCE THERE IS A NEEDLE

In the immediate aftermath of 9/11, Hayden and Vice President Dick Cheney decided that more surveillance was necessary to deter another terrorist attack, and that the FISA warrant procedure was simply too laborious for the task. Rather than use emergency procedures built into FISA, or ask Congress to amend the law—even though, at that very moment, Congress was giving the administration most of what it wanted in the Patriot Act—the administration decided to go it alone. The president signed a secret authorization to allow the NSA to engage in an enormous data grab.[34]

The new program was code-named Stellar Wind. Within the closed circle, though, it was often called the President's Surveillance Program, or simply "PSP."[35]

Much of the fight has been about whether the president was authorized, on his own, to collect the information of Americans without probable cause or a warrant. Answering that question requires having a firm grasp of the almost unimaginable amount of data the executive branch has been collecting.

The first part of Stellar Wind is now common knowledge: the NSA's bulk collection of "metadata" concerning phone calls of all Americans. The program often is referred to as the "215" program, because when the FISA court finally was asked to (and did) bless this part of what the NSA was doing, it did so under Section 215 of FISA, which provides procedures for obtaining "business records." Under the 215 program, the government collected all the call records from communications providers. For example, AT&T—which, as we have seen, is famously complicit with the government—built a secret room through which information was shuttled to NSA servers.[36]

But Stellar Wind went far beyond Americans' phone calls; it also included their e-mail addressing information, and the websites they were visiting. The government said it had abandoned Internet metadata collection in 2011; the NSA explained that the project was not valuable enough to justify the cost. But the real problem seems to be that the NSA could not get this information from U.S. Internet companies in ways that met the FISA court's privacy requirements. What the NSA cannot collect legally domestically, however, it finds ways of gathering abroad.[37]

In the early days after the Snowden revelations, the government was quick to dismiss this sort of bulk collection as inconsequential because it was only collecting metadata, and not the actual "content" of communications. As we've come to understand by now, though, the distinction between content and metadata is in many ways a facile one: possessing information about every call anyone makes, as well as who they email with and which URLs they visit, can give a very complete picture of a person's life.[38]

In any event, the government has been telling half-truths: the NSA was and still is collecting content as well, despite claims to the contrary. Consider, as an example, the NSA's wry reaction when it was finally able to nab Skype video: "The audio portions of these sessions have been processed correctly all along, but without the accompanying video. Now, analysts will have the complete 'picture.'"[39]

Although the government tells us that it is collecting content only on bad guys—or, at least, maybe just foreigners—that's not true either. Under the "702 program"—so named because section 702 of the 2008 FISA Amendments Act allowed this part of the President's Surveillance Program to continue once it became public—the NSA gets communications companies to turn over all the content associated with foreign targets (i.e., it can wiretap phones or read email). Included in the 702 program, however, is "upstream" collection, which involves getting huge amounts of data from a variety of foreign *sources*. That collection unequivocally includes Americans' content. That's because the FISA court signed off on procedures that required the NSA to be only 51 percent sure its target is foreign and not a U.S. person. (As John Oliver quipped,

"That's basically flipping a coin, plus one percent.") In addition, anytime the NSA is collecting information on a foreigner communicating *with* a U.S. person, the NSA gets to keep that as "incidental" collection. "Incidental" makes it sound like, oops, we just happened to get that information. In truth, though, this is a major purpose of the program—to collect all U.S. communications with any foreign individual the NSA targets.[40]

There's more: even today, after all this became public, the executive branch has claimed its own prerogative to collect our data. Ronald Reagan, in an attempt to regulate those forms of surveillance excluded from FISA, issued Executive Order 12333. This authority allows the executive branch to gather information without warrants, ostensibly because (again) it targets only foreign nationals. But, yet again, that is not true. John Tye, who served as the State Department's Internet freedom chief, blew the whistle on 12333 activities in a July 2014 *Washington Post* editorial. (Tye, unlike Snowden, cleared what he would say beforehand.) Tye's plain message was that both the metadata and content of Americans' communications are being collected and held under 12333, including in ways the government publicly says it has abandoned. Tye wrote, "Americans deserve an honest answer to the simple question: What kind of data is the NSA collecting on millions or hundreds of millions of Americans?"[41]

Perhaps more troubling even than what the government is collecting is how that information is accessed and searched: again, without warrants. Because, unlike the NSA and CIA, the FBI's mission is both foreign intelligence and criminal investigation, FBI agents apparently can search the 702 data for both. The Privacy and Civil Liberties Oversight Board (PCLOB), the federal agency charged with monitoring intelligence gathering, and a special Privacy Review Board appointed by the president after the Snowden revelations, said FBI searching of Americans without a warrant should come to a halt, but it has not. The volume of searches of U.S. persons in the 702 data is so large that a former FISA judge actually urged Congress not to require warrants because the number of requests would swamp the FISA court. That's pretty revealing, even if does seem to miss the entire purpose of having the FISA court in the first place.[42]

Finally, it appears the government also is aggregating the data it collects in ways that look very much like the Total Information Awareness program Congress supposedly killed. In 2010, NSA analysts began to create social network charts of Americans based on phone calls and email logs. The NSA can "augment" that information with all the other information it has in its vast databases, including "bank codes, insurance information, Facebook profiles, passenger manifests, voter registration rolls, and GPS location information, as well as property records and unspecified tax data." Obama administration officials acknowledged this has been done for Americans as well as foreigners—and all without any sort of warrant or oversight outside the executive branch.[43]

Hayden's successor at the NSA, General Keith Alexander, was known to say, "You need the haystack to find the needle." Even if this "build a haystack" approach makes sense—and, as we will see, there is plenty of reason to question its efficacy—the haystack simply was not built in the way the Constitution requires.[44]

UNCONSTITUTIONAL AUTHORIZATION

The scope of this data grab is so large as to be almost beyond comprehension. What's critical to see is how the whole thing went on for so long without proper democratic approval.

In March 2004, a constitutional crisis was brewing over the President's Surveillance Program. By its own terms Stellar Wind required reauthorization every thirty to forty-five days, and this time the Attorney General refused to sign off. There had been a change of leadership at the Department of Justice's Office of Legal Counsel, the top lawyers for the executive branch. OLC's new head, Jack Goldsmith, concluded that Stellar Wind suffered from serious legal deficiencies. Attorney General John Ashcroft was hospitalized at the time, gravely ill from acute pancreatitis, and had stepped aside in favor of his number two, James Comey—who later became the head of the FBI. Comey agreed with Goldsmith that aspects of Stellar Wind could not be justified under existing law, and refused to sign the authorization. At 7:35 p.m. on the evening of March 10, the White House dispatched minions to Ashcroft's hospital bedside in an attempt to get his signature on the document. Ashcroft refused. Following a dramatic meeting at the White House, Comey then sent the president a letter stating his objections formally.

In a chilly reply, White House Counsel Alberto Gonzalez wrote to say the president was going ahead on his own say-so. At which point Comey, FBI Director Robert Mueller, and other top DOJ officials prepared to resign in protest. The crisis was avoided only when the president agreed to two modifications to the existing programs six days later.[45]

This is the sort of constitutional crisis that occurs when officials push their lawful authority well past any plausible bounds. The president never was on a sound constitutional footing in launching Stellar Wind. And when the executive branch finally accepted that, and decided to come to the FISA judges to ask permission, they never should have granted it. None of it ever was remotely consistent with the FISA law itself, not to speak of the Constitution—which requires warrants before Americans' data is searched.

The Executive Branch Lacked Power to Go It Alone

The highly irregular way this massive surveillance was implemented in the immediate aftermath of 9/11 should have signaled to all concerned that things were awry. Only one lawyer at the Office of Legal Counsel was read into the program: an academic on temporary assignment named John Yoo. Even Yoo's boss, Jay Bybee, the head of OLC, was kept in the dark. The NSA's legal counsel also was not consulted. The authorization for Stellar Wind was kept secreted away, in Hayden's safe. In a scathing report years later, the NSA's Inspector General deemed it "strange that NSA was told to execute a secret program that everyone knew presented legal questions, without being told the underpinning legal theory."[46]

This secret and irregular authorization process was a power grab. Since 1947, the National Security Act had mandated Congress be kept "fully informed" of intelligence activity. At the least, the president should have briefed the Gang of Eight—the top congressional leaders on intelligence matters—at the outset. But Vice President Dick Cheney didn't like the idea that the executive branch should have to ask for permission. He not only wanted more surveillance, he was seeking to establish a precedent regarding presidential power.[47]

When Jack Goldsmith replaced Bybee as head of OLC on October 6, 2003, and read Yoo's legal opinions justifying Stellar Wind, he balked at the errors of legal analysis. Yoo later became notorious for his "torture memos," which justified the aggressive treatment of prisoners in CIA hands, and Yoo's memos on the President's Surveillance Program were no better. For example, Yoo advised that absent a "clear statement" from Congress that the executive could not move ahead in an emergency situation without warrants, the NSA was good to go. The problem, as Goldsmith instantly recognized, was that Congress *had* made a perfectly clear statement. FISA contained an explicit fifteen-day emergency exception, the clear inference being that if the executive wanted to wiretap Americans for a longer period, it needed a warrant from the FISA court.[48]

Goldsmith fixed Yoo's errors, but ultimately he, too, concluded that the executive branch was on firm legal ground in capturing the communications of Americans without a warrant. In times of war, Goldsmith reasoned, presidents have always exercised the power to intercept communications, even of Americans. Goldsmith also had a backup argument that Congress had authorized the executive branch's conduct in its post–September 11 Authorization for Use of Military Force.[49]

The difficulty with Goldsmith's arguments is that in FISA Congress had said as plainly as one could that there was to be no gathering of any American's communications without a warrant. That clarity mattered hugely under the chief Supreme Court precedent in the area— *Youngstown Sheet & Tube Co. v. Sawyer. Youngstown* involved Harry Truman's decision to seize the U.S. steel mills during the Korean War, when a union dispute threatened to shut them down. Truman argued that his seizure of the property of U.S. citizens was entirely legitimate, emphasizing his role as commander in chief, and the need for uninterrupted steel production to support the war effort. Justice Robert Jackson's famous opinion in *Youngstown* set out a three-part test for analyzing claims of executive power. If Congress had approved what the president did, the executive was at its greatest power—most likely the executive's actions were lawful. If Congress was silent, there was a complicated gray area. But if Congress had said no to the executive—as the Supreme Court concluded in *Youngstown* that Congress had, invalidating Truman's actions—then the executive's power was at its "lowest ebb." In the face of an explicit congressional no, it required an extraordinary determination of presidential power to conclude that no matter what, the president could go it alone.[50]

Just think about it for a minute. How plausible is it that—as a constitutional matter—the executive branch could proceed to collect the communications and other private information on hundreds of millions of Americans, in secret, after Congress had explicitly prohibited it? At the very, very least, it was beyond the extraordinary, and deeply ill advised.

Confirmation of this comes from none other than Jack Goldsmith. In October 2007, some three years after he left government service, Goldsmith was asked to testify before the Senate Judiciary Committee on the subject of "Preserving the Rule of Law in the Fight Against Terrorism." Goldsmith is a bright, talented, and dedicated man who rightly saw his job as supporting the president's goals to the extent remotely plausible, while still refusing to wander beyond the pale as Yoo had. But in his congressional testimony he was direct in criticizing the Bush administration as "excessively secretive." The ill effects of this secrecy were "exacerbated by the fact that the people inside the small circle of lawyers working on these issues shared remarkably like-minded and sometimes unusual views about the law. Close-looped decision-making by like-minded lawyers resulted in legal and political errors."[51]

What the president should have done, Goldsmith concluded, was ask Congress for explicit approval. Goldsmith acknowledged that "[f]orcing Congress to assume joint responsibility for counterterrorism policy weakens presidential prerogatives to act unilaterally." But there are higher and more long-term goals. "When the Executive branch forces Congress to deliberate, argue, and take a stand, it spreads accountability." That is exactly right.[52]

The FISA Court Should Never Have Approved Stellar Wind

The DOJ, at Goldsmith's urging, ultimately persuaded the president to seek FISA court approval. But the statutes that the administration now claimed gave it authority just didn't. The FISA judges should have sent the executive packing to Congress for approval, just as Goldsmith himself later suggested. Instead, they gave a judicial thumbs-up to the President's Surveillance Programs.[53]

The FISA judges were well aware they were being asked to allow something unprecedented. In 2004, for example, the court was asked to authorize the Stellar Wind program under FISA, forcing telecommunications and Internet companies to turn over vast amounts of information on targets. It described its order as one of "first impression," "resulting in the collection of metadata from an enormous volume of communications, the large majority of which will be unrelated to international terrorism."[54]

Still, the judges went ahead, although it was perfectly apparent that they were being asked to squeeze a large square peg into a much smaller round hole. For example, surveillance orders are supposed to specify "the identity, if known, of the person" to whose line the surveillance device is to be attached. But the administration was, as we all now know, not specifying any person whatsoever: it was collecting data on everyone. The gap between FISA's text and the executive's request was so wide that the court should then and there have required the executive to go to Congress. Instead, the FISA court simply waved the problem away, saying (remarkably) "there is no requirement to state the identity of such a person if it is not 'known.'"[55]

Most extraordinarily, the FISA court signed off on the NSA collecting all our phone metadata—without writing any legal opinion at all. That is just not done. It is a fundamental canon of judging that consequential decisions are accompanied by a written legal justification, one that is subject to critique and appeal. The fact that the FISA judges did not write the requisite opinion serves to underscore the difficulty they must have understood they had in justifying the program under existing law.[56]

When the FISA court finally felt forced to explain its approval in writing—*after* Snowden's disclosures—its opinion was threadbare, to say the least. Section 215 of FISA requires the government to show that the information being requested is "relevant" to an ongoing international terrorism investigation. How was the phone information of every American "relevant" to such an investigation? The court simply bought the government's argument that "[a]nalysts know that the terrorists' communications are located somewhere in the metadata," they just don't know where right now. So looking everywhere was apparently okay under the statute. As Congressman James Sensenbrenner, the author of the Patriot Act, points out, "The government may need the haystack to find the needle, but gathering the haystack without knowledge that it contains the needle is precisely what the relevance standard and Section 215 are supposed to prevent."[57]

Once caught in the act, the FISA court became defensive, blaming

Congress for the public brouhaha. It defended approving bulk collection by saying that even if the words of FISA don't bear the desired meaning, Congress reauthorized FISA in 2011 knowing full well what had been going on, so if anyone was at fault it was Congress. In support of this claim the court pointed to a briefing document that members of Congress got about the bulk telephone collection. It (and another, later, federal court opinion) basically called out members of Congress who claimed they did not know what was happening as incompetents, liars, or both. That was hardly fair: members of Congress were only allowed to look at the briefing document in a special secure space, with no staff to help them understand what was going on. Nothing like this has ever remotely counted in law as congressional authorization, nor should it. Congress can't strip our rights in secret.[58]

Why the judges acted as they did is difficult to fathom. Perhaps it was because they—being in no position to question the executive branch's claims of necessity—thought it better to try to bring the program within their notion of what was proper procedure, rather than letting it continue without any supervision.

In any event, it was simply wrong. When the FISA court finally had to justify its long negligence, it passed the buck: "[W]hether and to what extent the government seeks to continue the program . . . is a matter for the political branches to decide." That is what the court should have said when it was *first* asked to approve such extraordinary measures, not years later. Rather than approving an extraordinary program that defied existing law, it should have sent the administration immediately to Congress, thus forcing the very democratic deliberation the Constitution requires.[59]

Is the FISA Court a Court?

The FISA court had a far more profound reason to be defensive: It is a not a real law court, and thus should not be making legal determinations of such a serious magnitude anyway.

Law courts act in public. Under our justly famous adversarial system, judges hear all sides of an argument, not just the government's. They decide in written opinions that are open to public scrutiny and debate. Any affected party can appeal initial decisions. All these proceedings are open to public scrutiny.

None of this is true of the FISC, which was designed to act in secret.

As the FISA court was originally conceived, secrecy was just fine. The FISA court's imagined role was to act as a magistrate, granting warrant requests for searches of specific targets based on individualized suspicion. Magistrates typically consider particularized warrant requests in secret, hearing only from the government.[60]

But when it comes to deciding legal questions of great constitutional moment, the FISA judges—lacking all the accoutrements of a real court—were in over their head. The benefit of our public, adversarial system is that judges hear both sides of a tough question, and know their resultant opinion will have to stand up under public scrutiny.

The Fourth Amendment Failings of the FISA Opinions

The result of the FISA court's one-sided secret proceedings was a series of inadequate legal opinions, nowhere more so than regarding the constitutionality of the President's Surveillance Program under the Fourth Amendment.

Take the issue of bulk telephone data collection. The FISA court said the question was controlled by the Supreme Court's 1979 decision in *Smith v. Maryland*. That was the case involving the telephone stalker, critiqued in Chapter 10, in which the justices held that collecting the phone numbers dialed by one person (who there was cause to believe had committed the offense) was not a "search" within the meaning of the Fourth Amendment. It would seem perfectly obvious even to the greenest law student that there is a bit of distance between what got approved in *Smith*, and collecting the data of an entire nation. Yet all the FISA court could say was, "Whether a large number of persons are otherwise affected by the government's conduct is irrelevant."[61]

Courts that have handled this issue since, in public, with full briefing by both sides, have acknowledged that the question is considerably more difficult than the FISA court believed. The data from the *Smith* pen register was collected for a short time, and not retained; the bulk collection data is collected nonstop and retained for years. At the time of *Smith*, the information was collected from an independent third party, the phone company, while today the communications companies are so clearly in cahoots with the government that it is little different from the government simply gathering the data itself. The information collected under PSP was different than *Smith*: it included not just the number dialed, but also whether the call was completed, the call's duration, and the "trunk identifier" that can be used for location tracking. Since *Smith*, the Supreme Court itself has pointed to the perils of data collection that allows long-term location tracking. None of this, apparently, even occurred to the FISA court as worthy of discussion.[62]

Even more difficult to get one's head around—if that were possible—was the FISC Court of Review's decision that the executive branch could engage in surveillance of Americans, without warrants, so long as the purpose was foreign intelligence gathering. The case, *In re Directives*, arose when Yahoo balked at turning over data under a 2007 stopgap measure that allowed warrantless spying on Americans so long as they were "reasonably believed to be located outside the United States." Yahoo argued that allowing the executive branch to search on its own say-so invited "abuse." The Court of Review brushed aside Yahoo's argument, saying it is "little more than a lament about the risk that government officials will not operate in good faith." But isn't the whole point of the Constitution to trust in law rather than the good faith of government employees? As the Supreme Court in *Keith* pointed out—and it is awfully hard to square the Yahoo decision with *Keith*—"The Fourth Amendment contemplates a prior judicial judgment, not the risk that executive discretion may be reasonably exercised." Stated more plainly: Don't just trust in the good faith of the executive branch—get a warrant.[63]

UNCERTAIN EFFICACY

What the executive branch and the FISA court should have done was force Congress to decide in the first instance whether the sort of widespread surveillance of PSP was appropriate. When authorization is not sought, there is insufficient debate about the plusses and minuses, or the costs and benefits, of what government agencies wish to do. Bad decisions get made.

There are serious questions as to whether the government's bulk collection efforts—which occurred at breathtaking expense—make any sense. As the Privacy and Civil Liberties Oversight Board explained, in its skeptical review of the 215 bulk collection program, "[C]ounterterrorism resources are not unlimited, and if a program is not working those resources should be directed to other programs that are more effective in protecting us from terrorists."[64]

In the aftermath of the Snowden revelations, officials—including President Obama, General Keith Alexander, the NSA Director, and Representative Mike Rogers, the chair of the House Intelligence Committee—all claimed that bulk data collection had prevented some fifty terrorist incidents. The one federal judge outside the FISA court who upheld the bulk collection under the 215 program detailed three specific cases, including a plot to bomb New York's subways and another to attack the New York Stock Exchange.[65]

Under the cold eye of critical examination, however, the number of thwarted incidents dwindled pretty much to zero. The Privacy and Civil Liberties Oversight Board could find no instance of any threat where telephony data made a difference. The Privacy Review Board appointed by the president to review the PSP concluded the same. A joint report by the Inspectors General of the NSA, Department of Defense, CIA, Office of the Director of National Intelligence, and the DOJ determined that "most PSP leads were determined not to have any connection to terrorism." Even Matt Olsen, the lawyer at the DOJ who smoothed the path for FISC approval of bulk collection, conceded that it is really "a bit of an insurance policy . . . it's a way to do what we otherwise could do, but do it a little bit more quickly."[66]

The difficulty is that we are gathering vast amounts of information simply because we can. Technology has always been a driver of intelligence. In the 1960s, for example, advances in flight led to the U-2 spy plane and a greater emphasis on aerial surveillance. Similar advances in data collection, storage, and mining led to the PSP.[67]

When the 9/11 Commission member Richard Shelby called out the spy agencies for failing to connect the dots before the disaster, something serious was lost in translation. The first word in "connecting the dots" is connecting, not collecting. In his exhaustive and engrossing study of intelligence gathering post-9/11, Shane Harris concluded: "[T]he Watchers have become very good at collecting the dots and not very good at *connecting* them." Intelligence professionals and scholars worry we are drowning in a sea of data. Their oft-expressed concerns are about analytic capabilities, not data collection. Even an NSA internal report expressed concern that gathering location data was "outpacing our ability to ingest, process, and store that data." Today's mantra, "drowning in data, [yet] starving for wisdom," is as true in intelligence as elsewhere.[68]

There is, furthermore, good reason to be skeptical that the government's entire endeavor of predictive data mining can ever be successful. Jeff Jonas is a data engineer who has had great success with commercial data mining, and who worked for a time with Poindexter on TIA. Subsequently, he and his coauthor Jim Harper wrote a scathing denunciation of what was being done. For predictive data mining to work—as it does in fighting credit card fraud or targeting consumers—one needs a good model of what one is looking for. Yet terrorist plots come in so many varieties that it is ultimately impossible to find them in all the noise, quite unlike the submarines Poindexter hunted long ago. "[D]esign of a search algorithm based on anomaly is no more likely to turn up terrorists than twisting the end of a kaleidoscope is likely to draw an image of the Mona Lisa." Thus, they conclude, "pursuing this use of data mining wastes taxpayer dollars, needlessly infringes on privacy and civil liberties, and misdirects the valuable time and energy of the men and women in the national security community."[69]

WHAT'S CONSTITUTIONAL?

Whether efficacious or not, the American people are entitled to have the programs they want, so long as they are constitutional. That's what democracy is all about. What is notable here, however, is that when portions of the PSP *have* been debated publicly, judgments about what is constitutional and what is efficacious have altered. As we have seen time and again, policy changes when the public participates.

After intense national debate, in 2015 Congress adopted the USA Freedom Act. (Correcting, it should be noted, some of the abuses that occurred under the USA Patriot Act. There may be a message there.) Under the Freedom Act, the government is no longer permitted to collect and hold our information in bulk. Rather, that data rests with the telecom companies. More important, in order to access it the government now must have a court order, founded on reasonable suspicion.

These measures, readily approved after public debate, are all that the Constitution may require. Suspicionless *collection* of data is just fine so long as it is authorized by law, and the data of all of us is collected, in a nondiscriminatory manner. This was the lesson of Chapter 7, about suspicionless searches.

As for *searching* the data in government hands, that is fine too—so long as there is a warrant supported by cause whenever an American's data is being searched. That is the bedrock constitutional requirement, widely violated in the aftermath of 9/11. Voices on the left and right now agree that when the government searches United States persons, warrants should be required. The Privacy and Civil Liberties Oversight Board and the Privacy Review Board expressed this view in the strongest of terms.[70]

In other words, the government could have had much of what it wanted after 9/11 if it had only asked for prior approval. And it's not apparent why a congressional debate over those requests could not have been had publicly. With programs as general as these, it is difficult to know how public debate would have informed the terrorists of much of anything—except that they had better beware because the NSA has enormous capabilities, and has wide permission from the American people to exercise them. Indeed, it is a hallmark of deterrent programs that their existence is made public to put the bad guys on notice not to even try. Yes, there will be operational details we may not know—but we do not need to know so long as approval is sought and granted in general terms.

In sharp contrast to the national mood after 9/11, when the American people were—rightly or wrongly—prepared to give the government virtually all the tools it wanted, that is no longer the case. Today, pleas of necessity and good faith from the executive branch are met with skepticism, and moving legislation through Congress has proved extremely difficult. The cost of going it alone, it seems, has been a loss of the trust needed to govern, not of intelligence-gathering capability. And for that, we are all the poorer.

CONCLUSION:
THE CHALLENGES OF
DEMOCRATIC POLICING

As must be clear by now, achieving democratic and constitutional policing is not going to be easy. Moving policing to a democratic footing means fundamental change. That sort of change comes neither quickly nor easily. Still, there are promising signs from around the country that some policing agencies are endeavoring to engage with their communities over matters of policing policy and practice—and by doing so enhancing the legitimacy of, and public trust in, policing.

But here's the challenge: even as we move toward democratic engagement around policing, we still have to pause and reassure ourselves that is the correct path. Because democracy itself is fraught with dysfunction. Democratic governance has bequeathed us a destructive war on drugs. Democratic institutions tend to act precipitously under pressure—which has been all too evident at times in the fight against terrorism. And, importantly, majority rule does not always bode well for the treatment of minorities, racial, religious, or otherwise. The majority tends to want lower crime rates, and doesn't care who is inconvenienced—or worse—to get them.

The failings of democracy are so substantial that some might be skeptical of democratic policing altogether. In the end, though, what better option do we have, really? We have to move forward fully aware of democratic policing's challenges, as well as its benefits. That's what this concluding chapter is about.

Here's one last story, to bring us home. This one ended well. Still it, and its ironic aftermath, underscore both the possibilities and the cautions of democratic policing, within a framework of constitutional law.

WHO WILL WATCH THE WATCHERS?

At 7:00 a.m. on April 8, 2010, Anthony Graber—a twenty-five-year-old systems network engineer and reservist in the Air National Guard—was asleep in his parents' house in Abingdon, Maryland. He was recovering from two recent surgeries. His father, a twenty-six-year veteran of the Air Force, was already at work; his mom was up and getting ready to leave the house herself.[1]

Just then, the Maryland State Patrol came knocking, some five officers strong. They waved an unsigned copy of a warrant and proceeded to search the house for ninety minutes, going through closets and drawers. Before departing, they seized all the electronics from Graber's room, including a video recorder, four computers, and an external hard drive. They were supposed to have arrested Graber as well, but in light of his medical condition he was allowed to turn himself in a week later, at which time he spent a night in a Baltimore jail cell before posting the $15,000 bail that was set to assure his appearance.[2]

What crime had he committed that justified all of this? Graber, who never before had any brush with the law, had dared to record the police giving him a traffic ticket, and had posted the recording on YouTube. A month earlier Graber had been riding his motorcycle, testing out his new helmet-mounted video recorder. He had also been speeding—*really* speeding. As he exited the highway, a car cut him off and the driver jumped out, hollering at Graber and waving a pistol. It turns out the fellow brandishing the pistol was an off-duty member of the Maryland State Patrol, although the video shows a good five seconds of yelling and pistol-waving before the officer identifies himself as such. Graber was issued a speeding ticket and released. That would have been the end of it, but Graber's mother urged him to file a complaint. Graber, who is mild-mannered and quiet by nature, did not want to rock the boat. So he simply posted the video on YouTube with the caption "Motorcycle traffic violation—cop pulls out gun." (Note how factually accurate that is; Graber even concedes his own guilt.)[3]

A couple of weeks later the officer and other Maryland state troopers viewed the video—which someone unrelated to Graber had reposted, along with incendiary comments about the police—and launched a full-blown investigation. The result was that Graber was indicted by a grand jury on seven counts of violating Maryland law, including "unlawful interception of an oral communication" and possessing a device "primarily useful for the purpose of the surreptitious interception of oral communications." He faced up to sixteen years in prison.[4]

When it comes to being punished for recording the police, Graber's case is hardly an anomaly. Simon Glik, a lawyer with a Russian immigrant-makes-good story, was busted for video recording on his phone a police arrest he thought had gotten out of control. Kahliah Fitchette, a model student and junior class president at a Newark school, was hauled off a bus, handcuffed, had her cell phone erased, and was taken to an adult detention facility after she recorded police dealing with an apparently unwell bus passenger. In 2014, Karen Dziewit was arrested in Chicopee, Massachusetts, for drunk and disorderly, then charged with wiretapping for turning her smartphone on during the arrest.[5]

There have been so many prosecutions for recording the police that the United States Department of Justice ultimately felt compelled to weigh in. It filed a brief in 2013, in yet another Maryland case, *Garcia v. Montgomery County*. Garcia, a journalist, was placed in a chokehold, thrown to the ground, arrested, and had his camera confiscated—all for recording a public arrest he felt involved excessive force and other improprieties. In its brief, the DOJ argued that arrests and charges like these violate the First and Fourth Amendments. Their occurrence, the DOJ told the court, "erodes public confidence in our police departments, decreases accountability of our governmental officers, and conflicts with the liberties that the Constitution was designed to uphold."[6]

The good news is that Graber's story had exactly the ending it should. A Maryland judge, Emory A. Plitt, Jr., in a thoughtful opinion, dismissed all charges relating to the videotaping. He concluded that a public encounter involving the police could hardly be a private conversation subject to any of Maryland's prohibitions against surreptitious recording. "Those of us who are public officials and entrusted with the power of the state are ultimately accountable to the public . . . we should not expect our actions to be shielded from public observation." If people cannot observe and record the police, the judge asked, closing with the famous Latin phrase *Qui custodiet ipsos custodes* ("Who will watch the watchmen?").[7]

Despite the appropriate ending, Graber's story is ripe with instructive irony.

OF FORCE, AND SURVEILLANCE, AND POLICING OLD AND NEW

The first ironic thing about Graber's story is the strong position taken by the United States Department of Justice regarding the propriety of recording the police. The DOJ's brief in the *Garcia* case explained that the First Amendment both protects "the right to gather information critical of public officials" and "also prohibits government officials from 'punish[ing] the dissemination of information relating to alleged government misconduct.'" Uncovering such misconduct, the DOJ proclaimed, "has traditionally been recognized as lying at the core of the First Amendment."[8]

The DOJ's position favoring law enforcement transparency is a laudatory one; regrettably, it is not the stance the DOJ always maintains when federal officials are the ones the citizenry would hold accountable. The DOJ's filing in the *Garcia* case occurred just three months before Edward Snowden's first revelations of widespread secret government surveillance, which the DOJ itself had worked hard to keep under wraps. Similarly, one cannot help but recall the DOJ's cover-up of law enforcement use of Stingrays, or the Department's persistent opposition to disclosures about the use of National Security Letters and other tools in the war on terror.[9]

There are differences one can point to between what happened to Graber and these other examples, of course. As the DOJ said in its filing in the *Garcia* case, photographing "officers engaged in their duties on a public street" is the "archetype of a traditional public forum" where the First Amendment holds most sway. These other examples all involved government activity secreted from public view, not policing on public streets.[10]

However, this seeming distinction between street and secret policing only serves to underscore the challenge we face regulating policing in the future. The police use of force that citizens are filming on the streets, and the surveillance at issue with Stingrays and bulk data collection, are not really different things. They both are means of controlling the citizenry, of making them behave as the government wishes. That was the point of Orwell's *1984*.

As technology advances, we can expect the role of surveillance to increase, while the use of force may well diminish as a result. Policing is, as we have seen time and again, transforming before our very eyes. It continues to move from a model that requires force to forestall and apprehend the bad guys, to one in which widespread surveillance is used to detect and prevent bad acts before they occur. The government, in ways it deems entirely benevolent, is keeping tabs on all of us. It is looking for—as predictive policing would put it—signs of "abnormal" behavior. The hope and expectation is that all this monitoring will deter crime from happening, or allow the government to shut it down quickly before it does.[11]

As more and more policing takes the form of secret monitoring, it becomes increasingly difficult for the citizenry to monitor the government itself. When force is used, it often happens out in the open. (Not always, as the victims of aggressive interrogation can attest.) Surveillance, on the other hand, typically is designed and put into place behind closed doors. The debate about whether Edward Snowden is a hero or a villain is not because anyone countenances the theft and disclosure of government secrets as a general matter: that sort of conduct puts us all at risk. It is because in a world in which policing moves behind closed doors and happens surreptitiously, these sorts of leaks may be the only clue we get about what the government is doing. And we cannot govern without knowing.

Policing involves the use of force *and* surveillance. Transparency is necessary for both these activities, distinct in some ways though they may be. The use of surveillance on Americans is every bit as much a matter of public concern as the use of force. Democratic policing requires that the use of both tactics be debated, authorized, and monitored by the body politic. And that goes for the federal government as well.

RECORDING OF THE POLICE IS NOT GOVERNANCE

The second irony can hardly escape anyone's notice: in sharp contrast to what happened to Anthony Graber, cameras now seem to be the favored solution—including by many police officials themselves—for all the woes of street policing. Less than eighteen months after the DOJ filed its brief in the *Garcia* case defending the filming of the police, Michael Brown was killed in Ferguson, the militarized response to street protests began, and police use of force became a major and enduring media topic. To hear politicians tell it, the primary antidote to what is wrong with policing, and the best way for the police to regain trust, is body-worn cameras (BWCs).[12]

On the one hand, it's great, this sudden interest in transparency. Early studies suggest the cameras result in less use of force, better police conduct, and perhaps even fewer arrests.[13] When police officers in Rialto, California, were outfitted with body cameras, use of force by officers wearing cameras fell by almost 60 percent and complaints against officers plummeted by 87 percent compared with the year before. Mesa, Arizona, and San Diego reported similar dramatic reductions in citizen complaints and use of force. Whether these results will hold up under closer scrutiny is anyone's guess, but social science research does suggest that when people know they are being recorded, they often respond by altering their conduct. (Of course, this fact can cut both ways if it deters police from taking actions they otherwise should—which some people claim is the case, though there at present is insufficient data to back up the claim.)[14]

Still, before going gaga over the latest technological answer, it's important to pause and consider two things.

First, body-worn cameras are going to help with only a small percentage of perceived police misconduct. They're not going to do a thing to solve the problems of transparency present when police operate behind closed doors. And unless cameras are on all the time—more on this in a moment—there is still plenty of policing we won't catch on video.

More important, BWCs are *not* a substitute for democratic policing. Rather, they are a Band-Aid, yet one more after-the-fact substitute for regulating policing properly on the front end. Yes, the idea is that having the video available for after-the-fact review will cause the police to act better on the front end. That is precisely the theory of most after-the-fact solutions, be they judicial review, civilian complaint boards, or Inspectors General. None of these things is the same as the people regulating policing on the front end, the way all the rest of government is regulated.

What is needed are rules and policies that are transparent, and formulated with public input. That say how things should be done. Body cameras don't establish protocols: they simply are one other means to try to keep policing within bounds as it regulates itself.

No matter what the evidence proves over the long haul, the fundamental point is still the same: cameras are cameras; they are tools of assuring compliance, not governance.

GOVERNING CAMERAS

There's even irony regarding body cameras themselves: for although they are no substitute for democratic governance, there has been more democratic debate and policy-making around BWCs than any other aspect of policing in recent memory.

From Carrboro, North Carolina (pop. 20,000), to San Francisco, California, municipal authorities have worked with police to develop the rules and regulations as to how and when cameras will be deployed. Some of the processes have been extraordinarily involved. San Francisco's chief promised a body camera trial as early as 2011; in November 2015 a retinue of involved stakeholders—police officials, police unions, civic leaders, civil liberties advocates, and public defenders—still were fighting over the content of the BWC policy.[15]

There's good reason for all this debate; body cameras have promise, but still they pose significant risks. Some civil libertarians are rightly a bit dubious: they observe that the cameras are pointed at the public, not at the police, and may become yet one more tool for monitoring *by* the police. "There's a fine line between protection and surveillance," pointed out Alderwoman Randee Haven-O'Donnell of Carrboro, discussing the value of having the police notify people they are being filmed. That's one of the reasons some police have come to embrace BWCs: like cameras mounted on patrol car dashboards, these body cams can provide a trove of evidence to support the police. Indeed, some BWC policies allow officers to watch the video before they file an incident report or make a formal statement to investigators. The LAPD's draft policy requires it. Critics rightly point out we don't allow criminal defendants this opportunity to get their story "straight" before speaking—so why would we permit it of the police?[16]

Body cameras pose serious privacy concerns, a point that often seems overlooked in the face of demands to disclose the footage. The ACLU in Southern California challenged the LAPD's body camera policy on the grounds that it made no allowance for public viewing of the footage. In Hayward, California, the ACLU sued because it was charged almost three thousand dollars by the police to obtain video of police breaking up a demonstration. Whether that amount is right or not—and in the lawsuit the department documented its costs at great length—it can't possibly be the case that all footage the police capture must simply be turned over to the media or others, without reviewing it to ensure no one's privacy is at stake. What about when police enter private homes, interview rape and domestic violence victims, talk with confidential informants, or simply unwittingly capture people going about their private lives who would prefer it to remain that way?[17]

Beyond privacy, innumerable other issues loom. When should the cameras be turned on, and when may they be turned off? Giving individual officers the discretion to activate and deactivate the cameras won't work: research suggests that when police are able to control recording, important evidence—particularly evidence unfavorable to the police—goes missing. Turning a camera on late in an incident may provide a misleading impression of what occurred. On the other hand, requiring cameras always to be on would heighten privacy concerns and raise questions about interviews with confidential informants and some crime victims.[18]

For all these reasons it is both notable and commendable that so much citizen energy has gone into developing policy around the use of BWCs. The questions are hard, the evidence uncertain, and the values at stake often in tension. These are precisely the sorts of issues with which democracy regularly has to grapple.

What's unfathomable is why the same thing is not happening, then, with a host of other policing issues equally demanding of democracy's attention. Use of force is all over the news, but we haven't seen anything close to the same degree of formal public engagement with use-of-force policies. Facial recognition—and compiling recognition with other databases—is one of the looming privacy issues of our day. But the people of Carrboro and San Francisco have not organized to develop policies on these issues. And that doesn't begin to speak to all the aspects of policing to which we are not privy, but should be.[19]

To be clear, some of these other issues occasionally are matters of general public discussion—but that is not the same as democratic decision-making. Public debate is healthy, and can have an indirect influence on policy. What distinguishes what is happening regarding body cameras is that the policy itself—the actual legal rules to govern cameras—is being made with the involvement of an engaged citizenry. The rules are written down, debated, rewritten, and only then formally adopted. *That* is what democratic governance looks like.

THE COSTS OF DEMOCRACY

Even if we are inclined to pursue the democratic governance of policing—as we must—it is still going to prove difficult. One should not be naïve about the transition.

The first challenge of democratizing policing is one of "scale." Although it seems difficult to pinpoint the number with certainty—itself a telling fact—the Department of Justice's Census of State and Local Law Enforcement Agencies in 2008 put the number of law enforcement agencies at close to eighteen thousand. The largest force is New York City's with well over thirty thousand sworn officers. By contrast, Gaines Township, Michigan (pop. 7,000), has only one. (More than two thousand other communities have a single-member police department.) What's really stunning is that roughly half the police forces in this country have fewer than ten full-time sworn officers, and three quarters in the country have fewer than twenty-five.[20]

When it comes to governance of a police department, Los Angeles is a leader. For years LAPD has had a Police Commission composed of lay citizens. Pursuant to a settlement order with the U.S. Department of Justice, the Commission was turned into a real governing body. Any significant police policy is run through it. The Commission holds weekly meetings that are open to the public, and it solicits public input through notice-and-comment rule-making. As a result, there has been widespread democratic engagement in Los Angeles around issues involving use of force and surveillance.[21]

It's simply not realistic, though, to imagine every small hamlet and community in America engaging in quite the same degree of formal rule-making as Los Angeles. So what might be the best way to achieve local community governance of the police? Truth be told we have very little in the way of models. The President's Task Force on 21st Century Policing called for a host of community involvement in police policy-making, on everything from technology to setting enforcement priorities. Where the Task Force was silent is in how this is going to happen.[22]

There are some shortcuts available. Despite the huge amount of policy-making around body cams, it is worth asking whether every single community really needs to develop a unique policy on every policing subject. Certainly it should if community members want it. But we don't all write our own recipes; most of us pull something out of a cookbook or off the Internet, then alter it to shape our own tastes and dietary needs. What's true with cooking can be true of policing policy as well. There are many instances in which state and local governments borrow one another's legislation, tailoring it if necessary to a particular community's requirements. Why not the same with the law governing policing? Organizations such as the International Association of Chiefs of Police have a large store of policing policies for consideration; the American Law Institute is now drafting its Principles of Policing, which could be put to wide use.

The one thing that is not acceptable, though, is to excuse policing from the requirement of making policy on the front end simply because it is difficult and time-consuming, or ungainly in small jurisdictions. In many of the smallest communities in America, we manage to have school boards and zoning boards and other government bodies. As well we should; these are the sorts of things that matter to residents. But surely the same is true of the security and privacy of all members of the community, which are implicated by policing policies. Park Ridge, Illinois, a suburb of Chicago with a population of fewer than forty thousand people, has more than twenty commissions and task forces, including a Civil Service Commission, Historic Preservation Commission, Liquor License Review Board, and a Library Board of Trustees. The Library Trustees announce their meetings on the library website, post board meeting agendas and information packets in advance, and welcome comments on policies and public attendance at the meetings. Its sessions are broadcast live on a government access channel and recorded for later viewing. If it is possible for this level of civic engagement around libraries, it must be equally possible for law enforcement. Rather than simply telling the police to go forth and enforce the law as they choose, it is essential that we partner with them in determining how.[23]

THE PERILS OF DEMOCRACY

The last few years have looked like a magic moment for democracy and policing. Concerns about policing, from unwelcome surveillance to militarization to the tragic use of force, have brought together many well-meaning people from across the ideological spectrum. The banner once carried mostly by the progressive left now is held aloft by conservative groups such as Right on Crime as well. Working together, they are leading a consensus that mass incarceration must be reduced, that policing must occur with greater care and attention.[24]

Still, we should not delude ourselves: many of the ills of policing today are the product of democracy itself. As we discussed in Part I, there is a constant pressure from the public to keep crime in check. When this happens, politicians and the police respond, typically by favoring more aggressive policing. And this aggressive policing is tolerated by the community in part because its costs tend to be borne by minorities, not the rest of society. So if the goal is keeping policing within constitutional and sensible bounds, it is important to acknowledge that democracy actually can exacerbate the problem.

Take the war on drugs. Many of the difficulties with policing we are grappling with today are a result of our ill-conceived notion that force and imprisonment would rid society of drugs. They have not. We have spent a king's ransom in an attempt to reduce both supply and demand; yet data suggests drug usage has not responded significantly to these efforts, and where there is demand, there is supply as well. One tremendous cost of the failed drug war has been allowing policing tactics that are deeply destructive of our liberties. That is experienced by all of us to some extent, but in reality the burden of those tactics has fallen most heavily on racial minorities. We have imprisoned far too many of our youth, waged the drug war in a deeply racist way, and torn apart entire communities that already were marginalized. We would not have tolerated all this for so long if these costs were borne equally.[25]

The potential problem with democratic governance of policing is that policing does not fall equally on all parts of society. It never has. Whether it was plantation slave patrols, or union-busting Pinkertons, or Jim Crow police forces, policing often has been the tool of the ruling class. The Director of the FBI is but one of many public officials who have pointed out that policing can be an instrument of oppression. Even when it is not, the brunt of policing tends to land on the less well off, the disadvantaged, the marginalized, and racial minorities.[26]

When policing is not evenly distributed, there is the risk that democracy can be as much a problem as a solution. The people clamor for less crime, their leaders respond, the police enforce. And we are back in the same hole we've been trying to dig our way out of.

This challenge to the appeal of democratic policing is important. It requires a serious response. There are at least three.

WHAT DEMOCRACY ENTAILS

First, it is essential to distinguish between democracy at wholesale and democracy at retail. When it comes to policing, too often democracy has been at wholesale, offering no instructions to elected officials and the police other than to "reduce crime."

What is needed, what democratic policing requires, is a retail version of democratic policing, one in which the people must debate and decide— and take responsibility for—the actual practices that will be used to keep us safe. It is always more comfortable to set broad goals, and not ask messy questions about how they will be achieved, nowhere more so than when the government is being authorized to use force on someone else. But asking hard questions and directing policy is what responsible citizenship requires. People can't just demand the police "reduce crime" and then duck the question of how. They have to stand up and be counted on the tactics, be they aggressive use of stop-and-frisk, or SWAT, or racial profiling, or drones and facial recognition and predictive policing. The people, not the police, must decide as an initial matter if these things are in or out.

As we have seen time again, particularly in Chapter 4, when the people are asked to weigh in about the specifics of policing—which is to say, the question of what is permissible and what is not—policy changes dramatically. The difference between wholesale and retail democratic policing is palpable. New York City Mayor Michael Bloomberg credited aggressive stop-and-frisk for getting guns off the streets; despite this, in 2012 polls showed a majority of New Yorkers opposed the practice.[27] Similarly, polls show enormous public discomfort with police use of drones. And the public plainly opposed the use of indiscriminate power in the hands of the NSA to collect our data.[28]

In short, we don't think policing officials should be given the discretion to employ whatever tactics they choose in order to keep us safe. We care about the costs to our communities and our privacy. It is these retail views that must be translated into law, not the general preference we all share for being safe.

Indeed, one ray of sunshine here, ironic in itself, is that the new policing tends to affect all of us more often, rather than falling quite so unequally on minority and marginalized communities. Batons may land only on some heads, but CCTV—at least if distributed throughout the city—captures everyone. So do roadblocks on major highways and bulk collection of our data. To the extent that policing affects us personally, we all will be a bit more careful about the form it takes. We will ask harder questions about the benefits and the costs. We will engage more with what policing agencies are doing.

Still, the fact of the matter is, policing will follow crime, and crime does not necessarily distribute itself evenly. There is always the risk of inequality of treatment when it comes to policing. And to the extent that risk exists, at times democratic policing may aggravate it.[29]

WHAT IS THE ALTERNATIVE TO DEMOCRACY?

This brings us to the important second point about democracy, which is to ask precisely what those who are worried about the popular aspect of democratic policing would suggest as an alternative. It can't be that those who are concerned about minority rights would prefer to leave unconstrained, discretionary power in the hands of policing officials themselves. The system of very loose democratic supervision that we've had for some hundred years has not worked out so well for minority populations.

It may be trite to recur to Winston Churchill here, but Churchill had it right. "No one pretends," he said in Britain's House of Commons in 1947, "that democracy is perfect or all-wise. Indeed it has been said that democracy is the worst form of Government except for all those other forms that have been tried from time to time."[30]

It simply cannot be that because democracy can go astray at times, we should turn matters over to relatively unaccountable policing officials to decide how our laws will be enforced. Churchill's comment was made in the course of reflecting on how some of the world had for a time trusted in all-powerful totalitarian leaders rather than democratic governance. One hopes that by now the answer to that sort of claim is clear.

At bottom, we really have no good choice but to make democracy work, warts and all. Fortunately, we as a society are making progress: when debate happens in the open, publicly, as it should, politicians find it less acceptable to turn a blind eye to practices that have a discriminatory impact. That impact becomes a matter of public concern. Democracy may only be crawling its way toward equality, but that at least is the right direction.

THE ROLE OF COURTS (AGAIN)

Still, it bears recalling that policing does not rest in the hands of popular majorities alone. We live in a *constitutional* democracy in which the courts, and the state and federal constitutions, play an essential role. The suggestion—or rather, the insistence—that popular governance be given pride of place in policing in no way diminishes the important role that courts and constitutions must play. We need to restore democratic policymaking to policing; but we also need to do our best to ensure that after-the-fact remedies like judicial review work.

It cannot be gainsaid that the judges have made an embarrassment of their assignment. Throughout this account we've seen the reasons why it is difficult for the judiciary to police the police. And yet we should not be so quick to excuse them. The fact of the matter is that judges have had one job to do—to enforce the Constitution—and they have done it badly. Putting aside disagreement over the outcomes of particular cases, it is hard to miss the fact that too many judges have tried too hard to uphold some deeply unacceptable things the police have done.[31]

Hopefully, now, it is clear that the judges have an alternative. They need not, in the name of the Constitution, either bless police tactics or rule them absolutely out of bounds. Instead, they can act as agents of democracy, in effect forcing policing officials to get democratic approval before they proceed. Judicial review can—and should—force democracy and deliberation. The very form of democratic deliberation that will occur at retail, where we all will be required to come to grips with specific policing tactics. At the least, one can hope this will eliminate most of the crazy stuff.

When push comes to shove, though, if democracy goes off the rails, it is the job of the judges to step up, and here they simply need to do better. Part II made clear the relevant protections against errant policing. The judges need to insist on warrants when obtaining warrants is possible. They need to take the probable cause standard seriously. They need to learn to tell the difference between suspicion-based and suspicion-less searches, and to make sure adequate protections are in place for each.

And above all, sensitive and intelligent judging is needed when policing's heavy hand falls on racial and other minorities. The fact is that the judiciary's performance around issues of criminal justice and race has been altogether disappointing. Like a game of Go Ask Mom, Go Ask Pop, when discrimination is raised in policing cases the courts say that the Fourth Amendment's prohibition on unreasonable searches and seizures has no role; look to the equality principles of the Equal Protection Clause. But when the Equal Protection Clause is invoked, the proof presented to the courts is almost never enough to satisfy judges—even when the discrimination would be wildly obvious to anyone else.

It's not easy being a judge in a constitutional case. Courts are asked to do something that will be unpopular: rein in the police. But that's the job. People should not put on the robe if they aren't prepared to wield the gavel.

WE ARE THE POLICE

Ultimately, we have to recognize—and take responsibility for—the fact that we are the police. What is done by the police is done by all of us.

The patron saint of policing is Sir Robert Peel. He's why, as we learned in Chapter 3, English police are called "bobbies." It was his vision that gave birth to some of our larger metropolitan forces. In 1829, Peel authored *Principles of Law Enforcement*, a set of basic guidelines that remain remarkably germane to policing today.[32]

Peel's Principle 7 sounds the note on which we ought to conclude: "*[T]he police are the public and the public are the police.*" (That is his emphasis.) He elaborated: "the police being only members of the public who are paid to give full-time attention to duties which are incumbent on every citizen, in the interests of community welfare and existence."[33]

In a world drenched in vitriol and finger-pointing it is easy to lose sight of this all-important fact. "[T]he police are the public." Which is to say, when those men and women put on their blue uniforms and walk the streets, or sit at their desks as intelligence analysts, or conduct surveillance, they still are part of our body politic. We should not forget that, but they should not forget it either. On both sides of the divide—and the divide is the point—there is too much of an "us-them" perspective that interferes with the necessary empathy and judgment policing requires in order to do the job right.

We've seen a great deal of irresponsible policing, but we've also seen a real willingness to listen, and to engage in innovation. There is a new breed of policing leadership. It was policing's leaders who in 2015 called on Congress and the state legislatures to reform the criminal and sentencing laws to stop sending so many Americans to prison unnecessarily. It was that same leadership that huddled together to get militarized weapons off the streets. To be sure, these sorts of policing leaders may be too few, and times might change. But that leadership deserves our attention and support as it tries to do the right thing.[34]

Peel's admonition is two-sided, although it is easy to lose sight of the other half as well. "[T]he public are the police." By that he meant it is essential for all of us to pay attention to what the police do. "Incumbent" is the exact word he used, meaning we have no choice. Because when the police act, they do so in our name. We are the police—each and every one of us—and we are responsible for the turns policing takes.

Policing is one of the most dangerous jobs anyone in government does. It is also the most vital. It is fair to say that without policing, the rest of government would be for naught. And yet—to end where we began—policing has the capability to undermine the values of autonomy, liberty, and security it is pledged to protect. The very reasons we have government in the first place. That is what we must work together to avoid.

EPILOGUE

As I was putting the finishing touches on this manuscript, a series of horrific events again made policing *the* front-page story in the United States. Those events, and the conversations they sparked, only serve to underscore the need for us, as a country, to rethink the relationship between policing and our broader democracy.

In the early hours of July 5, 2016, outside a convenience store in Baton Rouge, Louisiana, police officers shot and killed Alton Sterling. Sterling was a familiar face on the block, where he sold CDs to passersby. The facts as we understand them now indicate that a person who was panhandling had approached Sterling. In response to the man's persistence, Sterling brandished a gun, which led the man to call 911. What happened next is familiar because, like so much else involving policing these days, it was caught on video. The officers who responded tackled Sterling to the ground; one officer unholstered his service weapon and fired several shots into Sterling's body, killing him. Sterling's death set off impassioned protests throughout the country, especially in Baton Rouge.

The next day, in Falcon Heights, Minnesota—a suburb of St. Paul—officers stopped the car Philando Castile was driving. Dispatch recordings have the officers saying, "The two occupants just look like people that were involved in a robbery. The driver looks more like one of our suspects, just 'cause of the wide-set nose."[1] The reason officers gave

Castile for pulling him over was that he had a broken taillight. Based on facts as they currently are understood, Officer Jeronimo Yanez asked Castile for his license and registration. Castile informed the officer he was licensed to carry a weapon and had one in the car. The officer instructed Castile not to move. Castile, who at that moment had been reaching to get his license, was then shot four to five times in the arm and chest by Officer Yanez. In the car with Castile was his girlfriend, Diamond Reynolds, and Reynolds's four-year-old daughter. Reynolds live-streamed the aftermath of the shooting on Facebook, a video that riveted the nation. The governor of Minnesota, Mark Dayton, issued a statement calling what happened "unacceptable," commenting, "Would this have happened if those passengers . . . were white? I don't think it would have."[2]

Street protests intensified in the wake of the Castile shooting, and President Barack Obama made a public statement: "All Americans should be deeply troubled by the fatal shootings of Alton Sterling . . . and Philando Castile." He went on to say that the deaths "are symptomatic of the broader challenges within our criminal justice system, the racial disparities that appear across the system year after year, and the resulting lack of trust that exists between law enforcement and too many of the communities they serve."[3]

Just one evening after the Castile shooting, a street protest in Dallas, Texas, turned into the deadliest day for American law enforcement since 9/11. The protest itself was peaceful; Dallas officers posted pictures of themselves posing with Black Lives Matter protesters. It was, as the president subsequently pointed out, a fine example of American democracy in action: police protecting protesters whose very complaints were aimed at policing. Then, all of a sudden, shots rang out. Micah Johnson, an army veteran who had expressed anger about police shootings, shot and killed five officers, and wounded seven more (as well as two civilians). The police cornered Johnson and a standoff ensued; eventually, the officers used a remote-controlled robot loaded with explosives to kill him.

The Dallas shooting triggered grief and recriminations. All well-meaning people deplored what happened in Dallas, but the country appeared deeply split between those who believed officer-involved shootings of African Americans were the result of unacceptable bias that needed dramatic and immediate attention, and those who felt the country's police were doing the job we wanted, and were unacceptably under attack. The president returned from a trip abroad to deliver a moving eulogy for the officers. He also hosted long meetings at the White House between activists and law enforcement, and a nationally televised Town Hall Meeting.

As if that were not already enough, on Sunday, July 17, a Missouri man, angry about police shootings of African Americans, traveled to Baton Rouge where—again, based on emerging facts—he ambushed officers, killing three and wounding three others.

All this was happening against the backdrop of a world in which terrorism continued to rear its ugly head, provoking ongoing discussion about what law enforcement could or should do to keep us safe. A few days earlier, on July 14, a man driving a truck and firing weapons from its cab plunged into a crowd in Nice, France, during Bastille Day celebrations, killing eighty-four and injuring over three hundred other people. France already was reeling from deadly coordinated attacks by Islamic State gunmen in Paris on November 13 of the prior year. Terrorist attacks were occurring with some regularity around the globe—from Afghanistan to Germany to Turkey—including the shooting and killing of forty-nine people in a gay nightclub in Orlando, Florida, in June 2016. Although some of these attacks appeared to be perpetrated by individuals acting alone, those individuals typically pledged fidelity to the Islamic State.

Insofar as this book is concerned, these tragic events represent a bitter irony. When I sent the proposal for this book to my publisher in 2012, the selling point was that no one seemed to care about what was going on with policing, and that we all should. I was hoping to raise the salience of the issue, to play some part, no matter how small, in moving it to the national agenda. As I worked on the manuscript, however, events clearly overtook me. Edward Snowden's revelations cast a bright spotlight on the emerging tools of government surveillance. Just months later, beginning with the unrest in Ferguson, Missouri, street policing—and all the questions it raises, from racial bias to militarization—came to the fore. Barely a day seemed to go by without some policing issue landing on the front pages of the country's papers. By July 2016, policing and race were Topic A in the United States.

As a consequence, to the extent that current events were part of my story, I could not possibly guarantee readers an up-to-date manuscript. Although most of the attention of late has been on the use of force by police, developments involving technology and surveillance also occur regularly. There have been many stories about the promise and perils of predictive policing, and soon enough we will be scrutinizing other technologies, such as license plate readers and facial recognition. Encryption is hotly debated.

With all this public concern about policing, however, we continue to miss the one thing that could make a big difference: we simply do not regulate policing like the rest of government. For the most part, we still are fixated on workarounds, or simply on assigning blame, rather than on how policing is governed.

What policing needs is democracy: popular engagement followed by decision-making. We need to turn all the talk and debate into action. We need policies—transparent rules adopted with public input—to deal with use of force, with implicit racial bias, with police adoption of new technologies.

I can anticipate the objection: the problems are really difficult, and there are not obvious solutions, so we should leave matters to the experts—the police.

Yes. And no. The issues *are* really hard, and that is exactly why we should *not* just leave their resolution to the police. The police have incredibly valuable expertise, and we unequivocally must consult with them. They must be part of the conversation. But precisely because there are no clear answers, it is our obligation as citizens to take responsibility. To make choices. What we decide, and what we do, may only be provisional. That is fine; that is how we learn and improve. But it cannot possibly be the answer that, because the issues are tough, we punt. As President Obama said in Dallas, "In the end, it's not about finding policies that work; it's about forging consensus, and fighting cynicism, and finding the will to make change."

There are hopeful signs that progress is being made; that the people are adopting measures, democratically, to regulate policing. As we saw in Chapter 4, after Ferguson, many jurisdictions began to limit militarization. Some states have enacted legislation on issues like racial bias in traffic stops, or drones, or other policing technologies. The American

Law Institute is working on use of force policies that seek to limit deadly encounters with the police. Police departments—some with the help of the Policing Project I run—have begun to engage their communities on matters of policy. Camden, New Jersey, was our first on-the-ground effort. The visionary police chief there, J. Scott Thomson, decided that rather than impose a body camera policy by fiat (as is common in policing), he would take the matter to the community. We held forums, did focus groups with officers, had the community fill out questionnaires, invited interest groups to send in comments. In response, Chief Thomson altered his policy and issued a report explaining to the public how he did so, and why. It also led New York City to try something similar, an effort that garnered tens of thousands of questionnaires from ordinary citizens weighing in on the NYPD's body camera policy.

Democracy is tough. It is time-consuming. And it can be contentious.

But what, after all, is more important, more basic and fundamental, than how we are policed? How the government conducts surveillance of us, how it uses force and coercion against us?

One thing surely has changed during the writing of this book. Although I remain troubled about policing, my confidence in police officials—at least some of them—has grown steadily. I have learned a great deal, and I keep encountering many fine, well-meaning people who have devoted their lives to public service. This is not to say that every cop or police chief is a good one—cops are human like the rest of us—and it remains the case that police culture can have corrosive effects at times. The real problem, however, as I said at the outset, is not the police. It is us. Police understand—or they need to, as do all officials in government— that they work for us: they *serve*, and they protect. It is time we do a better job of engaging with our policing officials, understanding the difficulties they face, making clear our wishes, and joining with them to adopt measures that keep us safe, while also making us proud.

NOTES

INTRODUCTION: THE PROBLEMS OF POLICING

1. Charles Carter Dep. at 6, *Carter v. Maryland State Police*, No. 03-C-96-000156 (Md. Cir. Ct., Aug. 1, 1996) (on file with author); Letter from Charles Carter and Etta Carter to Alfred Bailey, ACLU (1994) (on file with author); Etta Carter Dep. at 6, 10–11, 14–26, *Carter*, No. 03-C-96-000156 (Md. Cir. Ct., Aug. 1, 1996) (on file with author).

2. Etta Carter Dep. at 6, 45, 85; Quill Dep., pt. 1, at 68, 83, 86, 114; Charles Carter Dep. at 20, 33, 41–42, 55; Carter Letter to Bailey, ACLU.

3. Carter Letter to Bailey, ACLU; Etta Carter Dep. at 90, 92–94, 98; Quill Dep., pt. 1, at 67, 95, 124–25 (naming the dog as Spider, though Quill denies knowledge of the urination incident); Charles Carter Dep. at 42, 45–46, 48.

4. Mitchell Dep. at 103; Leatherbury Dep. at 20; Carter Letter to Bailey, ACLU.

5. Charles Carter Dep, at 104–6.

6. Charles Carter Aff. at ¶ 7.

7. *Floyd v. City of New York*, 959 F. Supp. 2d 540, 555, 572, 658–67 (S.D.N.Y. 2013); Conor Friedersdorf, "Eyes Over Compton: How Police Spied on a Whole City," *The Atlantic*, Apr. 21, 2014, www.theatlantic.com/national/archive/2014/04/sheriffs-deputy -compares-drone-surveillance-of-compton-to-big-brother/360954/. Email collection supposedly terminated in 2011, though there is evidence that this is not correct, and certainly does not include countless records of Americans being collected through overseas portals. Glenn Greenwald and Spencer Ackerman, "NSA Collected US Email Records in Bulk for More Than Two Years Under Obama," *The Guardian*, June 27, 2013, www.theguardian.com/world/2013/jun/27/nsa-data-mining-authorised-obama.

8. Julie Bosman and Matt Apuzzo, "In Wake of Clashes, Calls to Demilitarize Police," *N.Y. Times*, Aug. 14, 2014, www.nytimes.com/2014/08/15/us/ferguson-missouri-in-wake -of-clashes-calls-to-demilitarize-police.html; Joseph Goldstein and Marc Santora, "Staten Island Man Died from Chokehold During Arrest, Autopsy Finds," *N.Y. Times*, Aug. 1, 2014, www.nytimes.com/2014/08/02/nyregion/staten-island-man-died-from-officers -chokehold-autopsy-finds.html; Manny Fernandez, "North Charleston Police Shooting Not Justified, Experts Say," *N.Y. Times*, Apr. 9, 2015, www.nytimes.com/2015/04/10/us

/north-charleston-police-shooting-not-justified-experts-say.html; Annie Sweeney and Jason Meisner, "A Moment-by-Moment Account of What the Laquan McDonald Video Shows," *Chi. Trib.*, Nov. 25, 2015, 6:00 a.m., www.chicagotribune.com/news/ct-chicago -cop-shooting-video-release-laquan-mcdonald-20151124-story.html; Ben Austen, "Chicago After Laquan McDonald," *N.Y. Times Mag.*, Apr. 20, 2016, www.nytimes.com /2016/04/24/magazine/chicago-after-laquan-mcdonald.html; About, Million Hoodies Movement for Justice, http://millionhoodies.net/about/; Rachel Blade, "House Hearing on Police Turns Ugly," *Politico*, May 19, 2015, www.politico.com/story/2015/05/racial -epithets-mudslinging-house-hearing-police-reform-ghetto-118108; Press Release, Office of Public Affairs, U.S. Dep't of Justice, "Justice Department Announces Findings of Two Civil Rights Investigations in Ferguson, Missouri," Mar. 4, 2015, www.justice.gov /opa/pr/justice-department-announces-findings-two-civil-rights-investigations-ferguson -missouri; *Final Report of the President's Task Force on 21st Century Policing* (2015), www .cops.usdoj.gov/pdf/taskforce/taskforce_finalreport.pdf.

9. "How Much of an Iceberg Is Below the Water," Navigation Ctr., U.S. Coast Guard, www.navcen.uscg.gov/?pageName=iipHowMuchOfAnIcebergIsBelowTheWater; James B. Comey, Dir., Fed. Bureau of Investigation, Remarks at Georgetown University, "Hard Truths: Law Enforcement and Race," Feb. 12, 2015, www.fbi.gov/news/speeches /hard-truths-law-enforcement-and-race; Matt Apuzzo and Sarah Cohen, "Data on Use of Force by Police Across U.S. Proves Almost Useless," *N.Y. Times*, Aug. 11, 2015, www .nytimes.com/2015/08/12/us/data-on-use-of-force-by-police-across-us-proves-almost -useless.html; Alan Maimon, "National Data on Shootings by Police Not Collected," *Las Vegas Rev. J.*, Nov. 28, 2011, www.reviewjournal.com/news/deadly-force/142-dead -and-rising/national-data-shootings-police-not-collected; Naomi Shavin, "Our Government Has No Idea How Often Police Get Violent with Civilians," *New Republic*, Aug. 25, 2014, www.newrepublic.com/article/119192/police-use-force-stats-us-are -incomplete-and-unreliable. In May 2015, President Barack Obama announced a Police Data Initiative to help forces like that of Camden, New Jersey, make basic policing data available. Megan Smith and Roy L. Austin, Jr., "Launching the Police Data Initiative," *The White House Blog*, May 18, 2015, 6:00 a.m., www.whitehouse.gov/blog/2015 /05/18/launching-police-data-initiative. However, the program has "run into privacy hurdles" because some departments are reluctant to share data out of officers' privacy concerns. Gregory Korte, "White House Plan for Police Data Initiative Could Face Obstacles," *USA Today*, June 22, 2015, www.usatoday.com/story/news/politics/2015/06 /21/white-house-police-data-initiative-privacy-concerns/28952215. One department, Charlotte-Mecklenburg, successfully pressured its City Council to delay a vote agreeing to the data sharing initiative. Steve Harrison, "CMPD Postpones University Officer Study," *Charlotte Observer*, June 11, 2015, www.charlotteobserver.com/news/local /article23787358.html.

10. Jennifer Valentino-Devries, "Sealed Court Files Obscure Rise in Electronic Surveillance," *Wall St. J.*, June 2, 2014, 10:33 p.m., www.wsj.com/articles/sealed-court-files -obscure-rise-in-electronic-surveillance-1401761770; Rachel A. Harmon, "The Problem of Policing," *Mich. L. Rev.* 110 (2012): 808 (disciplinary records); Samuel Walker and Carol A. Archbold, *The New World of Police Accountability*, 2nd ed. (2013), 106– 15 (early intervention systems); Sam Adler-Bell, "Beware the 'Stingray,'" *U.S. News and World Rep.*, Mar. 13, 2015, 10:45 a.m., www.usnews.com/opinion/articles/2015/03/13 /stingray-lets-police-spy-on-cellphones-and-they-want-to-keep-it-secret; Kim Zetter, "Emails Show Feds Asking Florida Cops to Deceive Judges," *Wired*, June 19, 2014, 9:04 p.m., www.wired.com/2014/06/feds-told-cops-to-deceive-courts-about-stingray; Jeb Rubenfeld, "The End of Privacy," *Stan. L. Rev.* 61 (2008): 102 (emphasis in original), quoting Press Release, White House Office of the Press Sec'y, "President Bush: Infor-

mation Sharing, Patriot Act Vital to Homeland Security, Apr. 20, 2004, https://
georgewbush-whitehouse.archives.gov/news/releases/2004/04/20040420-2.html;
James Risen and Eric Lichtblau, "Bush Lets U.S. Spy on Callers Without Courts," *N.Y.
Times*, Dec. 16, 2005, www.nytimes.com/2005/12/16/politics/bush-lets-us-spy-on
-callers-without-courts.html.

11. Oren Bar-Gill and Barry Friedman, "Taking Warrants Seriously," *Nw. U. L. Rev.* 106
(2012): 1666.

12. Brief of American Civil Liberties Union et al. as Amicus Curiae in Support of Respondents, p. 15, *Florida v. Bostick*, citing *State v. Kerwick*, 512 So.2d 347, 349 (Fla. 4th
DCA 1987).

13. *Florida v. Bostick*, 501 U.S. 429, 431 (1991); Tia Mitchell, "Drug Agents Prowl City Bus
Stations," *Florida Times-Union*, Oct. 20, 2002, http://jacksonville.com/tu-online
/stories/102002/met_10741892.shtml#.VfRpN3t4iDp; Brief of American Civil Liberties Union et al. as Amicus Curiae in Support of Respondents at 5–15, *Florida v. Bostick*, 501 U.S. 429 (No. 89-1717) ("three thousand bags" [citing *State v. Kerwick*, 512
So.2d 347, 349 (Fla. 4th DCA 1987)]);. Brief of Petitioner at 3–5, *Bostick v. State*,
554 So.2d 1153 (Fla. 1989) (No. 70996) (78,000 bus passengers); Brief of Respondents
at 3n4, *United States v. Drayton*, 536 U.S. 194 (2002) (No. 01-631).

14. See *Florida v. Bostick*, 510 U.S. at 437–39; *U.S. v. Drayton*, 536 U.S. at 200, 207–208;
Ohio v. Robinette, 519 U.S. 33, 46–48 (1996) (Stevens, J., dissenting) ("Repeated decisions by ordinary citizens to surrender that interest cannot satisfactorily be explained
on any hypothesis other than an assumption that they believed they had a legal duty to
do so.") [citations omitted]); Los Angeles Police Department, Arrest, Discipline,
Use of Force, Field Data Capture and Audit Statistics and the City Status Report
Covering Period of January 1, 2006–June 30, 2006, at 8, 10 (2006), http://assets
.lapdonline.org/assets/pdf/consent_decree_rpt_jan_jun_2006.pdf (reporting that
36,583 out of 36,612 pedestrians granted consent to search). Accord Michelle Alexander, *The New Jim Crow: Mass Incarceration in the Age of Colorblindness* (2012),
63–86 (discussing law enforcement use of consent searches, and their close cousin,
pretext searches).

15. Brief of Respondents, at 3n4, *Drayton*, 536 U.S. 194; Charles Carter Dep. at 22–24.

16. Kimberly Kindy and Kennedy Elliott, "2015 Police Shootings Investigation," *Wash.
Post*, Dec. 26, 2015, www.washingtonpost.com/graphics/national/police-shootings
-year-end/; Officer Involved Shootings, City of Houston Police Department, http://
houstontx.gov/police/ois/index.htm; 2015 HPD Officer Involved Shootings, Homicide
Division, www.houstontx.gov/police/ois/2015.htm; 2014 HPD Officer Involved Shoot-
ings, Homicide Division, www.houstontx.gov/police/ois/2014.htm; 2013 HPD Officer
Involved Shootings, Homicide Division, www.houstontx.gov/police/ois/2013.htm; Sebastian Murdock, "Officer Juventino Castro Will Walk Free After Killing Unarmed
Man Jordan Baker," *Huffington Post*, Dec. 23, 2014, updated Dec. 24, 2014, 1:59 a.m.,
www.huffingtonpost.com/2014/12/23/jordan-baker-no-indictment_n_6373988.html;
James Pinkerton, "No Charges Against HPD Officer Who Killed Double Amputee in a
Wheelchair," *Houston Chron.*, June 13, 2013, www.chron.com/news/houston-texas
/houston/article/No-charges-against-HPD-officer-who-killed-double-4598518.php.

17. Larry Gordon, "Court Allows Release of Officers' Names in UC Davis Pepper-Spray
Case," *L.A. Times*, Aug. 21, 2014, 7:55 p.m., www.latimes.com/local/education/la-me
-ln-uc-pepper-spray-20140821-story.html; Dana Goldstein, "In Your Face," *The Marshall Project*, Jan. 26, 2015, 7:55 a.m., www.themarshallproject.org/2015/01/26/in-your
-face; "Stricter Limits Urged as Deaths Following Police Taser Use Reach 500," *Amnesty Int'l*, Nov. 19, 2014, www.amnesty.org/en/news/usa-stricter-limits-urged-deaths
-following-police-taser-use-reach-500-2012-02-15; Taser, *Advanced Taser M26C Op-*

erating Manual, www.taser.com/images/support/downloads/downloads/m26c_manual
.pdf; Adam Liptak, "A Ticket, 3 Taser Jolts and, Perhaps, a Trip to the Supreme Court,"
N.Y. Times, May 14, 2012, www.nytimes.com/2012/05/15/us/police-taser-use-on-pregnant
-woman-goes-before-supreme-court.html (pregnant woman); ACLU of Nebraska,
Dangerously Out of Bounds: Taser Use in Nebraska (2014), 14 (disabled person); Rhonda
Cook, "East Point Family to Sue City, Police in Taser Death," *Atl. J. Const.*, Aug. 7,
2014, www.ajc.com/news/news/lawsuit-to-be-filed-in-death-of-man-east-point-pol
/ngxgc (person in water); Mark Morgenstein, "Using a Taser on an 8-year-old? Mom
Sues Police, City," *CNN*, Aug. 9, 2014, www.cnn.com/2014/08/09/us/south-dakota-taser
-lawsuit; Sarah Solon and Heather Smith, "What Could Justify Using a Taser on an
8-Year-Old Girl?," ACLU, Oct. 11, 2013, 12:34 p.m., www.aclu.org/blog/what-could
-justify-using-taser-8-year-old-girl.

18. Radley Balko, "Shedding Light on the Use of SWAT Teams," *Wash. Post*, Feb. 17, 2014,
www.washingtonpost.com/news/the-watch/wp/2014/02/17/shedding-light-on-the-use
-of-swat-teams; Alex Horton, Opinion, "In Iraq, I Raided Insurgents. In Virginia, the
Police Raided Me," *Wash. Post*, July 24, 2015, www.washingtonpost.com/opinions/in
-iraq-i-raided-insurgents-in-virginia-the-police-raided-me/2015/07/24/2e114e54-2b02
-11e5-bd33-395c05608059_story.html; Eliott C. McLaughlin, "No Indictments for
Georgia SWAT Team That Burned Baby with Stun Grenade," *CNN*, Oct. 7, 2014,
www.cnn.com/2014/10/07/us/georgia-toddler-stun-grenade-no-indictment; Liz Fields,
"Toddler Maimed by SWAT Flash Grenade Sparks Georgia Bills on 'No-Knock'
Warrants," *Vice*, Jan. 23, 2015, https://news.vice.com/article/toddler-maimed-by-swat
-flash-grenade-sparks-georgia-bills-on-no-knock-warrants; Alison Lynn and Matt Gut-
man, "Family of Toddler Injured by SWAT 'Grenade' Faces $1M in Medical Bills,"
ABC News, Dec. 18, 2014, http://abcnews.go.com/US/family-toddler-injured-swat
-grenade-faces-1m-medical/story?id=27671521; Renee Lewis, "Georgia Toddler in
Coma After Stun Grenade Lands in Crib During SWAT Raid," *Al Jazeera Am.*, May 30,
2014, http://america.aljazeera.com/articles/2014/5/30/georgia-toddler-swat.html ("Is it
going to make us more careful in the next one? Yes ma'am it is.").

19. Glenn Greenwald, "NSA Collecting Phone Records of Millions of Verizon Customers
Daily," *The Guardian*, June 6, 2013, www.theguardian.com/world/2013/jun/06/nsa
-phone-records-verizon-court-order; Jason Leopold, "NSA Pushed 9/11 as Key 'Sound
Bite' to Justify Surveillance," *Al Jazeera Am.*, Oct. 30, 2013, http://america.aljazeera
.com/articles/2013/10/30/revealed-nsa-pushed911askeysoundbitetojustifysurveillance
.html; Scott Shane and Colin Moynihan, "Drug Agents Use Vast Phone Trove, Eclipsing N.S.A.'s," *N.Y. Times*, Sept. 1, 2013, www.nytimes.com/2013/09/02/us/drug-agents
-use-vast-phone-trove-eclipsing-nsas.html.

20. Brief of the National Association of Criminal Defense Lawyers & the Brennan Center
for Justice at New York University School of Law as Amici Curiae in Support of Petitioner at 23, Riley v. California, 134 S. Ct. 2473 (2014) (Nos. 13–132, 13–212) ("kiosks"); "Is the Government Spying on You Through Your Computer's Webcam or
Microphone?," *WashingtonBlog*, June 24, 2013, www.washingtonsblog.com/2013/06/is
-the-government-spying-on-you-through-your-own-webcam-or-microphone.html; Kim
Zetter, "How to Keep the NSA from Spying Through Your Webcam," *Wired*, Nov. 2,
2014, www.wired.com/2014/03/webcams-mics; Jay Stanley, "Mysterious Planes over
Baltimore Spark Surveillance Suspicions," *ACLU Free Future*, May 6, 2015, www.aclu
.org/blog/free-future/mysterious-planes-over-baltimore-spark-surveillance-suspicions;
Melanie Reid, "Grounding Drones: Big Brother's Tool Box Needs Regulation Not
Elimination," *Rich. J.L. & Tech.* 20 (2014): 8–9.

21. James Bamford, "The NSA Is Building the Country's Biggest Spy Center (Watch What
You Say)," *Wired*, Mar. 15, 2012, 7:24 p.m., www.wired.com/2012/03/ff_nsadatacenter;

Michael Price, Brennan Ctr. for Justice, *National Security and Local Police* (2013), 17–20, www.brennancenter.org/sites/default/files/publications/NationalSecurity_LocalPolice _web.pdf; Information Fusion Centers and Privacy, Electronic Privacy Information Ctr., www.epic.org/privacy/fusion/#background.

22. Jon B. Gould and Stephen D. Mastrofski, "Suspect Searches: Assessing Police Behavior Under the U.S. Constitution," *Criminology & Pub. Pol'y* 3 (2004): 325, 331, 351–52.

23. Jacob Sullum, "Why Is That Cop's Finger in Your Butt?," *Reason*, May 11, 2015, https:// reason.com/archives/2015/05/11/why-is-that-cops-finger-in-your-butt; Tim Zatzariny, Jr., "Suit Against O.C. Police, Hospital Raises Issue of Forced Testing in DWI Cases," *OCNJ Daily*, May 12, 2015, http://ocnjdaily.com/suit-against-o-c-police-hospital -raises-issue-of-forced-testing-in-dwi-cases; Ben Winslow, "Man Sues Police Over 'Forced Catheterization,'" Fox 13, May 24, 2012, updated May 25, 2012, 2:33 p.m., http://fox13now.com/2012/05/24/man-sues-police-over-forced-catheterization;   Anthony Colarossi and Pedro Ruz Gutierrez, "Orlando Police Use Stun Gun on Handcuffed Man," *Orlando Sentinel*, Mar. 9, 2005, http://articles.orlandosentinel.com/2005 -03-09/news/0503090380_1_wheeler-urinate-medical-staff; "Man in Hospital Bed Tasered to Force Urine Test," *Rense.com*, Mar. 10, 2005, http://rense.com/general63 /maninhospitalbedtasered.htm.

24. Jim Dwyer, "Police Video Caught a Couple's Intimate Moment on a Manhattan Rooftop," *N.Y. Times*, Dec. 22, 2005, www.nytimes.com/2005/12/22/nyregion/police-video -caught-a-couples-intimate-moment-on-a-manhattan-rooftop.html; Sarah Stillman, "The Throwaways," *New Yorker*, Sept. 3, 2012, www.newyorker.com/magazine/2012 /09/03/the-throwaways (teenage informants); Sari Horwitz, "Justice Dept. Will Review Practice of Creating Fake Facebook Profiles," *Wash. Post*, Oct. 7, 2014, www .washingtonpost.com/world/national-security/justice-dept-will-review-practice-of -creating-fake-facebook-profiles/2014/10/07/3f9a2fe8-4e57-11e4-aa5e-7153e466a02d _story.html.

25. Civil Rights Div., U.S. Dep't of Justice, *Investigation of the Ferguson Police Department* (2015), 2, www.justice.gov/sites/default/files/opa/press-releases/attachments/2015/03 /04/ferguson_police_department_report.pdf; Eli Yokley and Mitch Smith, "Contesting Traffic Fines, Missouri Sues 13 Suburbs of St. Louis," *N.Y. Times*, Dec. 18, 2014, www .nytimes.com/2014/12/19/us/missouri-sues-13-st-louis-suburbs-over-predatory-traffic -fines.html; Lawyers' Committee for Civil Rights of the San Francisco Bay Area et al., *Not Just a Ferguson Problem: How Traffic Courts Drive Inequality in California* (2015), www.lccr.com/wp-content/uploads/Not-Just-a-Ferguson-Problem-How-Traffic-Courts -Drive-Inequality-in-California-4.20.15.pdf; Jamilah King, "Driving While Poor Is Deepening Inequality in America," *Takepart*, May 8, 2015, www.takepart.com/article/2015/05 /08/traffic-court-one-cruelest-legal-systems-america; Aimee Picchi, "In Modern-Day Debtors' Prisons, Courts Team with Private Sector," *CBS News*, Mar. 25, 2015, www .cbsnews.com/news/the-rise-of-americas-debtor-prisons; Tiffany Roberts, "Fines, Fees, and Inequality," *Creative Loafing*, June 11, 2015, http://clatl.com/atlanta/fines-fees-and -inequality/Content?oid=14489691.

26. Sarah Stillman, "Taken," *New Yorker*, Aug. 12, 2013; Shaila Dewan, "Police Use Department Wish List When Deciding Which Assets to Seize," *N.Y. Times*, Nov. 9, 2014, www.nytimes.com/2014/11/10/us/police-use-department-wish-list-when-deciding -which-assets-to-seize.html; Marian R. Williams, Jefferson E. Holcomb, Tomislav V. Kovandzic, and Scott Bullock, Inst. for Justice, *Policing for Profit: The Abuse of Civil Asset Forfeiture* (2010), 20, 22–23, www.clinic.ij.org/images/pdf_folder/other _pubs/assetforfeituretoemail.pdf (hereinafter *Policing for Profit*); Stewart M. Powell, "Asset Forfeiture Both an Effective Tool, Civil-Liberties Nightmare," *SFGate*, May 26, 2013, www.sfgate.com/news/nation-world/article/Asset-forfeiture-both-an-effective-tool

-4546043.php (noting that roughly 1 percent of property seized by the feds makes it back to its former owners); Conor Friedersdorf, "The Injustice of Civil-Asset Forfeiture," *The Atlantic*, May 12, 2015, www.theatlantic.com/politics/archive/2015/05/the-glaring-injustice-of-civil-asset-forfeiture/392999 (citing Joline Gutierrez Krueger, "DEA to Traveler: Thanks, I'll Take That Cash," *Albuquerque J.*, May 6, 2015, www.abqjournal.com/580107/news/dea-agents-seize-16000-from-aspiring-music-video-producer.html) (Michigan man). For a vivid discussion of the value of forfeiture to law enforcement and its overuse, see Alexander, supra note 14 at 71–82.

27. *Policing for Profit*, supra note 26 at 18–19; Stillman, "Taken," supra note 26; Renée C. Lee, "Montgomery DA Says Funds Used for Liquor at Cook-Off," *Houston Chron.*, Mar. 18, 2008, www.chron.com/neighborhood/humble-news/article/Montgomery-DA-says-funds-used-for-liquor-at-1757341.php.

28. ACLU of Massachusetts, *Black, Brown and Targeted: A Report on Boston Police Department Street Encounters from 2007–2010* (2014), https://aclum.org/app/uploads/2015/06/reports-black-brown-and-targeted.pdf; NAACP, *Born Suspect: Stop-and-Frisk Abuses & the Continued Fight to End Racial Profiling in America* (2014), 10–16, 24, http://action.naacp.org/page/-/Criminal%20Justice/Born_Suspect_Report_final_web.pdf; David A. Harris, *Driving While Black: Racial Profiling on Our Nation's Highways* (1999), www.aclu.org/report/driving-while-black-racial-profiling-our-nations-highways; David A. Harris, "The Stories, the Statistics, and the Law: Why 'Driving While Black' Matters," *Minn. L. Rev.* 84 (1999): 277–80; Leatherbury Dep. at 62, 75–76; Comey, "Hard Truths," supra note 9.

29. For example, Derrick A. Bell, Jr., Comment, "*Brown v. Board of Education* and the Interest-Convergence Dilemma," *Harv. L. Rev.* 93 (1980): 518. Michelle Alexander's *The New Jim Crow* provides a vivid description of the impact of the criminal justice system on racial minorities, particularly African Americans. See Alexander, supra note 14. For a poignant account of its impact on individual members of minority groups, see Ta-Nehisi Coates, *Between the World and Me* (2015). Inter alia, Coates details the death of a friend in an officer-involved shooting, and how such incidents affect one's own sense of well-being.

30. Conor Friedersdorf, "How the DEA Harasses Amtrak Passengers," *The Atlantic*, May 19, 2015, www.theatlantic.com/politics/archive/2015/05/how-the-dea-harasses-amtrak-passengers/393230; Conor Friedersdorf, "Amtrak Passengers Share More Stories of Harassment," *The Atlantic*, May 22, 2015, www.theatlantic.com/politics/archive/2015/05/amtrak-reader-letters/393710.

31. Greenwald and Ackerman, "NSA Collected US Email Records in Bulk for More Than Two Years Under Obama," supra note 7.

32. Samuel R. Gross and Katherine Y. Barnes, "Road Work: Racial Profiling and Drug Interdiction on the Highway," *Mich. L. Rev.* 101 (2002): 670–77. See also Alexander, supra note 14 at 69–70 (discussing Operation Pipeline); id. at 60 ("Few legal rules meaningfully constrain the police in the War on Drugs.")

33. Kirk Simone, Kansas Highway Patrol, *EPIC Operation Pipeline: Passenger Vehicle Drug Interdiction*, 2, 4, http://norml.org/pdf_files/brief_bank/Operation_Pipeline_Manual.pdf; Samuel R. Gross and Katherine Y. Barnes, "Road Work: Racial Profiling and Drug Interdiction on the Highway," *Mich. L. Rev.* 101 (2002): 670–77, 685 (quoting Cal. State Assembly Democratic Caucus Task Force on Gov't Oversight, *Operation Pipeline: California Joint Legislative Task Force Report* (1999), 13, https://web.archive.org/web/20010127120300/www.aclunc.org/discrimination/webb-report.html); see also *Chavez v. Illinois State Police*, 251 F.3d 612, 621–22 (7th Cir. 2001):

> Once a vehicle is stopped, he explained, [Operation] Valkyrie officers look for indicators of drug trafficking. These indicators are numerous—

indeed there is a list of twenty-eight factors in the Operation Valkyrie training manual—and include such things as too little or too much luggage for the stated length of trip, maps from drug source cities or states, and air freshener. Officers are also trained to look for verbal and non-verbal signs of stress and deception, such as nervousness and an overly friendly demeanor. [Operation Valkyrie coordinator] Snyders testified that when Valkyrie officers observe these indicators, they are trained to request consent to search the vehicle. In 1992, Valkyrie officers requested permission to search in approximately fourteen percent of motorist stops, and when requested, over ninety-eight percent of motorists granted consent.

34. Mike German and Jay Stanley, *Fusion Center Update* (2008), 1–4, 6, www.aclu.org/files/pdfs/privacy/fusion_update_20080729.pdf; Complaint for Declaratory and Injunctive Relief at paras. 101–117, *Gill v. Dep't of Justice*, No. 3:14-cv-03120-RS (KAW) (N.D. Cal. filed July 10, 2014), 2014 WL 3374708 (Boston); About the NSI, National SAR Initiative, http://nsi.ncirc.gov/about_nsi.aspx.

35. Carter Letter to Bailey, ACLU.

36. See Civil Rights Div., U.S. Dep't of Justice, *Investigation of the Ferguson Police Department*, supra note 25 (focusing in part on the problem of implicit bias in policing); Chris Mooney, "The Science of Why Cops Shoot Young Black Men," *Mother Jones*, Dec. 1, 2014, www.motherjones.com/politics/2014/11/science-of-racism-prejudice (explaining the prevalence of implicit bias in policing); Jason Zengerle, "Michael Brown's Death Was Shocking. So Are the Racial Profiling Stats We've Been Ignoring," *New Republic*, Aug. 13, 2014, www.newrepublic.com/article/119071/michael-brown-shooting-we-know-about-racial-profiling-dont-act (noting incidence of racial profiling by Ferguson police in the wake of Michael Brown shooting); Friedersdorf, "Eyes Over Compton," supra note 7; Reid, "Grounding Drones," supra note 20; Bosman and Apuzzo, "In Wake of Clashes, Calls to Demilitarize Police," supra note 8; Stillman, "Taken," supra note 26, at 3 (highlighting abuses of civil forfeiture laws).

37. Nat'l Comm'n on Terrorist Attacks Upon the U.S., *The 9/11 Commission Report*, 400, 408 (2004) (using the phrase "connect the dots" to describe intelligence failure in the run-up to 9/11).

38. Cal. Code Regs. tit. 16, §§ 900–99; id. tit. 21 §§ 2205, 2207; Fla. Admin. Code Ann. R. 20; id. R.20-13,001,-32.006.

39. Florida's law contains a few scattered provisions giving guidance regarding warrantless searches, e.g. Fla. Stat. § 901.151 (governing stop and frisk); id. § 901.21 (regarding strip searches), but many are explicit or implicit codifications of Supreme Court precedent, e.g., id. § 901.21 (regarding search of arrestees); id. § 933.19 (regarding vehicle searches). In California, Governor Jerry Brown signed into law the California Electronic Communications Privacy Act, S.B. 178, which creates a warrant requirement for digital searches. Otherwise, the state laws remain largely devoid of guidance or restraint, with few exceptions such as the constitutionally required suppression of evidence obtained unreasonably without a warrant, Cal. Penal Code § 1538.5, and a prohibition against warrantless "physical body cavity search[es]" for infraction or misdemeanor arrestees. Cal. Penal Code § 4030(h).

40. See, e.g., 18 U.S.C. § 2511 (2012); 28 U.S.C. § 533(1); Nev. Rev. Stat. Ann. § 484B.570 (West); Or. Rev. Stat. Ann. § 837.310–65; N.Y.C. Law § 435.

41. Chi. Police Dep't, Chicago Police Department Directives System, http://directives.chicagopolice.org/directives; City of Seattle, Seattle Police Department Manual, www.seattle.gov/police-manual; The Function and Role of the Board of Police Commissioners, L.A. Police Dep't, www.lapdonline.org/police_commission/content_basic_view/900.

42. Carol S. Steiker, "Second Thoughts About First Principles," *Harv. L. Rev.* 107 (1994): 831, 834–35 (citing David R. Johnson, *Policing the Urban Underworld: The Impact of Crime on the Development of the American Police, 1800–1887* (1979), 48); Edward L. Ayers, *Vengeance and Justice: Crime and Punishment in the 19th Century American South* (1984), 88; Egon Bittner, *Aspects of Police Work* (1990), 117; Eric H. Monkkonen, *Police in Urban America, 1860–1920* (2004), 42–44; Samuel Walker, *A Critical History of Police Reform* (1977), 25–28, 39, 55–56, 70–75; Jerome H. Skolnick and James H. Fyfe, *Above the Law: Police and the Excessive Use of Force* (1993), 175.

43. Samuel Walker, *Popular Justice: A History of American Criminal Justice* (1998), 195–96; *The Kerner Report: The 1968 Report of the National Advisory Commission on Civil Disorders* (1968; repr. 1988), 206, 299; Skolnick and Fyfe, *Above the Law: Police and the Excessive Use of Force*, supra note 42, at 82–83; *The Challenge of Crime in a Free Society: A Report by the President's Commission on Law Enforcement and Administration of Justice* (1967), 99–102; Lee P. Brown, "Community Policing: A Practical Guide for Police Officials," *Perspectives on Policing*, Sept. 1989, at 5, www.ncjrs.gov/pdffiles1 /nij/118001.pdf.

44. Wesley G. Skogan, "Why Reform Fails," *Policing & Soc'y*, 28–29 (2008): 26; Dan Baum, "Legalize It All: How to Win the War on Drugs," *Harper's*, Apr. 2016, http://harpers.org /archive/2016/04/legalize-it-all/; Sandy Banks, "The Crack Epidemic's Toxic Legacy," *L.A. Times*, Aug. 7, 2010, http://articles.latimes.com/2010/aug/07/local/la-me-banks -20100807; Dennis Romero, "The Militarization of Police Started in Los Angeles," *L.A. Weekly*, Aug. 15, 2014, 6:04 a.m., www.laweekly.com/news/the-militarization-of -police-started-in-los-angeles-5010287.

45. Barry Friedman and Maria Ponomarenko, "Democratic Policing," *N.Y.U. L. Rev.* 90 (2015): 1871–73.

46. See, e.g., David Garland, *The Culture of Control: Crime and Social Order in Contemporary Society* (2001); Friedman and Ponomarenko, "Democratic Policing," supra note 45, at 1865–75; Reid, "Grounding Drones," supra note 20, at 1, 8, 9; Milton J. Valencia, "Police Defend Use of Military-Style Equipment," *Bos. Globe*, Aug. 16, 2014, at B1.

47. I am not alone in this, although my meaning is somewhat specific. For an excellent parallel approach to the question, see Christopher Stone and Heather H. Ward, "Democratic Policing: A Framework for Action," *Policing & Soc'y* 10 (2000): 11–45.

48. Office of the Federal Register, *A Guide to the Rulemaking Process*, www.federalregister .gov/uploads/2011/01/the_rulemaking_process.pdf.

49. U.S. Const. amend. IV.

50. Ta-Nehisi Coates makes this point, provocatively: "The problem with the police is not that they are fascist pigs, but that our country is ruled by majoritarian pigs." Coates, *Between the World and Me*, supra note 29 at 78.

51. That is the theme of Larry Kramer's book by this title. Larry Kramer, *The People Themselves: Popular Constitutionalism and Judicial Review* (2005).

52. *Katz v. United States*, 389 U.S. 347, 351 (1967) (citations omitted).

53. Daniel Solove, "'I've Got Nothing to Hide' and Other Misunderstandings of Privacy," *San Diego L. Rev.* 44 (2007): 746, 748–53; Daniel Solove, "Why Privacy Matters Even if You Have 'Nothing to Hide,'" *The Chronicle*, May 15, 2011, http://chronicle.com /article/Why-Privacy-Matters-Even-if/127461; CNBC Prime, "Inside the Mind of Google," *YouTube*, www.youtube.com/watch?v=u02h9LYYmuc.

54. Polly Sprenger, "Sun on Privacy: 'Get Over It,'" *Wired*, Jan. 26, 1999, http://archive .wired.com/politics/law/news/1999/01/17538; Natasha Singer, "Sharing Data, but Not Happily," *N.Y. Times*, June 4, 2015, www.nytimes.com/2015/06/05/technology/consu mers-conflicted-over-data-mining-policies-report-finds.html.

55. U.S. Const. amend. IV.
56. Richard A. Posner, *Not a Suicide Pact: The Constitution in a Time of National Emergency* (2006); see also *Terminiello v. City of Chicago*, 337 U.S. 1, 37 (1949) (Jackson, J. dissenting); *Ex Parte* Vallandingham, 68 U.S. 243 (1864); Letter from Thomas Jefferson to John B. Colvin, Sept. 20, 1810, in *The Works of Thomas Jefferson*, ed. Paul Leicester Ford (1905), 11:146, available at http://press-pubs.uchicago.edu/founders/documents /a2_3s8.html.
57. See, e.g., *The Federalist* No. 70 (Alexander Hamilton) (citing "[d]ecision, activity, secrecy, and dispatch" as advantages of a unitary executive that promote "energy" in that position). For more on the importance of constitutional commitments, the works of Stephen Holmes are instructive. E.g., Stephen Holmes, *Passions and Constraint: On the Theory of Liberal Democracy* (1995); Stephen Holmes, "In Case of Emergency: Misunderstanding Tradeoffs in the War on Terror," *Calif. L. Rev.* 97 (2009): 301.
58. Holmes, "In Case of Emergency," supra note 57, at 301–2. See generally Atul Gawande, *The Checklist Manifesto: How to Get Things Right* (2009).
59. Carl Matthies, Vera Institute of Justice, *Advancing the Quality of Cost-Benefit Analysis for Justice Programs* (2014), 1, www.vera.org/sites/default/files/resources/downloads /advancing-the-quality-of-cba.pdf.
60. See, e.g., Holmes, "In Case of Emergency," supra note 57.
61. E.g., Rachel Blade, "Criminal Justice Reform Gains Bipartisan Momentum," *Politico*, Jul. 15, 2015, 5:15 a.m., www.politico.com/story/2015/07/criminal-justice-reform-gains -bipartisan-momentum-120125.html.

1. POLICING IN SECRET

1. The Day We Fight Back, https://thedaywefightback.org; About Us: Restore the Fourth Chicago, http://rt4chicago.com/about.html; March & Dinner in Conjunction with "The Day We Fight Back," www.facebook.com/events/1438369666398805.
2. Interview by Barry Friedman with Freddy Martinez, Mar. 25, 2015 (hereinafter Martinez Interview); Sam Adler-Bell, "Beware the 'Stingray,'" *U.S. News & World Rep.*, Mar. 13, 2015, 10:45 a.m., www.usnews.com/opinion/articles/2015/03/13/stingray-lets -police-spy-on-cellphones-and-they-want-to-keep-it-secret.
3. Adler-Bell, "Beware the Stingray," supra note 2; Kim Zetter, "Turns Out Police Stingray Spy Tools Can Indeed Record Calls," *Wired*, Oct. 28, 2015, www.wired.com/2015 /10/stingray-government-spy-tools-can-record-calls-new-documents-confirm.
4. Chuck Sudo, "Is the Chicago Police Department Monitoring Occupy Chicago's Cell Phone Conversations?," *Chicagoist*, Nov. 7, 2011, 9:15 a.m., http://chicagoist.com/2011 /11/07/is_the_chicago_police_department_mo.php; John Kelly, "Cellphone Data Spying: It's Not Just the NSA," *USA Today*, May 20, 2014, 10:54 a.m., www.usatoday.com /story/news/nation/2013/12/08/cellphone-data-spying-nsa-police/3902809 (Miami police); Fruzsina Eördögh, "Evidence of 'Stingray' Phone Surveillance by Police Mounts in Chicago," *Christian Sci. Monitor*, Dec. 22, 2014, www.csmonitor.com/World /Passcode/2014/1222/Evidence-of-stingray-phone-surveillance-by-police-mounts-in -Chicago; Martinez Interview, supra note 2.
5. Martinez Interview, supra note 2; Complaint at 4, Ex. 7, *Martinez v. Chicago Police Dep't.* (*Martinez I*), No. 2014CH09565 (Ill Cir. Ct. filed June 6, 2014).
6. Interview by Barry Friedman with Matthew Topic, Mar. 13, 2015 (hereinafter Topic Interview); John Dodge, "After Denials, Chicago Police Department Admits Purchase of Cell-Phone Spying Devices," CBS Chicago, Oct. 1, 2014, 10:52 a.m., http://chicago .cbslocal.com/2014/10/01/chicago-police-department-admits-purchase-of-cell-phone -spying-devices.

7. Martinez filed four further FOIA requests with CPD seeking information on Stingrays. See Def.'s Notice of Supplemental Production in Response to FOIA Request at 2, *Martinez I*; Complaint at 3–4, Ex. E–F, *Martinez v. Chicago Police Dep't.* (*Martinez II*), No. 2014CH15338 (Ill. Cir. Ct. filed Sept. 23, 2014).

8. Invoice from Drinker Biddle & Reath LLP to City of Chicago (on file with author); Def.'s Motion to Dismiss at 4, 8, 14, *Martinez II* (Ill. Cir. Ct. filed Dec. 10, 2014); letter from Elizabeth V. Lopez, Drinker Biddle & Reath LLP, to Freddy Martinez, Nov. 13, 2014 (on file with author); letter from Jeffery D. Perconte, Drinker Biddle & Reath LLP, to Freddy Martinez, Feb. 10, 2015 (on file with author); letter from Jeffery D. Perconte, Drinker Biddle & Reath LLP, to Freddy Martinez, Feb. 5, 2015 (on file with author); letter from Jeffery D. Perconte, Drinker Biddle & Reath LLP, to Freddy Martinez, Jan. 22, 2015 (on file with author).

9. *Skolnick v. Altheimer & Gray*, 730 N.E.2d 4, 16 (Ill. 2000) (unsealed court records); Ryan Gallagher, "Meet the Machines That Steal Your Phone's Data," *Ars Technica*, Sep. 25, 2013, 1:00 p.m., http://arstechnica.com/tech-policy/2013/09/meet-the-machines -that-steal-your-phones-data/ (public patent documents).

10. Cyrus Farivar, "To Explain Stingrays, Local Cops Cribbed Letter Pre-Written by FBI," *Ars Technica*, Mar. 24, 2015, 7:00 a.m., http://arstechnica.com/tech-policy/2015/03/to -explain-stingrays-local-cops-cribbed-letter-likely-pre-written-by-feds/; Affidavit of Bradley S. Morrison, Def.'s Motion to Dismiss at Ex. 5, *Martinez II* (Ill. Cir. Ct. filed Dec. 10, 2014). Locales where the Morrison affidavit showed up include Tucson, Arizona; San Diego, California (where the City released the affidavit); and Virginia. See City Attorney Statement, City of San Diego, "City Attorney Releases Three Documents Related to Stingray Cell Site Simulator," Dec. 22, 2014, www.sandiego.gov /cityattorney/pdf/news/2014/nr141222.pdf; Jack Gillum and Eileen Sullivan, "US Pushing Local Cops to Stay Mum on Surveillance," *Yahoo Finance*, June 21, 2014, http://finance.yahoo.com/news/us-pushing-local-cops-stay-174613067.html; Matt Richtel, "A Police Gadget Tracks Phones? Shhh! It's Secret," *N.Y. Times*, Mar. 15, 2015, www.nytimes.com/2015/03/16/business/a-police-gadget-tracks-phones-shhh-its-secret .html.

11. Harris Government Communications Systems Terms and Conditions of Sale for Domestic Wireless Equipment, Software, and Services (on file with author) ("The customer shall not disclose . . . any information regarding Customer's purchase or use . . . to the public in any manner including but not limited to: in press releases, in court documents and/or proceedings, internet, or during other public forums or proceedings."); Jessica Glenza and Nicky Woolf, "Stingray Spying: FBI's Secret Deal with Police Hides Phone Dragnet from Courts," *The Guardian*, Apr. 10, 2015, www .theguardian.com/us-news/2015/apr/10/stingray-spying-fbi-phone-dragnet-police.

12. Affidavit of Bradley S. Morrison, Def.'s Motion to Dismiss at Ex. 5, *Martinez II* (Ill. Cir. Ct. filed Dec. 10, 2014) ("jigsaw puzzle"); Farivar, "To Explain Stingrays," supra note 10 ("circumvent"); Jessica Lussenhop, "St. Louis Police Have Used Stingray Technology for Years—They Just Won't Talk About It," *Riverfront Times*, May 20, 2015, 8:00 a.m., www.riverfronttimes.com/newsblog/2015/05/20/st-louis-police-have -used-stingray-technology-for-years-they-just-wont-talk-about-it (quoting Hanni Fakhoury).

13. Lussenhop, "St. Louis Police Have Used Stingray Technology for Years," supra note 12; Jason Koebler, "The FBI Admits It Uses Fake Cell Phone Towers to Track You," *Vice*, Feb. 16, 2015, http://motherboard.vice.com/read/fbi-admits-it-uses-fake-cell-phone -towers-to-track-you.

14. *Alliance to End Repression v. City of Chicago*, 237 F.3d 799, 801 (7th Cir. 2001) (Posner, J.); Martinez Interview, supra note 2; Topic Interview, supra note 6.

15. Fred Clasen-Kelly, "Secrecy Lifts in CMPD Stingray Phone Tracking," *Charlotte Observer*, Feb. 15, 2015, 6:00 a.m., www.charlotteobserver.com/latest-news/article10435436 .html#.VONYcy4YEsJ; Fred Clasen-Kelly, "Mecklenburg County District Attorney's Office to Review Surveillance Cases," *Charlotte Observer*, Nov. 20, 2014, www .charlotteobserver.com/news/local/crime/article9234986.html.

16. Clasen-Kelly, "Mecklenburg County, District Attorney's Office to Review Surveillance Cases," supra note 15; Adam Lynn, "Tacoma Police Change How They Seek Permission to Use Cellphone Tracker," *News Trib.*, Nov. 15, 2014, 12:00 a.m., www .thenewstribune.com/news/local/crime/article25894096.html.

17. Cyrus Farivar, "FBI Would Rather Prosecutors Drop Cases Than Disclose Stingray Details," *Ars Technica*, Apr. 7, 2015, 5:35 p.m., http://arstechnica.com/tech-policy/2015 /04/fbi-would-rather-prosecutors-drop-cases-than-disclose-stingray-details/ (FBI can force prosecutors to drop cases under NDAs); Lussenhop, "St. Louis Police Have Used Stingray Technology for Years," supra note 12 (cases actually dropped or generous plea agreements notwithstanding FBI denial); Ellen Nakashima, "Secrecy Around Police Surveillance Proves a Case's Undoing," *Wash. Post*, Feb. 22, 2015, www.washingtonpost .com/world/national-security/secrecy-around-police-surveillance-equipment-proves-a -cases-undoing/2015/02/22/ce72308a-b7ac-11e4-aa05-1ce812b3fdd2_story.html (Tallahassee).

18. Topic Interview, supra note 6; Justin Fenton, "Baltimore Police Used Secret Technology to Track Cellphones in Thousands of Cases," *Balt. Sun*, Apr. 9, 2015, www .baltimoresun.com/news/maryland/baltimore-city/bs-md-ci-stingray-case-20150408 -story.html (Baltimore records and contempt threat); Adler-Bell, "Beware the 'Stingray,'" supra note 2 (decision to proceed without evidence); Justin Fenton, "Maryland Appellate Court: Warrant Required for 'Stingray' Phone Tracking," *Balt. Sun*, Mar. 31, 2016, www.baltimoresun.com/news/maryland/crime/bs-md-ci-stingray-court-decision -20160331-story.html; Nakashima, "Secrecy Around Police Surveillance," supra note 17 (quoting Judge Frank Sheffield).

19. Glenza and Woolf, "Stingray Spying," supra note 11 (quoting Bruce Jacob); *N.Y. Civil Liberties Union v. Erie Cty. Sheriff's Office*, 15 N.Y.S.3d 713, 2015 WL 1295966, at *11 (N.Y. Sup. Ct. Mar. 17, 2015) (unreported table decision).

20. CPD supplemented its initial response with another disclosure on December 8, 2014. Letter from Elizabeth Lopez, Drinker Biddle & Reath LLP, to Freddy Martinez, Dec. 8, 2014 (on file with author) (Chicago had Stingrays as early as 2005); Martinez Interview, supra note 2; Topic Interview, supra note 6.

21. Douglas Greenberg, "The Effectiveness of Law Enforcement in Eighteenth-Century New York," *Am. J. Legal Hist.* 19 (1975): 177–78 (Schuyler); Eric H. Monkkonen, *Crime, Justice, History* (2012), 174 (*New York Gazette* (citing Arthur E. Peterson and George W. Edwards, *New York as an Eighteenth Century Municipality*, 2nd ed. (1967), 324)); Eric H. Monkkonen, *Police in Urban America, 1860–1920* (2004), 32 (*Louisiana Gazette* (citing George A. Ketcham, *Municipal Police Reform: A Comparative Study of Law Enforcement in Cincinnati, Chicago, New Orleans, New York, and St. Louis, 1844–1877* (1967), 48)).

22. James F. Richardson, *The New York Police: Colonial Times to 1901* (1970), 42 ("absolute police despotism"); Carol S. Steiker, "Second Thoughts About First Principles," *Harv. L. Rev.* 107 (1994): 831 (1833 report) (citing David R. Johnson, *Policing the Urban Underworld: The Impact of Crime on the Development of the American Police, 1800–1887* (1979), 48); Roger Roots, "Are Cops Constitutional?," *Seton Hall Const. L.J.* 11 (2001): 695 & 695n57 ("bobbies").

23. Monkkonen, *Crime, Justice, History*, supra note 21, at 175; Samuel Walker, *Popular Justice: A History of American Criminal Justice* (1998), 57, 63 ("in restaurants, asleep, or

otherwise away from their posts"); H. Paul Jeffers, *Commissioner Roosevelt: The Story of Theodore Roosevelt and the New York City Police, 1895–1897* (1994), 107 ("asleep on a butter-tub").

24. Allen Steinberg, *The Transformation of Criminal Justice: Philadelphia 1800–1880* (2000), 152, 177.

25. "Farewell to Williams," *N.Y. Times*, May 25, 1895, http://query.nytimes.com/mem /archive-free/pdf?res=9405E6D7133DE433A25756C2A9639C94649ED7CF; "Williams, 'Ex-Czar' of Tenderloin, Dies," *N.Y. Times*, Mar. 26, 1917, http://query .nytimes.com/mem/archive-free/pdf?res=9901E5D9143AE433A25755C2A9659C9 46696D6CF.

26. "Farewell to Williams," supra note 25 ("energetic action at popular gatherings"); *The Yale Book of Quotations*, ed. Fred. R. Shapiro (2006), 810 (attributing the "nightstick" quotation to Williams and noting Grover A. Whalen uttered a similar phrase decades later); "Williams, 'Ex-Czar' of Tenderloin, Dies," supra note 25 ("Just ask the Mayor"). Note, however, that Samuel Walker, *A Critical History of Police Reform* (1977), 8, attributes a similar quote about nightsticks and the Supreme Court to Thomas Byrnes.

27. "Williams, 'Ex-Czar' of Tenderloin, Dies," supra note 25.

28. Walker, *Popular Justice*, supra note 23, at 64 (quoting the Reverend Charles Henry Parkhurst); Richardson, *The New York Police*, supra note 22, at 234–40 (explaining the formation of the Lexow Commission and Parkhurst's role). See generally Charles H. Parkhurst, *Our Fight with Tammany* (1895).

29. *Report of the Special Committee Appointed to Investigate the Police Department of the City of New York*, S. 118–25 (N.Y., 1895), 25, 28, 34–35, 40, 44–45.

30. Id. at 15 (emphasis added).

31. Id. at 15–20, 29, 32–51.

32. On the politicization of the police, see Edward L. Ayers, *Vengeance and Justice: Crime and Punishment in the 19th Century American South* (1984), 88; Egon Bittner, *Aspects of Police Work* (1990), 117; Monkkonen, *Police in Urban America*, supra note 21, at 42–44; Walker, *A Critical History of Police Reform*, supra note 26, at 25–28; Steiker, "Second Thoughts About First Principles," supra note 22, at 834–35. For background on Vollmer, see Walker, *A Critical History of Police Reform*, supra note 26, at 70–73; O. W. Wilson, "August Vollmer," *J. Crim. L. & Criminology* 44 (1953): 94. The 1917 report is August Vollmer and Albert Schneider, "The School for Police as Planned at Berkley," *J. Crim L. & Criminology* 7 (1917): 877.

33. Walker, *A Critical History of Police Reform*, supra note 26, at 39, 70–75.

34. Id. at 70–75, 143 ("scientific"); Walker, *Popular Justice*, supra note 23, at 172–73 ("efficient").

35. Jerome H. Skolnick and James H. Fyfe, *Above the Law: Police and the Excessive Use of Force* (1993), 45–46 ("fixed" charges, "shakedown arrests"); National Comm'n on Law Observance and Enforcement, *Report on Lawlessness in Law Enforcement* (1931), 38–52 ("third degree," "torture").

36. *Brown v. Mississippi*, 297 U.S. 278, 281, 287 (1936). On the Isaac Woodard story, see "Aiken Is Angered at Welles Charge," *N.Y. Times*, Aug. 9, 1946; "Federal Help Sought for Blinded Veteran," *N.Y. Times*, July 25, 1946.

37. These developments are described in Skolnick and Fyfe, *Above the Law*, supra note 35, at 175; Walker, *A Critical History of Police Reform*, supra note 26, at ix, 55–56.

38. Walker, *Popular Justice*, supra note 23, at 60 (social services); Walker, *A Critical History of Police Reform*, supra note 26, at 139, 149–60 (going after the bad guys).

39. Bittner, *Aspects of Police Work*, supra note 32, at 6–7 (the shiny squad car, with its two-way radio); Walker, *Popular Justice*, supra note 23, at 165–67 (call response times and crime rates).

40. Walker, *Popular Justice*, supra note 23, at 195–96 ("long, hot summers"); *The Kerner Report: The 1968 Report of the National Advisory Commission on Civil Disorders* (1968; repr. 1988), 206, 299.

41. Skolnick and Fyfe, *Above the Law*, supra note 35, at 82–83, (quoting Daniel Bell, "Columbia and the New Left," *The Public Interest*, Fall 1968, at 81).

42. Id. at 75–76, 81 (quoting Daniel Walker, *Rights in Conflict: The Violent Confrontation of Demonstrators and Police in the Parks and Streets of Chicago During the Week of the Democratic National Convention of 1968: A Report to the National Commission on the Causes and Prevention of Violence* (1968), xv); see also Walker, *Popular Justice*, supra note 23, at 172–74 (discussing the events of the 1968 Democratic Convention in Chicago).

43. Barry Friedman, *The Will of the People: How Public Opinion Has Influenced the Supreme Court and Shaped the Meaning of the Constitution* (2009), 276.

44. Nicholas deB. Katzenbach, Foreword to *The Challenge of Crime in a Free Society: A Report by the President's Commission on Law Enforcement and Administration of Justice* (1967).

45. *The Challenge of Crime in a Free Society*, supra note 44, at 99–100, 102.

46. Id. at 100–101.

47. Lee P. Brown, "Community Policing: A Practical Guide for Police Officials," *Perspectives on Policing*, Sept. 1989, at 5, www.ncjrs.gov/pdffiles1/nij/118001.pdf.

48. William J. Clinton, "Address Before a Joint Session of the Congress on the State of the Union," Jan. 25, 1994, in *Weekly Compilation of Presidential Documents* 30 (1994): 155–56; COPS Office: Mission History, www.cops.usdoj.gov/default.asp?Item=2754; Michael D. Reisig, "Community and Problem-Oriented Policing," *Crime & Just.* 39 (2010): 19–20 (disbursements); Matthew J. Hickman and Brian A. Reaves, Bureau of Justice Statistics, *Special Report: Community Policing in Local Police Departments, 1997 and 1999* (2001), 1–2. See generally Tracey L. Meares, "Praying for Community Policing," *Calif. L. Rev.* 90 (2002): 1596–97.

49. Robert M. Morgenthau, "Does Community Policing Work? Beware of Its Limits," *N.Y. Times*, Dec. 30, 1990.

50. Id.

51. John Crank and Robert Langworthy, "Fragmented Centralization and the Organization of the Police," *Policing & Soc'y* 6 (1996): 213 ("hodge-podge"); Jerome H. Skolnick and David H. Bayley, "Theme and Variation in Community Policing," *Crime & Just.* 10 (1988): 4 ("buzzword"); Radley Balko, *Rise of the Warrior Cop: The Militarization of America's Police Forces* (2013), 220 (citing Peter B. Kraska and Victor E. Kappeler, "Militarizing American Police: The Rise and Normalization of Paramilitary Units," *Soc. Probs.* 44 [1997]: 13) (SWAT).

52. Deborah Spence, "Colorado Springs PD Takes Home 2010 Goldstein Award," *Community Policing Dispatch*, Nov. 2010, http://cops.usdoj.gov/html/dispatch/November_2010/index.asp.; Colorado Springs Police Dep't, *Homeless Outreach Team, Center for Problem-Oriented Policing* (2010), www.popcenter.org/conference/conferencepapers/2010/Colorado-Homeless-Winner.pdf; Los Angeles County Chief Executive Office, *Los Angeles County Regional Gang Violence Reduction Initiative: Semi-Annual Progress Report, April–September 2010* (2010), http://publichealth.lacounty.gov/ivpp/injury_topics/GangAwarenessPrevention/GVRI%20Compiled%20Report%20FINAL.pdf; About Us, National Association of Police Athletic/Activities Leagues, Inc., www.nationalpal.org/Default.aspx?tabid=784239.

53. George L. Kelling and James Q. Wilson, "Broken Windows," *Atlantic Monthly*, Mar. 1982, at 29–38, available at www.theatlantic.com/magazine/archive/1982/03/broken-windows/304465/?single_page=true.

54. K. Babe Howell, "Broken Lives from Broken Windows: The Hidden Costs of Aggressive Order-Maintenance Policing," *N.Y.U. Rev. L. & Soc. Change* 33 (2009): 274 ("undermine[d] the legitimacy of the criminal justice system"); Broken Windows Policing, Center for Evidence-Based Crime Policy, http://cebcp.org/evidence-based-policing/what-works-in-policing/research-evidence-review/broken-windows-policing/. On the New York City experience with order-maintenance policing under Mayor Giuliani, see, for example, New York City Police Department, *Police Strategy No. 5: Reclaiming the Public Spaces of New York* (1994), www.ncjrs.gov/pdffiles1/Photocopy/167807NCJRS.pdf; Jeffrey A. Fagan and Garth Davies, "Policing Guns: Order Maintenance and Crime Control in New York," in *Guns, Crime, and Punishment in America*, ed. Bernard E. Harcourt (2003), 193–96; Bernard E. Harcourt and Jens Ludwig, "Broken Windows: New Evidence for New York City and a Five-City Social Experiment," *U. Chi. L. Rev.* 73 (2006): 286.

55. Wesley G. Skogan, "Why Reform Fails," *Policing & Soc'y* 18 (2008): 26. In 1988, Jerome Skolnick, one of the academy's most admired scholars of policing, conducted a field study of the concept in action. He, along with his co-author, wrote: "[L]eaders talk a good game, but they rarely follow through." In practice, "[t]he old concept of professionalism is maintained, with the police firmly in charge and the public kept at arm's length until needed." Skolnick and Bayley, "Theme and Variation in Community Policing," supra note 51, at 16–17. That same year, a full generation after the professionalism movement was discredited, George Kelling and Mark Moore noted the "dominant trend" still "guiding today's police executives," one that "encourages the pursuit of independent, professional autonomy for police departments." They urged a pivot toward a broader understanding of the "police function" to include "order maintenance, conflict resolution, problem solving through the organization, and provision of services, as well as other activities." George L. Kelling and Mark H. Moore, "The Evolving Strategy of Policing," *Perspectives on Policing*, Nov. 1988, at 1, 11, www.ncjrs.gov/pdffiles1/nij/114213.pdf.

56. Exec. Order No. 13684, 79 Fed. Reg. 76865 (Dec. 18, 2014) (appointing the Task Force); *Final Report of the President's Task Force on 21st Century Policing* (2015), iii, 1, 11, www.cops.usdoj.gov/pdf/taskforce/taskforce_finalreport.pdf.

57. Angel Jennings, Richard Winton, and James Rainey, "L.A. County Sheriff's Dept. Used Spy Plane to Watch Compton," *L.A. Times*, Apr. 23, 2014, www.latimes.com/local/la-me-compton-surveillance-20140424-story.html; Conor Friedersdorf, "Eyes Over Compton: How Police Spied on a Whole City," *The Atlantic*, Apr. 21, 2014, www.theatlantic.com/national/archive/2014/04/sheriffs-deputy-compares-drone-surveillance-of-compton-to-big-brother/360954/ (quoting LASD Sergeant Douglas Iketani).

58. Friedersdorf, "Eyes Over Compton," supra note 57.

59. Commission to Investigate Allegations of Police Corruption and the Anti-Corruption Procedures of the Police Department, City of New York, *Commission Report* (1994), 36, 41 ("testilying," "God's work," "most common form of police corruption"); Christopher Slobogin, "Testilying: Police Perjury and What to Do About It," *U. Colo. L. Rev.* 67 (1996): 1041–48; Myron W. Orfield, Jr., "The Exclusionary Rule and Deterrence: An Empirical Study of Chicago Narcotics Officers," *U. Chi. L. Rev.* 54 (1987): 1050; Myron W. Orfield, Jr., "Deterrence, Perjury, and the Heater Factor: An Exclusionary Rule in the Chicago Criminal Courts," *U. Colo. L. Rev.* 63 (1992): 107; Michael Pearson, "Obama: No One is Listening to Your Calls," CNN, Jun. 9, 2013, 8:26 p.m., www.cnn.com/2013/06/07/politics/nsa-data-mining; *Current and Projected National Security Threats to the United States: Hearing Before the S. Select Comm. on Intelligence*, 113th Cong. 66 (2013) (statement of James R, Clapper, Dir. of Nat'l Intelligence).

60. Bill Berkowitz, "The Blue Wall of Silence Among Police Enables Cop Brutality," *TruthOut*, Mar. 5, 2015, 8:43 a.m., www.truth-out.org/buzzflash/commentary/the-blue -wall-of-silence-among-police-enables-cop-brutality/19187-the-blue-wall-of-silence -among-police-enables-cop-brutality (discussing the Seifert case); *Bowling v. United States*, 740 F. Supp. 2d 1240, 1262 & 1262n75 (D. Kan. 2010); Mark Karlin, "Federal Jury Finds City of Chicago Responsible for 'Code of Silence' in Chicago Police Department," *TruthOut*, Dec. 24, 2012, 11:43 a.m., www.truth-out.org/news/item/13510-in -significant-precedent-federal-jury-finds-city-of-chicago-responsible-for-code-of -silence-in-chicago-police-department; David Barstow and David Kocieniewski, "Records Show New Jersey Police Withheld Data on Race Profiling," *N.Y. Times*, Oct. 12, 2000, at B8.

61. *Final Report of the President's Task Force on 21st Century Policing*, supra note 56, at 21; Oliver Laughland, Jon Swaine, Ciara McCarthy, and Jamiles Lartey, "Justice Department Trials System to Count Killings by US Law Enforcement," *The Guardian*, Oct. 5, 2015, www.theguardian.com/us-news/2015/oct/05/justice-department-trials -system-count-killings-us-law-enforcement-the-counted; "The Counted," *The Guardian*, www.theguardian.com/us-news/series/counted-us-police-killings; "Fatal Force," *Wash. Post*, www.washingtonpost.com/graphics/national/police-shootings-2016/; Christine Hauser, "Police Told to Give Street-Stop Data," *N.Y. Times*, May 31, 2008, at B5 ("give away information"); ACLU, *War Comes Home: The Excessive Militarization of American Policing* (2014), 27–28, https://aclu.org/sites/default/files/field_document /jus14-warcomeshome-report-web-rel1_1.pdf; Joanna C. Schwartz, "Police Indemnification," *N.Y.U. L. Rev.* 89 (2014): 903–04.

62. Jeremy Waldron, "Accountability and Insolence," in *Political Political Theory: Essays on Institutions* (2016).

63. Kenneth Culp Davis, *Police Discretion* (1975), 72.

64. Jennifer Valentino-Devries, "Police Snap Up Cheap Cell Phone Trackers," *Wall St. J.*, Aug. 19, 2015 12:57 PM, www.wsj.com/articles/police-snap-up-cheap-cellphone -trackers-1439933271.

65. This argument is especially prevalent in the context of intelligence gathering, see, e.g., Emily Berman, "Regulating Domestic Intelligence Collection," *Wash. & Lee L. Rev.* 71 (2014): 29, 38, but is also frequently made in the context of ordinary policing.

66. See, e.g., *Lewis-Bey v. U.S. Dep't of Justice*, 595 F. Supp. 2d. 120, 137–38 (D.D.C. 2009) (protecting details of electronic surveillance techniques, including "timing of their use, and the specific location where they were employed" [internal quotation marks omitted]); *LaRouche v. U.S. Dep't of Justice*, No. 90-2753, slip op. at 21 (D.D.C. Nov. 17, 2000) (allowing department to withhold details regarding undercover investigative techniques); 18 U.S.C. § 2516 (2012) (defining categories of offenses for which wiretaps may be obtained).

67. See, e.g., Dell Cameron, "Feds Must Now Get a Warrant to Spy on Your Phone with a Stingray Device," *The Daily Dot*, Sept. 3, 2015, www.dailydot.com/politics/doj-stingray -policy/; Fenton, "Maryland Appellate Court: Warrant Required for 'Stingray' Phone Tracking," supra note 18.

68. Martinez Interview, supra note 2; Topic Interview, supra note 6.

69. Letter from Patrick J. Leahy, Chairman, and Charles E. Grassley, Ranking Member, Comm. on the Judiciary, U.S. Senate, to Eric H. Holder, Attorney General, and Jeh Johnson, Sec'y of Homeland Security, Dec. 23, 2014, www.grassley.senate.gov/sites /default/files/news/upload/2014-12-23%20PJL%20and%20CEG%20to%20DOJ%20 and%20DHS%20%28cell-site%20simulators%29.pdf. Political scorecards offer evidence of Senators Leahy and Grassley's ideological misalignment. Compare, e.g., Heritage Action Scorecard: Sen. Charles Grassley, www.heritageactionscorecard.com/members

/member/G000386, with Heritage Action Scorecard: Sen. Patrick Leahy, www
.heritageactionscorecard.com/members/member/L000174.

70. Cyrus Farivar, "FBI Now Claims Its Stingray NDA Means the Opposite of What It
Says," *Ars Technica*, May 15, 2015, http://arstechnica.com/tech-policy/2015/05/fbi-now
-claims-its-stingray-nda-means-the-opposite-of-what-it-says/; Cyrus Farivar, "Department of Justice Will Review How It Deploys Cell Phone Snooping Tech," *Ars Technica*,
May 3, 2015, http://arstechnica.com/tech-policy/2015/05/department-of-justice-will
-review-how-it-deploys-cell-phone-snooping-tech/; Cyrus Farivar, "FBI, DEA and
Others Will Now Have to Get a Warrant to Use Stingrays," *Ars Technica*, Sept. 3, 2015,
http://arstechnica.com/tech-policy/2015/09/fbi-dea-and-others-will-now-have-to-get-a
-warrant-to-use-stingrays/.

2. LEGISLATURES THAT WON'T LEGISLATE

1. Scarlata Dep. at 1, 8, 13, 92, 141, *Calvo v. Maryland*, CAL09-18584, 2011 WL 2437307
(Md. Cir. Ct. Jan. 1, 2011); Doug Donovan, "Prince George's Raid Prompts Call
for Probe," *Balt. Sun*, Aug. 8, 2008, articles.baltimoresun.com/2008-08-08/news
/0808070248_1_berwyn-heights-mayor-cheye-calvo-prince-george.

2. Scarlata Dep. at 14, 16–17, 88, 92, 130; Martini Dep. at 153, *Calvo v. Maryland*; Yarbrough Dep. at 176, *Calvo v. Maryland*; April Witt, "Deadly Force," *Wash. Post*, Feb. 1,
2009, www.washingtonpost.com/wp-dyn/content/article/2009/01/23/AR2009012302935
.html.

3. Sagin Dep. at 79, *Calvo v. Maryland*; Yarbrough Dep. at 78; Scarlata Dep. at 103; Martini Dep. at 61.

4. Martini Dep. at 78–79, 82, 87; Sagin Dep. at 82, 86–87; Scarlata Dep. at 189.

5. Martini Dep. at 85–89, 160.

6. Yarbourgh Dep. at 79, 83, 92, 107, 114, 173; Sagin Dep. at 119, 128–131, 143.

7. Yarbrough Dep. at 33, 91, 179, 222; Sagin Dep. at 119, 133, 142, 147–148; Sagin Dep. at
153; Witt, "Deadly Force," supra note 2.

8. Yarbrough Dep. at 117, 127, 138; Sagin Dep. at 102, 133; Daniel Valentine, "Sheriff
Says Deputies Were Justified in Shooting Mayor's Dogs," *The Gazette*, June 19, 2009,
http://ww2.gazette.net/stories/06192009/prinnew131944_32546.shtml; Witt, "Deadly
Force," supra note 2; Donovan, "Prince George's Raid Prompts Call for Probe," supra
note 1.

9. Sagin Dep. at 134, 135, 179. A veterinarian's report concluded that Chase had been
shot twice, once in the chest and once in the rear legs, and that the shot to the rear legs
had been fired from behind. He bled to death after the shot to the chest. Witt, "Deadly
Force," supra note 2.

10. New Hampshire Liberty Alliance, "Cheye Calvo Speaks on the Mundane Nature of
State Violence," YouTube, July 16, 2012, at11:23–16:30, www.youtube.com/watch?v
=yUTSehSF6pA (hereinafter "Calvo Liberty Alliance Speech").

11. Witt, "Deadly Force," supra note 2; Sagin Dep. at 192–93.

12. Donovan, "Prince George's Raid Prompts Call for Probe," supra note 1 (remaining
bound for two hours); "Calvo Liberty Alliance Speech," supra note 10, at 11:23–16:30
(tracking the dogs' blood through the house); Witt, "Deadly Force," supra note 2 (within
sight of the dead dogs); Scarlata Dep. at 157, 170–75 ("emotionally erratic"); Martini
Dep. at 169–171 ("too calm").

13. Witt, "Deadly Force," supra note 2.

14. Martini also discussed the topic with other officers at the debriefing after the raid. See
Scarlata Dep. at 100–105, 161; Martini Dep. at 63–64, 65, 133.

15. Witt, "Deadly Force," supra note 2; Scarlata Dep. at 188.

16. Scarlata Dep. at 68, 72–73, 75, 77, 87.
17. Witt, "Deadly Force," supra note 2. Undercover agents ultimately delivered the package to the Calvo-Tomsic residence. Scarlata Dep. at 68–69.
18. Id.; Scarlata Dep. at 227–28.
19. "Calvo Liberty Alliance Speech," supra note 10, at 18:00–23:00; Witt, "Deadly Force," supra note 2.
20. "Calvo Liberty Alliance Speech," supra note 10, at 15:00–16:30, 19:00–20:10, 27:00–39:00.
21. Radley Balko, Overkill: The Rise of Paramilitary Police Raids in America (2006), 4, 6–8, http://object.cato.org/sites/cato.org/files/pubs/pdf/balko_whitepaper_2006.pdf (origins of SWAT and rise in late 1980s); Karan R. Singh, "Treading the Thin Blue Line: Military Special-Operations Trained Police Swat Teams and the Constitution," Wm. & Mary Bill Rts. J. 9 (2001): 676 (origins of SWAT); "Oversight of Federal Programs for Equipping State and Local Law Enforcement Agencies," Hearing Before the S. Comm. on Homeland Security and Governmental Affairs, 113th Cong. 36 (2014) (statement of Peter B. Kraska, Ph.D., Professor, School of Justice Studies, University of Eastern Kentucky); ACLU, Excessive Militarization of American Policing (2015), 1, www.aclu.org/files/field_document/ACLU%20-%20%20Militarization%20of%20Policing.pdf; ACLU, War Comes Home: The Excessive Militarization of American Policing (2014), 19, www.aclu.org/sites/default/files/assets/jus14-warcomeshome-report-web-rel1.pdf; Scarlata Dep. at 122.
22. Michelle Alexander, The New Jim Crow: Mass Incarceration in the Age of Colorblindness (2012), 73–75 (describing the use of SWAT teams primarily to serve narcotics warrants); Balko, Overkill, supra note 21, at 1, 6, 25; ACLU, Excessive Militarization, supra note 21, at 1; Radley Balko, "Shedding Light on the Use of SWAT Teams," Wash. Post, Feb. 17, 2014, www.washingtonpost.com/news/the-watch/wp/2014/02/17/shedding-light-on-the-use-of-swat-teams/; Matthew Harwood, "One Nation Under SWAT: How America's Police Became an Occupying Force," Salon, Aug. 14, 2014, www.salon.com/2014/08/14/one_nation_under_swat_how_americas_police_became_an_occupying_force_partner/; Maryland Statistical Analysis Center, Governor's Office of Crime Control & Prevention, Maryland Fiscal Year 2014 SWAT Team Deployment Data Analysis (2014), 6; Scarlata Dep. at 44–47; Radley Balko, Rise of the Warrior Cop: The Militarization of America's Police Forces (2014), 319; Witt, "Deadly Force," supra note 2.
23. Yarbrough Dep. at 12–13, 16, 35, 44, 46, 248–49; Sagin Dep. at 53–54; Martini Dep. at 77.
24. Martini Dep. at 52, 86–88; Sagin Dep. at 66, 81, 119, 149–51; Yarbrough Dep. at 122, 123, 127, 144.
25. Balko, Overkill, supra note 21, at 22 (Reverend Williams); "Botched Paramilitary Police Raids: An Epidemic of 'Isolated Incidents,'" Cato Institute, www.cato.org/raidmap (Agee, Cohn); ACLU, War Comes Home, supra note 21, at 9, 17 (grandfather, veteran).
26. Scarlata Dep. at 60–61, 64; Sagin Dep. at 166, 237.
27. Balko, Overkill, supra note 21, at 4; Cato Institute, "Cheye Calvo Explores the Money Behind SWAT Raids," YouTube, Aug. 4, 2009, at 5:35–5:40, www.youtube.com/watch?v=1OPv_1YpqWQ.
28. Calvo Liberty Alliance Speech, supra note 10.
29. Id.
30. Mass. Const. pt. 1, art. XXX; S. B. Benjamin, "The Significance of the Massachusetts Constitution of 1780," Temp. L. Rev. 70 (1997): 885; Thomas Paine, Common Sense (1776), in Rights of Man, Common Sense, and Other Political Writings, ed. Mark Philp, Oxford World's Classics ed. (1998), 34.
31. See, e.g., Declaration of Independence para. 2 (U.S. 1776) ("Governments are instituted

among Men, deriving their just powers from the consent of the governed."); John Milton, "The Tenure of Kings and Magistrates," 1643, in *The Works of John Milton, Historical, Political and Miscellaneous*, ed. A. Millar (1753), Univ. of Mich. digitized ed. (2011), 345 ("[T]he power of kings and magistrates . . . is only . . . committed to them in trust from the people to the common good of them all.").

32. This is simply operationalizing the two core requirements of American democracy: democratic accountability and the rule of law. The basic idea of accountability is that government officials are accountable to us (the people) and we, in turn, are responsible for controlling them. See, e.g., Jeremy Waldron, "Accountability and Insolence" (using a principal-agent model to describe a system of democratic accountability), in *Political Political Theory: Essays on Institutions* (2016), 167. See generally *Democracy, Accountability, and Representation*, eds. Adam Przeworski et al. (1999) (describing various models of democratic accountability). The most famous elaboration of the rule of law (though there are many) probably comes from Lon Fuller, who "argued that the Rule of Law requires publicly promulgated rules, laid down in advance, and adherence to at least some natural-law values." Richard H. Fallon, Jr., "'The Rule of Law' as a Concept in Constitutional Discourse," *Colum. L. Rev.* 97 (1997): 2 (citing Lon L. Fuller, *The Morality of Law*, rev. ed. (1964), 42–44).

33. 28 U.S.C. §§ 531, 533(1) (2012); New York City, N.Y., Charter § 435.

34. See Sagin Dep. at 63, 71, 81, 92, 116–18 (explaining the improvisation with pepper spray for the dogs, but offering no explanation for why he didn't carry a baton on SWAT raids); Yarbrough Dep. at 61–65 (saying that Tasers, batons, and pepper spray were part of the "regular equipment" during the routine line of duty, but offering no explanation for why he didn't carry such equipment on SWAT raids).

35. See, e.g., Sagin Dep. at 63, 11, 117–18, 120–26 (revealing that there was no formal training or instruction that led Sagin to adopt a practice of disregarding the knocking requirement of a knock-and-announce warrant when being spotted by a resident); Scarlatta Dep. at 20–21; Yarbrough Dep. at 61–65, 116–17, 236–37, 242.

36. See Daniel A. Farber and Philip P. Frickey, *Law and Public Choice: A Critical Introduction* (1991), 14–24; William J. Stuntz, "The Pathological Politics of Criminal Law," *Mich. L. Rev.* 100 (2001): 505, 530–36, 545 ("Advancing police and prosecutors' goals usually means advancing legislators' goals as well.").

37. See William N. Eskridge, Jr., et al., *Cases and Materials on Legislation, Statutes and the Creation of Public Policy*, 4th ed. (2007), 49–50.

38. Donald A. Dripps, "Criminal Procedure, Footnote Four, and the Theory of Public Choice; or, Why Don't Legislatures Give a Damn About the Rights of the Accused?," *Syracuse L. Rev.* 44 (1993): 1081, 1091–92 (1993) (stating that the strength of the law enforcement lobby, which Dripps says includes local police unions, "can be seen in its relatively even matches with the NRA—the lobby that many in Washington regard as the most efficient pressure group this side of the AARP"); Radley Balko, "Militarized Police Overreach: 'Oh, God, I Thought They Were Going to Shoot Me Next,'" *Salon*, July 10, 2013, www.salon.com/2013/07/10/militarized_police_overreach_oh_god_i _thought_they_were_going_to_shoot_me_next/ (noting that a proposed Maryland law was vehemently opposed by law enforcement groups but was ultimately passed over the objection of "every police organization in the state"); Stuntz, "The Pathological Politics of Criminal Law," supra note 36, at 539.

39. See, e.g., Dripps, "Criminal Procedure," supra note 38, at 1089–91 ("[E]ven when legislatures authorize broad law enforcement powers, police and prosecutors face a substantial incentive to limit the application of those powers to the least politically influential segments of society."). For a more detailed discussion of discrimination and policing, see infra Chapter 8.

40. See, e.g., Dripps, "Criminal Procedure," supra note 38, at 1089; Jonathan Simon, *Governing Through Crime: How the War on Crime Transformed American Democracy and Created a Culture of Fear* (2007), 3–12; Rachel E. Barkow, "Administering Crime," *UCLA L. Rev.* 52 (2005): 751 ("[P]oliticians respond to the perception of rising crime rates created by the media and sensational cases . . . They must appear to be taking direct action against a perceived crime problem—and harsh sentencing creates the appearance of an immediate response."); Rachel E. Barkow, "Institutional Design and the Policing of Prosecutors: Lessons from Administrative Law," *Stan. L. Rev.* 61 (2009): 880; William J. Stuntz, "The Political Constitution of Criminal Justice," *Harv. L. Rev.* 119 (2006): 807.

41. Even today, the name of "Willie Horton . . . is enough to make a politician blanch." Beth Schwartzapfel and Bill Keller, "Willie Horton Revisited," *The Marshall Project*, May 13, 2015, www.themarshallproject.org/2015/05/13/willie-horton-revisited. William Horton was an African American man who committed rape while on furlough from a Massachusetts prison. During the 1988 presidential campaign, opponents of Governor Michael Dukakis of Massachusetts ran commercials featuring Horton and painting Dukakis as weak on crime. Eleanor Randolph, Op-Ed, "The Political Legacy of Baaad Boy Atwater," *N.Y. Times*, Sept. 19, 2008, www.nytimes.com/2008/09/20/opinion/20sat3.html. The Horton commercials likely contributed to what became a landslide defeat for Dukakis. Barkow, "Administering Crime," supra note 40, at 747.

42. See Debra Livingston, "Police Discretion and the Quality of Life in Public Places: Courts, Communities, and the New Policing," *Colum. L. Rev.* 97 (1997): 657 ("Policing is a risky business, and distance between politicians and the police helps the former avoid blame when the latter become ensnared in controversy.").

43. Act of May 19, 2009, ch. 542, 2009 Md. Laws 3034, http://msa.maryland.gov/megafile/msa/speccol/sc5300/sc5339/000113/017000/017812/unrestricted/20131824e-004.pdf (abrogated 2014) (requiring law enforcement agencies to report, every six months, the number of SWAT team deployments, the locations of the deployments, the reason and legal authority for each deployment, and the result of each deployment); Phillip Smith, "Reining in SWAT—Towards Effective Oversight of Paramilitary Police Units," *Drug War Chronicle*, May 27, 2010, http://stopthedrugwar.org/chronicle/2010/may/28/feature_reining_swat_towards_eff (quoting Eric Sterling); Justin George, "Police Agencies No Longer Need to Report Race, SWAT Deployments," *Balt. Sun*, July 5, 2014, http://articles.baltimoresun.com/2014-07-05/news/bs-md-sun-investigates-race-law-20140705_1_law-enforcement-agencies-deborah-jeon.

44. See Constitutionality of Legislation Extending the Term of the FBI Director, 2011 WL 2566125, at *4 (O.L.C. June 20, 2011).

45. See Stuntz, "The Pathological Politics of Criminal Law," supra note 36, at 529–30 ("[C]rime is one of those matters about which most voters care a great deal. Today it is regularly a major issue in elections at all levels of government, and it has been an issue in local elections for more than a century. If there is any sphere in which politicians would have an incentive simply to please the majority of voters, it's criminal law."); id. at 532 ("Rising crime generates demands from voters for legislative action, and often there is little in the way of legislative action that would be productive in the near term."); Herman Goldstein, *Policing a Free Society* (1977), 135 (noting that "[m]ayors often take pains to disassociate themselves from decisions upon which controversial police actions are based" and that as a result police often "have greater autonomy than other agencies of government that exercise much less authority."); Samuel Walker, *The New World of Police Accountability*, 1st ed. (2005), 8 (arguing that most elected officials are not very knowledgeable about police matters and are reluctant to provide guidance to law enforcement officials); Livingston, "Police Discretion," supra note 42

at 657 (explaining that by distancing themselves from police administration, politicians are able to insulate themselves from controversial police practices).

46. Michael Barbaro and David W. Chen, "De Blasio Is Elected New York City Mayor in Landslide," *N.Y. Times*, Nov. 5, 2013, www.nytimes.com/2013/11/06/nyregion/de-blasio-is-elected-new-york-city-mayor.html; Rebecca Kaplan, "Bill de Blasio Wins New York City Mayoral Race in Landslide," CBS News, Nov. 6, 2013, www.cbsnews.com/news/bill-de-blasio-wins-new-york-city-mayoral-race-in-landslide/; Adam Gabbatt, "Bill de Blasio Wins by a Landslide to Become New York City Mayor," *The Guardian*, Nov. 6, 2013, www.theguardian.com/world/2013/nov/06/bill-de-blasio-wins-new-york-mayoral-election; J. David Goodman and Kirk Semple, "Another Silent Protest of Mayor de Blasio as Officer Liu Is Laid to Rest," *N.Y. Times*, Jan. 4, 2015, www.nytimes.com/2015/01/05/nyregion/police-officers-gather-for-the-funeral-of-wenjian-liu-killed-in-an-ambush.html; Dean Schabner, "Hundreds Turn Their Back on de Blasio at NYPD Officer's Funeral," ABC News, Dec. 27, 2014, http://abcnews.go.com/US/nypd-officers-turn-back-de-blasio-cops-funeral/story?id=27851746.

47. John F. Manning and Matthew C. Stephenson, *Legislation and Regulation*, 2nd ed. (2013), 351; Richard J. Pierce, *Administrative Law Treatise*, 5th ed. (2010), 1: § 8.1; Rachel A. Harmon, "The Problem of Policing," *Mich. L. Rev.* 110 (2012): 763; Christopher Slobogin, "Panvasive Surveillance, Political Process Theory, and the Nondelegation Doctrine," *Geo. L.J.* 102 (2014): 1721; Richard B. Stewart, "The Reformation of American Administrative Law," *Harv. L. Rev.* 88 (1975): 1671–76.

48. Tracey Maclin, "The Central Meaning of the Fourth Amendment," *Wm. & Mary L. Rev.* 35 (1993): 248–49; Carl McGowan, "Rulemaking and the Police," *Mich. L. Rev.* 70 (1972): 673 ("semi-military tradition").

49. Samuel Walker, "Origins of the Contemporary Criminal Justice Paradigm: The American Bar Foundation Survey, 1953–1969," *Just. Q.* 9 (1992): 50–52, 57–59 (1992).

50. Id. at 56–58, 64–65; *The Challenge of Crime in a Free Society: A Report by the President's Commission on Law Enforcement and Administration of Justice* (1967), 103–06.

51. *The Challenge of Crime in a Free Society*, supra note 50, at 94, 104.

52. See Kenneth Culp Davis, *Police Discretion* (1975), 98–120 (arguing that rule-making is necessary to curb police discretion); Anthony G. Amsterdam, "Perspectives on the Fourth Amendment," *Minn. L. Rev.* 58 (1974): 416–28 (arguing in favor of police rule-making for searches and seizures); Sheldon Krantz et al., *Police Policymaking: The Boston Experience* (1979); Model Rules: Warrantless Searches of Persons and Places (*Project on Law Enforcement and Rulemaking* 1974) (Arizona State University); *A Model Code of Pre-Arraignment Procedure* (*Am. Law. Inst.* 1975); Standards Relating to the Administration of Criminal Justice (*Am. Bar Ass'n* 1974); Symposium, "The American Bar Association Standards Relating to the Administration of Criminal Justice," *Am. Crim. L. Rev.* 12 (1974): 251.

53. See, e.g., Samuel Walker, "Controlling the Cops: A Legislative Approach to Police Rulemaking," *U. Det. L. Rev.* 63 (1986): 361–63 (detailing the history of efforts to control police behavior and noting that "[d]espite the broad consensus over the potential effectiveness of administrative rulemaking, progress in that direction has been sporadic at best"); David A. Sklansky, "Quasi-Affirmative Rights in Constitutional Criminal Procedure," *Va. L. Rev.* 88 (2002): 1272–73 (noting limited progress on administrative or legislative rule-making).

54. See, e.g., Samuel Walker, "The New Paradigm of Police Accountability: The U.S. Justice Department 'Pattern or Practice' Suits in Context," *St. Louis U. Pub. L. Rev.* 22 (2003): 17 ("Many critical areas of police work remain ungoverned by rules (e.g., the use of informants, other undercover tactics, deployment of the canine unit, etc.). Many departments, meanwhile, have rules on the use of force that are not as comprehensive

as they could be . . ."); ACLU of N. Cal., *Stun Gun Fallacy: How the Lack of Taser Regulation Endangers Lives* (2005), www.aclunc.org/publications/stun-gun-fallacy-how -lack-taser-regulation-endangers-lives (noting gaps in police regulations governing use of tasers); John Rappaport, "Second-Order Regulation of Law Enforcement," *Calif. L. Rev.* 103 (2015): 214 (noting that 84 percent of law enforcement agencies lack rules on lineup procedures). For example, the Chicago Police Department (CPD) has guide-lines governing the use of both deadly and nondeadly force, the seizure and forfeiture of vehicles, vessels, and aircraft in the event of an arrest, and the strip searches of ar-restees (which require reasonable suspicion). See Chi. Police Dep't, General Order Nos. G03-02 to G03-02-07, http://directives.chicagopolice.org/directives/ (last visited Aug. 16, 2015) (use of force); Chi. Police Dep't, Special Order No. S07-03-06 (2014), http://directives.chicagopolice.org/directives/data/a7a57bf0-1348fc77-5f913-4901 -b8eedf1b08ca4714.pdf (confiscated property); Chi. Police Dep't, General Order No. G06-01-03 (2012), http://directives.chicagopolice.org/directives/data/a7a56e4b -12ccbe26-df812-ccbe-2c1daf267a24daeb.pdf (strip search of an arrestee). Yet the CPD places virtually no limits on the use of informants, has no policy on drones or aerial sur-veillance, and specifically exempts consent searches during routine traffic or pedestrian stops from department rules and regulations. See Chi. Police Dep't, General Order No. G02-01-01 (1989), http://directives.chicagopolice.org/directives/data/a7a57be2-12be97cf -78912-bea6-a75df41ea0024729.pdf (informants); Chi. Police Dep't, Special Order No. S04-19-01 (2015), http://directives.chicagopolice.org/directives/data/a7a57be2-12a76ce1 -24512-a773-3e562b92ee0b017f.pdf (consent searches). It is worth noting, though, that Illinois recently adopted a statute regulating drone use. Freedom from Drone Surveil-lance Act, 2013 Ill. Legis. Serv. 3930 (West) (codified at 725 Ill. Comp. Stat. Ann. 167/1 (West 2008 & Supp. 2015)).

55. Int'l Assoc. of Chiefs of Police, *Recommended Guidelines for the Use of Unmanned Aircraft* (2012), www.theiacp.org/portals/0/pdfs/IACP_UAGuidelines.pdf.

56. Adam Liptak, "A Ticket, 3 Taser Jolts and, Perhaps, a Trip to the Supreme Court," *N.Y. Times*, May 14, 2012, www.nytimes.com/2012/05/15/us/police-taser-use-on-pregnant -woman-goes-before-supreme-court.html; *2011 Electronic Control Weapon Guidelines* (Police Executive Research Forum & Office of Community Oriented Policing Ser-vices, U.S. Dep't of Justice, 2011), 20; ACLU of Nebraska, *Dangerously Out of Bounds: Taser Use in Nebraska* (2014), 5. www.aclunebraska.org/sites/default/files/field_ documents/dangerously_out_of_bounds_tasers_2014.pdf.

57. U.S. Dep't of Justice, *The Attorney General's Guidelines for Domestic FBI Operations* (2008), 8, www.justice.gov/sites/default/files/ag/legacy/2008/10/03/guidelines.pdf (here-inafter *2008 AG Guidelines*); Fed. Bureau of Investigations, *Domestic Investigations and Operations Guide (DIOG)*, Nov. 7, 2011, http://vault.fbi.gov/FBI%20Domestic%20Inves tigations%20and%20Operations%20Guide%20%28DIOG%29.

58. See Office of the Inspector General, U.S. Dep't of Justice, *A Review of the FBI's Inves-tigations of Certain Domestic Advocacy Groups* (2010), 30, 34 (describing the memo on "Pittsburgh anti-war activity") (hereinafter OIG, *Review*); *FBI Oversight: Hearing Be-fore the S. Comm. on the Judiciary*, 109th Cong. (2006) (statement of Sen. Patrick J. Leahy); John O'Neil, "F.B.I. Director Is Bombarded by Stinging Questions at Senate Hearing," *N.Y. Times*, May 3, 2006, www.nytimes.com/2006/05/03/washington/03fbi .html.

59. OIG, *Review*, supra note 58, at 46–47.

60. Id. at 31.

61. Id. at 36–38, 42–47, 63–65, 190.

62. Id. at 189–90; Eric Lichtblau, "Justice Dept. Completes Revision of F.B.I. Guidelines for Terrorism Investigations," *N.Y. Times*, Oct. 3, 2008, www.nytimes.com/2008/10/04

/washington/04fbi.html; *2008 AG Guidelines*, supra note 57, at 16 ("critical informa-tion"). In promulgating the 2008 Guidelines, there was some limited public participa-tion. An earlier draft was circulated, and met opposition from civil liberties groups. In response, the Justice Department included in the final rule "restrictions on the tactics that agents can use in handling large-scale demonstrations and civil disturbances" and required that such investigations be limited to thirty days. Civil rights groups still op-posed the final rule, and controversial provisions remained unchanged between the draft and final guidelines. Lichtblau, "Justice Dept. Completes Revision," supra.

63. See generally *2008 AG Guidelines*, supra note 57, at 17; Emily Berman, Brennan Ctr. for Justice, *Domestic Intelligence: New Powers, New Risks* (2011), 2, 17, 22, 28. On the episode in Orange County, see Berman, *Domestic Intelligence*, supra, at 4; Victoria Kim, "Federal Judge Throws Out Lawsuit Over Spying on O.C. Muslims," *L.A. Times*, Aug. 15, 2012, http://articles.latimes.com/2012/aug/15/local/la-me-mosque-spying -20120815; Paul Harris, "The Ex-FBI Informant with a Change Of Heart: 'There Is No Real Hunt. It's Fixed,'" *The Guardian*, Mar. 20, 2012, www.theguardian.com/world /2012/mar/20/fbi-informant.

64. First Amendment Rights and Police Standards Act of 2004, 52 D.C. Reg. 2296 (2005); Mary M. Cheh, "Legislative Oversight of Police: Lessons Learned from an Investigation of Police Handling of Demonstrations in Washington, D.C.," *J. Legis.* 32 (2005): 4; Emily Berman, "Regulating Domestic Intelligence Collection," *Wash & Lee L. Rev.* 71 (2014): 25 (DIOG); Berman, *Domestic Intelligence*, supra note 63, at 24 (LAPD).

65. The federal Administrative Procedure Act (APA) authorizes courts to set aside agency action found to be "arbitrary, capricious"—not the product of reasoned decision-making. 5 U.S.C. § 706(2)(A); see also Manning and Stephenson, *Legislation and Regulation*, supra note 47, at 669.

66. *2008 AG Guidelines*, supra note 57, at 17. On the shift from the old rules to the new rules, see Berman, *Domestic Intelligence*, supra note 63, at 22; OIG, *Review*, supra note 57, at 8–9 ("detecting and interrupting").

67. Berman, *Domestic Intelligence*, supra note 63, at 21. On concern whether unfocused antiterrorism efforts are making us safer, see infra Chapter 12.

68. See, e.g., ACLU, *Excessive Militarization*, supra note 21, at 1; Harwood, "One Nation Under SWAT," supra note 22; "Paramilitary Police: Cops or Soldiers?: America's Police Have Become Too Militarised," *The Economist*, Mar. 22, 2014, www.economist.com /news/united-states/21599349-americas-police-have-become-too-militarised-cops-or -soldiers.

69. See Carl Matthies, Vera Inst. of Justice, *Advancing the Quality of Cost-Benefit Analysis for Justice Programs* (2014), 40; ACLU, *War Comes Home*, supra note 21, at 27 ("[D]ata collecting and reporting in the context of SWAT was at best sporadic and at worst vir-tually nonexistent."); Joanna Schwartz, "Police Indemnification," *N.Y.U. L. Rev.* 89 (2014): 903–904 (detailing problems author encountered in gathering data on police settlements and indemnification policies).

70. ACLU, *War Comes Home*, supra note 21, at 23 (knock and wait); *Wilson v. Arkansas*, 514 U.S. 927, 930, 933 (1997) (same); Kevin Flynn and Lou Kilzer, "No-Knocks Net Little Jail Time," *Rocky Mountain News*, March 12, 2000 (on file with author).

71. Balko, *Overkill*, supra note 21, at 27; Smith, "Reining in SWAT," supra note 43 ("con-tain and call-out").

72. Gerald M. Caplan, "The Case for Rulemaking by Law Enforcement Agencies," *Law & Contemp. Probs.* 36 (1971): 509.

3. COURTS THAT CAN'T JUDGE

1. *Thomas* ex rel. *Thomas v. Roberts*, 261 F.3d 1160, 1163 (11th Cir. 2001).

2. Id. at 1164.

3. Id. at 1168–69. One judge did note, however, that the search only "*probably* went too far," and urged caution in interpreting the scope of constitutional protection in the school environment too broadly. Id. at 1177 (Roney, J., concurring specially) (emphasis added).

4. Id. at 1170–77 (majority opinion); *Jenkins* ex rel. *Hall v. Talladega City Bd. of Educ.*, 115 F.3d 821, 825–26 (11th Cir. 1997) ("In the absence of detailed guidance, no reasonable school official could glean . . . what constitutes an infraction great enough to warrant a constitutionally reasonable search or, conversely, minor enough such that a search of property or person would be characterized as unreasonable.").

5. *D.H.* ex rel. *Dawson v. Clayton Cty. Sch. Dist.*, 904 F. Supp. 2d 1301, 1304 (N.D. Ga. 2012); Complaint at paras. 11, 13, 15, *D.H.* ex rel. *Dawson*, 904 F. Supp. 2d 1301 (No. 1:12-CV-00478-AT).

6. Billingslea eventually was fired, though not so much for the search as for claiming that he had not been penalized for his conduct in an interview with the local paper. *Thomas v. Clayton Cty. Bd. of Educ.*, 94 F. Supp. 2d 1290, 1298 (N.D. Ga. 1999). The investigators found that Billingslea had violated departmental policy and existing law, searched without probable cause, acted unprofessionally in dropping his pants in front of the students, and improperly used threatening tactics to get the kids to pull down their pants. Id. at 1297, n. 9.

7. *Hearring v. Sliwowski*, 806 F.3d 864, 865 (6th Cir. 2015) (first grade); *Phaneuf v. Fraikin*, 448 F.3d 591 (2d Cir. 2006) (twelfth grade); *Dubbs v. Head Start, Inc.*, 336 F.3d 1194, 1200 (10th Cir. 2003) (preschool); *Tenenbaum v. Williams*, 193 F.3d 581 (2d Cir. 1999) (kindergarten); *S.S.* ex rel. *Sandidge v. Turner Unified Sch. Dist. # 202*, 12-CV-02346-CM, 2012 WL 6561525, at *1 (D. Kan. Dec. 14, 2012) (strip search by two school officials); *Bellnier v. Lund*, 438 F. Supp. 47, 50 (N.D.N.Y. 1977) (strip search by multiple school officials in front of other students in search of missing $3); *Cornfield* ex rel. *Lewis v. Consol. High Sch. Dist. No. 230*, 991 F.2d 1316, 1319 (7th Cir. 1993) ("well-endowed").

8. *Safford Unified Sch. Dist. No. 1 v. Redding*, 557 U.S. 364, 368–69, 378–79 (2009); id. at 380 (Stevens, J., concurring in part and dissenting in part) (quoting *N.J. v. T.L.O.*, 469 U.S. 325, 382n25 (1985) (Stevens, J. concurring in part and dissenting in part)).

9. Barry Friedman, *The Will of the People: How Public Opinion Has Influenced the Supreme Court and Shaped the Meaning of the Constitution* (2009), 270–77.

10. Herbert L. Packer, "Policing the Police: Nine Men Are Not Enough," *New Republic*, Sept. 4, 1965, at 19.

11. See John Hart Ely, *Democracy and Distrust: A Theory of Judicial Review* (1980), 73–75 (describing the Warren Court as largely motivated by a concern with correcting racial injustice); Burt Neuborne, "The Gravitational Pull of Race on the Warren Court," *Sup. Ct. Rev.*, 2010: 85–86 ("It is hard to overstate the sense of urgency driving the [Warren] Court's concern over racial discrimination in the enforcement of the criminal law.").

12. Friedman, *The Will of the People*, supra note 9, at 271–75 (quoting Governor Farris Bryant of Florida and describing the contemporaneous popularity of a number of the Warren Court's seminal criminal procedure decisions); Corinna Barrett Lain, "Countermajoritarian Hero or Zero? Rethinking the Warren Court's Role in the Criminal Procedure Revolution," *U. Pa. L. Rev.* 152 (2004): 1383, 1389–99 (quoting Anthony Lewis and discussing *Gideon*).

13. Friedman, *The Will of the People*, supra note 9, at 276.

14. Id. at 276–77.
15. Id. at 283.
16. See Daryl J. Levinson, "Rights Essentialism," *Colum. L. Rev.* 99 (1999): 904–905 ("At least since Legal Realism, no one has missed the point that the value of a right is a function of the consequences that will be brought to bear when the right is violated."); Barry Friedman, "When Rights Encounter Reality: Enforcing Federal Remedies," *S. Cal. L. Rev.* 65 (1992): 735–36 (describing the legal realist insight that "[w]ithout an available and enforceable remedy, a right may be nothing more than a nice idea").
17. Ann Woolhandler, "Patterns of Official Immunity and Accountability," *Case W. Res. L. Rev.* 37 (1987): 414–16 (describing the prevalence of damages actions against state agents throughout the nineteenth and early twentieth centuries, including the role of good-faith reliance in precluding punitive damages); *Coryell v. Colbaugh*, 1 N.J.L. 77, 77 (1791) (describing punitive, or exemplary, damages as "damages for example's sake, to prevent such offences in future").
18. *Little v. Barreme*, 6 U.S. (2 Cranch) 170, 170–72, 175–79 (1804). For the model used to calculate present value, see Robert C. Sahr, *Consumer Price Index (CPI) Conversion Factors for Years 1774 to Estimated 2026 to Convert to Dollars of 2015* (2016), http://liberalarts.oregonstate.edu/sites/liberalarts.oregonstate.edu/files/polisci/faculty-research/sahr/inflation-conversion/pdf/cv2015.pdf.
19. Katharine A. Wagner, "*Little v. Barreme*: The Little Case Caught in the Middle of a Big War Powers Debate," *J. L. Soc'y* 10 (2008): 78; Thomas Y. Davies, "Recovering the Original Fourth Amendment," *Mich. L. Rev.* 98 (1999): 588–89 (explaining that a peace officer was liable if he was the complainant in a specific warrant, while the magistrate or the peace officer could be liable if the warrant was general).
20. David E. Engdahl, "Immunity and Accountability for Positive Government Wrongs," *U. Colo. L. Rev.* 44 (1972): 21–56 (describing the gradual elimination of effective remedies in suits against state actors, and arguing that the breakdown was an "inadvertent" result of "pragmatic case-by-case adjudication"); *Mapp v. Ohio*, 367 U.S. 643, 651–52 (1961) (describing the states' experience of "other remedies hav[ing] completely failed to secure compliance with the constitutional provisions" (quoting *People v. Cahan*, 282 P. 2d 905, 911 (1955))); *Cahan*, 282 P. 2d at 906 (discussing police testimony in which "forcible entries and seizures were candidly admitted").
21. *Mapp*, 367 U.S at 644; Carolyn Long, Mapp v. Ohio: *Guarding Against Unreasonable Searches and Seizures* (2006), 2, 7 ("cunning" and "audacious").
22. Long, *Mapp v. Ohio*, supra note 21, at 5–6; *Mapp*, 367 U.S at 667, 669 (Douglas, J., concurring).
23. Long, Mapp v. Ohio, supra note 21, at 6–8, 66. The government still maintained throughout litigation that it did have *a* warrant, just not one that covered the evidence obtained. Supplemental Brief of Appellee on the Merits, *Mapp v. Ohio*, 367 U.S. 643 (No. 60-236), 1961 WL 101784, at *3. Delau, however, admitted twenty years later that there was no warrant at all. Long, *Mapp v. Ohio*, supra note 21, at 13.
24. Long, Mapp v. Ohio, supra note 21, at 8, 15.
25. Id. at 9, 13, 21.
26. Id. at 29, 63, 68.
27. *Weeks v. United States*, 232 U.S. 383, 393 (1914) (adopting the exclusionary rule); *Wolf v. Colorado*, 338 U.S 25 (1949).
28. *Mapp*, 367 U.S at 654–55.
29. Akhil Reed Amar, "Fourth Amendment First Principles," *Harv. L. Rev.* 107 (1994): 785–800 (describing the exclusionary rule as an "awkward and embarrassing remedy"); Richard A. Posner, "Rethinking the Fourth Amendment," *Sup. Ct. Rev.* 1981: 49 (critiquing

the exclusionary as an often clumsy deterrence mechanism); Potter Stewart, "The Road to *Mapp v. Ohio* and Beyond: The Origins, Development and Future of the Exclusionary Rule in Search-and-Seizure Cases," *Colum. L. Rev.* 83 (1983): 1393 ("technicality").

30. Michael J. Murphy, "Judicial Review of Police Methods in Law Enforcement: The Problem of Compliance by Police Departments," *Tex. L. Rev.* 44 (1966): 941; Sidney E. Zion, "Detectives Get a Course in Law," *N.Y. Times*, Apr. 28 1965, at A50 (Riesman).

31. See, e.g., *Herring v. United States*, 555 U.S. 135, 139 (2009) ("[The exclusionary rule] is 'designed to safeguard Fourth Amendment rights generally through its deterrent effect.'" (quoting *United States v. Calandra*, 414 U. S. 338, 348 (1974))); *Mapp*, 367 U.S at 656 ("[T]he purpose of the exclusionary rule 'is to deter—to compel respect for the constitutional guaranty in the only effectively available way—by removing the incentive to disregard it.'" (quoting *Elkins v. United States*, 364 U.S. 206, 217 (1960))).

32. Oren Bar-Gill and Barry Friedman, "Taking Warrants Seriously," *Nw. U. L. Rev.* 106 (2012): 1623.

33. Id. at 1623–24 (describing the general problem of the biased sample); *Murray v. United States*, 487 U.S. 533, 535–36 (1988). In the kind of truly twisted logic that gives lawyers a bad name, Justice Scalia wrote that because the police didn't tell the magistrate who gave them the warrant that they'd already broken in and seen drugs, the warrant they did get was still valid. *Murray*, 487 U.S. at 542–43.

34. *Murray*, 487 U.S. at 544 (Marshall, J., dissenting).

35. Tia Mitchell, "Drug Agents Prowl City Bus Stations," *Fla. Times-Union*, Oct. 20, 2002, http://jacksonville.com/tu-online/stories/102002/met_10741892.shtml.

36. See *Nix v. Williams*, 467 U.S. 431 (1984) (announcing the "inevitable discovery" exception to the exclusionary rule); *Herring*, 555 U.S. at 147 (holding that good-faith reliance on another police department's error meant evidence was admitted); *United States v. Leon*, 468 U.S. 897, 926 (1984) (holding that good-faith reliance on a warrant issued with insufficient probable cause meant evidence was admitted); *Davis v. United States*, 564 U.S. 229, 237 (2011) (citation omitted).

37. See, e.g., Amar, "Fourth Amendment First Principles," supra note 29, at 785–800 ("On efficiency grounds, money damages are often far superior to exclusion. Money is infinitely divisible; exclusion is clunky."); Posner, "Rethinking the Fourth Amendment," supra note 29 (advocating for money damages as a more natural and effective remedy).

38. See *Bivens v. Six Unknown Named Agents of Fed. Bureau of Narcotics*, 403 U.S. 388 (1971) (holding that federal officers may be sued for damages directly under the Fourth Amendment); Monroe v. Pape, 365 U.S. 167 (1961) (interpreting 42 U.S.C. § 1983 to provide a cause of action against officials acting under color of state law for violations of constitutional rights).

39. See Bar-Gill and Friedman, "Taking Warrants Seriously," supra note 32, at 1626–34 (describing the challenge of properly calibrating money damages).

40. See *Harlow v. Fitzgerald*, 457 U.S. 800, 818–19 (1982) ("[G]overnment officials performing discretionary functions, generally are shielded from liability for civil damages insofar as their conduct does not violate clearly established statutory or constitutional rights of which a reasonable person would have known.").

41. *Mattos v. Agarano*, 661 F.3d 433, 448 (9th Cir. 2011) (internal quotation marks omitted) (Malaika Brooks); *Miller v. Idaho State Patrol*, 252 P.3d 1274, 1279 (Idaho 2011); *Steen v. City of Pensacola*, 809 F. Supp. 2d 1342, 1344–45, 1353 (N.D. Fla. 2011) (internal quotation marks omitted); *S.S. ex rel. Sandidge*, 2012 WL 6561525, at *1, *4 (Kansas).

42. *Alden v. Maine*, 527 U.S. 706 (1999) (prohibiting Congress from abrogating state sovereign immunity in state court); *Seminole Tribe of Florida v. Florida*, 517 U.S. 44 (1996) (prohibiting Congress from abrogating state sovereign immunity in federal court); *Hans v. Louisiana*, 134 U.S. 1 (1890) (interpreting the Eleventh Amendment to prohibit a

citizen of a state from suing any state in federal court); *Monell v. Dep't of Soc. Servs.*, 436 U.S. 658, 690 (1978) (requiring an official policy to hold a local government or police force liable).

43. *Maryland v. Wilson*, 519 U.S. 408 (1997) (ordering everyone out of the car); *Atwater v. Lago Vista*, 532 U.S. 318 (2001) (arresting the driver); *United States v. Robinson*, 414 U.S. 218 (1973) (conducting a search incident to the arrest); *Florence v. Board of Chosen Freeholders* 132 S. Ct. 1510 (2012) (conducing a strip search and visual cavity search upon placing a person into a facility).

44. *New York v. Belton*, 453 U.S. 454, 458 (1981) (quoting *Dunaway v. New York*, 442 U.S. 200, 213–14 (1979)); see also Id. at 458 ("A highly sophisticated set of rules, qualified by all sorts of ifs, ands, and buts and requiring the drawing of subtle nuances and hairline distinctions, may be the sort of heady stuff upon which the facile minds of lawyers and judges eagerly feed, but they may be literally impossible of application by the officer in the field." (quoting Wayne R. LaFave, "'Case-by-Case Adjudication' Versus 'Standardized Procedures': The *Robinson* Dilemma," *Sup. Ct. Rev.* 1974: 141)); *Florence*, 132 S. Ct. at 1522 ("Officers who interact with those suspected of violating the law have an 'essential interest in readily administrable rules.'" [quoting *Atwater*, 532 U.S. at 347]); *Atwater*, 532 U.S. at 347 ("[T]he Fourth Amendment has to be applied on the spur (and in the heat) of the moment, and the object in implementing its command of reasonableness is to draw standards sufficiently clear and simple to be applied with a fair prospect of surviving judicial second-guessing months and years after an arrest or search is made.").

45. *Schneckloth v. Bustamonte*, 412 U.S. 218, 227 (1973) ("totality of the circumstances"); *Florida v. Harris*, 133 S. Ct. 1050, 1055 (2013) ("all-things-considered approach").

46. *Ohio v. Robinette*, 519 U.S. 33, 48 (1996) (Stevens, J., dissenting).

47. See, e.g., *Virginia v. Moore*, 553 U.S. 164 (2008) (rejecting the Supreme Court of Virginia's holding that a search incident to an arrest in violation of state law is a violation of the Fourth Amendment); *Robinette*, 519 U.S. (rejecting the Ohio Supreme Court's holding that police must inform motorists that they are free to leave before seeking their consent to search); *California v. Greenwood*, 486 U.S. 35 (1988) (rejecting the California Court of Appeals' holding that warrantless searches of people's trash violates the Fourth Amendment); *South Dakota v. Opperman*, 428 U.S. 364 (1976) (rejecting the Supreme Court of South Dakota's holding that a warrantless inventory search of an impounded car violates the Fourth Amendment); *Cooper v. California* 386 U.S. 58 (1967) (rejecting the California Court of Appeal's holding that a warrantless glovebox search of an impounded car violates the Fourth Amendment).

48. Barry Friedman and Maria Ponomarenko, "Democratic Policing," *N.Y.U. L. Rev.* 90 (2015): 1871–75.

49. Christopher Slobogin, "Panvasive Surveillance, Political Process Theory, and the Nondelegation Doctrine," *Geo. L.J.* 102 (2014): 1723.

50. See, e.g., *Wyoming v. Houghton*, 526 U.S. 295, 299–300 (1999); *Michigan Dep't of State Police v. Sitz*, 496 U.S. 444, 455 (1990).

51. T. Alexander Aleinikoff, "Constitutional Law in the Age of Balancing," *Yale L.J.* 96 (1987): 972–73 (discussing the incommensurability problem); Tracey Maclin, "Constructing Fourth Amendment Principles from the Government Perspective: Whose Amendment Is It, Anyway?," *Am. Crim. L. Rev.* 25 (1988): 669 (arguing that the Fourth Amendment balancing test skews in favor of government interests).

52. Christopher Slobogin and Joseph E. Schumacher, "Reasonable Expectations of Privacy and Autonomy in Fourth Amendment Cases: An Empirical Look at Understandings Recognized and Permitted by Society," *Duke L.J.* 42 (1993): 733–42; *United States v. Place*, 462 U.S. 696, 707 (1983) (dog sniff); *Bd. of Educ. v. Earls*, 536 U.S. 822, 833

(2002) (quoting Vernonia School District 47J v. Acton, 515 U.S. 646, 658 (1995)) (compelled urine test).

53. *Earls*, 536 U.S. at 837–38; Pieter S. de Ganon, Note, "Noticing Crisis," *N.Y.U. L. Rev.* 86 (2001): 573, 598 (discussing the paperwork submitted by the school district to the federal government). *All* there was in the way of evidence was teachers who said they had heard students talking about drugs, or had allegedly seen students under the influence, one single incident in which the police had found "drugs or drug paraphernalia in a car driven by a Future Farmers of America member," and one occasion in which "marijuana cigarettes" were found near a school parking lot—with no idea how they got there. *Earls*, 536 U.S. at 835. For this, all students involved in extracurricular activities were forced to undergo drug testing. Id.

54. *Earls*, 536 U.S. at 834 (school drug testing); *Sitz*, 496 U.S. at 451–52 (drunk-driving roadblock).

55. *United States v. White*, 401 U.S. 745, 756 (1971) (Douglas, J., dissenting).

56. Bill Status: SB-914 Search warrants: portable electronic devices, http://leginfo.legislature .ca.gov/faces/billStatusClient.xhtml?bill_id=201120120SB914; Bill Status: AB-1327 Unmanned aircraft systems, https://leginfo.legislature.ca.gov/faces/billStatusClient.xhtml ?bill_id=201320140AB1327

4. FOSTERING DEMOCRATIC POLICING

1. See, e.g., Wesley Lowery, *Ferguson: Three Minutes That Changed America* (2015); Jessica Lussenhop, "Ferguson: The Other Young Black Lives Laid to Rest in Michael Brown's Cemetery," *BBC News*, Aug. 7, 2015, www.bbc.com/news/magazine-33765871; John Eligon, "A Year After Ferguson, Housing Segregation Defies Tools to Erase It," *N.Y. Times*, Aug. 8, 2015, www.nytimes.com/2015/08/09/us/a-year-after-ferguson-housing -segregation-defies-tools-to-erase-it.html; Jake Halpern, "The Cop," *New Yorker*, Aug. 10 & 17, 2015, www.newyorker.com/magazine/2015/08/10/the-cop; Kelsey Proud, "Ferguson, One Year Later: What Others Are Reporting," St. Louis Public Radio, Aug. 9, 2015, http://news.stlpublicradio.org/post/ferguson-one-year-later-what-others-are -reporting.

2. "Michael Brown's Shooting and Its Immediate Aftermath in Ferguson," *N.Y. Times*, Aug. 25, 2014, www.nytimes.com/interactive/2014/08/12/us/13police-shooting-of -black-teenager-michael-brown.html.

3. Jamelle Bouie, "The Militarization of the Police," *Slate*, Aug. 13, 2014, www.slate.com /articles/news_and_politics/politics/2014/08/police_in_ferguson_military_weapons _threaten_protesters.html; see also Bradley Campbell and Nina Porzucki, "Why Are Police Using Military Gear in Ferguson and How Did They Get It?," *PRI*, Aug. 14, 2014, www.pri.org/stories/2014-08-14/why-are-police-using-military-gear-ferguson -and-how-did-they-get-it; Jay Caspian Kang, "A Militarized Night in Ferguson," *New Yorker*, Aug. 12, 2015, www.newyorker.com/news/news-desk/militarized-night-fer guson; Paul D. Shinkman, "Ferguson and the Militarization of Police," *U.S. News & World Rep.*, Aug. 14, 2014, www.usnews.com/news/articles/2014/08/14/ferguson-and-the -shocking-nature-of-us-police-militarization; Francesca Trianni, "Watch: Protesters Hit With Tear Gas and Rubber Bullets During Ferguson Unrest," *Time*, Aug. 14, 2014, http://time.com/3111829/ferguson-tear-gas-rubber-bullets-protests/.

4. Julie Bosman and Matt Apuzzo, "In Wake of Clashes, Calls to Demilitarize Police," *N.Y. Times*, Aug. 14, 2014, www.nytimes.com/2014/08/15/us/ferguson-missouri-in -wake-of-clashes-calls-to-demilitarize-police.html ("chaos stricken corner of Eastern Europe"); Jake Grovum, "Can States Slow the Flow of Military Equipment to Police?," *Stateline*, Mar. 24, 2015, www.pewtrusts.org/en/research-and-analysis/blogs/stateline

/2015/3/24/can-states-slow-the-flow-of-military-equipment-to-police (quoting Branden Peters); John Schwartz, Michael D. Shear, and Michael Paulson, "New Tack on Unrest Eases Tension in Missouri," *N.Y. Times*, Aug. 14, 2014, www.nytimes.com/2014 /08/15/us/ferguson-missouri-police-shooting.html (quoting Rand Paul). Those "voices in the wilderness" included the CATO Institute's Radley Balko, author of *Overkill: The Rise of Paramilitary Police Raids in America* (2006); the ACLU with its damning report, *War Comes Home: The Excessive Militarization of American Policing* (2014), www.aclu.org/sites/default/files/assets/jus14-warcomeshome-report-web-rel1.pdf; the civil rights advocate Michelle Alexander in her important book *The New Jim Crow: Mass Incarceration in the Age of Colorblindness* (2012), 73–75; and a few members of Congress, such as Hank Johnson of Georgia; Hank Johnson and Michael Shank, Opinion, "Small Town America Shouldn't Resemble War Zone," *USA Today*, Mar. 10, 2014, www.usatoday.com/story/opinion/2014/03/10/america-police-military -weapons-column/5789445/.

5. Benjamin Bell, "Missouri Gov. Jay Nixon 'Thunderstruck' by Images of Ferguson Police," ABCNews, Aug. 17, 2014, http://abcnews.go.com/blogs/politics/2014/08/missouri-gov -jay-nixon-thunderstruck-by-images-of-ferguson-police/; Everett Rosenfeld, "Where Ferguson's 'Military' Police Get Their Gear," *CNBC*, Aug. 14, 2014, www.cnbc.com/2014 /08/14/ferguson-missouri-protests-where-fergusons-military-cops-get-their-gear.html (MRAP/BearCat); David Nakamura and Wesley Lowery, "Obama Administration Bans Some Military-Style Assault Gear from Local Police Departments," *Wash. Post*, May 18, 2015, www.washingtonpost.com/news/post-politics/wp/2015/05/18/obama-to-visit -camden-n-j-to-tout-community-policing-reforms/ (quoting Wm. Lacy Clay); Burgess Everett, "Claire McCaskill: 'We Need to Demilitarize,'" *Politico*, Aug. 14, 2014, www .politico.com/story/2014/08/ferguson-claire-mccaskill-demilitarize-110013; Bosman and Apuzzo, "In Wake of Clashes, Calls to Demilitarize Police," supra note 4 (quoting Eric Holder); Zeke J. Miller, "Obama: 'No Excuse' for Ferguson Violence," *Time*, Aug. 14, 2014, http://time.com/3111730/barack-obama-ferguson-michael-brown/.

6. Bosman and Apuzzo, "In Wake of Clashes, Calls to Demilitarize Police," supra note 4 (quoting Nick Gragnani). On the various transfers of funds and materiel from the federal government to domestic policing agencies, see Executive Office of the President, *Review: Federal Support for Local Law Enforcement Equipment Acquisition* (2014), 3, 7–19, www.whitehouse.gov/sites/default/files/docs/federal_support_for_local_law _enforcement_equipment_acquisition.pdf (2014) (hereinafter *Review: Federal Support for Local Law Enforcement*); ACLU, *War Comes Home*, supra note 4, at 17, 24; Balko, *Overkill*, supra note 4, at 7–8.

7. *Review: Federal Support for Local Law Enforcement*, supra note 6, at 3, 7–9 (describing the "controlled equipment"); Jeff Schogol, "Can You Use the .50-Caliber on Human Targets?," *Stars and Stripes*, Feb. 9, 2011, www.stripes.com/blogs/the-rumor-doctor/the -rumor-doctor-1.104348/can-you-use-the-50-caliber-on-human-targets-1.134278; Law Enforcement Equipment Working Group, *Recommendations Pursuant to Executive Order 13688: Federal Support for Local Law Enforcement Equipment Acquisition* (2015), 13, www.whitehouse.gov/sites/default/files/docs/le_equipment_wg_final_report_final .pdf ("[T]his type of firearm, which is typically used for military operations, is very destructive and capable of penetrating structures and lightly armored vehicles.") (hereinafter *Recommendations Pursuant to E.O. 13688*); ACLU, *War Comes Home*, supra note 4, at 13 ("[A] .50 caliber machine gun . . . shoots bullets powerful enough to blast through the buildings on multiple city blocks.") The President's Working Group ultimately put bayonets on their "Prohibited Equipment List." *Recommendations Pursuant to E.O. 13688*, supra, at 13.

8. Grovum, supra note 4 (North Carolina, Tennessee, Florida); Molly Knefel, "Why Are Police Using Military-Grade Weapons in High Schools?," *Rolling Stone*, Oct. 8, 2014,

www.rollingstone.com/politics/news/why-are-police-using-military-grade-weapons-in
-high-schools-20141008 (Texas, California); Niraj Chokshi, "School Police Across the
Country Receive Excess Military Weapons and Gear," *Wash. Post*, Sept. 16, 2014,
www.washingtonpost.com/blogs/govbeat/wp/2014/09/16/school-police-across-the
-country-receive-excess-military-weapons-and-gear/ (grenade launchers, Mississippi
Hinds Community College, University of Central Florida).

9. *Review: Federal Support for Local Law Enforcement*, supra note 6, at 3.

10. Id. at 2, 4, 7.

11. Id. at 7. ("Property obtained through the 1033 Program must be placed into use within
one year of receipt . . .").

12. Troy Carter, "Obama's Anti-Police Militarization Order Slightly Overlaps New Montana Law," *Bozeman Daily Chronicle*, May 22, 2015, www.bozemandailychronicle.com
/news/politics/obama-s-anti-police-militarization-order-slightly-overlaps-new-montana
/article_32a01ca3-d822-5ee2-9fd7-d191ac66a492.html.

13. Nia H. Gill Esq. (D), New Jersey Legislature, www.njleg.state.nj.us/members/bio.asp
?Leg=126; Nia Gill, New Jersey Council of Teaching Hospitals, www.njcth.org
/PublicInnerPage/Legislative-Profiles/New-Jersey-Senate/Nia-Gill.aspx; interview by
Barry Friedman with Nia Gill, Aug. 6, 2015 (hereinafter Gill Interview).

14. Gill Interview, supra note 13.

15. "ACLU-NJ Lauds NJ's First-in-the-Nation Police Militarization Law," *ACLU-NJ*,
Mar. 19, 2015, www.aclu-nj.org/news/2015/03/19/aclu-nj-lauds-njs-first-nation-police
-militarization-law; Michael Symons, "Lawmakers Want More Scrutiny of Police Military Gear," *Asbury Park Press*, Jan. 12, 2015, www.app.com/story/news/politics/new
-jersey/2015/01/12/nj-police-surplus-military-equipment/21655389/; N.J. Stat. Ann.
§ 40A:5-30.1 (2016), www.njleg.state.nj.us/2014/Bills/PL15/23_.HTM; Gill Interview,
supra note 13.

16. Bob Adelmann, "Montana Is Second State to Slow Police Militarization," *The New
American*, Apr. 27, 2015, www.thenewamerican.com/usnews/crime/item/20748
-montana-is-second-state-to-slow-police-militarization; Nicholas Schwaderer (R), Montana Legislature, http://leg.mt.gov/css/Sessions/63rd/leg_info.asp?HouseID=1&SessionID
=107&LAWSID=15240; Mont. Code Ann. §§ 7-32-401 to-402 (2015).

17. Adam Nagourney, "Police Armored Vehicle Is Unwelcome in California College
Town," *N.Y. Times*, Sept. 13, 2014, http://nyti.ms/1q24csk (Davis); Susan Shroder, "SD
Unified to Return Armored Vehicle: Military Appearance of the Federal Surplus
Vehicle Created Uneasiness," *San Diego Union-Tribune*, Sept. 18, 2014, www
.sandiegouniontribune.com/news/2014/sep/18/san-diego-unified-to-return-armored
-vehicle/; Nick Henderson, "Town Board Declares It Will Never Accept Any Defense
Weapons," *Woodstock Times*, Aug. 22, 2014 (on file with author).

18. Grovum, supra note 4 ("backed by Democrats and Republicans, in red states and blue
states); "ACLU-NJ Lauds NJ's First-in-the-Nation Police Militarization Law," supra
note 15; interview by Barry Friedman with Ari Rosmarin, Aug. 6, 2015 (hereinafter
Rosmarin Interview); Mike Maharrey, "Montana Law Taking on Federal Militarization
of Police Now in Effect," *Tenth Amendment Ctr.*, Oct. 1, 2015, http://blog.tenth
amendmentcenter.com/2015/10/montana-law-taking-on-federal-militarization-of
-police-now-in-effect/; Mike Maharrey, "First in the Country: New Jersey Law a First
Step to Stop Federal Militarization of Local Police," *Tenth Amendment Ctr.*, Mar. 18,
2015, http://blog.tenthamendmentcenter.com/2015/03/first-in-the-country-new-jersey
-law-a-first-step-to-stop-federal-militarization-of-local-police/; Monica Davey and
Shaila Dewan, "Law Enforcement Concerns Create Unlikely Alliances in Missouri
and Beyond," *N.Y. Times*, Feb. 13, 2015, www.nytimes.com/2015/02/15/us/law
-enforcement-issues-in-missouri-and-other-states-spur-unlikely-alliances.html (quoting Bill Hennessy).

19. Rick Anderson, "Game of Drones: How LAPD Quietly Acquired the Spy Birds Shunned by Seattle," *L.A. Weekly*, June 19, 2014, www.laweekly.com/news/game-of -drones-how-lapd-quietly-acquired-the-spy-birds-shunned-by-seattle-4794894.

20. Katherine Hafner, "Coalition Continues Protest of LAPD's New Drone Policy with Downtown LA Town Hall," NBC L.A., Nov. 8, 2014, www.nbclosangeles.com/news /local/Coalition-Continues-to-Protest-LAPD-Acqusition-of-Aerial-Drones-282030421 .html (quoting Chief Beck and noting the formation of Drone-Free LAPD No Drones, LA!); Melissa Pamer and Mark Mester, "LAPD's 2 Drones Will Remain Grounded During Policy Review, Police Commission Says Amid Protest," KTLA 5, Sept. 15, 2014, http://ktla.com/2014/09/15/anti-spying-group-drone-free-lapd-to-protest-state -bill-that-would-allow-police-drones/ (noting that the drones were handed over to the Inspector General and reporting the L.A. Police Commission's tweet); see also Jim Newton, Opinion, "Drones and the LAPD," *L.A. Times*, Nov. 16, 2014, www.latimes .com/opinion/op-ed/la-oe-newton-column-lapd-drones-20141117-column.html. In June 2014 the LAPD announced it would not do anything with the drones until further public input. As of October 2015 there were no further developments after the LAPD chief handed the drones over to the department's Inspector General in September 2014. See Shawn Musgrave, "Los Angeles Police Have Spent a Year Figuring Out How to Use Their Drones," *Vice*, Oct. 1, 2015, http://motherboard.vice.com/read/los-angeles -police-have-spent-a-year-figuring-out-how-to-use-their-drones.

21. See Robert Salonga, "San Jose: Police Apologize for Drone Secrecy, Promise Transparency," *Mercury News*, Aug. 5, 2014, www.mercurynews.com/crime-courts/ci_2627 9254/san-jose-police-apologize-secret-drone-purchase-promise; Robert Salonga, "San Jose: Drone Debate Continues as SJPD Details Proposed Use Guidelines," *Mercury News*, Dec. 6, 2014, www.mercurynews.com/crime-courts/ci_27083927/san-jose -drone-debate-continues-sjpd-details-proposed; Robert Salonga, "San Jose: Commission to Endorse One-Year Pilot for Police Drone," *Mercury News*, Apr. 9, 2015, www .mercurynews.com/crime-courts/ci_27875047/san-jose-commission-endorse-one-year -pilot-police.

22. Bonnie Eslinger, "Menlo Park: Council Approves Ordinance Regulating Police Use of Surveillance Data," *Mercury News*, May 14, 2014, www.mercurynews.com/breaking -news/ci_25766277/menlo-park-council-approves-ordinance-regulating-police-use; Richard A. Oppel, Jr., "Activists Wield Search Data to Challenge and Change Police Policy," *N.Y. Times*, Nov. 20, 2014, www.nytimes.com/2014/11/21/us/activists-wield -search-data-to-challenge-and-change-police-policy.html (Durham).

23. Gill Interview, supra note 13; Chokshi, "School Police Across the Country Receive Excess Military Weapons and Gear," supra note 8 (quoting Michael Heidingsfield); *Recommendations Pursuant to E.O. 13688*, supra note 7, at 17 ("Emergency Rescue"). On the use of military vehicles for rescues during extreme weather, see, for example, "NJ Shore Town Receives 5 Surplus Military Vehicles," *AP*, Aug. 6, 2015, www.app.com /story/news/local/new-jersey/2015/08/06/nj-shore-town-receives-surplus-military -vehicles/31247845/; Ken Baker, "Armored Vehicles Credited to Saving Flood Victims," WMBF News, Oct. 14, 2015, www.wmbfnews.com/story/30264283/armored-vehicles -credited-to-saving-flood-victims.

24. Gill Interview, supra note 13; Nagourney, "Police Armored Vehicle Is Unwelcome in California College Town," supra note 17X (Davis); John Reynolds, "Sangamon County Gets Rid of MRAP Military Vehicle," *State Journal-Register*, Feb. 24, 2016, www.sj-r.com /article/20160224/ENTERTAINMENTLIFE/160229764; Jessica Mendoza, "Obama Moves to Curb 'Militarization' of Police: A Shift in Law Enforcement's Role?," *Christian Sci. Monitor*, May 18, 2015, www.csmonitor.com/USA/USA-Update/2015/0518 /Obama-moves-to-curb-militarization-of-police-A-shift-in-law-enforcement-s-role

-video (Edinburg); Ben Kesling, Miguel Bustillo, and Tamara Audi, "Federal Program Supplies Surplus Military Gear to Schools," *Wall St. J.*, Sept. 17, 2014, www.wsj.com /articles/federal-program-supplies-surplus-military-gear-to-schools-1410884584 (Edinburg, Los Angeles, Utah); Tami Abdollah, "L.A. School District to Give Up Three Grenade Launchers, Keep 60 M16 Rifles," *Mercury News*, Sep. 18, 2014, www.mercurynews .com/california/ci_26559699/l-school-district-give-up-three-grenade-launchers (Los Angeles, Utah, Nevada); Aaron Mendelson, "LAUSD Cuts Ties to Military Weapons Program," 89.3 KPCC, July 30, 2015, www.scpr.org/news/2015/07/30/53478/lausd-cuts-ties -to-military-weapons-program/ (Los Angeles); Knefel, "Why Are Police Using Military-Grade Weapons in High Schools?," supra note 8 (Aledo).

25. Chokshi, "School Police Across the Country Receive Excess Military Weapons and Gear," supra note 8.

26. Cyrus Farivar, "Cops Must Now Get a Warrant to Use Stingrays in Washington State," *Ars Technica*, May 12, 2015, http://arstechnica.com/tech-policy/2015/05/cops-must -now-get-a-warrant-to-use-stingrays-in-washington-state/; Jacob Sullum, "Texas Legislators Vote to Ban Roadside Sexual Assaults by Police," *Reason*, Apr. 30, 2015, http:// reason.com/blog/2015/04/30/texas-legislators-vote-to-ban-roadside-s.

27. See Barry Friedman and Maria Ponomarenko, "Democratic Policing," *N.Y.U. L. Rev.* 90 (2015): 1843–48 (identifying areas where policing policies are missing).

28. Rosmarin Interview, supra note 18.

29. Id.

30. See Donald A. Dripps, "Criminal Procedure, Footnote Four, and the Theory of Public Choice; Or, Why Don't Legislatures Give a Damn About the Rights of the Accused?," *Syracuse L. Rev.* 44 (1993): 1081, 1085–86 ("[T]elephone companies resented the expense and inconvenience of installing [pen-registers or trap-and-trace devices] at the whim of police officers, and joined the ACLU in urging that some hurdle be set up between the cop-on-the-beat and the telephone company's time and trouble."); 132 Cong. Rec. H4045-46 (daily ed. June 23, 1986) (statement of Rep. Kastenmeier) (citing support from a "coalition of business, Government and civil liberties groups"); H.R. Rep. No. 99–647, at 29–30 (1986) (listing the organizations and corporations that supported the legislation). For more on the Electronic Communications Privacy Act, see infra Chapter 10.

31. See, e.g., letter from ACT et al. to Robert W. Goodlatte, Chairman, and John Conyers, Jr., Ranking Member, House Judiciary Committee, Jan. 22, 2015, www.digital4th.org /wp-content/uploads/2015/02/ECPA-support-letter-House-judiciaryjan2015-v2-clean .pdf; letter from Mary Jo White, Chair, Securities and Exchange Commission, to Patrick J. Leahy, Chairman, Senate Judiciary Committee, Apr. 24, 2013, www.cdt.org /files/file/SEC%20ECPA%20Letter.pdf. Recently, the House unanimously passed the Email Privacy Act, which requires government officials to obtain a warrant before gaining access to users' email, but the legislation may encounter difficulties in the Senate. See Andrea Noble, "Email Privacy Act May Face Hurdles in Senate After Unanimous House Passage," *Wash. Times*, Apr. 28, 2016, www.washingtontimes.com/news /2016/apr/28/email-privacy-act-may-face-hurdles-senate-after-un/ ("'Members of this committee on both sides of the aisle have expressed concerns about the details of this reform, and whether it's balanced to reflect issues raised by law enforcement,' said Sen. Charles Grassley, the chairman of the Senate Judiciary Committee.").

32. Rosmarin Interview, supra note 18.

33. Id.

34. Gill Interview, supra note 13.

35. Daniel Justin Solove, GW Law, www.law.gwu.edu/daniel-justin-solove; Orin S. Kerr, GW Law, www.law.gwu.edu/orin-s-kerr.

36. See Orin S. Kerr, "The Fourth Amendment and New Technologies: Constitutional Myths and the Case for Caution," *Mich. L. Rev.* 102 (2004): 858–59 (2004); Daniel J. Solove, "Fourth Amendment Codification and Professor Kerr's Misguided Call for Judicial Deference," *Fordham L. Rev.* 74 (2005): 747.

37. See Stuart Elliott, "A Campaign for Miller Lite Goes Back to Basics and Beyond the Appeal to Younger Consumers," *N.Y. Times*, Mar. 5, 1999, www.nytimes.com/1999/03/05/business/media-business-advertising-campaign-for-miller-lite-goes-back-basics-beyond.html.

38. *Olmstead v. United States*, 277 U.S. 438, 466 (1928); *Berger v. New York*, 388 U.S. 41, 51 (1967).

39. *Berger*, 388 U.S. at 44; S. Rep. No. 90-1097, at 2155–56 ("[T]he Supreme Court has effectively prevented the use in both Federal and State courts of intercepted communications by wiretapping . . . but in doing so has laid out guidelines for the Congress and State legislatures to follow in enacting wiretapping and electronic eavesdropping statutes . . . Even . . . existing statutes . . . must now be reformed in light of the standards for constitutional electronic surveillance laid down by the Supreme Court in *Berger*."); see also Erin Murphy, "The Politics of Privacy in the Criminal Justice System: Information Disclosure, the Fourth Amendment, and Statutory Law Enforcement Exemptions," *Mich. L. Rev.* 111 (2013): 538 ("[T]he *Berger* opinion . . . exemplif[ies] a process by which the Court declares that an investigative method implicates a Fourth Amendment interest and then sketches the contours of a constitutional statute regulating the activity."); Donald A. Dripps, "Justice Harlan on Criminal Procedure: Two Cheers for the Legal Process School," *Ohio St. J. Crim. L.* 3 (2005): 148 ("Those sympathetic to law enforcement feared that *Berger v. New York* and *Katz v. United States* meant the end of electronic surveillance. The objective of Title III's proponents was to provide procedural safeguards that would survive constitutional challenge in the Supreme Court . . .").

40. See *Olmstead*, 277 U.S. at 466; *Berger*, 388 U.S. at 44.

41. See Dripps, supra note 30 at 1091–92; William J. Stuntz, "The Pathological Politics of Criminal Law," *Mich. L. Rev.* 100 (2001): 539.

42. See, e.g., *Mich. Dep't of State Police v. Sitz*, 496 U.S. 444, 453–54 (1990). For more on this point, see supra Chapter 3.

43. The factual account is taken from the reported decisions in *Utah v. Sims* (*Sims I*), 808 P.2d 141 (Utah Ct. App. 1991), and *Sims v. Collection Division of the Utah State Tax Commission* (*Sims II*), 841 P.2d 6 (Utah 1992).

44. *Sims I*, 808 P.2d at 142–46.

45. Id. at 147–48 ("Sims argues that the lack of statutory authority renders suspicionless roadblocks improper under the Utah Constitution."); *Sims II*, 841 P.2d at 9 ("Other states have inferred legislative authority to conduct roadblocks from such statutory grants of general police powers.").

46. *Sims I*, 808 P.2d at 147–49; see also *Sims II*, 841 P.2d at 7, 9n4.

47. *Sims II*, 841 P.2d at 9; *Sims I*, 808 P.2d at 141, 142–43, 148, 149.

48. *R. v. Spencer*, 2014 S.C.C. 43 ¶¶ 2, 68 (Can.).

49. On these broad grants of authority, see supra Introduction, Chapter 2.

50. *Kent v. Dulles*, 357 U.S. 116, 128–129 (1958).

51. *Spencer*, 2014 S.C.C. at ¶¶ 36, 62, 71.

52. U.S. Const. amend. IV ("The right of the people to be secure in their persons, houses, papers, and effects, against unreasonable searches and seizures, shall not be violated . . ."); *Virginia v. Moore*, 553 U.S. 167, 168 (2008).

53. E.g., *California v. Greenwood*, 486 U.S. 35, 43–44 (1988) ("We reject . . . Greenwood's . . . argument . . . that his expectation of privacy in his garbage should be deemed reasonable as a matter of federal constitutional law because the warrantless search and sei-

zure of his garbage was impermissible as a matter of California law . . . We have never intimated . . . that whether or not a search is reasonable within the meaning of the Fourth Amendment depends on the law of the particular State in which the search occurs."); see also, e.g., *Moore*, 553 U.S. at 176 (2008) ("[W]hile States are free to regulate such arrests however they desire, state restrictions do not alter the Fourth Amendment's protections."); *Katz v. United States*, 389 U.S. 347, 360 (1967) (establishing the "reasonable expectation of privacy" standard); William Baude and James Y. Stern, "The Positive Law Model of the Fourth Amendment," *Harv. L. Rev.* 129 (2016): 1823 ("Fourth Amendment protection should depend on . . . legislation . . . statutes, and other provisions of law generally applicable to private actors, rather than a freestanding doctrine of privacy fashioned by courts on the fly."). The question of what constitutes a search is discussed further in Chapter 9.

54. *Berger*, 388 U.S. at 58–62; *United States v. United States Dist. Ct. (Keith)*, 407 U.S. 297, 322; see also Samuel J. Rascoff, "Domesticating Intelligence," *S. Cal. L. Rev.* 83 (2010): 589–90 ("[I]n the *Keith* case, the Supreme Court expressed the view that the Fourth Amendment does apply in cases 'deemed necessary to protect the nation from attempts of *domestic organizations* to attack and subvert the existing structure of government.' But . . . the Court . . . express[ed] 'no judgment on the scope of the President's surveillance power with respect to the activities of foreign powers, within or without this country.' As a practical matter, Congress partially plugged this gap in 1978 when it passed [FISA]. . . ." (quoting *Keith*, 407 U.S. at 308, 309 (1972)).

55. See H.R. 4952—Electronic Communications Privacy Act of 1986, List of Sponsors, Congress.gov, www.congress.gov/bill/99th-congress/house-bill/4952/cosponsors (last visited Apr. 25, 2016) (showing a mix of Republican and Democratic cosponsors); To Pass H.R. 5037, After Substituting for Its Text the Language of S. 917 as Amended, GovTrack.us, www.govtrack.us/congress/votes/90-1968/s439 (showing a bipartisan 72–4 Senate vote to pass the Omnibus Crime Control and Safe Streets Act of 1968).

56. On deference, see supra Introduction, Chapter 3.

57. *Ornelas v. United States*, 517 U.S. 690, 699 (1996).

58. *United States. v. Perry*, 449 F.2d 1026, 1037 (D.C. Cir. 1971), quoted in Gerald M. Caplan, "The Case for Rulemaking by Law Enforcement Agencies," *Law & Contemp. Probs.* 36 (1971): 504.

59. Gill Interview, supra note 13.

60. Id.; see also, e.g., Sandra M. Stevenson, *Antieau on Local Government Law*, 2nd ed. (2015), § 1.01 ("The term 'local government' . . . refers to local entities that have been organized to exercise governing authority, delegated by the state through charter, state constitution or statute.").

5. SEARCHES WITHOUT WARRANT

1. *Frunz v. City of Tacoma*, 468 F.3d 1141, 1142 (9th Cir. 2006).

2. See Transcript of Trial at 20:24–21:2; 37:6–39:25, 40:16–17, 184:22–185:6, *Frunz*, 468 F.3d 1141 (No. 05-35302); *Frunz*, 468 F.3d at 1142.

3. See Transcript of Trial at 19:14–17, 75:18–21, 76:13–15,76:18–77:12, 357:4–13, *Frunz*, 468 F.3d 1141 (No. 05-35302); *Frunz*, 468 F.3d at 1142–43.

4. See Transcript of Trial at 185:9–11, 186:15–18, 187:2–12, 308:7–24, 338:10–15, 343:11–14, *Frunz*, 468 F.3d 1141 (No. 05-35302).

5. Transcript of Trial at 190:22–191–25, 192:7–17, 193:10–194:2, *Frunz*, 468 F.3d 1141 (No. 05-35302).

6. Transcript of Trial at 195:7–18, 197:18–25, *Frunz*, 468 F.3d 1141 (No. 05-35302).

7. *Frunz*, 468 F.3d at 1146.

8. *Frunz*, 468 F.3d at 1146.

9. *Frunz*, 468 F.3d at 1144, 1147 (damages, "the citizens of Tacoma"); Transcript of Oral Argument at 11:09, *Frunz*, 468 F.3d 1141 (No. 05-35302) ("You had a jury and for me it sounded like the jury gave your clients a hug and kiss for what they did. Boy was this a parsimonious jury. You should have thanked them."); *Frunz v. City of Tacoma*, 476 F.3d 661, 665 (9th Cir. 2007).

10. Oren Bar-Gill and Barry Friedman, "Taking Warrants Seriously," *Nw. U. L. Rev.* 106 (2012): 1664–66 (citing studies indicating police rarely obtain warrants in advance of searches); Richard Van Duizend et al., *The Search Warrant Process: Preconceptions, Perceptions, Practices* (1985), 17; Craig D. Uchida and Timothy S. Bynum, "Search Warrants, Motions to Suppress and 'Lost Cases': The Effects of the Exclusionary Rule in Seven Jurisdictions," *J. Crim. L. & Criminology* 81 (1991): 1051; Jon B. Gould and Stephen D. Mastrofski, "Suspect Searches: Assessing Police Behavior Under the U.S. Constitution," *Criminology & Pub. Pol'y* 3 (2004): 334 ("[I]t is notable that not a single search in the sample of 115 was conducted by warrant. Although search warrants are rare in other jurisdictions . . . the pattern in [the city being studied] appears to be exceptional."). On warrantless entries of the home, see, for example, *Mitchell v. City of Henderson*, No. 13-01154, 2015 WL 427835, at *17 (D. Nev. Feb. 2, 2015) (denying defendants' motion to dismiss plaintiffs' § 1983 claims regarding police forcibly entering and searching their homes without a warrant where plaintiffs were home at the time of entry); Carlos Miller, "Watch New York Cops Force Way into Woman's Home Without Warrant," *PINAC*, Apr. 10, 2015, http://photographyisnotacrime.com/2015/04/watch-new-york-cops-force-way-into-womans-home-without-warrant/ (describing police officers forcing their way into a woman's home in search of a felon who was not found; video footage was taken); "Video: Man Refuses to Let Cops Search House Without Warrant," *RT*, Sept. 3, 2014, www.rt.com/usa/185084-homeowner-police-enter-warrant/.

11. *The Maltese Falcon* (Warner Bros., 1941).

12. *Ex parte* Jackson, 96 U.S. 727, 733 (1877).

13. *Johnson v. United States*, 333 U.S. 10, 14 (1948).

14. *United States v. Lefkowitz*, 285 U.S. 452, 465 (1932).

15. See Bar-Gill and Friedman, "Taking Warrants Seriously," supra note 10, at 1643 & 1643n136 (citing studies on accountability and belief perseverance); Linda Babcock et al., "Creating Convergence: Debiasing Biased Litigants," *Law & Soc. Inquiry* 22 (1997): 918 (settlement). Similarly, deliberation, which requires individuals to convince each other, filters out bias, prejudice, and irrational motives. See Bar-Gill and Friedman, "Taking Warrants Seriously," supra note 10, at 1643 & 1643 n137.

16. *Katz v. United States*, 389 U.S. 347, 357 (1967).

17. See Christopher Slobogin, "Why Liberals Should Chuck the Exclusionary Rule," *Ill. L. Rev.* 1999: 375 ("[T]oday's swiss cheese exclusionary rule is a mere shadow of what it could be.").

18. See, e.g., *Frunz*, 468 F.3d at 1145 ("In such exigent circumstances, the police are entitled to enter immediately, using all appropriate force.").

19. See Thomas Y. Davies, "Recovering the Original Fourth Amendment," *Mich. L. Rev.* 98 (1999): 628–34 (discussing three justifications for warrantless arrests at common law in 1791: when (1) the offense was committed/attempted in view of the officer; (2) the person arrested committed a felony; and (3) the officer had reasonable cause to believe arrested individual committed a known crime); *People v. Chiagles*, 237 N.Y. 193, 195 (1923) (Cardozo, J.) ("[T]here is one exception [to the Fourth Amendment] that has been established as firmly as the rule itself. The government may 'search the person of the accused when legally arrested to discover and seize the fruits or evidences of crime.'" (quoting *Weeks v. United States*, 232 U.S. 383, 392 (1914))); id. at

196 ("The right goes back beyond doubt to the days of the hue and cry, when there was short shrift for the thief who was caught with the mainour, still in seisin of his crime." (internal quotation marks omitted)).

20. On quantifying the exceptions, see, for example, David C. Behar, "An Exception to an Exception: Officer Inadvertence as a Requirement to Plain View Seizures in the Computer Context," *U. Miami L. Rev.* 66 (2012): 472 ("[T]he Court has also carved a vast number of exceptions to whether and when a warrant is required . . . [w]ith all these exceptions, one must wonder whether Fourth Amendment protections are a rule or an exception itself."); Thomas Y. Davies, "The Supreme Court Giveth and the Supreme Court Taketh Away: The Century of Fourth Amendment 'Search and Seizure' Doctrine," *J. Crim. L. & Criminology* 100 (2010): 939 ("[Crime-control justices] have . . . expand[ed] law enforcement search powers by announcing a multitude of doctrinal limitations and exceptions that make the earlier protections largely meaningless in practice."); *California v. Acevedo*, 500 U.S. 565, 582–83 (1991) (Scalia, J., concurring in judgment). On the exceptions themselves, see *United States v. Martinez-Fuerte*, 428 U.S. 543 (1976) (approving an unwarranted search by Border Patrol at a checkpoint forty-three air miles from the nearest Mexican border); *United States v. Biswell*, 406 U.S. 311 (1972) (permitting a search of gun dealer's locked storeroom as part of an authorized inspection did not require a warrant); *Wyman v. James*, 400 U.S. 309 (1971) (finding home visits prescribed by statute as condition for welfare assistance is not a search covered by the Fourth Amendment); *New Jersey v. T.L.O.*, 469 U.S. 325, 340 (1985) ("[S]chool officials need not obtain a warrant before searching a student who is under their authority."); *United States v. Knights*, 534 U.S. 112 (2001) (approving a warrantless search of probationer's apartment); *City of Ontario v. Quon*, 560 U.S. 746 (2010) (permitting a warrantless search of a city employee's city-issued cell phone); *South Dakota v. Opperman*, 428 U.S. 364 (1976) (finding an inventory search of defendant's locked but impounded car reasonable for Fourth Amendment purposes); *Carroll v. United States*, 267 U.S. 312 (1925) (approving a warrantless search of a car); *Acevedo*, 500 U.S. 565 (holding police may conduct warrantless searches of containers in cars, where police have probable cause to search the car or container); *Michigan v. Tyler*, 436 U.S. 499 (1978) (permitting warrantless entry into a building to fight a fire and officers to remain in the building to investigate the fire).

21. *Cardwell v. Lewis*, 417 U.S. 583, 587–88 (1974).

22. See id. at 590 (explaining the automobile exception is due in part to the fact that (1) "[a car] travels through public thoroughfares where its occupants and contents are in plain view" and (2) "[a car's] function is transportation and it seldom serves as one's residence or the repository of personal effects"); *United States v. Chadwick*, 433 U.S. 1, 12–13 (1977) (arguing that reduced "automobile privacy" is due in part to the fact that "[a]ll states require vehicles to be registered and operators to be licensed").

23. U.S. Const. amend. IV.

24. Joint Comm. on Continuing Legal Educ. of the Am. Law Inst. and the Am. Bar Ass'n, *Trial Manual for the Defense of Criminal Cases* (Preliminary Draft No. 1, Sept. 29, 1966), 28, quoted in Telford Taylor, *Two Studies in Constitutional Interpretation* (1969), 23 & 182n12.

25. See Taylor, *Two Studies in Constitutional Interpretation*, supra note 24, at 21, 43; Akhil Reed Amar, "Fourth Amendment First Principles," *Harv. L. Rev.* 107 (1994): 761.

26. See Taylor, *Two Studies in Constitutional Interpretation*, supra note 24, at 41–43; Amar, "Fourth Amendment First Principles," supra note 25, at 774, 778, 798.

27. See William J. Cuddihy, *The Fourth Amendment: Origins and Original Meaning 602–1791* (2009), 232–52 (discussing the use of search warrants in the colonies and noting their indiscriminate issuance); Leonard Levy, "Origins of the Fourth Amendment,"

Pol. Sci. Q. 114 (1999): 92 (quoting "The Rights of the Colonies," 1772, reprinted in *The Bill of Rights: A Documentary History*, ed. Bernard Schwartz (1971), 1:206) (Boston Town Meeting).

28. *Acevedo*, 500 U.S. at 581 (Scalia, J., concurring in judgment).

29. *Wyoming v. Houghton*, 526 U.S. 295, 299–300 (1999) (citations omitted).

30. *United States v. Davis*, 785 F. 3d 498, 516–17 (11th Cir. 2015) (cell site data searches); *Maryland v. King*, 133 S. Ct. 1958, 1970 (2013) (post-arrest buccal swab); *Reynolds v. City of Anchorage*, 379 F. 3d 358, 367 (6th Cir. 2004) (search of juvenile in group home).

31. See Amar, "Fourth Amendment First Principles," supra note 25, at 772 & 772n54 (suppression of Wilkes and others); Levy, "Origins of the Fourth Amendment," supra note 27, at 87 ("Wilkes and Liberty"); Akhil Reed Amar, "The Fourth Amendment, Boston, and the Writs of Assistance," *Suffolk U. L. Rev.* 30 (1997): 65–66 (importance of the Wilkesite cases).

32. George Rudé, *Wilkes and Liberty: A Social Study of 1763 to 1774* (1962), xiii, 17–19.

33. Id. at 20–22 (describing *The North Briton*); George Nobbe, *The North Briton: A Study in Political Propaganda* (1939), 206 ("I cannot tell, but I am trying to know.").

34. Rudé, *Wilkes and Liberty: A Social Study of 1763 to 1774*, supra note 32, at 22–23 (describing the response to issue Number 45); Nobbe, *The North Briton: A Study in Political Propaganda*, supra note 33, at 214 (quoting Lord Halifax).

35. Cuddihy, *The Fourth Amendment: Origins and Original Meaning 602–1791*, supra note 27, at 441–43 (describing the searches and seizures); Rudé, *Wilkes and Liberty: A Social Study of 1763 to 1774*, supra note 32, at 24–26 (Tower of London and ascension to stardom).

36. Levy, "Origins of the Fourth Amendment," supra note 27, at 88. One estimate puts the number of suits and trials at more than forty-six. Cuddihy, *The Fourth Amendment: Origins and Original Meaning 602–1791*, supra note 27, at 443.

37. Rudé, *Wilkes and Liberty: A Social Study of 1763 to 1774*, supra note 32, at 29 (internal quotation marks omitted) ("extraordinary"); *Wilkes v. Wood*, 98 Eng. Rep. 489, 498 (C.B. 1763) (totally subversive).

38. They exercised particular care not because a general warrant was of significance—it wasn't—but because Wilkes himself was a Member of Parliament and privileged as such. See Rudé, *Wilkes and Liberty: A Social Study of 1763 to 1774*, supra note 32, at 24. Thus, the usual form of the warrant was altered to include "treasonable" activities to get around the parliamentary privilege. Nobbe, *The North Briton: A Study in Political Propaganda*, supra note 33, at 214.

39. M. H. Smith, *The Writs of Assistance Case* (1978), 336 (discussing the use of general warrants for 150 years before the Wilkesite cases); *Wood*, 98 Eng. Rep. at 498 (noting lawyers' reliance on precedents approving general warrants); Rudé, *Wilkes and Liberty: A Social Study of 1763 to 1774*, supra note 32, at 29 (quoting letter from the Duke of Newcastle to Devonshire, May 2, 1763); *Money v. Leach*, 1 Black W. 555, 558 (1765); Cuddihy, *The Fourth Amendment: Origins and Original Meaning 602–1791*, supra note 27, at 449 (noting Pratt's issuance of a general warrant).

40. *Leach*, 1 Black W. at 562 (Mansfield); id. at 558 (Yates); *Wood*, 98 Eng. Rep. at 498 (Pratt).

41. See Joseph Story, "Codification of the Common Law," in *Miscellaneous Writings of Joseph Story*, ed. William Story (1852), 701–02 (recognizing that some common law rules "are of such high antiquity, that the time cannot be assigned, when they had not an existence and use" while others "have been developed with the gradual progress of society"). For a framing-era view, see Zachariah Swift, *A System of the Laws of Connecticut* (1795–1796), 1:41 ("Courts however are not absolutely bound by the authority of precedents. If a determination has been founded upon mistaken principles, or the rule

adopted by it be inconvenient, or repugnant to the general tenor of the law, a subsequent court assumes the power to vary from or contradict it."), quoted in Charles W. Wolfram, "The Constitutional History of the Seventh Amendment," *Minn. L. Rev.* 57 (1973): 736n289. See also Morton J. Horwitz, *The Transformation of American Law 1780–1860* (1977), 23 ("Theoretically courts make no law . . . but in point of fact they are legislators . . . How can [common law rules] be said to have existed from time immemorial, when there [sic] origin is notorious." (quoting the 1813 instructions of Judges Trapping Reeve and James Gould at Litchfield Law School)). Such a view was understood as early as the seventeenth century by Matthew Hale, who recognized both the constancy and the mutability of the common law: "[T]hey are the same English Laws now, that they were six hundred years since, in the general. As the Argonauts Ship was the same when it returned home, as it was when it went out; though in that long voyage it had successive amendments, and scarce came back with any of its former materials." Matthew Hale, *The History of the Common Law of England*, 6th ed. (1820), 84.

42. Story, "Codification of the Common Law," supra note 41, at 702; Frederick Pollock, "The Genius of the Common Law," *Colum. L. Rev.* 12 (1912): 291 (ability to evolve).

43. *Riley v. California*, 134 S. Ct. 2473, 2484 (2014); Amar, "Fourth Amendment First Principles," supra note 25, at 818.

44. *Leach*, 3 Burr. 1743, 1766, 97 Eng. Rep. 1075, 1088 (1765) (narrowing Pratt's decisions on appeal); Cuddihy, *The Fourth Amendment: Origins and Original Meaning 602–1791*, supra note 27, at 475 ("except in cases provided for by act of Parliament" (quoting Procs., 25 Apr. 1766, C. J., vol. 30 (1765–66))). See generally Cuddihy, *The Fourth Amendment: Origins and Original Meaning 602–1791*, supra note 27, at 469–76 (describing the fighting in Parliament over general warrants).

45. William Blackstone, *Commentaries*, 1:*91, *161.

46. See Nelson Lasson, *The History and Development of the Fourth Amendment of the United States Constitution* (1937), 51 (describing the use of writs of assistance).

47. Thomas Hutchinson, *The History of the Colony of Massachusetts-Bay*, 92–93 (1764); Smith, *The Writs of Assistance Case*, supra note 39, at 97; Cuddihy, *The Fourth Amendment: Origins and Original Meaning 602–1791*, supra note 27, at 381. In the intervening few years, the authority of the Superior Court to issue the writs lapsed when the sitting King passed away. Before that authority could be restored by the new monarch, the merchants sued. See Cuddihy, *The Fourth Amendment: Origins and Original Meaning 602–1791*, supra note 27, at 380–81; Smith, *The Writs of Assistance Case*, supra note 39, at 130.

48. Hutchinson, *The History of the Colony of Massachusetts-Bay*, supra note 47, at 93–94; Smith, *The Writs of Assistance Case*, supra note 39, at 332, 551–55 (Otis).

49. Smith, *The Writs of Assistance Case*, supra note 39, at 555 (internal quotation marks omitted) (reprinting Adams's later account of Otis's speech). On the revolutionary conception of constitutional supremacy in the American colonies, see, for example, Barry Friedman, *The Will of the People: How Public Opinion Has Influenced the Supreme Court and Shaped the Meaning of the Constitution* (2009), 391n17; Gordon S. Wood, *The Creation of the American Republic 1776–1787* (1969), 266 ("Americans were determined to provide for the protection of . . . fundamental rights and moves . . . toward a definition of a constitution as something distinct from and superior to the entire government."); Larry D. Kramer, "The Supreme Court 2000 Term, Foreword: We the Court," *Harv. L. Rev.* 115 (2001): 73 ("The colonial experience of resisting King and Parliament served as the model from which the Founders constructed their theories, and the Revolution itself . . . provided their blueprint for opposing a government that exceeded its constitutional authority."); Samuel Adams, *Massachusetts Circular Letter*

of 1768, quoted in Wood, *The Creation of the American Republic 1776–1787*, supra, at 266 ("[I]n all free States the Constitution is fixed; and as the supreme Legislative derives its Power and Authority from the Constitution, it cannot overleap the Bounds of it without destroying its own foundation.") (internal quotation marks omitted)).

50. Smith, *The Writs of Assistance Case*, supra note 39, at 253 (quoting letter from John Adams to William Tudor, Mar. 29, 1817); Cuddihy, *The Fourth Amendment: Origins and Original Meaning 602–1791*, supra note 27, at 490–501 (discussing "liberations" and other incidents of resistance); id. at 438–64, 503–7 (Townshend Revenue Act); Lasson, *The History and Development of the Fourth Amendment of the United States Constitution*, supra note 46, at 75 (emphasis added) (Continental Congress). For an argument that, fifty-six years after the case, "Adams's memory may have been faulty and that he was indulging in a forgiveable [sic] bit of late-life romanticizing," see Kramer, "The Supreme Court 2000 Term, Foreword: We the Court," supra note 49, at 30n105.

51. Cuddihy, *The Fourth Amendment: Origins and Original Meaning 602–1791*, supra note 27, at 522.

52. Hutchinson, *The History of the Colony of Massachusetts-Bay*, supra note 47, at 93 (summarizing Otis's speech about "special warrants"); Smith, *The Writs of Assistance Case*, supra note 39, at 336 (quoting Otis, based on Adam's later account, as stating "*that special warrants only are legal*").

53. See generally Cuddihy, *The Fourth Amendment: Origins and Original Meaning 602–1791*, supra note 27, at 634–58 (noting the statutory shift to specific warrants in the majority of states post-Revolution).

54. Cuddihy, *The Fourth Amendment: Origins and Original Meaning 602–1791*, supra note 27, at 176–90, 192,–356–63.

55. Cuddihy, *The Fourth Amendment: Origins and Original Meaning 602–1791*, supra note 27, at 520 (Sift case). On colonial courts' resistance to the writs and willingness to issue them in specific form, see id. at 513–26; Lasson, *The History and Development of the Fourth Amendment of the United States Constitution*, supra note 46, at 73–76; Levy, "Origins of the Fourth Amendment," supra note 27, at 90–91.

56. Cuddihy, *The Fourth Amendment: Origins and Original Meaning 602–1791*, supra note 27, at 633–68 (specific warrants in the states following the American Revolution); see also Davies, "Recovering the Original Fourth Amendment," supra note 19, at 577–79 (arguing that ratifiers of the Fourth Amendment strongly condemned warrantless searches due in large part to their distaste for "the character and judgment of ordinary [police] officers"). Massachusetts presents an example of this switch from general to specific warrants. "General warrants were an everyday fact of life for over three years in revolutionary Massachusetts." Though as a colony Massachusetts abolished general warrants, as a state it reinstated their use. In 1777, in order to confiscate Loyalists' weapons, the state allowed its council "to declare any person dangerous to the state, and authorized warrants by which the sheriffs could break open any dwelling house or other building in which they suspected that such a person was concealed." In 1778, general warrants were mentioned twelve times in the state council's notes. Such warrants were used to search and apprehend political dissidents, but even before the state ratified its constitution, general warrants for on land searches "were far less common than specific search warrants and warrants to apprehend particular persons." John Adams then drafted the 1780 Massachusetts constitution to protect people from unreasonable searches and seizures and in 1781 "state law reverted to multiple-specific search warrants for deserters." Cuddihy, *The Fourth Amendment: Origins and Original Meaning 602–1791*, supra note 27, at 613–16. Similarly, in New Hampshire, general warrants enacted in 1777 lasted only eleven weeks before the General Court's next session replaced them with specific warrants. In 1778, the legislature permitted war-

rantless searches, but towns "almost never appointed the officials who were responsible for performing these searches." In the five years after establishing a right to be free from unreasonable searches and seizures, in 1784, New Hampshire's legislature passed no laws permitting an official to search a house. The next warrants created by state law, in 1791, were specific. Id. at 638–39.

57. See Cuddihy, *The Fourth Amendment: Origins and Original Meaning 602–1791*, supra note 27, at 602–68 (discussing in detail the general preference for specific warrants, as well as notable exceptions, in the period between the Revolution and 1791).

58. Id. at 670–72 (describing how the move toward a federal constitution led to an even greater preference for specific warrants); Levy, "Origins of the Fourth Amendment," supra note 27, at 96–97 (same); George C. Thomas III, "Time Travel, Hovercrafts, and the Framers: James Madison Sees the Future and Rewrites the Fourth Amendment," *Notre Dame L. Rev.* 80 (2005): 1767n126 (quoting Patrick Henry's remarks from Virginia ratifying convention on June 14, 1788, as reported in *The Debates in the Several State Conventions on the Adoption of the Federal Constitution as Recommended by the General Convention at Philadelphia in 1787*, ed. Jonathan Elliot, J. B. Lippincott Co., 2nd ed. (1836), 265). To be fair, opponents of the federal government were not crazy about excise searches altogether. Cuddihy, *The Fourth Amendment: Origins and Original Meaning 602–1791*, supra note 27, at 742 ("While the Constitution was being ratified, moreover, nearly as many authors had execrated general excise searches without warrant as had similar searches by warrant . . .").

59. St. George Tucker, *Blackstone's Commentaries with Notes of Reference, to the Constitution and Laws of the Federal Government of United States and of the Commonwealth of Virginia* (1803), 302 (emphasis added); David T. Hardy, "The Lecture Notes of St. George Tucker: A Framing Era View of the Bill of Rights," *Nw. U. L. Rev.* 103 (2008): 1535 (emphasis added) (transcribing from Tucker's original lecture notes, dating from around 1791–92, which preserved and archived in the Tucker-Coleman Collection of the Earl Gregg Swem Library at the College of William and Mary, where Tucker was professor of law from 1790 until 1804). Some of Tucker's lecture notes and other legal papers have since been edited and published in *St. George Tucker's Law Reports and Selected Papers, 1782–1825*, ed. Charles F. Hobson (2013).

60. William Rawle, *A View of the Constitution*, 2nd ed. (1829), 127 (emphasis added).

61. One of the two historians who developed the argument relied upon by Justice Scalia—Akhil Amar—has an answer: Warrants were unnecessary, but those who searched unlawfully were subject to liability without immunity. Amar argues there is "no evidence" that early Americans "*preached* a 'warrant preference' or a 'warrant requirement.'" Amar, "The Fourth Amendment, Boston, and the Writs of Assistance," supra note 31, at 73. But he fails to account for all the evidence above, such as St. George Tucker's treatise. The compiler of Tucker's notes observes quite aptly that "Professor Akhil Reed Amar has argued that . . . warrantless searches need only be 'reasonable' . . . [but] Tucker's discussion appears to be to the contrary, treating probable cause and warrants as components of reasonableness." Hardy, "The Lecture Notes of St. George Tucker: A Framing Era View of the Bill of Rights," supra note 59, at 1535. Worse yet, in a sense Amar has been had. Justice Scalia adopted only half of his view of the Fourth Amendment, the part that lets officers run free without warrants. But Scalia and his colleagues never adopted Amar's view that strict money damages should follow for unwarranted unlawful searches. To the contrary, as Chapter 3 explains, the justices have avoided imposing this liability. Absent warrants and damages, there is no restraint on unlawful searches.

62. Davies, "Recovering the Original Fourth Amendment," supra note 19, at 552.

63. *Gouled v. United States*, 255 U.S. 298, 308 (1921) (emphasis added).

64. See generally Bar-Gill and Friedman, "Taking Warrants Seriously," supra note 10, at 1638–46 (discussing the benefits of warrants).

65. See, e.g., Note, "Police Practices and the Threatened Destruction of Tangible Evidence," *Harv. L. Rev.* 84 (1971): 1478–79 and 1478–79nn61–63 (noting the time necessary to get a warrant can range from one and a half hours in Denver, to six hours in Los Angeles, to over a day in a rural community in some circumstances).

66. *Frunz,* 468 F.3d at 1146; Cal. Penal Code §1526(b) (West 1970) ("In lieu of the written affidavit . . . the magistrate may take an oral statement under oath which shall be recorded and transcribed."); People v. Peck, 113 Cal. Rptr. 806, 810 (Ct. App. 1974) ("In our view the telephonic search warrant statute provides for adequate judicial supervision and control and sufficient protective measures to withstand constitutional challenge."). The Federal Rules of Criminal Procedure were amended in 1977 to allow warrants "based upon sworn oral testimony communicated by telephone or other appropriate means." Fed. R. Crim. P. 41(c)(2)(A) (1977). In 2011, the advisory committee moved the procedures governing search warrants by electronic means to a new rule, "support[ing] the extension of these procedures to arrest warrants, complaints, and summonses." Fed. R. Crim. P. 4.1 committee's notes to 2011 amendment.

67. Sarah Lundy, "Palm Bay Police Use Skype to Obtain Warrants," *Orlando Sentinel,* Mar. 28, 2011, http://articles.orlandosentinel.com/2011-03-28/business/os-police-skype -20110328_1_skype-arrest-warrants-judge-signs; Ken Thomas, "Agency Urges 'No-Refusal' DWI Policies, *AP,* Dec. 13, 2010, www.msnbc.msn.com/id/40646098/ns/us _news-crime_and_courts/t/govt-urges-no-refusal-policy-drunken-driving/ (Louisiana); Press Release, Michael Ramsey, Butte County District Attorney, "Butte County Law Enforcement First in State to Use Digital Signature on Search Warrant," Apr. 2, 2012, www.buttecounty.net/da/Press%20Releases/Search%20Warrant%20-%20 Electronic%20-%20Press%20Release.pdf; Missouri v. McNeely, 133 S. Ct. 1552, 1562 (2013).

68. See *McNeely,* 133 S. Ct. at 1556, 1562–63 (discussing changes in technology in the context of a drunk driving case); *Riley,* 134 S.Ct. at 2482 (Roberts, C. J.) (alterations in original) (quoting *Vernonia School Dist. 47J v. Acton,* 515 U.S. 646, 653 (1995)).

6. SEARCHES WITHOUT PROBABLE CAUSE

1. Interview by Barry Friedman with Nicholas Peart, Apr. 5, 2012 (hereinafter Peart Interview).

2. Nicholas K. Peart, "Why Is the N.Y.P.D. After Me?," *N.Y. Times,* Dec. 18, 2011, at SR6.

3. Id.; see also *Floyd v. City of New York,* 959 F. Supp. 2d 540, 633–37 (S.D.N.Y. 2013) (making mixed findings of fact and law regarding unconstitutional stops and frisks of Nicholas Peart).

4. *Floyd,* 959 F. Supp. 2d at 573 (noting 4.4 million stops followed by more than 2.2 million frisks, 1.5 percent of which led to finding guns); Rachel A. Harmon, "The Problem of Policing," *Mich. L. Rev.* 110 (2012): 779 (reporting 4 million stops); Al Baker and J. David Goodman, "Police Are Undercounting Street Stops, U.S. Monitor Finds," *N.Y. Times,* July 10, 2015, at A22 (undocumented stops); *Floyd v. City of New York,* 283 F.R.D. 153, 166n68 (S.D.N.Y. 2012) (quoting recorded statements by NYPD supervisors).

5. Compare *Floyd,* 283 F.R.D. at 164 (acknowledging NYPD rejection of the characterization of its stop-and-frisk program as a quota), with id. at 163n40 (quoting Ray Kelly).

6. Though no single nationwide database tracks the stop-and-frisk statistics of the nation's thousands of police agencies, other major cities documenting their policies exhibit trends paralleling New York, where 4.4 million stops were documented from

January 2004 to June 2012. *Floyd*, 959 F. Supp. 2d at 573. In 2012, Philadelphia police stopped over 215,000 pedestrians in six months, finding only three guns. Id. Boston police the same year stopped 123,000 people, turning up nine guns and a knife. NAACP, *Born Suspect: Stop-and-Frisk Abuses & the Continued Fight to End Racial Profiling in America* (2014), 24, http://naacp.3cdn.net/443b9cbc69a3ef1aab _ygfm66yd7.pdf.

7. Peart Interview, supra note 1; see also *City of Indianapolis v. Edmond*, 531 U.S. 32, 56 (2000) (Thomas, J., dissenting) ("I rather doubt that the Framers of the Fourth Amendment would have considered 'reasonable' a program of indiscriminate stops of individuals not suspected of wrongdoing.").

.8. *Sir Anthony Ashley's Case* (1611) 77 Eng. Rep. 1366, 1367-68 (KB).

9. *Henry v. United States*, 361 U.S. 98, 104 (1959) ("Under our system suspicion is not enough for an officer to lay hands on a citizen. It is better, so the Fourth Amendment teaches, that the guilty sometimes go free than that citizens be subject to easy arrest."); William Blackstone, *Commentaries*, 4:*290 (probable suspicion); id. at 4:*287 ("cause and probability of suspecting the party"); Nathan Dane, *A General Abridgment and Digest of Law* (1824), 5:588 ("reasonable cause").

10. *Brinegar v. United States*, 338 U.S. 160, 162–64, 169, 175–76 (1949) (quoting *Carroll v. United States*, 267 U.S. 132, 162 (1925)). On the continued vitality of *Brinegar's* definition of probable cause, see, for example, *Green v. Missouri*, 734 F. Supp. 2d 814, 832 (2010).

11. *Terry v. Ohio*, 392 U.S. 1, 5 (1968) (noting McFadden was patrolling his usual beat in plainclothes); "*State of Ohio v. Richard D. Chilton* and *State of Ohio v. John W. Terry*: Suppression Hearing and Trial Transcripts," ed. John Q. Barrett, St. John's L. Rev. 72 (1998): app. B at 1420 (reprinted the suppression hearing testimony of Detective McFadden) (hereinafter "*Terry* Transcripts").

12. "*Terry* Transcripts," supra note 11, at 1456.

13. Id. at 1418, 1456.

14. Id. at 1411, 1418.

15. Id. at 1413.

16. Id. at 1416, 1429, 1444.

17. See Barry Friedman, *The Will of the People: How Public Opinion Has Influenced the Supreme Court and Shaped the Meaning of the Constitution* (2009), 275–78; Risa Goluboff, *Vagrant Nation* (2016), 216–17; Earl C. Dudley, Jr., "*Terry v. Ohio*, the Warren Court, and the Fourth Amendment: A Law Clerk's Perspective," St. John's L. Rev. 72 (1998): 892.

18. Goluboff, *Vagrant Nation*, supra note 17, at 216 (describing the political climate leading up to *Terry*); Lewis R. Katz, "*Terry v. Ohio* at Thirty-Five: A Revisionist View," *Miss. L.J.* 74 (2004): 438 (noting the proximity of the decision to the Kennedy assassination); *Terry*, 392 U.S. at 10 ("[I]t is frequently argued that in dealing with the rapidly unfolding and often dangerous situations on city streets the police are in need of an escalating set of flexible responses, graduated in relation to the amount of information they possess."); *The Challenge of Crime in a Free Society: A Report by the President's Commission on Law Enforcement and Administration of Justice* (1967); *The Kerner Report: The 1968 Report of the National Advisory Commission on Civil Disorders* (1968).

19. "*Terry* Transcripts," supra note 11, at 1444.

20. *Terry*, 392 U.S. at 17 (quoting L. L. Priar and T. F. Martin, "Searching and Disarming Criminals," *J. Crim. L. Criminology & Police Sci.* 45 (1954): 481).

21. Id. at 24; id. at 36 (Douglas, J., dissenting).

22. Id. at 20 (majority opinion).

23. Id. at 15 (emphasis added).

24. Id. at 27, 30; id. at 31–32 (Harlan, J., concurring).
25. See generally Kimberly J. Winbush, Annotation, "Propriety of Stop and Search by Law Enforcement Officers Based Solely on Drug Courier Profile," *A.L.R.* 5th 37 (1996): 1.
26. *United States v. Condelee*, 915 F.2d 1206, 1208–09 (8th Cir. 1990).
27. Id. at 1209–10.
28. Id. at 1209; id. at 1211 (Gibson, J., dissenting).
29. *United States v. Weaver*, 966 F.2d 391, 397 (8th Cir. 1992) (Arnold, J., dissenting). For another "drug courier profile" case invovlving Agent Hicks, see *United States v. McKines*, 933 F.2d 1412 (8th Cir. 1991).
30. *United States v. Hooper*, 935 F.2d 484, 499 (2d Cir. 1991) (Pratt, J., dissenting).
31. Id. at 499–500.
32. Id. at 500.
33. *Floyd*, 959 F. Supp. 2d at 558–59.
34. *Navarette v. California*, 134 S. Ct. 1683, 1686–87 (2014).
35. Compare *Williams v. Adams*, 436 F.2d 30, 38 (2d Cir. 1970) (Friendly, J., dissenting) ("There is too much danger that instead of the stop being the object and the protective frisk an incident thereto, the reverse will be true."), rev'd en banc, 441 F.2d 394 (2d Cir. 1971), rev'd, 407 U.S. 143 (1972), with David M. Dorsen, *Henry Friendly* (2012), 214–15, 219 (highlighting the influence of Judge Friendly's relatively conservative emphasis on actual innocence in habeas corpus inquiries), Henry J. Friendly, "Is Innocence Irrelevant? Collateral Attack on Criminal Judgments," *U. Chi. L. Rev.* 38 (1970): 142 (taking a more conservative stance on habeas review), Henry Friendly, "The Fifth Amendment Tomorrow: The Case for Constitutional Change," *U. Cin. L. Rev.* 37 (1968): 671 (criticizing the Warren Court's modern interpretations of the right against self-incrimination), and Yale Kamisar, "The Warren Court and Criminal Justice: A Quarter-Century Retrospective," *Tulsa L.J.* 31 (1995): 1 (referring to Judge Friendly as "perhaps the most formidable critic of the Warren Court's criminal procedure cases").
36. David A. Harris, "Frisking Every Suspect: The Withering of *Terry*," *U.C. Davis L. Rev.* 28 (1994): 24–26 (describing courts' rationales in approving frisks for weapons based on suspected drug transactions and citing numerous examples); *United States v. Clark*, 24 F.3d 299, 301 (D.C. Cir. 1994).
37. Id. at 302–304.
38. N.Y. Penal Law § 221.05 (McKinney) (punishing simple possession of marijuana by only a fine, with possible imprisonment for recidivists); N.Y. Penal Law § 221.10 (McKinney) (punishing possession of marijuana as a class B misdemeanor when in public view or when the amount possessed exceeds 25 grams). Editorial, "No Crime, Real Punishment," *N.Y. Times*, June 5, 2012, www.nytimes.com/2012/06/05/opinion /no-crime-real-punishment.html (describing the practice of making the marijuana "public").
39. Plaintiff's Third Report to Court and Monitor on Stop and Frisk Practices at 9, *Bailey v. City of Philadelphia*, No. 10-cv-5952 (E.D. Pa. Mar. 19, 2013) (indicating, that in the first half of 2012, Philadelphia police made 215,000 stops, and recovered contraband of any kind in 1.57 percent of stops and guns in 0.16 percent of stops, only three weapons total); ACLU of Massachusetts, *Black Brown and Targeted* (2014), 1–2, https:// aclum.org/app/uploads/2015/06/reports-black-brown-and-targeted.pdf (study of Boston stop-and-frisk analyzing over 200,000 encounters between 2007 and 2010; only 2.5 percent resulted in seizure of contraband); Ian Ayres and Jonathan Borowsky, *A Study of Racially Disparate Outcomes in the Los Angeles Police Department* (2008), i, http://islandia.law.yale.edu/ayres/Ayres%20LAPD%20Report.pdf (reporting that stopped blacks were 127 percent more likely to be frisked than stopped whites, but were 42.3 percent less likely to be found with a weapon after they were frisked, 25

percent less likely to be found with drugs, and 33 percent less likely to be found with other contraband, and reporting similar findings for Hispanics).

40. See, e.g., Anthony G. Amsterdam, "Perspectives on the Fourth Amendment," *Minn. L. Rev.* 58 (1974): 356–60 (noting relative stability of the Fourth Amendment before *Katz* and discussing the requirements for *Terry* stops).

41. See, e.g., id. at 413 (noting that exceptions to the warrant requirement should still be founded on determinations of probable cause in the case of arrests).

42. *Terry*, 392 U.S. at 26–27.

43. See Goluboff, *Vagrant Nation*, supra note 17, at 186–88 (noting that conventional wisdom says *Terry* was a response to the end of vagrancy laws, but arguing that vagrancy laws actually continued past the 1960s); David A. Harris, "Factors for Reasonable Suspicion: When Black and Poor Means Stopped and Frisked," *Ind. L.J.* 69 (1994): 659, 683 (suggesting that of the justices then on the Court, only Justice Scalia would be amenable to a return to pre-*Terry* law); David A. Harris, "Frisking Every Suspect: The Withering of *Terry*," *U.C. Davis L. Rev.* 28 (1994): 39–40 (explaining that the doctrine is more likely to go the other direction, i.e., that the limits *Terry* placed on automatic frisking will likely soon be dispensed with); *Terry*, 392 U.S. at 10 ("[I]t is frequently argued that in dealing with the rapidly unfolding and often dangerous situations on city streets the police are in need of an escalating set of flexible responses, graduated in relation to the amount of information they possess."); Jeffrey Fagan and Amanda Geller, "Following the Script: Narratives of Suspicion in *Terry* Stops in Street Policing," *U. Chi. L. Rev.* 82 (2015): 51 (surveying studies of police officer behavior in the 1960s and 1970s); Craig S. Lerner, "Reasonable Suspicion and Mere Hunches," *Vand. L. Rev.* 59 (2006): 427–28 (describing the leeway given to government officials in American history). New York and Rhode Island legislatures passed stop-and-frisk laws in 1964 and 1956, respectively. Goluboff, *Vagrant Nation*, supra note 17, at 202–203.

44. *Terry*, 392 U.S. at 14, 20 (acknowledging that the law "is powerless to deter invasions of other constitutionally guaranteed rights where the police either have no interest in prosecuting or are willing to forgo successful prosecution in the interest of serving some other goal"); see also Harris, "Frisking Every Suspect," supra note 36, at 13–14 (arguing that *Terry* was a practical concession to give power back to the police as a compromise after *Mapp v. Ohio*, 367 U.S. 643, 655 (1961), which extended the Fourth Amendment's exclusionary rule—"all evidence obtained by an unconstitutional search and seizure [i]s inadmissible"—to the states).

45. See Sherry Colb, "The Qualitative Dimension of Fourth Amendment Reasonableness," *Colum. L. Rev.* 98 (1998): 1691–93 (contending that fidelity to *Terry* would cabin permissible stops to the originally announced rationale of preventing crime and protecting police in dangerous situations and rejecting expansion to completed felonies or trivial offenses); David Keenan and Tina M. Thomas, Note, "An Offense-Severity Model for Stop-and-Frisks," *Yale L.J.* 123 (2014): 1452–53 (suggesting that *Terry* stops for petty offenses should be presumptively invalid); Harris, "Frisking Every Suspect," supra note 36, at 48–49 (proposing that *Terry* be limited to situations where the suspected crime involves the use of force, violence, or weapons); Memorandum Submitting Consensus Seattle Police Department Policies and Order Approving Same at 3–5, *United States v. City of Seattle*, No. C12-1282JLR (W.D. Wash., Jan. 17, 2014), www.justice.gov/crt/about/spl/documents/spd_docket118.pdf (approving a consent decree, following a DOJ investigation, under which police cannot stop and frisk on reasonable suspicion of a misdemeanor unless there is reason to believe the suspect poses a public safety risk and must also keep detailed records, including demographic information, about each stop); *Commonwealth v. Cruz*, 945 N.E.2d 899, 908 (Md. 2011) (holding that an officer cannot order a person out of a car without suspicion of a

criminal—rather than civil—offense); Consent Decree at 20, *United States v. City of Newark*, No. 16-cv-01731 (D.N.J. May. 5, 2016), www.justice.gov/opa/file/836901/download (providing that Newark police must collect and analyze "the age, race, ethnicity, gender, location, time of day, reason for stop, post-stop activity, duration, and result or outcome of each encounter"); David A. Harris, "How Accountability-Based Policing Can Reinforce—or Replace—the Fourth Amendment Exclusionary Rule," *Ohio St. J. Crim. L.* 7 (2009): 166–68, 173–75 (encouraging a more robust review of citizen complaints, as well as improved departmental policies and procedures); Andrew Guthrie Ferguson, "Policing 'Stop and Frisk' with 'Stop and Track' Policing," *Huffington Post*, Aug. 17, 2014, www.huffingtonpost.com/andrew-guthrie-ferguson/policing-stop-and-frisk-w_b_5686208.html (proposing "random audits of people stopped . . . to compare the reported sentiment with the actual sentiment"); "America's Police on Trial," *Economist*, Dec. 13, 2014, www.economist.com/news/leaders/21636033-united-states-needs-overhaul-its-law-enforcement-system-americas-police-trial ("It must be easier to sack bad cops."). According to one study, 90 percent of Americans support the use of body cameras, and President Obama recently designated $74 million to the cause. Justin T. Ready and Jacob T. N. Young, "A Tale of Two Cities," *Slate*, Dec. 10, 2014, www.slate.com/articles/technology/future_tense/2014/12/police_body_cams_won_t_help_unless_they_come_with_the_right_policies.html. Cameras are not an antidote to bad police behavior, as countless YouTube videos are testament, but they do facilitate data collection and resolve factual disputes when officer conduct is challenged. See id.; David A. Harris, "Picture This: Body-Worn Video Devices (Head Cams) as Tools for Ensuring Fourth Amendment Compliance by Police," *Tex. Tech L. Rev.* 43 (2010): 369–70 (discussing how cameras improve officer behavior).

46. *Terry*, 392 U.S. at 6, 21, 23.
47. *Floyd*, 959 F. Supp. 2d at 559.
48. Id. at 575, 614.
49. *Terry*, 392 U.S. at 22. Applying strict scrutiny to investigations rooted in a suspect description or profile including a suspect classification would address this concern as it would require officers to explain precisely why the classification is relevant. Cf. *Brown v. City of Oneonta*, 235 F.3d 769, 774, 777 (2d Cir. 2000) (Walker, J., concurring in denial of rehearing en banc) (explaining that if equal protection doctrine were extended to policing, "[o]fficers would be forced to justify" their "non-articulable hunches, . . . intuition, and sense impressions," but finding such an approach "unworkable").
50. *Terry*, 392 U.S. at 22, 24. See generally Harris, "Frisking Every Suspect," supra note 36, at 24–26.
51. For courts applying a "reasonable suspicion" standard to auto stops, see, for example, *United States v. Jenkins*, 452 F.3d 207, 212 (2d Cir. 2006); *United States v. Cortez-Galaviz*, 495 F.3d 1203, 1206 (10th Cir. 2007); *Weaver v. Shadoan*, 340 F.3d 398, 407 (6th Cir. 2003).
52. Jeffrey Toobin, *The Nine: Inside the Secret World of the Supreme Court* (2007), 79.
53. *Weaver*, 966 F.2d at 397 (Arnold, J., dissenting).
54. Id.

7. GENERAL SEARCHES

1. *Bruce v. Beary*, 498 F.3d 1232, 1236 (11th Cir. 2007); Root Dep. at 27, 36–38, 92–93, *Bruce v. Beary*, No. 6:04-cv-1595-Orl-22DAB slip op. at 37 (M.D. Fla. Aug. 16, 2006), *vacated* 498 F.3d 1232 (2007) (Bloomberg Law, Litigation and Dockets); Bass Dep. at 3, 6 *Bruce*, (M.D. Fla. Aug. 16, 2006).

2. Bass Dep. at 2–3, 5–6.

3. Root Dep. at 44, 60–68.

4. Root Dep. at 33, 95–96; Bruce Dep. at 84, *Bruce*, (M.D. Fla. Aug. 16, 2006). The basis for charging Bruce initially was for violating Florida law prohibiting having loose VINs. But see Fla. Stat. § 319.30(5)(c) (exempting from prosecution anyone "who removes, possesses, or replaces a manufacturer's or state-assigned identification number plate, in the course of performing repairs on a vehicle").

5. *Bruce*, 498 F.3d at 1238. The exceptions were a former employee's car, and another for which the documents could not be found.

6. *Bruce*, 498 F.3d at 1238 ("In March, the Orange County state attorney dropped all criminal charges against Bruce. Beary did not, however, return Bruce's property."); Bruce Dep. at 86–87.

7. *Bruce*, 498 F.3d at 1245, 1250.

8. Id. at 1235–36.

9. Bruce Dep. at 53–57, 163–66, 167–68.

10. Root Dep. at 23, 25; *Bruce*, 498 F.3d at 1242.

11. Root Dep. at 21–23.

12. *Bruce*, 498 F.3d at 1250 (Carnes, J., concurring).

13. Id. at 1241, 1248 (majority opinion).

14. See generally Edwin J. Butterfoss, "A Suspicionless Search and Seizure Quagmire: The Supreme Court Revives the Pretext Doctrine and Creates Another Fine Fourth Amendment Mess," *Creighton L. Rev.* 40 (2007): 419 (detailing the Court's fractured jurisprudence in suspicionless search cases).

15. *Terry v. Ohio*, 392 U.S. 1, 27 (1968).

16. *Terry*, 392 U.S. at 21 (quoting *Camara v. Mun. Ct. of S.F.*, 387 U.S. 523, 534–535, 536–537 (1967) (balancing)); *United States v. Martinez-Fuerte*, 428 U.S. 543, 557, 559 (1976) (roadblocks).

17. *New Jersey v. T.L.O.*, 469 U.S. 325, 327–28, 336, 338 (1985).

18. *Board of Education v. Earls*, 536 U.S. 822, 828 (2002) (emphasis added) ("Searches by public school officials, such as the collection of urine samples, implicate Fourth Amendment interests.").

19. See, e.g., *Mich. Dep't of State Police v. Sitz*, 496 U.S. 444, 455 (1990) (approving the use of drunk-driving roadblocks); *New York v. Burger*, 482 U.S. 691, 703 (1987) (upholding the constitutionality of warrantless inspections of vehicle-dismantling businesses); In re Sealed Case, 310 F.3d 717, 745-46 (FISA Ct. Rev. 2002) (eliminating the need for particularized suspicion for data collection under FISA because "FISA's general programmatic purpose" is foreign intelligence gathering, as distinguished from "ordinary crime control"); *United States v. Duka*, 671 F.3d 329, 340–46 (3d Cir. 2011) (upholding the constitutionality of suspicionless electronic surveillance "given the government's special interest in collecting foreign intelligence information"); *Haskell v. Harris*, 669 F.3d 1049, 1056–57 (9th Cir. 2012) (upholding a California DNA-testing statute because testing was "programmatic and applie[d] to all felony arrestees," and did not "single out one individual"). On Earls, see *Earls*, 536 U.S. at 826; David Shipler, *The Rights of the People: How Our Search for Safety Invades Our Liberties* (2012), 190 ("Goody Two-Shoes").

20. *Measuring Community Building Involving the Police: The Final Research Report of the Police-Community Interaction Project* (2001), 5.7, www.ncjrs.gov/pdffiles1/nij/grants /213135.pdf.

21. Rodger Birchfield, "Roadblocks Will Feature Drug Dogs," *Indianapolis Star*, Sept. 22, 1995, at E1; R. Joseph Gelarden, "19 Suspects Nabbed in I-65 Drug Roadblock," *Indianapolis Star*, Aug. 14, 1998, at A1.

22. Birchfield, "Roadblocks Will Feature Drug Dogs," supra note 21 (press conference); Office of Juvenile Justice & Delinquency Prevention, U.S. Dept. of Justice, *Promising Strategies to Reduce Gun Violence* (1999), 53, www.ojjdp.gov/pubs/gun_violence /173950.pdf (reporting slightly more than 1,000 stops and just over 100 arrests); Gelarden, "19 Suspects Nabbed in I-65 Drug Roadblock," supra note 21 (marijuana).

23. Birchfield, "Roadblocks Will Feature Drug Dogs," supra note 21 ("deter people"); Stephen Beaver, "IPD Roadblock Draws Big Crowd, Mixed Reviews," *Indianapolis Star*, Oct. 16, 1998, at C1 ("It's not just the statistics." "It's the message." "It made a statement."); Stephen Beaver, "Police Roadblock Results in 29 Arrests," *Indianapolis Star*, Sept. 30, 1998, at B5 ("You're not going to be totally safe . . ."). On the shift from investigative to deterrent-based police practices, see Barry Friedman and Maria Ponomarenko, "Democratic Policing," *N.Y.U. L. Rev.* 90 (2015): 1871–75.

24. R. Joseph Gelarden, "ICLU's Roadblock Sparks Lawsuit," *Indianapolis Star*, Oct. 21, 1998, at B1.

25. *Sitz*, 496 U.S. at 449–52, 455 (weighing the intrusion on the "average motorist" against the "magnitude of the drunken driving problem [and] the States' interest in eradicating it").

26. *City of Indianapolis v. Edmond*, 531 U.S. 32, 42, 52 (2000) ("The seizure is objectively reasonable as it lasts, on average, two to three minutes and does not involve a search."). *Compare* id. at 35, 41–42 (finding the roadblock unreasonable despite an overall hit rate of approximately 4.7 percent for narcotics offenses and 9 percent for all crimes), with *Sitz*, 496 U.S. at 454–55 (finding the roadblock reasonable with a hit rate for DUI arrests of 1.6%).

27. *Edmond*, 531 U.S. at 37, 41–42.

28. Compare *Ferguson v. City of Charleston*, 532 U.S. 67, 83–84 (2001) ("While the ultimate goal of the program may well have been to get the women in question into substance abuse treatment and off of drugs, the immediate objective of the searches was to generate evidence *for law enforcement purposes*"), with id. at 86–87 (Kennedy, J., concurring) (disagreeing with the majority's distinction between "immediate" and "ultimate" law enforcement objectives in interpreting *Edmond*).

29. Compare *Davis v. State*, 788 So. 2d 1064, 1065–66 (Fla. Dist. Ct. App. 2001) (drawing a distinction, in a case out of Tampa involving a driver's license checkpoint, between checkpoints to arrest people and checkpoints to improve roadway safety), with *United States v. Funaro*, 253 F. Supp. 2d 286, 296–97 (D. Conn. 2003) ("[DEA] agents may conduct an administrative inspection for the simultaneous pursuit of an administrative objective and the gathering of evidence for criminal purposes if the administrative inspection is authorized and legitimate."). There has been rampant confusion among the lower courts. See, e.g., *Mills v. District of Columbia*, 584 F. Supp. 2d 47, 56–57 (D.D.C. 2008) (approving a system of checkpoints outside high-crime neighborhoods because the goal was deterrence, not "mak[ing] arrests" or "detect[ing] evidence of ordinary criminal wrongdoing"), rev'd, 571 F.3d 1304, 1311–12 (D.C. Cir. 2009) (holding that the distinction between ordinary law enforcement and special needs does *not* turn on whether the goal is evidence gathering or deterrence, but rather whether the objectives are criminal versus regulatory); *People v. Jackson*, 782 N.E.2d 67, 71–72 & n.2 (N.Y. 2002) (rejecting roadblocks with purposes including general crime control but lacking a clear primary purpose, and explicitly avoiding a decision as to whether it would be lawful if the asserted primary purpose was to *prevent*, rather than investigate, carjacking and taxi robbery); cf. *City of Overland Park v. Rhodes*, 257 P.3d 864, 871, 875 (Kan. Ct. App. 2011) (Atcheson, J., dissenting) (deeming a DUI checkpoint designed to "educat[e] the public as a whole as far as the effects of alcohol on their driving" impermissible because, while a primary purpose cannot be ordinary law enforcement, it cannot be too

far from ordinary law enforcement either). For scholarship challenging the logic of *Edmond*'s distinction, see Barry Friedman and Cynthia Benin Stein, "Redefining What's 'Reasonable': The Protections for Policing," *Geo. Wash. L. Rev.* 84 (2016): 293–97.

30. *Camera*, 387 U.S. at 536–38.

31. *Delaware v. Prouse*, 440 U.S. 648, 650–51 (1979).

32. Id. at 657–59 (considering the state's interest in road safety against the intrusion and effectiveness of spot checks).

33. Id. at 659–60.

34. Id. at 657, 659–60 (finding its "incremental contribution to highway safety" insufficient to justify the stop under the Fourth Amendment).

35. Id. at 663 (emphasis added).

36. Id. at 664 (Rehnquist, J., dissenting); *Leo Sheep Co. v. United States*, 440 U.S. 668 (1979).

37. *Prouse*, 440 U.S. at 653–54 (footnote omitted) (quoting Marshall v. Barlow's Inc., 436 U.S. 307, 312 (1978)); *Camara*, 387 U.S. at 528 (1967) ("The basic purpose of [the Fourth] Amendment . . . is to safeguard the privacy and security of individuals against arbitrary invasions by governmental officials.").

38. James Otis, "Speech Against the Writs of Assistance," Feb. 24, 1761, reprinted in John Wesley Hall, Jr., *Search and Seizure*, 2nd ed. (1991), 1:8; *Wilkes v. Wood*, (1763) 98 Eng. Rep. 489, 498 (K.B.); see, e.g., *Skinner*, 489 U.S. at 621–22 ("An essential purpose of a warrant requirement is to protect privacy interests by assuring citizens subject to a search or seizure that such intrusions are not the random or arbitrary acts of government agents."); *United States v. Cannon*, 29 F.3d 472, 475 (9th Cir. 1994) ("Courts have long recognized that . . . arbitrariness is unreasonable within the meaning of the Fourth Amendment."); *United States v. Guzman*, 864 F.2d 1512, 1516 (10th Cir. 1988) ("It is the need to restrain the arbitrary exercise of discretionary police power that has been the driving force behind the Court's decisions forbidding police practices not amenable to objective review."); Anthony G. Amsterdam, "Perspectives on the Fourth Amendment," *Minn. L. Rev.* 58 (1974): 417 ("A paramount purpose of the fourth amendment is to prohibit arbitrary searches and seizures as well as unjustified searches and seizures."); Monrad G. Paulsen, "The Exclusionary Rule and Misconduct by the Police," *J. Crim. L. & Criminology* 52 (1961): 264 ("All the other freedoms, freedom of speech, of assembly, of religion, of political action, presuppose that arbitrary and capricious police action has been restrained."); M. Blane Michael, Lecture, "Reading the Fourth Amendment: Guidance from the Mischief That Gave It Birth," *N.Y.U. L. Rev.* 85 (2010): 921 ("[T]he mischief that gave birth to the Fourth Amendment was the oppressive general search, executed through the use of writs of assistance and general warrants. The lesson from this mischief is that granting unlimited discretion to customs agents and constables inevitably leads to incursions on privacy and liberty.").

39. *Camara*, 387 U.S. at 532; *Prouse*, 440 U.S. at 661.

40. *Camara*, 387 U.S. at 535 ("[T]he agency's decision to conduct an area inspection is unavoidably based on its appraisal of conditions in the area as a whole, not on its knowledge of conditions in each particular building."); id. at 538–39 ("[Standards for inspection] may be based upon the passage of time, the nature of the building (e.g., a multi-family apartment house), or the condition of the entire area. . . . Such an approach . . . best fulfills the historic purpose behind the constitutional right to be free from unreasonable government invasions of privacy."); id. at 533–34 (holding that safety inspection schemes nevertheless require the "individualized review" of a magistrate to adequately safeguard against Fourth Amendment intrusions).

41. *Prouse*, 440 U.S. at 657 ("[A]nd he is much less likely to be frightened or annoyed by the intrusion.").

42. Cf. Kimberlianne Podlas, "Guilty on All Accounts: *Law & Order*'s Impact on Public Perception of Law and Order," *Seton Hall J. Sports & Ent. L.* 18 (2008): 1 (discussing the cumulative influence of crime entertainment on viewer knowledge).

43. See Randy W. Elder et al., *Effectiveness of Sobriety Checkpoints for Reducing Alcohol-Involved Crashes* (2002), 266–67, www.wrap.org/pdfs/2010TIPElderCDCPaper.pdf ("Although sobriety checkpoints remove some drinking drivers from the road, their primary goal is to deter driving after drinking by increasing the perceived risk of arrest."); Office of Nat'l Drug Control Policy, *Measuring the Deterrent Effect of Enforcement Operations on Drug Smuggling, 1991–1999* (2001), 1–3, www.ncjrs.gov/ondcppubs/publications/pdf/measure_deter_effct.pdf.

44. There are other sorts of regulatory goals that police are permitted to further as well: for example, the police can require a driver to get out of a car they've stopped to ensure the safety of officers. *See Pennsylvania v. Mimms*, 434 U.S. 106, 111 (1977) (justifying the Court's rule in the face of "legitimate concerns for the officer's safety").

45. See *Camara*, 387 U.S. at 532–33 (describing the protections provided by the warrant requirement); *Brinegar v. United States*, 338 U.S. 160, 175–76 (1949) (describing the protections provided by probable cause). For responses to the arguments that warrants are not required by the Fourth Amendment and that probable cause is not always the appropriate standard, see supra Chapters 5 and 6.

46. *Burger*, 482 U.S. at 691, 693–96.

47. Id. at 696, 710 ("[S]urprise is crucial if the regulatory scheme aimed at remedying this major social problem is to function at all.").

48. Id. at 703, 711–12 (holding that the regulatory statute must serve as an "adequate substitute for a warrant" by having a "properly defined scope" and "limit[ing] the discretion of the inspecting officers").

49. Id. at 694n2; id. at 725–26 (Brennan, J., dissenting) ("[I]t is factually impossible that the search was intended to discover wrongdoing subject to administrative sanction.").

50. *Brinegar*, 338 U.S. at 181 (Jackson, J., dissenting).

51. See, e.g., Thomas K. Clancy, "The Role of Individualized Suspicion in Assessing the Reasonableness of Searches and Seizures," *U. Mem. L. Rev.* 25 (1995): 517–20, 626–32 (framing the preference for warrants and probable cause, as articulated by Justice Frankfurter).

52. *Prouse*, 440 U.S. at 663 (permitting the "[q]uestioning of all oncoming traffic at roadblock-type stops" as a measure free from individual discretion).

53. Id. at 663–64 (Blackmun, J., concurring) (noting that the majority opinion does not foreclose spot checks "that do not involve the unconstrained exercise of discretion").

54. Cf. Max Minzner, "Putting Probability Back into Probable Cause," *Tex. L. Rev.* 87 (2009): 913 (comparing the high hit rates in searches pursuant to warrants to the lower hit rates in warrantless searches). As the mayor said in *Edmond*, if publicity around the program was successful, they might catch only a few people at the roadblocks precisely because the roadblocks are working at deterring the prohibited activity. Birchfield, "Roadblocks Will Feature Drug Dogs," supra note 21 (quoting former Mayor Stephen Goldsmith as acknowledging that the roadblocks may not catch a lot of offenders, but they may "deter people from engaging in activity that could land them in jail").

55. See Christopher Slobogin, "Panvasive Surveillance, Political Process Theory, and the Nondelegation Doctrine," *Geo. L.J.* 102 (2014): 1733–45 (explaining political process theory and its applicability to searches and seizure affecting large groups that have access to the legislature); William J. Stuntz, "Implicit Bargains, Government Power, and the Fourth Amendment," *Stan. L. Rev.* 44 (1992): 588 ("Fourth Amendment regulation is usually unnecessary where large numbers of affected parties are involved. Citizens can protect themselves in the same way that they protect themselves against most

kinds of government misconduct—they can throw the rascals out."); Richard C. Worf, "The Case for Rational Basis Review of General Suspicionless Searches and Seizures," *Touro L. Rev.* 23 (2007): 93, 115 (arguing that courts should defer to legislative judgments about society-wide group search and seizure practices, and that "so long as there is *significant* spreading of costs . . . the theoretical possibilities of different preferences, concentrated costs, and collective action problems do not justify the costs of judicial review . . ."); Tracey L. Meares and Dan M. Kahan, "The Wages of Antiquated Procedural Thinking: A Critique of Chicago v Morales," *U. Chi. Legal F.* 1998: 209–10 (concluding that the political process should govern where a community has internalized the burden of law enforcement techniques).

56. See FAA Modernization and Reform Act of 2012, § 826, 49 U.S.C. § 44901 (2012) (prohibiting the TSA from using body scanners that do not incorporate privacy filters); Ron Nixon, "Unpopular Full-Body Scanners to Be Removed from Airports," *N.Y. Times*, Jan. 18, 2013, www.nytimes.com/2013/01/19/us/tsa-to-remove-invasive-body -scanners.html (reporting that the TSA would remove the controversial body scanners from airports).

57. Affidavit of Marshall DePew at ¶ 3, *Edmond v. Goldsmith*, 38 F. Supp. 2d 1016 (S.D. Ind. 1998); Drug Checkpoint Contact Officer Directives by Order of the Chief of Police at ¶¶ 8–9, Stipulation of the Parties, *Edmond v. Goldsmith*, 38 F. Supp. 2d 1016 (S.D. Ind. 1998).

8. DISCRIMINATORY SEARCHES

1. Samuel R. Gross and Debra Livingston, "Racial Profiling Under Attack," *Colum. L. Rev.* 102 (2002): 1415 ("[R]acial profiling occurs whenever a law enforcement officer . . . investigates a person because the officer believes that members of that person's racial or ethnic group are more likely than the population at large to commit the sort of crime the officer is investigating.").

2. Interview by Barry Friedman with Linda Sarsour, Nov. 3, 2014 (hereinafter Sarsour Interview); Champions of Change, The White House, www.whitehouse.gov/champions /giving-back-to-community/linda-sarsour (last visited Feb. 22, 2016).

3. Sarsour Interview, supra note 2.

4. See, e.g., Matt Apuzzo and Adam Goldman, "Inside the Spy Unit that NYPD Says Doesn't Exist," *AP*, Aug. 31, 2011, www.ap.org/Content/AP-In-The-News/2011/Inside -the-spy-unit-that-NYPD-says-doesnt-exist ("mapping"); Adam Goldman and Matt Apuzzo, "With Cameras, Informants, NYPD Eyed Mosques," *AP*, Feb. 23, 2012, www .ap.org/Content/AP-In-The-News/2012/Newark-mayor-seeks-probe-of-NYPD -Muslim-spying; Matt Apuzzo and Adam Goldman, "Documents Show NY Police Watched Devout Muslims," *AP*, Sept. 6, 2011, www.ap.org/Content/AP-In-The-News /2011/Documents-show-NY-police-watched-devout-Muslims; NYPD Intelligence Division, Intelligence Collection Coordinator, "Deputy Commissioner's Briefing," Apr. 25, 2008, http://hosted.ap.org/specials/interactives/documents/nypd/dci-briefing -04252008.pdf (describing informants' activities and reports); Muslim American Civil Liberties Coalition et al., *Mapping Muslims: NYPD Spying and Its Impact on American Muslims* (2013), 12–15, 39–40, http://aaldef.org/Mapping%20Muslims%20NYPD%20 Spying%20and%20its%20Impacts%20on%20American%20Muslims.pdf (describing the impact on mosque activities and student groups) (hereinafter *Mapping Muslims*).

5. Sarsour Interview, supra note 2; NYPD Intelligence Division, *Debriefing Initiative: CI Profiles* (2009), 2, http://hosted.ap.org/specials/interactives/documents/nypd/Informant _Profiles.pdf (noting the desirability of getting a confidential informant "on the board of . . . the Arab American Association of New York [AAANY]").

6. Sarsour Interview, supra note 2; Mitchell D. Silber and Arvin Bhatt, NYPD Intelligence Division, *Radicalization in the West: The Homegrown Threat* (2007), www .brennancenter.org/sites/default/files/legacy/Justice/20070816.NYPD.Radicalization .in.the.West.pdf. Pursuant to the settlement in *Raza v. City of New York*, the materials have been removed from the NYPD's website. Settlement Stipulation and Order at Ex. A, *Raza v. City of New York*, No.13-3448 (S.D.N.Y. 2016), available at www.aclu.org /legal-document/raza-v-city-new-york-exhibit-settlement-stipulation-and-order -proposed-modified.

7. For a discussion of FBI and CIA spying in the 1960s and 1970s, see infra Chapter 12.

8. Al Baker and Kate Taylor, "Bloomberg Defends Police's Monitoring of Muslim Students on Web," *N.Y. Times*, Feb. 21, 2012, www.nytimes.com/2012/02/22/nyregion/bloomberg -defends-polices-monitoring-of-muslim-student-web-sites.html; Hina Shamsi, "Landmark Settlement in Challenge to NYPD Surveillance of New York Muslims: What You Need to Know," *ACLU: Speak Freely*, Jan 7. 2016, www.aclu.org/blog/speak-freely /landmark-settlement-challenge-nypd-surveillance-new-york-muslims-what-you-need (describing the settlement agreement in *Raza*, which includes—subject to court approval—the appointment of an independent civilian monitor and a limitation on the use of undercover officers); Settlement Stipulation and Order at Ex. A, *Raza v. City of New York*, No.13-3448 (S.D.N.Y. 2016), available at www.aclu.org/legal-document/raza -v-city-new-york-exhibit-settlement-stipulation-and-order-proposed-modified; Paul J. Browne, "NYPD's 'Muslim Mapping' Saved Lives," *N.Y. Post*, Apr. 20, 2014, http:// nypost.com/2014/04/20/nypds-muslim-mapping-saved-lives/ (arguing that the Demographics Unit was instrumental in thwarting some of "terrorists' relentless post-9/11 efforts to again target New York"); Charles Krauthammer, "The Case for Profiling," *Time*, Mar. 10, 2002, http://content.time.com/time/magazine/article/0,9171,216319,00 .html; Michael Kinsley, "When Is Racial Profiling Okay?," *Wash. Post*, Sept. 30, 2001, www.washingtonpost.com/archive/opinions/2001/09/30/when-is-racial-profiling-okay /4fdb1630-d0b1-4810-aa11-8237c5bbbafc/.

9. Krauthammer, "The Case for Profiling," supra note 8.

10. National Institute of Justice, DNA Sample Collection from Arrestees (last visited Apr. 8, 2016), www.nij.gov/topics/forensics/evidence/dna/pages/collection-from-arrestees .aspx.

11. Drug Testing for Welfare Recipients and Public Assistance, National Conference of State Legislatures, www.ncsl.org/research/human-services/drug-testing-and-public -assistance.aspx (noting that more than a dozen states have approved some form of welfare drug testing since 2010); Marc Lacey, "U.S. Finds Pervasive Bias Against Latinos by Arizona Sheriff," *N.Y. Times*, Dec. 15, 2011, www.nytimes.com/2011/12/16/us /arizona-sheriffs-office-unfairly-targeted-latinos-justice-department-says.html; Matt Apuzzo and Michael S. Schmidt, "U.S. to Continue Racial, Ethnic Profiling in Border Policy," *N.Y. Times*, Dec. 5, 2014, www.nytimes.com/2014/12/06/us/politics/obama-to -impose-racial-profiling-curbs-with-exceptions.html; National Institute of Justice, DNA Sample Collection from Arrestees, www.nij.gov/topics/forensics/evidence/dna /pages/collection-from-arrestees.aspx.

12. *United States v. Brignoni-Ponce*, 422 U.S. 873 (1973); *Maryland v. King*, 133 S. Ct. 1958, 1967 (2013) (upholding Maryland's collection of DNA from those arrested only for serious crimes and categorizing the testing as an identification procedure); *Bd. of Educ. of Independent School District No. 92 v. Earls*, 536 U.S. 822, 826 (2002) (approving a drug-testing program for students involved in extracurricular activities, despite no evidence of a drug problem unique to that population, and categorizing the testing as a special need).

13. For a discussion of how the Fourth Amendment's purpose is to prevent arbitrary policing, see supra Chapter 6.

14. Chisun Lee, "In Search of a Right," *Village Voice*, July 26, 2005, www.villagevoice.com /news/in-search-of-a-right-6399394.

15. *Brown v. City of Oneonta*, 221 F.3d 329, 334 (2d Cir. 1999); Diana Jean Schemo, "College Town in Uproar Over 'Black List' Search," *N.Y. Times*, Sept. 27, 1992; Lee, "In Search of a Right," supra note 13 (dorm rooms, admissions officer). Other sources vary on the exact numbers involved. See, e.g., Bob Herbert, *In America; Breathing While Black*, Nov. 4, 1999 (14,000 residents, fewer than 500 black residents, and around 150 black students); Lee, "In Search of a Right," supra note 13 (400 black students and several hundred black residents).

16. Lee, "In Search of a Right," supra note 13.

17. *City of Oneonta*, 221 F.3d at 337, 339.

18. See, e.g., id. at 337–39. Compare *United States v. Avery*, 137 F.3d 343, 354 (6th Cir. 1997) (holding that the equal protection clause prohibits "investigative surveillance" based solely on race), with *United States v. Travis*, 62 F.3d 170, 176 (6th Cir. 1995) (Batchelder, J., concurring in judgment) (deeming the equal protection analysis "simply not germane" to consensual encounters).

19. See Erwin Chemerinsky, *Constitutional Law: Principles and Policies*, 5th ed. (2015), 697.

20. See, e.g., *NYC Transit Auth. v. Beazer*, 440 U.S. 568, 592–93 (1979) (upholding a New York City Transit Authority hiring policy that distinguished between people who regularly use narcotics, including methadone primarily used as treatment, and those who don't); *Ry. Express Agency v. New York*, 336 U.S. 106, 109–110 (1949) (upholding a New York law distinguishing between advertisements on delivery trucks and on all other vehicles).

21. See, e.g., *Beazer*, 440 U.S. at 594 ("No matter how unwise it may be for TA to refuse employment to individual car cleaners, track repairmen, or bus drivers simply because they are receiving methadone treatment, the Constitution does not authorize a federal court to interfere in that policy decision."); *Ry. Express Agency*, 336 U.S. at 110 (deferring to the government's conclusion that advertisements on delivery vehicles present less of a traffic problem because "[i]t would take a degree of omniscience which we lack to say that such is not the case").

22. *Korematsu v. United States*, 323 U.S. 214, 216 (1944) (noting that racial classifications are "immediately suspect" and subject to "the most rigid scrutiny"); *City of Richmond v. J.A. Croson Co.*, 488 U.S. 469, 493 (1989) ("[T]he purpose of strict scrutiny is to 'smoke' out illegitimate uses of race. . . . The test also ensures that the means chosen 'fit' this compelling goal so closely that there is little or no possibility that the motive for the classification was illegitimate racial prejudice or stereotype.").

23. See, e.g., *Craig v. Boren*, 429 U.S. 190, 201–202 (1976) (applying intermediate scrutiny and explaining that using "maleness . . . as a proxy for drinking and driving" by eighteen- to twenty-year-olds was an "unduly tenuous fit" where just 2 percent of males in that age group were arrested for that offense). See generally Chemerinsky, *Constitutional Law: Principles and Policies*, supra note 19, at 699; Joseph Tussman and Jacobus ten-Broek, "The Equal Protection of the Laws," *Calif. L. Rev.* 37 (1949): 348–53.

24. See, e.g., *City of Oneonta*, 221 F.3d at 337 ("In acting on a description provided by the victim of the assault . . . defendants did not engage in a suspect racial classification that would draw strict scrutiny"); *Monroe v. City of Charlottesville*, 579 F.3d 380, 388 (4th Cir. 2009) (upholding a DNA dragnet because although the Equal Protection Clause comes into play when "*the government* distinguishes among the citizenry on the basis of race," in that case "any descriptive categorization came from the rape victims who described their assailant").

25. Brothers of the Blacklist (Whatnot Productions 2014) ("[T]he only list I ever wanted to be on was the Dean's List."); Lee, "In Search of a Right," supra note 13 (quoting Eliot Spitzer).

26. Peter Verniero and Paul H. Zoubek, *Interim Report of the State Police Review Team Regarding Allegations of Racial Profiling* (1999), 4, 24–25, www.state.nj.us/lps/intm _419.pdf.

27. *State v. Soto*, 734 A.2d 350, 353, 355, 360 (N.J. Super. Ct. Law Div. 1996).

28. *Report of the New Jersey Senate Judiciary Committee's Investigation of Racial Profiling and the New Jersey State Police* (2001), 17–18 ("[T]he minority arrest rates for troopers involved in the *Soto* appeal were: 63%, 80%, 79%, 84%, 100%, 90%, 84% and 92%."); Imani Perry, *More Beautiful and More Terrible: The Embrace and Transcendence of Racial Inequality in the United States* (2011), 102 (quoting Colonel Carl Williams); Robert D. McFadden, "Whitman Dismisses State Police Chief for Race Remarks," *N.Y. Times*, Mar. 1, 1999, www.nytimes.com/1999/03/01/nyregion/whitman-dismisses -state-police-chief-for-race-remarks.html. For a discussion of the DOJ investigation and the hiding of data by state officials, see *Report of the New Jersey Senate Judiciary Committee's Investigation*, supra, at 19–32. Also note that "[t]he fact that the arrest rates for whites [were] comparatively low does not mean that white motorists are less likely to be transporting drugs, but rather that they were less likely to be suspected of being drug traffickers in the first place and, thus, less likely to be subjected to probing investigative tactics designed to confirm suspicions of criminal activity." Verniero and Zoubek, *Interim Report*, supra note 26, at 36.

29. Verniero and Zoubek, *Interim Report*, supra note 26, at 33–34.

30. Report of John Lamberth, Ph.D. at 5, *Wilkins v. Md. State Police*, No. CCB-93-483 (D. Md. 1993); Albert J. Meehan and Michael C. Ponder, "Race and Place: The Ecology of Racial Profiling African American Motorists," *Just. Q.* 19 (2002): 422 (Michigan); David A. Harris, *Profiles in Injustice: Why Racial Profiling Cannot Work* (2002), 70, 81 (Michigan and North Carolina); David A. Harris, ACLU, *Driving While Black: Racial Profiling on Our Nation's Highways* (1999), www.aclu.org/report/driving-while-black -racial-profiling-our-nations-highways (Colorado).

31. Ian Ayres and Jonathan Borowsky, *A Study of Racially Disparate Outcomes in the Los Angeles Police Department* (2008), 5, 8, http://islandia.law.yale.edu/ayres/Ayres%20 LAPD%20Report.pdf; *Floyd v. City of New York*, 959 F. Supp. 2d 540, 573, 584 (S.D.N.Y. 2013); Jeffrey Fagan et al., *Final Report: An Analysis of Race and Ethnicity in Boston Police Department Field Interrogation, Observation, Frisk, and/or Search Reports* (2015), 2; Travis Anderson, "Boston Police Release New Data on FIO stops," *Bos. Globe*, Jan. 9, 2016, www.bostonglobe.com/metro/2016/01/08/boston-police-release -new-data-fio-stops/6iPbS7E0QEYjLJIut5KnxL/story.html.

32. L. Song Richardson, "Arrest Efficiency and the Fourth Amendment," *Minn. L. Rev.* 95 (2011): 2037–38 (hit rates); Harris, "Profiles in Injustice," supra note 30, at 79–84 (discussing the disparity in hit rates across various contexts and states, including North Carolina); Illinois Dep't of Transp., *Illinois Traffic Stop Study: 2014 Annual Report* (2015), 11–12, https://idot.illinois.gov/Assets/uploads/files/Transportation-System /Reports/Safety/Traffic-Stop-Studies/2014/2014%20ITSS%20Executive%20Summary .pdf; Ayres and Borowsky, "A Study of Racially Disparate Outcomes in the Los Angeles Police Department," supra note 31, at i; Verniero and Zoubek, *Interim Report*, supra note 26, at 66.

33. See Harris, *Profiles in Injustice*, supra note 30, at 76–78; Richardson, "Arrest Efficiency and the Fourth Amendment," supra note 32, at 2039 ("[I]mplicit stereotypes can cause an officer who harbors no conscious racial animosity and who rejects using race as a proxy for criminality to unintentionally treat individuals differently based solely upon their physical appearance.").

34. Verniero and Zoubek, "Interim Report of the State Police Review Team Regarding Allegations of Racial Profiling," supra note 26, at 68.

35. Albert W. Alschuler, "Racial Profiling and the Constitution," *U. Chi. Legal F.* 2002: 163 (noting widespread condemnation of racial profiling prior to the terrorist attacks of September 11, 2001); Gross and Livingston, "Racial Profiling Under Attack," supra note 1, at 1413–14 (same); End Racial Profiling Act of 2001, S. 989, 107th Cong. (2001); Frank Newport, "Racial Profiling Is Seen as Widespread, Particularly Among Young Black Men," *Gallup,* Dec. 9, 1999, www.gallup.com/poll/3421/racial-profiling-seen-widespread-particularly-among-young-black-men.aspx.

36. Kathy Barrett Carter, "Some See New Need for Racial Profiling—Threats to Security Alter State National Debate," *Star-Ledger,* Sept. 20, 2001, at 21 (describing Farmer's experience on September 11, 2001 and the initial impact of 9/11 on racial profiling); John Farmer, Jr., "Rethinking Racial Profiling," *Star-Ledger,* Sept. 23, 2001 (Perspective), at 1.

37. See, e.g., *Village of Arlington Heights v. Metro. Hous. Dev. Corp.,* 429 U.S. 252, 265–66 (1977).

38. *Weaver v. United States,* 966 F.2d 391, 392–93 (8th Cir. 1992).

39. *Weaver,* 966 F.2d at 394 n.2; see also, e.g., Michelle Alexander, *The New Jim Crow: Mass Incarceration in the Age of Colorblindness* (2012), 128–30 (describing how the "solely" test effectively endorses racial profiling).

40. Tussman and tenBroek, "The Equal Protection of the Laws," supra note 23, at 348–53.

41. *Weaver,* 966 F.2d at 397 (Arnold, J., dissenting).

42. See, e.g., *United States v. Jennings,* No. 91-5942, 1993 WL 5927, at *4 (6th Cir. Jan. 13, 1993) (describing a DEA officer who "admit[ted] that half the people he stops at the Cincinnati airport are either Hispanic or Black," even though "Blacks and Hispanics comprise far less than fifty percent of the airline passengers using the Cincinnati airport"). *Jennings* also notes other Sixth Circuit cases, two of which implicated the same officers, "involving airport narcotics agents stopping an allegedly disproportionate number of persons of color while purporting to act in accordance with drug courier profiles." Id. at *14n3.

43. *J.A. Croson Co.,* 488 U.S. at 493 ("[T]he purpose of strict scrutiny is to 'smoke out' illegitimate uses of race . . . The test also ensures that the means chosen 'fit' this compelling goal so closely that there is little or no possibility that the motive for the classification was illegitimate racial prejudice or stereotype."). The figure for Muslims is from Besheer Mohamed, "A New Estimate of the U.S. Muslim Population," Pew Research Ctr., Jan. 6, 2016, www.pewresearch.org/fact-tank/2016/01/06/a-new-estimate-of-the-u-s-muslim-population/. The number of Arab Americans is subject to debate: The U.S. Census estimates there are 1.8 million, while the Arab American Institute Foundation estimates almost 3.7 million Arab Americans in the United States. Jens Manuel Krogstad, "Census Bureau Explores New Middle East/North Africa Ethnic Category," Pew Research Ctr., Mar. 24, 2014, www.pewresearch.org/fact-tank/2014/03/24/census-bureau-explores-new-middle-eastnorth-africa-ethnic-category/.

44. *Vernonia School District 47J v. Acton,* 515 U.S. 646 (1995) (drug testing); Michelle Hibbert, "DNA Databanks: Law Enforcement's Greatest Surveillance Tool?," *Wake Forest L. Rev.* 34 (1999): 771 n.12 (DNA testing).

45. See, e.g., *Griffin v. Wisconsin,* 483 U.S. 868, 876 (1987) (permitting the search of a probationer's home, balancing invasion of defendant's reduced expectation of privacy and government's need in an effective probation system); *New Jersey v. T.L.O.,* 469 U.S. 325, 337–42 (1985) (permitting a search of student's property by school officials, balancing slight invasion of children's expectation of privacy and school administrators' interest in maintaining discipline); *Bell v. Wolfish,* 441 U.S. 520, 558–60 (1979) (permitting body cavity searches of pretrial detainees, balancing high intrusion of pretrial

detainees' diminished expectation of privacy and government's significant security interests).

46. *Von Raab*, 489 U.S. at 660.

47. Id. at 660, 673; id. at 682–84 (Scalia, J., dissenting).

48. Id. at 671 (majority opinion).

49. Id.

50. Id. at 686 (Scalia, J., dissenting).

51. *Skinner v. Ry. Labor Execs.' Ass'n*, 489 U.S. 602, 610–11 (1989).

52. Id. at 607, 628–29. Though the government met the burden imposed by the equal protection clause, the Court did not engage in a Fourteenth Amendment analysis. It instead relied on a Fourth Amendment balancing analysis. Id. at 624. Justice Stevens's concurrence argued that there was no evidence testing for impairment would deter employees when the worry about an accident did not. Id. at 634 (Stevens, J., concurring in part and concurring in judgment). But it seems evident that the possibility one is going to be dismissed or prosecuted immediately upon an accident—and indeed to have blame fixed squarely on one's shoulders—adds to the consequences of one's actions and, therefore, increases deterrence.

53. One might argue that the analysis here is circular: the very question is whether Fourth Amendment rights are being violated, so one can't rely on the fact of violation to set the level of scrutiny. The Fourth Amendment only prohibits "unreasonable" searches and seizures, and until scrutiny is applied, there is no conclusion as to what is unreasonable. This argument proves too much, for the level of scrutiny typically is set as a function of the underlying interests or rights that potentially are infringed. When the government chooses among people on the basis of race, it has not necessarily violated the equal protection clause. That is the question we are trying to answer—just as in the Fourth Amendment context. But because we are concerned about racial discrimination we set the level of scrutiny high. So, too, when the worry is government arbitrariness in policing.

54. *District of Columbia v. Heller*, 554 U.S. 570, 628n27 (2008); *Plyler v. Doe*, 457 U.S. 202, 223 (1982). For an argument that education *is* a fundamental right and effectively has been recognized as such, see Barry Friedman and Sara Solow, "The Federal Right to an Adequate Education," *Geo. Wash. L. Rev.* 81 (2013): 92.

55. *Wolf v. Colorado*, 338 U.S. 25, 27 (1949), overruled on other grounds by *Mapp v. Ohio*, 367 U.S. 643 (1961); see also Nadine Strossen, "The Fourth Amendment in the Balance: Accurately Setting the Scales Through the Least Intrusive Alternative Analysis," *N.Y.U. L. Rev.* 63 (1988): 1187–91 (arguing that infringements upon Fourth Amendment liberties deserve more intense scrutiny because such liberties are fundamental, such infringements typically harm communities unpopular with police, and law enforcement agencies are nondemocratic bodies); Wayne D. Holly, "The Fourth Amendment Hangs in the Balance: Resurrecting the Warrant Requirement Through Strict Scrutiny," *N.Y.L. Sch. J. Hum. Rts.* 13 (1997): 562–66 (arguing for strict scrutiny review of warrantless searches as the Fourth Amendment right is "unquestionably fundamental"); Cynthia Lee, "Package Bombs, Footlockers, and Laptops: What the Disappearing Container Doctrine Can Tell Us About the Fourth Amendment," *J. Crim. L. & Criminology* 100 (2010): 1482–83 (arguing for a "non-deferential inquiry" into the reasonableness of warrantless searches of containers because such searches disproportionately hurt poor communities of color).

56. Matt Apuzzo and Joseph Goldstein, "New York Drops Unit That Spied on Muslims," *N.Y. Times*, Apr. 15, 2014, www.nytimes.com/2014/04/16/nyregion/police-unit-that-spied-on-muslims-is-disbanded.html; *Mapping Muslims*, supra note 4, at 9, 12, 20 ("helped thwart"); Galati Dep. at 128–29, June 28, 2012, *Handschu v. Special Servs. Div.*, 727 F. Supp. 2d 239 (S.D.N.Y. 2010) 71 Civ. 2203, www.nyclu.org/files/releases/Galati_EBT

_6.28.12.pdf ("I have never made a lead from the rhetoric that came from a Demographics Unit report and I'm here since 2006.").

9. SURVEILLANCE TECHNOLOGY

1. P. D. Eastman, *Are You My Mother?* (1998).
2. Interview by Barry Friedman with Abdo Alwareeth, Mar. 17, 2015.
3. Id.
4. Id.
5. Id.
6. Id.
7. Id.
8. *United States v. Pineda-Moreno*, 591 F.3d 1212, 1216 (9th Cir. 2010).
9. Id. at 1121, 1124, 1126 (Kozinski, J., dissenting).
10. Lindsay Miller et al., *Implementing a Body-Worn Camera Program: Recommendations and Lessons Learned* (2014), 1, www.justice.gov/iso/opa/resources/4720149121347 15246869.pdf (quoting Charles Ramsey); *Kyllo v. United States*, 533 U.S. 27, 37 n.3 (2001) (citing National Law Enforcement and Correction Technology Center, www .nlectc.org/techproj/) (radar flashlights); Jay Stanley and Catherine Crump, ACLU, *Protecting Privacy from Aerial Surveillance: Recommendations for Government Use of Drone Aircraft* (2011), 68, www.aclu.org/files/assets/protectingprivacyfromaerialsurvei llance.pdf; Conor Friedersdorf, "Eyes Over Compton: How Police Spied on a Whole City," *The Atlantic*, Apr. 21, 2014 ("We literally watched all of Compton during the times that we were flying." (quoting Ross McNutt of Persistence Surveillance Systems)); Ted Bridis, "FBI Is Building a 'Magic Lantern,'" *Wash. Post*, Nov. 23, 2001, at A15, www.washingtonpost.com/archive/politics/2001/11/23/fbi-is-building-a-magic -lantern/ca972123-83a8-46d8-b95c-c2edafda0fea/; John Schwartz, "Privacy Debate Focuses on F.B.I. Use of an Internet Wiretap," *N.Y. Times*, Oct. 13, 2001, www.nytimes .com/2001/10/13/us/nation-challenged-legislation-privacy-debate-focuses-fbi-use -internet-wiretap.html; Craig Timberg and Ellen Nakashima, "FBI's Search for 'Mo,' Suspect in Bomb Threats, Highlights Use of Malware for Surveillance," *Wash. Post*, Dec. 6, 2013, www.washingtonpost.com/business/technology/2013/12/06/352ba174-5397-11e3 -9e2c-e1d01116fd98_story.html; Christopher Soghoian, "Caught in the Cloud: Privacy, Encryption, and Government Back Doors in the Web 2.0 Era," *J. on Telecomm. & High Tech. L.* 8 (2010): 401–402 (cell phone microphone); *Pineda-Moreno*, 617 F.3d at 1121 (Kozinski, J., dissenting).
11. See *United States v. Jones*, 132 S. Ct. 945, 957 (2012) (Sotomayor, J., concurring); id. at 962 (Alito, J., concurring in judgment).
12. Id. at 964 (Alito, J., concurring in judgment).
13. *Olmstead v. United States*, 277 U.S. 438, 456 (1928).
14. John Kobler, *Ardent Spirits: The Rise and Fall of Prohibition* (1993), 329 ("baby lieutenant"); Phillip Metcalfe, *Whispering Wires: The Tragic Tale of an American Bootlegger* (2007), 8, 19 (quoting Mayor Doc Brown).
15. Kobler, *Ardent Spirits*, supra note 14, at 329–30; Metcalfe, *Whispering Wires*, supra note 14, at 52–53; *Olmstead*, 277 U.S. at 457.
16. Kobler, *Ardent Spirits*, supra note 14, at 331; Metcalfe, *Whispering Wires*, supra note 14, at 94. The moniker may have had its roots in a detective novel, based on a *Saturday Evening Post* story, published in 1918. That book's central mystery was the identity of a "whispering voice of low pitch and timber." Henry Leverage, *Whispering Wires* (1918), 120. The defense attorney on Olmstead's case also used the phrase. Metcalfe, *Whispering Wires*, supra note 14, at 206.

17. *Olmstead*, 277 U.S. at 464–65; Robert Post, "Federalism, Positive Law, and the Emergence of the American Administrative State: Prohibition in the Taft Court Era," *Wm. & Mary L. Rev.* 48 (2006): 42 ("The Taft Court would be widely and correctly perceived as a 'bone dry' institution grimly committed to the success of prohibition.").

18. *Olmstead*, 277 U.S. at 464–66.

19. *Olmstead*, 277 U.S. at 473–74, 476, 479 (Brandeis, J., dissenting) ("Discovery and invention have made it possible for the government, by means far more effective than stretching upon the rack, to obtain disclosure in court of what is whispered in the closet."). One commentator argues that even though Brandeis was committed to enforcing Prohibition, he was equally "vehement on the question of preserving the integrity of law enforcement practices." Post, "Federalism, Positive Law, and the Emergence of the American Administrative State," supra note 17, at 138, 142.

20. *Olmstead*, 277 U.S. at 474 (Brandeis, J., dissenting); Eric Lichtblau, "Police Are Using Phone Tracking as a Routine Tool," *N.Y. Times*, Mar. 21, 2012, www.nytimes.com /2012/04/01/us/police-tracking-of-cellphones-raises-privacy-fears.html (describing the California manual).

21. *Goldman v. United States*, 316 U.S. 129, 135 (1942) (upholding use of the "detecta-phone"); id. at 139, 141 (Murphy, J., dissenting); *Silverman v. United States*, 365 U.S. 505, 506, 512 (1961) (quoting *Silverman v. United States*, 275 F.2d 173, 178 (D.C. Cir. 1960)).

22. Harvey A. Schneider, "*Katz v. United States*: The Untold Story," *McGeorge L. Rev.* 40 (2009): 13.

23. Id. at 13–14.

24. *Katz v. United States*, 389 U.S. 347, 351–53 (1967) ("The Government's activities in electronically listening to and recording the petitioner's words violated the privacy upon which he justifiably relied . . ."); see also Jed Rubenfeld, "The End of Privacy," *Stan. L. Rev.* 61 (2008): 105 ("Modern Fourth Amendment doctrine begins with *Katz v. United States*.").

25. See Orin Kerr, "Four Models of Fourth Amendment Protection," *Stan. L. Rev.* 60 (2007): 504 ("[F]our decades have passed since Justice Harlan introduced the test in his concurrence in *Katz v. United States*, the meaning of 'reasonable expectation of privacy' remains remarkably opaque."); Sherry F. Colb, "What Is a Search? Two Conceptual Flaws in Fourth Amendment Doctrine and Some Hints of a Remedy," *Stan. L. Rev.* 55 (2002): 123 (noting that the Court must address "the instability and poverty of Fourth Amendment doctrine").

26. *Katz*, 389 U.S. at 351. The iconic language of a "reasonable expectation of privacy" actually comes from the concurring opinion of Justice John Marshall Harlan II. Id. at 360 (Harlan, J., concurring).

27. See Colb, "What Is a Search?," supra note 25, at 122 (arguing that the Court treats the risk of exposure "as tantamount to an invitation for that exposure" and treats "exposure to a limited audience as morally equivalent to exposure to the whole world"); *California v. Ciraolo*, 476 U.S. 207, 209, 211–14 (1986); id. at 224 (Powell, J., dissenting).

28. *California v. Greenwood*, 486 U.S. 35, 38, 40–41 (1988).

29. *United States v. Knotts*, 460 U.S. 276, 278, 281–82 (1983).

30. *Dow Chemical Co. v. United States*, 476 U.S. 227, 229–31 (1986) (emphasis added); id. at 242n4 (Powell, J., concurring in part and dissenting in part) (quoting *Dow Chemical Co. v. United States*, 536 F. Supp. 1355, 1357n2 (E.D. Mich. 1982)).

31. *Knotts*, 460 U.S. at 284–85.

32. See id. at 288 (Stevens, J., concurring in judgment) ("[The majority] suggests that the Fourth Amendment does not inhibit the police from augmenting the sensory faculties bestowed upon them at birth with such enhancement as science and technology af-

forded them. But the Court held to the contrary in *Katz v. United States.*" (internal quotation marks omitted) (citations omitted)).

33. *Kyllo*, 533 U.S. at 29 (thermal heat detector); id. at 43 (Stevens, J., dissenting).

34. Id. at 34 (majority opinion).

35. Id. at 40.

36. See Jeffrey W. Childers, "*Kyllo v. United States*: A Temporary Repreive from Technology-Enhanced Surveillance of the Home," *N.C. L. Rev.* 81 (2003): 759–62 (arguing that the thermal-imaging devices at issue in *Kyllo* are becoming more prevalent and reasonably priced and should that continue "the 'not in general public use' standard could very soon undermine the Fourth Amendment protection that *Kyllo* purportedly provides"); Peter Swire, "Proportionality for High-Tech Searches," *Ohio St. J. Crim. L.* 6 (2009): 752 (reviewing Christopher Slobogin, *Privacy at Risk: The New Government Surveillance and the Fourth Amendment* (2007)) (explaining that Slobogin calls the "general public use" test the "Wal-Mart test" because "the cutting edge technology of one year is on the discount shelf at Wal-Mart the next"); Rhett Allain, "The Seek Thermal Infrared Camera for iPhone and Android," *Wired*, Oct. 17, 2014, www.wired.com /2014/10/seek-thermal-infrared-camera-iphone-android/; *Kyllo*, 533 U.S. at 37 n.3 (quoting National Law Enforcement and Correction Technology Center, www.nlectc .org/techproj/); Melanie Reid, "Grounding Drones: Big Brother's Tool Box Needs Regulation Not Elimination," *Rich. J.L. & Tech.* 20, art. 9 (2014): 3 (citing the many ways in which domestic drones are used); see also William Baude and James Y. Stern, "The Positive Law Model of the Fourth Amendment," *Harv. L. Rev.* 129 (2016): 1831 (arguing that whether the Fourth Amendment applies to government use of thermal-imaging cameras should depend "on whether an ordinary citizen would breach any legal duty by attempting to do the same thing in the same circumstances"); Laura Sydell, "As Drones Fly in Cities and Yards, So Do Complaints," NPR, May 12, 2014, www.npr.org/sections /alltechconsidered/2014/05/12/311154242/as-drones-fly-in-cities-and-yards-so-do-the =complaints (discussing the prevalence of drones in San Francisco).

37. *Jones*, 132 S. Ct. at 948.

38. See id. at 952n6 (leaving open the question of the constitutionality of "dragnet type law enforcement practices" like twenty-four-hour surveillance); id. at 956 (Sotomayor, J., concurring) (arguing for the relevance of the length of GPS monitoring and the robustness of the data captured by GPS tracking, but giving no indication of how long is too long or how much data is too much); id. at 964 (Alito, J., concurring in judgment) (arguing that long-term GPS tracking crosses a line, but giving no indication of when GPS tracking becomes long-term).

39. Id. at 940–51 (majority opinion).

40. See, e.g., Matt Taibbi, "Apocalypse, New Jersey: A Dispatch from America's Most Desperate Town," *Rolling Stone*, Dec. 11, 2013, www.rollingstone.com/culture/news /apocalypse-new-jersey-a-dispatch-from-americas-most-desperate-town-20131211 ("One hundred and twenty-one cameras cover virtually every inch of sidewalk [in Camden, New Jersey] . . . Planted on the backs of a fleet of new cruisers are *Minority Report*–style scanners that read license plates and automatically generate warning letters . . ."); William M. Bulkeley, "Business Technology: Chicago's Camera Network Is Everywhere," *Wall St. J.*, Nov. 17, 2009, www.wsj.com/articles/SB10001424052748704 538404574539910412824756 (explaining that Chicago's police department links its own 1,500 cameras with thousands of other cameras placed throughout the city by other government agencies and the private sector); Chris Woodyard and Jayne O'Donnell, "Your Car May Be Invading Your Privacy," *USA Today*, Mar. 25, 2013, www.usatoday .com/story/money/cars/2013/03/24/car-spying-edr-data-privacy/1991751/.

41. *Jones*, 132 S. Ct. at 964 (Alito, J., concurring in judgment) ("We need not identify with

precision the point at which the tracking of this vehicle became a search . . .") Equally mysterious was Justice Alito's suggestion that the test for what constitutes a "search" might vary from one offense to the next, an entirely novel proposition. Id. The confusion among lower courts post-*Jones* is considerable. Compare, e.g., *United States v. Skinner*, 690 F. 3d 772, 779–80 (6th Cir. 2012) (holding that three days of tracking cell phone location data is not a search and that no warrant is required), and *United States v. Davis*, 785 F. 3d 498, 513, 515–16 (11th Cir. 2015) (holding that the release of historical cell site data is not a search and that no warrant required), with *Tracey v. State*, 152 So. 3d 504, 525–26 (Fla. 2014) (holding that the use of cell phone location data is a search and that a warrant required), and *United States v. Graham*, No. 12-4659, 2015 WL 4637931, at *11–12 (4th Cir. 2015) (holding that the release of more than two hundred days of historical cell site location data constitutes a search and that a warrant is required).

42. *Jones*, 132 S. Ct. at 963–64 (Alito, J., concurring in judgment); W. H. Parker, "Surveillance by Wiretap or Dictograph: Threat or Protection?: A Police Chief's Opinion," *Calif. L. Rev.* 42 (1954): 734.

43. *Katz*, 389 U.S. at 361 (Harlan, J., concurring); see also Rubenfeld, "The End of Privacy," supra note 24, at 107 (arguing that the Court escaped the circularity of the *Katz* test by "root[ing] individuals' privacy expectations in widespread social norms drawn from 'outside of the Fourth Amendment'" (quoting *Rakas v. Illinois*, 439 U.S. 128, 143n12 (1978))); David Alan Sklansky, "Too Much Information: How Not to Think About Privacy and the Fourth Amendment," *Calif. L. Rev.* 102 (2014): 1119–20 (arguing that the best way to understand *Katz*'s reasonable expectations test is to understand privacy as respect for a socially constructed "sphere of individual sovereignty" and to define "what counts as disrespect" for the sphere as "to a great extent, a matter of convention."). See generally, Robert C. Post, "The Social Foundations of Privacy," *Calif. L. Rev.* 77 (1989): 962 (arguing that the common law tort of the invasion of privacy protects social norms); Lior Jacob Strahilevitz, "A Social Networks Theory of Privacy," *U. Chi. L. Rev.* 72 (2005): 930–31 (arguing that in the context of tort law, the social norms of dissemination inform what courts consider "highly offensive to a reasonable person," the standard for a violation of the tort law of privacy).

44. See Katherine J. Strandburg, "Home, Home on the Web and Other Fourth Amendment Implications of Technosocial Change," *Md. L. Rev.* 70 (2011): 114–16 (arguing that the distinction between *Katz* and *Olmstead* was that the former Court recognized "the need to adopt the Fourth Amendment's protections to technology-mediated social change," like the ubiquity of the telephone and its use for deep and private conversations, while the latter Court did not); Ric Simmons, "Why 2007 Is Not Like 1984: A Broader Perspective on Technology's Effect on Privacy and Fourth Amendment Jurisprudence," *J. Crim. L & Criminology* 97 (2007): 535 (party lines); Susan W. Brenner, "The Fourth Amendment in an Era of Ubiquitous Technology," *Miss. L.J.* 75 (2005): 20 (quoting Arthur Woods, "Police Espionage in a Democracy," *The Outlook*, May 31, 1916, 113: 235); *Katz*, 389 U.S. at 352.

45. *State v. Rose*, 909 P. 2d 280, 282, 285–86 (Wash. 1996); id. at 288–89 (Johnson, J., dissenting).

46. *Greenwood*, 486 U.S. at 40n4 (alteration in original) (quoting Editorial, "Trash," *Wash. Post*, July 10, 1975, at A18); id. at 52 (Brennan, J., dissenting) (second alteration in original) (quoting Howard Flieger, "Investigative Trash," *U.S. News & World Rep.*, July 28, 1975, at 72; Editorial, "Trash," supra); see also, e.g., *Florida v. Riley*, 488 U.S. 445, 450 (1989) (holding as not a search an officer's flyover, in a helicopter at 400 feet, of the defendant's greenhouse, located on his property); *United States v. Anderson-Bagshaw*, 509 Fed. App'x 396, 404–405 (6th Cir. 2012) (finding pole video camera

overlooking Bagshaw's backyard constitutionally permissible because it was visible from the publicly accessible lot where the pole was placed); *United States v. Brooks*, 911 F. Supp. 2d 836, 843 (D. Ariz. 2012) (denying motion to suppress evidence because the government had permission to install its camera, which only acted to "enhance their sense of sight"); *People v. Lieng*, 119 Cal. Rptr. 3d 200, 211 (Ct. App. 2010) (finding night vision goggles "do not penetrate walls, detect something that would otherwise be invisible, or provide information that would otherwise require physical intrusion"); *United States v. Vogel*, 428 N.W. 2d 272, 275 (S.D. 1998) (finding it permissible for a state trooper to fly over the defendant's geodesic dome home with a zoom lens camera). But see, e.g., *United States v. Houston*, No. 13-09, 2014 WL 259085, at *3 (E.D. Tenn., Jan. 23, 2014) (finding video pole camera's surveillance of the rear of Houston's mobile home unreasonable because it continued for ten weeks).

47. Chris Lydgate and Nick Budnick, "RUBBISH! Portland's Top Brass Said It Was OK to Swipe Your Garbage—So We Grabbed Theirs," *Willamette Week*, Dec. 24, 2002, www .wweek.com/portland/article-1616-rubbish.html; *State v. Galloway*, 109 P. 3d 383, 383–84 (Or. App. 2005) (finding the Portland Police Department's search and seizure of Officer Gina Marie Hoesly's garbage violated Article I, Section 9 of the Oregon Constitution).

48. Noam Cohen, "Law Students Teach Scalia About Privacy and the Web," *N.Y. Times*, May 17, 2009, www.nytimes.com/2009/05/18/technology/internet/18link.html; Kashmir Hill, "Justice Scalia Responds to Fordham Privacy Invasion!," *Above the Law*, Apr. 29, 2009, 9:52 a.m., http://abovethelaw.com/2009/04/justice-scalia-responds-to-fordham -privacy-invasion/ (quoting Justice Scalia).

49. See Colb, "What Is a Search?," supra note 25, at 126 (2002) (critiquing *Smayda v. United States*, 352 F.2d 251 (9th Cir. 1965), which deemed public bathroom stalls a "public space" and accordingly found that evidence obtained by park rangers by cutting a hole over each stall and photographing patrons was admissible); *Pineda-Moreno*, 617 F.3d at 1123 (Kozinski, J., dissenting).

50. *Jones*, 132 S. Ct. at 948; *Rose*, 909 P.2d at 282.

51. See Reid, "Grounding Drones," supra note 36, at 3–5.

52. David J. Roberts and Meghann Casanova, Int'l Ass'n of Chiefs of Police, *Automated License Plate Recognition Systems: Policy and Operational Guidance for Law Enforcement* (2012), 5, 23, www.iacp.org/Portals/0/pdfs/IACP_ALPR_Policy_Operational _Guidance.pdf; ACLU, *You Are Being Tracked: How License Plate Readers Are Being Used to Record Americans' Movements* (2013), 7, www.aclu.org/files/assets/071613-aclu -alprreport-opt-v05.pdf.

53. International Association of Chiefs of Police, *Privacy Impact Assessment Report for the Utilization of License Plate Readers* (2009), 21, www.theiacp.org/Portals/0/pdfs/LPR _Privacy_Impact_Assessment.pdf; Jon Campbell, "License Plate Recognition Logs Our Lives Long Before We Sin," *L.A. Weekly*, June 21, 2012, www.laweekly.com/news /license-plate-recognition-logs-our-lives-long-before-we-sin-2175357.

54. *Jones*, 132 S. Ct. at 964 (Alito J., concurring); Timberg and Nakashima, "FBI's Search for 'Mo,'" supra note 10 (quoting Christopher Soghoian).

55. Timberg and Nakashima, "FBI's Search for 'Mo,'" supra note 10 (quoting Christopher Soghoian); *Jones*, 132 S. Ct. at 964 (Alito, J. concurring in judgment).

56. *Greenwood*, 486 U.S. at 43 (citing *People v. Krivda*, 486 P.2d 1262 (Cal. 1971)); *United States v. Dunn*, 480 U.S. 294, 297–98, 303 (1987).

57. Guido Calabresi, *A Common Law for the Age of Statutes* (1982), 91–119.

58. Roberts and Casanova, *Automated License Plate Recognition Systems: Policy and Operational Guidance for Law Enforcement*, supra note 52, at 28 & 45nn66–67 (citing *Me. Rev. Stat. Ann.* tit. 29-A, §2117-A[5] (2009); Paula T. Dow, N.J. Att'y Gen., *Attorney*

General Guidelines for the Use of Automated License Plate Readers [ALPRs] and Stored ALPR Data (2010) (effective Jan. 18, 2011)); Jeffery Rosen, *The Naked Crowd: Reclaiming Security and Freedom in an Anxious Age* (2005), 57–59 (discussing the Washington Metropolitan Police Department's proposed regulations); *Joint Hearing on Video Technology in Police Surveillance and Traffic Control Before the Council of the District of Columbia Comm. on the Judiciary and Comm. on Public Works and the Env't* (2002) (statement of Margret Kellems, Deputy Mayor for Public Safety & Justice), www .dcwatch.com/issues/privacy10.htm ("[W]e have prepared draft regulations for the operation of CCTV by MPD in the District for which we will be seeking public comment and Council approval.").

59. *City of Ontario v. Quon,* 560 U.S. 746, 759–60 (2010) (ruling on narrow grounds in part because "the Court would have difficulty predicting . . . the degree to which society will be prepared to recognize [employee's privacy] expectations as reasonable" in light of "[r]apid changes in the dynamics of communication and information transmission").

10. THIRD-PARTY INFORMATION AND THE CLOUD

1. This chapter treats several interconnected topics, on which there is a great deal of scholarship. Here is a sampler of relevant sources.

Subpoenas: Christopher Slobogin, "Subpoenas and Privacy," *DePaul L. Rev.* 54 (2005): 805; William J. Stuntz, Commentary, "O. J. Simpson, Bill Clinton, and the Trans-Substantive Fourth Amendment," *Harv. L. Rev.* 114 (2001): 842.

Electronic Communications Privacy Act (ECPA): Patricia L. Bellia, "Surveillance Law Through Cyberlaw's Lens," *Geo. Wash. L. Rev.* 72 (2004): 1375; Orin S. Kerr, "A User's Guide to the Stored Communications Act, and a Legislator's Guide to Amending It," *Geo. Wash. L. Rev.* 72 (2004): 1208; Orin S. Kerr, "Lifting the 'Fog' of Internet Surveillance: How a Suppression Remedy Would Change Computer Crime Law," *Hastings L.J.* 54 (2003): 805; Dierdre K. Mulligan, "Reasonable Expectations in Electronic Communications: A Critical Perspective on the Electronic Communications Privacy Act," *Geo. Wash. L. Rev.* 72 (2004): 1557.

Cell phone location tracking: Brian L. Owsley, "The Fourth Amendment Implications of the Government's Use of Cell Tower Dumps in Its Electronic Surveillance," *U. Pa. J. Const. L.* 16 (2013): 1; Haley Plourde-Cole, "Back to *Katz*: Reasonable Expectation of Privacy in the Facebook Age," *Fordham Urb. L.J.* 38 (2010): 571; Ian James Samuel, Note, "Warrantless Location Tracking," *N.Y.U. L. Rev.* 83 (2008): 1324.

National Security Letters (NSLs): Andrew E. Nieland, Note, "National Security Letters and the Amended Patriot Act," *Cornell L. Rev.* 92 (2007): 1208.

Encryption: Steven M. Bellovin, Matt Blaze, Sandy Clark, and Susan Landau, "Lawful Hacking: Using Existing Vulnerabilities for Wiretapping on the Internet," *Nw. J. Tech. & Intell. Prop.* 12 (2014): 1; Christopher Soghoian, "Caught in the Cloud: Privacy, Encryption, and Government Back Doors in the Web 2.0 Era," *J. Telecomm. & High Tech. L.* 8 (2010): 359; Steven M. Bellovin, Matt Blaze, Sandy Clark, and Susan Landau, "Going Bright: Wiretapping Without Weakening Communications Infrastructure," *IEEE Security & Privacy,* Jan./Feb. 2013, at 62, available at www.cs .columbia.edu/~smb/papers/GoingBright.pdf.

2. See Soghoian, "Caught in the Cloud: Privacy, Encryption, and Government Back Doors in the Web 2.0 Era," supra note 1, at 424 (noting that the combination of the third-party doctrine and the widespread adoption of cloud computing services makes it very easy for law enforcement to obtain digital data).

3. *In re* § 2703(d) Order, 787 F. Supp. 2d 430 (E.D. Va. 2011); *In re* Application of the

United States of America for an Order Pursuant to 18 U.S.C. § 2703(d), 830 F. Supp. 2d 114, 121 (E.D. Va. 2011). The government's order also sought account information for each account registered to or associated with WikiLeaks; Julian Assange; and Bradley Manning. Only Appelbaum, Gonggrijp, and Jonsdottir fought the D-order in this case.

4. See "Who Has Your Back?," Elec. Frontier Found., 2011, www.eff.org/who-has-your -back-2011 (grading technology companies on defense of consumer privacy from government intrusions); Interview by Barry Friedman with Ben Lee, June 2, 2015 (hereafter Lee Interview).

5. *In re § 2703(d) Order*, 787 F. Supp. 2d at 434 (secret court filing); *In re Application*, 830 F. Supp. 2d at 139 ("[It is difficult] to oppose an order because the individual does not know about it."); Scott Shane and John F. Burns, "Twitter Records in Wikileaks Case Are Subpoenaed," *N.Y. Times*, Jan. 9, 2011, at A1 (front-page news); Barton Gellman, "Twitter, Wikileaks and the Broken Market for Consumer Privacy," *Time*, Jan. 14, 2011, http://techland.time.com/2011/01/14/twitter-wikileaks-and-the-broken-market -for-consumer-privacy/. It is Twitter's policy to disclose law enforcement requests to its users, but this is unusual; most requests remain secret. Somini Sengupta, "Twitter's Free Speech Defender," *N.Y. Times*, Sept. 3, 2012, at B1 (profiling Twitter's erstwhile head lawyer and describing Twitter's defense of user privacy as a business policy; contrasting other social networks and tech giants that have violated user privacy to comply with government demands); Declan McCullagh, "DOJ Sends Order to Twitter for WikiLeaks-Related Account Info," CNET, Jan. 7, 2011, http://news.cnet.com/8301 -31921_3-20027893-281.html (recounting Gonggrijp's belief that, unlike Twitter, other companies quietly complied with requests for information without notifying users).

6. *In re § 2703(d)*, 787 F. Supp. 2d at 435, 437, 439.

7. *In re* Application, 830 F. Supp. 2d at 129 (ruling Twitter lacked standing); Lee Interview, supra note 4; Memorandum in Support of Non-Party Twitter, Inc.'s Motion to Quash § 2703(d) Order at 1, *People v. Harris*, No. 2011NY080152 (N.Y. Crim. Ct., May 7, 2012), 2012 WL 1644956 ("Twitter will often know little or nothing about the underlying facts . . ."); Naomi Gilens, ACLU Speech, Privacy and Technology Project, "Twitter Forced to Hand Over Occupy Wall Street Protester Info," Sept. 14, 2012, 5:28 p.m., www.aclu.org/blog/twitter-forced-hand-over-occupy-wall-street-protester-info (commenting on third-party companies in the context of another case in which Twitter was forced to supply the tweets of a protester to facilitate his prosecution).

8. That said, Twitter played a key role in the Arab Spring, and in the Occupy movement in the United States, as well as in many protests around 'officer-involved shootings. The profound importance of social networking and mass texts to the nascent Egyptian revolution in 2011 led to the government's ill-fated attempt to undermine protests by shutting down Internet access. See, e.g., Matt Richtel, "Egypt Halts Most Internet and Cell Service, and Scale of Shutdown Surprises Experts," *N.Y.Times*, Jan. 29, 2011, at A13.

9. *In re* Application, 830 F. Supp. 2d at 133.

10. See Alex Kozinski and Eric S. Nguyen, "Has Technology Killed the Fourth Amendment?" *Cato Sup. Ct. Rev.* 2011–2012: 18–19; Soghoian, "Caught in the Cloud," supra note 1, at 424. Some privacy advocates have noted the potentially invasive use of energy data. See, e.g., Matthew Cagle, ACLU Blog, "Call Logs? Try Kilowatts: Reports Reveal Demands for California Energy Data," June 18, 2013, 4:34 p.m., www.aclu.org /blog/call-logs-try-kilowatts-reports-reveal-demands-california-energy-data (reporting thousands of requests for customer energy usage data disclosed by California utility companies pursuant to legal demands).

11. *In re* Application, 830 F. Supp. 2d at 117 ("The purpose of a criminal investigation is to

find out whether crimes have occurred."); *People v. Harris*, 945 N.Y.S.2d 505, 512 (Crim. Ct. 2012) ("[T]he legal threshold for issuing a subpoena is low,"); James B. Comey, Director, Federal Bureau of Investigation, Remarks at the Brookings Inst., Oct. 16, 2014, www.fbi.gov/news/speeches/going-dark-are-technology-privacy-and -public-safety-on-a-collision-course (hereinafter Comey Remarks).

12. Sengupta, "Twitter's Free Speech Defender," supra note 5; Interview by Barry Friedman with Marc Rotenberg, Sept. 18, 2015 (hereinafter Rotenberg Interview).

13. *Hoffa v. United States*, 385 U.S. 293, 302–303 (1966) ("'The risk of being overheard by an eavesdropper or betrayed by an informer or deceived as to the identity of one with whom one deals is probably inherent in the conditions of human society. It is the kind of risk we necessarily assume whenever we speak." (quoting *Lopez v. United States*, 373 U.S. 427, 465 (1963) (Brennan, J., dissenting))); see also *United States v. White*, 401 U.S. 745, 764–65, (1971) (Douglas, J., dissenting) ("I can imagine nothing that has a more chilling effect on people speaking their minds and expressing their views on important matters. The advocates of that regime should spend some time in totalitarian countries and learn firsthand the kind of regime they are creating here.").

14. *United States v. Miller*, 425 U.S. 435, 436–37, 442–43 (1976).

15. Id. at 438.

16. *Smith v. Maryland*, 442 U.S. 735, 737 (1979).

17. Id. at 744–45.

18. *Smith*, 442 U.S. at 748 (Stewart, J., dissenting). On *Katz v. United States*, 389 U.S. 347 (1967), see supra Chapter 9.

19. See *In re* Application of the United States of America for Historical Cell Site Data, 724 F.3d 600, 611–13 (5th Cir. 2013) (using *Smith* as a basis for permitting location tracking); *Liberty and Security in a Changing World: Report and Recommendations of the President's Review Group on Intelligence and Communications Technologies* (2013), 83, www.whitehouse.gov/sites/default/files/docs/2013-12-12_rg_final_report.pdf (noting Congress's reliance on *Smith* in authorizing the Foreign Intelligence Surveillance Court to order phone service providers to enable call information tracking, but acknowledging that "there is some question today whether [*Smith* is] still good law); Memorandum from Jack L. Goldsmith, III, Ass't Att'y Gen., for the Att'y Gen., Review of the Legality of the STELLAR WIND Program, May 6, 2004, at 101, 106–107, https://fas.org/irp/agency/doj/olc/stellar.pdf (citing *Smith* in justification of NSA collection of email metadata); Eric Lichtblau, "More Demands on Cell Carriers in Surveillance," *N.Y. Times*, July 9, 2012, at A1 (cell phone companies); Michael Isikoff, "FBI Tracks Suspects' Cell Phones Without a Warrant," *Newsweek*, Feb. 18, 2010, 7:00 p.m., www.newsweek.com/fbi-tracks-suspects-cell-phones-without-warrant-75099 (quoting Sprint Nextel's "manager of electronic surveillance").

20. *Miller*, 425 U.S. at 437 (emphasis added).

21. *United States v. Morton Salt Co.*, 338 U.S. 632, 642–43 (1950) ("merely on suspicion"); *Branzburg v. Hayes*, 408 U.S. 665, 701 (1972) (quoting *United States v. Stone*, 429 F.2d 138, 140 (2d Cir. 1970) ("not fully carried out")); *United States v. R. Enterprises, Inc.*, 498 U.S. 292, 297 (1991) ("broad brush"); *In re* Application, 830 F. Supp. 2d at 117 ("The purpose of a criminal investigation is to find out whether crimes have occurred."). On the history of grand juries, see generally Mark Kadish, "Behind the Locked Door of an American Grand Jury: Its History, Its Secrecy, and Its Process," *Fla. St. U. L. Rev.* 24 (1996): 5–6; Roger Roots, "If It's Not a Runaway, It's Not a Real Grand Jury," *Creighton L. Rev.* 33 (2000): 830.

22. Roots, "If It's Not a Runaway, It's Not a Real Grand Jury," supra note 21, at 822; *Hale v. Henkel*, 201 U.S. 43, 59 (1906) ("most valuable function").

23. Kadish, "Behind the Locked Door of an American Grand Jury," supra note 21, at 11 (Zenger); Kevin K. Washburn, "Restoring the Grand Jury," *Fordham L. Rev.* 76 (2008):

2344 (Stamp Act); Roots, "If It's Not a Runaway, It's Not a Real Grand Jury," supra note 21, at 833 (Boss Tweed).

24. See *United States v. Dionisio*, 410 U.S. 19, 23 (1973) (Douglas, J., dissenting) ("It is, indeed, common knowledge that the grand jury, having been conceived as a bulwark between the citizen and the Government, is now a tool of the Executive."); Roots, "If It's Not a Runaway, It's Not a Real Grand Jury," supra note 21, at 823–27 (describing the waning independence of grand juries); Stuntz, "O. J. Simpson, Bill Clinton, and the Trans-Substantive Fourth Amendment," supra note 1, at 864n81. The "ham sandwich" saying originates with Chief Judge Sol Wachtler of the New York Court of Appeals, and was first quoted in Marcia Kramer and Frank Lombardi, "New Top State Judge: Abolish Grand Juries and Let Us Decide," *N.Y. Daily News*, Jan. 31, 1985, at 3 ("Wachtler, who became the state's top judge earlier this month, said district attorneys now have so much influence on grand juries that 'by and large' they could get them to 'indict a ham sandwich.'").

25. Slobogin, "Subpoenas and Privacy," supra note 1, at 814–16 (explaining the development of administrative subpoenas as a means of allowing regulators to enforce business laws); Stuntz, "O. J. Simpson, Bill Clinton, and the Trans-Substantive Fourth Amendment," supra note 1, at 859–60 (noting the historical requirement that administrative officials have probable cause to investigate); 18 U.S.C. § 3486 (2012) (authorizing administrative subpoenas; *Doe v. United States*, 253 F.3d 256, 260–61 (6th Cir. 2001) (financial records, patient records, lists of magazines and journals they read, information about courses they take, and the financial records of their children)); *In re* Subpoena Duces Tecum 228 F.3d 341, 347 (4th Cir. 2000) (warrant-subpoena comparison).

26. See Nieland, "National Security Letters and the Amended Patriot Act," supra note 1, at 1209–12, 1214 (narrating the origins of NSL authority through stages of congressional legislation and highlighting the expanding license granted the FBI at each stage); Electronic Communications Privacy Act of 1986, Pub. L. No. 99-508, § 201, 100 Stat. 1848, 1867 (1986) ("specific and articulable facts"); 18 U.S.C. § 2709(a)–(b) (2012) (setting forth the current requirements for NSLs); Office of the Inspector Gen., U.S. Dep't of Justice, *A Review of the Federal Bureau of Investigation's Use of National Security Letters* (2007), xvi–xvii, https://oig.justice.gov/special/s0703b/final .pdf (reporting the number of NSLs); Office of the Inspector Gen., U.S. Dep't. of Justice, *A Review of the Federal Bureau of Investigation's Use of Exigent Letters and Other Informal Requests for Telephone Records* (2010), 2, https://oig.justice.gov/special/s1001r .pdf; *Liberty and Security in a Changing World*, supra note 19, at 92 (discussing "exigent letters").

27. *Liberty and Security in a Changing World*, supra note 19, at 91, 93; see also Nieland, "National Security Letters and the Amended Patriot Act," supra note 1, at 1202.

28. See, e.g., *Doe v. Gonzales*, 500 F. Supp. 2d 379, 409 (S.D.N.Y. 2007) aff'd in part, rev'd in part, and remanded sub nom. *John Doe, Inc. v. Mukasey*, 549 F.3d 861 (2d Cir. 2008), as modified (Mar. 26, 2009) ("[T]he best protection against abuse of the FBI's discretion in certifying nondisclosure is to ensure that such discretion is checked by meaningful and reasonably expeditious judicial review.")

29. See, e.g., *Morton Salt Co.*, 338 U.S. at 652 ("It is sufficient if the inquiry is within the authority of the agency, the demand is not too indefinite and the information sought is reasonably relevant"); Stuntz, "O. J. Simpson, Bill Clinton, and the Trans-Substantive Fourth Amendment," supra note 1, at 864 ("blank check").

30. *In re* Search Warrant for [Redacted]@hotmail.com, 74 F. Supp. 3d 1184, 1185 (N.D. Cal. 2014). For laws with such "gag" provisions, see, for example, 18 U.S.C. §§ 2703(d), 2709(c) (2012).

31. Nieland, "National Security Letters and the Amended Patriot Act," supra note 1, at 1209 (describing early recognition of the need for legislation); Mulligan, "Reasonable

Expectations in Electronic Communications," supra note 1, at 1561–62 (noting the pre-ECPA asymmetry between the "superwarrant" requirement for wiretaps and the vulnerability of email and other electronic communications); H.R. Rep. No. 99-647, at 26–27 (1986) ("At the state level, some states have placed limits on access to telephone toll records by state and local law enforcement. Colorado, California, Pennsylvania, and New Jersey have all required that a court order be obtained before access to telephone-created transactional information can be granted.") (citations omitted); 132 Cong. Rec. H4045-46 (daily ed. June 23, 1986) (statement of Rep. Kastenmeier) (citing support from a "coalition of business, Government and civil liberties groups").

32. Electronic Communication Privacy Act of 1986, Pub. L. No. 99-508 § 201, 100 Stat. 1848, 1867 (1986) (codified as amended in scattered sections of 18 U.S.C.); Orin S. Kerr, "Internet Surveillance Law After the USA Patriot Act: The Big Brother That Isn't," *Nw. U. L. Rev.* 97 (2003): 611–12, 620, 662; 18 U.S.C. § 2703(d) (requiring "specific and articulable facts" showing the information is potentially "relevant and material" to a criminal investigation).

33. Mulligan, "Reasonable Expectations in Electronic Communications," supra note 1, at 1584.

34. Noncommunications such as photos, diaries, and documents stored in the cloud fall under ECPA's weaker protections of "Remote Computing Services," rather than "Electronic Communications Services." See, e.g., Kerr, "A User's Guide to the Stored Communications Act, and a Legislator's Guide to Amending It," supra note 1, at 1214; Theodoric Meyer, "No Warrant, No Problem: How the Government Can Still Get Your Digital Data," *ProPublica*, June 27, 2014, www.propublica.org/special/no-warrant-no -problem-how-the-government-can-still-get-your-digital-data (noting that unsent email drafts, as well as documents and photos on services like Dropbox and SkyDrive, require no more than a subpoena or court order).

35. Rotenberg Interview, supra note 12.

36. Editorial, "The End of Privacy," *N.Y. Times*, July 15, 2012, at SR10. On government requests for cell phone location data, see, for example, *In re Search Warrant*, 74 F. Supp. 3d at 1185–86.

37. The Mosaic Web browser was released in 1993. See J. Beckwith Burr, "The Electronic Communications Privacy Act of 1986: Principles for Reform," at 8 n.30 (2010).

38. Mulligan, "Reasonable Expectations in Electronic Communications," supra note 1, at 1560 (personal computers); J. Beckwith Burr, "The Electronic Communications Privacy Act of 1986: Principles for Reform," Mar. 30, 2010, at 8, http://digitaldueprocess .org/files/DDP_Burr_Memo.pdf (web browser); *In re* Application, 747 F.Supp.2d at 832 (cell sites).

39. Paul Ohm, "Probably Probable Cause," *Minn. L. Rev.* 94 (2010): 1551n182 ("changing it in fairly significant ways"); Who We Are, Digital Due Process, www.digitaldueprocess .org/index.cfm?objectid=DF652CE0-2552-11DF-B455000C296BA163; Our Principles, Digital Due Process, http://digitaldueprocess.org/index.cfm?objectid=A77781D0 -2551-11DF-8E02000C296BA163.

40. Comey Remarks, supra note 11.

41. Id.

42. Id.

43. Id.

44. Privacy Built In, Apple, www.apple.com/privacy/privacy-built-in/; Comey Remarks, supra note 11.

45. See Eric Lichtblau, "Judge Tells Apple to Help Unlock iPhone Used by San Bernardino Gunman," *N.Y. Times*, Feb. 16, 2016, www.nytimes.com/2016/02/17/us/judge-tells -apple-to-help-unlock-san-bernardino-gunmans-iphone.html; Eric Lichtblau and Kate

Brenner, "Apple Fights Order to Unlock San Bernardino Gunman's iPhone," *N.Y. Times*, Feb. 17, 2016, www.nytimes.com/2016/02/18/technology/apple-timothy-cook -fbi-san-bernardino.html; Kate Brenner and Eric Lichtblau, "U.S. Says It Has Unlocked iPhone Without Apple," *N.Y. Times*, Mar. 28, 2016, www.nytimes.com/2016/03 /29/technology/apple-iphone-fbi-justice-department-case.html.

46. Comey Remarks, supra note 11.

47. Long after everyone else could see the insanity of it, the government continued to insist it should be able to get emails left on a server more than six months without a warrant or probable cause. It also argued that the moment an email was opened, it should be able to use D-order rather than a warrant. Kerr, "User's Guide," supra note 1, at 1219. And even though, in 2015, virtually everyone agreed the ECPA's email rules were wildly out of sync with actual social practice, federal enforcement agencies such as the Securities and Exchange Commission and the Department of Justice continued to fight ECPA reform arguing they should be able to get emails—the content of communications— via subpoena.

48. Comey Remarks, supra note 11 (emphasis added); *Going Dark: Encryption, Technology, and the Balance Between Public Safety and Privacy, Hearing Before the S. Comm. on the Judiciary*, 114th Cong. (2015), at 1, 3, 5 (joint statement of James B. Comey, Dir., Fed. Bureau of investigation, and Sally Quillian Yates, Dep. Att'y Gen., U.S. Dep't of Justice) (emphasis added) (hereinafter Comey-Yates Joint Statement).

49. Reforming the Electronic Communications Privacy Act, Hearing Before the S. Comm. on the Judiciary, 114th Cong. (2015), at 2 (statement of Elana Tyrangiel, Principal Dep. Ass't Att'y Gen., U.S. Dep't of Justice) (hereinafter Tyrangiel Statement).

50. Id. at 2–3; Jack Gillum and Eric Tucker, "Do Cases FBI Cites Support Encryption Worries?" AP, Oct. 18, 2014, http://bigstory.ap.org/article/e03177df2c9a4e0ebe5b584c 909218bf/do-cases-fbi-cites-support-encryption-worries (showing that content on the phones of perpetrators was "at best, supplementary" to law enforcement's investigations in cited examples); Marcy Wheeler, "Jim Comey's Confused Defense of Front Door Back Doors and Storage Intercepts," *Emptywheel*, Oct. 16, 2014, www.emptywheel .net/2014/10/16/jim-comeys-confused-defense-of-front-back-doors-and-storage -intercepts/ (pointing out that law enforcement in Comey's proffered anecdotes did not require access to the phones, and most digital evidence was accessible to law enforcement via service providers); Mike Masnick, "Everybody Knows FBI Director James Comey Is Wrong About Encryption, Even the FBI," *Techdirt*, Oct. 20, 2014, www .techdirt.com/articles/20141019/07115528878/everybody-knows-fbi-director-james -comey-is-wrong-about-encryption-even-fbi.shtml (same); Mike Masnick, "FUD: Former FBI Guy Lies, Claiming New Mobile Encryption Would Have Resulted in Dead Kidnap Subject," *Techdirt*, Sept. 24, 2014, www.techdirt.com/articles/20140923 /17483528611/fud-former-fbi-guy-lies-claiming-new-mobile-encryption-would-have -resulted-dead-kidnap-suspect.shtml (disputing another official's claim that encryption would have hindered law enforcement in another case, because the relevant information was transmitted content available to the service provider rather than stored content limited to the customer's physical device); Mike Masnick, "Manhattan District Attorney Ratchets Up the 'Going Dark' FUD; Leaves Out Its Connection to Shady Hacking Team," *Techdirt*, Aug. 12, 2015, www.techdirt.com/articles/20150812 /06530731921/manhattan-district-attorney-ratchets-up-going-dark-fud-leaves-out -connection-to-shady-hacking-team.shtml#comments (dismissing the possibility that default smartphone encryption settings were a factor in law enforcement's inability to solve a murder).

51. Scott Shane and Colin Moynihan, "Drug Agents Use Vast Phone Trove, Eclipsing N.S.A.'s," *N.Y. Times*, Sept. 2, 2013, at A1.

52. Compare "Who Has Your Back?," Elec. Frontier Found., www.eff.org/who-has-your-back-government-data-requests-2015, with "Who Has Your Back?," Elec. Frontier Found., 2011, www.eff.org/who-has-your-back-2011.

53. Lee Interview, supra note 4.

54. *United States v. Skinner*, 690 F.3d 772, 777 (6th Cir. 2012).

55. Katherine J. Strandburg, "Home, Home on the Web and Other Fourth Amendment Implications of Technosocial Change," *Md. L. Rev.* 70 (2011): 614, 629–30, 639.

56. Comey-Yates Joint Statement, supra note 48, at 3; *United States v. Warshak*, 631 F.3d 266, 288 (6th Cir. 2010). Note that the government cannot search your rental unit *even if* the landlord consents to the search. See *Chapman v. United States*, 365 U.S. 610, 616–17, (1961) ("[T]o uphold such an entry, search and seizure 'without a warrant would reduce the [Fourth] Amendment to a nullity and leave [tenants'] homes secure only in the discretion of [landlords].'") (quoting *Johnson v. United States*, 333 U.S. 10, 14 [1948]).

57. Tyrangiel Statement, supra note 49, at 7.

58. *Riley v. California*, 134 S. Ct. 2473, 2490 (2014).

59. For example, in holding that the Constitution requires probable cause and a warrant before the government can collect our email from cyberspace, the Sixth Circuit said emails are not like the bank statements and slips that could be subpoenaed in *Miller*, see supra notes 14–15 and accompanying text, because "the bank depositor in *Miller* conveyed information to the bank so that the bank could put the information to use in the ordinary course of business. By contrast, Warshak received his emails through NuVox. NuVox was an intermediary, not the intended recipient of the emails." *Warshak*, 631 F.3d at 288 (internal quotation marks omitted) (citations omitted): see also Patricia L. Bellia and Susan Freiwald, "Fourth Amendment Protection for Stored E-Mail," *U. Chi. Legal F.* 2008: 165 ("[W]e view the best analogy for this scenario as the cases in which a third party carries, transports, or stores property for another. In these cases, as in the stored email case, the customer grants access to the ISP because it is essential to the customer's interests."), quoted in *Warshak*, 631 F.3d at 288.

60. Richard Posner, *Not a Suicide Pact: The Constitution in a Time of National Emergency* (2006), 140; Helen Nissenbaum, "Protecting Privacy in an Information Age: The Problem of Privacy in Public," *L. & Phil.* 17 (1998): 581–82.

61. See, e.g., *Chapman*, 365 U.S. at 616–17 (1961) ("[T]o uphold such an entry, search and seizure 'without a warrant would reduce the [Fourth] Amendment to a nullity and leave [tenants'] homes secure only in the discretion of [landlords].'") (quoting *Johnson v. United States*, 333 U.S. 10, 14 [1948]); Strandburg, "Home, Home on the Web," supra note 55, at 650; Bellia, "Surveillance Law Through Cyberlaw's Lens," supra note 1, at 1405n185.

62. *Miller*, 425 U.S. at 440; En Banc Brief of the United States of America, *United States v. Davis*, 785 F.3d 498 (11th Cir. 2015) No. 12–12928, 2014 WL 7232613, at *21–22 ("Like the bank customer in *Miller* and the phone customer in *Smith*, Davis can assert neither ownership nor possession of the third-party records he sought to suppress. Instead, those records were generated by MetroPCS, stored on its own premises, and subject to its control. Cell tower records are not the private papers of the subscriber; indeed, customers "do not generally have access to those records." (citations omitted)).

63. See, e.g., Claire Cain Miller, "N.S.A. Spying Imposing Cost on Tech Firms," *N.Y. Times*, Mar. 22, 2014, at A1 (reporting on the substantial losses American tech firms incurred after the Snowden revelations, and the emerging benefits to more privacy-oriented European firms).

64. Michael V. Hayden, Opinion, "Getting Past the Zero-Sum Game Online," *Wash. Post*,

Apr. 2, 2015, www.washingtonpost.com/opinions/dont-let-america-be-boxed-in-by-its-own-computers/2015/04/02/30742192-cc04-11e4-8a46-b1dc9be5a8ff_story.html.

11. GOVERNMENT DATABASES

1. Abe Mashal, *No Spy No Fly* (2011), 150–51.
2. Id. at 151.
3. Id. at 151–52.
4. Id. at 27, 32, 34, 49, 57–60.
5. Id. at 74–76, 79.
6. Id. at 114, 137–38, 146; Interview by Barry Friedman with Abe Mashal, Jan. 9, 2014 (hereinafter Mashal Interview).
7. Mashal, *No Spy No Fly*, supra note 1, at 152.
8. Id. at 161–62.
9. Mashal, *No Spy No Fly*, supra note 1, at 162; Mashal Interview, supra note 6.
10. Mashal, *No Spy No Fly*, supra note 1, at 10–12, 140–46, 161.
11. Susan Stellin, "Security Check Now Starts Long Before You Fly," *N.Y Times*, Oct. 22, 2013, at A1.
12. Susan N. Herman, *Taking Liberties: The War on Terror and the Erosion of American Democracy* (2011), 66; Sara Kehaulani Goo, "Sen. Kennedy Flagged by No-Fly List," *Wash. Post*, Aug. 20, 2004, www.washingtonpost.com/wp-dyn/articles/A17073-2004Aug19.html; Rick Bowmer, "Terror List Snag Nearly Grounded Ted Kennedy," *USA Today*, Aug. 19, 2004 8:27 p.m., http://usatoday30.usatoday.com/news/washington/2004-08-19-kennedy-list_x.htm (quoting Senator Kennedy).
13. Simon Chesterman, *One Nation Under Surveillance: A New Social Contract to Defend Freedom Without Sacrificing Liberty* (2011), 231 ("link government databases" (citing Charles Sykes, *The End of Privacy: The Attack on Personal Rights at Home, at Work, On-Line, and in Court* (1999)); Stellin, "Security Check Now Starts Long Before You Fly," supra note 11 (EPIC lawyer).
14. Stellin, "Security Check Now Starts Long Before You Fly," supra note 11; Erin Murphy, "The Politics of Privacy in the Criminal Justice System: Information Disclosure, the Fourth Amendment, and Statutory Law Enforcement Exemptions," *Mich. L. Rev.* 111 (2013): 504.
15. Integrated Automated Fingerprint Identification System, FBI, www.fbi.gov/about-us/cjis/fingerprints_biometrics/iafis/iafis; James B. Jacobs, *The Eternal Criminal Record* (2015), 39; Leon Neyfakh, "The Future of Getting Arrested," *The Atlantic*, Dec. 28, 2014, 7:43 p.m., www.theatlantic.com/magazine/archive/2015/01/the-future-of-getting-arrested/383507. Much of this account comes from my colleague Erin Murphy's article "Databases, Doctrine and Constitutional Criminal Procedure," *Fordham Urb. L.J.* 37 (2010): 806–808.
16. *Data Mining: Federal Efforts Cover a Wide Range of Uses*, GAO-04-548 (2004) (database revolution); Thomas Friedman, "Moore's Law Turns 50," *N.Y. Times*, May 13, 2015, www.nytimes.com/2015/05/13/opinion/thomas-friedman-moores-law-turns-50.html (Intel); James Bamford, "The NSA Is Building the Country's Biggest Spy Center (Watch What You Say)," *Wired*, Mar. 15, 2015, 7:24 p.m., www.wired.com/2012/03/ff_nsadatacenter; Lucas Mearian, "By 2020 There Will Be 5,200 GB of Data for Every Person on Earth," *Computerworld*, Dec. 11, 2012, 5:29 a.m., www.computerworld.com/article/2493701/data-center/by-2020-there-will-be-5-200-gb-of-data-for-every-person-on-earth.html; "What Is Big Data?," IBM, www-01.ibm.com/software/data/bigdata/what-is-big-data.html; Sebastian Anthony, "Samsung Unveils 2.5-inch 16TB SSD: The World's Largest Hard Drive," *Ars Technica*, Aug. 13, 2015, 9:14 a.m., http://

arstechnica.com/gadgets/2015/08/samsung-unveils-2-5-inch-16tb-ssd-the-worlds -largest-hard-drive/; "What's a Byte?," www.whatsabyte.com/.

17. National Crime Information Center, FBI, www.fbi.gov/about-us/cjis/ncic; *Terrorism Identities Datasmart Environment (TIDE)* (2014), www.nctc.gov/docs/tidefactsheet _aug12014.pdf; Karen DeYoung, "Terror Database Has Quadrupled in Four Years," *Wash. Post*, Mar. 25, 2007, www.washingtonpost.com/wp-dyn/content/article/2007/03 /24/AR2007032400944.html.

18. Stellin, "Security Check Now Starts Long Before You Fly," supra note 11; see also Ryan Singel, "U.S. Airport Screeners Are Watching What You Read," *Wired*, Sept. 20, 2007, http://archive.wired.com/politics/onlinerights/news/2007/09/flight_tracking; Automated Targeting System, Electronic Privacy Information Center, https://epic.org/privacy /travel/ats/.

19. Permanent Subcomm. on Investigations of the S. Comm. on Homeland Sec. & Gov't Aff., *Federal Support for and Involvement in State and Local Fusion Centers* (2012), 5, www.hsgac.senate.gov/download/?id=49139e81-1dd7-4788-a3bb-d6e7d97dde04 (hereafter *Federal Support for State and Local Fusion Centers*); National Commission on Terrorist Attacks upon the United States, *The 9/11 Commission Report* (2004), 416– 19; Homeland Security Act of 2002, Pub. L. No. 107-296, §§ 111–113, 116 Stat. 2135, 2142–45 (codified at 6 U.S.C. §§111–113 (2006)) (establishing the Department of Homeland Security); John D. Negroponte, Dir. Nat'l Intelligence, "Remarks to the FBI National Academy," Oct. 3, 2006, www.dni.gov/files/documents/Newsroom/Speeches and Interviews/20061003_speech.pdf.

20. Danielle Keats Citron and Frank Pasquale, "Network Accountability for the Domestic Intelligence Apparatus," *Hastings L.J.* 62 (2011): 1458 ("all hazards, all crimes, all threats"); Michael Price, Brennan Ctr. for Justice, *National Security and Local Police* (2013), 20, www.brennancenter.org/sites/default/files/publications/NationalSecurity _LocalPolice_web.pdf ("skills would atrophy"); John W. Whitehead, *A Government of Wolves: The Emerging American Police State* (2013), 118; James B. Perrine, Verne H. Speirs, and Jonah J. Horwitz, *Fusion Centers and the Fourth Amendment: Application of the Exclusionary Rule in the Post-9/11 Age of Information Sharing*, Cap. U. L. Rev. 38 (2010): 735; Alice Lipowicz, Boeing to Staff FBI Fusion Center, *Wash. Tech.*, June 1, 2007, https://washingtontechnology.com/articles/2007/06/01/Boeing-to-staff -FBi-Fusion-Center.aspx; Colin Wood, "New Partnership to Help Fusion Centers Streamline Intelligence Gathering, Dissemination," *Gov't Tech.*, July 16, 2015, www .govtech.com/public-safety/New-Partnership-to-Help-Fusion-Centers-Streamline -Intelligence-Gathering-Dissemination.html.

21. Michael German and Jay Stanley, ACLU, *What's Wrong with Fusion Centers?* (2007), 16, www.aclu.org/files/pdfs/privacy/fusioncenter_20071212.pdf (Bill Harris); Citron and Pasquale, "Network Accountability for the Domestic Intelligence Apparatus," supra note 20, at 1451 (R.I. State Patrol).

22. Information Sharing Environment Functional Standard Suspicious Activity Reporting Version 1.5.5 42-51, 55, https://nsi.ncirc.gov/documents/SAR_FS_1.5.5_PMISE.pdf; Mike German and Jay Stanley, ACLU, *Fusion Center Update* (2008), 2, www.aclu.org /files/pdfs/privacy/fusion_update_20080729.pdf (LAPD).

23. Reed Elsevier to Acquire Choicepoint for 3.6 billion, *N.Y. Times*, Feb. 21, 2008, www .nytimes.com/2008/02/21/technology/21iht-reed.4.10279549.html; RELX Group, *Annual Reports and Financial Statements* (2014), 5, www.relx.com/investorcentre /reports%202007/Documents/2014/relxgroup_ar_2014.pdf; Steve Kroft, "The Data Brokers: Selling Your Personal Information," CBS News, Mar. 9, 2014, www.cbsnews .com/news/the-data-brokers-selling-your-personal-information/; Ryan Gallagher, "De- fense Giant Builds 'Google for Spies' to Track Social Networking Users," *The Guard-*

ian, Feb. 11, 2013, at p.1; Brian Urch, "How Raytheon Software Tracks You Online—Video," *The Guardian*, Feb. 10, 2013, www.theguardian.com/world/video /2013/feb/10/raytheon-software-tracks-online-video.

24. Jacob Goodwin, "Intrado Accesses Personal Data Quickly to Assist Law Enforcement," *Gov't Sec. News*, Oct. 15, 2012, 10:46 a.m., http://gsnmagazine.com/article/27594 /intrado_accesses_personal_data_quickly_assist_law_; Daniel J. Steinbock, "Data Matching, Data Mining, and Due Process," *Ga. L. Rev.* 40 (2005): 13–16 (citing *Data Mining*, supra note 16); Walter L. Perry et al., *Predictive Policing: The Role of Crime Forecasting in Law Enforcement Operations* (2013), 36–41, www.rand.org/content/dam /rand/pubs/research_reports/RR200/RR233/RAND_RR233.pdf; Brent Skorup, "Cops Scan Social Media to Help Assess Their 'Threat Rating,'" Reuters, Dec. 12, 2014, http://blogs.reuters.com/great-debate/2014/12/12/police-data-mining-looks-through -social-media-assigns-you-a-threat-level/.

25. Matt Stroud, "The Minority Report: Chicago's New Police Computer Predicts Crimes, but Is It Racist?," *The Verge*, Feb. 19, 2014, 9:31 a.m., www.theverge.com/2014/2/19 /5419854/the-minority-report-this-computer-predicts-crime-but-is-it-racist; David Smiley, "Not Science Fiction: Miami Wants to Predict When and Where Crime Will Occur," *Miami Herald*, Apr. 23, 2015, 8:21 a.m., www.miamiherald.com/news/local/community /miami-dade/article19256145.html.

26. Urch, "How Raytheon Software Tracks You Online—Video," supra note 23.

27. Goodwin, "Intrado Accesses Personal Data Quickly to Assist Law Enforcement," supra note 24.

28. DeYoung, "Terror Database Has Quadrupled in Four Years," supra note 17.

29. Jacobs, *The Eternal Criminal Record*, supra note 15, at 25 ("baggy pants and tight shirts"); Doreen Carvajal, "O.C. Girl Challenges Police Photo Policy: Lawsuit: Attorneys Contend Youths' Attire, Race Made Them Targets of Mug Shots for Gang File," *L.A. Times*, May 20, 1994, http://articles.latimes.com/1994-05-20/news/mn-60111_1 _police-department ("If you have a problem with this, then don't come to my city."); Emily Thode, "San Diegans Say Police Wrongly Documented Them as Gang Members Because of Neighborhood," *ABC10 News*, May 3, 2015, www.10news.com/news/san -diegans-say-police-wrongly-documented-them-as-as-gang-members-because-of -neighborhood.

30. Citron and Pasquale, "Network Accountability for the Domestic Intelligence Apparatus," supra note 20, at 1444–45, 1458–59 (Bob Barr and Ron Paul); Brandon Ellington Patterson, "Black Lives Matter Organizers Labeled as Threat Actors," *Mother Jones*, Aug. 3, 2015, www.motherjones.com/politics/2015/07/zerofox-report-baltimore-black -lives-matter; George Joseph, "Feds Regularly Monitored Black Lives Matter," *The Intercept*, July 24, 2015, https://theintercept.com/2015/07/24/documents-show-department -homeland-security-monitoring-black-lives-matter-since-ferguson/.

31. Audit Division, Office of the Inspector General, U.S. Dep't of Justice, *Follow-Up Audit of the Terrorist Screening Center* (2007), xiii, https://oig.justice.gov/reports/FBI/a0741 /final.pdf ("individuals could present an immediate threat"); *Terrorist Watchlist: Routinely Assessing Impacts of Agency Actions Since the December 25, 2009, Attempted Attack Could Help Inform Future Efforts*, GAO-12-476 (2012), 15, www.gao.gov/assets /600/591312.pdf.

32. Amy B. Zegart, *Eyes on Spies: Congress and the United States Intelligence Community* (2011), 2; see also DeYoung, "Terror Database Has Quadrupled in Four Years," supra note 17; Mark Hosenball, "Information-Sharing Guru Becomes Chief Leak Plugger," Reuters, Dec. 2, 2010, http://blogs.reuters.com/talesfromthetrail/2010/12/02/information -sharing-guru-becomes-chief-leak-plugger/.

33. Paul Ohm, "Probably Probable Cause: The Diminishing Importance of Justification

Standards," *Minn. L. Rev.* 95 (2010): 1548 ("entirely unregulated"); Murphy, "The Politics of Privacy in the Criminal Justice System," supra note 14, at 495 ("comprehensive privacy laws" (quoting Paul M. Schwartz, "Privacy and Democracy in Cyberspace," *Vand. L. Rev.* 52 (1999): 1632)).

34. *Herring v. U.S.*, 555 U.S. 135, 136–37, 146, 155 (2009).

35. Id. at 153–54.

36. Stewart A. Baker, *Skating on Stilts: Why We Aren't Stopping Tomorrow's Terrorism* (2010), 326, 332, 334.

37. Id. at 336; see also Murphy, "Databases, Doctrine, and Constitutional Criminal Procedure," supra note 15, at 829.

38. Citron and Pasquale, "Network Accountability for the Domestic Intelligence Apparatus," supra note 20, at 1470–74.

39. Alvaro M. Bedoya, "Big Data and the Underground Railroad," *Slate*, Nov. 7, 2014, 10:10 a.m., www.slate.com/articles/technology/future_tense/2014/11/big_data_underground _railroad_history_says_unfettered_collection_of_data.html.

40. Douglas J. Sylvester and Sharon Lohr, "Counting on Confidentiality: Legal and Statistical Approaches to Federal Privacy Law After the USA PATRIOT Act," *Wis. L. Rev.* 2005: 1043 (citing Lynette Clementson, "Homeland Security Given Data on Arab-Americans," *N.Y. Times*, July 30, 2004, at A14).

41. *Federal Support for State and Local Fusion Centers*, supra note 19, at 5; Colo. Rev. State. § 24-33.5-1604(8) (2013), cited in Christopher Slobogin, "Panvasive Surveillance, Political Process Theory, and the Nondelegation Doctrine," *Geo. L.J.* 102 (2014): 1766–67 (2014); Price, *National Security and Local Police*, supra note 20, at 3–4.

42. *Federal Support for State and Local Fusion Centers*, supra note 19, at 27, 85.

43. Id. at 1, 35, 38.

44. Id. at 1, 94.

45. German and Stanley, *Fusion Center Update*, supra note 22, at 7 ("one-way mirror"); Slobogin, "Panvasive Surveillance, Political Process Theory, and the Nondelegation Doctrine," supra note 41, at 1750 ("throw a fit" [quoting Torin Monahan and Neal A. Palmer, "The Emerging Politics of DHS Fusion Centers," *Sec. Dialogue* 40 (2009): 625]). German and Stanley, "What's Wrong with Fusion Centers?," supra note 21, at 9 (citing Adena Schulzberg, "MetaCarta Users Tap Unstructured Data for New Geographic Uses," *Directions Magazine*, May 30, 2007, www.directionsmag.com/article /php?article_id=2478&trv=1 ("Wild West").

46. Maryland DNA Collection Act, 2010 Maryland Code, §2-504.

47. *Maryland v. King*, 133 S. Ct. 1958, 1962, 1965–66 (2013) (quoting *Dist. Att'y's Office for the Third Judicial Dist. v. Osborne*, 557 U.S. 52, 55 (2009)).

48. Id. at 1976; id. at 1980–90 (Scalia, J., dissenting).

49. Id. at 1985 (quoting Md. Code § 2-505(a)(2); Jean Marbella, "Supreme Court Will Review Md. DNA Law," *Balt. Sun*, Nov. 9, 2012, http://articles.baltimoresun.com /2012-11-09/news/bs-md-scotus-dna-20121109_1_violent-crime-or-burglary-dna -samples-jay-king-jr).

50. *Haskell v. Brown*, 677 F.Supp.2d 1187, 1191–92 (N.D. Cal. 2009), aff'd sub nom. *Haskell v. Harris*, 745 F.3d 1269 (9th. Cir. 2014); see also *People v. Buza*, 342 P.3d 415 (Cal. 2015); *Haskell v. Harris*, ACLU of Northern California (Dec. 13 2014), https:// aclunc.org/our-work/legal-docket/haskell-v-harris.

51. See Christine Rosen, "Liberty, Privacy, and DNA Databases," *The New Atlantis*, Spring 2003, at 43 (military); Susan Essoyan, "2 Marines Challenge Pentagon Order to Give DNA Samples: Defense Dept. Says Its Goal Is to Identify Bodies in Wartime. But Enlisted Men Tell Court Their Privacy Is Being Violated," *L.A. Times*, Dec. 27, 1995, http://articles.latimes.com/1995-12-27/news/mn-18238_1_dna-sample; *Amato v. Dist.*

Att'y for Cape & Islands Dist., 80 Mass. App. Ct. 230, 231–34 (2011); Amy Anthony, "DBA Deal Reached in Christa Worthington Murder Case," *Cape Cod Times*, May 6, 2014, www.capecodtimes.com/article/20140506/NEWS/405060325; D. H. Kaye and Michael E. Smith, "DNA Identification Databases: Legality, Legitimacy, and the Case for Population-Wide Coverage," *Wis. L. Rev.* 2003: 435; *People v. Thomas*, 200 Cal. App. 4th 338, 340 (2011); *State v. Buckman*, 613 N.W.3d 463, 474 (Neb. 2000).

52. Akhil Reed Amar, Op-Ed, "A Search for Justice in Our Genes," *N.Y. Times*, May 8, 2002, www.nytimes.com/2002/05/07/opinion/a-search-for-justice-in-our-genes.html; Rosen, "Liberty, Privacy, and DNA Databases," supra note 51, at 44 (quoting Alec Jeffreys).

53. Kevin Lapp and Joy Radice, "A Better Balancing: Reconsidering Pre-Conviction DNA Extraction from Federal Arrestees," *N.C. L. Rev.* Addendum 90 (2012): 163.

54. Erin Murphy, "Relative Doubt: Familial Searches of DNA Databases," *Mich. L. Rev.* 109 (2010): 316, 321–23 (2010) (citing Gautam Naik, "To Sketch a Thief," *Wall St. J.*, Mar. 27, 2009, www.wsj.com/articles/SB123810863649052551); Jeffrey Rosen, "Genetic Surveillance for All?," *Slate*, Mar. 17, 2009, 4:52 p.m., www.slate.com/articles/news _and_politics/jurisprudence/2009/03/genetic_surveillance_for_all.html; Rosen, "Liberty, Privacy, and DNA Databases," supra note 51, at 41 (quoting Alec Jeffreys).

55. Kaye and Smith, "DNA Identification Databases," supra note 51, at 436; "Frequently Asked Questions (FAQs) on the CODIS Program and National DNA Index System," FBI, www.fbi.gov/about-us/lab/biometric-analysis/codis/codis-and-ndis-fact-sheet; Nat'l Ctr. for Victims of Crime, *Evidence Retention Laws: A State by State Comparison* (2013), http://victimsofcrime.org/docs/default-source/dna-resource-center-documents /evidence-retention-check-chart-9-5.pdf.

56. See Murphy, "Relative Doubt," supra note 54, at 293, 297–300, 314–15, 346 ("cloud of suspicion"); Ellen Nakashima, "From DNA of Family, a Tool to Make Arrests," *Wash. Post*, Apr. 21, 2008, www.washingtonpost.com/wp-dyn/content/article/2008/04/20 /AR2008042002388.html; Rosen, "Genetic Surveillance for All?," supra note 54.

57. Perhaps not that far away "[a]s genetic research . . . reveals increasing ties between genes and predisposition to violence and other antisocial behavior." Rosen, "Genetic Surveillance for All?," supra note 54.

58. Rosen, "Liberty, Privacy, and DNA Databases," supra note 51, at 44 (Iceland); *King*, 133 S.Ct. at 1989 (Scalia, J., dissenting).

59. Matthew R. Durose, Alexia D. Cooper, and Howard N. Snyder, Bureau of Justice Statistics, *Recidivism of Prisoners Released in 30 States in 2005: Patterns from 2005 to 2010* (2014), www.bjs.gov/content/pub/pdf/rprts05p0510.pdf; *U.S. v. Kriesel*, 508 F.3d 941, 957 (9th Cir. 2007) (Fletcher, J., dissenting) (citing U.S. Sentencing Comm'n, *Measuring Recidivism: The Criminal History and Computation of the Federal Sentencing Guidelines* (2004), 13, www.ussc.gov/sites/default/files/pdf/research-and -publications/research-publications/2004/200405_Recidivism_Criminal_History .pdf); William J. Sabol et al., Bureau of Justice Statistics, *Offenders Returning to Federal Prison, 1986–97* (2000), 1, 3, http://bjs.gov/content/pub/pdf/orfp97.pdf; Rosen, "Liberty, Privacy, and DNA Databases," supra note 51, at 40 (quoting Benjamin Keehn).

60. Jeremiah Goulka, Carl Matthies, Emma Disley, and Paul Steinberg, RAND Center, *Toward a Comparison of DNA Profiling and Databases in the United States and England* (2010), 8, 18, 20, www.rand.org/content/dam/rand/pubs/technical_reports/2010/RAND _TR918.pdf.

61. Erin E. Murphy, *Inside the Cell: The Dark Side of Forensic DNA* (2015), 65–67; Martin Kaste, "'Great Pause' Among Prosecutors as DNA Proves Fallible," NPR, Oct. 9, 2015, 5:30 p.m., www.npr.org/2015/10/09/447202433/-great-pause-among-forensic-scientists -as-dna-proves-fallible.

62. *Latif v. Holder*, No. 3:10-CV-00750-BR, 2015 WL 1883890 (D. Or. Apr. 24, 2015); Mashal Interview, *supra* note 6.

63. Hina Shamsi, "The U.S. Government Is Putting Americans on Its No-Fly List on a Hunch," *Slate*, Aug. 12, 2015, 4:19 p.m., www.slate.com/articles/news_and_politics /politics/2015/08/the_u_s_government_is_putting_americans_on_its_no_fly_list_on _a_hunch_and.html.

64. Spencer S. Hsu, "FBI Notifies Crime Labs of Errors Used in DNA Match Calculations Since 1999," *Wash. Post*, May 29, 2015, www.washingtonpost.com/local/crime/fbi -notifies-crime-labs-of-errors-used-in-dna-match-calculations-since-1999/2015/05/29 /f04234fc-0591-11e5-8bda-c7b4e9a8f7ac_story.html; Louis Brandeis, *Other People's Money and How the Bankers Use It* (1913), 92.

65. Mashal Interview, *supra* note 6.

12. COUNTERTERRORISM AND NATIONAL SECURITY

1. This account is taken from the video of *The Daily Show*, "Good News! You're Not Paranoid," Comedy Central, June 10, 2013, http://thedailyshow.cc.com/videos/cthyr1/good -news—you-re-not-paranoid—nsa-oversight.

2. See Ron Wyden, "DNI Clapper Tells Wyden the NSA Does Not Collect Data on Millions of Americans," YouTube, www.youtube.com/watch?v=QwiUVUJmGjs&feature =youtu.be&t=6m9s; letter from James R. Clapper, Dir. Nat'l Intelligence, to Senator Diane Feinstein, Chairwoman, Senate Comm. on Intelligence, Jun 21, 2013, www.dni .gov/files/documents/2013-06-21%20DNI%20Ltr%20to%20Sen.%20Feinstein.pdf (quoting Senator Wyden's question and Director Clapper's answer).

3. Glenn Greenwald, "NSA Collecting Phone Records of Millions of Verizon Customers Daily," *The Guardian*, June 6, 2013, www.theguardian.com/world/2013/jun/06/nsa -phone-records-verizon-court-order; Barton Gellman and Laura Poitras, "U.S., British Intelligence Mining Data from Nine U.S. Internet Companies in Broad Secret Program," *Wash. Post*, June 7, 2013, www.washingtonpost.com/investigations/us -intelligence-mining-data-from-nine-us-internet-companies-in-broad-secret-program /2013/06/06/3a0c0da8-cebf-11e2-8845-d970ccb04497_story.html.; Glenn Greenwald and Ewen MacAskill, "NSA Prism Program Taps in to User Data of Apple, Google and Others," *The Guardian*, June 7, 2013, www.theguardian.com/world/2013/jun/06/us -tech-giants-nsa-data; Paul Szoldra, "SNOWDEN: Here's Everything We've Learned in One Year of Unprecedented Top-Secret Leaks," *Bus. Insider*, June 7, 2014, www .businessinsider.com/snowden-leaks-timeline-2014-6 (describing the leaks of these programs). Muscular "infiltrates and copies data flowing out of Yahoo and Google's overseas data centers"; EvilOlive "collects and stores large quantities of Americans' internet metadata"; and Royal Concierge "monitored the booking systems of 350 high-end hotels." HappyFoot monitors applications that "transmit their locations to Google and other Internet companies . . . to [discover] a mobile device's precise physical location." Ashkan Soltani, "NSA uses Google cookies to pinpoint targets for hacking," *Wash. Post*, Dec. 10, 2013, www.washingtonpost.com/news/the-switch/wp/2013/12/10/nsa -uses-google-cookies-to-pinpoint-targets-for-hacking/. On Snowden, see, for example, Mirren Gidda, "Edward Snowden and the NSA Files—Timeline," *The Guardian*, Aug. 21, 2013, www.theguardian.com/world/2013/jun/23/edward-snowden-nsa-files -timeline.

4. See Janet Reitman, "Q&A: Senator Ron Wyden on NSA Surveillance and Government Transparency," *Rolling Stone*, Aug. 15, 2013, www.rollingstone.com/politics/news/q-a -senator-ron-wyden-on-nsa-surveillance-and-government-transparency-20130815 (interviewing Senator Wyden about his thoughts on NSA surveillance); Zoe Carpenter,

"Can Congress Oversee the NSA?," *The Nation*, Jan. 30, 2014, 1:19 p.m. ET, www .thenation.com/article/can-congress-oversee-nsa/ (quoting Senator Wyden in describing how difficult it will be to fix the "culture of misinformation" surrounding NSA programs); 157 Cong Rec. S3386 (daily ed. May 26, 2011) (statement of Sen. Wyden) (hereinafter Wyden Statement).

5. Reitman, supra note 4 ("fundamentally inconsistent"); Wyden Statement supra note 4, at S3388.

6. Lecture of Senator Wyden at First Congressional Church, Portland, Oregon, March 18, 2014, at 15, www.scribd.com/doc/213525546/Wyden-Speech-at-Wayne-Morse-Legacy -Series.

7. Gregory Moore, "A History of U.S. Intelligence," in *Homeland Security and Intelligence*, ed. Keith Gregory Logan (2010), 5, 10, 13.

8. See *The National Security Agency and Fourth Amendment Rights: Hearing on S.R. 21 Before the S. Select Comm. to Study Governmental Operations with Respect to Intelligence Activities*, 94th Cong. (1975), 6 (explaining how the United States "intercepted . . . analyzed, and . . . decoded" foreign communications to produce intelligence during the Revolutionary War, used wire telegrams to send foreign communications during the Civil War and World War I, and relied on decoding radio messages during World War II); President Barack Obama, "Remarks by the President on Review of Signals Intelligence," January 17, 2014, www.whitehouse.gov/the-press-office/2014 /01/17/remarks-president-review-signals-intelligence (describing "Union balloon reconnaissance" in the Civil War and "code-breakers" in World War II).

9. James B. Bruce, "The Missing Link: The Analyst-Collector Relationship," in *Analyzing Intelligence: Origins, Obstacles, and Innovations*, eds. Roger Z. George and James B. Bruce (2008), 19 (explaining the "signal-to-noise ratio" problem causing intelligence failure in Pearl Harbor); National Commission on Terrorist Attacks upon the United States, *The 9/11 Commission Report* (2004), 255–63 (detailing intelligence known to the government in 2001) (hereinafter *9/11 Commission Report*); S. Rep No. 108-301 at 14–35 (2004) (discussing the sources of intelligence failures leading up to the war in Iraq).

10. Seymour M. Hersh, "Huge C.I.A. Operation Reported in U.S. Against Antiwar Forces, Other Dissidents in Nixon Years," *N.Y. Times*, Dec. 22, 1974, http://s3.documentcloud .org/documents/238963/huge-c-i-a-operation-reported-in-u-s-against.pdf.

11. *Intelligence Activities and the Rights of Americans: Final Report of the Select Committee to Study Governmental Operations with Respect to Intelligence Activities*, S. Rep. No. 94-755, at 4–20, 100–102, 167, 170, 172, 174–75, 180–82 (2d Sess. 1976), www .intelligence.senate.gov/sites/default/files/94755_II.pdf (hereinafter Church Committee Report).

12. Id. at 14, 177 (witness, head of FBI Intelligence Division); Frederick A. O. Schwarz, Jr., "The Church Committee and a New Era of Intelligence Oversight," *Intel. & Nat'l. Sec.* 22 (2007): 277 (Phillip Hart).

13. Church Committee Report, supra note 11, at 20; Schwarz, Jr., "The Church Committee," supra note 12, at 291–92. ("natural tendency of Government," "secrecy has been extended").

14. "The Church Committee," supra note 12, at 279–88 (discussing the evolution of wiretapping policy in subsequent presidential administrations, including proposed bills that ultimately did not pass related to restrictions on wiretapping under President Roosevelt and President Eisenhower).

15. *United States v. U.S. District Court (Keith)*, 407 U.S. 297 (1972).

16. Christopher Zbrozek, "The Bombing of the A2 CIA Office," *Mich. Daily*, Oct. 24, 2006, www.michigandaily.com/content/bombing-a2-cia-office; "Ten Most Wanted

Fugitives" Program Frequently Asked Questions, FBI, www.fbi.gov/wanted/topten/ten
-most-wanted-fugitives-faq; *Keith*, 407 U.S. at 300–301.

17. *Keith*, 407 U.S. at 300–301; Peter P. Swire, "The System of Foreign Intelligence Surveillance Law," *Geo. Wash. L. Rev.* 72 (2004): 1314.

18. *Keith*, 407 U.S. at 299, 308–309, 317 (discussing the president's surveillance powers
with respect to suspected activities of foreign powers and noting that it "may well be
that, in the instant case, the Government's surveillance of Plamondon's conversations
was a reasonable one which readily would have gained prior judicial approval").

19. *Id.* at 318–19 ("We are told further that these surveillances are directed primarily to
the collecting and maintaining of intelligence with respect to subversive forces, and
are not an attempt to gather evidence for specific criminal prosecutions."); *Administration White Paper: Bulk Collection of Telephony Metadata under Section 215 of the USA
PATRIOT Act* (2013), 12, www.eff.org/files/filenode/section215.pdf (characterizing the
government's bulk metadata collection programs as "*preventing* threats to national
security" as opposed to civil or criminal investigations).

20. Id. at 320.

21. Id. at 315–16.

22. Id. at 321–23; ("Given those potential distinctions between Title III criminal surveillances and those involving the domestic security, Congress may wish to consider protective standards for the latter which differ from those already prescribed for specified
crimes in Title III . . . It may be that Congress, for example, would judge that the application and affidavit showing probable cause need not follow the exact requirements of
§ 2518 but should allege other circumstances more appropriate to domestic security
cases. . . .").

23. *ACLU v. Clapper*, 785 F.3d 787, 793 (2d Cir. 2015), *staying mandate*, 2015 WL
4196833, *lifting stay*, 804 F.3d 617 (explaining the role *Keith* and the Church Commission played in the genesis of FISA); 50 U.S.C. §§ 1801(b), 1803(a) (2012); see also
Legal Standards for the Intelligence Community in Conducting Electronic Surveillance, Federation of American Scientists, http://fas.org/irp/nsa/standards.html (2000)
(explaining the requirements for electronic surveillance under FISA).

24. Daniel J. Solove, "Reconstructing Electronic Surveillance Law," *Geo. Wash. L. Rev.* 72
(2004): 1716 ("The [USA Patriot] Act was . . . actually a DOJ wish list from before
September 11.")

25. David S. Kris, "The Rise and Fall of the FISA Wall" *Stan. L. & Pol'y Rev.* 17 (2006):
501–508 (discussing "judicial concerns on the FISA surveillance of any target who had
not been a Title III target (or whose Title III surveillance was not strongly supported)
on the theory that the government had resorted to FISA because it could not satisfy
the requirements of Title III"). The Department of Justice worked out guidelines that
did permit information sharing when intelligence agents had some reason to believe
that significant federal crimes had been, were being, or may have been committed,
subject to approval by the Office of Intelligence Policy and Review. *Id.*

26. Stewart A. Baker, *Skating on Stilts: Why We Aren't Stopping Tomorrow's Terrorism*,
66–69, 74–75 (2010) (FBI); *9/11 Commission Report*, supra note 9, at 158, 181–82, 239
(CIA).

27. 50 U.S.C. § 1804(a)(6)(B) (requiring "that a significant purpose of the surveillance is to
obtain foreign intelligence information"); Kris, supra note 25, at 508–509 (quoting
50 U.S.C. §§ 1806[k], 1825[k]) (providing that "'[f]ederal officers' who conduct electronic surveillance or physical searches 'to acquire foreign intelligence information'
'may consult with Federal law enforcement officers to coordinate efforts to investigate
or protect against' the threats to national security specified in the definition of 'foreign
intelligence information.'").

28. *In re* Sealed Case, 310 F.3d 717, 735, 746 (FISA Ct. Rev. 2002).

29. Id. at 737–42.

30. Ryan Lizza, "State of Deception," *New Yorker*, Dec. 16, 2013, at 48, 53 (Total Information Awareness); Shane Harris, *The Watchers: The Rise of America's Surveillance State* (2010), 27–28 (Reagan's National Security Advisor); *9/11 Commission Report*, supra note 9, at 99 (Iran-Contra); William Safire, "You Are a Suspect," *N.Y. Times*, Nov. 14, 2002 (Information Awareness Office).

31. See Gina Marie Stevens, Cong. Research Serv., RL31730, *Privacy: Total Information Awareness Programs and Related Information Access, Collection, and Protection Laws* (2010), 2–3, http://fas.org/irp/crs/RL31730.pdf; Harris, *The Watchers*, supra note 30, at 146–48.

32. Safire, "You Are a Suspect," supra note 30; "Total Information Awareness," *Wash. Post*, Nov. 16, 2002, at A20; see also Baker, *Skating on Stilts*, supra note 26, at 191–92; Stevens, *Privacy*, supra note 31, at 2.

33. Carl Hulse, "Congress Shuts Pentagon Unit Over Privacy," *N.Y. Times*, Sept. 26, 2003 (describing termination of TIA program); Nicole Perlroth and John Markoff, "N.S.A. May Have Hit Internet Companies at a Weak Spot," *N.Y. Times*, Nov. 25, 2013, www.nytimes.com/2013/11/26/technology/a-peephole-for-the-nsa.html (explaining similarity of NSA program to the canceled TIA plan); *Nomination of General Michael V. Hayden, USAF to be Director of the Central Intelligence Agency: Hearing Before the S. Select Comm. on Intelligence*, 109th Cong. (2006), 88 ("frankly played a bit back from the line"); "Fareed Zakaria GPS: Beyond the Manhunts: How to Stop Terror" (CNN television broadcast, May 24, 2013), http://edition.cnn.com/TRANSCRIPTS/1305/24/fzgps.01.html ("[W]e're going to play inside the foul lines, but there's going to be chalk dust on our cleats.").

34. Lizza, "State of Deception," supra note 30, at 51–52 ("Hayden noted the limitations of the FISA law, which prevented the N.S.A. from indiscriminately collecting electronic communications of Americans.").

35. Id.

36. Id. (describing the "Business Records Order" as a victory for the NSA and the metadata program, as well as explaining that "the FISA court issued a secret opinion ratifying the N.S.A.'s" argument that it should be able to "force phone companies to regularly hand over their entire databases"); Perlroth and Markoff, "N.S.A. May Have Hit Internet Companies at a Weak Spot," supra note 33.

37. Lizza, "State of Deception," supra note 30, at 50 ("Internet metadata can include e-mail and I.P. addresses, along with location information, Web sites visited, and many other electronic traces left when a person goes online."); id. at 60 (explaining that the NSA notified the Intelligence Committee "it was indefinitely suspending the program" while providing "little explanation" for its change of heart); "John Inglis Explains Why (US-Based Collection of) Internet Metadata Doesn't Work," *emptywheel*, Jan. 10, 2014, www.emptywheel.net/2014/01/10/john-inglis-explains-why-us-based-collection-of-internet-metadata-doesnt-work/ ("NSA couldn't meet the Court's requirements that it not collect content that is also routing information, because the telecoms, from which NSA collected this data, only had access to the data the NSA wanted at a content level.").

38. See, e.g. James Ball, "NSA Stores Metadata of Millions of Web Users for up to a Year, Secret Files Show," *The Guardian*, Sept. 30, 2013, www.theguardian.com/world/2013/sep/30/nsa-americans-metadata-year-documents.

39. Glenn Greenwald et al., "Microsoft Handed the NSA Access to Encrypted Messages," *The Guardian*, July 11, 2013, www.theguardian.com/world/2013/jul/11/microsoft-nsa-collaboration-user-data.

40. See, e.g., James Ball and Spencer Ackerman, "NSA Loophole Allows Warrantless Search for US Citizens' Emails and Phone Calls," *The Guardian*, August 9, 2013, www .theguardian.com/world/2013/aug/09/nsa-loophole-warrantless-searches-email-calls (quoting government officials stating U.S. persons are not targeted under 702 and that the program is focused on foreign targets); Privacy and Civil Liberties Oversight Board, *Report on the Surveillance Program Operated Pursuant to Section 702* (2014), 7, 82–83 (describing this "incidental" collection of U.S. persons' information as "clearly contemplated by Congress at the time of drafting" and is neither "accidental, or . . . inadvertent") (hereinafter PCLOB, *702 Report*); [Redacted], 2011 WL 10945618, at *1 (FISA Ct. Oct. 3, 2011), https://lawfare.s3-us-west-2.amazonaws.com/staging/s3fs-public /uploads/2013/08/162016974-FISA-court-opinion-with-exemptions.pdf (approving minimization procedures that are "limited to 'the targeting of non-United States persons reasonably believed to be located outside the United States'" [quoting Certification (redacted)]); Brett Logiurato, "John Oliver's First Night Hosting 'The Daily Show' Was Brilliant," *Bus. Insider*, Jun. 11, 2013, 8:53 a.m., www.businessinsider.com/john-oliver -daily-show-debut-june-10-jon-stewart-nsa-scandal-2013-6. Several sources indicate that the NSA applies this standard in a 51 percent foreignness test. See, e.g., Joshua A. T. Fairfield and Erik Luna, "Digital Innocence," *Cornell L. Rev.* 99 (2014): 1024 ("Reportedly, NSA analysts use search terms designed to create at least 51% confidence in a target's 'foreignness'—hardly a rigorous standard and one virtually guaranteed to collect domestic communications." (footnote omitted) (quoting Barton Gellman and Laura Poitras, "U.S., British Intelligence Mining Data from Nine U.S. Internet Companies in Broad Secret Program," supra note 3)). But see Kenneth Anderson, "Readings: NSA Report on the 702 Program," *Lawfare*, April 19, 2014, www.lawfareblog.com/readings -nsa-report-702-program ("This is not a 51% to 49% 'foreignness' test. Rather the NSA analyst will check multiple sources and make a decision based on the totality of the information available.").

41. Laura K. Donohue, "Section 702 and the Collection of International Telephone and Internet Data," *Harv. J.L. & Pub. Pol'y* 38 (2015): 144–46 (describing E.O. 12333's approval procedures); Nate Raymond and Aruna Viswanatha, "New Documents Show Legal Basis for NSA Surveillance Programs," Reuters, Sept. 29, 2014, www.reuters .com/article/2014/09/29/us-nsa-surveillance-idUSKCN0HO1YQ20140929 (explaining that E.O. 12333 "was intended to give the government broad authority over surveillance of international targets"); John Napier Tye, "Meet Executive Order 12333: The Reagan Rule That Lets the NSA Spy on Americans," *Wash. Post*, July 18, 2014, www .washingtonpost.com/opinions/meet-executive-order-12333-the-reagan-rule-that-lets -the-nsa-spy-on-americans/2014/07/18/93d2ac22-0b93-11e4-b8e5-d0de80767fc2 _story.html ("No warrant or court approval is required, and such collection never need be reported to Congress."); Charlie Savage, "Reagan-Era Order on Surveillance Violates Rights, Says Departing Aide," *N.Y. Times*, Aug. 13, 2014, www.nytimes.com/2014 /08/14/us/politics/reagan-era-order-on-surveillance-violates-rights-says-departing-aide .html ("Unlike Section 215, the executive order authorizes collection of the content of communications, not just metadata, even for U.S. persons. Such persons cannot be individually targeted under 12333 without a court order. However, if the contents of a U.S. person's communications are "incidentally" collected (an NSA term of art) in the course of a lawful overseas foreign intelligence investigation, then Section 2.3(c) of the executive order explicitly authorizes their retention. It does not require that the affected U.S. persons be suspected of wrongdoing and places no limits on the volume of communications by U.S. persons that may be collected and retained."); see also id. ("Aware of leak prosecutions . . . [Tye] has spent $13,000 on lawyers to make sure he stays within the lines.").

42. PCLOB, *702 Report*, supra note 40, at 137–38, 159 (describing the FBI's use of 702 data for criminal prosecutions and recommending placing limits on what FBI can do with information intercepted under 702); *Liberty and Security in a Changing World: Report and Recommendations of the President's Review Group on Intelligence and Communications Technologies* (2013), 145–50, (providing recommendations for improving privacy of intercepted communications of U.S. persons); letter from Hon. John D. Bates, Dir., Admin. Office of the U.S. Courts, to Sen. Dianne Feinstein, Chairman, U.S. Senate Select Comm. on Intelligence, Jan. 13, 2014, at 2, www.feinstein.senate.gov/public /index.cfm/files/serve/?File_id=3bcc8fbc-d13c-4f95-8aa9-09887d6e90ed.

43. See, e.g., James Ball, "NSA Stores Metadata of Millions of Web Users for up to a Year, Secret Files Show," *The Guardian*, Sept. 30, 2013, www.theguardian.com/world/2013 /sep/30/nsa-americans-metadata-year-documents; James Risen, "N.S.A. Gathers Data on Social Connections of U.S. Citizens," *N.Y. Times*, Sept. 28, 2013, www.nytimes .com/2013/09/29/us/nsa-examines-social-networks-of-us-citizens.html (discussing the "social network diagrams" created using "bank codes, insurance information, Facebook profiles, passenger manifests, voter registration rolls, and GPS location information, as well as property records and unspecified tax data" and citing NSA officials).

44. Barton Gellman and Ashkan Soltani, "NSA Collects Millions of E-mail Address Books Globally," *Wash. Post*, Oct. 14, 2013, www.washingtonpost.com/world/national -security/nsa-collects-millions-of-e-mail-address-books-globally/2013/10/14/8e58b5be -34f9-11e3-80c6-7e6dd8d22d8f_story.html.

45. See *Unclassified Report on the President's Surveillance Program* (2009), 19–30, https:// fas.org/irp/eprint/psp.pdf; Lizza, "State of Deception," supra note 30, at 53.

46. *Unclassified Report on the President's Surveillance Program*, supra note 45, at 10, 13; Lizza, "State of Deception," supra note 30, at 53; Office of the Inspector General, National Security Agency, *ST-09-0002 Working Draft* (2009), 25, http://nsarchive.gwu .edu/NSAEBB/NSAEBB436/docs/EBB-023.pdf.

47. See Jack Goldsmith, *The Terror Presidency* (2007), 85–90 (describing the views of Cheney and his Counsel, David Addington, on the need to restore the power of the presidency); *Preserving the Rule of Law in the Fight Against Terrorism: Hearing Before the S. Comm. on the Judiciary*, 110th Cong. 60 (2007) (statement of Jack Landman Goldsmith) ("One of the reasons that the administration did not consult more with Congress is that it believed doing so on any particular issue would imply a lack of inherent or exclusive Executive power, and might result in restrictions imposed by Congress that tied the President's hands in ways that prevented him from thwarting the terrorists."). The president is required to keep Congress informed of intelligence activities, 50 U.S.C. § 3091(a)(1) (2012). If the president determines that information involved in a required brief to Congress is extraordinarily sensitive, he may limit reporting to only "the chairmen and ranking minority members of the congressional intelligence committees, the Speaker and minority leader of the House of Representatives, the majority and minority leaders of the Senate," id. § 3093(c)(2), a group informally called the "Gang of Eight"; Kathleen Clark, "The Architecture of Accountability: A Case Study of the Warrantless Surveillance Program" *B.Y.U. L. Rev.* 2010: 395n173.

48. *Unclassified Report on the President's Surveillance Program*, supra note 45, at 12, 19–20.

49. Id. at 11.

50. *Youngstown Sheet & Tube Co. v. Sawyer*, 343 U.S. 579, 582–84, 587, 590–91 (1952); id. at 635–38, 645–46 (Jackson, J. concurring) ("When the President acts in absence of either a congressional grant or denial of authority, he can only rely upon his own independent powers, but there is a zone of twilight in which he and Congress may have concurrent authority, or in which its distribution is uncertain.").

51. "Preserving the Rule of Law in the Fight Against Terrorism," supra note 47, at 57–58.
52. Id. at 59.
53. Id. at 63 (suggesting courts lack the intelligence expertise, access to information, and political accountability required to make the "hard tradeoffs" of modern counterterrorism policy).
54. See, e.g., [Redacted], No. PR/TT, slip op. at 2–4, 28 (FISA Ct. 2004), www.aclu.org /files/assets/FISC%20Opinion%20Granting%20Government%20Application%20Pursuant%20to%20Section%20402.pdf.
55. Id. at 21 (quoting FISA, 50 U.S.C. § 1842[d] [2] [A] [ii]); Lizza, "State of Deception," supra note 30, at 50.
56. PCLOB, 702 Report, supra note 40, at 9 (explaining that "this was the first judicial opinion explaining the FISA court's legal reasoning in authorizing the bulk records collection").
57. 50 U.S.C. § 1851(b)(2)(A) (2012) (requiring "a statement of facts showing that there are reasonable grounds to believe that the tangible things sought are relevant to an authorized investigation [other than a threat assessment] conducted in accordance with subsection [a][2] to obtain foreign intelligence information not concerning a United States person or to protect against international terrorism or clandestine intelligence activities"); In re Application of the F.B.I. for an Order Requiring Prod. of Tangible Things from [Redacted], No. BR 13-109, 2013 WL 5741573, at *7 (FISA Ct. Aug. 29, 2013) (alteration in original) (internal quotation marks omitted) ("somewhere in the metadata"); Jim Sensenbrenner, "How Obama Has Abused the Patriot Act," L.A. Times, Aug. 19, 2013, http://articles.latimes.com/2013/aug/19/opinion/la-oe-sensen brenner-data-patriot-act-obama-20130819.
58. In re Application, 2013 WL 5741573, at *8–9 (finding "legislative re-enactment" because Congress had access to a report describing "the nature and scope of [the FISA] Court's approval of the implementation of Section 215 concerning bulk telephone metadata"); ACLU v. Clapper, 959 F. Supp. 2d 724, 743–46 (S.D.N.Y. 2013), aff'd in part, vacating in part, 785 F.3d 787 staying mandate, 2015 WL 4196833, lifting stay, 804 F.3d 617 (finding that Congress had access to the document prior to reauthorizing 215 and thus ratified the law's interpretation).
59. In re Application, 2013 WL 5741573, at *9.
60. Id.
61. [Redacted], slip op. at 22, 62.
62. ACLU v. Clapper, 785 F.3d 787, 822–25 (2d Cir. 2015) (discussing the "weighty constitutional issues" invoked by the volume of metadata but not deciding whether the volume would transform the collection into a search); Klayman v. Obama, 957 F. Supp. 2d 1, 31–32, 35n57 (D.D.C. 2013) ("[T]he Court in Smith was not confronted with the NSA's Bulk Telephony Metadata Program. Nor could the Court in 1979 have ever imagined how the citizens of 2013 would interact with their phones. For the many reasons discussed below, I am convinced that the surveillance program now before me is so different from a simple pen register that Smith is of little value in assessing whether the Bulk Telephony Metadata Program constitutes a Fourth Amendment search."), vacated and remanded, 800 F.3d 559 (D.C. Cir. 2015).
63. In re Directives Pursuant to Section 105B of Foreign Intelligence Surveillance Act, 551 F.3d 1004, 1006, 1012, 1014 (FISA Ct. 2008) (quoting 50 U.S.C. § 1806b(a)) ("[W]e hold that a foreign intelligence exception to the Fourth Amendment's warrant requirement exists when surveillance is conducted to obtain foreign intelligence for national security purposes and is directed against foreign powers or agents of foreign powers reasonably believed to be located outside the United States."); Keith, 407 U.S. at 317 (footnote omitted).

64. PCLOB, *702 Report*, supra note 40, at 148.

65. See, e.g., John R. Parkinson, "NSA: 'Over 50' Terror Plots Foiled by Data Dragnets," ABC News, June 18, 2013, http://abcnews.go.com/Politics/nsa-director-50-potential -terrorist-attacks-thwarted-controversial/story?id=19428148 ("In recent years, these programs, together with other intelligence, have protected the U.S and our allies from terrorist threats across the globe to include helping prevent the potential terrorist events over 50 times since 9/11." [quoting General Keith Alexander's testimony during a House Committee meeting]); Justin Elliott and Theodoric Meyer, "Claim on 'Attacks Thwarted' by NSA Spreads Despite Lack of Evidence," *ProPublica*, Oct. 23, 2013, 8:59 a.m., www.propublica.org/article/claim-on-attacks-thwarted-by-nsa-spreads -despite-lack-of-evidence (quoting Representative Rogers on the House floor stating the program prevented "fifty-four" attacks); "Obama on NSA Spying: 'We Have Struck the Appropriate Balance' of Privacy and Security," *RealClearPolitics*, www.realclearpolitics .com/video/2013/06/19/obama_on_nsa_spying_we_have_struck_the_appropriate _balance_of_privacy_and_security.html; *Clapper*, 959 F. Supp. 2d at 755.

66. PCLOB, *702 Report*, supra note 40, at 146 ("Based on the information provided to the Board, we have not identified a single instance involving a threat to the United States in which the telephone records program made a concrete difference in the outcome of a counterterrorism investigation. Moreover, we are aware of no instance in which the program directly contributed to the discovery of a previously unknown terrorist plot or the disruption of a terrorist attack."); *Liberty and Security in a Changing World*, supra note 42, at 119–20 n.119 (comparing 215 to 702 and finding that "section 215 has generated relevant information in only a small number of cases, and there has been no instance in which NSA could say with confidence that the outcome would have been different without the section 215 telephony meta-data program"); *Unclassified Report on the President's Surveillance Program*, supra note 45, at 32; Lizza, "State of Deception," supra note 30, at 61 (quoting Matt Olsen).

67. John H. Hedley, "The Evolution of Intelligence Analysis," in *Analyzing Intelligence*, supra note 9, at 26.

68. Richard C. Shelby, Vice Chairman, Senate Select committee on Intelligence, *September 11 and the Imperative of Reform in the U.S. Intelligence Community*, 23–31 (Dec. 10, 2002), www.intelligence.senate.gov/shelby.pdf (criticizing the intelligence community for failure to "connect the dots" on several incidents prior to 9/11); Harris, *The Watchers*, supra note 30, at 5; Carmen A. Medina, "The New Analysis," in *Analyzing Intelligence*, supra note 9, at 240–41 (discussing the proliferation of data and the analyst's difficulty in processing it); Gregory F. Treverton, "Intelligence Analysis Between 'Politicization' and Irrelevance," in *Analyzing Intelligence*, supra note 9, at 97 (discussing the problem of "too much [data] to sift through"); Barton Gellman and Ashkan Soltani, "NSA Tracking Cellphone Locations Worldwide, Snowden Documents Show," *Wash. Post*, Dec. 4, 2013, www.washingtonpost.com/world/national-security/nsa-tracking -cellphone-locations-worldwide-snowden-documents-show/2013/12/04/5492873a -5cf2-11e3-bc56-c6ca94801fac_story.html; Keith Gregory Logan, *Homeland Security and Intelligence* (2010), 205 (featuring a chapter titled "Drowning in Data While Starving for Wisdom").

69. Harris, *The Watchers*, supra note 30, in Jeff Jonas and Jim Harper, *Effective Counterterrorism and the Limited Role of Predictive Data Mining* (2006), at 1, 7–8, http://object .cato.org/sites/cato.org/files/pubs/pdf/pa584.pdf (explaining that data mining "relies on models constructed using many thousands of known examples of fraud per year"); Katherine J. Strandburg, "Freedom of Association in a Networked World: First Amendment Regulation of Relational Surveillance," *Boston Coll. L. Rev.* 49 (2008): 765–68; Jeffrey Rosen, *The Naked Crowd: Reclaiming Security and Freedom in an Anx-*

ious Age (2013), 104 ("Unlike people who commit credit card fraud—a form of system-atic, repetitive, and predictable behavior that fits a consistent profile identified by millions of transactions—there is no reason to believe that terrorists in the future will resemble those in the past."); Susan N. Herman, *Taking Liberties: The War on Terror and the Erosion of American Democracy* (2011), 98 (citing a 2008 report by the National Research Council of the National Academy of Sciences that "concluded that there was simply no scientific consensus that contemporary data mining techniques were ready for use in terrorism investigations . . . [because] we know very little about how to recognize potential terrorists because our information about patterns of terrorism is so sparse.").

70. See PCLOB, *702 Report*, supra note 40, at 2, 9, 12–14; *Liberty and Security in a Changing World*, supra note 42, at 146–50 (recommending "the government may not search the contents of communications acquired under section 702, or under any other authority covered by this recommendation, in an effort to identify communications of particular United States persons, except . . . when the government obtains a warrant based on probable cause to believe that the United States person is planning or is engaged in acts of international terrorism"); Glenn Harlan Reynolds, "NSA Spying Undermines Separation of Powers," *USA Today*, Feb. 10, 2014, www.usatoday.com/story /opinion/2014/02/10/nsa-spying-surveillance-congress-column/5340281/.

CONCLUSION: THE CHALLENGES OF DEMOCRATIC POLICING

1. Annys Shin, "Traffic Stop Video on YouTube Sparks Debate on Police Use of Md. Wiretap Laws," *Wash. Post*, June 16, 2010, www.washingtonpost.com/wp-dyn/content/article/2010 /06/15/AR2010061505556.html; "Wrongful Charges Dropped Against Motorcyclist Prosecuted for Videotaping Encounter with Police," ACLU, Sept. 27, 2010, www.aclu .org/news/wrongful-charges-dropped-against-motorcyclist-prosecuted-videotaping -encounter-police. This account also is based on an interview by Barry Friedman with Anthony Graber.

2. Peter Hermann, "ACLU Lawyers Seek to Quash Wiretapping Charges," *Balt. Sun*, Sept. 3, 2010, http://articles.baltimoresun.com/2010-09-03/news/bs-md-police-cameras -graber-20100903_1_traffic-stop-trooper-j-d-uhler-anthony-graber.

3. Anthony Graber, "Motorcycle Traffic Violation—Cop Pulls Out Gun (Extended No Sound)," YouTube, Mar. 12, 2010, www.youtube.com/watch?v=G7PC9cZEWCQ; State's Answer to Def.'s Mot. to Suppress at 11, *State v. Graber*, No. K-IO-647, 2010 Md. Cir. Ct. LEXIS 7 (Md. Cir. Ct. Sept. 27, 2010).

4. *Graber*, 2010 Md. Cir. Ct. LEXIS 7, at *1–2; Hermann, "ACLU Lawyers," supra note 2.

5. Toni Waterman, "Boston Court Ruling Affirms Citizens' Right to Record Officials," WGBH, Sept. 23, 2011, www.wgbh.org/articles/Boston-Court-Ruling-Affirms-Citizens -Right-To-Record-Officials-4342 (Glik); *Glik v. Cunniffe*, 655 F.3d 78 (1st Cir. 2011); James Queally, "Newark Police Settle Case with Teen Illegally Detained for Filming Cops," *Star-Ledger*, Nov. 28, 2012, 12:24 p.m., www.nj.com/news/index.ssf/2012/11 /newark_police_settle_case_with.html; AP, "Mass. Woman Charged with Recording Her Own Arrest," WBUR, May 12, 2014, www.wbur.org/2014/05/12/record-arrest -chicopee (Karen Dziewit).

6. Statement of Interest of the United States at 2, *Garcia v. Montgomery County*, No. 8:12-cv-03592 (D. Md. Mar. 4, 2013).

7. *Graber*, 2010 Md. Cir. Ct. LEXIS 7, at *35–36.

8. Statement of Interest at 6–7, *Garcia*, No. 8:12-cv-03592 (quoting *Gentile v. State Bar of Nev.* 501 U.S. 1030, 1034 (1991); *Butterworth v. Smith*, 494 U.S. 624, 632 (1990)).

9. Devlin Barrett, "U.S. Will Change Stance on Phone Tracking," *Wall St. J.*, May 3, 2015, 7:46 p.m., www.wsj.com/articles/u-s-will-change-stance-on-secret-phone-tracking

-1430696796; Office of the Inspector General, *A Review of the Federal Bureau of Investigation's Use of National Security Letters* (2007), 7, 31, https://oig.justice.gov/special/s0703b/final.pdf. For a discussion of the Department of Justice's role in keeping the NSA's mass surveillance programs secret, see supra Chapter 12.

10. Statement of Interest at 5, *Garcia*, No. 8:12-cv-03592.

11. Matt Stroud, "The Minority Report: Chicago's New Police Computer Predicts Crimes, but Is It Racist?," *The Verge*, Feb. 19, 2014, 9:31 a.m., www.theverge.com/2014/2/19/5419854/the-minority-report-this-computer-predicts-crime-but-is-it-racist.

12. Developments in the Law, "Policing, Chapter Four: Considering Police Body Cameras," *Harv. L. Rev.* 128 (2015): 1794–95.

13. See, e.g., Michael D. White, *Police Officer Body-Worn Cameras: Assessing the Evidence* (2014), 17, https://ojpdiagnosticcenter.org/sites/default/files/spotlight/download/Police%20Officer%20Body-Worn%20Cameras.pdf (reviewing preliminary results of BWC studies). Although comprehensive, White himself notes that the cited studies suffer significant methodological limitations, including lack of comparative design, overreliance on police officer surveys about perceptions and attitudes, and the fact that many were carried out by law enforcement agencies who were themselves deploying the technology.

14. Barak Ariel et al., "The Effect of Police Body-Worn Cameras on Use of Force and Citizens' Complaints Against the Police: A Randomized Controlled Trial," *J. Quantitative Criminology* 31 (2015): 509 (Rialto); Justin T. Ready and Jacob T. N. Young, "The Impact of On-Officer Video Cameras on Police–Citizen Contacts: Findings from a Controlled Experiment in Mesa, AZ," *J. Experimental Criminology* 11 (2015): 445–47 (noting that presence of cameras altered the behavior of both police and civilians); *San Diego Police Department Body Worn Camera Program Update* (2015), http://docs.sandiego.gov/councilcomm_agendas_attach/2015/psln_150318_2.pdf ("Body worn camera technology is a win-win for both the officer and the community. Although only implemented for a relatively short period of time, the results are very promising, showing a reduction in citizen complaints, allegations, and a reduction of some use of force applications."); Barak Ariel and Tony Farrar, *Self-Awareness to Being Watched and Socially-Desirable Behavior: A Field Experiment on the Effect of Body-Worn Cameras on Police Use-Of-Force* (2013), 8, www.policefoundation.org/sites/g/files/g798246/f/201303/The%20Effect%20of%20Body-Worn%20Cameras%20on%20Police%20Use-of-Force.pdf (finding that shifts without cameras experienced twice as many incidents of use of force as shifts with cameras, and that the rate of use of force incidents per 1,000 contacts was reduced by 2.5 times). FBI Director James Comey has said that ubiquitous recording makes some cops more reluctant to aggressively pursue crime. Martin Kaste, "FBI Director Connects Heightened Police Scrutiny to Violent Crime Spike," NPR, Oct. 26, 2015 4:25 p.m., www.npr.org/2015/10/26/452012194/fbi-director-connects-heightened-police-scrutiny-to-violent-crime-spike ("They described a feeling of being under siege and were honest and said, we don't feel much like getting out of our cars."). See generally Heather MacDonald, *The War on Cops: How the New Attack on Law and Order Makes Everyone Less Safe* (2016).

15. Lauren Miller, "Police, ACLU Draft New Body Camera Policy for Carrboro," *Daily Tarheel*, Mar. 25, 2015, 12:33 a.m., www.dailytarheel.com/article/2015/03/police-aclu-draft-new-body-camera-policy-for-carrboro; Vivian Ho, "S.F. Panel Votes on Body Camera Policy," *SFGate*, Dec. 3, 2015, 7:06 a.m., www.sfgate.com/crime/article/S-F-panel-votes-on-body-camera-policy-6672070.php.

16. Miller, "Police, ACLU Draft New Body Camera Policy for Carrboro," supra note 15; Los Angeles Police Department, *Body Worn Video Procedures* (2015), www.lapdpolicecom.lacity.org/042815/BPC_15-0115.pdf; letter from Peter Bibring, Director

of Police Practices, ACLU, to Denise E. O'Donnell, Director, Bureau of Justice Assistance, Sep. 3, 2015, www.aele.org/aclu2doj-lapd$.pdf.

17. Letter from Peter Bibring, supra note 16; Bob Egelko, "ACLU Sues Hayward over $2,938 Fee for Protest Video," *SFGate*, Sep. 15, 2015, 6:00 p.m., www.sfgate.com /bayarea/article/ACLU-sues-Hayward-over-2-938-fee-for-protest-6507262.php. Similarly, when a New York City TV station requested footage from the NYPD's body camera pilot program, they were told the editing bill would be $36,000. David Kravets, "Police Department Charging TV News Network $36,000 for Body Cam Footage," *Ars Technica*, Jan. 17, 2016, 12:40 p.m., http://arstechnica.com/tech-policy/2016/01/police -department-charging-tv-news-network-36000-for-body-cam-footage/;   Respondents City of Hayward, Adam Perez and Diane Urban's Opposition to Petitioner's Motion for Injunctive and Declaratory Relief and Preemptory Writ of Mandate at 5–7, *Nat'l Lawyer's Guild San Francisco Bay Area Chapter v. City of Hayward*, No. RG15785743 (Cal. Super. Ct. Feb. 25, 2016) (documenting the efforts made by the City to comply with a public records request for BWC footage).

18. See, e.g., Martina Kitzmueller, "Are You Recording This? Enforcement of Police Video-taping," *Conn. L. Rev.* 47 (2014): 170 and 170n8 ("Of the fifty-nine DUI and domestic violence cases handled by my students in the spring semester of 2014, ten cases had an issue with video that was lost or destroyed, or where no video had been taken at all."); Ken Daley, "Cameras Not On Most of the Time When NOPD Uses Force, Monitor Finds," *Times Picayune*, Sept. 4, 2014, 10:05 p.m., www.nola.com/crime/index.ssf /2014/09/cameras_not_on_most_of_the_tim.html (noting that only 34 percent of the 145 use-of-force events in New Orleans had preserved video of the event). For example, it's hard to argue that cops shouldn't be able to turn the camera off when talking to an underage sex crime victim.

19. Beau Hodai, "The Homeland Security Apparatus: Fusion Centers, Data Mining and Private Sector Partners," *PR Watch*, May 22, 2013, www.prwatch.org/news/2013/05/12122 /homeland-security-apparatus-fusion-centers-data-mining-and-private-sector-partner.

20. Brian A. Reaves, *Census of State and Local Law Enforcement Agencies, 2008* (2011), 2 & 2tbl.2, www.bjs.gov/content/pub/pdf/csllea08.pdf (tallying 17,985 state and local law enforcement agencies).

21. Consent Decree, *United States v. City of Los Angeles*, No. 00-CV-11769 (C.D. Cal. June 15, 2001), http://assets.lapdonline.org/assets/pdf/final_consent_decree.pdf; Kate Mather, "The LAPD Is Officially Suggesting a Few Things Officers Can Try to Do Before Pulling the Trigger," *L.A. Times*, Mar. 15, 2016, 9:34 p.m., www.latimes.com /local/lanow/la-me-ln-lapd-rules-change-20160315-story.html (discussing the Police Commission's changes to LA's use of force policy); Sid Garcia, "LA Police Commission to Hold Public Hearings on LAPD Drone Use," *ABC7*, June 3, 2014, http://abc7.com /news/commission-to-hold-public-hearings-on-lapd-drones/92193/ (discussing upcoming meeting on drone use).

22. *Final Report of the President's Task Force on 21st Century Policing* (2015), 15, www.cops .usdoj.gov/pdf/taskforce/taskforce_finalreport.pdf.

23. Boards, Commissions, Committees and Task Forces, City of Park Ridge, www .parkridge.us/government/committees_commissions_and_boards.aspx; Meetings, Library Board of Trustees, Park Ridge Public Library, www.parkridgelibrary.org/about _us/meetings.aspx

24. See "The Conservative Case for Reform," Right on Crime, http://rightoncrime.com/the -conservative-case-for-reform/ (using conservative principles to advocate for penal reform).

25. Efforts to reduce drug use and its consequences resulted in $30.6 billion in direct federal expenditures in 2016 alone. Executive Office of the President, *National Drug*

Control Budget FY 2017 Funding Highlights (2016), 2, www.whitehouse.gov/sites/default/files/ondcp/press-releases/fy_2017_budget_highlights.pdf. At the same time, the National Institutes of Health have reported an 8.3 percent increase in the use of illicit drugs by Americans between 2002 and 2012. National Institute on Drug Abuse, *Drug Facts* (2015), 1, www.drugabuse.gov/sites/default/files/drugfacts_nationtrends_6_15.pdf. For an investigation of the drug war's impact on aggressive policing and its effect on minority communities see Samuel R. Gross and Katherine Y. Barnes, "Road Work: Racial Profiling and Drug Interdiction on the Highway," *Mich. L. Rev.* 101 (2002): 670–77.

26. Stephen A. Berrey, *The Jim Crow Routine* (2015), 138–42 (discussing the racial aspects of policing during the Jim Crow era in Mississippi and Alabama); David A. Sklansky, "The Fourth Amendment and Common Law," *Colum. L. Rev.* 100 (2000): 1806 (describing slave patrols); David A. Slansky, "The Private Police," *UCLA L. Rev.* 46 (1999): 1213–16 (describing the Pinkerton Agency's activities in support of management during labor disputes); James Comey, Director, FBI, "Hard Truths: Law Enforcement and Race," Address at Georgetown University, Feb. 12, 2015, www.fbi.gov/news/speeches/hard-truths-law-enforcement-and-race ("[A]ll of us in law enforcement must be honest enough to acknowledge that much of our history is not pretty. At many points in American history, law enforcement enforced the status quo, a status quo that was often brutally unfair to disfavored groups.").

27. "Poll: NYC Split on Stop and Frisk," *Politico*, Aug. 16, 2012, 6:31 a.m., www.politico.com/story/2012/08/poll-nyc-racially-divided-over-stop-and-frisk-079781. There is reason to question Bloomberg's claim of the effectiveness of the program. See NYCLU, *Stop & Frisk During the Bloomberg Administration 2002–2013* (2014), 1, www.nyclu.org/files/publications/stopandfrisk_briefer_2002-2013_final.pdf (arguing that as the number of stops and frisks decreased, violent crime also decreased).

28. Joan Lowy, "AP-NCC Poll: A Third of the Public Fears Police Use of Drones for Surveillance Will Erode Their Privacy," AP-GFK, Sept. 27, 2012, http://ap-gfkpoll.com/uncategorized/our-latest-poll-findings-13. Fifty-four perecent of Americans disapprove of the government's collection of telephone and Internet data as part of antiterrorism efforts. George Gao, "What Americans Think About NSA Surveillance, National Security, and Privacy," Pew Research Center, May 29, 2015, www.pewresearch.org/fact-tank/2015/05/29/what-americans-think-about-nsa-surveillance-national-security-and-privacy/.

29. Allen E. Liska and Paul E. Bellair, "Violent Crime Rates and Racial Composition: Convergence over Time," *Am. J. Soc.* 101 (1995), 586–88 (finding nonwhites to be more likely to live in areas affected by violent crime); Ingrid Gould Ellen and Katherine O'Regan, "Crime and U.S. Cities: Recent Patterns and Implications," *Annals Am. Acad. Pol. & Soc. Sci.* 626 (2009): 26–27 (finding minority populations also disproportionately benefiting from reduced crime rates).

30. Robert T. de George, "Democracy as a Social Myth," in *Philosophical Perspectives on Democracy in the 21st Century*, eds. Ann E. Cudd and Sally J. Scholz (2013), 43 n.2.

31. See generally Seth Stoughton, "Policing Facts," *Tulane L. Rev.* 88 (2014): 847 (arguing that courts' perception of what policing entails differs widely from what policing actually is, which hampers courts' ability to regulate the constitutionality of policing).

32. See Jonathan Stewart, "Peel's Principles of Law Enforcement," *Marron Inst. of Urban Mgmt.*, Sep. 18, 2013, http://marroninstitute.nyu.edu/content/blog/peels-principles-of-law-enforcement.

33. Id.

34. See Timothy Williams, "Police Leaders Join Call to Cut Prison Rosters," *N.Y. Times*, Oct. 20, 2015, www.nytimes.com/2015/10/21/us/police-leaders-join-call-to-cut-prison

-rosters.html; Radley Balko "Former Cops Speak Out About Police Militarization," *Huffington Post*, Aug. 1, 2013 11:09 p.m., www.huffingtonpost.com/2013/08/01/cops -speak-out-on-police-_n_3688999.html/ ("Older and retired cops don't seem to like where policing is headed . . . Younger cops, who are nudging policing in a more militaristic direction, are naturally fine with it.").

EPILOGUE

1. Victoria M. Massie, "What Philando Castile's Death Says About the Dangers of Driving While Black," *VICE*, July 11, 2016, 3:20 p.m., www.vox.com/2016/7/11/12147878 /philando-castile-driving-while-black.

2. Aaron Rupar, "Minnesota Governor on Philando Castile's Death: He'd Still Be Alive Had He Been White," *ThinkProgress*, July 7, 2016, 5:11 p.m., http://thinkprogress.org /justice/2016/07/07/3796518/mark-dayton-philando-castile-racism.

3. Melanie Garunay, "President Obama on the Fatal Shootings of Alton Sterling and Philando Castile," *The White House Blog*, July 7, 2016, 2:12 p.m., www.whitehouse.gov /blog/2016/07/07/president-obama-fatal-shootings-alton-sterling-and-philando-castile.

ACKNOWLEDGMENTS

I procrastinated in writing these acknowledgments. It is because so many people and institutions contributed to this project, in so many ways, that I have had to live with the deep sense of dread that I would omit someone important, and that in any event I could not possibly recall or thank everyone who touched some aspect of this work, let alone thank some people enough.

I want to start with my family. Barely a day goes by that I don't think how blessed I am to have the life I do—that they give me each and every day. It is difficult to imagine any person being more supportive than my wife, Jill Anton. She is the one who creates the space that allows the writing to get done, and who pays the price as I neglect other responsibilities. I count my lucky stars that she not only puts up with me, but actually seems okay with it. Samara and Simon, you got the front of the book the old-fashioned way: by providing an environment of unrelenting chaos, with huge doses of hilarity mixed in. Each and every day you amaze me with your energy, your curiosity, your thoughts, and your love. My in-laws, Gloria and Saul Anton, are a vital part of my life. My mom, Sally Friedman, has been the same combination of fiercely loyal and proud for literally as long as I can remember. My father, Benjamin Friedman—Papa to the kids—passed away while I was working on this book. An auditor by training, my dad spent the latter part of his career working in Inspectors General offices in the federal government. This book was the very sort of project that drew him in completely, and I have missed horribly the many conversations we never got to have.

I owe a special debt of gratitude to the people whose stories I have told here. They, or in some instances their lawyers or loved ones, were generous with their time. They assembled files, sent me materials, and answered a flood of questions. But most important, they agreed to relive one of the most difficult moments of their lives. Listening to those stories brought home to me the profound and often incalculable injury that follows from innocent people being cast under suspicion by their government, and being subjected to surveillance and state-sanctioned force. As a society, we unequivocally need to ensure our public safety. But we also have to take seriously the responsibility to minimize the trauma, injury, indignity, and humiliation that accompany encounters such as these.

This is the second book I've written with the dynamic duo of Christy Fletcher and Eric Chinski by my side. Christy, my literary agent, believed in this book, and was fascinated by its subject matter, from the start. She constantly read drafts, pushed me to make the narrative sharper and more accessible, and provided an invaluable stream of advice and support. Eric—and his colleagues at Farrar, Straus and Giroux—decided the subject matter was too compelling not to publish, even at a time when no one seemed to care a whit about policing (which, as Eric pointed out to me, was not a prescription for selling books). Eric is a rock; I'm again grateful for his sharp and questioning eye, his gentle but firm editorial hand. I love talking with him about ideas. Additional thanks to the whole team at FSG, including Laird Gallagher, Susan Goldfarb, Jeff Seroy, and Lottchen Shivers.

It is said that there is nothing new under the sun. My hat is, and remains, off to Anthony Amsterdam. From the time I began teaching Criminal Procedure, over thirty years ago, his extraordinary published lectures—*Perspectives on the Fourth Amendment*—have been the very best thing written on this subject. Tony is a wonder of care, brilliance, and passion. Much of what I've done here is derivative of his work. He was generous and meticulous (as always) in offering help when asked.

Similar grace and generosity was exhibited by two of the leading figures in this field, Orin Kerr and Chris Slobogin. Without their quite knowing it, they have been my go-to guys. I have stepped all over their turf, and they have repaid me by providing unending assistance.

I worked many of these ideas out in articles I was fortunate to coauthor with Oren Bar-Gill, Cynthia Stein, and Maria Ponomarenko. Oren taught me a great deal, a store of insight on which I keep drawing. I really can't capture the debt I owe Maria in particular. She is, and has been, my partner in crime—or at least policing and criminal procedure—for years now. Once my talented student—she did research for this book beginning in her 1L year—she now coteaches the Democratic Policing seminar with me, where the ideas here are refined, and serves as the Deputy Director of the Policing Project, where we labor side by side daily to put these ideas into action. Most important, Maria read every word of this book, sometimes two or three times.

I am lucky to teach at a school that must have the largest and most talented collection of criminal justice, policing, administrative, and constitutional law experts in the country, if not the world. I can't measure their contributions but to say that this book was vastly improved by the countless conversations we had, the many chances they give me to present parts of the manuscript, and their generosity in reading and commenting on it. A special shout-out to Daryl Levinson and Rachel Barkow, who read every word of the manuscript and provided extensive comments. And then there are (and here is where I start worrying I'm missing people) Adam Cox, Michael Farbiarz, David Garland, Deb Gramiccioni, Randy Hertz, Rick Hills, Dan Hulsebosch, Jim Jacobs, Michael Levine, Erin Murphy, Burt Neuborne, Sam Rascoff, Adam Samaha, Andy Schaffer, Steve Schulhofer, Kathy Strandburg, Tony Thompson, Jeremy Waldron, and Andrew Weissmann.

I got similar help from friends and colleagues everywhere. The Austin family spent a few days obsessed with stop-and-frisk. Many people read portions of the book in progress or talked with me at length about the ideas: Miriam Baer, Sandy Baggett, Emily Berman, Kiel Brennan-Marquez, Sam Buell, Bethany Chaney, Simon Chesterman, Doug Cohen, Andrew Crespo, John Cuti, Herman Goldstein, Risa Goluboff, Michael Jones, Nancy King, Anne Kornhauser, Genevieve Lakier, Rob Lax, Dahlia Lithwick, Mary Moore, Eve Primus, John Rappaport, Daphna Renan, Erin Scharff, Joanna Schwartz, Geoff Smith, Lior Strahelivitz,

Scott Sundby, Sam Walker, and Dan Wilhelm. Various and sundry members of my lifelong friends, the Tenenbaum clan, read pieces of the manuscript and commented, no one more so than Mike Eisner, an author himself. Special thanks to Eberhardt Schmidt-Assman, who connected me to the German policing-law tradition.

I've talked about the ideas here in many forums, whether it was this book or the articles that preceded it. In addition to my gratitude for any number of workshops at NYU, I'd like to express my appreciation to the law faculties at Vanderbilt (my former home, which will always hold a special place in my heart), as well as American University, the University of Chicago, Northwestern University, Georgetown University, and the University of Miami. I particularly enjoyed an early conversation about this project with prosecutors and top police in Singapore; thanks to Sandy Baggett for that. I enjoyed and learned from a lecture at the UC-Irvine Law School at the start of the project, and the Hoffinger Colloquium at NYU Law toward the end. As I labored to finish the book, I profited from a remarkable stay at NYU's Paris campus. That is what the writing life should always be like. I'm grateful to all who arranged and nurtured that stay. And I spent a terrific, deeply intellectual couple of weeks at the Max Planck Institute at Heidelberg. It is a great place, in no small part because of its remarkable codirector, Armin von Bogdandy. Finally, there are the years of students on whom I tried out these ideas—you have enriched me more than you will ever know.

Books like this aren't written without support. NYU Law School has had a succession of deans who seem to say yes to anything that fosters faculty research. I thank Ricky Revesz and Trevor Morrison for seeing that this project got done. I've continually drawn from the generosity of the Filomen D'Agostino and Max E. Greenburg Faculty Research Fund. We have an incredible library support team, with Dana Rubin getting the special note here for all her help. A line of talented and dedicated administrative assistants kept things going: Jesus Ballivian, Alex Lu, Kristin Slater, and now Claire Duleba, whose level of commitment is beyond. There were myriad research assistants who made this happen, from those who initially found and investigated the stories I tell, to those who located my many sources, to those who kept me honest in the claims and endnotes. I lack the space to thank you all here—and many were thanked in the law review articles that preceded this—but you know who you are, and I am grateful to you. I do want to single out a few students for special recognition, because you gave more than I reasonably should have asked. Rebecca Talbott for the first Fourth Amendment seminar, Sean Childers for the crazy data project. For research: Nick Axelrod, Tommy Bennett, Hannah Bloch-Wehba, David Carey, Christina Dahlman, Jon Daniels, Peter Dubrowski, Kevin Friedl, Dan Haaren, Ian Herbert, Bradley Markano, Neal Perlman, Lance Polivy, Matt Robinson, Colin Roth, and Nik Williams. The footnote crew pulled it together at the end: Getzy Berger, Anna Estevao, Juan Gascon, Ranit Patel, Alex Peacocke, Eric Phillips, Alex Schindler, Stephanie Spies, Daniel Thomson, and Max Yoeli. Mitchell Stern gets bountiful thanks for bringing the manuscript home, making sure all the endnotes (and some of the text) were in perfect order.

As usual, Mitchell Charap and Adam Steinlauf kept me going. So did Tamar Amitay, Sinead Fitzgibbon, and Elizabeth Houchins.

About three-quarters of the way through this book, I began to work to put the ideas here into action. In that work I've had remarkable colleagues, many of whom shaped what got published here. There aren't thanks enough for Anne Milgram, who helped launch the Policing Project and serves as advisor-in-chief. The American Law Institute launched its Principles of the Law: Policing project; my fellow Reporters— Brandon Garrett, Rachel Harmon, Tracey Meares, and Chris Slobogin— are a constant source of intellectual inspiration. (We eat well, too.) Rebekah Carmichael and the communications team at NYU Law have been extraordinary in their support and ingenuity. Tolga Ergunay and the IT crew have made so much happen The externs and interns at the Policing Project have accomplished amazing things in a short period of time, and—again—that work influenced where this project ended up.

The world is changed by people who labor to change it. The events described in this book have triggered studies, conferences, debates, and— yes—protests from people across the ideological spectrum. I have learned a terrific amount from all those who, in the streets, in public interest groups, and in government, have pushed back against government overreaching, whether it was surveillance or the use of force. Eternal vigilance is indeed the price of liberty, and in moments of quiet reflection we should all thank you for your work. It's not always popular, but it is so essential.

And then there are the police. If you'd asked me at the start of this project if I predicted I'd be spending large swaths of my life with law enforcement, I'd have chuckled. I chuckle no more. I have learned from— and this book was enormously influenced by—so many fine public servants. At a time of great turmoil in your profession, you have exhibited vision, balance, and a willingness to examine all you do. I'm lucky to be working each day with so many of you. Particular thanks to the signatories of the original Statement of Democratic Policing Principles, who attended the Democratic Policing conference at NYU in November 2015 and collectively demanded that we produce it. And abundant gratitude to my now dear friend and counselor, Camden County Police Chief J. Scott Thomson.

INDEX